Challenges, Performances and Tendencies in Organisation Management

Challenges, Performances and Tendencies in Organisation Management

Editors

Ovidiu Nicolescu
The Bucharest University of Economic Studies, Romania

Lester Lloyd-Reason
Anglia Ruskin University, UK

Romanian Scientific Management Society

World Scientific

Published by

World Scientific Publishing Co. Pte. Ltd.
5 Toh Tuck Link, Singapore 596224
USA office: 27 Warren Street, Suite 401-402, Hackensack, NJ 07601
UK office: 57 Shelton Street, Covent Garden, London WC2H 9HE

Library of Congress Cataloging-in-Publication Data
Challenges, performances and tendencies in organisation management / edited by Ovidiu Nicolescu (The Bucharest University of Economic Studies, Romania) & Lester Lloyd-Reason (Anglia Ruskin University, UK).
   pages cm
  Includes bibliographical references and index.
  ISBN 978-9814656016 (alk. paper)
  1. Management. 2. International business enterprises--Management. I. Nicolescu, Ovidiu. II. Lloyd-Reason, Lester.
  HD31.C424 2015
  658--dc23
                                                                                2015009071

British Library Cataloguing-in-Publication Data
A catalogue record for this book is available from the British Library.

Copyright © 2016 by World Scientific Publishing Co. Pte. Ltd.

All rights reserved. This book, or parts thereof, may not be reproduced in any form or by any means, electronic or mechanical, including photocopying, recording or any information storage and retrieval system now known or to be invented, without written permission from the publisher.

For photocopying of material in this volume, please pay a copying fee through the Copyright Clearance Center, Inc., 222 Rosewood Drive, Danvers, MA 01923, USA. In this case permission to photocopy is not required from the publisher.

In-house Editors: Dipasri Sardar/Li Hongyan

Typeset by Stallion Press
Email: enquiries@stallionpress.com

Printed in Singapore

Board Members

Coordinators:

Prof. Ovidiu Nicolescu, The Bucharest University of Economic Studies, Bucharest, Romania

Prof. Lester Lloyd-Reason, Anglia Ruskin University, Cambridge, United Kingdom

Editors:

Prof. Ovidiu Nicolescu, The Bucharest University of Economic Studies, Bucharest, Romania

Prof. Lester Lloyd Reason, Anglia Ruskin University, Cambridge, United Kingdom

Scientific Board:

Prof. Doina Banciu, National Institute for Research & Development in Informatics, Romania

Prof. Mihai Bocarnea, Regent University, USA

Prof. Zbigniew Bochniarz, Evans School of Public Affairs, University of Washington, Seattle, USA

Prof. Constantin Bratianu, Bucharest University of Economic Studies, Romania

Prof. Dan Candea, Technical University of Cluj-Napoca, Romania

Prof. Martin Henson, University of Essex, United Kingdom

Prof. Norbert Grunwald, Wiesmar University of Technology, Germany

Prof. Lars Hulgard, Roskilde University, Denmark

Prof. Soulla Louca, University of Nicosia, Cyprus

Prof. Dumitru Miron, Bucharest University of Economic Studies, Romania

Prof. Ovidiu Nicolescu, Bucharest University of Economic Studies, Romania

Associate Prof. Marian Nastase, Bucharest University of Economic Studies, Romania

Prof. Constantin Oprean, România, University "Lucian Blaga" of Sibiu, Romania

Prof. Hanns Pitchler, Wien Economics University

Prof. George Plesoianu, Bucharest University of Economic Studies, Romania

Prof. Lester Lloyd-Reason, Anglia Ruskin University, Cambridge, UK

Prof. Victoria Seitz, California State University, USA

Prof. Ion Stegaroiu, "Valahia" University of Targoviste, Romania

Prof. Lajos Szabo, University of Pannonia, Veszprem, Hungary

Prof. Blandine Vanderlinden, MIME-ICHEC, Brussels, Belgium

Scientific Secretary:

Lecturer Eduard Ceptureanu

Contents

Foreword	xi
About the Editor	xiii

Part I. International Management and Cultural Diversity — 1

Chapter 1. The Role of Large Corporate Boards in the Context of Globalization and Smart Economy: Creating Value for All Stakeholders — 3
Mariana Gheorghe

Chapter 2. New Management Tendencies and Their Impact on the Form of Capitalism — 11
Maria Negreponti-Delivanis

Chapter 3. Trends and Developments of Diversity Management at the Global level — 19
Stegăroiu Ion, Mubeen Ştefania, Istrate Ciprian, Lile Ramona

Chapter 4. Corporate Social Responsibility or Corporate Sustainability of Romanian Enterprises? — 25
Zaiţ Dumitru, Onea Angelica, Tătăruşanu Maria, Ciulu Ruxandra

Chapter 5. Re-Thinking Our Model of Management in the Light of the Cultural Dimension — A Systemic Approach to the Company — 35
Blandine Vanderlinden

Part II. Sustainable Development and Business Sustainability — 45

Chapter 6. Social Capital and Business Sustainability: Defining, Measuring, and Assessing its Impact on Cluster Performance in the Podkarpackie Region of Poland — 47
Zbigniew Bochniarz

Chapter 7. Integrating Corporate and Academic Alumni into the Drive toward Sustainability — 55
Rodica Stefănescu

Part III. University Governance and Management — 65

Chapter 8. Taxonomies of Internationalization for Higher Education — 67
Martin Henson

Chapter 9. The Most Pressing Challenges for Romanian Higher Education System in Line with the Bologna Process Values — 79
Dumitru Miron

Chapter 10. University Governance and Competitive Advantage 89
Mihai Korka

Chapter 11. Study Programs in English in Non-Anglophone Countries:
Looking at Impacts and Challenges from a Romanian Perspective 97
Mariana Nicolae

Chapter 12. Romanian Private Higher Education in the Current European Context 107
Folcuț Ovidiu, Grigore Ramona

**Part IV. Knowledge-Based Organization, Intellectual Capital,
Information, and Management Documents** **115**

Chapter 13. Contributions to the Evaluation of e-Learning Processes in Higher Education 117
Doina Banciu, Monica Florea

Chapter 14. Evaluation of Knowledge Processes Within the Learning Organization 125
Constantin Bratianu, Ruxandra Bejinaru

Chapter 15. Universities in Transition: Are Library Directors Facing Changed Demands? 137
Arja Mäntykangas

Chapter 16. Knowledge Management in the Information Society — Case Study on e-Services 143
Monica Anghel

Chapter 17. Risk Awareness as Key Success Factor for more Efficient Management
for Local Public Administrations 151
Markus Bodemann, Marieta Olaru, Ionela Carmen Pirnea

Chapter 18. Information and its Entropy — A Measure of Market Complexity 159
Camelia Oprean

Part V. Entrepreneurship, Social Enterprise, and SMEs **167**

Chapter 19. SME-Conducive Policy Formulation under Systemic Perspectives 169
J. Hanns Pichler

Chapter 20. Particularities of the Procesual Organisation in the Medium Knowledge-Based Enterprise 175
Ovidiu Nicolescu

Chapter 21. Preparing Our Students for an Entrepreneurial Life: Are Universities Part of the Solution
or Part of the Problem 185
Lester Lloyd-Reason

Chapter 22. Difficulties in Improving Romanian Companies Management 195
Corneliu Russu

Chapter 23. Contributions to Redesigning the Management System in Medium-Sized Enterprises 203
Ion Verboncu, Ciprian Nicolescu

Chapter 24. The New Paradigm of Social Enterprise 213
Ana-Maria Grigore

Chapter 25. Realities and Peculiarities of the Entrepreneurship in Brasov, Romania *Camelia Dragomir, Stelian Panzaru, Carmen Lis*	219
Chapter 26. ESF Interventions for Promoting Entrepreneurship in Romania *Daniela Manuc*	227
Chapter 27. Contributions to the Development and Use of Information Programs Dealing With Human Resources in the Rural Area *Simona Biriescu, Mariana Predişcan, Marian Năstase*	235
Chapter 28. Management Particularities of the Romanian Social Enterprise *Bibu Nicolae, Lisetchi Mihai, Nastase Marian*	243
Chapter 29. The Evolution of the Romanian SMEs' Perceptions Over the Last Decade *Luminiţa Nicolescu, Ciprian Nicolescu*	261

Part VI. Leadership and Human Resources Management — 273

Chapter 30. The Relationship between Leadership Styles, Leader Communication Style, and Impact on Leader–Member Exchange Relationship within the Banking Sector in the United States *Theodore G. Pacleb, Mihai C. Bocarnea*	275
Chapter 31. The Effect of Organizational Culture on the Responsiveness of Small and Medium-Sized Enterprises to Environmental Change: An Empirical Study in Romania *Michael Stoica, Liviu Florea, Edit Lukacs*	289
Chapter 32. Model Proposal for Cluster Implementation in Romania *Ion Popa, Cristina Vlăsceanu*	297
Chapter 33. Aspects of Human Resources' Management within Organizations in Braşov, Romania *Stelian Panzaru, Camelia-Cristina Dragomir, Tudor Pendiuc, Dan Cojocaru*	303
Chapter 34. Managing Individual Performance Appraisal in Project Teams *Florin-Ioan Petean, Bogdan Bâlc, Horaţiu Cătălin Sălăgean, Răzvan Dimitrie Gârbacea, Diana Sopon*	313
Chapter 35. The Relation between Labor Force Profitability and the Firm's Personnel Policy *Gabriel Sorin Badea, Constanta Popescu, Silvia Elena Iacob*	319
Chapter 36. Analysis of Multinational Companies in Romania *Eduard Ceptureanu, Sebastian Ceptureanu*	329

Part VII. Management of Change, Innovation, and Quality — 339

Chapter 37. Study Regarding the Correlation between the Changes in the Energy Economy and the Competitiveness of Companies in Germany and Romania *Gregor Johannes Weber, Marieta Olaru, Georgiana Marin*	341
Chapter 38. Management of Intangible Assets Valorization in Small and Medium Enterprises *Constantin Oprean, Mihail Aurel Ţîţu, Claudiu Vasile Kifor*	349

Chapter 39. Comparative Management in the Field of Extracurricular Activities, Highlighting Instrument of Potential Change 355
Oana Dumitraşcu, Emanoil Muscalu

Chapter 40. Study for Creating and Developing Regional Agrifood Markets in Romania 363
Nicolae Istudor, George Plesoianu, Bogdan Bazga, Oana Georgiana Stanila, St. Alexandru Costin Cirstea

Chapter 41. Comparative Analysis of the Factors Influencing the Development and Implementation of European Projects 373
Diana Elena Ranf, Liana Marcu, Dănut Dumitru Dumitraşcu

Chapter 42. Organizational Change — Managing Employees Resistance 381
Viorel Cornescu, Roxana Adam

Chapter 43. How to Reduce Supplemental Claims in Construction Industry — Selected Management Tools to Implement a Systematic Anti-Claim Management 391
Martin Heinisch, Jörg-U. Muckenfuß, Dan Miricescu

Chapter 44. Implementation of Quality Management for Ecotouristic Operators in the Danube Delta 399
Virgil Nicula, Simona Spânu

Chapter 45. Romanian Pre-University Educational Management in the Context of European Integration 409
Ana Tuşa, Claudiu Sorin Voinia, Oana Dumitraşcu

Chapter 46. Study on the Promotion and Implementation of Sustainable Development in Modern Management in National and Regional Economies, Case Study: Romania as EU Member 417
George Plesoianu, St. Alexandru Costin Cirstea

Index 427

Foreword

The management is — without any doubt — one of the most important and the fast changing fields of the society. There is no component of the human activity — family, enterprise, town region, industry, country, a.s.o — which can perform without a good management. For this reason there are a lot of resources allocated to improve the management in the largest companies and to provide management research/education and training.

Transition to the knowledge-based economy, to the "smart economy" — the crucial mutation of our times — generates new requirements and opportunities for all management components. It is now under construction a new type of management, i.e., knowledge-based management.

The present book incorporates 46 chapters from more than 110, presented to the international conference **"Challenges, Performances and Tendencies in the Organization Management"** organized by Romanian Scientific Management Society — the most elitist Romanian professional management association, from June 22–24, 2014 in Danube Delta, Romania. The chapters have been selected by 20 scientific board members from 9 countries — USA, UK, Austria, Belgium, Germany, Denmark, Hungary, Cyprus, and Romania.

The book is structured in seven parts referring to the major management fields:

— International management and cultural diversity.
— Sustainable development and business sustainability.
— University governance and management.
— Knowledge based organization, intellectual capital, information, and management documents.
— Entrepreneurship, social enterprise and SMEs.
— Leadership and human resource management.
— Management of change, innovation and quality.

In each part there are several chapters dealing with significant elements of the management topics, having new theoretical and/or pragmatic contributions.

Every chapter is very methodically structured: introduction, theoretical background, methodology used, scientific and/or pragmatic management elements analyzed, and conclusions. Without any doubt the most part of chapters contain new or less known management elements referring especially to the management in Central, Eastern, and Western Europe in a modern approach. Many chapters there are based on the recent empirical research in the companies.

This book presents major interest and utility for:

— Management professors, students, trainers, and consultants.
— Managers and management specialists from the companies and public administration.
— Persons interested in management evolution in the last years in Europe and, especially, in the Central and Eastern Europe.

Despite of the author's efforts, of the scientific board members implication and of the book scientific coordinators contribution, the book is not perfect and it could be further improved. Reader's suggestions and observations are welcome.

Finally, we want to thank to each participant in this scientific work for their contribution and implication. Special thanks to the Romanian Scientific Management Society which made this book possible, to the scientific board, and to my colleagues in coordinating this book and to the scientific secretary, last but not least our thanks to the prestigious World Scientific Publishing specialists who have published the book.

September 22, 2014
Prof. PhD Ovidiu Nicolescu
President Romanian Scientific Management Society
Bucharest, Romania

About the Editor

OVIDIU NICOLESCU

Professor PhD Ovidiu Nicolescu from Economic University of Bucharest is President of Romanian Scientific Management Society, President of National Council of SMEs of Romania, the largest Romanian employers confederation, Vice President of European Association of Craft, Small and Medium-sized Enterprises, Vice President of World Association for Small and Medium Enterprises. He has published 43 books as single or main author, 507 studies in Romania and other 22 countries and he has implemented in Romania 6 new university courses. In 1990 he has founded in Romania the first private management-consultancy company — Manager Institute. His last book co-authored in 2015 is White Charter of SMEs from Romania — 13 yearly research report.

LESTER LLOYD-REASON

Professor PhD Lester Lloyd-Reason from Anglia Ruskin University, Lord Ashcroft International Business School in Cambridge, UK is Director of the Center for Enterprise Development and Research CEDAR. His areas of expertise are Strategic Management, Small and Medium-sized Enterprises, Transition Economies, and Arts Management. Professor Lester Lloyd-Reason has published 3 books and more than 101 papers in books and reviews from 16 countries. He is a member of the European and International Council for Small Business, member of the Board of Directors of the Institute of Small Business Affairs. During the last 20 years he has been involved in many international activities of OECD, ASEAN, APO, WASME, a.s.o.

Part I

International Management and Cultural Diversity

Chapter 1

The Role of Large Corporate Boards in the Context of Globalization and Smart Economy: Creating Value for All Stakeholders

Mariana Gheorghe

CEO of OMV PETROM

In the context of globalization and smart economy, large corporate boards are very important for the development of a company. The chapter aims to analyze the way in which a company can advance due to the vision of Corporate Boards. The used research methodology is the case study. The case study distinctly presents the way in which OMV Petrom managed to deal with the new challenges arising from the privatization of the company. The analysis is carried forward in three dimensions: the complex socio-economic context, along with the more demanding stakeholders' environment; adopting new technology and innovating; people changes and challenges. For the last 10 years, since privatization, the company has adapted itself through an almost radical and complex process of transformation and has created new opportunities for all of its stakeholders, while facing the challenges of this new era: the new economic and social order, both locally as well as internationally.

1. Introduction

Our new reality is shaped by three key dimensions that put a lot of pressure on all organizations and companies:

1.1. *The complex socio-economic context and more demanding stakeholders' environment*

It is well known that we operate in an increasingly complex socio-economic context and a generally more demanding stakeholders' environment, as we moved from a resource based economy to a knowledge based economy. Companies worldwide needed to adapt their strategies to this changing context and new solutions emerged as a result, in order to deal with the new priorities of the corporate world. "Boards of directors perform a monitoring and advising role and ensure that management is making decisions in a way that is consistent with organizational objectives" (Eccles *et al.*, 2012: 7).

The financial crisis in recent years has brought a set of special circumstances and conditions that have also clearly put a mark on the general context and have influenced the behavior of companies and their stakeholders, with a generally increased concern for imposing stricter financial and operational discipline. "Researchers have also found correlations between stakeholder performance indicators and conventional measures of corporate profitability and growth" (Global Corporate Governance Forum, 2009: 9).

As a regional company based in Eastern Europe, with presence in Romania, Moldavia, Bulgaria, Serbia, and Kazakhstan, OMV Petrom has also had to additionally face the inherent pressure coming from the general context of transition economies and the deep reforms undertaken to emerge from the socialist command based position to the market economy status.

The main stakeholders, all the parties impacting and driving our business in addition to the employees are: investors, authorities, banks, society, media, customers and suppliers, our partner universities, which are constantly changing and evolving and we have noticed a major shift in their priorities. To give an example: the company's customers were primarily interested in price before, but they became more sophisticated, with women and young generations being nowadays more of a decisive factor in the household purchase decisions, constantly seeking, in addition to product quality and prices, suppliers that are socially responsible and that have a reduced carbon footprint in society.

1.2. Adopting new technology and innovating

"Industries and companies tend to globalize in stages, and at each stage, there are different opportunities for, and challenges associated with, creating value" (Kluyver, 2010: 41). The economic globalization and the development of an economy where knowledge is prevalent could not have manifested without the platform offered by technology. What strikes business corporate boards across the world nowadays is, however, the extremely rapid and intense pace of the development of new technologies and the information revolution creating a new dimension of organizational transparency and communication. "The company provides timely disclosure of information about its products, services, and activities, thus permitting stakeholders to make informed decisions" (Epstein & Rejc-Buhovac, 2014: 22). The depth of the current levels of understanding real-time business operational information, empathizing with consumers and building a universe of connections with the environment in which the company operates was never seen before. This constant challenge to keep the pace with the rapid change of technologies and information creates a different scope of work for the business managers operating in the new economy.

The prerequisite for the development of the new economy and of all the technological and informational advancements remains energy — we cannot conceive of a modern society without having sustainable and affordable energy sources.

1.3. People changes and challenges

"One of the primary duties of every board is to ensure that its enterprise is heading in the right direction" (Tricker, 2012: 176). The last challenge is represented by the people dimension, present in all business aspects. The generation Y of our employees is no longer satisfied with just having an interesting job, they are looking for quick results, rapid evolution, and on-the-spot reward and feedback. They are technologically savvy, more mobile, and constantly seek for a better work–life balance. Balancing between the need for speed of the generation Y employees and the more experienced generation X baby boomers puts additional pressure on boards and business executives in planning the workforce development by increasing motivational actions, and it will go a long way towards determining a company's success in the future.

2. OMV Petrom Case Topics

The chapter will focus next on bringing to attention the OMV Petrom transformation case study, as this year it celebrates 10 years since its privatization, along the three dimensions identified before:

(a) Context: The evolution of Petrom with a strong impact on the Romanian transition economy;
(b) Integrating innovation and technology (owned and through partnerships);
(c) Stakeholders' engagement and performance culture.

2.1. *Context*: *The evolution of Petrom with a strong impact on the Romanian transition economy*

Romania is one of the earliest historically attested oil providers in the world, as in Romania the first oil exploration was documented 150 years ago, earlier than those of US or Russia. So we hold the record for the first documented oil production in the world.

Today, OMV Petrom is an operationally integrated oil and gas player, with a market capitalization of around EUR 6 bn, ranking as the largest company in South Eastern Europe and 16th in Central Eastern Europe. The Group turnover is EUR 5.5 bn and the total shareholders return based on dividend yield plus share price increase stands at 16% in 2013.

OMV Petrom has a complex shareholders structure: 51% OMV — Austria's largest listed industrial company, an integrated oil and gas corporation with international presence; 20% the Romanian state, around 19% Property Fund — a close end fund managed by Franklin Templeton from US, and around 10% Bucharest Stock Exchange Free Float.

OMV Petrom represents a challenging business proposition and epitomizes a player with strong economic and social impact. It is the largest private employer in Romania, with over 20,000 direct employees and more than 60,000 indirect jobs created, at the same time being the main energy supplier accounting for almost 40% of oil, gas, and fuel supply and up to 10% of the power generating capacity.

OMV Petrom has a strong impact on the Romanian state budget, being the largest contributor, with a significant equivalent of 11% contribution to the non-consolidated annual revenues budget. This also represents a big responsibility for us, as the company generated and collected taxes amounting to around EUR 16 bn cumulated since 2005, the first year after the privatization.

OMV Petrom is also the largest investor in Romania, with EUR 10 bn cumulated investments over the past nine years, as almost 90% of company's operational profit is reinvested each year.

These key performance indicators (KPIs) illustrate the successful turnaround of a state company into a performing privately owned, competitive company.

How was this transformation possible? Through a determined and dynamic change management process and a comprehensive risk management approach. As Board members of a large corporation, we are accustomed to deal with change and risk daily in our operations and in our decision-making, particularly in the dynamic global and European context mentioned earlier.

To make this turnaround possible, we have managed our corporation through thousands of change projects: after privatization in December 2004, we identified all the dimensions of the organization which were not in line with what the market and the society required and with what the industry's best practices were at the time. We have taken all our activities from operational processes to corporate functions, identified *status quos* and the best practice of the industry in each area and then implemented the required change, in order to take the organization to that ideal position.

As this continuous effort for change became the standard norm, I was afraid, as the chief executive officer (CEO), of maybe pushing the organization too hard and I felt at times that we almost had a fatigue of change. But this is what it takes to turn around a large organization, as Petrom was before the privatization, into a very successful, competitive, dynamic company that has now become a role model for the Romanian economy.

The main dimensions of our change journey cover the areas of operational efficiency, management turnaround, and corporate governance.

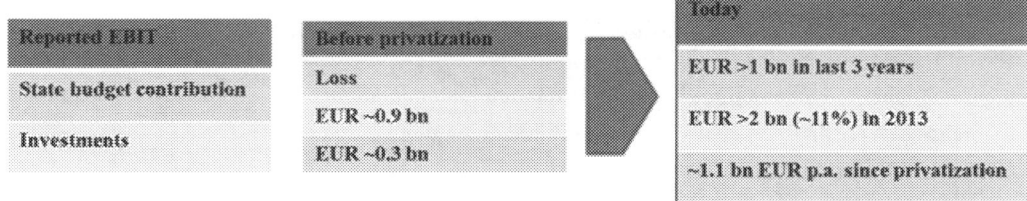

Fig. 1. The economic situation of the company before and after privatization
Source: Created by the author.

First, the company concentrated its operations on its oil and gas core and divested from large non-core businesses, at the same time embracing the latest technologies, modernizing facilities and processes.

Concurrently, the health, safety, security, and environmental standards were always in its focus and, as a result, the performance of these indicators improved dramatically over time. Given the concentration on core business and improved operational efficiency, ROACE[1] ratio reached 19% in 2013.

But the basic, fundamental change of this company has been possible because of the management turnaround. From the composition of the management team, to attracting and developing the right qualities and capabilities of the managers, to the management systems which we put in place and through the programs we initiated — all of these measures helped build a Performance mind-set in our management team and consolidated their commitment to excellence.

2.1.1. Corporate governance

The quality of the management was also manifested through diligent measures taken for the prevention of unethical behavior and improving corporate governance in general, adhering to international standards and best practices and generally increasing transparency in order to protect stakeholders' rights and interests, safeguard business value, and manage risks. These sustained efforts enabled us to build a professional organization based on a long term strategy, best practices in process management, clear procedures, and clear decision-making processes, translated into a positive work environment and responsible external relationships with all company stakeholders.

OMV Petrom has a two-tier management system since 2007: a Supervisory Board representing key shareholders and an Executive Board providing strategy and organizational direction and having overall a business administration role. Audit and Risk Committees manage the financials and also the risks of the business. Internal rules and procedures and management systems adhering to the highest industry standards ensure an optimal level of transparency and business ethics.

One of the most significant shifts in the organization was the evolution from a state company mind-set, without a long term view, to a company with a long term vision and a strategy for the next decade, incorporating sustainability and cascaded through KPIs to all levels of the organization. OMV Petrom strategy includes not only operational and financial business objectives, but also integrates sustainability and people development goals.

One of the company's success stories proving the benefits achieved by having strong corporate governance in our organization was recorded in the peak of the recent financial crisis. In 2008, Petrom had already exhausted the capital advanced at the time of the privatization and developed an ambitious project portfolio, ready to take the company to the next level of development. As the crisis hit, we have seen a collapse of our cash flows due to the decline from USD 140 price per barrel of crude oil to USD 35 per barrel. So, although the company faced a major challenge, under this changed general business environment, we were still able to raise over 1.5 billion in bank financing, due to the credibility of the company's management and its strategy. OMV Petrom has been recognized internationally, as well as nationally, for its corporate governance standards:

- Best Corporate Governance in Romania (World Finance, 2013);
- Most valuable company in Romania (ZF, 2007–2013);
- Most appreciated company in applying Corporate Governance (2011) — Romanian Brokers' Association (public's vote);
- Most convincing and coherent strategy in Romania (2010) — Euromoney survey.

2.1.2. Risk management framework

Another management challenge for the company and the Board, was to manage complex strategic and

---

[1] Return on Average Capital Employed.

operational risks and to develop a framework, process, and a reporting function in a company and in a country where the concept of risk management did not exist before 1989. In order to cope with the volatility and uncertainty of the global and European markets, but also to mitigate the business volatility factors, the company has spent a lot of efforts in identifying, assessing, reviewing impact on cash flows and mitigating strategic and operational risks. This approach has ensured a solid base for our successful results.

2.2. Integrating innovation and technology (owned and through partnerships)

This is the story of a transformation that has taken OMV Petrom, as an organization, 10 years to achieve, but this would not have been possible without having a very clear focus on technology and innovation. The company has built an innovative culture throughout the organization and an approach where we always try to better ourselves and to increase our performance compared to the previous year, by continuously improving technologies, processes, and operations. The company develops and runs operational excellence and idea management programs to increase our efficiency and reduce waste in our operations.

OMV Petrom invests substantially in training and developing our people, spending more than EUR 10 mn annually on the training budget and we also develop R&D partnerships with universities to raise the skills and capabilities of our staff and of our company to cope with the challenges of the new economy. We now focus on creating the right organizational context in order for our people to be able to reach their full potential and to have the flexibility to cope with change. The company realizes that it can no longer predict what set of skills and abilities will be required in the next era, everybody knows how volatile, how uncertain the future is, therefore what we want is more of a mental readiness of our people to cope with the change and adapt to the new realities.

OMV Petrom integrates innovation opportunities also through our strategic partnerships with reputable

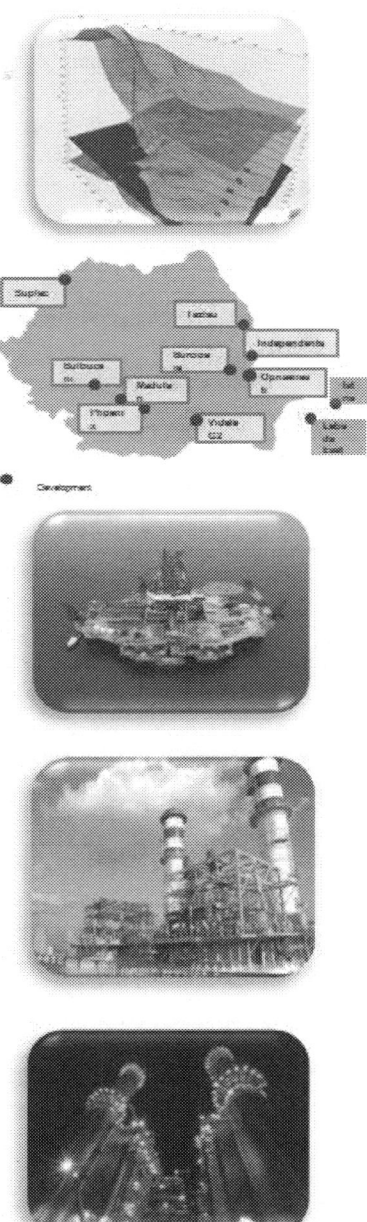

Fig. 2. Innovation and technology within OMV Petrom
Source: Created by the author.

international players: ExxonMobil, Hunt Oil, Repsol, Petrofac, PetroSantander, Expert Petroleum, in various onshore and offshore projects.

At the core of its operations, the company relies on values such as: Professionalism, Partnership, and Pioneering, and they represent our invigorated spirit and readiness to adapt to change.

OMV Petrom has a strong track record of integrating innovation and technology, owned and through partnerships:

- **World record in shallow horizontal drilling:** Suplacu de Barcau — mature oil field (NW Romania), on which the exploitation began in 1960 and supplies around 10% of Petrom's oil production.
- **Latest mature field technologies:** steam, polymer, water injections;
- A total of 11 field redevelopment projects in development phase aimed at maximizing ultimate recovery totaling: EUR 550 million investments.
- **Deep water drilling:** first exploration well in Neptun Deep successful, following largest 3D seismic program in the Romanian Black Sea, 1 billion to be spent before final reinvestment decision.
- **CCPP Brazi power plant, EUR 530 mn:** largest private Greenfield power generation project in Romania and the first of this size in the last 20 years;
- State-of-the-art, best available technical solutions in the field, energy efficient and flexible.
- **Petrobrazi refinery modernization:** Maximized integration value from conversion of Romanian crude only;
- 2010–2014 investments of EUR 600 mn.

2.3. Stakeholders engagement and performance culture

In the first years after the privatization, as OMV Petrom had embarked on its journey to increase performance, the initial focus has been on delivering results against stretched financial targets. But that was not enough, doing just what was required from a business and financial perspective does not build the differentiating factors in a company for the market place and for the community. So, in the next phase, the company focused on our pool of 1,100 managers, structured on six levels, as they constitute the driving engine of the business, cornerstone for building a solid organizational DNA that can take the company to the next level of development.

The company aimed to grow and develop a strong, diverse and sustainable local managerial base, with 60% of our top and executive levels being represented by Romanian managers, but also incorporated gender, age, and nationality diversity programs in our workforce strategy: 30% of our managers are women, although we are an industrial company; 28 nationalities work together in our headquarters: Petrom City, each bringing their own cultural and professional heritage, but together achieving the best results.

The company identified seven levers of intervention, which were structured into change management projects, through which the company was able to start building the Performance Culture within the organization:

(1) Developing a vision and focused strategy and communicating it to all managers and the organization;
(2) Streamline decision processes;
(3) Communicate successes, as well as learning from mistakes;
(4) Make people development objectives as important as business objectives;
(5) Performance management based on measurable KPIs;
(6) Talent Management programs;
(7) Close the gap between headquarters and territories, as our organization has 1,600 working points throughout the country.

The next dimension of the company's stakeholder engagement focus was translated in Resourcefulness — our concept of sustainability and responsible behavior. As an energy company administering natural resources, but also financial and human capital, we structure our approach to sustainability on three pillars: **Eco-Innovation, Eco-Efficiency,** and **Skills to Succeed** — volunteering and local community programs. OMV Petrom developed an online platform for the dialogue and programs dedicated to support the 340 local communities in which we operate. "Andrei's Country" is our online community, a collection of programs through which citizens can concretely redesign the life of their community through:

(1) **Ideas from Andrei's Country** — projects competition;
(2) **Andrei's School** — national yearly schools program and competition, including Andrei's Camp for the winning teams;

(3) **Made in Andrei's Country** — the first social business entrepreneurship program which attracted 500 project proposals, trained social entrepreneurs to build and implement business plans, and financed 10 of those projects.

More than EUR 5 mn overall financing has been granted in the four years of activity at this platform, over 2,500 projects were submitted and over 6,300 volunteers participated in community projects. What was extremely important to us were the projects with schools and students: over 25,000 pupils and 1,700 teachers learned about civic involvement, entrepreneurship, project management, and even business communication.

These results not only give the company the comfort to claim a license to operate in the communities where we work, but also an opportunity for Romania to convert into a high performing economy through the development of entrepreneurship, small businesses, and local communities. OMV Petrom has received many prizes in recognition of its efforts for constantly developing its people but also mobilizing and bringing along other stakeholders and communities and raising the competitiveness of our economy:

- Best online community in Europe — European Digital Awards, Berlin 2013;
- Best volunteer program — PR Daily's Corporate Social Responsibility Awards, USA 2013;
- Honorable mention for "Stakeholder engagement" — PR News CSR Awards, USA 2014.

3. Conclusions

It is obvious that we operate in an increasingly complex socio-economic context in which globalization conditions affect the activity of any company, fact that implies more and more knowledge of and alignment with the rules applicable at a global level. Basically, in order to become and remain competitive, it is required to take more and more into consideration the global climate in which we carry out our activities, without which we are doomed to self-isolation and low performance. Another fact worth mentioning is that the economic and financial crisis of the recent years has had a major impact over the developmental strategies of any company, especially over a company with a significant regional role like OMV Petrom.

It is inconceivable to promote a sustainable development strategy without considering the dialogue with the company's stakeholders which, depending on the specificity of business, are more or less complex. Promoting a knowledge-based economy requires actions that call for high organizational transparency and continuous dialogue with stakeholders, these being also dependent on the environment in which a company conducts its activity.

All these elements enforce any company to promote the principles of a sustainable development, and to permanently take into consideration its decisional process on the environment, the social, and the economic factors.

The development of any company is only viable if it uses the most precious resource it has, the human resource, especially by increasing the staff motivational activities. The focused case study of OMV Petrom reveals a number of lessons to be learned when it comes to the transformations it suffered, given the fact that it functioned in a transition economy. Therefore, in order to lead the transformation to a good direction, some actions were required, as follows:

— Identification of the organizational issues that were not aligned with market mechanisms requirements;
— Evaluation, in order to find out the best international industry practices, both at operational and at corporate functions level and establish the most appropriate actions and changes for implementing them;
— Focusing on operational efficiency, management, and corporate governance, as areas that suffered major changes, in order to support building a Performance mind-set in our management team and consolidate their commitment to excellence;
— Adopting measures to ensure the promotion of the principles and specific Business Ethics rules and to improve the corporate governance in general, according to international standards. Thus, this led to the achievement of a company based on a long term strategy, on the best management practices, on

clear procedures and mechanisms in order to adopt efficient and performance-oriented decisions;
— Assuring the transparency of implemented processes and their adequate communication, which led to national and international recognition of OMV Petrom for its corporate governance standards;
— Adopting a management and risk mitigation framework both at operational and strategic level, so that this approach allows the company to obtain successful results;
— Elaborating and implementing a well-defined program which allows innovation and modernization at organizational level. For this purpose, OMV Petrom invested significant amounts for training and developing its own employees, as well as through its strategic partnerships with reputable international players in various onshore and offshore projects;
— Constantly promoting a change in management aspects, in order to enable the company to build the Performance Culture within the organization;
— Permanently improving the dialogue with the communities in which the company operates, thus promoting the concept of a sustainable and responsible conduct. This way, the company became known and appreciated for the projects it promotes in relation to communities, in various areas such as: education, health, social business programs, and developing entrepreneurship, small businesses at local communities' level.

For final conclusions, it is safe to say one of the main lessons learnt from transforming a large corporation like OMV Petrom and all the work it has taken the company over the last 10 years is that large Corporate Boards need to focus towards managing more complex strategic risks, be more technologically wise, and focus more on its people and stakeholders' matters to adequately meet the challenges of the current markets and socio-economic and environmental changes.

At the same time, large organizations have a long term vocation and responsibility, having a strong impact on the social-economic indicators (such as economic growth, state budget contributions, jobs' creation, role models in the business environment, etc.). In addition, the corporate boards in Eastern Europe also have a role to bring their contribution to close the gap with the West and assist in the transformation of economies.

Studies show that those who take an active role in people development and in their communities tend to deliver higher capital returns. Large corporations are well placed to fulfill this role: they have significant research and innovation capabilities, a deep capacity to scale and mobilize, and a growing understanding of what it takes to build alliances across multiple stakeholders.

References

Clarke, T. & Rama, M. (2008), *Fundamentals of Corporate Governance*, London: Sage Publications.

Eccles, R., Ioannou, I., & Serafeim, G. (2012), *The Impact of Corporate Sustainability on Organizational Processes and Performance*, Cambridge: National Bureau of Economic Research Working Paper Series.

Global Corporate Governance Forum (2009), *Stakeholder Engagement and the Board: Integrating Best Governance Practices*, Washington: Focus 8.

Kluyver, C. (2010), *Fundamentals of Global Strategy. A Business Model Approach*, New York: Business Expert Press.

Rodriguez-Melo, A. & Mansouri, A. (2011), *Stakeholder Engagement: Defining Strategic Advantage for Sustainable Construction, Business Strategy and the Environment*.

Chapter 2

New Management Tendencies and Their Impact on the Form of Capitalism

Maria Negreponti-Delivanis

Docteur ès Sciences Economiques de la Sorbonne
University of Macedonia
Académie des Sciences de la Roumanie
Delivanis' Foundation

The chapter presents a new kind of hybrid company, which appeared and developed rapidly after 1980 and came to be known under the characteristic name of "distorporation". The main difference between this new form of companies and the traditional ones with limited liability is the treatment of the shareholders who are losing their old privileges. These privileges are assured only for a few among them, called oligarchs. But the most important change concerning the management of this new kind of companies is the fact that they do not keep any profit for investment, but distribute the whole to a few shareholders. As the profits are no longer channeled towards investment, the distorporation companies are trying to cover the need of financing thanks to their presence on the Stock Exchange and no longer thanks to the saving of small savers. No problem was encountered during the high phase of economic cycle, but the same was not true during recession. It is certainly clear that this new management is just trying to avoid taxes and it was very successful until now. However, the distorporation has negative results as it intensifies inequalities which have reached unacceptable levels everywhere, thus destabilizing modern economies, encouraging recession because of insufficient demand, weakening the welfare state, and disrupting social cohesion. The higher profits assured by those companies and the almost complete avoidance of taxation, lead to a rapid increase of their number as the political parties of both sides, republican and democratic show no interest in distorporation businesses.

1. Introduction

Simultaneously with the prevalence of globalization in the 1980s, mainly due to its combination with a fanatical form of neo-liberalism, which has been characterized by the author as "conspiratorial", a new form of business emerged in the US. It is a type of business known as distorporation, or hybrid enterprise, because of its peculiar structure but mainly, because of its unprecedented type of management. This kind of business, which developed rapidly after 1980, mainly in America, includes elements of traditional enterprises, such as the limited liability company, combined with important new additions, however, which are responsible for its generic title of distorporation. The spectacular growth of these firms since, which marginalized the presence and number of traditional companies with limited liability (MLP = master limited partnership), is the by-product of basic beliefs and extreme neo-liberal views. More specifically:

→ Taxation limits the freedom of individuals, with the consequence that institutions and measures aiming at reducing it or even eliminating it are favored.
→ The state is generally vicious and ineffective, contrary to the private sector, and therefore should refrain from any form of intervention in the economy.
→ Savage capitalism,[1] in spite of leading to disparities of uncontrollable extent and intensity, is nevertheless valuable for the US, because it ensures the conduct of innovations, which does not remain within the borders of America, but spreads across the globe.

These distorporations, which as we shall see, are closely related to tax havens and perhaps even to the new digital currency Bitcoin,[2] met the indifference of most politicians of both right and left wing parties. This lack of criticism as to the operation of distorporations, as well as to their significant macroeconomic implications, leaves the way open to their undoubtedly impressive expansion, which thus manages to essentially remain in the shade. In seeking possible interpretations of this political lack of involvement with distorporations, one could argue that their successful, up to now attempts to intertwine themselves with the respective governments, and conceal their objectives, contribute to leaving them untouched for the time being. Also, the fact that any sort of discussion about this business is very recent, and is possibly linked to the public debt problem which is obviously becoming worse due to the fact that distorporations are able to evade taxes.

I will structure my chapter around two main parts. In the first part, I will try to highlight the key features, particularly those differentiating distorporations from traditional enterprises. The second part of my chapter will attempt to identify the changes which distorporations are expected to conduct — or have already conducted — as to the mode of income and wealth distribution and the general form of capitalism now prevailing.

---
[1] Edsall (2013).
[2] Tabuchi (2014).

2. The Characteristics and Aspirations of Distorporations

The choice of the combination of characteristics, and the constant addition of new ones, if applicable, is directly linked to their aspirations, first and foremost of which is total tax evasion. Zero taxation, if possible. It is therefore not too extreme to argue that distorporations are only marginally legitimate and that their existence is ensured only through the allocation of significant monetary sums to lawyers, accountants, and even politicians, in an attempt to circumvent the law. The activities of these enterprises, encouraging and somehow legitimizing speculation are generally justified under well-known arguments such as the state regulation of businesses is time-consuming, bureaucratic, and exhaustive, and even that a high corporate tax discourages entrepreneurship.

Let us now briefly look at the distinguishing features of these distorporations:[3]

→ I would first like to mention that the defining feature and what distinguishes them from traditional enterprises is the total downgrading of the importance of shareholders in the management and decision-making of these new businesses. Indeed, in contrast to traditional enterprises, shareholders do not participate or participate minimally in the management, they have no voice, their demands are not met in general, their opinion is not taken into account, and they receive limited dividends.
→ The reduction of the importance of shareholders is mainly due to the different structure of distorporations, which in spite of maintaining the traditional element of limited liability partnership, nevertheless participate in the stock market. Their involvement in the stock market ensures, under certain competitive conditions, the ability to accumulate large investment funds. Thus, investment on the

---
[3] An important point to mention is that, due to the fact that the operation of distorporations remains in the shadows, there is no relevant literature. In fact, only one relevant article has been published citing the various views of a number of researchers on the subject, under the title of: 'Rise of the Distorporation' (2013), *The Economist* (October 26).

part of distorporations is no longer dependent on small scale investors.

→ Another, particularly important feature of distorporations is that they do not accumulate profits in order to invest them, but on the contrary, annually distribute the totality of their profits to their partners — not to all of them, but to a select few who constitute the "oligarchy". In this case, dividends are double or triple the size of the market average, they are not subject to regulations and controls and most importantly, are not subject to taxes. Tax avoidance is generally achieved, by representing dividends not as profits but as a return on capital.

The management of distorporations is almost omnipotent and has significantly more freedom of action in relation to traditional limited liability companies. But it would be wrong to assume that the management of these new businesses is totally unregulated. This is due to the fact that, as long as distorporations are under the obligation of distributing all of their profits, they are under the constant need of raising new funds for investment. These funds are the product of the distorporation's shares in the stock market and their price depends on what those doing businesses think of its performance. The goal is obviously raising the highest possible funds from the stock market, in relation to the dividends paid. As an example, it is estimated that in 2012, this new form of business paid out 10% of total dividends, but raised approximately 30% of equity in the stock market.[4]

Their ability to raise money from the stock market relies on the fact that these companies function as a kind of fund or banks, capable of attracting substantial amounts even when representing small firms. And because they are willing to take high risks, which existing regulations prevent banks from taking, they fulfill the desires of Americans and not only, as to the achievement of high returns. It is obvious that all these hybrid enterprises exhibit varying degrees of risk and returns. Some promise a minimum return, up to 19% in many cases. Hi-Crush f.i. promised a minimum payout of 11%, which eventually exceeded 28%.

Other similar businesses do not promise specific returns, but in some cases, such as the groups of Acon Investments and TPG Capital LLC, these may shoot up to 45%, or in other cases, drop below 13%. In spite of the differences inevitably existing among these companies, their return is on average 6%, i.e., three times higher than the corresponding market average which does not exceed 2%. The high returns of hybrid cooperatives represent the main reason why they are high in the preference of investors. Obviously, the danger lurking for these hybrid businesses is the difficulty of securing funds, especially apparent in periods of economic recession.

The expansion of distorporations has indeed been spectacular since 1980 and was at the expense of traditional limited liability corporations. It is estimated that their total value already exceeds USD 1 trn, while they represent 9% of companies listed in the stock exchange. Also, based on estimates — since, due to the complex structure of these businesses, it is quite hard to acquire official data on them — distorporations already represent 2/3 of new businesses[5] in the US. An additional indication of the rising importance of distorporations is the dramatic decline of traditional businesses, from 7,306 recorded in 1997 to only 1,369[6] today, precisely because of the rapid shift to new, non-traditional forms of business. According to other estimates,[7] the percentage of distorporations represents 23% of the total companies listed and 63% of total profits. The collective market-capitalization of MLPs now exceeds that of Exxon Mobil, the most highly valued energy company on the New York Stock Exchange.

The sectors, mainly incorporating this type of distorporations are primarily capital-intensive industries such as energy, which even during the great crisis of 2007 and up to now, managed to attract enormous funds. Another industry within which these new types of business have developed is real estate. The facilities of Walmart and New York Times, for example, belong to Real Estate Investment Funds.[8]

---

[4] Extract from 'Hot New Wall Street Investment', *Investment Management Review*, January 2013.

[5] According to estimates by Professor Rodney Chrisman, Liberty University School of Law.
[6] Based on the Vanguard index.
[7] Inland Revenue Service.
[8] *The Economist*, (October 26, 2013), *op cit*.

I believe that a partial conclusion of the first part of my chapter should be the realization of an essentially unpleasant truth concerning these new types of business. By this, I mean the realization that their existence is ensured through continuous efforts to circumvent the laws and rules that govern traditional businesses. Distorporations therefore, resort to an effort to conceal the details of their operation and their overall status through a number of complex and hard to understand details, making reporting them for illegal practices almost impossible. It is clear that, under these circumstances, distorporations operating on the margin between what is considered legitimate and illegitimate manage to remain afloat only thanks to their links with members of the respective governments, who take upon themselves to circumstantially regulate the legal framework of their operation.

3. The Effects of Distorporations on the Form of Capitalism

These major changes in the field of American business[9] and not only, as long as the US is the leading economy in the international arena and as such leads the way of change across the globe, result into numerous and complex consequences throughout the macroeconomic spectrum of individual national economies. In particular, it would be interesting to investigate the possible changes in the fields of income distribution, tax evasion, and the mutations which the form of capitalism itself seems to undergo.

3.1. *Distribution of income and wealth*

Following the establishment of globalization on earth, hand in hand with a fanatic form of neo-liberalism, there was a rapid deterioration of the mode of income distribution, with unprecedented inequalities of unimaginable scale. And while the neo-liberals have been trying to ease these sad developments through the endearing, but due to several reasons of unfounded argument that "what is important is the increase of income, not its distribution,"[10] the alarm is already ringing, even from where least expected, such as the annual Davos summit of 2013.[11] This is because the realization is dawning that the adverse effects of inequality are not confined to the social realm, but also pose a risk to the smooth functioning of the economy when they rise past a critical threshold. And, furthermore, these disparities exacerbate the problem of unemployment and underemployment, which thus appears even more threatening for the future, given the fact that according to estimates, 230 million staff posts in the US — and not only — representing an income of approximately USD 9 trillion, are expected to mutate downward, thus decimating the middle class.[12] The following overwhelming data show that this limit has long since been surpassed. These may be expressed through two essentially different approaches. The first is related to personal income distribution whose inequalities are measured by the well-known Gini indicators, and range from 0–1, while the second is related to the Cobb–Douglas function, representing the national income shares of labor and capital.

(a) Personal income distribution has witnessed crushing developments after the imposition of globalization and neo-liberalism, with 1% of the wealthiest people on earth controlling 45% of global wealth and 50% of the poorest people on earth having to share 1% of global wealth. Moreover, during the present crisis, the richest 1% of the world population has increased its average income by 31.4%. It is predicted that the rate of control of the global elite will grow further after the crisis. Specifically, according to a relevant survey, global wealth will grow at an annual rate equal to 4.8% over the next five years.[13] Another aspect of these uncontrollable disparities is expressed in the realization that the 400 wealthiest Americans possess greater wealth than the poorest, amounting to USD 150 mn. The 15% representing the poorest population segment, approximately 46 million people, belong to households earning less than USD 22,050 a year. In 2012, global wealth amounted to USD 135 trn. Around

---

[9] As briefly outlined in part I.
[10] Krugman (2013).
[11] L'édition 2014 du World Economic Forum de Davos débute cette semaine. Lauener (2013).
[12] Foroohar (2014).
[13] Boston Consulting Group.

1% of the wealthiest segment of the global population controls USD 52.8 trillion of this sum. Furthermore, the 100 richest people in the world increased their wealth by USD 212 billion in 2012. This unchecked increase in the wealth of the world's oligarchy, which is obviously reflected in the bankruptcy and impoverishment of large socio-economic groups, originates — as might be expected — mainly in the price rise of shares in the telecommunications sector. The assets of these 100 tycoons are estimated at USD 1.9 trillion. Before we leave the subject of these incredible disparities, let us also mention the following: on a global level, it has been estimated that 29 million people possess a wealth greater than USD 1 mn and they represent 0.6% of the world population. The total fortune of these few is therefore estimated at USD 87.5 trillion. Let us now consider those who could be defined as the sum of the wealthy of the world, i.e., those with assets between USD 100,000 and USD 1 mn. They are estimated to represent 7.5% of the world's adult population and to own 43.1% of global wealth. If we now continue adding the wealthy and millionaires, we will reach the really creepy conclusion according to which 8.1% of the world population dominates 82.4% of global wealth, while the remaining 92% of the world population is obliged to survive and be content with 18% of global wealth. Going further down, i.e., to the poor, who consist of more than 3 billion or 69.3% of the total adult population, with a fortune of USD 10,000, we are led to the horrifying conclusion that they must survive on just 3.3% of global wealth.[14] *The culmination of these disparities, condemned on all sides, has serious adverse effects on the global economy*, as I will mention in the following paragraphs. Also, the contribution of distorporations in creating these disparities is undeniable and constantly rising. The distortions of these businesses, which assure returns of up to 50%, do not affect all the partners, but only a small group of select few who contribute to the excessive concentration of wealth in very small numbers. *With the rapid pace at which distorporations displace traditional corporations, it should be considered certain that their influence will continue growing in the future.*

(b) The shares of labor and capital in national income, as expressed in the Cobb–Douglas function were considered as stable and non-changing up to 1980s, or else, up to the emergence of globalization and the developments that accompanied it. However, the substitution of the primary aim of economic science, which was the welfare of the individual, for an aggressive form of competitiveness, completely overturned the foundations of the Cobb–Douglas function, especially the assumption concerning the stability of the shares of the two major production factors — labor and capital — in national income. Thus, the share of labor in global GDP, as well as in the GDP of individual national economies has declined dramatically in favor of capital, especially financial capital. Based on International Monetary Fund (IMF) estimates,[15] the share of wages in the member countries of the G7 fell by 5.8% in the period 1983 to 2006, and more specifically by 8.8% in the member states of the EU,[16] by 9.3 points in France and 13[17] points in Greece, respectively. In 51 of the 73 countries for which statistical data were available, the share of wages has been declining over the last 20 years. The largest reduction in this share is witnessed in Latin America and the Caribbean (−13 points), followed by Asia and the Pacific (−10 points), while in the case of advanced economies this same study concludes that the reduction amounts to an average of 9 points. Rising unemployment which as I have been arguing for a long time[18] is quite deliberate, undoubtedly contributes significantly to this decline.

3.2. *Tax evasion*

Through the emergence, but especially with the dramatic growth of distorporations in the USA — and not only — are two very different categories of companies created: those that pay the legally prescribed corporate taxes, and those who systematically evade them. It is

---

[14] Bloomberg and Crédit Suisse.

[15] March 2008.
[16] Commission Européenne.
[17] 1995–2004, INE-Labor Institute ΓΣΕΕ-ΑΔΕΔΥ.
[18] Negreponti-Delivanis (1995).

clear that the very essence of competition is thus altered, both between firms operating within the same national market, but also internationally. Those not burdened with taxes are able to secure special privileges over traditional companies and compete unfairly at the expense of the latter. Their coexistence is only possible because of the fact that, for the time being, they are largely operating in different business areas. Furthermore, the tolerance of the American government towards distorporations can only be explained on the basis of the inherent dislike of neo-liberal views to the obligation of paying taxes. It can effortlessly be assumed that with the predominance of conservatives across the globe, minimal taxation would have prevailed, in the absence of the relentless problem of public debt.

Tax evasion on the part of distorporations, especially as the latter are rapidly replacing traditional companies, risks having — and may already have — a very negative impact on the operation and sustainability of the welfare state. It is an undeniable fact that the latter is being challenged and restricted on all sides, not just in the US, where it never adequately developed, in contrast to Europe, where *capitalism with a human face* was something to make it rightfully proud of.

The very probable prevalence of distorporations in the future — when and if the debt problem has been successfully addressed — will most likely result in the end of the welfare state and the return to Middle Ages societies.

3.3. *The mutation of capitalism*

Capitalism is undoubtedly undergoing dramatic changes in the last few decades, mainly under the influence of unprecedented measures which individual national governments consider — rightly or wrongly — that they are forced to impose in order to deal with the debt problem. To these we shall now have to add all those resulting from the gradual prevalence of distorporations, which we shall address in this section. First, the operation mode of distorporations and the special privileges they enjoy hinders accessibility to them, since this is only possible for the select few. However, the provision of no barriers to entry and exit of firms in the industry, is a *sine qua non* condition of free competition, which in turn is recognized as a cornerstone of capitalism and the free market. An *oligarchic* capitalism is thus established, which is not justified on the basis of higher qualifications on the part of the oligarchs, but rather on privileges secured largely thanks to their complex interrelations. Please note that the oligarchs of distorporations are not related to the respective oligarchs in Herodotus, who were tolerated because they were recognized as the best of all.[19] Another element of capitalist differentiation resulting from distorporations is the non-financing of corporations through profits, and the need to raise investment funds in the stock exchange. Numerous questions naturally arise such as where these profits are channeled, as long as they are not re-invested but paid out to the select few, as well as what are the consequences of raising extra funds in the stock market. The profits of distorporations thus acquire a speculative origin and non-productive disposal, as long as they are not channeled into productive uses but, most probably towards hoarding or tax havens. At the same time however, probably because of the network of complex interrelations in which they operate, distorporations manage to acquire additional investment funds, taking them away from other alternative uses, and thus, necessarily limiting the intensity of potential economic activity.

4. Conclusions

Opponents of state intervention in the economy argue that the creation and rapid growth of distorporations may have positive effects on the economy such as allowing capital to move where yields are higher, instead of remaining inactive in the form of retained earnings, as in the case of traditional businesses. This feature appears as the most attractive of all those defining the American model and enabling it to be productive and innovative. However, the extensive interplay between business and government in question, which seems to form the foundations of the distorporate system, results in far-reaching phenomena of corruption, which are formalized and explain many of the problems of modern economies. Moreover, distorporations intensify inequalities which have reached unacceptable levels everywhere, and which destabilize modern economies, are at the root of the second Great Depression, as in that of 1929,[20] encourage recession because of insufficient demand,

---

[19] Kemp (2011).
[20] Negreponti-Delivanis (2008).

weaken the welfare state, and disrupt social cohesion. Any weak and uncertain positive consequences of distorporations however, are only visible when addressed in a fragmentary manner and not as developments of the economy as a whole, which is being robbed of the public sector. No type of economy however can function in a fair way if deprived of the cooperation and complementarities between private and public sector.

References

Edsall, T. B. (2013), Why can't America be Sweden opiniator, 19/5 (based on a paper by Daron Acemoglu "We cannot all be like the Nordics," declaring, in a 2012 "Choosing Your Own Capitalism in a Globalized World".

Foroohar, R. (2014), Time to talk about I World-Inequality isn't just a social issue-it's putting the future of the world economy in peril, *Time* 10/2.

Kemp, H. (2011), *L'Oligarchie ça Suffit, Vive l'Oligarchie*, p. 46, Paris: Seuil.

Krugman, P. (2013), Why inequality matters, *International New York Times* (December 17).

Lauener, P. (2013), La question des inégalités sera au cœur du prochain Forum économique mondial de Davos qui se déroule du 22 au 25 janvier, *Reuters*.

Negreponti-Delivanis, M. (1995), *Chômage-Un Faux Problème*, Thessaloniki: Editions Sakkoulas (in Greek).

Negreponti-Delivanis, M. (2002), *Globalisation Conspiratrice*, Paris: L'Harmattan (in Greek), and *Mondializarea Conspiratoare*, Bucurest: Editura Eficient (in Romanian).

Negreponti-Delivanis, M. (2008), *The Lethal Crisis*, F. Delivanis and Livanis (eds.) (in Greek), also electronic publication in Lulu.

Tabuchi, H. (2014), Collapse of Bitcoin exchange brings both hope and caution, *International New York Times* (February 27).

Chapter 3

Trends and Developments of Diversity Management at the Global Level

Stegăroiu Ion, Mubeen Ştefania and Istrate Ciprian

Valahia University of Targoviste

Lile Ramona

"Aurel Vlaicu" University of Arad

Diversity management has become a necessity in this era of knowledge. This chapter attempts to capture which are the global developments in this area. We will highlight the changes taking place in an organization from the perspective of several reasons, namely: respecting the law, ethics, the need for proximity to consumer (client), the need to create a climate of innovation and creativity in organizations, the need of change, not least the organizational performance. All these aspects will be analyzed from the perspective of 2020 strategy.

1. Introduction

The report "Trends and Developments of Diversity Management at the Global Level" is the point of view, intentionally speaking, of a research team from the Centre for Applied Scientific Research in the Field of Management and Marketing" (CASRMM) — "Valahia" University of Targoviste that has proposed to itself to make a more extensive research referring to the dimension, diversity of human resource management. It has been identified a causal relationship between diversity and organizational performance.

The report outlines the structure of the scientific approach:

- ➔ A — presentation of the European context of achieving the scientific approach;
- ➔ B — identification of the main categories of diversity and the way how the integration of personnel is made in an organization;
- ➔ C — determine the impact of diversity on human resource management by emphasizing its strategic dimension: recognizing diversity and cultural dimension (universal values and local values);
- ➔ D — framing priority directions of action from the perspective of social responsibility of the organization and establishing the strategies of diversity management.

2. Research Methodology

The scientific approach is conducted in the context of the 2020 Strategy, in the idea that we want to make a comparison between how the diversity is perceived in Romania and most of the other European Union (EU) member states.

The study will identify the contribution of organizations to create a smart, sustainable, and inclusive growth. The objective is to obtain a high level of labor employment, productivity, and social cohesion.

Research method: sociological survey based on questionnaire; the analysis based on scores studied population:

→ 67 superior managers and 904 middle managers
→ Sample size — 971.
→ Number of organizations — 25 multinational firms from Region 3 South-Muntenia.
→ Epistemological positioning: positivist current, constructivist current.

Achieving the aimed scientific approach involves the dichotomy (exploration and test), to justify the steps that have to be taken in the reasoning that must be adopted:

— **The first one**, of inductive type and/or abductive. Inductive, in this case, refers to a circumstantial analysis, that means an analysis through which are identified and observed the facts from the environment under review. The exploration of the complex context occurs, setting as objective the proposal of new valid and strong theoretical conceptualizations, developed in a rigorous way (Thiétart, 2007: 61). They speak about an approach in four directions:

- From particular to general;
- From facts to law;
- From the effect to the cause;
- From consequence to principles.

— **The second one**, of abductive type, that allows the researcher in management, using the analogy or metaphor, to form a judgement based on probable inference that establishes similarities between facts and processes that lead to the formulation of generalizations in the efforts of finding optimal solutions for achieving some objectives (Delattre & Thellier, 1979). Abduction is the making of observations on circumstances that agree to test the working hypotheses and making the actual scientific research. (König, 1993: 7). In order to raise the qualitative level of the research, the use of the metaphor

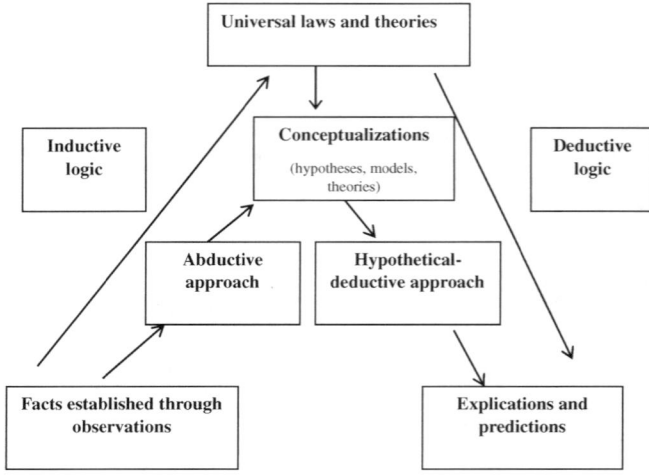

Fig. 1. Ways of judgement and scientific knowledge
Source: Chalmars (2007).

becomes, even, a necessity. This approach consists in describing a fact or phenomenon in the terms of another, highlighting the similarities and differences that will be the basis of some relevant conclusions. The use of the metaphor in management science allows the analysis of the organization in all its complexity through the decoding of all its components. The metaphor is seen as an effective tool raised at the level of research device: a machine, a body, a brain, and a culture (Morgan, 1990).

The aim is to achieve a scientific complementarity, the synthesis being presented as in Fig. 1.

3. Results and Discussions

3.1. *Identification of main diversity categories*

In an increasingly globalized world and in an expanding era of knowledge getting organizational performance is part of quite a difficult approach for an enterprise. The questions we ask ourselves are: What do we have to do in order to perform?, what are the factors that must be taken into account? In this sense the report presents, actually a scenario that has set itself as objective of the approach of getting organizational performance from the perspective of perceiving diversity by the employees of an organization.

Thus, the main categories of diversity have been identified: diversity of ages; diversity of ethnic origins; diversity of health; religious diversity; diversity of sexual orientations; diversity of formal levels; diversity of clients; diversity of involved parties; diversity of jobs.

By diversity we understand what distinguishes one individual from another, one community from another, which means the differences of identity such as: age, sex, ethnicity, health status, education, and religion, etc.

The concept of diversity, from the point of view of managerial practice, is associated with the concept of integration which reflects the approach of implementation of diversity and the approach of getting organizational performance. This means creating a sense of value, respect, and commitment that represent the content of valorization, respect, commitment (VRC) paradigm.

3.2. *The impact of diversity on human resource management*

The impact of diversity on human resource management is approached from a double perspective:

→ Recognizing diversity as experiments of solidarity, as an argument of equality, and freedom in an organization.
→ Of the cultural dimension of diversity by identifying universal values (human rights) and local values shared by members of the organization (trust, recognition, self-esteem, social integration, reciprocity, etc.).

The impact of diversity on human resource management means respecting, in the organization, some principles such as:

→ The principle of mutualism;
→ The principle of collaboration between all the employees;
→ The principle of listening to the employees.

The assessment of the impact of diversity on management is materialized in the following priority actions that can be undertaken in the organization:

→ Elaborating a charter of diversity;
→ Elaborating diversity politics;
→ Insuring an organizational environment favorable to the development of work under mutual respect conditions.

3.3. *Classification of the priority directions of action from the perspective of social responsibility of the organization*

Classification of the priority directions of action from the perspective of social responsibility of the organization becomes a necessity for establishing the strategies of improving the management of diversity in an organization. The achievement of this objective is based on the fundamental question: Why the management of diversity? The answer for this question is rooted in the changes that took place in contemporary society, that means what it is today and where we are going in terms of an uncertain future for the safety of individuals. The following aspects will be taken into consideration:

→ The demographic and composition changes of labor market with impact on the organization;
→ The changes in the structure of society and in family structures. In Romania there is a latent demographic crisis;
→ The changes in the assembly of the needs, desires and expectations of the people, and the implications in the organizational behavior.

Developing a strategy to improve the management of diversity means knowing how it should be promoted from the perspective of several aspects:

→ Of the variety of behaviors in an organization that, many times, leads to differentiation and induces a specific manner of valuation of all involved parties;
→ Of practicing a flexible management by the organization that must keep awake the feeling of integration and motivation of the employees within an organization from the perspective of optimal balance between their interests and the interests of the organization;
→ Of the organizational culture, by promoting these values shared by all of them, values that generate innovation and creativity;

→ Of the professional development through promoting efficient and competent policies of personnel by the organization.

All these issues will be the four major themes of achieving the scientific approach proposed.

Another issue is the wage in terms of expression "from equal to equity pay" and has become a general principle in labor law. Equality must be understood in terms of a program of measures, increasingly more complex and complete that allows correction of inequalities.

First, equal pay is not equal work equally paid. Equal pay must be ensured by equal qualifications:

→ Between men and women;
→ Between employees with permanent contract and fixed-term employees;
→ Between fulltime employees and employees' part-time proportion to the time worked.

Secondly, appears the issue of the non-discrimination regarding union membership and strike.

Thirdly, the labor of "equal value, equal pay". This refers to the production of inequality due to disability age.

EU labor codes provide a hierarchical level identity (classification, responsibility) and similar importance in the functioning of the company, any work involving load capacity and is a nervous comparable identical, if we talk about a work of equal value.

In this area we can draw payroll conclusions

→ The need to establish a trend of transition from logic of equality of payment inter-categorical equal treatment;
→ The equal opportunities and actions that target a potential group discriminated against, like between male–female equality, integration of people with disabilities, seniors, and taking account of the origins of social, ethnic, and geographic entity;
→ Doing a very fine segmentation of employees (each person in part) based on the peculiarities of labor (autonomy, responsibility) and taking care of the compliance of requirements on constraints, schedules etc.;

→ Human resource management should focus on managing that singularity of every employee is treated in all the characteristics.

There are four criteria that must be taken into account (Peretti, 2012: 130)

→ Identify some situations when professional knowledge are required for a particular function, title, degree, or professional practice;
→ Identify the situations when the capabilities are required for the performance of certain functions, capabilities arising from the experience gained over time;
→ Identify professional responsibilities;
→ Evaluation of candidates' physical load or nerve arising from the exercise.

These criteria may be supplemented by two: seniority and level of study. Differences result from work-related goals made, professional experiential, level of responsibility, possession of a proper workstation requirements, and actual responsibilities.

Case study 1

Creation of social networks

— The usefulness of professional networks and women's access to networks;
— The need for feminine social networks;
— Creating internal and external networks by increasing the access of women.

Case study 2

Proposals to promote policies of social dialogue

— Regulations in the EU;
— Proposal for national agreement on inter-professional diversity.

Case study 3

Study regarding recruitment

— Identify the multiplicity of possible attitudes on diversity;
— Confronting the candidates' abilities with the exigencies of the organization;

— Identify the obstacles to increasing the quality of development;
— Evaluation of the risk of conflict of interests;
— Ethical issues regarding the recruiter;
— Aspects regarding the management of diversity and recruitment.

Multidisciplinary Design Optimization (MDO) is based on the idea that the recruitment process is the one that provides an identical tool for all the individuals in the group, that there are guidelines and identical behaviors. It aims to strengthen the visibility of the organization and its impact on the labor market. It is determined from the following principles:

— Professional treatment of the candidates;
— Preparing the recruiters for the meeting with the candidates;
— The candidate receiving a report on the organization;
— Presentation and representation of the organization by the recruiter.

> **The fundamental principle = a uniform ethics for all the candidates from all recruiters**

The main stages of achieving the recruitment process are:

— Identifying the vacant positions;
— Attracting and managing applications;
— Assessment of the candidates;
— Selecting and making proposals; and
— Employment.

The scientific research will conclude with guide of good practices of diversity in an organization that will allow the realization of an efficient management of human resource within it.

The guide of good practices will be designed on three dimensions: professional equality (gender), age, disability, cultural differences.

> **Diversity management must be, above all, a management of the people**

4. Conclusions

The scientific research will materialize in a model of organizational diversity (MOD) whose implementation will allow the 25 multinationals from the Region 3 South-Muntenia to promote the principle of non-discrimination in all departments of human resource management (recruitment, training, advancement, promotion). We will have to find answers to several questions: What is the current situation in the field of diversity? To what extent are the enterprises prepared in this area? The two major dimensions that will be taken into account in the design of MOD are: the establishment of a variable equality of chances within the organization (from diversity to equal opportunities, making a social organizational balance that generates economic performance); taking pragmatic measures to facilitate the integration and management of differences (using the reporting indicators); communication and awareness of stakeholders in order to reach the highest level of social responsibility of the organization and association of managers in this approach is more than necessary; professional training is considered a key factor given the fact that the population of target enterprises is, in proportion of 62% under 40 years, 36% having medium education and knowing the fact that, often university graduates leave with qualifications and skills that are not relevant on labor market.

Achieving performance in diversity management represents a way through which the organization achieves its set goals referring to: the need to respect the legal frame, ethical exigency, the need for proximity to consumers, encouraging innovation and creativity, diversity as factor of change.

Therefore, results the necessity in the organization to create a pro-diversity system of piloting capable and ensuring the promotion of integration, coordination, motivation, and conflict management strategies. The final conclusion that can be drawn is "diversity becomes a managerial tool in achieving performance of the organization".

An enterprise can develop sustainably only by practicing an effective management (a balanced management of economic and social performances) and taking into account the needs and aspirations, sometimes contradictory, of all the stakeholders (customers, employees, shareholders, suppliers, civil society, environment).

Now the enterprise, assuming responsibility in the field of human resources and practicing a discretionary commitment to freedom, carries two main types of action (Peretti, 2012: 141).

- Cross-cutting actions involving all employees and focus on business processes and practices, like:
    — Securing and adapting HR processes (recruitment, assessment career, development, remuneration);
    — Training and awareness (managers, human resources, partners, not involved parties);
    — Communication throughout the all approach;
    — Encouraging social dialogue regarding diversity;
- Implementation of cross-cutting measures (marketing, purchases).

References

Baranga, L. (2013), *The Social Responsibility of the Organization*, Târgoviște: Bibliotheca Publishing.

Burlea Schiopoiu, A. (2007), *The Communications Process in Virtual Teams, Economics Informatics*, Paris: Senil.

Chalmars, A. (1987), *What is Science*, Paris: La Decouverte.

Delattre, P. & Théllier, M. (1979), *Development and Justification of Models*, Paris: Maloine.

Delmas Marty, M. (2010), Liberty and security in a dangerous world, toward a community of values.

Gavard-Perret, M.-L. *et al.* (2008), *Research Methodology*, Paris: Pearson Education.

Gravitz, M. (1996), *Methods of Social Science* (10th edn.), Paris: Précis Dalloz.

König, G. Production of knowledge and constitution of organizational practices, *Revue de Gestion des Ressources Humaines*.

Martis, D. & Sorescu, I. (2008), How do we promote diversity management in the organization, CPE.

Morgan, G. (1986), *Images of Organization*, Beverly Hills: Sage Publications, translated into French, *Images de l'Organisation*, Québec: Presse de l'Université de Laval, 1990.

Novethic (2006), *Diversity: Ethnic Statistics Remain a Sensitive Topic*, Paris:

Pauget, J. (2010), *Integrate and Manage the Y Generation*, Vuibert.

Peretti, J. M. (2006), *Richness of Diversity*, Vuibert.

Peretti, J. M. (2012), *The Encyclopaedia of Diversity*, Paris: EMS Edition.

Rojot, J. (2005), *The Theory of Organizations*, Paris: SSKA Edition.

Thiétart, R. A. (2007), *Methods and Research in Management*, Paris: Dunod.

Vagu, P. & Stegăroiu, I. (2007), *Motivation at Work*, Târgoviște: Bibliotheca Publishing.

x x x — The RBC Strategy in Diversity 2002–2015.

Chapter 4

Corporate Social Responsibility or Corporate Sustainability of Romanian Enterprises?*

Zaiț Dumitru, Onea Angelica, Tătărușanu Maria and Ciulu Ruxandra

"Alexandru Ioan Cuza" University of Iași

The purpose of this chapter is to identify the relationship and the differences between the concepts of corporate social responsibility (CSR) and corporate sustainability (CS), as well as the manner in which they are applied in the practice of Romanian enterprises. The approach is based on the extensive literature in the field and on the perceived insufficient cohesion and correlation between the two concepts. For this purpose, we used a methodology that includes qualitative methods, such as the critical analysis of Romanian and international literature on the topic, syntheses by various authors and abstraction. Results can be used by organizations and by people interested in understanding the interconnections between the two manners of expressing the concern for obtaining increased performance (corporate social responsibility [CSR] and corporate sustainability [CS]) in certain fields (social, economic, environmental) in order to ensure the development and even survival of Romanian enterprises in the long term.

---

*This research was conducted within the activities related to the project "Sustainable development, social responsibility, organizational culture and performance", Cooperation project Wallonia-Brussels/Romania 2012–2014, Reference WBI: GL/AS/CAS/SOR/2012/70098.

1. Introduction

The theme of corporate responsibility towards the environment, community, employees, society as a whole has had a major impact in the economic literature in the past few years, even if the first concerns appeared in ancient times (Wilson, 2003). As "social responsibility" it was approached almost 100 years ago, became an area of interest about 50 years ago. It has even become fashionable in the past 20 years, not to mention compulsory for big companies in India (*The Economic Times*, 2014). Arguments for a behavior which would take into account the interests of other people/institutions affected by company actions reside in a few philosophical theories (Wilson, 2003). Therefore, *the social contract theory* states that companies engage in contracts with other members of the society and receive resources, societal approval for operating in exchange of good behavior. The *social justice theory* takes into account the needs of all members of a society in order to build a fair society. At corporate level, it relies on equitable allocation of resources and results. *The rights theory*, considered as source of the corporate responsibility concept, is focused on human rights and property rights, the latter always coming in second place. When applied in the field of corporate responsibility, we note that, when companies base their actions on property rights (shareholders), they must take into account other stakeholder rights (local community, employees, etc.), which rank first. The deontological theory is based on the belief that everyone, including corporations, has the moral duty of treating others respectfully, to listen, and to observe their needs.

Many terms have been used to define ethic company responsibilities in relation with their environment, but some of the most successful ones in the past few years have been CSR and CS. Other terms refer to sustainable development (SD), durability, but these are used in relation with the general model of development at society level and with a way of approaching business on the long-term, a new paradigm of social and economic development.

In the current chapter, we synthesized the literature in the field of corporate responsibility, we tried to clarify the terms and the relation among them, but we also analyzed the way in which Romanian companies interpret and apply the concepts, starting from a study performed on three representative companies from three different sectors in Romania.

2. What About CSR?

Literature on CSR is extensive and highly fragmented. A large number of authors around the world have been trying to clarify concepts such as CSR, CS, or SD. Carroll's work (1979, 1983, 1991, 1999) on CSR is often cited (Sabadoz, 2011; Wang, 2011; Hediger, 2010; Garriga & Mele, 2004) and has become a benchmark in this field, Carroll being considered as one of the most prestigious specialists in the field of CSR (Garriga & Mele, 2004). In 1983, Carroll stated that CSR is composed of the four parts largely used nowadays: economic, legal, ethical, and voluntary or philanthropic, while, in 1984, Drucker made it very clear that organizations need to convert social responsibilities into business opportunities (Drucker, 1984).

One of the definitions provided by official bodies, such as the European Commission (2006) is highly referred to. The European Commission regards Corporate Responsibility as 'a concept whereby companies integrate social and environmental concerns in their business operations and in their interaction with their stakeholders on a voluntary basis' (European Commission, 2006). It becomes of interest to analyze the effect of making CSR compulsory in India for large companies and, basically, eliminating the 'voluntary' approach of CSR. More recently, Aguinis (2011: 855) states that CSR is about "context-specific organizational actions and policies that take into account stakeholders' expectations and the triple bottom line of economic, social, and environmental performance." Regardless of definitions and various approaches towards CSR, the concept is a reality of everyday life in most organizations worldwide and, moreover, Carroll (1999: 292) believes that it "has a bright future because at its core, it addresses and captures the most important concerns of the public regarding business and society relationships".

3. CSR or CS: Together, but Separate

Wilson (2003) proves that CS takes over a few elements which belong to different concepts: SD, CSR, stakeholder theory, and corporate accountability theory. According to the same author, CS can be seen as a new paradigm of corporate management, a counterpart to the traditional model of growth and profit maximization. He proves that CS acknowledges the importance of profit and growth, but requires taking into consideration other objectives (social, linked to SD — environmental protection, social justice, equitableness, and economic development). The author performs a synthesis for the evolution of the concept from the point of view of fields involved and sources where different concepts evolved (Fig. 1).

The relationship CS–CSR is also analyzed, especially from the point of view of SD: if the need for SD is accepted, then companies have the ethical duty to act for this purpose. The author proves that the CSR concept is based on philosophy and morals, sources that generated responsible corporate behaviors towards the society where they operate and obtain profits. Wilson defines CSR as a broad concept, which 'deals with the role of the business in the society' (Wilson, 2003), being focused rather on how much companies should take into account societal needs than on debating if they should or not have this duty.

Lately, the terms of CSR, CS, and SD have been present in the literature, as well as in actions considered imperative by international organizations and governments. Basically, SD has become a need: nowadays, businesses must take into account the need to contribute to ensuring the reach of long-term ecologic balance (from resource point of view), economic balance, international organizations objectives working for economic development (that refer to reduction of poverty, involving local communities into company activity), while simultaneously observing objectives of economic growth and long-term company development.

Nowadays, CS is intermingled with CSR or includes CSR elements, being distinguished only based on the fact that any corporation needs to behave responsibly towards its environment. At European level, there is the same substitution of CSR and CS. The CSR definition (European Commission, 2006) accentuates the voluntary action of companies and the willingness to contribute to solving social and environmental issues, as well as taking into account other stakeholders. In 2011, the European Commission redefined CSR and showed that ~CSR is increasingly important to the competitiveness of enterprises. It can bring benefits in terms of risk management, cost savings, access to capital, customer relationships, human resource management, and innovation capacity (EC, 2011). In this approach, CSR is a means of supporting SD objectives of the EU, especially connected to the need to improve competitiveness, while solving issues that affect economy and society as a whole (unemployment, environmental pollution, need of social cohesion). Companies should create a process to integrate social, environmental, ethical, as well as human rights and consumer rights aspects into their business operations and global strategy, closely linked to their stakeholders (EC, 2011).

4. CSR and CS in Romania

In our attempt to distinguish between CSR and CS, we generally noted that Romanian authors adopt or adapt the concepts present in the international literature. Therefore, our purpose is to extract the meaning they provide for the concepts, relying more on the context, on the manner of approaching the topic rather than on their definitions.

Inspired by European documents and foreign literature, Romanian authors (Stancu & Orzan, 2007; Dinu, 2011; Borțun et al., 2011; Vintilă et al., 2012; Barbu et al., 2011; Hristea, 2011; Mihăilă, op cit.; Dobrea, 2006) present the CSR concept in a similar manner with the one provided by the European Commission (2006). Still, there is a focus on multidimensional definitions of CSR, somehow neglecting those based on social marketing by accentuating economic, legal, ethical, and philanthropic responsibilities. The dimensions of

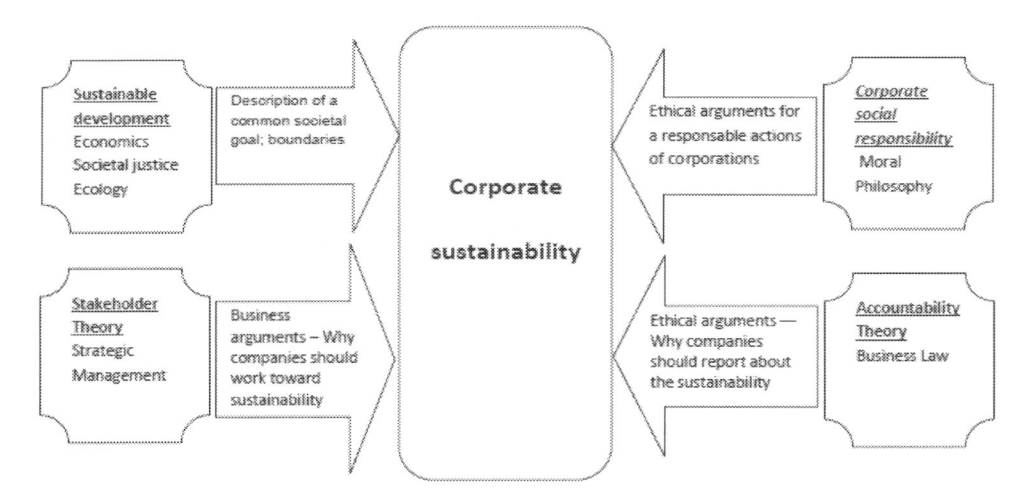

Fig. 1. Sources of CS concept
Source: Adapted after Wilson (2003).

the CSR in the Romanian literature, based on the international literature in the field are Stancu & Orzan, 2007; Covaş & Braguţa, 2009; Dinu, 2011; Hristea, 2011; Barbu et al., 2011; Mihăilă, op cit.; Dobrea, 2006):

→ CSR issues refer to community problems and environmental problems;
→ CSR involves integrating elements into the business strategy and operations; it is not a separate component, but one which is created by appropriate integration at each organizational level;
→ CSR is displayed through voluntary actions;
→ CSR takes into account the stakeholders;
→ CSR involves harmonizing company activity with social values by bringing together economic, social, and environmental interests;
→ CSR is not confounded with philanthropy, involving strategies which lead to gains for all stakeholders;
→ CSR measures several types of results: financial, social, environmental;
→ CSR is defined by transparency;
→ CSR's purpose is to be successful in business while being socially responsible and positively impacting on society; through CSR, companies go beyond legal requirements, being sensitive to social needs.

Also, we notice the association of CSR with long-term orientation of the company (Gănescu, 2012; Hristea, 2011; Stancu & Orzan, 2007, etc.). Therefore, they suggest that through permanent CSR actions there can be reached SD of the company (see Fig. 2), the point where some authors confound CSR to CS and they do not obviously distinguish them. Benefits presented by the authors (good relations with the community, influencing target audience, image improvement, better positioning, consumer fidelity, employee motivation, etc. — Toma, 2006) seen as CSR effects on the long-term confirm the idea that CS is seen rather as an advanced phase of CS or as strategic and long-term activity (Cristiana et al., 2011). Other authors simply present that, in the international literature, the terms CSR and CS have a rather similar meaning (Barbu et al., 2011, Gănescu, 2012). Also, Romanian authors fully understand that CSR can provide financial benefits and that it can be used as an instrument for strategic marketing, having multiple roles and objectives (Dobrea, 2006).

The CS terms is rather seldom used by Romanian authors, who generally associate and analyze the CSR–SD relationship or the CSR–corporate governance relationship. The CS content seems frequently equivalent to SD by means of translation, some authors omitting to define the level of analysis (micro or macro), which is why we will also analyze the SD meaning in the Romanian literature. For example, according to the European Commission (apud Borţun, 2011) SD refers to meeting society needs by honoring the natural environment and without jeopardizing the needs of future generations. On the other hand, CS refers to applying business strategies and performing activities that refer to the current needs of the organization and its

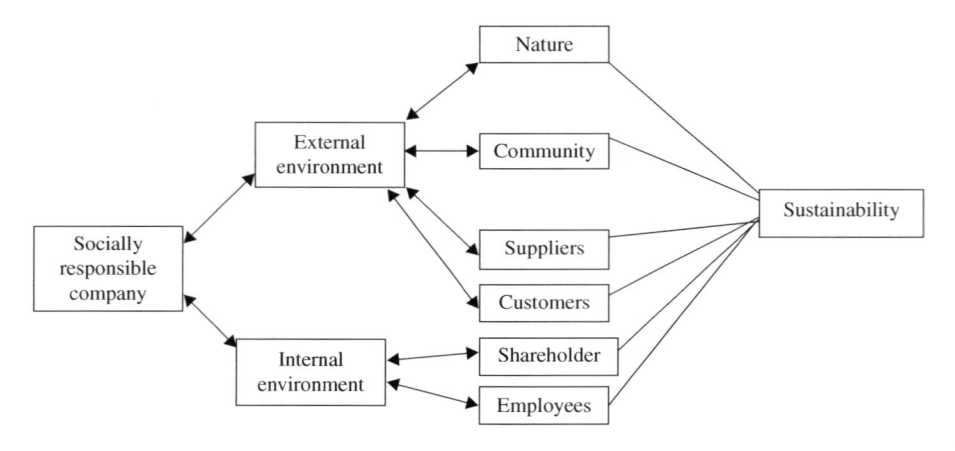

Fig. 2. Interaction between a responsible company and the environment
Source: Hristea (2011).

stakeholders, while protecting human resources and natural resources needed in the future (International Institute for Sustainable Development, 1992 *apud* Gănescu, 2012). These definitions are undertaken and do not clearly describe differences, even though the context created by the authors is rather clear. We also notice that, in most works of Romanian authors, SD is focused on environmental issues (Bejan & Rusu, 2007; Ștefănescu & Coturbaș, 2009; Manoleli, 2000). This can also be due to its dual character, *anthropocentric* (humans survival, continuous development of human kind, intergenerational equitableness) and *biospheric* (preserving the biosphere). The vision for the concept being influenced by the focus on one aspect or on the overall vision, which results also from one SD definition: development of a society which does not push the limits of the biosphere and does not destroy the natural basis of human life reproduction (Danilov-Dănilean *apud* Rusandu, 2008). Also, we notice that ecological systems are regarded as life support system, thereby the importance of their protection. Another explanation is linked to the SD vision: economical (at global level) or ecological. The integrative meaning of SD is interesting, being understood as future form of co-evolutionary interaction of nature and society, which ensures their mutual existence (Rusandu, 2008). Where CS appears, it has either a connotation closer to the responsibility towards the environment, focusing moreover on the impact of company actions on the environment (while CSR is focused on the social aspects) or it is seen as an advanced stage of CSR (as in Fig. 2). Therefore, authors do not distinguish CSR and CS, CS being the purpose of the CSR actions (Hristea, 2011, Barbu et al., 2011). Also, we encounter the vision that CS is a corporate approach to SD (Gănescu, 2012).

We can distinguish between CSR, CS, and SD based on the stakeholder categories involved (Werther & Chandler *apud* Borțun, 2011): organizational (employees, managers, shareholders, unions); economic (customers, lenders, distributors, suppliers); social (communities, government, other organisms, not-for-profit organizations, environment). If CSR and CS appear to be linked rather to the first two categories of stakeholders (micro level or micro–macro, connecting the micro and macro levels), SD is more about the third category.

5. CSR and CS Applied to Romanian Enterprises

Hesitations or divergent opinions concerning the meaning of different concepts presented in the literature or in established research in the field almost naturally relate to the activity of the Romanian enterprises nowadays. Still, there are significant differences between enterprises and the most obvious ones seem to distinguish current approaches and practices in those organizations based on their experience in the field, their field of activity, as well as the national or international coverage of their activities. Next to these three main variables, the profile of the top managers is always an essential element, providing or even imposing the position towards CSR, CS, or SD. In order to test the connection between the three main variables and the position of the enterprise towards the three concepts, as well as the manner of putting them into practice, we used the same three enterprises included in a previous study concerning the CSR–performance relationship in Romania.[1] We maintained their symbols for this study: A for the pharmaceutical company; B for the metallurgical company; and C for the textile company. The three enterprises meet the requirements imposed in the selection: belonging to different sectors of activity, their experience in the field and the extent of their activities. Moreover, the three can be significantly differentiated through the profiles of their main managers.

To identify the positions of the three enterprises and their management concerning their approach and the specific actions towards the three concepts we performed in-depth interviews based on a special guide, conceived and applied during a period of six months through direct meetings with a total number of eight top managers (at least two from each company). Generally, the dominant positions identified during the interviews outlined an accentuated preference for the CSR concept, while the other two concepts were rather present in their comments, without outlining or identifying potential differences in any way. This is the reason why we felt the need to resume the synthetic table from our earlier chapter, a table expressing the position of the

---
[1] See Zaiț et al. (2013).

managers towards CSR (see Table 1). Therefore, we have a rather clear image about what those managers consider to be CSR.

In order to identify the dominating aspects regarding the three concepts for the three companies, we deductively separated the corresponding elements from Table 1, according to the definitions of CSR, CS, and SD (see Chapters 1 to 3). We systemized the specific aspects of CSR, CS, and SD into Table 2. In our attempt to distinguish between specific actions and practices, we delimited based on micro and macro-economic traits, as well as strategic and operational actions, that the interviewees identified in their answers or comments.

As we can notice, even based on our potentially subjective analysis, the aspects related to CS can be identified as following:

→ Company A, a Romanian company, is concerned mainly by social responsibility towards the community, missing the connection with the benefits it may record from increasing CS based on CSR actions. At least for the moment, the company sees

Table 1. The synthesis of positioning towards CSR

	Enterprise A	Enterprise B	Enterprise C	Observations
Employees	Recruitment, selection, training, health and security, performance Explicit (productivity increase)	Training, recruitment, security and protection Explicit (productivity increase)	Encouragement, rewards, special interest Explicit (productivity increase)	Explicit positioning — productivity increase
Natural environment	Integrated management system, waste collection, reducing polluting factors Explicit (cost reduction, revenue increase)	Anti-pollution investments, using forms of renewable energy Explicit (cost reduction)	Regulations, cost reduction Implicit (cost reduction, customer satisfaction)	Dominantly explicit (cost reduction, revenue increase)
Community	Charity, philanthropy, image Low impact	Help, support for local development, involvement in education Explicit (formation facilities, mentality change, diminished losses and costs)	Charity, philanthropy, ethics, image Mediated perception, low subjective impact	Diffuse — hesitation between favorable influence and image
Culture	Scholarships, book launches, conferences Mediated perception	Education, local events Mediated perception	Education, ethics, image Mediated perception, low impact	Mediated perception — positive role through generated effects
Health	First care, blood donations, modernizing hospitals (image) Implicit (productivity)	Caring for the employees, security and protection Implicit (productivity)	Routine check, care and hospitalization, insurance payment Explicit (productivity, cost reduction)	Dominantly implicit — image, health of employees and of the community, cost reduction
Others (customers, suppliers, partners)	Sports Mediated perception, image	Requests from partners, customers, local development actions Implicit (revenue increase)	Requests from partners, customers, suppliers, social awareness and image Explicit (revenue increase, improving market relations)	Diffuse — image, improving relations, revenue increase

Table 2. Systematic actions and practices related to CSR and CS

Company	Company A		Company B		Company C	
Field of action	Strategic	Operational	Strategic	Operational	Strategic	Operational
Macro Explicit	—	—	—	—	—	—
Implicit	—	Employees Environment Community Culture Health Other **CSR**	Environment Community **SD**	Employees Environment Community Culture Health Other **CSR**	—	Environment Employees Other **CSR**
Micro Explicit	Employees Environment **CS**	Employees Environment Culture Health Other **CSR**	Employees Environment Culture Health Other **CS**	Employees Environment Culture Health Other **CSR**	Employees Environment Health Other **CS**	Employees Environment Community **CSR**
Implicit	—	Employees Environment Culture Health Other **CSR**	—	Employees Environment Culture Health Other **CSR**	Employees Environment Health Other **CSR**	Employees Environment Community Other **CSR**

CSR actions mainly as a cost, arguing that it is extremely difficult to quantify the benefits generated through CSR actions. In the past few years, the corporate strategy became more complex, incorporating CSR, and CS referred to mainly as SD.

→ For company B, subsidiary of a well-known multinational company, the CS component has a strategic role, being generally present in the micro–macro area of influence of the company (macro especially based on the effect generated by the company as a whole, through all of its subsidiaries), being extremely important, regarded as a purpose and integrated in all activities. This integration is made possible with the help of the operational level, which includes all CSR actions and serves as basis for CS and SD. Therefore, we can conclude that the company understood that only the continuous strategic orientation towards responsibility (as a whole) can generate consistent positive results on the long term for the entity and for the environment in which it acts and voluntary assumes its mission.

→ Within company C, manufacturer of textile with a national and international presence, we can identify predominantly CSR elements referring to the level of impact and period for observing consequences of their actions. Also, elements concerning the attitude towards responsible behaviors regarding the social, economic, and natural environment are integrated at strategic level. The adoption of the CS concept in the current practice of this company can be reached in time, but the lack of CSR strategy and the punctual actions in the field (even the ones on the long-term are moreover a response to regulations and partners' demands) prove the lack of explicit interest at the moment.

Also potentially impaired, the aspects referring precisely to SD can be summarized as following:

→ Company A sees itself as being on a mission for improving life in the communities where it is present. Locally or internationally, it gets involved into actions and projects to support communities (at operational level) and, more and more often, it integrates these actions into strategies. Still, it seems to lack a clear vision of its true ability to improve lives and of positively/negatively impacting the world we live in.

→ For company B, SD is the result of getting involved at local, national and global levels (through the mother company). This component is also based on CSR activities, extended regionally and becoming permanent through CS. Unlike institutional, political (national, regional) entities, who provide regulations/strategic milestones about SD, company B assumes its strategic-operational role every time, being interested by putting into practice strategic plans of its own or in cooperation.

→ In company C, we encounter CSR actions as unconscious support for SD objectives. Basically, the strategic plan includes elements that refer to partner dialogue, innovation, recruitment through long-term partnerships with educational organizations, training programs for the unemployed, investments in equipment for reducing pollution, which are all steps towards SD.

By overlapping the ensembles of specific elements for all three concepts, we can identify commonalities and differences in terms of CSR, CS, and SD for all three companies, which can even lead to an acceptable generalization for the moment regarding the way this issue is perceived and approached. A suggestive figure (see Fig. 3) can visually represent the few significant fields of the relation between elements included in the three concepts in the case of the Romanian enterprise nowadays.

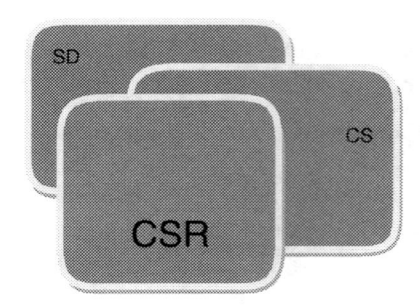

Fig. 3. Differentiating CSR, CS, and SD actions and practices at the level of the Romanian enterprise nowadays (representation that could be generalized)

6. Conclusions

Company A is still in search of its true identity in terms of CSR, CS, and SD. While it does have a clear strategic vision, its connection with CSR is still not clearly established. Even if it has been performing CSR actions for many years and it has been involved in the lives of the communities in which it has been present, it needs to build a clearer vision for what CSR really stands for, as well as its connections with CS and SD. It needs to have a deeper understanding of the reasons for getting involved in CSR actions, to understand that CSR is more about benefits than costs and to clearly understand its role in SD.

Company B benefits from the strategic vision and the expertise of the mother company. CS is the result of CSR actions on the long-term, organizationally and locally, while SD is the CS vision extended regionally. Strategic vision is obvious in all company activities. Differentiation between CS and SD is deducted from the area of influence of CSR activities, from a strategic point of view: internal and local environment in the first case; external and regional environment in the second case. All CSR components (economic, social, and environmental) are considered by the firm, which proves the multidimensional vision for these concepts.

In the case of company C, we observe the orientation of CSR actions towards the internal environment, some of them being expressed as long-term goals and included in the company strategy. Also, the consequences of some actions that refer to the company responsibility towards the environment can be regarded locally (philanthropy, partnerships with local organizations ...), but also regionally, nationally or internationally through the behavioral model used with business partners (paying the dues, reducing pollution, innovation).

As a basic idea for our study, we can conclude that both the Romanian literature in the field and the practice of Romanian companies prove, on one hand, good knowledge of concepts and ideas regarding CSR, CS, and SD, these constantly being updated. On the other hand, the acknowledgement of its importance for practice, the growingly intense concern for developing CSR activities (many already having a strategic role), which leads to CS (at organizational level) and SD (at macroeconomic level). Even if for most Romanian companies (especially SMEs) activities are not highly extensive, the cumulative effect is worth to be taken into account.

References

Aguinis, H. (2011), Organizational responsibility: Doing good and doing well. In *APA Handbook of Industrial and Organizational Psychology*, S. Zedeck (ed.), pp. 855–879. Washington: American Psychological Association.

Barbu, I. A., Chirea, G., & Constantinescu, L. (2011), Caracteristicile responsabilității sociale corporative: De la etică și transparență la performanță, *Revista de Marketing Online*, 5(4), 94–103. Available at http://www.edituraauranus.ro/marketing-online/54/pdf/8.pdf (Accessed 7 May 2014).

Bejan, M. & Rusu, T. (2007), Exploatarea resurselor naturale și conceptul de dezvoltare durabilă, *Buletinul AGIR*, 1, 20–24. Available at http://www.agir.ro/buletine/245.pdf (Accessed 7 May 2014).

Borțun, D. (coord.), (2011), *Parteneriate Sustenabile și Bune Practici în Responsabilitatea Social*, București: JCI România.

Carroll, A. B. (1979), A three-dimensional conceptual model of corporate social performance, *Academy of Management Review*, 4, 497–505.

Carroll, A. B. (1983), Corporate social responsibility: Will industry respond to cutbacks in social program funding? *Vital Speeches of the Day*, 49, 604–608.

Carroll, A. B. (1991), The pyramid of corporate social responsibility: Toward the moral management of organizational stakeholders, *Business Horizons*, 34(4), 39–48.

Carroll, A. B. (1999), Corporate social responsibility evolution of a definitional construct, *Business & Society*, 38(3), 268–295.

Corporate Knights (2013), Corporate knights global 100 most sustainable corporations announced in Davos. Available at http://www.corporateknights.com/article/corporate-knights-global-100-most-sustainable-corporations-announced-davos (Accessed 10 May 2014).

Covaș, L. & Braguța, A. (2009), *Responsabilitatea Socială Corporativă — Aspecte Practice*. Chișinău: Ivesa Grup.

Dinu, V. (2011), Responsabilitatea socială corporativă — oportunitate de reconciliere a intereselor economice cu cele sociale și de mediu, *Amfiteatrul Economic*, XIII(29), 6–7.

Dobrea, R. C. (2006), Managementul organizațiilor și responsabilitatea socială corporativă, *Administrație Și Management Public*, 7, 89–93.

Drucker, P. F. (1984), The new meaning of corporate social responsibility, *California Management Review*, 26, 53–63.

EU (2014), A renewed EU strategy 2011–2014 for Corporate Social Responsibility, Brussels. Available at http://eur-lex.europa.eu/LexUriServ/LexUriServ.do?uri=COM:2011:0681:FIN:EN:PDF (Accessed 10 May 2014).

EU (2014), Corporate social responsibility (CSR). Available at http://ec.europa.eu/enterprise/policies/sustainable-business/corporate-social-responsibility/index_en.htm (Accessed 10 May 2014).

European Commission (2006), Implementing the partnership for growth and jobs: Making Europe a pole of excellence on corporate social responsibility. Available at http://www.csreurope.org/data/files/eucommision_csr_strategy_march_2006.pdf (Accessed 12 February 2013).

Forbes (2014), The most responsible companies: Another ranking. Available at http://www.forbes.com/sites/susanadams/2011/09/16/the-most-responsible-companies-another-ranking/ (Accessed 15 May 2014).

Garriga, E. & Melé, D. (2004), Corporate social responsibility theories: Mapping the territory, *Journal of Business Ethics*, 53, 51–71.

Gănescu, M. C. (2012), Responsabilitatea socială a întreprinderii ca strategie de creare și consolidare a unor afaceri sustenabile, *Economie Teoretică și Aplicată*, XIX, 11(576), 93–109. Available at http://store.ectap.ro/articole/799_ro.pdf (Accessed 16 May 2014).

Global Reporting Initiative (2014), Reporting framework overview. Available at https://www.globalreporting.org/reporting/reporting-framework-overview/Pages/default.aspx (Accessed 15 May 2014).

Hediger, W. (2010), Welfare and capital-theoretic foundations of corporate social responsibility and corporate sustainability, *The Journal of Socio-Economics*, 39, 518–526.

Hristea, A. M. (2011), Responsabilitatea socială corporativă — între deziderat și realitate, *Economie Teoretică și Aplicată*, XVIII, 10(563), 56–73. Available at http://store.ectap.ro/articole/650_ro.pdf (Accessed 7 May 2014).

Manoleli, D. (2000), Dezvoltarea durabilă (suport de curs). Available at http://lefo.ro/carmensylva/Carmensylva/ppap/2000/an2/sem1/manolelidezdur.pdf (Accessed 7 May 2014).

Mihăilă, G. Responsabilitatea socială a întreprinderilor. Available at http://www.readbag.com/antreprenoriateractivroconsult-ro-fw-files-file-iasi-responsabilitatea-sociala-a-intreprinderilor-iasi (Accessed 2 May 2014).

Rusandu, I. (2008), Probleme filosofice și metodologice ale dezvoltării durabile (DD), *Revista de Filosofie, Sociologie și Stiințe Politice*, 3(148), 19–29. Available at http://iiesp.asm.md/wp-content/uploads/2010/12/Revista-2008-3-JIS-B5.pdf#page=19 (Accessed 2 May 2014).

Sabadoz, C. (2011), Between profit-seeking and prosociality: Corporate social responsibility as Derridean supplement, *Journal of Business Ethics*, 104, 77–91.

Stancu, A. & Orzan, M. (2007), Responsabilitatea socială a companiilor românești — un pas pentru dezvoltarea durabilă/Social responsibility of Romanian companies: A stepping stone for national sustainable development, *Revista de Marketing Online*, 1(2), 49–53. Available at http://www.edumark.ase.ro/RePEc/rmko/2/6.pdf (Accessed 7 May 2014).

Ştefănescu, F. & Coturbaş, L. (2009), Sustainable development and life quality, *Annals: Economics Science Series*, (XV), 530–537.

The Economic Times (2014), Corporate social responsibility mandatory for corporates from April 1. Available at http://articles.economictimes.indiatimes.com/2014-01-29/news/46782747_1_csr-policy-csr-committee-new-companies-act (Accessed 15 May 2014).

Toma, S. G. (2006), De la calitate la responsabilitatea socială corporatistă, *Amfiteatrul Economic*, 20, 1–6. Available at http://www.amfiteatrueconomic.ase.ro/arhiva/pdf/no20/articol_fulltext_pag145.pdf (Accessed 7 May 2014).

Vintilă, G., Armeanu, Ş. D., Filipescu, M. O., Moscalu, M., & Lazăr, P. (2012), Studiu privind corelația politică fiscală — responsabilitate socială corporativă, *Economie Teoretică și Aplicată* XIX, 4(569), 3–14.

Wang, Y. G. (2011), Corporate social responsibility and stock performance — evidence from Taiwan, *Modern Economy*, 2, 788–799.

Wilson, M. (2003), Corporate sustainability: What is it and where does it come from, *Ivey Business Journal*, 67(6), 1–5.

Zaiț, D., Onea, A., Tătărușanu, M., & Ciulu, R. (2013), The social responsibility and competitiveness of the Romania firm, *Procedia Economics and Finance*, Special edition for the GEBA conference.

Chapter 5

Re-Thinking Our Model of Management in the Light of the Cultural Dimension — A Systemic Approach to the Company

Blandine Vanderlinden

MIME-ICHEC

The hierarchical, mechanical, and rational model of management is no longer suited to our present complex and unpredictable business context. We propose that the current concerns of managers such as the style of management, change, innovation, organizational learning, cultural diversity, multicultural team management, corporate social responsibility (CSR), etc. be discussed in the light of a systemic approach to the organization where the cultural dimension is situated. Culture is a complex concept that is not something that can be assessed as different, but as "Sensemaking". Corporate culture is more than just a set of values; it fulfills a double role with regard to construction of identity and to integration. The systemic approach views the organization in a holistic way and tries to see the various components of the company as a part of the whole (instead of looking at them separately), focusing particularly on their interactions and consistency in a clear and expressed global vision. All business functions can be seen in this double reading, the cornerstone of organizational analysis. This chapter is a condensed version of major ideas taken from an extensive research project conducted over several years by the team of MIME of the ICHEC, Brussels Management School. We invite the reader to read the book *Au Coeur de la Dimension Culturelle du Management*, by the authors Pierre Dupriez and Blandine Vanderlinden (under the supervision of), to be published soon.

1. The Relevant Managerial Issues

To meet contemporary managerial concerns, this chapter proposes viewing organizations and management differently. Firstly, it clarifies the concept of culture and corporate culture as applied to management issues. Culture will not be considered as "difference" as it is more often presented in the literature and used by practitioners, but as "Sensemaking". Major methodological challenges will stem from this comprehensive approach to culture. Secondly, it proposes to address managerial concerns in a systemic approach, which is radically different from the classical, analytical, and mechanical perspectives.

We can observe that many companies, particularly in Eastern European countries, still work according to traditional models of management. They generally fit into a hierarchical, rational, and mechanical management approach in line with the teachings of famous "Organizational theories". These theories,[1] developed by the Cartesian minds of Westerners,

---
[1] OST: Scientific Organization of Labor.

adopt a "scientific" approach (OST) looking for the "One Best Way". They were developed at the beginning of the industrial era in a stable and controllable context of relative certainty and are based on the major assumption of rationality. They considered that the best way to organize work is through "performance". In that context, it was sufficient that the decision maker — in sole command — make the "right" decisions in a framework of humanly acceptable knowledge, that he optimize the division and coordination of labor, make a good product or provide a good service for success to be guaranteed.

In this line of thinking, we find among others, Fayol (1916), whose main functionalist discourse shows that managerial responsibilities are essentially to produce, to organize, to direct, and to control. The human being is a "tool", malleable and compliant ("the right man in the right place"). It is true that these early theories were subsequently complemented by more humanizing ones, called "human relations theories", but the human being is represented as a contingent variable and the organization remains a "machine", however human; this is sometimes called a "soft-Taylorist" view of work.

However, the world and the context of business have changed radically since that time and as regards management, globalization has radically altered these first premises.

This period of globalization is characterized by complexity and uncertainty, the more so because information technology is constantly innovating and technological tools enable us to reach the entire planet at any level. All companies (even small and medium-sized enterprises (SMEs) working at a local level) are forced to operate at a global level and to be on constant standby, proactive, or very quickly react to the evolutions of competitors and markets. In short, nothing is safe and everything changes all the time.

At an organizational level, in addition to the need for learning and for flexibility, companies face the challenges of differentiation to suit local markets coupled with the need for integration. Trying to find a balance, they often adopt contradictory approaches. On the one hand, to motivate the troops and be close to the markets, top managers talk about decentralized decision-making, accountability, autonomy, creativity, ...; on the other hand, to maintain the ship's course and to ensure control, they develop and implement a panoply of procedures and processes that bureaucratizes and weighs down the system. If control is vital to avoid the risk of fragmentation, it is even more difficult to ensure when partners are scattered all over the world and can be driven by interests that may be different because of geographical remoteness and particular interests. Furthermore, internet resources and social networks allow anyone to access information that can have an impact on the course of business and internal competition does not always get on well with cooperation.

At an individual level, in this context of constant change, people lose their bearings. On the one hand, they are asked to be open, learning, creative, flexible, autonomous,... and, on the other hand, they must constantly be accountable for their performance at work (individual and collective) and they are stifled by the procedures, the rules, and standards they have to follow, as well as by the constant controls. Under this contradictory pressures, workers do only what they are asked to do, and keep their nose to the grindstone, changing only because they have to. They no longer have the energy to step back and distance themselves from their work. The risks are high and they often fall into depression, burn-out, or even attempt suicide from simple exhaustion.

This context is well-known and academics, consultants, and companies are trying their best to find solutions. They all come up with good ideas and good practices, and articles, books, conferences and training courses are available in abundance. There are also fashions. Until recently we heard a lot about reengineering, quality, change management, etc.; today, discussions focus much more on leadership style and collaborative management, team management (multicultural), organizational learning, social responsibility, innovation, etc. We are convinced that all these thoughts and discussions are appropriate, necessary, and very interesting and that they provide solutions, in their own way, to certain corporate challenges. Our proposal is that all of them be integrated into a global approach which, as we will see, renews management.

On the one hand, it is a matter of taking into account the cultural dimension and in particular corporate culture that we will define as construction of meaning and that produces a double effect, identity, and integration (2.1) and, on the other hand, of adopting a systemic reading of the organization which enables us to focus attention both on the vision that directs and gives meaning and on the interactions and their coherence (2.2).

2. Rethinking Management: Systemic Approach and Cultural Dimension

The new additions to this chapter aim to take into account the cultural dimension within a systemic approach to the company. We will see that all business functions may be found in this double reading, which is the keystone of organizational analysis in its search for coherence and meaning. Concerning culture, given the diversity of approaches and the difficulty of grasping it, we want to start by reviewing its meaning and scope.[2] Corporate culture will be then considered as a major company-system component.

2.1. *Culture and corporate culture: Construction of meaning*

In the private, social, and business field, we can observe an intensification of the interactions between people of different cultural origins, and backgrounds. "Culture" and "cultural diversity" are words which are now on everyone's lips. Yet, the concept is clear to very few people and if we ask people what culture is, answers are likely to be very vague and inconsistent. Answers tend to be about feelings "I can't say, it is different" and experiences "they do/say/think differently from us". Is not culture more than a simple matter of difference? At the company level, we speak about culture casually, and we would be able to enumerate a number of values, those that are overt. But what about culture as it is experienced? It therefore seems important to us to clarify the concept of culture and to show the scope of corporate culture.

[2] To be brief in the context of an article, we invite the reader to look at Chapters 2, 3, and 4 of the book by Pierre Dupriez and Blandine Vanderlinden titled *Au Coeur de la Dimension Culturelle du Management*, forthcoming.

2.1.1. *Culture does not have to be perceived as different but as "Sensemaking"*

It is widely accepted that culture is a coherent social construction, related to the action of humans on their environment and their relationships with others. This social construction is forged in early childhood in the relationship with parents and continues throughout life. How each person will respond to the questions of life depends on their system of values, and is the heart of any culture. This system of values appear both as a protection against external elements and as a condition of maintaining the internal balance of social relations (Dupriez, 2014: 10); and it is expressed through different signs characteristic of the group culture.

From different responses to similar concerns related to management, Hofstede[3] sought to identify some values that might explain those differences and he identified a number of well-known cultural dimensions (hierarchical distance, uncertainty avoidance, individualism/collectivism, femininity/masculinity, long/short term orientation, …). Hofstede went a part of the way in this, and his work is very interesting; he also recognized the limits of his research. However, those limits are most often forgotten and the figures he provided are used inappropriately.

In his research, Hofstede sought to describe cultures by comparison; his approach is comparative and is based on quantitative method using questionnaires. These choices have their limits. The questionnaires have been designed by Westerners; are they are thus able to consider the specificities of other ways of life, thoughts, and behaviors? Can questions that use Western concepts be understood in the same way by people from other cultures? Can those questionnaires take into account the complexities inherent in any culture? Can Hofstede's dimensions enable us to understand what underlies the thoughts and behaviors? Raising these issues that obviously demand negative answers reveal that Hofstede's dimensions can only show some "indications", which may be useful but not sufficient to explain culture.

[3] The early work of Geert Hosftede date from the 1970s; he conducted a survey (more than 100,000 questionnaires) to IBM employees in over 70 different countries.

Moreover, culture is a coherent construction, and as Marcel Mauss recalled, a "total social fact". This means that no aspect of social life can be understood alone "each of them has reality because each one is integrated in a system" (Dupriez, 2014: 7). Therefore, taking into account one dimension or other in an isolated way cannot explain the observed reality and get to the heart of culture. Finally, culture also has its "hidden dimension" (Hall, 1971, 1984) and in addition to the observed facts there is a whole world which belongs to the imagination (Godelier, 2007), to thought, and to the informal which need to be decoded rather than observed and which are understandable only by their cultural references.

In the footsteps of the anthropologists, the MIME of ICHEC offer a radically different approach to culture. It defines culture as "what makes sense" (Sensemaking). Looking for the meaning of social practices and questioning why specific behaviors occur, enables us to get to the heart of culture. "I use the word 'culture' to refer to the set of representations and principles that consciously organize the different areas of social life, as well as the values attached to these ways of acting and thinking. We see therefore that a culture arises first from the domain of the ideal but that it does not really exist until the elements of the ideal — principles, representations, values — are linked firmly to social and material practices to which they give meaning" (Godelier, 2007: 96).

This approach, opens to interdisciplinarity and is linked, among others, to psychology. "Culture operates in a fundamental domain for humans: units of meaning or of significations, which constitute the obligatory mediation for our access to reality; because no stimulus acts on us directly, but through the intermediary of a sense in which it is inevitably wrapped, consciously or unconsciously. So we are constantly moving in a symbolic universe becoming variable. And it is this sense that decides, ultimately, our actions: we do not act the same way with adults, children, nature, the multitude of objects, disease, according to the meaning which we give them" (Camilleri, 1989: 24).

Ultimately, and regardless of the discipline within which the question is asked, addressing the notion of culture always brings us back to wondering what makes sense (Dupriez, 2014: 10).

This approach also has its methodological requirements and limitations. First, any field of study is unique and the criteria can only refer to the emic perspective: "each cultural unit must be understood and judged by its own logic in relation to its model which is a matter of emic perspective, as opposed to the etic perspective which makes judgments from outside" (Camilleri, 1996). Secondly, it can only be appreciated through an anthropological approach using qualitative methods of data collection.

2.1.2. *Corporate culture is not just a question of values*: *It exercises a double function of construction of identity and integration*

Our major concern being the company of what importance is its cultural dimension? Our detour via the general concept of culture is not without purpose because our approach to it will also be a construction of meaning.

To start, let us emphasize that the company is a receptacle of many cultural influences in interaction with each other coming from the national culture where it is located, professional cultures, micro-cultures forged in social groups (for example, the departments), and the cultures of individuals (identities). These cultural references may be conflicting or a source of tension and it is necessary to identify them. Secondly, by the intensity, the duration, and the complexity of human relationships being developed by the company while carrying out its functions also creates and embodies culture. "Corporate culture means then a set of standards, often implicit, organizing the relationships within a particular group, of modes of action and thought, invented by this group to meet its specific problems" (Dupriez, 2000).

"If we talk about corporate culture, it is ultimately because there is a continuing need to produce sense and meaning to act. Daily technical problems as much as the organizational complexities and commercial constraints force us to engage in reflection, to call upon beliefs and motivating values, to subscribe to a mesh of solidarity and representations of those with whom it should collaborate. Without production of meaning, the company doesn't coordinate its members in the same direction of economic objectives"

(Sainsaulieu, 1990: 58). How can we indicate more clearly the continuity between the two concepts, culture in the general sense and corporate culture, each one conveying and creating sense? We are thus immersed in the heart of "*Sensemaking*" and here the contribution of Karl Weick is fundamental.[4]

The creation of meaning is a highly social process (Weick, 1995) and this design leads us to review the traditional definition of the organization. "To act together, it is necessary to have not only a common goal, but at least a minimum agreement on the meaning of the situation, to allow the co-orientation of minds and the coordination of actions. Organizing oneself means (according to Weick) making sense together in and by means of joint activities" (Giroux, 2006: 32). So, as much as being a system of production of goods and services, and according to Weick even more than being that, the organization should be a system facilitating the collective production of meaning (Giroux, 2006).

When corporate culture is discussed as a historical process and when we are interested in the experienced culture of the members of the organization, corporate culture tends to produce a double effect, of integration and of identity.

Integration implies a reciprocal loyalty of the workers toward the company and the company towards its members (Dupriez, 2000). From the point of view that concerns us, participation in the collective creation of sense can explain individuals' engagement in, or the disengagement from, operational, managerial, or strategic actions (Vandangeon-Deng & Autissier, 2006: 170).

The expected identity effect of a culture searching for meaning is no longer the identification of the individual with his or her company. In fact, this illusion is more utopian than real and it is interesting to remember the failures encountered by Westerners attempting to reproduce certain practices of socialization imported from other cultural areas. The expected effect is rather the individual construction of identity made up of recognition and belonging (Sainsaulieu, 1990), being recognized for what we are and for what we do; belonging to a group that shares the same search for meanings. We could thus claim that the issue of the production of sense is not only to understand what is happening in this or that situation, but that it could equally be, if not more likely to be, to produce a representation of what happens that conforms to what the person wants to be or wants to appear to be (Vidaillet, 2006: 117).

2.1.3. *Researching the cultural dimension of organizations also calls for a specific approach*

Referring to this approach of culture within an organization, it is clear that corporate culture stems from a historical process rooted in a history and context which is unique in evolution. Therefore, our concern is to read corporate culture for what it is.

Decoding corporate culture is more complex than a simple survey of some items described as "cultural". To do an in-depth study, it is necessary to move in stages and to use tools consistent with an anthropological approach which proceeds from the explicit to the implicit. That is to say, after recording cultural traits, we still need to consider what they mean to those who expressed them. Here, any researcher has to be extremely careful not to confuse the "stated" culture, the one the organization displays and that it wants to promote among its members and outside, with the "experienced" culture which is even more internalized than the "effective" culture and the only one in which reside the factors of group cohesion and adherence to the project of the company (Vanderlinden, 2009).

Identifying the cultural elements should be followed by analysis. To do this, we need reading guidelines or models of analysis that place the observed elements in a cultural typology which, subsequently, enables us to point each type of culture in its organizational context. The MIME of ICHEC suggests tools, or rather an approach based on criteria recognized as relevant to read the corporate culture in the specific context of a given company. Indeed, as these tools cannot be universal, they have to be re-calibrated for each situation (Vanderlinden, 2009).[5]

---

[4] The synthesis presented by Giroux (2006) has been a guide in the exploration of the paradoxical approach of Karl Weick; it highlights his original conception of creation of sense, of the organization and of the learning process.

[5] Tools have been proposed to read some company's situations in Romania; their making process is explained.

2.2. The company, an open system

"I hold it to be equally impossible to know the parts without knowing the whole, and to know the whole without knowing the parts." It is from this dilemma stated by Pascal that the systemic approach was born. Our aim is to show that a systemic approach to organizations can provide a response to contemporary managerial challenges. But, first of all what is a systemic approach to organizations and what place does the cultural dimension have in this?

2.2.1. *Systemic approach: A search for coherence within a shared vision that gives sense*

Joël de Rosnay defines the system as "a set of elements in dynamic interaction with each other organized so as to reach an objective" (de Rosnay, 1975). Concerning organizations, Morel and Ramanujal add: "Organizations are now routinely viewed as dynamic systems of adaptation and evolution that contain multiple parts which interact with one another and environment. Such a representation is so common that it has acquired the status of a self-evident fact" (Morel & Ramanjual, 1999, cited by Fillol, 2006: 30) emphasizing here the interaction of the system with its environment.

The richness of the systemic approach is already evident. First of all, the system is perceived as a whole and with Edgar Morin, we bear in mind that "the whole is simultaneously greater and smaller than the sum of its parts" (Morin, 1990). Consequently, the organization is teleological and the system is purpose-driven; the company participates in this logic (Moilanen, 2001). Finally, Gérard Donnadieu recalls that openness is a major feature of complex systems (Donnadieu, 1985; Donnadieu & Karsky, 2002).

Thus, adopting a systemic approach means adopting an approach that, instead of considering the different parts separately, strives to understand holistically all the components of the system by focusing on their connections and their interactions. It also seeks to understand how each element contributes to the purpose of the system while preserving its own identity (Yatchinovsky, 1999).

Applied to management, this approach leads us to consider that "any organization composed of people in relationship to each other is a system" (Bériot, 2006: 294).

Systems composed of human beings focus primarily on the relationships between these people even if inert elements, such as technology and conceptual tools, can interact with users; these will be considered only in their relationships with the living elements, such as individuals, groups, or professional categories. Because they are alive, they may behave differently depending on the system of values to which they belong and their behavior will depend on the relationships they maintain with the other elements of the system (Bériot, 2006).

Now we turn to the notion of ramification of the systems. Any human system is always a subsystem of another broader system (Passet, 1979). Thus, a company consists of a set of subsystems one above the other: a team project is often more important than individual projects and this team project must fit into the company's project. But at the same time a kind of reverse direction is in operation: each overarching project gives meaning to the ones beneath it (Yatchinovsky, 1999).

Thus, we can consider any organization as a system which is *complex*, *open* to its environment, *purpose-driven* and composed of subsystems in *interrelations*. We can represent it by the following Fig. 1.

A company lives in an environment that influences it, has a purpose, determines strategic choices (strategy), organizes itself to implement them (structure), benefits from skills (financial tools, legal, technological, commercial,...) (techno structure) and is motivated by a culture (corporate culture).[6]

The interest of this approach comes from the dynamics inherent in any system. Indeed, one of its

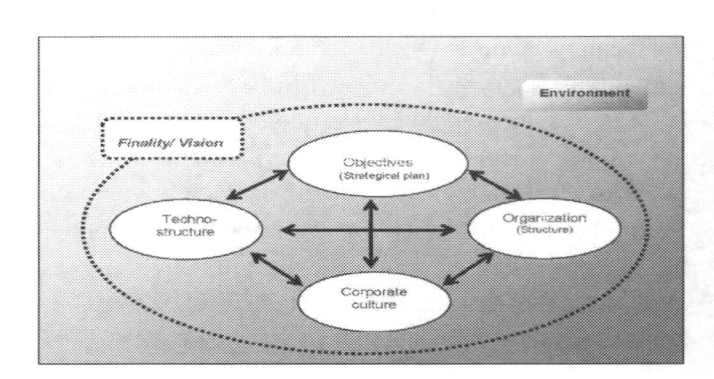

Fig. 1. A systemic approach of the company
Source: MIME, ICHEC.

---

[6] The figure can be completed by any other subsystem that concern management issues.

major properties is its adaptability and therefore its ability to change but with a safeguard. A major condition for its survival, and its performance, is maintaining its consistency.

In practice, this means that managers' main focus should be on the interactions between subsystems and on ensuring their consistency. That is, when a change is made in the system, at any level, it is essential to look at its potential impact on other subsystems. Thus, a change will only operate permanently in the company if it is done in an overall consistent way and if it meets the goals that the organization had clearly expressed in advance. It is the vision that will ultimately give meaning to the actions.

2.2.2. Culture is a component of the system

In this systemic vision of the organization, the cultural dimension is taken into account at two different levels that complement each other. On the one hand, corporate culture is a subsystem of the complex system that is the company as a whole. On the other hand, culture acts on the system in its entirety since its role is to indicate the sense that the concrete actions and the proposed goals can have.

Ultimately, the concept of meaning is inseparable from that of globality. There is a possible meaning only when the actions and everyday daily life take place in a coherent whole. In a way, the need for meaning arises out of a need for consistency, which brings us back to the system as a whole.

Culture also intervenes at the level of individuals and their interactions, first through their cultural sensitivity (Bennett, 1986, 1994),[7] and then through the cultural traits that characterize them.

2.2.3. Systemic approach, a key to approach all managerial concerns

The systemic approach invites us to take a holistic look at the company. To check the consistency of the system, a necessary condition for its performance, it is necessary to develop tools allowing the relationships between its various components to be analyzed on the one hand and on the other hand to be acted on.

MIME-ICHEC team has proposed a model of interpretation by mobilizing various tools suggested in the literature. It is the result of a theoretical study which reviewed the compatibility or incompatibility[8] between typologies for reading the strategy, the structure and the culture. This model is an operational tool enabling us to verify the consistency peculiar to any organizational system (Vanderlinden, 2009). But above all, it invites us to retain the method. In a very concrete way, within the system that is a company, for each business concern we must consider its interactions and effects with the various other subsystems.

Let us take some examples. To speak about cooperative management essentially means that all stakeholders are driven by a common goal that transcends their individual objectives. Therefore, it can only be considered within an organization that shares a strong culture of belonging, characterized by mutual trust, and constant interactions. At the same time strategy, structure, culture, human resources management, etc. must be mobilized adequately to promote this style of leadership.

To speak about a "learning company" also calls to mind a shared vision, a flexible structure encouraging teamwork and learning, a techno-structure allowing information to be easily shared, a culture based on strong relationships, sense of community, confidence, and cultural sensitivity.

To speak about CSR and not lapsing into superficial actions that have more to do with image, requires the concept to be closely integrated in the system.

We could give examples ad infinitum. Each company situation being unique, there is no master key and no one managerial model is better than the other. What matters here is the approach and we believe that, regardless of the chosen options, the coherence of the system must be present consistently at all levels of the company. With the vision as the starting point and passing through the teams it should be reflected in practices, tasks, and actions of each player/actor.

---

[7] Milton Bennett proposed a model with six sensitivity levels corresponding to the degree of openness to cultural differences; they go from refusal and negation of the differences to acceptance and integration of cultural specificities.

[8] Bartlett & Ghoshal's typology (1986, 1991) has been mobilized to examine international strategies.

3. Contributions and Openings

We have tried to propose two new ideas. One concerns the concept of culture and corporate culture and the other aims to address the current companies' concerns according to a systemic approach.

Thus, firstly, and against the currents of thought that have dominated the literature for decades, the MIME-ICHEC team suggests approaching culture as being what gives sense to the relationship of one person with other people and with their environment (Weick, 1995; Dupriez & Simons, 2000; D'Iribarne, 2003, 2008; Dupriez, 2006). Isn't making sense, following an expression of Karl Weick's "transforming a universe of experience into an intelligible world?" (Weick, 1993, cited by Giroux, 2006). Understanding a culture, is thus trying to find out what interpretation those who share this culture give to situations, events, and actions of others and to their own, and how they react to them (D'Iribarne, 2003; Sauquet & Vielajus, 2014).

The cultural dimension of management can be seen in the continuity of this approach. Producing meaning and coordinating the activities of its members in one direction is without doubt the primary function of what has been called corporate culture (Sainsaulieu, 1990). The two concepts that of culture in its general sense and business culture, are not all two carriers and creators of meaning? (Dupriez & Vanderlinden, 2008, 2009, 2014).

At a research level, this way of addressing the cultural dimension results in methodological choices that often vary from traditional practices. Going to the heart of culture and discovering what makes sense implies a deep and complex study that cannot be accomplished using ready-made tools. Going against the flow of the hypothetical-deductive approach, we adopt an abductive approach where, instead of being given, the theory is to be discovered. This leads to the use of a contextual approach, a constructivist and interpretative epistemological attitude, a data collection methodology which focuses on observation and interviews, and a qualitative processing of the information gathered (Dupriez & Vanderlinden, 2013, 2014).

Secondly, to answer the current concerns of the companies that are evolving in a context characterized by complexity and uncertainty, we have proposed a radically different approach to the current hierarchical, rational, and mechanical type of management.

The systemic approach strives to describe, to understand, and to support the interactions and their successive adaptations of all the components of the system that contribute to the same purpose. On the one hand, these components which constitute subsystems must form a coherent whole to respond to the constraints and opportunities of the environment and, on the other hand, the system can only be consistent if it clearly defines its purpose. Corporate culture cannot be isolated from the other elements in which it operates and is constructed. As a creator of meaning, it is a key component of the company: it mobilizes, channelizes and has a double effect, it helps in the construction of identity and integration.

The systemic approach is therefore presented as a framework that allows us to express the implemented logic. Management style, change management, organizational learning, management teams, and all other managerial concerns will be able to find an answer to their integration in this approach.

References

Bartlett, C. A. (1986), Building and managing the transnational: The new organizational challenge. In *Competition in Global Industries*, M. E. Porter (ed.), pp. 367–401, Boston: Harvard Business School Press.

Bartlett, C. A. & Ghoshal, S. (1991), *Le Management Sans Frontières*, Paris: Éditions d'Organisation.

Bartlett, C. A. & Ghoshal, S. (1998/2002), *Managing Across Borders: The Transnational Solution*, Massachusetts: Harvard Business School Press.

Bériot, D. (2006), *Manager par L'Approche Systémique*, Paris, Eyrolles: Éditions d'Organisation.

Bollinger, D. & Hofstede, G. (1987), *Les Différences Culturelles Dans le Management: Comment Chaque Pays Gère-t-il ses Hommes* ? Paris: Éditions d'Organisation.

Camilleri, C. (1989), La culture et l'identité culturelle: Champ notionnel et devenir. In *Chocs de Cultures: Concepts et Enjeux Pratiques de L'Interculturel*, C. Carmel and M. Cohen-Emerique (eds.), Paris: L'Harmattan, coll. Espaces culturels.

Camilleri, C. & Vinsonneau, G. (1996), *Psychologie et Culture*, Paris: Armand Colin.

De Rosnay, J. (1975), *Le Macroscope: Vers Une Vision Globale*, Paris: Seuil.

D'Iribarne, P. (1977), The usefulness of an ethnographic approach to the international comparison of organisation, *International Studies of Management and Organisations*, 26(4), 30–47.

D'Iribarne, P. (1989), *La Logique de L'Honneur, Gestion des Entreprises et Traditions Nationales*, Paris: Seuil.

D'Iribarne, P. (2003), *Le Tiers-Monde qui Réussit: Nouveaux Modèles*, Paris: Odile Jacob.

D'Iribarne, P. (2008), *Penser la Diversité du Monde*, Paris: Seuil.

D'Iribarne, P. (avec Henry A., Segal, J.-P., Chevrier, S., & Globokar, T.) (1998), *Cultures et Mondialisation: Gérer Par-delà les Frontières*, Paris: Seuil.

Donnadieu, G. (1985), L'approche systémique: De quoi s'agit-il?, *Arts et Métiers Magazine* (November).

Donnadieu, G. & Karsky, M. (2002), *La Systémique, Penser et Agir Dans la Complexité*, Paris: Éditions Liaisons.

Dupriez, P. (2000), Culture et management, un vieux couple pour le meilleur et pour le pire. In *La Résistance Culturelle: Fondements, Applications e Implications du Management Interculturel*, P. Dupriez and S. Simons (eds.), Bruxelles: De Boeck, 2 ème édition, 2002.

Dupriez, P. (2005), Le couple culture et management dans un contexte de transition. In *Entreprises Roumaines en Transition: Études de Cultures Organisationnelles*, P. Dupriez (sous la direction de), Paris: L'Harmattan, Cedimes.

Dupriez, P. (2006), *De Culture et de Sens: Orientations de Recherches en Management Interculturel, Textes et Réflexions*, Bruxelles: MIME.

Dupriez, P. (2014), Culture et cultures. In *Au Cœur de la Dimension Culturelle du Management*, D. Pierre and B. Vanderlinden (eds.), à paraître.

Dupriez, P. & Simons, S. (2000), *La Résistance Culturelle: Fondements, Applications e Implications du Management Interculturel*, Bruxelles: De Boeck, 2 ème édn., 2002.

Dupriez, P. & Vanderlinden, B. (sous la direction de) (2014), *Au Cœur de la Dimension Culturelle du Management*, à paraître.

Dupriez, P. & Vanderlinden, B. (2014), Culture d'entreprise, le dit et le vécu. In *Au Cœur de la Dimension Culturelle du Management*, D. Pierre and B. Vanderlinden (eds.), à paraître.

Fillol, C. (2006), L'émergence de l'entreprise apprenante et son instrumentalisation: Études de cas chez EDF, Thèse de doctorat, Université Paris Dauphine.

Giroux, N. (2006), La démarche paradoxale de Karl E. Weick. In *Les Défis du Sensemaking en Entreprise*, D. Autissier and F. Bensebaa (eds.), Paris: Economica.

Godelier, M. (1984), *L'idéel et le Matériel: Pensée, Économie, Sociétés*, Paris: Fayard.

Godelier, M. (2007), *Au Fondement des Sociétés Humaines: Ce Que Nous Apprend L'Anthropologie*, Paris: Albin Michel.

Hall, E. T. (1971), *La Dimension Cachée*, Paris: Seuil.

Hall, E. T. (1979), *Au-Delà de la Culture*, Paris: Seuil.

Hall, E. T. (1984), *Le Langage Silencieux*, Paris: Seuil. Traduction française de 'The Silent'.

Hofstede, G. (1984), *Culture Consequences*, Beverly Hills: Sage Publications.

Hofstede, G., Neuijen, B., Daval-Ohayv, D., & Sanders, G. (1990), Measuring organisational culture: A qualitative and quantitative study across twenty cases, *Administrative Science Quarterly*, (2), 286–316.

Hofstede, G. (1994), *Cultures and Organizations: Software of the Mind*, London: Harper Collins.

Le Moigne, J.-L. (1990), Systémique et Complexité. In *Numéro Spécial de la Revue Internationale de Systémique*, co-direction avec M. Orillard (ed.).

Le Moigne, J.-L. (1995), Intelligence stratégique de la complexité. In *Numéro Spécial de la Revue Internationale de Systémique*, co-direction avec M. Orillard.

Le Moigne, J.-L. & Morin, E. (1999), *L'Intelligence de la Complexité*, Paris: L'Harmattan.

Levi-Strauss, C. (1950), Introduction à l'œuvre de Marcel Mauss. In *Sociologie et Anthropologie*, M. Mauss (ed.). Paris: PUF.

Levi-Strauss, C. (1974), *Anthropologie Structurale*, Paris: Plon.

Livian, Y.-F. (2013), Pour en finir avec Hofstede: Renouveler les recherches en management intercultural. In *Nouveaux Défis du Management International*, V. Carbonne, S. Nivoix, and J.P. Lemaire (coordinateurs), Paris: Gualino et Atlas-AFMI.

Mauss, M. (1950), *Sociologie et Anthropologie*, Paris: PUF.

Meier, O. (2004), *Management Interculturel. Stratégie: Organisation. Performance*, Paris: Dunod.

Mintzberg, H. (1982), *Structure et Dynamique des Organisations*, Paris: Éditions d'Organisation.

Moilanen, R. L. (2001), Diagnostic tools for learning organizations. In *The Learning Organization*, pp. 6–20.

Moran, R. T. & Xardel, D. (1994), *Au-delà des Cultures: Les Enjeux du Management Interculturel*, Paris: Interéditions.

Morin, E. (1990), *Introduction à La Pensée Complexe*, Paris: ESF.

Morin, P. & Delavallée É. (2000), *Le Manager à L'Ecoute des Sociologues*, Paris: Éditions d'Organisation.

Passet, R. (1979), *L'Économique et le Vivant*, Paris: Payot.

Quinn, R. E. (1991), *Beyond Rational Management, Mastering the Paradoxes and Competing Demands of*

High Performance, San Francisco: Jossey-Bass (first published in 1988).

Quinn, R. E. & Spreitzer, G. M. (1991), The psychometrics of the competing values culture instrument and an analysis of the impact of organizational culture on quality of live, *Research in Organizational Change and Development*, 5, 115–142.

Quinn, R. E., Faerman, S. R., Thompson, M. P., & McGran, M. R. (2002), *Becoming a Master Manager: A Competency Framework* (3rd edn.), Hoboken: John Wiley and Sons Inc. (first published 1990).

Sainsaulieu, R. (1987), *Sociologie de L'Organisation et de L'Entreprise*, Paris: Dalloz.

Sainsaulieu, R. (1990), *Culture-Entreprise-Société*. In *Cultures d'Entreprise: Vous Avez dit Cultures?* Louvain-la-Neuve: UCL, Institut des sciences du travail.

Sauquet, M. & Vielajus, M. (2014), La démarche d'intelligence de l'autre: Observer, questionner, prendre en compte. In *Au Cœur de la Dimension Culturelle du Management*, P. Dupriez and B. Vanderlinden (eds.), à paraître.

Schein, E. (1985), *Organizational Culture and Leadership*, San Francisco: Jossey-Bass.

Schneider, S. & Barsoux, J.-L. (1997), *Managing Across Cultures*, Englewood Cliffs: Prentice Hall, Pearson Education Limited.

Schneider, S. & Barsoux, J.-L. (2003), *Management Interculturel* (2nd edn.), France: Pearson Education Limited.

Selznick, P. (1957), *Leadership in Administration: A Sociological Interpretation*, New York: Harper & Row.

Skinner, B. F. (1971), *Beyond Freedom and Dignity*, New York: Knopf.

Sonnenfeld, J. A. (1988), *The Hero's Farewell: What Happens When CEOs Retire*, New York: Oxford University Press.

Sonnenfeld, J. A., Peiperl, M. A., & Kotter, J. P. (1992), Strategic determinants of managerial labor markets: A career systems view. In *Human Resource Strategies*, G. Salaman *et al.* (eds.), London: Sage Publications (reprinted 1999).

Thevenet, M. (1986), Audit de la Culture D'Entreprise, Paris: Éditions d'Organisation.

Thevenet, M. (1993), *La Culture D'Entreprise, Que Sais-Je?* Paris: PUF.

Triandis, H. C. (1972), *The Analysis of Subjective Culture*, New York: Wiley.

Triandis, H. C. (1994), *Culture and Social Behavior*, New York: McGraw-Hill.

Triandis, H. C. (1995), *Individualism and Collectivism*, Boulder: Westview.

Triandis, H. C. (2002), Subjective culture. In *Online Readings in Psychology and Culture*, W. J. Lonner, D. L. Dinnel, S. A. Hayes and D. N. Sattler (eds.), Bellingham: Center for Cross-Cultural Research, Western Washington University.

Trompenaars, F. (1993), *L'Entreprise Multiculturelle*, Paris: Maxima.

Vandangeon-Derumez, I. & Autissier, D. (2006), Construire du sens pour réussir les projets de changement. In *Les Défis du Sensemaking en Entreprise*, D. Autissier and F. Bensebaa (eds.), Paris: Economica.

Vanderlinden, B. (2002), Expliciter l'implicite. À propos des structures implicites d'organisation. In *Communication & Organisation*, Bordeaux, Greco, (2nd trimester), pp. 98–119.

Vanderlinden, B. (2005), Outils d'analyse et d'interprétation des cultures organisationnelles. In *Entreprises Roumaines en Transition. Études de Cultures Organisationnelles*, P. Dupriez (ed.), Paris: L'Harmattan, Cedimes.

Vanderlinden, B. (2009), *Cultures, Management et Performance: Leçons de Quelques Situations Roumaines*, Târgoviste: Bibliotheca.

Vanderlinden, B. (2014), La culture, composante d'un système ouvert. In *Au Cœur de la Dimension Culturelle du Management*, P. Dupriez and B. Vanderlinden (eds.), à paraître.

Vanderlinden, B. & Dupriez, P. (2009), *Aux Sources du Management Interculturel*, Brussels: ICHEC–MIME.

Vanderlinden, B., Fratila, C., & Croitoru, G. (2005), Privatisées ou nouvelle, trois sas d'entreprises. In *Entreprises Roumaines en Transition. Études de Cultures Organisationnelles*, P. Dupriez (ed.), Paris: L'Harmattan, Cedimes.

Vidaillet, B. (2006), Comment l'envie déclenche des processus de sensemaking dans les organisations. In *Les Défis du Sensemaking en Entreprise*, D. Autissier and F. Bensebaa (eds.), Paris: Economica.

Walker, D. M., Walker, T., & Schmitz, J. (2003), *Doing Business Internationally: The Guide to Cross-Cultural Success* (2nd edn.), New York: McGraw-Hill.

Weick, K. E. (1993), Sensemaking in organizations: Small structures with large consequences. In *Social Psychology in Organizations: Advances in Theory and Research*, K. J. Murnighan (ed.), pp. 10–37, Englewood Cliffs: Prentice Hall.

Weick, K. E. (1995), *Sensemaking in Organizations*, London: Sage Publications.

Weick, K. E. & Quinn, E. (1999), Organizational change and development, *Annual Review of Psychology*, 361–386.

Yatchinovsky, A. (1999), *L'Approche Systémique: Pour Gérer L'Incertitude et la Complexité*, Paris: ESF.

Part II

Sustainable Development and Business Sustainability

Chapter 6

Social Capital and Business Sustainability: Defining, Measuring, and Assessing Its Impact on Cluster Performance in the Podkarpackie Region of Poland

Zbigniew Bochniarz

Evans School of Public Affairs, University of Washington

Over the last 30 years, social capital (SC) has become a popular subject of studies in social sciences. In developmental and regional economics, as well as in management, the category of SC is usually linked with development of industrial clusters and their performance. In 2006, the European Commission decided to allocate a significant portion of the European Union (EU) Regional Development Fund to support cluster initiatives in its financial perspective of 2007–2013. Since then, the category of SC, as a catalyst of clustering, became important for EU policy makers in both the public and private sectors when attempting to determine how to allocate limited resources effectively and efficiently.

The objectives of this chapter are to define what SC means for economists and business leaders; how to measure its growth and assess its impact on cluster performance, particularly for business sustainability and regional prosperity; and how to improve policy making processes in resource allocation for cluster support in public and business sectors.

The first part of this chapter will clarify basic definitions of SC, sustainability, and sustainable business. Based on the proposed definition, the main hypothesis will be presented: the size of accumulated SC and its growth positively impacts cluster performance producing synergetic effects — positive externalities — resulting from better cooperation and more trust among major actors within the cluster. In order to prove such a hypothesis, measurements of social capital will be proposed and verified through the 2014 pilot survey conducted by researchers in the Podkarpackie Region of Poland. This chapter will summarize the pilot survey conducted, present methodological recommendations for further research on social capital, and will elaborate initial policy recommendations on assessing cluster performance, particularly cluster initiatives.

1. Introduction

There are thousands of publications devoted to examining SC and its roles in families, communities, and nations as well as regional and national economies. This has been a trendy subject investigated intensely by sociologists, ecologists, political scientists, and economists over the past 30 years. This chapter focuses on SC from the point of view of an economist involved in institutional and policy design, as well as management and ecology. The inspiration for this chapter was the desire to reflect on the author's experiences in designing and implementing an international research project on "Effective Clusters — the Base for Innovation and the Source of Sustainable Regional Development." This research began last fall in the Podkarpackie Region of Poland and is scheduled to continue in Washington State, USA in the Spring and Summer of 2014 and summarized at an international conference planned in Poland for Spring 2015. The project is hosted by the Rzeszow School of Business (*Wyzsza Szkola Zarzadzania w Rzeszowie*) and the Evans School of Public Affairs at the University of Washington (Seattle), in collaboration with the Adam Mickiewicz University in Poznan (Poland) and the Free University of Amsterdam (The Netherlands).

The main goal of this research project is to develop a methodology to analyze and evaluate cluster performance and apply it to aerospace clusters in Poland (Dolina Lotnicza) and the US (Washington State Aerospace Cluster). The new cluster evaluation methodology will identify effective clusters and collect their best practices and problem solving procedures for key aerospace cluster stakeholders — business, public, and non-governmental sector leaders. These two clusters are the most advanced in their respective regions and are the major contributors to their regional economies. For that reason, the application of research findings should lead not only to significant improvement in these clusters' performance, but also significantly contribute to sustainable regional development and prosperity.

Despite the growing significance of industrial clusters in the Polish economy, their potential is still far behind the world's leading economies. Effective cluster policy is particularly critical for the poorest European regions — among them the Podkarpackie Voivodship (one of 16 administrative regions in Poland) which had the country's lowest GDP per capita in 2012. In order to help these regions improve competitiveness and innovation, the European Commission modified the rules of regional policy and decided to re-allocate the bulk of its resources to support existing and emerging clusters in its financial perspective for 2007–2013. This policy change significantly boosted the numbers of emerging clusters or cluster initiatives throughout the European Union (EU). In Poland, for instance, this new policy resulted in the establishment of about 250 clusters and cluster initiatives by the end of 2012.

Unfortunately, according to the Polish Agency for Enterprise Development (PARP), about 75% of their support for about 80 cluster initiatives failed to meet the promised objectives (PARP, 2012; Zachariasz, 2012). France experienced a similar "success" ratio as Poland, while Finland, Germany and the UK reached at least 75–80% effectiveness in cluster support (Czyzewska, 2013). These facts from the EU cluster support policy motivated the research team to begin developing a new evaluation methodology and collection of best practices.

Ineffective cluster support was not a problem in the Podkarpackie Region, which at the turn of the 21st century began to develop faster than most of the other poorest regions in Europe, thanks to visionary leadership and entrepreneurship in all sectors and good governance at the local and regional levels (Bochniarz & Sienko, 2008). As a result, industrial clusters started to emerge in the region and were further supported by the EU's structural funds. One of the most dynamic and high-tech clusters in the region is called Dolina Lotnicza (Aviation Valley), with over 100 firms and over USD 1 bn in revenue in 2012. It is worth mentioning that the initial resources for the Aviation Valley cluster support came out not from the governmental but from the corporate sector — from the United Technology Corporation (UTC), which owned several large manufacturing firms in this region — with initial funding of USD 300,000 (split equally at USD 60,000) for five years since 2003.

Today, Dolina Lotnicza hosts representatives of the major global aviation manufacturers (e.g., Airbus, Boeing, GE, Goodrich, Sikorsky, Whitney and Pratt, etc.) and is regarded as the future regional flagship. However, it is still far from reaching the necessary level of synergy to realize its full potential. Internal communication, management, and innovation are not yet operating at levels expected by its major stakeholders.

2. Defining Social Capital, Sustainability and Effective Clusters

Although the term SC appeared sporadically in social science literature in the 1970s, the real breakthrough in defining this category happened in the 1980s with contributions from Bourdieu (1986), Coleman (1988), and

Lin (1986). The following decades saw an explosion of studies on SC. There is also an ongoing process of institutionalization of the category of SC as an important factor influencing social and economic development by international organizations such as the United Nations, International Monetary Fund (IMF), World Bank and Organization for Economic Co-operation and Development (OECD).

In a comprehensive study on SC, Lin (2001) defines *capital* as "*investment of resources with expected returns in the marketplace*" (Lin, 2001: 3). Making a clear distinction between **capital** and **human capital**, he then defines **SC** as "*investment in social relations with expected returns in the marketplace*" (*op cit.*: 19).

In a similar way, Pierre Bourdieu defined the SC as a private investment in social networks that brings the owner expected benefits such as wealth, and "symbolic capital" — representing symbols of social position/strata (1986). Also James Coleman regarded SC as an individual good that could be traded through social networks for the advance of human capital or for getting things done (1988).

Contrary to earlier researchers treating SC as an individual or private good, there is another group of authors defining SC as a collective or even public good: Fukuyama (1997, 2000), Grootaert (1997), Huber (2008), Putnam (2000, 2003), Rosenfeld (2007), Roman (2007), and Woolcock & Narayan (2000).

For Francis Fukuyama, SC is a set of informal norms and rules as well as ethical values shared by individuals and social groups that enable them to cooperate effectively (1999, 2002). For Robert Putnam, SC does not belong to anybody but is a public good representing a set of social norms and civic attitudes supporting common actions and trust — both interpersonal and in public institutions (1993). In a similar way, SC is defined by experts from the OECD as, "networks together with shared norms, values, and understanding that facilitate cooperation within or among groups" (OECD, 2001). The World Bank team expands this definition further by adding "institutions, relationships, attitudes, and values that govern interactions among people and contribute to economic and social development." (Grootaert & van Bestelaer, 2002).

Interesting proposition of the SC concept offers Franz Huber defining it as "… resources embedded in social networks which can be potentially accessed or are actually used by individuals for action …" (Huber, 2008: 19). Then he proposes in addition to this "internal social capital (resources mobilized through relationships between members of the collectivity)" an "… external social capital (resources mobilized through relationships between members of the collectivity and actors outside of the collectivity)" (*ibid.*: 20). As an example for this dual character of SC Huber uses economic clusters, which depends on both — access to knowledge within the cluster and from other clusters and individuals outside.

Phil Cook adds notions of reciprocity, trust and "… exchange for political or economic purposes" to his definition of SC (Cooke, 2007: 102), arguing that in knowledge-based industries businesses are more engaged than others in building and performing SC.

SC is defined in a similar way by Carlos Roman — a system of social relationships based on trust and working according to well-known rules (Roman, 2007). Roman's methods of measurements of SC will be discussed later this chapter.

Finally, Stuart Rosenfeld summarizes the notion of SC in clusters that gives opportunities to "know-who" leading to build "know-how" (2003). He also classifies SC from the point of view of openness as positive and negative SC (Rosenfeld, 2007). Positive SC creates economic advantages that are major forces for clustering. Negative SC could start developing when there are efforts to limit membership in clusters and cultivate insularity or lock-in.

In summary, we may conclude: **SC is defined as a special type of capital resulting from investments in building relations, institutions and networks that produce collaborative attitudes, shared norms and values, mutual understanding and trust.** These are critical factors for cooperation with other types of capital and thus contribute to sustainable development (SD).

There are many definitions of sustainability. Often the term "sustainability" is used as a substitute for "sustainable development" (Adams, 2006) or as an intergenerational equity (Ott, 2003). In fact, **sustainability applied in many disciplines means maintaining a state of a dynamic balance in a system with its major elements interacting with each other and its relations with the higher system.**

In a biological system, sustainability is related to securing necessary diversity and reproductive capacity. For the global environment, sustainability means that earth's basic ecosystems are dynamically balanced and life on the planet is secure.

For human beings, sustainability means the long-term maintenance of their carrying capacity (life supporting ecosystem) that secures their non-declining wealth and reproduction with limitation to natural endowments (natural capital), making the foundation for carrying capacity to secure intergenerational equity (Pezzey & Toman, 2002).

Economists have addressed conceptual problems of SD with respect to intergenerational equity (Solow, 1974; Hartwick, 1977), by requiring non-declining resource endowment and introducing the "Hartwick Rule".

The UN World Commission on Environment and Development report defined SD as "development that meets the needs of the present without compromising the ability of future generations to meet their own needs" (Brundtland, 1987: 43).

In order to operationalize, there are two approaches to sustainability: (i) maximizing wealth (usually based on GDP); and (ii) maintaining non-declining capital (non-declining total capital).

Non-declining wealth is often measured by one of the two sustainability indicators:

- Non-declining income per capita (mostly GDP (PPP) per capita);
- Non-declining genuine (adjusted net) savings (genuine domestic savings (GDS) or adjusted net savings (ANS)).

David Pearce introduced the *GDS* indicator in 1994 and the United Nations adapted it in the *UN Statistical Yearbook* in 1999:

$$GDS = GDP - C - K_{mf}D + EdI - EngD - MinD - ForD - CDD,$$

where GDS = genuine domestic savings; GDP = gross domestic product; C = annual consumption; $K_{mf}D$ = capital fixed depreciation; EdI = education expenditures (investment in human capital); EngD = energy resource depletion (depreciation of natural capital); MinD = mineral resource depletion (depreciation of natural capital); ForD = forest depletion (depreciation of natural capital); CDD = damage to the environment due to carbon dioxide emission (depreciation of natural capital).

Expanding the original concepts of Solow (1974), Hartwick (1977) and Pearce (1989), Bochniarz & Bolan (2005) introduced the *Non-Declining Total Capital* sustainability indicator which is based on four types of capital:

$$TK = K_m + K_n + K_h + K_s = \text{constant (non-declining)},$$

where K_m = man-made capital (physical and financial); K_n = natural capital; K_h = human capital; K_s = social capital.

Sustainable business (SB), often referred to as green business, is an enterprise that is globally and locally environment friendly, socially responsible, and economically sound. For that reason SB is also described as an enterprise that strives to meet this triple bottom line.

In a popular definition endorsed by International Union for Conservation of Nature (IUCN) (Adams & Jeanrenaud, 2008), an SB or green business should match the following four criteria (Coon, 2009): (i) it incorporates principles of sustainability into each of its business decisions; (ii) it supplies environmentally friendly products or services that replaces demand for non-green products and/or services; (iii) it is greener than traditional competition; (iv) it has made an enduring commitment to environmental principles in its business operations.

From an **economics point of view, SB means an enterprise that maintains its** competitive advantage **coming from its unique value chain** (Porter, 2008). It requires a strategic approach to SB, including optimization of the firms value chain and diamond of competition (Porter & Kramer, 2006).

The last category that has to be defined is clusters. The research project embraced the most popular definition, credited to Michael Porter: **Clusters are geographic concentrations of interconnected companies, specialized suppliers, service providers, firms in related industries, and associated institutions that can cooperate and compete in particular fields** (Porter, 2008: 213).

There is an interesting dynamics in cluster development based on their integration from functional clusters through clumps to working clusters described (Fig. 1) by Derik Andreoli (Bochniarz, *et al.*, 2008).

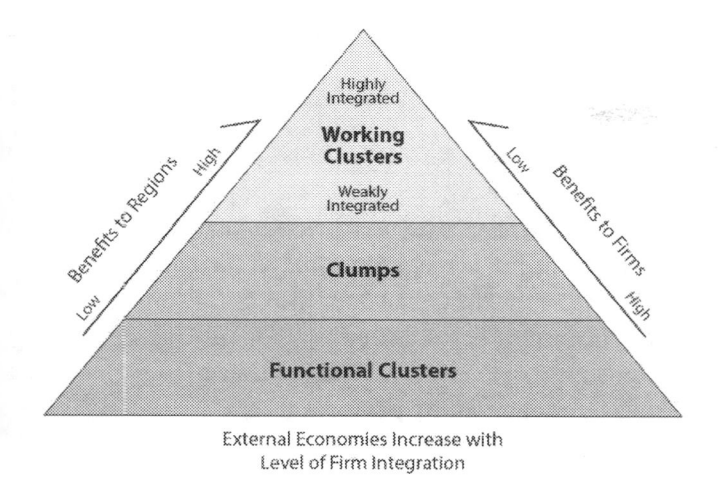

Fig. 1. Dynamics of cluster development
Sources: Andreoli (Bochniarz *et al.*, 2008).

Functional clusters are spatial networks of like and functionally linked industries, which enjoy the basic positive externalities coming from co-location known in economics literature as **Marshallian externalities** (Runiewicz-Wardyn, 2013). The higher level of integration represent **clumps**, represented by groups of functionally linked firms in which the physical distance separating member firms does not prohibit the range of benefits that are made possible through frequent interactions. The progress of integration moves up to the level of **working clusters**, where firms and other organizations, including academic, governmental, and other institutions, maximize benefits from synergetic effects coming from integration, cooperation, and competition within the clusters — **Porterian externalities** (*ibid.*). Finally, there are some other externalities coming from urbanization diversity, creating benefits from cluster openness and innovation spillover between co-located clusters — **Jacobsian externalities** (*ibid.*).

Taking into account the dynamics of cluster development and growing synergy along with cluster integration we came to formulate the following definition: The **effective cluster** is characterized by rich SC that enables all participants to efficiently cooperate, which leads to maximum generation of positive externalities coming not only from co-location but also from building collaborative synergy within the cluster and its openness for cooperation with other clusters, leading to knowledge spillovers among them and increasing innovations.

3. Research Hypothesis

Based on the above-mentioned assumptions and definitions of the basic categories, as well as on several studies in this field including a.o. Kourtit & Nijkamp (2012), Caragliu & Nijkamp (2011), Westlund & Adam (2010), the researchers formulated the following three hypotheses to be verified:

- Hypothesis 1: The process of cluster development from its functional stage to the stage of the effective cluster is strongly influenced by increases in SC.
- Hypothesis 2: The integration process of a cluster fueled by SC has a positive effect on its economic performance.
- Hypothesis 3: The progress in cluster development accompanied by growing SC contributes to the sustainability of the regional economy.

At the end of February 2014, a field research project began work to test these hypotheses.

4. The Applied System of Measurements

There are two basic approaches to measure the SC value — according to Fukuyama (1999) — either by conducting census of groups and their members or by using surveys (1999: 6). He proposed a third method based on a metrics, which could be applied within a private firm. Due to the interests of the project in measuring SC within clusters, a combination of survey and census method will be applied.

The economic value of SC depends on time invested in developing relations and networks, institutions and shared values, attitudes and trust within a certain group of people. This begins at the micro level, for example a family, and continues through firms, clusters and regions, to the macro level of a nation or even global community (Bochniarz *et al.*, 2008). A very similar approach to the measurement of SC was published by Roman (2007), with a set of complex indicators assessing its value mainly through surveys. For that reason, the research team adapted Roman's following indicators and applied them to the Podkarpackie Region to verify their usefulness.

There are four groups of indicators for measuring SC:

- Indicators measuring associations: assessing the size of the investment in SC.
- Indicators measuring trust: assessing one of the most desired impact of SC.
- Indicators measuring existing institutions: assessing business and political environment.
- Indicators measuring results: assessing the impact of SC.

The four groups of indicators were split into a series of specific questions which included a variety of research methods — from simple surveys through in-depth interviews and participatory assessment workshops. In addition to primary information collection, a comprehensive desk study is underway based on the secondary data.

5. Assessing Initial Results

The first two stages of the field research — surveys and interviews — in the Podkarpackie Region have been recently completed. The initial results indicate that there has been a significant investment in SC by business leaders of the Aviation Valley cluster in order to move toward the goal of higher efficiency. The initial interviews indicated that the top business leaders invested about 12.5% of their time for cluster activities, which was the equivalent of USD 900,000 in 2013. The cluster association hold regular monthly meetings, established many working groups to resolve emerging problems and/or to respond to future challenges and opportunities. As the result of their activities the trust in the association has significantly increased and is well illustrated by the number of cluster members, which has quadrupled since 2003, reaching 120 in April 2014. The monetary value of the SC created in 2013 measured by the time invested in building cluster relations, participating in joint activities, and resolving problems was 3,180,000 PLN or over USD 1 mn. Taking these facts into account, we came to conclusions that this type of investment in SC supports the Hypothesis 1: **increasing SC supports integration of the cluster and increases its synergies and positive externalities.**

In terms of economic performance, the cluster has been growing drastically, with sales quadrupling during the period of 2003–2008 (Polish Information and Foreign Investment Agency *et al.*, 2012). This unprecedented growth is closely tied to foreign direct investment (FDI), since the majority of sales came out of companies that were privatized by large multinational corporations. They invested more than USD 2 bn in new machines and technologies and introduced thousands of new patents since 2003 (ResEco Firma, 2014). This information contributes to verification of Hypothesis 2: **progressing integration of the cluster improves its economic performance.**

Finally, one might notice that Polish aviation companies from this poorest (according to GDP per capita) Polish region offer advanced products and services and are present in all major supply chains, to the extent that almost every passenger aircraft in the world is equipped with at least one part manufactured in Poland. Aviation Valley represents a very sophisticated and technologically advanced industry with over 90% of production targeted toward the most competitive global markets. It also means that this cluster has a well-educated and skilled workforce that is earning decent salaries and thus contributing to the wealth of the region and its sustainability. The number of employees in the cluster has increased significantly, from 9,000 in 2003 to 23,000 in 2014. This positive picture is illustrated in economic terms by the total export sales from USD 250 mn in 2003 to USD 2 bn in 2013 (*ibid.*). All these facts contribute to the verification of Hypothesis 3: **progress in cluster development accompanied by growth of its SC contributes to SD of the whole region.**

6. Conclusions

The descriptive analysis of the initial results from the field looks promising, but it should be further verified by more rigorous quantitative analysis of the three hypotheses. There is no doubt that the cluster and the region as a whole are moving toward a more sustainable path of development. Completing the field research and desk studies will lay the foundation for deeper analysis and design of an appropriate cluster upgrading policy. This policy will be focused on further decreasing the weak links within the cluster and enhancing its strengths to improve its competitiveness. It will also include the elimination of existing bottlenecks and unnecessary red tape, and investment in necessary types of capital, including human and social ones.

There is hope that this project will convince business and political leaders that investing in SC helps the participating actors to advance from a functional cluster to an effective one by reaching a higher level of development, better economic performance, and more effective contributions to the prosperity of the regional community.

References

Adams, W. M. (2006), The future of sustainability: Re-thinking environment and development in the twenty-first century, Report of the IUCN Renowned Thinkers Meeting, January 29–31.

Adams, W. M. & Jeanrenaud, S. J. (2008), *Transition to Sustainability: Towards a Humane and Diverse World*, p. 108, Gland, Switzerland: IUCN.

Bochniarz, Z. et al. (2008), Clustering and social capital: Past and current research at the University of Washington and unanswered questions, at the Annual MOC Faculty Workshop of the Harvard Business School, December 7.

Bochniarz, Z. & Bolan, R. (2004), Building institutional capacity for biodiversity and rural sustainability. In *The Role of Biodiversity Conservation in Rural Sustainability*, S. Light (ed.), pp. 79–94, Amsterdam: IOS Press.

Bochniarz, Z. & Sienko, B. (2008), Globalization, clustering and innovation: Some regional aspects. In *Enterprise Towards Global Challenges*, A. Herman and Szablewski (eds.), pp. 152–168, Warsaw: SGH.

Bourdieu, P. (1986), *The Forms of Capital, Handbook of Theory and Research for Sociology of Education*. In *Handbook of Theory and Research for the Sociology of Education*, J. G. Richardson (ed.), New York: Greenwood Press.

Brundtland, G. H. (1987), *Our Common Future*, Oxford: Oxford University Press.

Caragliu, A. & Nijkamp, P. (2011), The impact of regional absorptive capacity on spatial knowledge spillovers: The Cohen and Levinthal model revisited, *Applied Economics*, 44(11), 1363–1374.

Coleman, J. (1988), Social capital in the creation of human capital, *American Journal of Sociology*, 94(95), 121.

Cooke, P. (2007), Social capital, embeddedness, and regional innovation. In *Europe Reflection On Social Capital, Innovation And Regional Development: The Ostuni Consensus*, A. Kuklinski, M. Landabaso, and C. Roman (eds.), pp. 162–175, Nowy Sącz: Wyższa Szkoła Biznesu- National-Louis University w Nowym Sączu, Oficyna Wydawnicza Rewasz.

Cooney, S. (2009), *Build A Green Small Business: Profitable Ways to Become an Ecopreneur*, New York: McGraw-Hill.

Czyzewska, D. (2013), Empirical evidence and first assessment of the competitiveness clusters policy in France, *International Journal of Management and Economics*, 39.

Dasgupta, P. & Serageldin, I. (2000), *Social Capital: A Multifaceted Perspective*, Washington, D.C.: The World Bank.

Flap, H. D. & Völker, B. (2005), *Creation and Returns of Social Capital*, London: Routledge.

Francois, P. (2002), *Social Capital and Economic Development*, London: Routledge.

Franke, S. (2005), *Measurement of Social Capital: Reference Document for Public Policy Research, Development, and Evaluation. PRI Project Social Capital as a Public Policy Tool*, Canada: Policy Research Initiative.

Fukuyama, F. (1999), Social capital and civil society. IMF lecture.

Fukuyama, F. (2002), Social capital and development: The coming agenda, *SAIS Review*, 22(1).

Grootaert, C. (1997), *Social Capital: The Missing Link? World Bank, Expanding the Measure of Wealth: Indicators of Environmentally Sustainable Development*, Washington, D.C.: World Bank.

Grootaert, C. & Van Bastelaer, T. (2002), Conclusion: Measuring impact and drawing policy implications. In *The Role of Social Capital in Development*, T. Van Bestelaer (ed.), Melbourne: Cambridge University Press.

Hartwick, J. M. (1977), Intergenerational equity and the investing of rents from exhaustible resources, *American Economic Review*, 67(5), 972–974.

Huber, F. (2008), Social capital of economic clusters: Toward a network-based conception of social resources, Economic Geography Research Group, Working Paper Series No. 02.08, Cambridge.

Jacobs, J. (2000), *The Nature of Economies*, New York: Random House.

Kourtit, K. & Nijkamp, P. (2012), Creative firms as change agents in creative spaces, *Quaestiones Geographicae*, December.

Lin, N. et al. (eds.) (1986), *Conceptualizing Social Support, Social Support, Life Events and Depression*, Orlando: Academic Press.

Lin, N. (2001), *Social Capital: A Theory of Social Structure and Action*, Cambridge: Cambridge University Press.

Marshall, A. (1920), *Principles of Economics* (8th edn.), London: Macmillan.

Nijkamp, P. (2003), Entrepreneurship in a modern network economy, *Regional Studies*, 37, 395–405.

OECD (2001), *The Well-Being of Nations: The Role of Human and Social Capital*, Paris: OECD.

Ott, K. (2003), The Case for Strong Sustainability. In *Greifswald's Environmental Ethics*, K. Ott and P. Thapa (eds.). Greifswald: Steinbecker Verlag Ulrich Rose.

PARP (2012), Cluster Benchmarking in Poland.

Pearce, D. (1989), Energy and environment: Editor's introduction, *Energy Policy*, Elsevier, 17(2), 82–83.

Pezzey, J. & Toman, M. A. (2002), Progress and problems in the economics of sustainability. In *International Yearbook of Environmental and Resource Economics*, T. Tietenberg and H. Folmer (eds.), pp. 265–232, Cheltenham: Edward Elgar.

Polish Information and Foreign Investment Agency (2012), Invest in Poland. Available at http://www.paiz.gov.pl/sectors/aviation.

Porter, M. (2008), *On Competition: Updated and Expanded Edition*, Boston: HBS Publishing.

Porter, M. & Kramer. M. (2011), Big idea: Creating shared value, *Harvard Business Review*, January–February.

Putnam, R. (1995), Bowling alone: America's declining social capital, *Journal of Democracy*, 6, 65–78.

Putnam, R. (2000), *Bowling Alone: The Collapse and Survival of American Community*, New York: Simon and Schuster.

ResEco Firma (2014), Raport koncowy z badan w malych i srednich przedsiebiorstwach klastra lotniczego (Final Report from the Aviation Cluster SME) — Effective Clusters Project's study.

Roman, C. (2007), Why social capital? What social capital? In A. Kuklinski, pp. 80–92.

Rosenfeld S. A. (1997), Bringing business clusters into the mainstream of economic development, *European Planning Studies*, 5, 3–23.

Rosenfeld, S. (2007), The social imperatives of clusters. In A. Kuklinski, pp. 176–182.

Runiewicz-Wardyn, M. (2013), *Knowledge Flows, Technological Change and Regional Growth in the European Union*, New York: Springer.

Sobel, J. (2002), Can we trust social capital?, *Journal of Economic Literature*, 40, 139–154.

Solow, R. M. (1974), Intergenerational equity and exhaustible resources, *Review of Economic Studies*, Symposium.

Sommers, P. (1998), Rural networks in the United States: Lessons from three experiments, *Economic Development Quarterly*, 12, 54–67.

Westlund, H. & Adam, F. (2010), Social capital and economic performance: A meta-analysis of 65 studies, *European Planning Studies*, 18(6), 893–919.

Woolcock, M. & Narayan, D. (2000), Social capital: Implications for development theory, research, and policy, *World Bank Research Observer*, 15(2), 225–250.

Zachariasz, K. (2012), Pół miliarda I ... zaklajstrowane Klastry, *Gazeta Wyborcza* (December 1).

Chapter 7

Integrating Corporate and Academic Alumni into the Drive toward Sustainability

Rodica Stefănescu

Certified Independent Senior Consultant in Management

The chapter presents how alumni — both corporate and university, resources' proper capitalization may sustain the respective organizations' pursue towards sustainability. More, by integrating those two alumni categories and their management approaches in each of the two organizations' cultures, each of them may increase their respective chances to sustainability, and also those of better contribution to sustainable development.

Corporate and university alumni concepts are, thus far, developed separately. It is our conviction that they can be joined together, in an integrative management approach. Both universities and corporations may learn from each other's knowledge, experience, best practices, managerial instruments' use, attitudes and skills, in their quest for improved capabilities and performance. Alumni are just a human resource and capital, that each of the two types of organizations may hire, value and use, both for their benefit and for that of society at large.

Our research is based on literature, websites' data, and case studies survey, from both worldwide and Romanian experience, regarding corporate and university's current stage and methods in managing their respective specific alumni resources. The conclusion of the research is based on the idea that learning organizations and those which can best capitalize on all their resources may have better chances for sustainability.

The chapter represents a theoretical approach, based on existing practices. Looking at ways to improve the capitalization of the alumni potentials through integrated management approaches, addressing a merge of both corporation and university attempts in this respect, is a fresh view. Especially in the globalization era, it can offer both corporations and universities even broader resources and largely improved competitive advantages. In addition, with joint efforts, through partnerships, in this respect, both sectors can grow in becoming stronger pillars of the society in its pathway towards sustainable development.

1. Introduction

If the notion of alumni defines the quality of graduates of a type of school (Webster, 2000), then corporate alumni refers to former employees of a company (Business Dictionary, 2009). From our point of view, beyond highlighting, in a brief manner, the need and organizational benefits of creating, maintaining, preserving, and developing the relationship with specific alumni, we believe that it is important to point out two aspects of the necessary overcoming of the conceptual limitations associated with those two notions. Thus, we consider that, if companies will be able to perceive and cultivate the notion of corporate alumni in the sense of "former" — not just employees, but also the collaborators, customers, suppliers, partners, associates, consultants or experts, financiers, founders, honorary members, applicants for vacancies and interviews, maybe even competitors, etc., their interrelation basis would be much wider, and of a higher potential of benefits and of competitive advantage provision, at least at the social capital level.

We consider the same kind of conceptual approach useful for educational structures as well. Their alumni are not only graduates but also former students, as well as all stakeholders with whom they were related at one time and whom they can attract and train towards the same aim of development and strengthening of their respective social capital (Stefanescu *et al.*, 2010).

In this sense, any organization should focus on the formation and cultivation of the sense and feeling of community (Williams, 2009), of belonging to a family, both organizational as well as in regards to social responsibility, with, and towards all those with whom it interacts, as well as with and towards all those it serves.

The justification for this approach of extending the notion of alumni would be based on the educational dimension which any organization has, directly or indirectly, willingly or unconsciously, over any category of its stakeholders, through its way of relating with them and as impact of its interactions. This educational component, of a training as well as learning nature, determines both the drive towards sustainability of any organization, as well as its role and contributions to the sustainable development of society (Candea, 2007a), including through its members, be they internal or external.

From the two standpoints of extending the definition and the common perception of the concepts regarding alumni, in a dynamic and flexible approach more suited to the evolutions marked by information technology and communication, globalization, and of the influences of boundless interactions caused by these two coordinates of the present, including the impact of chrysies (economical, political, social, environmental, etc.), we consider that it becomes evident and logical that the two conceptual approaches should merge, being integrated into a management of excellence and in the sustainability strategy of any organizational structure.

We must not lose sight of the fact that, both university and corporate alumni are not only presented with (other) multiple possibilities of affirmation and evolution, but they represent, wherever they may be found, members of society and contributors to its becoming. That is why, once more, the way these "alumni" are trained in this sense of their role is also important, (especially in the extended view of the notion) by the organizations they have gone through at one time, but also in what way these organizations continue keeping them in their connection and attention network, including in the sense of consciously assuming their own social responsibility (Candea, 2010).

If the universities are already beginning to acquire and apply corporate managerial approaches, for a prosperous existence, for unlimited time (Stefanescu *et al.*, 2011), we consider that corporations can also learn some practices that are useful for their evolution from university management, including regarding liaising with the alumni. In fact, any organization which, at the sustainability management of excellence level integrates the understanding and conscious attitude of a learning organization, staying open to the accumulation of information and practices, from any area, at the same time sharing their own accumulated values, is an organization committed to a prosperous evolution, for unlimited time (Oncica & Candea, 2010).

Therefore, in the following, we will attempt a rundown of the advantages of capitalizing on corporate and academic alumni, as it manifests at present, both worldwide and in Romania, then presenting how we view the possibility of integrating these management approaches, both for higher organizational benefits, and for their increased input in supporting the sustainable development of society.

2. Corporate and University Alumni — Conceptual and in Practice Differentiation and Similarities

By definition, corporate alumni means former employees, with whom the organization maintains connectivity. It can be said that using the notion of alumni, in this acceptability too, is justified by keeping, to an extent, the sense of the basic definition of alumni (The American Heritage Dictionary, 2000), namely that of a "product" of an educational (institutionalized) process. In fact, as in the case of university alumni, as long as some people have functioned within an organization, those members or employees have acquired a certain experience, had access to some information, were taught and learned certain rules, procedures, techniques, and technologies, as well as many other things, it was invested in them through programmatic training, experience exchanges, involvement in various contexts of connections, and responsibilities etc. Therefore, we consider it very natural that at the departure of any person from an organization (corporate, educational, or of any other nature), its management should make every effort to keep in touch with them. It is an already earned, trained, and known human and social capital, which only needs to be cultivated and capitalized further.

As in the case of university alumni, people who leave an organization already know the institution to which they belonged at one time, from the inside, from most points of view. Thus, in case of a need for hiring or collaborations, the institution in question can call upon former members, as known and accepted people, if not directly for employment, at least to make recommendations, or to guide a new employee as a mentor (Spencer Lee, 2008).

Former employees or members can be of three types: unemployed, retired or active, steering towards new steps in their career (obviously we do not consider the negative cases of terminated collaborations). With all these, the organization will have to keep and maintain the connection, if it desires certain benefits. In any of the three posts, such persons may also be useful to the organization, providing both feedback and information from its external reality, and as a resource of ideas, new collaborations, and possible partnerships, but, more importantly, in strengthening the organization's social capital and image, especially in knowledge based economy (McNamara & McLaughlin, 2009). Therefore, the way in which an organization structures its sustainability strategy (Candea, 2007b), based on developing or strengthening its organizational culture, its human resource management (current and potential — to create and/or to attract), and its communication with stakeholders (Candea & Candea, 2009), can insure its thriving viability indefinitely or it can doom it to failure (Candea, 2009).

Thus, regarding the relationship with alumni, the organization will have to take into account both an anti-breakup strategy for its employees or members, concerning the maintenance of a communication and collaboration relationship, as well as a one after terminating contractual ties (Koc-Menard, 2009). And this is valid and must also be transposed for universities, in regard to both their relationship with the students as well as to their staff or other stakeholders.

This preoccupation and responsibility has as its aim that the mentality created within the organization will act in furthering natural cooperation and team relationships with all its members, for the entire duration of their existence, be they within the organization, or not, and beyond these, even regarding their family members, acquaintances, as well as their various community involvement and correlations. And that is because, as for university alumni, corporate alumni can also play a role of organizations' relevant stakeholders, due to their double quality of ex-interns, operating as externals.

As well, the same as for university alumni, corporate ones can also be agents of the organization as its representation in the society, marketers for it, and endorsers of its image and factors of its integration into society (Stefanescu et al., 2009). Therefore, the same as for universities, in the same capacity of multi-role stakeholders, corporate alumni also represent an organizational resource that provides benefits, which the organization can draw on, and it would be very beneficial for it to do so. McKinsey & Company (2013), for example, said that "Our alumni number nearly 27,000 and work in virtually every business sector in 120 countries. Through formal events and informal networking, former McKinsey consultants make and sustain professional relationships. This dynamic network is a lasting benefit of a McKinsey career."

As in the case of university alumni, the benefits of cultivating a relationship with corporate alumni, in particular as regards the recruitment of talents, have become so apparent, especially in statistical references, that it led to a rapid development of both a number of companies providing services in maintaining databases associated with the capitalization of corporate alumni resources communities (Expert Alumni, 2014), as well as the IT programs and consultancy in this regard. The slogan of one such service company (Insala, 2014), for example, is "Your Current Employees Are Your Future Alumni", stating that "Ultimately, the success of any organization comes down to one thing: the engagement of its people, by expanding vision to include corporate alumni in the HRM strategy." At the same time, field-specific studies exist or are being developed by groups of experts in the field (Xing, 2006).

The analysis of the similarities between the way in which both corporate and university alumni can be useful to the organizations that they are affiliates to can continue. What we consider important to remember is that both communities are valuable resources to be capitalized, both to the benefit of such organizations, as well as that of their respective alumni, and together, contributing to that of society.

Beyond the conceptual definition, specific differences between corporate and university alumni (also) consist of:

- The number of members that each of these communities can have and its growth rate (if for universities the growth is annual and continues with each new promotion of graduates, for corporations that number is significantly low and random);
- The number of alma-maters (between 1 to 3–4 or so, if a person graduates more universities and/or also takes Masters, or PhD degrees too), versus corporate-mothers (which could be from 1 to as many as an individual's career shall gather);
- History and the complexity of the range of means and methods by which each of these communities of alumni are capitalized.

2.1. Benefits of cultivating the corporation — corporate alumni relationship

Benefits for the corporation

- Alumni may represent a pool of already known, tested, and trained specialists from which to re-recruit, to get recommendations for fresh recruitments from, to receive feed-back information from the external environment, to use as mentors, councilors or support staff, with experience, in guiding new employees, or as consultants in particular projects, or even trainers for youth talents (Lorenz, 2014);
- They may also facilitate connection with potential business partners, or to come up with creative ideas and innovative approaches in how to further develop the corporate business;
- They could (now) have time or opportunity to become (more or less occasional) vendors, promoters, or suppliers of some goods and services for the corporate business (Jones, 2010), especially if specifically further trained on;
- They may become company's ambassadors and its advocacy representatives, if well prepared to and properly treated for (Hoey, 2011);
- They could possibly also undertake (now) an advisory role of pointing out weaknesses and strengths of the company, up to their direct perceptions, which, most probably, they did not share with their leaders, during their employment;
- At the same time, this could also be a way in which the company may gain credit and trust on the line of social responsibility (Sullivan, 2009).

As Jones (2009) said: "The time has come for businesses to view ex-employees, as a commodity that can continue to be of value even after they have left". As Laurano (2009) put it "Leveraging an alumni community can be a win–win for an organization". And, as an international report (IPR, 2003) states "Companies that are not actively viewing and treating their former employees as "alumni" — that is, staying in touch with, reaching out to, and providing networking and educational opportunities to former employees — are actually creating a competitive advantage for companies that do institute "alumni" programs. Progressive companies — ones that are, in many cases, the leaders in their industries — are beginning to view former employees as stakeholders and are leading a shift in the way human assets are approached."

And, this is perfectly in line with what we have stated about the university alumni — they are a strategic resource of competitive advantage for their alma-mater (Stefanescu et al., 2010), as they also are to be found in all type of stakeholder categories (Stefanescu et al., 2011), so that they should be included in the human resources management strategy (Stefanescu et al., 2013), as well as in the university's strategy for sustainability (Stefanescu et al., 2012). Adding here the alumni contribution to creativity and innovation (Stefanescu, 2012), the picture of similarities between the way corporate alumni can be assets for a firm, as the university alumni are a strategic resource for the sustainable university (Stefanescu, 2011), is almost complete.

Benefits for the corporate alumni

- By setting up corporate alumni networks, these may further benefit of involvement in further professional training sessions that the company may organize; keeping in touch among themselves, as well as with former colleagues; participating in corporate events or occasional community activities (the procedures in the army system, in this respect, for instance, may set an example of such a fruitful management of keeping together all category members of their respective community);
- Recognition of professional capabilities and potential, including support in finding new jobs;
- Free invitations to company fairs or congresses, or discounts to the firm products (per life), thus making them clients, as Microsoft does, for instance (Glazer, 2013).

Currently, most corporate alumni networks are managed as LinkedIn or Facebook groups, hosted on the company servers (Doyle, 2014). Tracking which are the big corporations in the world that have developed the most comprehensive and visible public relations programs with their alumni, one can easily conclude that, renowned IT firms have the top places, or ones that have developed broad cooperative platforms and social networks through IT, or working in the field of information and communication technology services (Microsoft, IBM, Apple Inc., Google, Buzz Allen Hamilton, McKinsey, Accenture, Ernst & Young, KPMG, Deloitte & Touche, AT&T, Alcatel-Lucent, etc.).

Exactly like in the case of university alumni management (Stefanescu, 2013), corporate alumni management means having a strategy, a program, a designated responsibility, personnel trained in dealing with this community, a database and online networking platform — institutionalization. A differentiation of particularities between corporate and university alumni management is highlighted in the IPR report (2003) as "the need to compete to be the" alma mater. "Unlike academic institutions, whose alumni have only attended one or two other schools, companies have alumni who may have worked for five, six, or more organizations, many of which are competitors. This situation means that companies will be competing for the affinity of a former employee who may belong to multiple communities. Hence, the fast have a real advantage over the sluggish."

3. Corporate and University Alumni Programs in Romania

From public information on company websites, mentions regarding corporate alumni, in Romania, are encountered only sporadically and in particular at companies operating as representatives of foreign groups. More specifically, there appear present at companies where this trend towards corporate alumni comes from the mother-company's policy and organizational culture. The following are to be mentioned in this respect: KPMG (2012) — that has created an association of alumni and issued a magazine intended for them, but also developed various activities, requesting that the 2% contribution from the tax revenue be steered towards the company's foundation, then Accenture (2014), Ernst & Young (2014), INSEAD (2013), Deloitte (2014), and even IBM (2014).

On April 23, 2012, IBM opens CCS–Corporate Service Corps Romania (IBM–CSC, 2012), meant to facilitate networking between the IBMers interested in finding out about the unique IBM volunteering program. On April 9, 2009, in Romania, the LinkedIn group for the alumni of Hachette Distribution Services — Romania under the brands of Inmedio, Relay and MOA (HDS, 2009) team is created. A special case is the group of alumni of Japan International Cooperation Agency — JICA (2014), whose purpose is the support of ideas of new cooperation and programs (Japan–Romania). We should also mention Entrepreneur of the Year (EY), which launched in Romania a LinkedIn group for the EY/AA Alumni (2013), "to share their news, business achievements, and personal stories and to keep in touch as part of an online community", numbering, at present, 147 members.

As it regards university alumni, our research and doctoral studies have highlighted the fact that the mention of alumni on institutional websites is found in 72%

of the around 120 universities in Romania, but only approximately 10% of them also carry out some activities concerning liaising with the alumni, without, however, being a main incumbent concern of university strategy or to any formally assumed responsibility of its leadership (Stefanescu et al., 2011). But it is salutary to note the fact that, to date, there are at least 3–4 programs with financing from European funds that took place in Romania, through university's consortiums, on goals underwriting the idea to facilitate a connection (post graduate) of alumni with the university and between them.

4. What Could Integrative Corporate and University Alumni Concepts Merging Bring in for the Organizational Pursue to Sustainability

If the universities, especially those of world renown, are already familiar with the idea of the need to capitalize on the potential of their graduate community, a rich tradition and experience already existing, in this sense, they do not register official, programmatic, and systematic actions of capitalizing on the potential of former employees. Moreover, neither the managerial approach of the universities of investing in their employees, with respect to training and gaining their loyalty as members of an organizational family, is not very manifest, nor frequent. We believe strongly, however, that such a cultural dimension of the management of their own human resources, to which to add an extension of concern in the sense of programs regarding corporate alumni (the university also being a corporation, in fact), could only bring additional benefits to the university (Laufer, 2009), in providing resources along the line of creating a competitive advantage and providing multi-talent support in its efforts toward sustainability. Anyway, it is already shown (in theory, in practice, and in statistics), that interaction between and over generations of people belonging to the same organization, especially as a training environment, is emulative and beneficial to all those involved. Enthusiasm merges with experience, the creative energies being stimulated by the conjugation of the efforts and expertise of the parties involved in dialogue and cooperation. And, of course, the wider the community of those involved in achieving the same objectives, the greater the chances of synergistic, constructive effects.

In addition, because the tendency, natural in our times, is for universities to be managed more and more by adapting methods and tools, approaches and concepts from corporate management (Stefanescu, 2012), we do not see why the idea of developing programs relating to the capitalization of former employees and collaborators communities' resources would not be part of this. The university, as a learning organization, which is also concerned with sustainability, is characterized by a visionary, excellence management, which should harness all resources — both those available, as well as the ones that it can create, and those it can attract, to the up most (Stefanescu et al., 2010b).

On the other hand, we believe that no matter how aware is the organizational strategy and strongly manifest is the management programs, liaising with corporate alumni, at companies, and institutions outside of schools, corporate management would also have much to learn from the practices and working methods of universities in their relationship with graduates (alumni, regarded as former students).

An interface area is the role that corporate alumni can have in influencing students towards specific professional paths (Davis, 2014), including by promoting employment at companies they can represent, as well as in favor of recruiting young specialists. The practice of some companies to get involved in the recruitment of talent from universities, starting at the time they are still students is already known and quite widespread. Add to this the fact that many universities are both financially supported through donations from companies, as is the case with the University of Alabama, with the "corporate matching gift" program, carried out through its Alumni Association (UA Alumni, 2014), for example, but also involved in relationships of scientific and technical cooperation relating to their educational programs, with companies in the business sector, as is the case at Dalhousie University (Peters, 2013), for example. It would only seem very natural that, from and through such partnerships, both organizations to be able to share from their own managerial experience, including on the liaising with specific alumni, and to teach each other, and to evolve, in this way, also as institutional structures. Moreover, because the university prepares experts on various fields, it would be a gift for them to also institutionally apply what they impart during their training process and to continue to then receive, especially through networking with alumni, feedback from the practical reality. This would lead to both an increase in the pertinence of the educational process, as well as of the organizational evolution towards sustainability. And the same thing is true in the case of corporations (Vermeiren, 2009), or any other organizations. Continuous learning and integrated management of all resources imparts efficiency.

It is essential to highlight that sustainable development cannot be aimed without relying on sustainable organizations (Candea, 2006). However, this means, among other things, openness towards communication, sharing of knowledge and practices, cooperation, partnerships and consortiums, including interdisciplinary ones, to learn and adapt, permanently, from own experiences and from that of others, from anywhere, but also to join individual efforts into a chain of synergistic accomplishments, for global benefits.

So, with the strict applicability to universities and corporations concerning the capitalization of specific alumni communities, incorporating within a unified strategic vision, customized for each organization, the capitalization of the resources that the alumni communities in their extended sense represent, cannot but serve, every structure in increasing their capabilities and in turn, of their respective chances and opportunities towards sustainability. And, through this, also those of every individual and every organization to become significant pillars in the efforts (in common, but also joint) towards sustainable development.

5. Conclusion

Summarizing the above-mentioned sections:

(a) Both corporate and university alumni:

- Possess the special feature of being a strategic resource of the organizations to which they may be affiliated, as ex-internal and (then) external stakeholders — who can also enter and fit into any category of capital (human, informational, relational, financial, of creativity and innovation, promotional, voluntary, social, of branding, mentoring, community integration, and trust building etc.) that the organization may benefit from, being, at the same time, a most at hand resource, which can also, the easiest, be capitalized;
- Represent a continuous potential source of competitive advantages (for their respective organization) and, thus, the most available resource that the organization can relay on in its' drive towards sustainability.

(b) Improved capitalization of their (extended) alumni resources, by any organization, presupposes going with an all resources integrative management of excellence, which involves, among others, to:

- Establish an organizational culture of sustainability;
- Keep learning (individually, as organization, as society);
- Maintaining uninterrupted open communication and sharing (of information, knowledge and experience — individually, as organization, as society);
- Invest in human capital development, through education;
- Maintain the "family" (individual, organizational, and social) sustainable.

Therefore, both corporate alumni, and university alumni are representatives (in society) of the organizations to which they belonged at one time. It is up to each individual organization how much it recognizes the importance and role of alumni, including as an extension of the sense of the notion, and to what extent they manage to capitalize the resources potential of these communities (both as human resources and as social capital).

"Brand ambassadors cannot be created overnight. Nor can they be created from a group of people who are disengaged and disconnected from your brand and your organization. If you are serious about your corporate alumni program, you have to be serious about your brand, your culture, and your employees' level of engagement with both" (Insala, 2014b).

A corporate alumni program, exactly like in the case of the university alumni strategy and program should be about: the organizational culture, its branding and the human resources (including alumni) forming and involving management. In essence, the internal culture comes out into the external brand — be it of an individual, an organization, or a nation.

In maintaining the organization — alumni relationship and of communication with them, it is essential to keep the alumni interested in the network and in the organization. Keeping updated and relevant content on the website and on the online dialogue would be a must. Keeping them involved and participative could make the difference.

And, last but not least, maintaining the openness of the organization's management and that of its entire team (of current, former and future members) towards continuous learning is defining for the quest toward sustainability, both individual and collective, as well as in the joint efforts towards sustainable development.

References

Accenture (2014), Alumni network. Available at https://www.accenturealumni.com/web/guest/home (Accessed 17 January 2014).

Alumni at KPMG in Romania (2012), Forget me not. Available at http://www.kpmg.com/RO/en/Alumni/Documents/alumni_web.pdf (Accessed 11 March 2014).

American Heritage Dictionary of the English Language: Fourth Edition (2000), Boston: Houghton Mifflin Harcourt.

Business Dictionary — online (2014), Available at http://www.businessdictionary.com/definition/alumni.html (Accessed 23 January 2014).

Candea, D. (2006), From sustainable development to the sustainable corporation, *Intreprinderea Sustenabila*, 1, iii, vi.

Candea, D. (2007a), Sustenabilitatea intreprinderii si responsabilitatea sociala, *Intreprinderea Sustenabila*, 2, 1–6.

Candea, D. (2007b), Conjectures about the relationship among business sustainability, learning organization, and management systems integration, Keynote speaker address to the International Conference on Business Excellence ICBE-2007, Brasov, Romania.

Candea, D. (2009), Organizational challenges in building a sustainable enterprise, Keynote address at the 7th International symposium of the Romanian Regional Science Association, Universitatea de Nord, Baia Mare, Romania, June 12–13.

Candea, R. & Candea, D. (2009), Comunicare corporativa integrata pentru sustenabilitatea afacerii, *Intreprinderea Sustenabila*, 4, 39–54. Available at https://sites.google.com/site/organizatiasustenabila/.

Davis, C. (2014), Corporate alumni offer students networking opportunity, *Finance & Investment*, Features. Available at http://www.theaggie.org/2014/02/06/corporate-alumni-offer-students-networking-opportunity/ (Accessed 1 March 2014).

Deloitte Romania Alumni (2014), Available at https://www.deloitte.com/view/en_RO/ro/alumni/index.htm (Accessed 11 February 2014).

Doyle, A. (2014), How to use corporate alumni networks to stay connected. Available at http://jobsearch.about.com/od/networking-tips/a/corporate-alumni-networks.htm (Accessed 1 March 2014).

Expert Alumni, The Value of Experience (2014), Designing, developing and launching a corporate alumni programme Available at http://www.expertalumni.com/support-your-corporate-alumni/ (Accessed 28 January 2014).

EY Romania Alumni (2013), Available at https://www.linkedin.com/groups?gid=5191191 (Accessed 3 July 2014).

Glazer, E. (2013), Leave the company, but stay in touch, *Careers, The Wall Street Journal*, April 12.

Hachette Distribution Services Romania (HDS) (2009), HDS inmedio alumni. Available at http://www.linkedin.com/groups/HDS-Inmedio-Romania-Alumni-1893875/about.

Hoey, J. K. (2011), Corporate alumni programs: Maintaining relationships & amp, enhancing reputation. Available at http://www.slideshare.net/JKHoey/corporate-alumni-programs-maintaining-relationships-amp-enhancing-reputation (Accessed 19 July 2014).

IBM– CSC Romania (2012), CSC alumni. Available at http://www.linkedin.com/groups/IBM-Romania-CSC-alumni-4391270? (Accessed 3 March 2014).

Insala (2014a), What your corporate alumni program has to do with employee engagement. Available at http://www.insala.com/Articles/career-development/what-your-corporate-alumni-program-has-to-do-with-employee-engagement.asp (Accessed 18 February 2014).

Insala (2014b), Corporate alumni: Targeted programs. Available at https://www.insala.com/corporate-alumni-targeted-programs.asp (Accessed 2 March 2014).

INSEAD (2013), iConnect-INSEAD Community IAA Romania. Available at https://iconnect.insead.edu/iaa/ROU/Pages/Default.aspx (Accessed 12 January 2013).

IPR Strategic Business Information Database (2003), World: Hidden value of corporate alumni networks. Available at http://alumnichannel.com/blog/wp-content/uploads/

2008/09/hidden-value-of-corporate-alumni-networks.pdf (Accessed 18 January 2014).

JICA (2008), Alumni Romania. Available at http://www.jica-alumni.ro/ (Accessed 10 February 2014).

Jones, D. (2009), How to win back lost talent, *HR Management*.

Jones, S. (2010), Maintaining relationships with former employees: A look into corporate alumni networks: Managing Information for Innovation. Available at http://infomgmt.wordpress.com/2010/02/09/ei2-maintaining-relationships-with-former-employees-a-look-into-corporate-alumni-networks/ (Accessed 26 February 2014).

Koc-Menard, S. (2009), Knowledge transfer after retirement: The role of corporate alumni networks, *Development and Learning in Organizations*, 23(2), 9–11.

Laufer, J. (2009), What universities can learn from corporate alumni programs, slides presentation at the *Corporate Alumni Programmes — Nuffic Holland Alumni Conference*. Available at http://www.slideshare.net/joeinholland/what-universities-can-learn-from-corporate-alumni-programs (Accessed 9 March 2014).

Laurano, M. (2009), Keep in touch: The power of alumni programs, *Bersin by Deloitte* (February 2).

Lorenz, M. (2014), "Grey's Anatomy" and the case for corporate alumni programs; employment branding, referral programs, talent pipeline. Available at http://thehiringsite.careerbuilder.com/2014/03/10/greys-anatomy-case-corporate-alumni-programs/ (Accessed 20 July 2014).

McKinsey & Company (2014), Alumni. Available at http://www.mckinsey.com/alumni? (Accessed 23 February 2014).

McNamara, Y. & McLaughlin, D. P. (2009), Corporate alumni networks and knowledge flows. Available at http://impgroup.org/uploads/papers/5906.pdf (Accessed 18 July 2014).

Oncica-Stanislav, D. & Candea, D. (2010), The learning organization, a strategic dimension of the sustainable enterprise? *Proceedings of the 6th European Conference on Management, Leadership, and Governance*, Wroclaw, Poland.

Peters, K. (2013), Merging science and business, Dalhousie University, Canada. Available at http://alumni.dal.ca/alumni-story/merging-science-and-business-kelly-peters/ (Accessed 18 July 2014).

Spencer Lee, K. (2006), The value of corporate alumni networks: Communication for information technology leaders. Available at http://www.cioupdate.com/career/article.php/3602391/The-Value-of-Corporate-Alumni-Networks.htm (Accessed 26 February 2014).

Sullivan. J. (2009), Corporate alumni and boomerang recruiting programs are hot due to layoffs. Available at http://www.ere.net/2009/03/02/corporate-alumni-and-boomerang-recruiting-programs-are-hot-due-to-layoffs/ (Accessed 19 July 2014).

Stefanescu, R., Candea, D., & Candea, R. (2009), Alumni — a strategic resource for universities, *Proceedings of The 5th Balcanic and 2nd International Conference on Engineering and Business Education*, 2, pp. 557–561, BRCEE&ICEBE — LBU Sibiu 2009/Romania. Available at http://www.cedc.ro/pages/english/conference-and-journal/brcebe/the-5th-brcee.php.

Stefanescu, R., Candea, D., & Candea, R. (2010a), Alumni — a university's resource for competitive advantage, *Proceedings of the 6th International Seminar on Quality Management in Higher Education — QMHE 2010*, pp. 343–346, Cluj-Napoca, Romania.

Stefanescu, R., Candea, D., & Candea, R. (2010b), The sustainable university, *Review of International Comparative Management*, 11(5), 841–852. Available at http://www.rmci.ase.ro/.

Stefanescu, R., Candea, D., & Candea, R. (2011), A model for managing the university — alumni relationship strategically for sustainability, *Proceedings of the 7th International Conference on Management of Technological Changes — MTC 2011*, pp. 213–216, Alexandroupolis/Greece: Democritus University of Thrace, Book 2.

Stefanesu, R., Candea, D., Candea, R., & Manolache, R. (2011), Relatia universitate — alumni, in opinia unor romani, din mediul academic autohton si international, *Intreprinderea Sustenabila*, 6, 65–106. Available at https://sites.google.com/site/organizatiasustenabila/.

Stefanescu, R. (2012), Managing university through business approaches, *Proceedings of The 6th Balkan Region Conference and 5th International Conference on Engineering & Business Education, and 4th International Conference on Innovation and Entrepreneurship*, pp. 247–252, BRCEE, ICEBE & ICIE — LBU Sibiu/Romania. Available at http://www.cedc.ro/pages/english/conference-and-journal/brcebe/the-6th-brcee.php.

Stefanescu, R. & Candea, R. (2012), Alumni inclusion as human resources into the strategic management of the university, *Proceedings of the 5th International Management Conference on Managerial Challenges of the Contemporary Society — MCCS 2012*, 4, pp. 17–175. FSEGA, Babes-Bolyai University of Cluj-Napoca.

Stefanescu, R., Candea, D., & Candea, R. (2012), The sustainable university: Adopting and adapting business management practices, *Management of Sustainable Development Journal*, 4. Available at http://www.cedc.ro/pages/english/conference-and-journal/msd-journal/papers/volume-4-no-22012.php.

Stefanescu, R. & Manolache, R. (2012a), Organizational creativity and idea generation through investing in alumni potentials capitalization, *Journal of International Scientific Publications: Educational Alternatives*, 10(1), 212–219. Available at http://www.science-journals.eu/.

Stefanescu, R. (2013), Alumni si universitatea sustenabila, *Intreprinderea Sustenabila*, 7, 163. Available at https://sites.google.com/site/organizatiasustenabila/.

University of Alabama (UA) (2014), Corporate matching gift program. Available at http://alumni.ua.edu/membership/corporate-matching/ (Accessed 4 July 2014).

Vermeiren, J. (2009), What any organization can learn from great alumni programs. Available at http://janvermeiren.wordpress.com/2009/03/28/what-any-organisation-can-learn-from-great-alumni-programs/ (Accessed 22 July 2014).

Wilson, G. (2009), Corporate alumni networks. Available at http://www.corporate-alumni.info/Corporate%20Alumni%20Networks%20-%20overview%202.pdf (Accessed 14 January 2014).

XING (2006), Corporate alumni networks: leveraging intangible assets, Gottlieb Duttweiler Institute (GDI), Rüschlikon, Zurich, Austria. Available at https://corporate.xing.com/fileadmin/image_archive/survey_corporate_alumni_networks_summary_english.pdf (Accessed 25 February 2014).

Part III

University Governance and Management

Chapter 8

Taxonomies of Internationalization for Higher Education

Martin Henson

University of Essex

Internationalization is now of central importance for higher education institutions across the world, and the development of an international strategy is high on the agenda. In this chapter we look at the complexities of globalization and internationalization as they play out in the particular circumstances of higher education, and provide a number of taxonomic approaches that can serve to organize the range of responses to globalization's challenges, as possible precursors to strategy development and as aids to strategy revision and implementation.

1. Introduction

Internationalization is now of central importance for higher education institutions across the world, and the development of an appropriate international strategy is a matter that is high on the institutional agenda.

The external driver for internationalization is globalization. In this chapter we describe and establish some taxonomic approaches that aim to provide mechanisms by which an institution of higher education might organize its response to globalization's challenges and to develop the architecture of an internationalization strategy — a strategy that aligns with the pressures of globalization as they apply to the particular circumstances of that institution.

We begin in the next section by setting out the background and the context in which higher education institutions now find themselves, and we move on, in Sec. 3, to examine the special complexities of globalization and internationalization in higher education, by undertaking a very brief comparison with the retail sector. The remainder of the chapter then explores and evaluates taxonomies for organizing approaches and responses to globalization, classification schemes that can be adapted to the very different circumstances of institutions in different higher education sectors and at different levels of maturity. In Sec. 4, we examine four possible taxonomies for classifying international responses to global drivers: the first, based on the location of those responses; the second, based on the nature of the relationship between the international partners involved; the third, based on the approach taken to internationalization; and the fourth, based on the complexity of the partnership arrangements that pertain. We draw some conclusions in Sec. 5 and then our references to the literature complete the chapter.

2. Background and Context

The higher education community faces an uncertain future. No serious commentator, however, disputes that internationalization will be central to that future and key to the resolution of its current difficulties.

> "*An academic revolution has taken place in higher education in the past half century marked by transformations unprecedented in scope and diversity. Comprehending this on-going and dynamic process while being in the midst of it is not an easy task.*"

Universities, wherever they are located, are looking to secure themselves for the long term while simultaneously rethinking their purpose and reorienting their vision, so that these are appropriate for this uncertain future. In doing so they are recognizing that they operate in an increasingly global context, and that they are competing not solely within their regions or countries, but increasingly and inevitably on an international stage.

> "*... going it alone is increasingly difficult, and ... partnerships ... build capacity and strength that few institutions can muster on their own. Paradoxically, 'cooperation redefines the space in which higher education competes'.*"

Internationalization can be thought of as the *internal response* to globalization's *external threat* (or, more optimistically: *opportunity*). It is not uncommon for the higher education sector to be viewed as lagging behind business and commerce, but here are some interesting facts: only 1% of US companies have an international presence (though the figure is somewhat higher elsewhere in the developed world); only 3% of the workforce comes from outside the country; and only 20% of Internet traffic crosses the national boundary. In stark contrast, the proportion of faculty members at most universities far exceeds 1% — for example, even by the academic year 2005–2006 there were 31,477 non-UK nationals holding academic positions in UK higher education institutions; this represents 19.1% of total academic staff. Furthermore, it hardly merits mentioning that almost all, if not all, higher education institutions engage in *some* form of international activity — if restricted in type and lacking strategic oversight. And the idea that only one in five web pages consulted by faculty members and students comes from within country, is absurd.

In the area of internationalization then, universities are not so much trailing in the wake of business and commerce, as leading from the front. Indeed, the levels of participation, in terms of international students, international faculty, and international activities, are generally so high that the one might be inclined to conclude that the gap between the external pressure of globalization and the internal move towards internationalization has more or less collapsed — that the boundary between the institution and its international context is already so transparent that there is no special strategic imperative to address. This, however, seriously underestimates the complexities of globalization and internationalization in the higher education context.

These complexities, however, needs some unpacking before we can usefully organize and evaluate possible responses in Sec. 4. So we first undertake a very brief comparison between the retail and higher education sectors.

3. Global and International in Retail and Higher Education

3.1. *Globalization*

Let us begin with globalization. While complex enough outside the world of higher education, the situation inside is more complex still. If we take first-world retailing as a (counter) example, we find that the global forces at play are the pull factors of the increased purchasing power of foreign consumers and the underdeveloped retail sector in their countries. On the other hand the key push factors are the saturated retail markets of Europe and the US. Something analogous also operates within Higher Education — pull factors certainly include the increased capacity of the "consumers" of education in less-developed regions to pay for "products" from more-developed regions, and the push factors do indeed include a form of home-market saturation — in this case arising from the gradual withdrawal of public/state funding for higher education and, in some jurisdictions, artificial caps on (national) students numbers. But this misses so much more. The less-developed higher education sectors are themselves developing rapidly — thus giving consumers a choice of where to spend their resources. Perhaps there is an analogy between designer brands in the retail sector and highly-ranked universities — but the quality issues (and so the structure of decision-making) is very likely quite different.

More significantly, the direct analogy here accords only with the recruitment of students which, while critical to institutional success, forces attention on the wrong target: the core businesses of higher education institutions are education and research, for which there are no direct comparisons at all in the retail sector. The very broad range of activities we encounter in higher education lead to a variety of *value outcomes* — extending financial outcomes, something we will explore in more detail later. To make matters worse, there are significant differences between disciplinary areas and there are interactions between education and research that further complicate the picture.

3.2. *Internationalization*

Turning now to internationalization. For most higher education institutions, the majority of international activities are narrowly based and bilateral (we will explore this more in Sec. 4.4.1) and they are essentially unplanned — at least at the level of the institution as a whole. In terms of human resources, the *proportions* of international students and faculty members turn out to be a poor surrogate as a measure of internationalization "at home". Such measures are, however, part of the methodology of international institutional rankings, such as the *QS Top Universities* ranking, so that higher proportions contribute to a higher score under the subheading "internationalization". However, many Middle East and North Africa (MENA) countries, for example, lack a sufficient number of qualified faculty, and rely on ex-patriot labor — while compared to institutions in more developed higher education sectors, MENA higher education institutions are much less engaged internationally. As we will see in the sequel, these few indicators (unplanned international activities, proportions of foreign faculty and students) barely scratch the surface of what is on offer under the rubric "internationalization" for universities and higher colleges.

Responses to global forces have led to a distinction between market-seeking and efficiency-seeking internationalization strategies. Furthermore, internationalization can be classified according to the direction of the process as out-facing or in-facing. The former includes exporting and production overseas, including licensing and franchising. In-facing internationalization would include the sourcing of materials from overseas.

Again, at the level of student recruitment, we can see similar processes at play in Higher Education. In-facing responses include the direct recruitment of faculty from overseas, whereas out-facing responses include the creation of branch campuses, validated degree programs, and franchised degree programs overseas. We will examine these options in more detail later.

However, the points at which this general model aligns with features of internationalization within Higher Education do not exhaust the full range of activities and responses to globalization. We noted that the global push/pull factors in retail do not cover other core activities that exist within Higher Education, such as research, and the interaction between them. Unsurprisingly, therefore, these additional activities are not well covered by either the market seeking/efficiency seeking models, or simply by asymmetric in-facing/out-facing process flows.

Neither does this general model even properly account for student recruitment within Higher Education. To see this, imagine a manufacturer that imports raw fabric from an international supplier. This establishes two asymmetric internationalization strategies — in-facing for the importing organization and out-facing for the exporter. The importer may subsequently export finished garments back to the international market — thus enriching its internationalization strategy with out-facing activities. This looks tantalizingly similar to the education of international students in Higher Education. However, appearances can be deceptive — it is a false analogy.

The situation is particularly complicated because, while the geographic movement and in/out-facing flows in the manufacturing example aforementioned are covariant, the same flows in Higher Education are contra-variant, at least where international students are concerned: the movement of uneducated students (raw fabric) is, in fact, in-facing for the supplier and out-facing for the institution which undertakes the education (which may import the students but is exporting education — consider the finances). And the return of educated students (the finished garments) involves no further financial transaction — and appears, therefore, not to be a feature of anyone's international strategy. But of course it is — because the value of the returning student (perhaps with a PhD) is not measured in financial terms, but in terms of the capacities the returner has to teach, lead, and research: a variety of non-financial value outcomes arising from value propositions offered by the educator. It is worth noting that this also illustrates the interactions between distinct aspects of core business. Finally, to completely undermine the false analogy: the institution that imports the students is, in fact, also engaged in a covariant in-facing activity. While the finance flows contra-variantly with the geographical movements, there are value propositions offered by the supplier to the educator that do not involve money. The incoming students enrich the culture in which they are educated and provide access to other value outcomes in the international market — as ambassadors, providing access to researchers, and other partners of value. And as we saw earlier, the presence of international students within an institution makes a net positive contribution to scores in international league tables.

There is one further difference between internationalization in retail and in higher education. This concerns the value of intellectual resources within and between higher education sectors. The term *intellectual arbitrage* has been coined to capture the idea that a resource (which might be expertise rather than physical) has a value to a partner that lacks it that is vastly greater than it has for a partner who possesses it. So much is true in the retail sector — a company that lacks resources that are readily available only overseas will import them — and may attach them a value that may be significantly higher than might apply within the foreign market itself. However, the value of the transaction is purely financial — and the asymmetry is such that it is the importer (the in-facing flow) that is the typical focus of the international activity in the literature, despite the fact that there is an exporter (the out-facing flow) — presumably because power in the transaction is more often located with the importer and the exporter is very much the dependent partner.

In higher education, however, there are many significant value outcomes — finance being only one. Less well-developed higher education sectors often possess significant value even when they are more financially dependent. As a consequence, even when engaged in an asymmetric international partnership — one in which the in-facing and out-facing processes differ — the less well-developed partner is often not as dependent as may be imagined through the partial analogy with business generally — as described earlier.

Consider, for example, the value of an Indian university's access to the dying languages of the Andaman Islands to a western department of linguistics — or the value of access to desert plants in Saudi Arabia to plant biologists outside the region. Consider also the value of academic expertise in the social anthropology of Inuit culture to social scientists who lack that — or details of the study of micro-financed and social-sector-inspired business models that have gained such traction in Latin America, and Africa. On the other hand, there are developing higher education sectors, notably in the Gulf Cooperation Council (GCC), where finance is actually a strength, even compared to Western systems, but which are otherwise situated amidst weaknesses in capacity and resources — that is: other important value outcomes. The international playing field is, therefore, much more level than might be imagined at first glance.

In conclusion, we have illustrated that the drivers of globalization and the responses of internationalization are both different from and more complex than those to be found in more traditional business contexts. As a consequence, even though, there are markers of internationalization in higher education that appear to be better developed than in the general context, the gap between global pressures and the responses of internationalization remains significant. In order to meet the challenges effectively, we need to understand the complexities of the tools of, and approaches to, internationalization that we might deploy in response to globalization's challenges. We now turn to that.

4. Taxonomies of Internationalization

4.1. *Internationalization at home and abroad*

Someone who have an interest in better understanding internationalization in Higher Education and in finding ways of organizing the options, make a first cut in terms of *internationalization at home* versus *internationalization abroad*.

4.1.1. Internationalization at home

At home we will interested in internationalizing the curriculum through the inclusion of international perspectives and relevant comparative content — making courses more interesting both for home and international students. It will also include mechanisms to support foreign language learning for local students, and support for the language of instruction, foundation programs, inward international mobility (for study, work, or volunteering), summer schools, and other specialist services to improve the experience of international students.

Internationalization at home also includes encouraging *internationally informed research*. That is, research that incorporates and is relevant to constituencies outside the national boundary and that considers questions of global significance.

Internationalization of the teaching and learning process will also feature at home. Such processes can incorporate appropriate pedagogies for differing educational cultures and make use of both international students' and international faculty members' expertise and experiences.

Where appropriate academic, administrative, and student services would be structured and delivered with a multicultural mix of stakeholders and core business activities in mind. Quality assurance processes, for example, would ensure that curricula and qualifications comply with international agreements, such as the diploma supplement and the ETCS credit system within the Bologna area.

Such internationalization — of curriculum, research, services, and educational approaches would naturally be supported by appropriate internationalization of professional development activities.

4.1.2. Internationalization abroad

Internationalization abroad covers more substantial activities and tends to appear after internationalization has taken place at home — just as out-facing internationalization activities tend to later follow in-facing internationalization activities in retail.

Under this rubric authors include the recruitment of international students, outward student mobility (local students travelling abroad for study, work placements, or volunteering), alumni activities, outward faculty mobility, and joint academic appointments.

Research is now encouraged to be *internationally engaged* — not simply informed — with corresponding support for international projects based on externally funded international strategic partnerships (academic, business, or governmental). This naturally leads to internationally co-authored publications — something that is now well known to add value through improved citation rates.

It is not only students and faculty members who can become internationally mobile, academic programs and indeed academic providers — institutions themselves — can become mobile.

Institutions can create mobile programs in a number of ways. First, they can *validate* the curricula of a foreign provider — awarding their own certification for study on a program designed and delivered by the foreign entity. Second, they can *franchise* their own programs to a foreign provider — awarding the same qualification for comparable (quality assured) study at an international site. Third, institutions can offer their programs, or courses from programs, at a distance through e-learning, supported by appropriate technology. Fourth, pairs (or larger networks) of institutions can offer joint or double degree programs, or joint courses within programs. These programs might involve a mandatory period of overseas study for students who are enrolled and they could lead to a single award — offered by the partners together, or a dual award — offered by the partners separately. Smaller, joint courses might be co-taught across national boundaries and involve only *virtual mobility* through an e-learning experience.

Institutions themselves can become mobile in a number of ways. First, they may set up regional offices overseas. These may serve as a mechanism for profile raising, marketing and recruitment. They may also provide limited academic services, such as teaching in the language of instruction. Second, and more significantly, they may set up a branch centre abroad — covering a limited number of courses or subjects. Third, they may establish a comprehensive branch campus abroad, offering a substantial range of subjects and courses.

In both these cases, the academic and administrative staff may be entirely local to the branch, or supported to a greater or lesser extent by personnel from the home campus. Branch campuses of these kinds may be set up independently or they may be undertaken in partnership with local providers or local businesses.

4.1.3. *Critique*

While useful, this binary division of internationalization in terms of in-facing and out-facing activities and processes is rather crude. Moreover, it is not entirely clear whether there should be a distinction between out-facing activities that involve the institution alone from those which involve one or more partners. A third category *internationalization together* might be introduced — though we will look at other means for capturing the spirit of cooperative ventures in Secs. 4.2 and 4.4.

In addition, from a strategic perspective, there are two further weaknesses of this classification. First, there is a very significant difference in complexity between activities that fall under the same heading, especially under the rubric of internationalization abroad: a branch campus is a major project, while a jointly taught course is quite simple. Second, there is a difference between activities according to their context. For example, outward student mobility may be a simple bilateral arrangement with another provider, or it may be one of a larger set of interacting activities with that provider or consortium. The manner in which such an activity is managed will differ accordingly. We will suggest an improved taxonomy in Sec. 4.4 to deal with this.

4.2. *Symmetry and asymmetry*

In Sec. 3, we recognized that each out-facing activity for one partner is an in-facing activity for another. Such, of course, is the case in Higher Education. In some cases, the activity may be both in-facing and out-facing — benefits and processes flowing seamlessly in both directions. One example of this might be airline alliances — where reciprocal arrangements are instituted between more-or-less equal partners.

This leads us to consider activities and processes distinguished according to whether the relationship between the partners is symmetric or asymmetric. We will see that items within the two categories discussed in Sec. 4.1 are now reassigned across this new classification.

4.2.1. *Asymmetric relationships*

An asymmetric relationship is one in which the activity or process involved appears quite different for each partner. For example, fee-paying study abroad packages do not involve student exchange and are thus quite different international activities for the supplier of services and for the supplier of students.

Similarly, institutions that make use of government scholarships to up-skill their staff, a situation that is currently operating in, for example, Indonesia (DIKTI scholarships), Saudi Arabia (King Abdullah Scholarship Program), and Brazil (Science Without Borders), create a partnership with overseas institutions in which they are the more dependent partner.

Franchise arrangements and validation arrangements, discussed in Sec. 4.1.2 are also examples of asymmetrical relationships — one in which the validated institution or franchisee are significantly dependent upon their international partners.

Moreover, the benefits, across the range of value outcomes, are also asymmetrical. For example, in franchise or validation arrangements, the franchiser or validator benefits mainly in financial terms, the franchisee or validated institution benefits in brand association and through offering highly-valued qualifications. In some cases, such an arrangement benefits the franchisee through the meeting of local regulations: in Oman, for example, private institutions must offer degrees in collaboration with a recognized international provider.

Clearly, setting up a branch campus in collaboration with an overseas partner — whether academic or business — is another example of an asymmetric arrangement.

4.2.2. *Symmetric relationships*

Symmetric relationships are those in which the activities and processes, and the value outcomes, are largely the same for the collaborating partners.

Faculty and student exchange programs — the latter most often undertaken on a no-fee basis — are example of symmetric relationships. Jointly run courses, and dual or joint degree programs are also examples.

Ambitious international alliances, whether bilateral or multi-lateral, are largely symmetric in nature. These we will describe in more detail in Sec. 4.4.

4.2.3. *Critique*

Once again, this classification does not capture the context within which a single activity takes place. From a strategic perspective, thinking about how the relationship, activity or process is managed, it makes a significant difference whether the activity is, or is not, among a larger set of arrangements with the same institution or consortium.

The situation, even for joint degrees, is more complex than the simple classification allows. For example, the recently completed Erasmus Mundus Program (Action 1 — joint programs) provided a means by which consortia made up of a number of institutions could design and deliver joint masters programs. This would seem to be a straightforward symmetric arrangement of the collaborating institutions. However, although the activities are symmetric, national policies create asymmetries in the value outcomes: in the UK students pay fees for their education — whether they are national or international students. In Germany, however, education is (mostly) free. This creates practical difficulties that are often unanticipated by consortia who assume that they are dealing with a symmetric arrangement.

4.3. *Internationalization by approach*

A somewhat different classification, seeks to categorize international activities and processes in terms of the *approach* to internationalization they adopt or which is appropriate.

Consideration of internationalization in terms of approach was initially introduced as a means by which an institution could characterize its *entire* attitude towards internationalization. The suggested categories are: Activity, Outcomes, Rationales, Process, Ethos, and Cross-border.

Each of these approaches could lead to a further classification under its separate rubric — as we will outline in a moment. However, there is no reason why a classification could not be devised based on the set of approaches — if an institution felt that its response to globalization required different approaches and different responses under these.

4.3.1. *Six approaches*

The *activity approach* simply classifies internationalization according to the activities it comprises — and we have already discussed many such activities: joint degree programs, international projects, student mobility, and so on. Many institutions already approach internationalization in this way, and there is, perhaps, an argument to be made that it is not so much an approach as simply a list that lacks overall strategic coherence.

The *outcomes approach* attempts to organize international activities in terms of desirable results. For example, a raised profile and better international visibility for the institution; internationalized qualifications; research projects and deliverables with international significance; income generation; students as global citizens; and so on.

The *rationales approach* considers the drivers of internationalization — that is, the global forces at play (even if some are locally generated). These may involve identity building at the national, not simply institutional, level; the development of multiculturalism at the level of the citizen or civic society; it could involve human capital development — to meet national as well as individual demands; and other local and regional drivers: economic development, nation building and identity, national security, and so forth.

The *process approach* considers the institution holistically, asking how internationalization integrates within all aspects of core business, and the structures and processes that support them. This approach raises interesting questions regarding the architecture of institutional strategy: should internationalization be a *core* strategy — perhaps sitting alongside an education and a research strategy, or a *supporting* strategy — perhaps sitting alongside a finance and a human resources strategy, or should it appear fully integrated within all core and supporting strategies, making an appearance within key strategic goals and objectives of each?

The *ethos approach* focuses primarily on internationalization at home — considering in particular the climate on the home campus, while the *cross-border approach* focuses on internationalization abroad, particularly the more adventurous asymmetric arrangements such as franchising and branch campuses.

4.3.2. Critique

As discussed earlier, it is not clear that the activities approach amounts to more than a list of responses to globalization's challenges, while the ethos/cross-border axis rather resembles the at-home versus abroad classification of Sec. 4.1, with its attendant limitations as discussed in Sec. 4.1.3.

There seems much to be commended in the outcomes and rationale approaches. Both keep globalization's imperatives in focus and so encourage responses that align with these.

Similarly, the process approach, while not perhaps providing a means to classify activities by scale or type, provides much encouragement towards a clear approach to institutional strategy development.

4.4. Types of partnership

Perhaps the main limitation that emerged from the discussion in Secs. 4.1.3 and 4.2.3 concerned the failure of those classifications to address the context in which specific international activities take place. Our final taxonomy seeks to address this weakness.

Figure 1, show a matrix in which the complexity of the international partnership appears along the *y*-axis and the complexity of the international activities appears along the *x*-axis. This gives us four cells in the matrix to serve as our classification. A word of caution: this is *not* a four-valued variant of the two-valued classification described in Sec. 4.1. As we will see in the sequel, and in contrast to the classification in Sec. 4.1, activities of a similar nature may appear in more than one cell of the matrix. This will become clearer as we proceed.

4.4.1. Narrowly-based bilateral partnerships

The bottom-left of the matrix concern narrowly-based bilateral activities. These are generally mobility arrangements, for example symmetric or asymmetric flows of mobile students on exchange programs, study abroad periods, work placements, volunteering, or attending summer schools. In addition, this cell also represents a kind of faculty mobility, in particular, the individual relationships that most academics routinely have with colleagues usually in order to pursue research. As we noted in Sec. 3.2, these faculty relationships are largely (and probably wisely) unmanaged and, indeed, most institutions do not know how many relationships of this kind exist, who is involved, and which partner institutions are implicated.

Another narrowly-based bilateral activity is the joint or dual degree offered in collaboration with a single partner.

Activities appear in this cell of the matrix when they are not sub-activities of some more comprehensive relationship. As such, the simple faculty-to-faculty relationships are important to institutional performance but the lack of strategic oversight is not simply forgivable, it is probably appropriate. Similarly, most universities with a healthy level of international student mobility will engage in a large number of bilateral mobility agreements. Taken together they almost certainly represent the implementation of a strategic aim: to improve academic standards and employability through an international experience — but the details of specific bilateral agreements are tactical rather than strategic.

4.4.2. Narrowly-based multi-lateral partnerships

Many institutions will be familiar with partnerships that occupy the top-left cell of the matrix. Examples here include research groups which have established

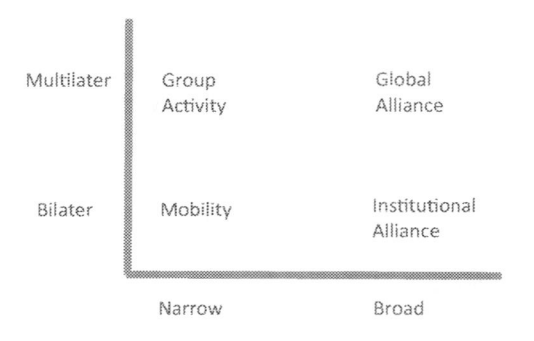

	Narrow	Broad
Multilater	Group Activity	Global Alliance
Bilater	Mobility	Institutional Alliance

Fig. 1.

partnerships with consortia of similar groups internationally — often supported by external funding.

Other examples include internationally engaged degree programs, offered by a consortium of institutions.

The *Global Studies Program* offered by the University of Freiburg and its partners is one such example.

> "The Global Studies Program is a two-year Master program initiated in 2002 followed by an optional PhD initiated in 2008. The mission of the program is to study social sciences in various cultures and regions focusing on the global South. It is conducted jointly by the University of Freiburg, the University of Cape Town, FLACSO-Argentina (Buenos Aires), Chulalongkorn University (Bangkok), and the Jawaharlal Nehru University (New Delhi). Each institution belongs to the best in its region."

Another more recent example is the *Center for Urban Science and Progress* (CUSP) which brings together seven higher education institutions, including New York University, from four countries, nine industry partners, and a number of civic/governmental agencies. It is located in Brooklyn and serves to create a hub for research and postgraduate study. It focuses on topics such as energy, infrastructure, and public safety.

CUSP currently awards a joint certificate in Applied Urban Science and Informatics while master-level degrees are awarded by the participating institutions separately. Students spend part of their study period in more than one geographic centre. CUSP is currently developing a PhD program and creating a research capacity. In this sense, it is beginning to move towards a Type 4 relationship — as described in Sec. 4.4.4.

4.4.3. *Broadly-based bilateral partnerships*

Partnerships that belong in the bottom-right cell are complex bilateral alliances between institutions. A recent example of such an alliance is the arrangement that has been established between the University of Warwick in the UK and Monash University in Australia.

> "... the partnership reveals a shift for the education sector. While it aims to deliver a seamless international experience for students, the advent of a range of jointly delivered degrees at both universities represents a departure from traditional educational partnerships and shows at least some of the hallmarks of cross-border collaboration more commonly seen in the private sector." Monish Paul and Anveeta Shrivastava, Deloitte, *Australian Financial Review*, April 2, 2012.

The two universities began this project by each committing a considerable financial investment. As a significant profile-raising project, the partnership rapidly secured further external funding from the UK and Australian governments. £500,000 was awarded by the UK Engineering and Physical Sciences Research Council (EPSRC) under its "Building Global Engagements" program to build connections in the physical sciences, £66,000 was received from the Australian Government to support student mobility, and £200,000 was committed by the Australian Research Council grant to build collaborations in engineering.

The relationship is bilateral but involves a large number of distinct activities: research in several areas, student mobility, a PhD program, joint degrees and other forms of student collaboration, including a peer-reviewed journal for students.

Such relationships challenge the traditional model of the university and offer a new set of possibilities that address globalization's challenges. Clearly, they set enormous challenges for management and governance. In this case, the two universities have made a joint senior-level appointment to manage the partnership.

4.4.4. *Broadly-based multi-lateral partnerships*

In principle these are the most complex of all partnerships. There are many of these, perhaps the oldest and most established being *Universitas 21*. These bring together often large numbers of institutions to cooperate over a large number of activities.

Universitas 21 is a consortium of 24 member universities from 16 countries and counts some half a million students under its members' jurisdiction. It was founded in 1997 and serves both as a "think-tank" on higher education as well as delivering collaborative education, research, and mobility programs.

In 2001, together with organizations outside higher education provision, the consortium launched an online university, *Universitas 21 Global*, based in Singapore.

The universities collaborate on many levels, undergraduate and postgraduate research, and several hundred students a year participate in the student exchange programs, the *U21 Student Mobility Program*. The management of this ambitious activity is so complex that a separate company *U21 Pedagogica* Ltd. was set up in the US to oversee the administration and quality assurance.

Other well established consortia are the *International Alliance of Research Universities*, the *League of European Research Universities*, and the *Worldwide Universities Network*. Some have a specific focus, for example, on research, others on the education or mobility of students. There is some doubt as to the productivity of the larger networks, as the space of potential collaborations is extremely high, and the resources and capacities available to negotiate the formidable range of interactions and differences in administration, policy and regulation, is limited. More recently, there has been more interest in growing much smaller partnerships — beginning, as Warwick and Monash have done, with a productive Type 3 arrangement.

4.4.5. *Critique*

As we have stressed, this final taxonomy is not a four-valued version of the two-valued classification provided in Sec. 4.1. In this matrix model, an activity or process belongs in a cell only when considered in relation to all activities with all partners. For example a mobility agreement belongs in the bottom-left cell just in case there are no other partners to that agreement and when there are no other activities with the partner to the agreement.

This approach addresses the weaknesses we observed in Secs. 4.1.3 and 4.2.3 — that we cannot evaluate the strategic significance of an international activity if we consider it in isolation. In this model each activity belongs with related partners and related activities with those partners.

The model is also helpful in tracking the migration of partnerships as they develop. In Sec. 4.4.2, we described the CUSP project and noted that although it is currently a Type 2 arrangement, it is on a trajectory towards a Type 4 partnership. As relationships evolve over time, their position in the taxonomy can be tracked — allowing appropriate changes to strategy to be triggered.

There does remain a weakness, one that we have not previously mentioned because the models of Secs. 4.1 and 4.2 do not begin to provide a classification that might address it. The issue concerns collections of related activities that lie within the bottom-left cell and, perhaps to a lesser extent, the top-left cell.

Although not a partnership, the collection of, for example, all bilateral student mobility agreements forms a natural type which requires strategic oversight, even though the individual agreements are essentially a tactical matter of implementation. Similarly, an individual joint or double degree certainly requires quality oversight — but the institution's *collection* of such degrees is a strategic matter and creates general liabilities for quality management with concomitant implications for planning and resourcing.

Perhaps this might be addressed by refining the matrix. Alternatively, a mixed-mode approach in which the matrix — which concentrates on the partnerships — is combined with aspects of the rationales and process approaches outlined in Sec. 4.3 to provide a means to organize activities across non-partnership dimensions.

4. Conclusions and Future Work

We have attempted in this chapter to show that globalization and internationalization in higher education have distinct contours and complexities when compared to more generic businesses. The complexities arise largely because the core business of institutions of higher education is multi-faceted and, even within one aspect such as research, has distinct strands (by disciplinary area and specific subject) that are subject to different global drivers, and require a differentiated response. They arise also because there are, in higher education, several value outcomes that transcend the purely financial.

A consequence of this complexity is that, despite being to a large extent inherently international organizations, it remains a significant challenge to find an appropriate international strategy that can successfully address the global externalities. There is, in particular, a very large space of potential activities and processes that can be deployed, each of which requiring a different level of strategic or tactical oversight.

A first step towards developing a strategy is a means by which this large space of activities can be tamed. We have looked, in this chapter, at a number of taxonomies that could be use to structure this organizational challenge, and evaluated them.

It is beyond the scope of this chapter to address the next stage which must, therefore, remain as future work: that is, to relate the taxonomic approaches described here to the activity of strategy development, revision and implementation. An audit of internationalization within one of more of these taxonomies will act, as a Strengths, Weaknesses, Opportunities, Threats (SWOT) analysis would also contribute, as a precursor to stating strategic goals and objectives. A continuing process of activity capture and development within a taxonomy can serve as an aid when strategies are evaluated and revised, and provide guidance for their operationalization. We have not touched upon many critical factors that need to be considered. The details are complex, requiring the further elaboration of issues of management and governance (in particular an unusual dynamic found in universities: the interaction between the academic core business activities and the professional services that support them), and of quality assurance and enhancement (which are fundamental to the success of complex partnership arrangements). We will cover all this in a separate publication.

References

Altbach, P. G., Reisberg, L., & Rumbley, L. E. (2009), Trends in global higher education: Tracking an academic revolution, A Report Prepared for the UNESCO World Conference on Higher Education.

Altbach, P. G. & Salmi, J. (eds.) (2011), The Road to academic excellence the making of world-class research universities, World Bank.

Coclanis, P. A. & Strauss, R. P. (2010), Partnerships: An alternative to branch campuses overseas, commentary, *The Chronicle*. Available at http://chronicle.com/article/Partnerships-a-Different-A/124286/ (consulted April 2014).

De Gruyter, J., Anna-Kaarina, A., Kairamo Use, K., de Beeck, O., Rintala, U., & Van Petegem, W. (2011), Virtual mobility — a contribution to the internationalization of higher education, Article D3.9 of Internationalisation of Higher Education — An EUA/ACA Handbook.

Diploma Supplement. Available at http://ec.europa.eu/education/lifelong-learning-policy/doc1239_en.htm (consulted April 2014).

Erasmus Mundus Action 1 — Joint programmes. Available at http://eacea.ec.europa.eu/erasmus_mundus/programme/action1_en.php.

European Credit Transfer and Accumulation System. Available at http://ec.europa.eu/education/lifelong-learning-policy/doc48_en.htm (consulted April 2014).

Ghemawat, P. (2011), World 3.0: Global Prosperity and how to Achieve it.

Global Studies Programme. Available at https://www.gsp.uni-freiburg.de/aboutgsp (consulted April 2014).

Grant, C. (2012), Losing our chains? Contexts and ethics of university internationalisation, Stimulus paper, Leadership Foundation for Higher Education.

Hanf, J. H. & Pall, Z. (2009), Is retailing really unique? Insights into retail internationalization using business theories, 113th EAAE Seminar "A resilient European food industry and food chain in a challenging world", Crete, Greece.

International Alliance of Research Universities. Available at http://www.iaruni.org (consulted April 2014).

Jaramillo, A. *et al.* (2011), Internationalization of higher education in mena: policy issues associated with skills formation and mobility, Report 63762-mna.

Kinser, K. & Green, M. F. (2009), *The power of partnerships: A transatlantic dialogue*, American Council on Education.

Knight, J. (2010), Internationalisation: Key concepts and elements, Article A1.1 of Internationalisation of Higher Education — An EUA/ACA Handbook.

Koutsantoni, D. (2006), Internationalisation in the UK: Leadership foundation for higher education, Briefing papers, London: Leadership Foundation for Higher Education.

Lawton, W. *et al.* (2014), Horizon Scanning: What will higher education look like in 2020?, Observatory on Borderless Higher Education Report 12, Available at http://www.obhe.ac.uk/documents/view_details?id=934 (consulted April 2014).

League of European Research Universities. http://www.leru.org/index.php/public/home/ (consulted April 2014).

Meyer, D. & O'Carroll, C. (2009), International collaboration: The lifeblood of research and innovation, Article C 1.1 of Internationalisation of Higher Education — An EUA/ACA Handbook.

Middlehurst, R. & Woodfield, S. (2007), Responding to the internationalisation agenda: Implications for institutional strategy, Research Report 05/06, New York: Higher Education Academy.

Pearce, R. (2006), Globalization and development: An international business strategy approach, *Transnational Corporations*, 15(1), 39–74.

Talent Wars (2007), The international market for academic staff, Universities UK Policy Briefing.

Understanding the Methodology: QS world university rankings, QS top universities. Available at http://www.topuniversities.com/university-rankings-articles/world-university-rankings/understanding-methodology-qs-world-university-rankings (consulted April 2014).

Universitas 21. Available at http://www.universitas21.com (consulted April 2014).

Warwick/Monash Institutional Alliance. Available at http://www2.warwick.ac.uk/about/partnerships/monash/ (consulted April 2014).

Welch, L. S. & Luostarinen, R. (1993), Inward–outward connections in internationalization, *Journal of International Marketing*, 1(1), 44–56.

Worldwide Universities Network. Available at http://www.wun.ac.uk (consulted April 2014).

Chapter 9

The Most Pressing Challenges for Romanian Higher Education System in Line with the Bologna Process Values

Dumitru Miron

Bucharest University of Economic Studies

In this chapter, there were analyzed a number of issues related to the implementation of few changes in Romanian educational system, in order to internalize the values of the Bologna Process. The chapter presents some evidences which proves that the evolutions taking place in Romania over the last decades continue some traditions, are justified by the need for paradigm change, but they can hardly become undeniable achievements. The chapter supports the idea that adopting a common action plan and putting into practice the commitments made in frame of Bologna Process, without having a highly professional academic management and without taking on the new university governance values, is not a smooth process and did not generate inspiring effects. The chapter will approach as main directions: the social dimension of education, continuous education and professional development, employability, student-centered education, multiple-sourced financing and improved academic governance, quality assurance in higher education.

1. Introduction

Depicting the manner in which the process of reform in the Romanian education is a complex endeavor, both provocative and useful. Besides the criticism regarding the quality and efficiency of tertiary education in Romania, we must point out that the Romanian higher education also capitalizes on a series of competitive advantages, some of them sustainable, which may become profitable only when their conditions are understood and actions are taken in the respective direction. Making higher education an active agent of the Romanian economic and social modernization depends on understanding and accepting the change in the dominant logics happening in the international and the European academic landscape. We need to be mainly concerned by the position in which we have to place the university in the process of modernization happening in education, especially now, when higher education is maybe the most globalized component of the social landscape. Enders & De Weert (2004) stated that "*although many universities still seem to perceive themselves rather as objects of processes of globalization, they are at the same time also key agents.*" This is very specific for a country which is on a complex and painful path of transition from a social-political system to another, and which greatly needs to use its education system as a modern driver of change at the level of the dominant social logics. The people who make decisions about public policies related to higher education and those who decide at the universities level must take into consideration that in order for these policies to have consistency they need to internalize good practices, to be based on successful experiences, and to be characterized by a dynamic continuity. The greatest attention must be paid to avoiding errors of interpretation of certain concepts and taken actions. The problem is more sensitive having in mind that Romania is an European Union (EU) member country being obliged to implement the *acquis communautaire*. Regarding higher education, where EU has no elements of *acquis communautaire*, the position of EU is more complex because, as Corbett (2004: 12) stated "*governments want to use Europe to introduce domestic reform. The Commission wishes to extend its competence in higher education. University presidents want recognition. They each bring elements of the solution, as embodied in Bologna.*"

2. The Need of an Appropriate Balance between More Harmonization and Traditional Benchmarks

Definitely, higher education is essential for creating knowledge, technological progress, communication, behavior change, and cultural mutation. After 1990, an important dilemma had to be handled with great sagacity: how one could keep the balance between more harmonization required by the acquiescence to the referential values of our European re-becoming and the obligation to maintain traditional benchmarks of the Romanian higher education. As it is shown in the specialized literature (Kurelic, 2009), the changes of landscape, fed by the logics of the Bologna Process, are not always meant to improve and modernize educational practices which have proved sustainable in time, but to bring new untested ones which can lead, under certain circumstances, to collateral effects difficult to manage. The efforts to introduce the values of the process in national education systems seem to have been configured as if they had already been tested and they had proved their competitive advantages. On the other hand, essential mutations at the level of education systems prove to be risky if the people required to enforce them are not seriously preoccupied by their urgency and relevance. From this perspective as well, the reality of the implementation in Romania of the reforms fed by the Bologna Process shows that the decision-makers have aligned themselves to most requirements without first doing an in-depth analysis which would accentuate the urgency, the direction, the costs and the effects of the transformation processes. The problem has acquired a relevant importance in Romania's efforts to try certain changes in paradigm.

Romania must move from a dominant logics based on conformity to one based on proactivity. Higher education is an area in which we can demonstrate this change. The process is not an easy one because the EU has become a major player on the stage of higher education, promoting the phrase 'the Europeanization of higher education' in logics of integration, the positive and the negative one. (Craig & de Burca, 2011). As it is stated in the Article 165(1) of the Treaty of European Union (TEU), the EU member states remain responsible for organizing the national higher education systems, but this competence must be carried out in strict accordance with the community right. Education has proved to be an important area for both the Lisbon Strategy and the 2020 Europe Strategy (European Commission, 2010). In order to achieve an intelligent, sustainable, and inclusive economic growth by 2020, the EU will have to focus on five major directions among which education. It is expected to reach at least 40% of 30–34-year-olds completing third level education. Although the European-level cooperation is mostly on a voluntary basis, it is clear that the Member States' education policies are becoming more and more Europeanized. Specialized literature highlights that the developments concerning the Bologna Process seem to contradict the "*traditional resistance of the EU Member States to any harmonization policy in education and to increased Community competence*" (Hackl, 2001: 2). Beyond rhetoric, close analysis of evolutions related to the Bologna Process shows that we can identify differentiation, as well as harmonization areas, perceived as standardization. This is the case of the educational scheme based on higher education cycles, which went beyond the limit of the vocational, as the study cycles and their length were agreed on. If some formal aspects were standardized, maintaining diversity is still possible in the case of curricula content. Close analysis of the relationship between the evolution of the European integration process and that of the Bologna Process is required to identify basic interferences and understand causalities appropriately. Although the Bologna Process is not under its direct supervision, the European Commission used it to increase its technocratic influence on various aspects of the education and professional development processes. As highlighted by Keeling (2006: 203), "*the Commission's dynamic association of the Bologna university reforms with its Lisbon research agenda and its successful appropriation of these as European-level issues has placed its perspectives firmly at the heart of higher education policy debates in Europe.*" In Romania's case the question is whether the originality elements of its higher education system should be kept or it would be more comfortable to increase even more the Community's involvement in this sensitive social and economic area. If one considers Romanian decision-makers' concerns, there seems to be no resistance to adopting the Community's regulations in this field. Overcoming the compliance-based approach requires public strategies and policies that are adopted and implemented professionally, coherently, and consistently by experts who are able to represent us where projects and framework documents are discussed, as well as behavioral changes to ensure a culture of quality, entrepreneurship, and efficiency. The Bologna Process is related not only to the European integration process — sometimes to the point of juxtaposition — but also to evolutions taking place at the level of multilateral trading system (Huisman & van de Wende, 2004: 34–35). It is possible to say that some operational entities from the European education system comply with the institutional format specific to the World Trade Organization (WTO). A good example in this respect is represented by the European Network of Quality Assurance Agencies (ENQA), which according to Furlong (2005: 5) have the features of the WTO operational system and an essential role in the framework of the Bologna philosophy.

In terms of rhetoric, governments support inter-governmental philosophy, pleading for maintaining the delimitation between the European integration process and the Bologna Process. In terms of practice, governments benefit from the increased convergence between education systems, a process which can stimulate and support achieving objectives related to intelligent and sustainable economic growth. Ravinet (2008: 357) showed that the difference between the objectives assumed in the framework of the Bologna Process and those derived from the dynamics of European economic integration is determined by "*where they derive their authority and importance from, at least partly explaining why their use contributes so much to a sense of bindingness.*" Similarly, Fejes (2005: 219) claims that "*planet speak rhetoric such as the ideas of the knowledge society, employability, lifelong learning, quality assurance and mobility [...] constitute a way of thinking that makes participation in the Bologna Process and the implementation of its objectives a rational way to act.*"

Taking into consideration concerns determined by the structural crisis of European welfare state, the employability of graduates and the need to create an educational model which is affordable and globally attractive, the Bologna Process became an interesting mix of inter-governmental and supranational elements due to which actions undertaken by EU organizations are influenced by cooperation between states. The main objectives of the European Higher Education Area (EHEA) are: to facilitate the speedy entrance of educated professionals into the job market through shortened degrees; to enhance the cross-border mobility of students and job seekers; to increase the competitiveness of European higher education internationally (Sedgwick, 2003). The comparative analysis of national educational policies and the values of the Bologna Process reveal many areas of compliance, but even more transgressions from the dominant values of the process. The first transgression from the intrinsic logic of the vocational character of the Bologna Process was that many times it seemed that the implementation of commitments assumed in the framework of this process was a precondition of a country's accession to the EU, which was not only untrue, but also sometimes counter-productive. Such an approach was adopted by Romania.

3. The Most Important Thematic Areas — Future Research Directions

The pivotal idea of the Bologna Process is the coagulation of EHEA having as referential drivers: the knowledge economy, European citizenship, employability, and cross-border mobility. Each state participating in this exercise of multi-level integration is committed to proceed autonomously in reforming their educational systems.

3.1. Social dimension of education: Access, equity, and studies graduation

This goal was scored for the first time, in the communication adopted at the Ministerial Conference in Prague in 2001 and was operationalized by educational policies focused towards equity, undistorted access, and graduation in higher education. What it desired to achieve was, *"strengthen policies of widening overall access and raising completion rates, including measures targeting the increased participation of underrepresented groups,"* ministers of the participating countries are committed to *"work to enhance employability, life-long learning, problem-solving and entrepreneurial skills through improved cooperation with employers, especially in the development of educational programs."* At the London Conference of 2007, participating States reaffirmed the principle of fairness and the need for students to be able to complete their studies without encountering obstacles related to their social and economic status. Challenges which we must respond and Romania aims: setting measurable targets for widening access to higher education and take appropriate measures to achieve these objectives, increasing graduation rates and scroll for university studies; increasing participation of under-represented groups in higher education; implementation of national strategies, action plans, and measures efficacy.

3.2. Education and life-long learning (LLL)

The Prague Communication in 2001 stated stringency of adoption of national strategies through which to face the challenges coming from the direction of the new competitiveness, the use of new technologies, social cohesion, equal opportunity, and improved quality of life. In the London Communication, in 2007, national delegations assumed recognition of life-long transferable credits, pledging to set clear and appropriate funding mechanisms and improving academic governance. Other commitments in this direction are to include the LLL in the European and national frameworks of qualifications. In Leuven in 2009 it was agreed that LLL encouraged by national policies to be reflected in the practices of higher educational institutions. The new legislation in higher education (National Education Law No. 1/2011) has provisions of consistency in this direction, but their consistency and especially insufficient methodological instructions make them unclear, unworkable, and ineffective.

3.3. Employability

This goal defined in the Bologna Follow Up Group (BFUG) as *"the ability to hold an initial job, to maintain the job and to be mobile on the labor market"* has been identified as a priority at ministerial conferences starting the London Communiqué (2007), in which the signatory states intends to improve the employment rate of graduates. Ministerial conferences that followed have been undertaken by both specific targets, such as those related to the employment in a compatible manner within the public sector with the three cycles system or reducing the rate of youth unemployment, and public policy commitments, such as those related to cooperation with representatives of employers or professional practice program integration in curriculum architectures or the compatibilization process of the careers in public administration with the new education system structured on three academic cycles. At Leuven, in 2009, the focus was on: including internship periods in university programs and workplace education, and improving career counseling services. At the Conference held in Bucharest in 2012, specific targets were assumed on reducing youth unemployment, improving employability, and personal and professional development of graduates, improving cooperation between employers, students and higher education institutions in order to develop programs of academic studies which will further stimulate the entrepreneurship, the innovation and the research potential of the graduates. In Romania, there remains a structural difference of perception between the representatives of academia and the ones of the business environment in relation to the compatibility between the requests of employers and competencies, cognitive skills, and abilities of the graduates of university programs; the employers considering them inappropriate. It overlooks the fact that, in order to maximize the compatibility level it is necessary for employers to anticipate and identify professional profile elements defining each skill, to discuss them with the decision-makers in academia so that they are included in the portfolio of skills, and to adopt curricular designs that contribute effectively to minimize this gap. And academia needs to be at the forefront of proactive referral trends occurring in human capital and contribute to the adequate preparation of graduates. Examination of the Romanian societal landscape indicates incoherence, inconsistency, lack of rigor, and reactive rather than pro-active habits at almost all levels of decision and action.

3.4. *The student-centered education*

An ongoing challenge that universities had to face was related to what a graduate student needs to know and be able to do after graduation, based on what the study programs offered. Student-centered education has not been a topic directly addressed at the beginning of the Bologna Process, but it was addressed as a transversal concept. With the adoption of the Leuven Communiqué, an increasing focus was put on the mission of teaching/learning of the institutions of higher education, the reform of university curricula and the introduction of learning outcomes as a tool in the teaching process. The Conference from Bucharest, in 2012, agreed to intensify efforts in order to ensure that: higher education institutions make the connection between study credits, learning outcomes, and effort of students and to include the acquisition of learning outcomes into assessment procedures; to promote innovative teaching methods and to involve students as active partners in their own training. In Romania, decision-makers often mistakenly believe that they have fulfilled all obligations with the implementation of the system of financing education-equivalent student. Academic staff remains tributary to the traditional teaching methods maintaining the teaching logic and being reluctant to move to learning logic. The students also have a simplified understanding of what student-centered learning really means and they are still maintaining low levels of proactivity, staying out of the development of the training process and being unconcerned for entrepreneurship, critical and creative thinking, innovation capabilities, and diversification of extracurricular and volunteering activities. Moving towards to a student-centered learning system involves changes in the strategies and policies at attitudinal level, at the educational infrastructure level, and in terms of relational mechanisms between the different categories of stakeholders.

3.5. *The international opening of education systems*

Given the challenges package fueled by globalization, the higher education institutions implementing the Bologna Process assumed, increasingly obvious, the internationalization process of their activities as a referential strategic component. In this respect, since the first ministerial statement it is assumed to promote the European dimension, in particular for the development of curricula, inter-institutional cooperation, or partnerships for mobility and joint degree programs. In Berlin in 2003, commitments were made to the implement scholarship programs for young people from outside Europe. In Bergen, in 2005, commitments were made to exchange best practices in collaborative programs with neighboring countries and in London in 2007, commitments concerned the exchange of information and further efforts to increase the attractiveness and competitiveness of the EHEA. At Leuven, in 2009, ministers have pledged to boost higher education institutions in their countries to internationalize their activities and to engage in global collaboration for sustainable development. Analysis reveals significant backlogs in this direction. The attractiveness of Romanian universities educational offer is extremely low due to the poor placement of their international rankings, the small number of join degree programs, and endemic parochialism of the behavior of decision-makers at the university level. Invoking financial reasons but sacrificing the strategic nature objectives, the Romanian universities seldom attend or are not attending at all in major international education fairs have less offensive promotional policies and often sacrifice long-term ambitions in favor of short-term goals. The main challenge that lies in front of universities in Romania refers to the dramatic fall in the number of potential students. The analysis of this phenomenon shows the complexity of its causalities. Often, the management of universities is limited to demographic reasons and seeks circumstantial solutions that will prove later on to be extremely expensive from medium and long term perspective. For treating those vulnerabilities it is necessary to move from university management to leadership and academic governance.

3.6. *The mobility of university community members*

The main challenges that the member states need to face are related to: the portability of grants study and loans; recognition of study periods in other universities; minimizing financial barriers for the mobility of students and teachers; increase the flexibility of learning paths. In London in 2007, it was revealed that it is the responsibility of governments to facilitate the granting of residence and work permits. By Leuven Communiqué of 2009, a clear target in the Bologna Process has been adopted, i.e., at least 20% of those who have completed a university program have to benefit by 2020 from a period of study or training abroad. On this occasion it was pointed out that career structures must be adapted to facilitate mobility of teachers, researchers, and administrative staff. Working conditions must be established in order to ensure appropriate access to social security and to facilitate the portability of pensions and of additional rights for staff involved in mobility. In Bucharest, in 2012, it was agreed to adopt the strategy of "Mobility for better learning." Ministers agreed that the requirements for mobility are: flexible learning paths, active information policies, full recognition of learning outcomes, study support and full portability of grants and loans. In this respect, Romania can act at the level of the promotion criteria and evaluation of academic performance by increasing indicators covering the period of study abroad, involvement in interdisciplinary research teams, visiting professor status. Romanian Universities should be encouraged through public funding schemes, to increase the proportion of teachers from other EU member states and their number of teachers who teach abroad. It is necessary to develop and operationalize motivational schemes that include financial incentives for intra-national and international mobility of academic staff. There is much to do in the direction of increasing the share of students attending one or more semesters of study at foreign universities partner. It is imperative to provide the academic curricula with mandatory periods of study or internship abroad.

3.7. *Improved academic governance*

Financing higher education system was central point of the Bologna Process with the adoption of the Leuven Communiqué, where the national delegations assumed that public funding remains the main priority which guarantees equitable and sustainable development of autonomous higher education institutions. At the same time, searching of other diversified funding sources and methods were also carried on. The Bucharest Communiqué reiterates the need for public funding at the highest possible level, while describing other appropriate sources. In terms of governance of higher education system, the Bologna Process states from the beginning the attendance of students, teachers, and non-teaching administrative staff to the decision-making process at all levels and the existence of a legal framework to ensure such participation. The Communiqué Budapest/Vienna, in 2010, referred to staff and student participation in decision-making at European, national, and institutional levels. Communique from Bucharest is the first programmatic document that makes clear reference to **governance structures**, noting the need to develop effective management structures. In the new conditions of inter-university competition, the development of the more effective governance management structures of higher education institutions becomes essential. At the magnitude of the economic and financial global crisis, Romania was among the EU member states that have reduced by over 20% allocations for education and academic research demonstrating that politicians and decision-makers did not understand that in times of crisis one should not operate pro-cyclical measures but inverse with anti-cyclical measures. The budget financial and statistical engineering will not replace the smart, structured, and consistently applied financing schemes and the non-switching process to the European logic of multi-annual financial perspectives in the financing of higher education, will deprive this sector from the strategic approach absolutely necessary to ensure the quality and sustainability at its level. One of the most significant vulnerabilities of the Romanian higher education system is the structural deficit in the university governance which makes the coexistence of at least three major confusion: the confusion between documents bearing the title and genuine political strategy or strategies and policies in education; confusion between real manager with management capabilities and complex educational process and people democratically elected or appointed to fill managerial functions and skills without binding it, the confusion of true educational paradigm shift that requires behavioral changes involving all stakeholders of education and cosmetic changes in the institutional and regulatory architectures which are not addressing the nuances of cultural nature.

3.8. Qualifications framework

One of the main objectives of the Bologna Process was the transition to three-cycle system, since 2005. The participating States have also undertaken the mission to develop and implement national qualifications frameworks compatible with the European Qualifications Framework, which describe what a student should know, understand, and be able to achieve on the basis of that qualification. The main purpose of implementing these measures is to ensure coherence, consistency, and international comparability of qualifications and titles acquired during higher education process in Europe. Even in 2003, in Berlin, it was expected that the first university course to provide access, for the purposes of the Lisbon Recognition Convention, to second cycle of studies and the second cycle to give access to doctoral studies. Within the Berlin Communiqué it is declared that "... *The quality of higher education has proven to beat the heart of the setting up of a European Higher Education Area*" (European Ministers of Education, Berlin, 2003). To the Bergen meeting it was stated that: "*We commit ourselves to introducing the proposed model for peer review of quality assurance agencies on a national basis, while respecting the commonly accepted guidelines and criteria*" (European Ministers of Education, Bergen, 2005). In London, in 2007, the commitments aimed: proper implementation of European Credit Transfer and Accumulation System (ECTS) based on the learning results and students workload and full implementation of national qualifications frameworks to the EQF certificate of EHEA by 2010 as preparing for self-certification QF–EHEA by 2012. In Bucharest, in 2012, participants were committed that the qualifications giving access to higher education should be considered as part of the European Qualifications Framework (EQF) level 4, or equivalent (for countries that are not related to EQF but include national frameworks) and award the first, second and third cycle, levels 6, 7, and 8 of the EQF. Nationally, there were developed and certified skills scales obtained through successful completion of a bachelor degree or Master program. Based on these skills grids (1), in case of certain university programs and grids 1 — *bis* there were assigned to each competence and adjacent descriptor, disciplines and their respective credit points. It's time to start the reverse process conducted to date, one in which, having as landmark the already nationally approved competences grids, the curricula programs should be revised and to further include in it those disciplines that really contribute to the announced competences, to carefully consider the intracurricular synergistic correlations and to eliminate redundancies which is also reflected in the records of disciplines (syllabus). It becomes mandatory to agree with representatives of employers the curriculum content, to early involve both specialists in science education and those from social and economic environment, in all stages of the ambitious process of development of a truly modern and consistent with best European and international practices, curricula architecture. Romanian educational reality show as time goes by that universities face more complex challenges. To be able to respond proactively and intelligently to this, universities need to know how to: be practical as well as transcendent, assist immediate needs and pursue knowledge for its own sake and both add and question value. Academic governance structures must find the means by which they make the community members understand that: *higher education is not about results in the next quarter, but about discoveries that may take-and last-decades or even centuries; higher education has the responsibility to serve not just as a source of economic growth, but as society's critic and conscience; universities are meant to be producers not just of knowledge but also of (often inconvenient) doubt.* In the last decade there has been a shift both in the political discourse and in the academic research from the process of education and implicitly of teaching requiring external intervention from a whole system, towards the learning process learning which is a profoundly individual act (Peter and Humes, 2003).

3.9. *Quality assurance in higher education system*

One of the most important objectives of the Bologna Process was to develop the aspects of quality assurance, in particular the common general criteria for compatibility of national systems of quality assurance. In the Berlin Communiqué, in 2003, it is predicted that by 2005 national quality assurance systems should include: a definition of the responsibilities of the stakeholders and institutions involved, an evaluation of programs or institutions including internal assessment, external student participation and publication of results, a system of accreditation, certification or comparable procedures, international participation, cooperation and networking. In this respect, the Bergen Communiqué adopted standards and trends for quality assurance in the EHEA, document designed by the European Association for Quality Assurance National Agencies which includes provisions on quality assurance at institutional level, external quality assurance and standards for national agencies. In London Communiqué, in 2007, the participating States decided to support the founding of a European register of quality assurance and in 2012, in the Bucharest Communiqué, the national agencies are encouraged to apply for registration. In Romania, it has been made important steps towards the operationalization of regulatory and institutional framework required to ensure the quality of education, the educational effectiveness and ensuring internal and external evaluation of compliance with quality criteria. From the formal point of view, the Romanian universities carry out self-evaluation quality assurance process of the study programs, have their own institutional structures required by the quality assurance and evaluation of study programs offered and they began to implement the vectors quality culture. Almost all Romanian universities proceeded external quality assessment procedures for higher education, went through institutional assessment and implement the recommendation of expert evaluators. What has to be done as next steps is overcoming the purely quantitative criteria check stage, that may be irrelevant, and passing to a prevalent qualitative assessment in order to certify that it has been made the move from teaching to learning, was enthroned a culture of quality of study programs whose values are assumed by all members of the university community and that the *status quo* has close connections with the process itself.

4. Conclusion

We can conclude the Bologna Process represents undoubtedly a revolution of European academic landscape meant to generate significant medium and long-term effects. The most important drivers of this process are: the enthronement and intelligent management of a new culture of quality in higher education and the contribution of tertiary education to the increase of flexibility and adaptability of intellectual capital. What should be regulatory clarified, understood at the academic governance level and implemented in the conduct of university community members is whether the values of this process should be regarded as endogenous factors of higher education systems or as their exogenous determinants. The central issue of this process remains the paradigm shift from a model of higher education systems based on the accumulation and transmission of knowledge to a new model of tertiary education based primarily on providing competencies (general, specialized and transverse competencies), cognitive skills and abilities. This fundamental change must take into account a number of transformations taking place at the Romanian educational landscape also. Among these, the most notable are: the massification and marketization of higher education; changing background of professional training processes nature, of the appetite for learning among young people and of their range of expectations; the deepening need for attracting in the functional and assessing decision-making process of a growing number of interest groups (stakeholders); deepening urgency to change the quality of the educational culture; the rapid advancement of the process of internationalization in higher education, which has generated greater mobility of the members of the university community and has sharpened the need for transparency of activities. The need to "*provide common European answers to common European challenges*", is more acute than ever.

For Romania, aligning with the European objective further requires: the adoption of a clear educational system, rigorous, logically articulated and feasible, taking into account the requirements of current and future human capital market and to internalize best practices enshrined at international and European level; promoting an international dimension to the higher education system and ensuring conditions for unrestricted mobility of Romanian students and those from other countries, of the teaching and research staff and of other members of the university community; promoting cooperation at European and international level in matters of ensuring high quality standards in higher education; promoting at all university cycles the defining values for the European identity; raising the attractiveness of Romanian universities for the citizens of the European Economic Area; modernization of doctoral programs in what their content and purpose is concerned, in order to ensure the desirable synergy between education and scientific research, essential in the context of an knowledge and creativity based economy.

References

Bucharest Communiqué (2012), Making the most of our potential: Consolidating the European Higher Education Area. Available at http://www.ehea.info/news-details.aspx?ArticleId=266.

Corbett, A. (2004), Europeanization and the Bologna Process — A preliminary to a British study, Paper presented to the One day conference co-sponsored by the ESRC and UACES.

Craig, P. & Burca, G. de. (2011), *EU Law, Text Cases and Materials* (5th edn.), Oxford: Oxford University Press.

Enders, J. & De Weert, E. (2004), The international attractiveness of the academic workplace in Europe — synopsis report. In *The International Attractiveness of the Academic Workplace in Europe*, J. Enders and E. de Weert (eds.), Frankfurt: Herausgeber und Bestelladresse.

European Ministers of Education (2003), *Realizing the European Higher Education Area*, Berlin: Communiqué of the conference of ministers responsible for higher education.

European Ministers of Education (2005), *The European Higher Education Area — Achieving the Goals*, Bergen: Communiqué of the conference of ministers responsible for higher education.

European Ministers of Education (2007), Towards the European higher education area: Responding to challenges in a globalized world, London.

European Commission (2010), Europe 2020: A strategy for smart, sustainable and inclusive growth, COM 2020, 3.

Fejes, A. (2005), The Bologna process — governing higher education in Europe through standardization. Paper presented at the third conference on Knowledge and Politics — the Bologna Process and the Shaping of the Future Knowledge Societies.

Feyerabend, P. (1987), *Science in a Free Society*, London: Verso.

Furlong, P. (2005), British higher education and the Bologna process: An interim assessment, *Politics*, 25(1), 53–61.

Garben, S. (2010), The Bologna process from a European law perspective, *European Law Journal*, 16(2), 186–210.

Garben, S. (2013), The Future of Higher education in Europe: The case for a stronger base in EU law. LEQS Paper No. 50.

Hackl, E. (2001), Towards a European area of higher education: Change and convergence in European Higher Education, EUI Working Paper, RSC No. 2001/09.

Huisman, J. & van de Wende, M. (2004), The EU and Bologna: Are supra- and international initiatives threatening domestic agendas? *European Journal of Education*, 39(3).

Keeling, R. (2006). The Bologna Process and the Lisbon Research Agenda: The European Commission's expanding role in higher education discourse, *European Journal of Education*, 41(2), 203–222.

Kuhn, T. (1970), *The Structure of Scientific Revolutions*, Chicago: The University of Chicago Press.

Kurelic, Z. (2009), How not to defend your tradition of higher education, *Političkamisao*, 46(5), 9–20.

Luijten-Lub, A. van der Wende, M., & Huisman, J. (2005), On cooperation and competition: A comparative analysis of national policies for internationalization of higher education in seven Western European countries, *Journal of Studies in Higher Education*, 9(2).

Marginson, S. (2004), Globalization and higher education: Global markets and public goods. In *The International Attractiveness of the Academic Workplace in Europe*, J. Enders and E. de Weert (eds.). Frankfurt: Herausgeber und Bestelladresse.

Ravinet, P. (2008), From voluntary participation to monitored coordination: Why European countries feel increasingly bound by their commitment to the Bologna Process, *European Journal of Education*, 43(3).

Reinalda, B. & Kulesza, E. (2005), *The Bologna Process — Harmonizing Europe's Higher Education*, Opladen & Bloomfield Hills: Barbara Budrich Publishers.

Chapter 10

University Governance and Competitive Advantage

Mihai Korka

Bucharest University of Economic Studies

Modern universities are complex institutions, with multiple functions in the society and specific organizational and managerial structures. Universities fulfill their public mission only by integrating into their respective civic, economic, cultural and scientific environment and playing an active role in the sustainable progress of the smaller or larger scale communities they serve. As society is under a continuing transformation and competition among the providers of higher education services becomes stronger, universities engaged a multifaceted modernization process as they wanted to keep their role as strong growth engines in the society. Changes might be observed in the way universities accomplish their mission and public functions. Changes are noticeable also in terms of management structure and decision-making, in organizational behavior and in the way universities connect with the world beyond their respective campuses. New university governance concepts and principles are discussed and implemented in a variety of models everywhere in the academic world. Even the ways of approaching competitive advantages of universities register a certain diversification as risks and opportunities are so different from a region to another, as internationalization is embedded in sustainable development strategies.

The chapter reiterates some of the observed changes in the university governance and discusses practices which trigger the competitive advantage of universities. As cost leadership appears to have limited application field, specialization of university functions and readiness for quick adaptation to the ever changing needs of the society are presented as possible ways of cultivating competitive advantage of institutions for their sustainable development. The background for the discussion on university governance and competitive advantage refers to existing positive and negative legal, institutional and behavioral factors in the Romanian higher education sector.

1. Introduction

Change is probably the single stable element of life on earth whether one looks to an individual or to a smaller or larger community. However, the speed and depth of the change register amazing dimensions at present and in the predictable future their intensification appears to be a normal extension of the current situation. Change will affect even more facets of human presence and life and will continue to shape the interaction of the society with the natural environment. Korka affirms that "on a 2025 horizon the society itself will continue to change. On one hand, individual interests and consumerism are becoming stronger but on the other hand social capital becomes more influential as awareness of ecological, civic and political rights for individuals and communities are on the agenda of each and everyone. Common interests and new communication channels supported by last generation hard- and software stimulate global interconnectedness in almost all the aspects of the day to day life and work" (2013: 49–59).

Universities have been created a millennium ago and still exist as constituent part of the society with specific public functions which answer current and future requirements of the society. In the dynamic and challenging context of the fast changing societal environment, universities have undergone more or less visible transformation processes. Some of the universities proofed to be more dynamic, showing an explicit propensity to change under the strain of the extra academic world. Some others were more rigid showing resistance to change. This is why these universities were qualified as ivory towers. The second part of the last century revealed the fact that even ivory towers were challenged by the society and invited to better respond to the needs and expectations of their stakeholders. By discussing the drivers of increased role of universities in the future progress of the society, Scott states that "The prospects for the next half century are for an acceleration of both drivers — to include access to higher education among the basic entitlements enjoyed by citizens in democratic societies; and to "put knowledge at work" in order to generate wealth and to improve the quality of life" (1998: 18–20).

Universities will continue and even strengthen the transformation process as they want to keep and demonstrate their real potential as growth and wealth engines in the society. The traditional competitive advantage of universities as knowledge and skills providers cannot be defended by stiff attitudes towards the multiple and complex changes in the society. Under the competition pressure of new innovative providers entering the higher education sector, many universities have engaged in consistent re-engineering of teaching and learning; there are also coherent attempts to re-organize the research activities and the provision of services to the local, regional, national, and/or global society. Changes in university life might be also observed in terms of management structure and decision-making, in organizational behavior and in operating the interface with the world of stakeholders and clients beyond the respective campuses. Additionally, new university governance concepts and principles are discussed and implemented in a variety of models everywhere in the world. Therefore, the purpose of this chapter is to discuss the impact of the changing world on Romanian universities in a prospective approach. Korka mentions five different dimensions of these changes: deep functional specialization, flexible and efficient organizational models, entrepreneurial spirit, systemic communication, and networking and performance oriented university governance (2013: 61–80). Specifically, the chapter offers a review of these predictable changes from the perspective of competitive advantage.

2. Deep Functional Specialization of Universities

The global changes in the social, cultural, natural, communication and information environment, the continuing evolution of the national and international legal, political and diplomatic setting in which universities exist and function generate numerous yet different responses. Some of these responses have already turned to practice in the most dynamic universities, others are only anticipated. Without doubt, some responses of the university communities are not or cannot be anticipated because the mix of factors and circumstances cannot be always predicted, nor can their results.

As they have been so far, universities will continue to operate as higher learning and training organizations, as research and innovation hubs which promote and disseminate science and culture, as service providers to the society or to the business community. In all these functions, universities fully apply and promote the human rights and the principles of democratic citizenship.

One of the outcomes of the transformations in the Romanian higher education after December 1989 is the increase of the number of public universities and the emergence of private providers. As a consequence, the study opportunities for Romanian and international students appear to be highly segmented and amazingly repetitive. Many study programs are operated by tens of higher education institutions. Even in the same town the same study profile is present in more than one university. The higher education applicants are confused by this multiplication of learning opportunities and, in the absence of transparent information regarding quality or learning outcomes differentiation, they might make inappropriate choices.

The Romanian National Education Law No. 1/2011 provides a grouping of Romanian universities into three categories according to the prevalence of research or higher education in the total volume of activities carried out by each of the organizations. The aim of the grouping is to offer a more substantial financial support to advanced research and education universities, and a less beneficial financing to the other two categories — education and research universities and, respectively to only education universities.

However this grouping proves to meet only partially the diversification expectations of the present and especially of the future society. A profound functional specialization could better answer the needs of the society than a grouping which appears to be too simple, too generalist when compared to the diversity of the present and future expectations and needs. On the other hand, this grouping generates an explicit disadvantage for most of the higher education institutions and ends up with a differentiated treatment of the right of applicants to a sound and quality education.

By the profile of their activity, advanced research and education universities do not have the capacity of enlisting for studies all the people interested in higher education, nor do they wish to sacrifice excellence in research in favor of initial training of a large number of students. In order to promote excellence in research, some of these universities have taken the step to significantly reduce the number of people enrolled in the first study cycle (undergraduate) alongside with the attraction of an increased number of Master and PhD students, with a careful selection of applicants based on intellectual performance. Other universities of the first group have introduced from the first study year disciplines or modules which develop research aptitudes in students and train them as research assistants. It means that advanced research and education universities trigger their competitive advantage by pointing on talent (research expertise of the staff and strong selection criteria of students) and/or on cost leadership (undergraduate students are trained to become from an early stage of their presence on campus competent, creative and entrepreneurial research assistants). Altbach & Salmi enumerate three pre-requisites for reaching academic excellence in research: talent, resources and governance. Their innovative mix could support a university on its road to academic excellence. The authors point to the fact that "a key success factor in building a top research university is the ability to attract, recruit, and retain leading academics" (2011: 323–333).

But society does not only need advanced research competencies, nor is the students' learning potential uniform. Alongside with the advanced research and education universities, society will always need other types of higher education institutions which should be capable to demonstrate excellence in their field of activity. The universities of education and research which offer excellence in higher education and professional training are already greatly appreciated in the society. Their main goal is the students' professional and intellectual development, so that they may prove the personal and social effectiveness of their training as specialists which are successfully entering the labour market based on their learning outcomes. They also successfully enter social life, having acquired the set of competencies and values which allow them to take roles and responsibilities in the democratic society. The competitive advantage of some of these education and research universities resides in diverse and flexible curricula and in the quality of the career orientation and assistance services provided throughout the study period, for acquiring knowledge and skills useful to society. Student-focused learning involves taking into consideration the individual or group demands and expectations of the students, who aim at an advanced professional training and also at their intellectual development, at cultivating their personality as a highly qualified specialist, critically-minded, bright, creative, capable to communicate in an intelligent manner, to assert themselves and to integrate at the workplace and in the community, to assume leadership and the results of their decisions. International experience points to the fact that the competitive advantage of this type of universities can also be strengthened by the quality of life and services on campus, by the diversity of the possibilities of (multi)cultural and artistic education, by sports and extra-curricular activities. Such a mission assumed by some of the education and research universities responds to the expectations of quite a number of students of today and much more of tomorrow. Besides strictly acquiring a professional qualification, they have other personal or societal motivations to attend higher education courses. In fact, the increased complexity of the future society recommends conceiving and implementing interdisciplinary curricula, which should develop inter-professional and inter-cultural competencies of communication and interaction.

The education-research binomial is and remains in the foreseeable future the only guarantee of a university's attractiveness and competitiveness in any domain of knowledge. As every element of the binomial will improve in complexity, due to the diversity of concrete elements assembled in the curricula and the adjustment to the requirements of society; a single university will not be able to concomitantly cover all the types of demands, either in the domain of higher education or in the domain of scientific research, without the risk of losing excellence. Competitive advantage of education and research universities can be strengthened by a balanced specialization of the public functions of the organization. The university management with the support of the academic community has to adapt to the long run specialization opportunities existing in the wider society the university serves and to face challenges build up by local and international competitors in each of the functions. Based on a sound analysis of the risks and advantages, the entire university community will have to make its choices in establishing those ones which better support the sustainable institutional development.

As regards the third type of higher education institutions, there will be no universities exclusively dedicated to education, without any research or knowledge development activity. Higher education simply does not exist without a concern for fundamental or applied research connected to the teaching activity. Every university will have to continue to identify human, informational, technical and financial resources in order to preserve and increase through research the value, relevance and quality of the training offered to students. Otherwise, it will be exposed to the risk of losing its identity and its role in the society.

The variety of requirements of people interested in initial and further higher education will determine both the flexibility of the study duration and the diversification of the study formats. The rigid duration of the study programs, formalized by the present national legal framework as well as by some international agreements will be reconsidered in the immediate future. More flexible pathways will be implemented in the initial higher education concomitantly with new teaching and learning methods. Evaluation of knowledge and skills will undergo a significant improvement focusing on the problem solving aptitudes and attitudes of students.

On the other hand, there are successful international examples of universities offering training programs to graduates which are interested to acquire useful competencies after they get work experience. These are life-long and life wide programs of variable duration and formats which are tailored according to the needs of the attendance. The interest for higher education of people belonging to different age-groups represents a reasonable motivation for Romanian universities to find appropriate and advantageous methods to make the tertiary professional and intellectual training more flexible in terms of access and delivery. In the context of the shrinking trend in new intakes from the regular student cohorts, some of the higher education institutions could even decide on for a specialization in tertiary lifelong study programs.

The variety of the local/regional or international/global opportunities of sustainable institutional development, the different visions of the university communities about their role and mission in the society as well as the human and financial resources which can be attracted to the institutional sustainable development project will determine a much deeper functional specialization of universities as in present days. The missions and functions of universities will be much more divers than they are today. The main drivers of the specialization are competition forces and the permanent search for competitive advantage.

Treacy & Wiersema analyze three main "value disciplines" assuring the competitive advantage of a company: product leadership, operational excellence and customer confidence (1993 and 1995). By adapting these concepts to the academic world, Korka observes that product leadership should be a permanent goal to be followed by the university management team along all the phases of the life-cycle of each study program (from the design of the curriculum, throughout delivery, quality control, and cost effectiveness), while operational excellence depends on the relevance of the learning outcomes, the variety of educational formats and the appropriateness of the internships. Finally, customer confidence can be nourished via soft or emotional arguments (satisfaction of graduates, success rates in entering the labor market, etc.) and hard or factual ones (international accreditation and recognition of diplomas and certificates). Showing readiness to adapt to the ever changing needs of the real and potential students and learners could also increase comfort and confidence of the customers (2011: 117–125).

3. Flexible and Efficient Organizational Models

The traditional organizational model of Romanian universities is based on rigid disciplinary division of the academic activity and on highly bureaucratic administration. Driven by the global race for students and resources, universities adopt different organizational models, which focus on the principles of organizational flexibility and efficiency.

Whatever the organizational model may be, university will have to take on the organizational behaviour of an enterprise confronted with competition, as it is, in fact, an organization which continuously strives for recognition and the promotion of its products (whether we mean graduation diplomas, registered patents or other research-development-innovation results, or the services rendered for the welfare of the community), for excellence and visibility in its field, for preserving and, if possible, for expanding its own activity of interaction with society in the country and/or abroad.

The universities of excellence promote the *adhocratic model*, respectively, the organization of their own employees and of those attracted to temporary teams centred on problem solving and interdisciplinary association of experts, which stimulates a strong creative-innovative spirit. From the perspective of the knowledge society, flexibility, and the permanent competition among specialists represent the fundamental principles of an efficient organization.

Already present in international practice, the *matrix model* makes a clear distinction between the role of departments, which pool human resources involved in academic activities according to subjects, and the interdisciplinary demand administered by schools and/or research centres. The department focuses on the affiliated disciplines and on continuous updating of disciplinary pedagogy, while the administration of the study programs and of the research projects is entrusted to centres, which are created ad hoc to cover the activities enlisted in the university portfolio. Actually, this model is based on the idea that a university cannot efficiently respond to the contextual needs of society other than by flexibility, by rapidly adjusting the internal organization of "production". The model of the universities organized on the matrix basis will gain ground in the future, but it will not be generally applied.

The alternative model of a *hybrid organizational structure* is present in most systems of higher education which are highly dependent on state financing. These universities show departments organized according to disciplines, consolidated administration structures of the study programs (faculties/schools) or of the research projects (centres of excellence) and a large bureaucratic sector of auxiliary services, which administrates the activities on the real or virtual campus and operates the financial — accounting department. The supremacy of rigid professional bureaucracy over the intellectual activity eliminates from the competition for excellence all those universities which apply this model. Recent years prove that even the success in the competition for students and for resources might be jeopardized by heavy bureaucratic procedures.

In order to avoid such a perspective, the organizational model adopted by the university community should rely on a simple, operational hierarchic structure, with minimum bureaucratic mechanisms, yet transparent and efficient, capable of adapting to the inevitable increase in the complexity of activities carried out in the university of a future society, with much more numerous and more varied needs and expectations (even including individual demands) than at present. The impeccable articulation and good functioning of the university management informational system represent a clear option for all the universities deciding to become involved, on the one hand, in the intra-sectoral competition for a better position and, on the other hand, in a dynamic international dialogue of turning to account the opportunities of inter-institutional cooperation.

To sum-up, a significant increase in the university's organizational complexity is anticipated, brought about by the diversification of the portfolio of activities and by the need for flexible structures involved in adequate and efficient solutions for the commitments made by the institution. This increase in organizational complexity goes hand in hand with the review of the internal quality management system and the gradual introduction of a new quality culture at institutional and individual level.

4. Entrepreneurship and Networking

Entrepreneurial esprit of the members of the academic community, excellent communication skills, and inter-institutional networking represent intangible assets with a strong contribution to the increase of the competitive advantage of a modern university.

Romanian universities' entrepreneurial propensity has developed under the conditions in which they realized that the resources distributed by the state can only partially cover the running costs, despite the internal efforts to prioritize the various categories of expenses. In the foreseeable future, the (co)financing of higher education from private sources will have a larger share than it has at present. In order to attract financial resources, all the functions of the universities in their interaction with the rest of the world will put at work.

In the initial higher education, (co)financing has become current practice in the late 1990's. The tertiary training of adults will become a significant source of complementary income with the specialization of some of the universities in this type of provision. The training of adults is financed by employers to a great extent, while further higher education with a view to satisfying personal interests will develop based on tuition/attendance fees. It is important for universities to implement flexible durations and appropriate forms of interaction with this heterogeneous category of clients.

On its side, scientific research of universities will continue to be financed from various public and private sources mobilized locally or internationally. The scarcity of available resources enhances the intensity of the competition but also nurtures the entrepreneurial spirit. The growth of the institutional and functional complexity of universities, the diversification of the communication channels, the increase in costs of scientific research and the expenses specific to internationalization point to the fact that Romanian universities will have to dedicate a part of their creativity–innovation effort to identify alternative sources for their own sustainable development. International experience underpins the positive role of the many services carried out for business partners and the applied research projects and civic services ordered and financed by the local and regional communities. They are an everlasting source of additional financing of universities, but they might increase both amplitude and thematic diversity of the intellectual work.

Unsurprisingly, the location of the university, its socio-economic, cultural and natural environment, the institutional, communication and transportation, infrastructure represent favoring premises for increased entrepreneurial spirit. However, the main source of entrepreneurship lies in the will of every community member to identify new means of solving the problems the university faces, to identify activities and action partners in diverse circumstances which could add to a better valorisation of the existing creative potential. It is anticipated that the current resistance to that diversification of goals and clientele will considerably decrease in Romanian universities. On the other hand, the interaction with the private investors will bring certain challenges to the university management, but this will not determine academic communities to give up their educational ideals, the ethical principles of scientific research dedicated to the progress of mankind.

Networking with other universities and with partners from the local and international businesses and/or institutions also helps a university to overcome shortages in human and financial resources, in getting involved in new projects. It also increases the visibility of the organization in the local and international market which strengthens its attractiveness and competitive advantage.

5. Institutional Governance

Successful universities have an efficient task solving structure, with a reduced formalization of conduct and of working relations among the members of the organization and the management team. Nevertheless, they show a high horizontal professional specialization of the academic and non-academic staff, which triggers the organizational flexibility and favor the interdisciplinary cooperation focusing on creativity and innovation. Such universities are genuine models of organizational behaviour comparable to successful companies of the knowledge society. In these academic communities teaching and research freedom as well as traditional values of universities are promoted by all members of the staff on each layer of the decision-making process. At the same time, high quality professional involvement and accountability are freely respected basic principles of life and work on campus.

The leaders of high performance universities increasingly rely on a flexible combination between professional management principles applied in complex multifunctional organizations with flexible academic coordination of teaching and research. In the design of sustainable development plans as well as in the strategic decision-making, leaders involve in a consultation process all the members of the academic community and as many as possible business and institutional stakeholders. University governance is based on this combination of top down professional management with bottom-up open consultation assure.

The university senate, consisting of professors, students, and researchers elected by their peers loses ground to university governance mostly because it enjoys visibility and recognition only in the academic environment, while in most cases it lacks the high professional competencies necessary for running in the most effective manner such a complex and dynamic organization as a university. Members of the university senate might show education and/or research excellence but usually they lack the competencies needed for decision-making in financial or accounting issues, in negotiating commercial contracts, in dealing with banking arrangements or in establishing partnerships which affect the university's tangible or intangible assets.

At the same time, the increasing diversity of problems a university has to cope with in its interaction with public administration institutions, with various categories of stakeholders and with the society in its whole ask for a professional management of the organization. The increasing costs of education and research as well as the legal, administrative, logistical and financial consequences of the internationalization of education and research also demand a professional management, capable to evaluate the present situation, to elaborate financial strategies and action plans aiming at attracting new institutional partners and stakeholders, as well as new resources which could contribute to the sustainable development of the university.

Obviously, such an "enterprise" needs a leader, respectively, a person endowed with personal authority, holding a set of professional and managerial competencies, which are freely recognized by the members of the academic community as being beneficial for the interests of the university. Korka observes (2003: 50–51) that a university leader should be not only in best health and showing a stable temperament; he or she should be a sociable, honest, modest person, and exhibit a strong and credible character, a visionary spirit and a strong entrepreneurial propensity, openness to new and creative solutions/ideas; the leader should be capable of coagulating the necessary critical mass in order to promote and administer change, of understanding the need for flexible structures in the organization and of sharing responsibility with the other members of the managing team. At the same time, the leadership should prove understanding, respect, and support for the mission assumed by the community, for the academic freedom and for the ethical conduct in research and education.

On the road to academic excellence, Romanian universities will appoint to a greater extent their leadership by means of competition based on public hearing and comparative analysis of institutional projects and managerial programs forwarded by aspirants. The winner of such a contest signs a management contract with the university senate. The provisions of the contract detail by means of objectives and performance indicators the role of the professional management in the accomplishment of the mission and functions of the university. The consequences of the contractual relation between the parties will acquire increased relevance in the dialogue between the university community and the leadership. The leading team will be responsible for possible adverse results and for not reaching the performance indicators. It can be dismissed by the university senate before the traditional four year term of office is over. Thus, public accountability will succeed in determining the rationality of the decisions referring to all financial and logistic aspects of university activity. On the other side, the management team will avert the university senate on the risks and cost consequences of some of its specialization options in the field of teaching programs or research networking. That dual decision-making process introduces equilibrium between the academic aspirations and the available means to be involved in their fulfilment and prevents universities from possible institutional risks.

6. Final Remarks

Romanian universities will differ functionally and organizationally in the foreseeable future from the present over standardized pattern. They will capitalize on the great number and variety of opportunities offered by the global knowledge society. While fundamental academic values will be preserved, the university governance will show much more interest for specialization and diversification of the public functions for the benefit of spiritual and material wealth of all the members of the academic community as well as for the sustainable development of the local, regional, national, and international/global society.

The concrete means of action of every university depend on the academic community and the professional leadership, on the vision, mission and functions assumed, on the art of combining resources in order to prove performance in every field of specialization, on the continuous and consistent inter-connectivity and communication both on campus and in the relation with the extra-university environment.

References

Altbach, P. & Salmi, J. (2011), *The Road to Academic Excellence*: *The Making of World-Class Research Universities*, Washington: The World Bank.

Korka, M. (2008), Re-engineering partnership and leadership in universities: Change leadership in Romania's new economy, *Theoretical and Applied Economics*, May Supplement.

Korka, M. (2011), Turning competitive master's degree programmes, *Quality Assurance Review for Higher Education*, 3(2), September.

Korka, M. (2013), *Viziune Asupra Mediului în Care Vor Acționa Universitățile și Asupra Stării Lor la Orizontul de Timp 2025, Viziunea "Universitatea Orientată Spre Tqm În Anul 2025"*, Iași: Sedcom Libris.

National Education Law No. 1/2011, Monitorul Oficial al Romaniei (Romanian Official Gazette), Year 179 (XXIII), No. 18, Bucharest, January 10.

Scott, P. (1998), *Shaking the Ivory Tower*, Paris: The UNESCO Courier.

Treacy, M. & Wiersema, F. (1993), Customer intimacy and other value disciplines, *Harvard Business Review*, Reprint 93107.

Treacy, M. & Wiersema, F. (1995), *The Discipline of Market Leaders*: *Choose Your Customers*, *Narrow Your Focus*, *Dominate Your Market*, Perseus Books Group.

Chapter 11

Study Programs in English in Non-Anglophone Countries: Looking at Impacts and Challenges from a Romanian Perspective

Mariana Nicolae

Bucharest University of Economic Studies

Developing new study programs required by the dynamically changing educational market is a matter of both university governance and faculty management. There has been lately a new and increasing trend to develop English language study programs as an answer to some university development issues. The background to this trend is the rapid pace of economic development that requires new language skills constantly. However, this language competence development involves on the one hand, very intimate processes that transcend the individual and belong to the capacity of societies to develop intelligently and, on the other, to the capacity of the educational system to be agile on the educational markets. This chapter will explore the tensions between offering study programs in English, which decrease in an unexpected way the language diversity of students, and the need for multilingual and multicultural graduates from our universities as the policies and jargon of the European Union suggest. The present study will also look at the complex competences needed in order to put together such study programs by university administrators and how to rally the important stakeholders into approving them. The issues are connected both with specific university structures and also with the larger educational system which, in Romania, seems unable to cater for interdisciplinarity other than in discourse. This chapter will explore some of the impacts and challenges that the author perceives as critical for the awareness of decision-makers in the educational field.

1. Introduction

The challenges of higher education in the whole world almost are important today. From the pressure of university rankings where the Anglophone countries are the most significantly represented to the constraints of financial accountability the types of pressure are varied and continually increasing. That is why in certain economic environments there are numerous discussions about the end of the university system as we know it today. The higher education bubble is already a common place in the mainstream discourse of most researchers, practitioners, or policy-makers (Leach, 2012). When and how the bubble will burst is a matter that keeps people and specialists guessing while various scenarios are being proposed and rejected. A larger and more refined range of stakeholders are increasingly concerned that what we still call higher education, with the university as its main representative but also including other types of institutions, has started on a clear road to become an organizational form that needs reinvention. Some people have called this process the democratization of higher education. Some others have preferred terms such as massification, or educational markets, competitive advantages of universities, entrepreneurial universities, quality assurance, ranking of universities, teaching and research higher education institutions, and the list can continue. For the general public as well as for the policy makers those concepts are generally positive and motivating building up a vision of an enlightened knowledge society in which innovation and creativity are key elements of social life. For an increasing number of people working within the various systems of higher education those concepts also carry darker connotations. They reveal the battles for university expansion. Those battles may be less evident than those in the economic field, but they are as impactful. And since policy and decision-makers have started giving increased importance to the profitability of higher education we are witnessing expansion in terms of number of students, geographical areas from where those students are drawn as well as in terms of the social prestige of their academics, prestige that is materialized in income and influence. And by academics the author understands teaching and, mainly, research staff. The emphasis on research staff and the devaluation of teaching, and by contagion of learning (Popenici, 2013), is relevant for the present chapter.

Peter Drucker (Forbes, 1997) was drawing attention to the high costs of running traditional campuses and of hiring academic and administrative staff. He was warning that big university campuses would become relics and universities would not survive in the form we know them today. What Drucker was saying was that continuously higher and "totally uncontrollable expenditures, without any visible improvement in either the content or the quality of education, means that the system is rapidly becoming untenable. Higher education is in deep crisis... Already we are beginning to deliver more lectures and classes off campus via satellite or two-way video at a fraction of the cost. The college will not survive as a residential institution." And this was before the arrival of the MOOCs (Massive Open Online Course) and their growing (*The Economist*, 2013) although the real influence of MOOCs over education is still under scrutiny.

Another significant challenge to education worldwide is a less mainstream theme for academic discussions, rather than a more specialized theme for applied linguistics. However the phenomenon that I have in mind is the one referred to as English as *lingua franca* of academias. The phenomenon refers to the fact that English has clearly become the *lingua franca* of academic exchange all over the world. Lecturers in a large diversity of subject areas are now more and more delivered in English. This is a consequence, among others, of the student and staff mobility which makes study program accommodate a highly diverse and international student audience. That student audience requires instruction through the medium of English. Therefore, English as Medium of Instruction (EMI) has become an important benchmark in the process of university internationalization. An advertisement for a British Council new course in EMI claims that "in 2012, 4,646 higher education institutions offered English taught master's courses across Europe. In 2013, that number has risen to 6,407." On the other hand, an issue of great concern to the universities, lecturers but mainly to the students is the quality of academic teaching and, consequently, learning that take place in this new context.

Another pressure on the way universities develop their strategies is demographics. Even from 2010, Standard & Poor's in their Global Ageing Report showed that "no other force is likely to shape the future of national economic health, public finances, and policymaking as the irreversible rate at which the world's population is aging". One answer to that challenge was the expansion of mainly western universities towards Asia and the emerging countries, with again the need for EMI. Another challenge is the realization of some regional or national universities that their pool of students is decreasing fast due to demographics, but also due to students' mobility and to the convenience to choose international universities.

2. Changes in Romanian Higher Education — To What Purpose?

The Romanian landscape of higher education has been changing rapidly and some stakeholders will say relatively chaotically as reactions to external political commands. Even during the period before 1989 there have been changes in the Romanian education system. Some of those significant changes were the introduction of national exams and standardized qualifications to enter university through an extremely selective and severe admission process. Due, however, to excessive central planning in all fields and consequently also in education, with the exception of a brief period of liberalization of the Romanian society of the early 1970s (Seitz & Nicolae, 2014), universities were forced to give up certain study program (sociology, psychology) and to reduce their enrolment capacity according to the quota allotted by the ministry of education. Consequently, after 1989 the country faced a shortage of experts in many subject areas mainly in social sciences and humanities which obviously had a negative impact on its capacity to engage in the international dialogue meaningfully in order to catch up with other countries.

This led, after 1989, to the realization that Romania needs state-of-the-art education. Therefore, the country started to implement, somehow naively, educational reforms based on the self-evident reasoning that one of the main drivers of economic and social development was higher education. Democratic societies of today can hope to become significant in the global market only with a competitive tertiary education. Various examples, such as South Korea (Johnson, 2002) and China (Narayana & Smyth, 2006), clearly point to the importance of serious investment in higher education, but also to a change in mentalities and values.

It is not easy, however, to make the right choices, when the Romanian society at large finds itself in continuous crises and there is an international concern about the direction that universities need to take in the future. Those choices need to be made not only by visionary leaders of the higher education system, but also by well-trained individuals who are able to cope with a system that has become more complex because of the pressures, among others, of the Bologna Process. What happens instead is that leadership positions are filled by elections in a collegial system of governance that allows at best dedicated researchers and at worst opportunistic academics promoting personal agendas. None of those are useful for the system of education, but among them manage to contribute to the complications of an already too complicated higher education system and to the perverse effects that initially well-intended actions actually have.

Seitz & Nicolae (2014) show that Romania was one of the first Central and Eastern European countries to set up in 1993, by law, a "quality assurance" institution (Damian, 2011). However, the curricula with the range of courses supplied and their contents continued to be approved by the Ministry of Education. Today, the higher education system in Romania is still centrally planned and although many of the provisions of the Bologna Process have been implemented, academic values have been adopted mainly as lip service to the official European discourse and as political clichés. The Law of National Education of 2011 introduces the concept of "values" for the first time in relation to education without identifying what they are. Article 2, para. 1 stipulates that "the law has as vision an education oriented to values" while in Article 3 it enumerates 21 "principles" governing education in Romania. Among those 21 principles academic autonomy and freedom are on position 11 and 12 respectively and their meaning is not clear. Why is this relevant for the present discussion? Because it explains the otherwise difficult to grasp bureaucratic difficulties to develop new study program. The law itself, in Article 131, para. 1, gives the authority to set up study programs to the faculty, even if in the next paragraphs cites exceptions that allow the government to propose such program. Since the law neither defines the values it mentions for education nor clarifies what the 21 principles actually mean in practical terms, it leaves room for speculation and interpretation. In practice it allows plenty of opportunities for administrative and bureaucratic hassle whenever initiatives are taken at the department or faculty levels. As an example, in the section referring specifically to higher education, there is an attempt to clarify university autonomy as "the right of university communities to establish their own mission, institutional strategy, structure, activities, organization and functioning, managing their own material and human resources, in strict compliance with the current legislation" (Article 123, para. 2). All the Articles that seem to allow and encourage decentralization are completed by variations of the phrase "in strict compliance with the current legislation". Most of the issues related to teaching staff recruitment, promotions, budgets and new study program must therefore be approved by the Ministry.

The author is well aware and firmly believes that university autonomy does not mean lack of accountability to higher bodies. It is, however, the author's understanding, based on her personal/international experience, that university autonomy means encouraging or at least allowing institutions to fulfill their mission based on their strengths. This obviously is not the case in Romania were the legislation continues to place the final approval for all university efforts with the Ministry of Education. As stipulated in the law, the Ministry "controls the way in which universities exercise their university autonomy and their public responsibility and assume the general mission as their own" (Law on National Education, 2011). True, some progress has been made and the law states that universities may "establish their own mission, institutional strategy, structure, activities, organizations, and operation and to manage their own material and human resources in strict compliance with the legislation in force." In other words, no matter how we look at things, the final decision regarding the development and execution of Romania's higher education policy rests with the Ministry of Education which is invested with the authority to set up, change and close down universities. This approach to university autonomy limits the potential of Romania's higher education system and the ability of its individual institutions to be agile on a dynamic international education market.

At present, Romania has over one hundred institutions of higher education. These very diverse organizations of higher education are still given all the responsibility but not the authority or, as important, the financial resources to function. The Ministry of Education should allow and trust institutions to establish their strategic mission within the limits of the Law of National Education. It is difficult to imagine an attempt at standardization at all levels. Each university has different strengths and resources. The university governance and administration should collaborate to establish and develop its overall priorities and define its profile, its lines of accountability, and its own human resource policies within the framework established by appropriate bodies within the respective institution. The many and diverse aspects regarding curriculum development, allocation of resources, staff recruitment, and promotion are best left in the care of the institution which knows them best. The Law of National Education (2011) provides an improved and healthy framework for the organization of universities. It has built in important check points to maintain balance within the institution through Board of administration, University Senate, and various faculty advisory groups. New study programs, curriculum development, staff recruitment, and promotions are internal to a university and need to be decided there.

One of the weakest areas for higher education in Romania has been the funding of institutions with all the issues that lack of adequate finance triggers. According to the Law of National Education (2011), Romania proposes to allocate 6% of its GDP from the state and local authorities for higher education and 1% to research. This again has been a political statement and this percentage has not been reached while universities continue to be underfunded (Duguleana & Duguleana, 2012). The aspects discussed earlier relative to university autonomy would also translate into institutional capacity to develop revenues that would, in turn, contribute to funding programs, updating curricula, supporting research and supporting students and teaching staff. Although higher education is still enjoying high esteem in Romania it is severely under-funded. The legislation provides the necessary framework, but the mechanisms of implementing the political decisions are not yet fully operational. The entrepreneurial efforts of individuals and institutions need encouragement and support from the state. Universities should be allowed to use the money they attract through partnerships with businesses, institutes, and fundraising efforts for their own programs.

Romania's higher education reform has been funded through various sources. Curaj et al. (2012) determined that there have been four periods of reform in the Romanian higher education system to this point: (i) between 1990–1995 reparatory reforms were initiated to clear the curriculum from its heavily inherited political components and to re-introduce study programs forbidden before 1989 (the faculties of sociology, psychology and international business were re-opened in the early 1990s); (ii) between 1995–2002 the first wave of systemic reforms were introduced and were aimed at developing higher education and research based on programs financed by the World Bank and by Phare and managed to put in place some autonomy for universities; (iii) between 2002 and 2009 was a period of fragmented changes triggered by the Bologna Process and a time known as the missing opportunities period; and lastly, (iv) from 2009 on the second wave of systemic reforms in Romania were implemented. These higher education reforms in Romania can be seen from different but overlapping perspectives: from a broad European perspective set by the Bologna Process and from Romania's own national perspective. The reforms of this second wave, still being implemented, are financed through structural funds that the European Union allows its newly accepted members to absorb to catch up with the development levels of older members.

The five strategic projects that had been financed through the European Social Fund include: (i) Quality and Leadership for Romanian Higher Education, (ii) Doctorate in Centers of Excellence, (iii) Doctoral Studies in Romania — Organization of the Doctoral Schools, (iv) Improving University Management and (v) National Student Enrollment Registry Project. Those projects attracted much participation among academics, key stakeholders of the Romanian higher education system, as well as international consultants which offered the hope that implementation of those reforms would align higher education to international quality standards and prepare to compete on the global education market. The very existence of those projects had been an attempt to recover the public trust in the Romanian education system, trust that continues to be seriously eroded due to complex causes from real problems in the system to the contribution of the media that covers mainly the critical incidents taking place particularly during the periods of national examination. Between 2012 and 2014 two more strategic projects are implemented with international involvement to support public policy making in Romania in the field of higher education. (i) "Performance in research, performance in teaching. Quality, Diversity and Innovation in Romanian Universities" and (ii) "Ready to innovate, ready to better answer local needs" are the two projects through which Romanian universities continue to align themselves to the European ones in an attempt to contribute to the education of the young as well as address the needs of the life-long learner.

The conclusion to this section of the present chapter is that the Romanian higher education went through a lot of change that had clear positive effects in aligning the system to international expectations, even though mainly at a declarative level, but had also created a lot of confusion among its various stakeholders. The author would attempt to state that all in all, given a wise, responsible and entrepreneurial management, the present situation of the Romanian higher education allows hopes for a significant contribution of the individual higher education institutions to the intelligent development not only of the Romanian society but, given the mechanisms of globalization, also of the European society at large.

3. Introducing New Study Programs — a Solution or Another Challenge?

The introduction of new study programs in the curriculum of Romanian universities has been considered an appropriate answer to the dynamics of the national labor market and to the changes in the international higher education landscape. The former is self-evident while the latter is manifested through the requests of candidates who are nowadays more internationally mobile and, therefore experienced and knowledgeable, but still prefer to study in their home country. This process of setting up new study programs has gone through multiple versions both in terms of getting approvals and also of quality assurance. The legal modifications after 1990 permitted the quick appearance of a large variety of private higher education institutions as well as the creation of campuses belonging to or associated with international providers of higher education. The university establishment answered to those market and political commands by introducing accreditation for the new higher education institutions, focusing heavily on capacity factors, especially staff numbers and appropriate facilities.

The various periods of changes in higher education that have been referred to in the previous section have led to a large number of regulations meant to provide order and transparency in what has become a chaotic system. This process is at present, in the author's opinion, over-regulated and highly centralized in Romania which does not mean that it is a process that should be left at the discretion of the individual higher education institutions, whether public or private. Also, the author firmly believes, that it is a healthy situation that new study programs have to go through a transparent, well-structured and public procedure of authorization and accreditation by an external, independent body or agency that has no direct invested interests in the processes that it evaluates.

The term university study program has been introduced in the Romanian higher education discourse and defined by the Law of National Education (2011, Article 137, para. 1) as "a group of teaching, learning, research, practical applications and evaluation curriculum units, designed to lead to a university qualification certified through a diploma and a diploma supplement". A study program can be, therefore, defined within the various education cycles. In this chapter we are looking at an undergraduate study program that has been designed and implemented by the Faculty of International Business and Economics of the Bucharest University of Economic Studies as an answer to the various signals coming towards the managerial team of the faculty. The study program we are considering here is called Applied Modern Languages to International Business and Economics and was authorized in May 2013 by ARACIS (The Romanian Agency for Quality Assurance in Higher Education). It was offered to the public in the admission sessions of July and September 2013 and is running at present having 60 students enrolled.

Why was such a program initiated and launched? The reasons have been various and have appeared and accumulated in time. Some of the reasons were due to external factors such as a pressure for the internationalization of universities, including the need for attracting foreign students both for the benefits of diversity and for institutional financial benefits as well. In terms of financial benefits the interest of Romanian universities is to attract foreign students as compared to international students. Foreign students are students who come from non-EU countries and have higher tuition fees than Romanian students, while international students are students who come from EU countries and have the same financial obligations as Romanians. At present this situation is more relevant at graduate and post-graduate levels rather than at undergraduate level, but there are indications that even undergraduate programs will attract international and foreign students if they are offered through the medium of English. Among the internal factors contributing to the setting up of the Applied Modern Languages (AML) study program was mainly the realization that the language skills of the graduates of the Faculty of International Business and Economics have on the general deteriorated due to the reduction in the curriculum of the school of the language study from 6 hours per week to 4 and starting with Bologna only 2 hours per week per language (Nicolae, 2013).

Another reason was the successful existence on the mature educational markets of interdisciplinary programs called International Business and Modern Languages or BSc in international business administration and modern Languages or International Business Communication with a Modern Foreign Language. These programs are offered, somehow expectedly, in the UK and/or the US, which use the advantage of using English as a first language, and have always had a more flexible educational offer in which students can choose their tracks of specialization, (http://www.aston.ac.uk/study/undergraduate/courses/school/aston-business-school/international-business-modern-languages/, http://www.uclan.ac.uk/courses/ba_hons_international_business_communication_with_a_modern_foreign_language.php), but also, and this comes as an interesting development, in non-Anglophone countries, which do not have the advantage of native English lecturers, like Denmark (http://www.sdu.dk/en/uddannelse/bachelor/bsc_in_international_business_administration_and_modern_languages), Germany (http://www.uni-giessen.de/cms/study/courses/ba/mlcb) or Latvia (http://www.lu.lv/eng/istudents/degree/study/bachelor-modernlanguage/).

Another reason for creating such a program in our university was the increasing demand for AML at other Romanian higher education institutions and the decision of those institutions to accept only a very small number of the applicants. In other words identifying a gap in the market and addressing it. Still another reason, this time from the perspective of the teaching staff, was the need to balance the drop in applications for higher education caused by demographic changes and to create new offers.

All the above reasons and some others led to the decision of the dean's office and the management of the Department of Modern Languages and Business Communication (DMLBC) in the Bucharest University of Economic Studies to start the internal process to get the approvals to ask for the authorization of such a program. The Dean asked the DMLBC to provide an offer for such a program. A task force was put together by the DMLBC, coordinated by a senior person, a reader in applied linguistics with a doctorate in the UK in applied linguistics, who had worked for a long period of time for the British Council Romania. The group worked under the direct supervision of the head of department and of the dean while consulting with a large number of experts. The result of their work was presented and approved at the various levels within the faculty (department and faculty councils) and then university (Board of Administration and university Senate). The following is an abstract and a discussion of the group's opportunity report on such a development.

The report states that "such an interdisciplinary program offers students a competitive set of abilities which combine the knowledge and use of English and other foreign languages in international business and entrepreneurship while understanding and applying business principles in corporations. The program offers integrated education in the theory and practice of applied linguistics combined with the theory of business, particularly international business administration. Advanced language skills will allow students to communicate effectively in a variety of professional situations — customer care, marketing and advertising, media and public relations."

The arguments were organized in two sets: academic and practical ones. The academic arguments are important and relevant for the present Romanian higher education system because of focusing the discussion on the presence and the status of applied linguistics in the Romanian academic landscape. Applied linguistics is a discipline that has been fully recognized in the large majority of the European educational contexts. Nevertheless the situation is different in Romania where the discipline is at best neglected or worse overlooked in the faculties of languages or linguistics in the country. This means that wherever it is acknowledged and exists, AML is a second-hand division in a larger administrative unit. There are still few undergraduate studies organized in the field, though the situation has improved lately, and those study programs are not continued with master and doctoral studies. This is a major handicap both for students and academics. There are only relatively few master programs in Romania in the field. One of the portals that offer students information on what is new on the Romanian higher education market lists 15 master programs under the title AML master (http://www.studentie.ro/Master/Master-limbi-moderne-aplicate-d3-s14). However, only some of them are clearly addressing their marketing title, while others have obviously another mission (Master in Comparative and World Literatures). For students who want to continue their specialization in relevant, pragmatic and industry oriented master programs it is a real challenge. The main challenge here is, however, the academics' own professional development which clearly starts from a philological background with a certain type of research interests which are not connected to what the field of AML considers as relevant research. Therefore, academics in the field that is still called in Romania with the umbrella term of philology, though the international research community considers that "philology" remains largely synonymous with "historical linguistics" or, more generally, with the study of language grammar, history and literary tradition (Morpurgo Davies, 1998), have an understandable reluctance to shift their life-long research focus to another area. This, however, reflects on the larger higher education management and administration policies as it is important to find a balanced way between personal research interests and the complexity and dynamics of the international field and is generally settled through the emergence of inter-disciplinarity. The issue of interdisciplinarity is however a difficult one from an administrative point of view in Romania and has been addressed in-depth by Cojanu (2014). For the present chapter what is important is the faculty decision to apply for the authorization of the AML program in the field of philology as there was no procedure to evaluate interdisciplinary programs by ARACIS (The Romanian Agency for Quality Assurance in Higher Education).

The author of this chapter together with the team leaders were advised to choose one of the already existing fields — either international business and economics or philology. Examples were provided underlining that what most similar international programs (presented earlier as examples in this chapter) have in common is the open acknowledgement of their interdisciplinary characteristic which is perceived and marketed as a plus. For example the Latvian program says on its website: "The program is interdisciplinary and is designed to prepare graduates for international careers in enterprises and organizations where knowledge of several languages and business is required. The program offers three language modules (…) as well as general and business aspects of the module language. The program provides cultural studies (…), business studies through the basic management courses such as Marketing, Management Theory, Accounting Theory, Entrepreneurship in the EU, as well as the EU and international market specific study courses. Upon graduation, students are able to continue education in Master degree programs and second level professional study programs."

After careful consideration and analysis the institutional choice was to ask for the authorization of the AML program in the field of philology — for a number of reasons that are outside the scope of the present chapter.

Another important argument for the setting up of the program was the lack of capacity to coordinate doctoral research in applied linguistics in Romania. This has a serious direct effect on the career path of teaching staff in non-philological university departments, like the one in our own university. In practical terms this means that young academics have to pursue doctoral research in areas with little if any relevance to their daily professional activity and, not less important, to their evaluation and promotion chances. The relevance of this issue for the setting up of an undergraduate program maybe not easily seen, but it exists. Romanian legislation and regulations require for granting institutional permission to organize doctoral studies in a certain field to have all also undergraduate study programs in that specialization. This provision is, therefore, relevant both for the teaching staff and for the students who can continue their studies in their chosen field. Since the beginning of the 1990s there were lots of efforts made in this respect both by the British Council and, later on, by the professional community of specialists in applied linguistics. The results are still almost non-existing.

The Bucharest University of Economic Studies has, within the Faculty of International Business and Economics, the largest and most diverse department of modern languages and business communication in Romania. With 65 full-time teaching staff (7 professors, 12 readers, 22 lecturers, and 24 teaching assistants), 20 associate/part-time teaching staff and 9 admin and support staff, the DMLBC has the professional capacity to develop study programs for applied linguistics in accordance with the present international best-practices (Nicolae, 2013).

The practical arguments start from acknowledging a clear and growing interest of university prospective candidates for applied studies of modern languages. The existence of a study program that combines language study and business studies fills a gap in the Romanian higher education market. The Bucharest University of Economic Studies has the obvious advantage of having academics from both areas and the institutional capacity to provide and promote such a program.

It is important to note at this point that the distinction between academic and practical arguments that the author has borrowed from the opportunity report of the task group is purely theoretical and was used for the sake of argumentation. It is clear that the two sets of arguments overlap being difficult to discuss in a chapter of this length the complexity of the mix of history developments, personal mentalities and organizational cultures and mainly of the Romanian legal environment.

4. Tensions between Study Programs in English and the Need for Multilingualism and Multiculturality?

The upward trend to establish English language study programs is clearly visible across Europe and beyond as already shown in the introduction to this chapter. However, the attitudes of individual academics from non-Anglophone countries towards this trend are diverse and belong as pointed out by Mureşan &

Llantada (2013) to realities shaped by the historical, political, social and linguistic, educational, socioeconomic and institutional local contexts. While Mureșan & Llantada (2013) focus on the attitudes and challenges of publishing internationally, Mureșan & Nicolae (2014) look closer at the Romanian context underlining new angles and presenting some of the tensions that arise between the various stakeholders of the process: the individual academic, the higher education institution and the larger research needs of the Romanian society. Those tensions take place against a background of continual changes in the Romanian higher education system which makes institutional development and career planning very difficult.

The international literature documenting the issues related to English as a medium for instruction is rich and growing. Starting with Krishnamurti (1990) who discusses the Indian dilemma of regional language versus English as the medium of instruction in higher education and up to the present moment there is a constantly growing body of research and articles as presented in the February 2013 reference list of TIRF, the International Research Foundation for English Language Education. The list, which is selective, includes 90 titles and points to a diversity of topics, approaches and geographies. TIRF is a non-profit organization whose mission is to generate new knowledge about English language teaching and learning as professed on their website http://www.tirfonline.org. From their mission statement one particular item is relevant for the present chapter by showing the concerns that the professional communities world-wide have towards EMI. TIRF acknowledge the tensions documented by the individual researchers and academics and set itself as a goal to "influence the formation and implementation of appropriate language education policies, recognizing the importance of indigenous languages and cultures worldwide, and of English as an international language" (http://www.tirfonline.org/about-us/).

Some of those tensions include, but are not limited to, the following: (a) multilingualism and multiculturalism as important values of the European Union are threatened by the use of only one language; (b) the optimism of using English as a *lingua franca* in the global village or merely in the single market of the European Union has various effects on both individuals and businesses; (c) communication is difficult and even distorted when those involved use another language than their own; (d) creativity and innovation as main drivers of progress are best functioning when people use their own language.

5. Conclusions

In this chapter, I have looked at the challenges and opportunities of developing new university study programs as required by the dynamics of the educational market. I have shown that in the Romanian higher education system this is not a simple process and it requires both good university governance and wise faculty management.

I have underlined that this is a process in line with the newest and increasing European trends to develop English language study programs as an answer to, basically, the general decrease in the number of potential students that universities can attract. This trend is powerful as it is backed by the rapid pace of international economic development that requires new language skills constantly. The chapter has explored the tensions between offering study programs in English, which decrease in an unexpected way the language diversity of students, and the need for multilingual and multicultural graduates of society. The chapter also looked at some of the competences needed by university staff and administrators in order to put together such study programs. I have underlined issues that are connected both with specific university structures and also with the larger educational system which, in Romania, seems still unable to cater for inter-disciplinarity other than in discourse.

As a general conclusion I would attempt to state that the Romanian higher education went through a lot of change in the last two decades that had clear positive effects in aligning the system to international expectations, even though mainly at a declarative level, but had also created a lot of confusion among its various stakeholders and affected in severe ways the academics themselves. However, as in most cases in the history of Romanian education, wise, responsible, and entrepreneurial individual academics, who make up the management of institutions if organizations have chosen in an educated way, demonstrate that things can be done even in an unpredictable system.

References

Cojanu, V. (2014), Interdisciplinaritatea în științele sociale ca problem, de management/ Interdisciplinarity in social sciences as a management problem, *Revista de Politica Științei si Scientometrie — Serie Noua*, 3(1), 30–35. Available at rpss.inoe.ro/articles/124/file.

Krishnamurti, B. (1990), The regional language vis-à-vis English as the medium of instruction in higher education: The Indian dilemma, *Multilingualism in India*, 61, 15–24. Available at apud http://www.tirfonline.org.

Leach, M. (2012), Bursting bubbles in higher education. In *Blue Skies*: *New Thinking about the Future of Higher Education. A Collection of Short Articles by Leading Commentators*, L. Coiffat (ed.), pp. 58–60, London: Pearson.

Morpurgo Davies, A. (1998), Nineteenth-century linguistics. In *History of Linguistics*, Vol. IV, G. Lepschy (ed.), London: Longman.

Mureşan, L. M. & Pérez-Llantada, C. (2013), English for research publication and dissemination in bi-/multiliterate environments: The case of Romanian academics, *Journal of English for Academic Purposes*, 2. Available at http://dx.doi.org/10.1016/j.jeap.2013.10.009.

Mureşan, L. M. & Nicolae, M. (2014). The Challenge of Publishing Internationally in a Non-Anglophone Academic Context: Romania — A Case in Point. In print.

Nicolae, M. & Maftei, M. M. (eds.) (2013), *Istoria Limbilor Moderne în ASE*: *O Perspectivă Centenară*, pp. 136–137. Bucharest: Editura ASE.

Popenici, S. (2013), Devaluation of teaching and learning: The Popenici blog. Available at http://popenici.com/2013/10/10/teaching/ (Accessed 21 March 2014).

Seitz, V. & Nicolae, M. (2014), The role of academic values in higher education convergence in Romania: A new approach. In *Handbook of Research on Trends in European Higher Education Convergence*, in publication with IGI Global. Available at http://www.igi-global.com/book/handbook-research-trends-european-higher/97340.

Standard & Poor's (2010), Global ageing report. Available at http://www.cfr.org/aging/standard-poors-global-aging-2010-irreversible-truth/p23299 (Accessed 19 March 2014).

The Attack of the MOOCS, *The Economist*, 20 July, 2013. Available at http://www.economist.com/news/business/21582001-army-new-online-courses-scaring-wits-out-traditional-universities-can-they (Accessed 21 March 2014).

Chapter 12

Romanian Private Higher Education in the Current European Context

Folcuț Ovidiu and Grigore Ramona

Romanian American University

European Union's (EU's) potential to generate smart growth depends on the quality of higher education system, contributing also to a sustainable and inclusive growth. In this context, the aim of this chapter is to present the main trends in European higher education and to assess the main challenges for Romanian private higher education providers in the current European economic, political and social environment. Since their emergence in the early nineties, the Romanian private higher education institutions have become an important feature of the higher education landscape, their fast expansion being a common trend among central and eastern European countries. The analysis highlights also some examples of good practices in the field that can contribute to the improvement of the Romanian private higher education outcomes, although "one size fits all" approach may not be appropriate for higher education.

1. Introduction

Since the Bologna Declaration has been signed, in 1999, the European higher education is continuously transforming, seeking for more quality, transparency and coordination within the European Higher Education Area (EHAE). Under the Bologna Declaration's provisions, all countries have made efforts to create a functional European Higher Education Area able to serve an increasing range of societal demands, promote and support staff and student mobility, develop appropriate quality assurance systems and efficient higher education structures, facilitate grater compatibility and comparability of higher education systems in order to increase the international competitiveness of European higher education (The Bologna Declaration (EHAE), 1999).

Although the Bologna process is considered the most important driving force behind the unprecedented reform dynamics both at European higher education level, but also at national level, contributing to more convergence within the EHEA, there is still a significant degree of diversity within and across higher educational systems. (OECD, 2009) Among them, the OECD report on higher education is mentioning: different lengths of cycles across countries and disciplines, different ways of using the degree titles and also different status of the bachelor degree in national systems, different supply systems for diploma supplements, different approaches regarding quality assurance mechanisms, some being based on institutional audits, while others on program accreditation, some with more emphasis on quality enhancement than quality control. Thus, in this context marked more by variety than convergence, the success of the next stage of the Bologna process is mostly determined by a series of factors, the most important being the need for coherence in establishing process's phases and priorities and correlate them with the appropriate financial support.

The level of variety that still exists among participants is to some extent understandable and foreseeable as long as the EHEA countries have to implement policies in different economic, political and social conditions. One of the diversity's components is represented by the type and number of higher education institutions. Thus, higher education institutions can be public or private, academically or professionally oriented, these typologies influencing the Bologna process's understanding and implementation.

In the last two decades, the mix between public and private higher educational institutions has gathered attention of many researchers, as long as for example in the vast majority of the EHEA countries there are both public and private higher education institutions, the weight of private institutions being different among countries (EHEA, 2012). Private higher education (PHE) has been gradually a permanent feature of the higher education landscape not only in developing countries, but also in many developed countries (OECD, 2009). Prior to 2010, many research studies emphasized, more or less enthusiastic, the unprecedented PHE's expansion, especially in central and Eastern Europe, as a regional component of a global trend towards higher education privatization (UNESCO, 2009; OECD, 2009). Since 2010, important declines in PHE have emerged, different social and political factors contributing to the magnitude of this process (Levy, 2011). Even if is going through a challenging period, PHE remains an important feature of many higher education systems in Central and Eastern Europe, consequently with an important contribution to the Bologna process' s success.

2. Private Higher Education in EU

The emergence of PHE in Europe is mainly a recent phenomenon with different growth paths from one country to another, due to different national economic, political and social conditions. After the fall of the communism system in 1989, a major surge in private institutions emerged in Central and Eastern Europe, private higher education gradually becoming a significant feature of the higher education system in this region. Prior to 1990, some forms of private higher institutions existed in Germany, Italy, Portugal, and Spain but also in Bulgaria (Wells *et al.*, 2007). However, analyzing the emergence and evolution of private higher institutions in Europe and worldwide is a challenging task as long as is becoming more and more difficult to make an accurate distinction between private and public higher institutions. According to the OECD definition, the distinction between public and private institutions is made by taking into account the conditions of operation and relationships to public authorities and their stakeholders but also the source of funding. Using the source of funding as the main distinction criteria seems the easiest way to make a clear distinction between public and private institutions, or not. Depending on their sources of funding, some private institutions are government-dependent while others are independent private institution. By OECD definition, government-dependent private institutions receive more than 50% of their core funding from government agencies, while independent private institutions are generally referred to as private. Usually, both public and government-dependent private institutions are generally perceived as public institution (OECD, 2009).

In the most part of the EHEA countries there are both private and public higher education institutions. All institutions are considered public in Denmark, Finland, Greece, Italy, and Belgium (French Community). (EHEA, 2012) A clear distinction between public and private is difficult to make, as long as, for example, in Italy there are also private higher institutions, but they are very similar with the public ones and thus assimilated to public higher institutions. In the United Kingdom, higher education institutions are considered public, even if they are mostly government-dependent private institutions. The same situation is in Netherlands, where public higher institutions have been gradually transformed after 2004 in government-dependent private institutions due to some chances in the composition of the governing boards of universities, the new legislation raising the number of the members coming from non-governmental organizations. (OECD, 2009) When referring to private higher institutions, the analysis in this chapter takes into account only independent private institutions.

Among EU member states, the weight of private higher institutions differs. In Western European countries, the contribution of private institutions to higher education is lower than in Central and Eastern European Countries, in which the general trend in the last 20 years has been towards more participation of private institutions to higher education.

As Table 1 shows, Portugal remains the only case in western Europe with a strong private higher education sector, which reached 27% of total enrolment in higher education in 2004, representing 106,754 enrolled students. In 1996, the share was even higher, reaching 36% after a continuous increase since 1971, when the private institutions emerged. Since 2004, the private enrolment has decreased to 24% in 2009 and 20% in 2012, representing 78,699 enrolled students. According to Teixeira & Amaral (2008) most Portuguese private institutions registered a rapid decline after the mid-1990s, in some cases the decrease being above 50% of their maximum enrolment. The most important factors that contributed to this decline were the demographic patterns, an increasing quality attitude of the policy-makers and also a market saturation for certain specializations, especially those in which the private sector was perceived as demand-absorbing — social sciences, commerce, law, and education. Facing these challenges, the Portuguese private sector seems to have limited survival alternatives. Finding some demand niches, restructuring through mergers and acquisitions, programs diversification, especially for mature students, developing research capacity are the main solutions proposed by Teixeira & Amaral (2008). No matter the alternatives chosen, the private institutions have to concentrate more on quality improving activities by investing in their academic staff and a stronger commitment to research activities. While in Portugal, the entire private sector is under pressure, in other western countries, the share of the private sector has increased in 2003–2012 period. Thus, in France the private sector reached 17% in 2012, in Spain the share of the private sector was 13% and in Italy it reached 9%. Although the shares of private higher education in these countries are lower than those presented for Portugal, the role of private higher education is rising even in regions traditionally associated with public

Table 1. Private enrolment in EU higher education institutions (%)

Country/Year	2003	2009	2012	Country/Year	2003	2009	2012
Austria	0	0	0	Bulgaria	13.4	21.3	18.5
Belgium	0	0	0	Croatia	2.5	6.9	7.1
Cyprus	70.3*	71.7	62.3	Czech Republic	3.8	12.1	12.2
Denmark	0	0.1	0.1	Estonia	20.3	18.0	11.0
Finland	0	0	0	Hungary	0	0	0
France	13.5	16.1	17.3	Latvia	22.9	32.6	28.7
Germany	0	0	0	Lithuania	5.0	12.1	10.8
Greece	0	0	0	Poland	28.3	33.4	29.6
Ireland	6.2	3.1	2.2	Romania	21.3*	42.3	22.9
Italy	6.5	7.6	9.4	Slovakia	0.4	13.2	17.9
Luxembourg	0	0	0	Slovenia	2.4	7.2	7.5
Malta	0	0	0				
Netherlands	0	0	13.4				
Portugal	27.0*	24.3	20.2				
Spain	11.4	9.7	13.0				
Sweden	1.2	0	0				
UK	0	0	0				

*2004.

education providers. For France, Italy, and Spain, among the factors that have contributed to this increase the most important can be related to the changes occurred in the finance and management of public institutions, but also to the steady attractiveness of provision, especially for foreign students. However, the existence of private higher institutions in western European countries remains minimal, despite the increasing willingness of policy-makers to adopt market-like mechanism in higher education (Teixeira et al., 2004). Nevertheless, the Portugal's case can offer some important lessons for some central and eastern European countries, private higher education facing multiple challenges in this region after almost 20 years of continuous expansion.

Looking at Table 1, the existence of private higher institutions seems a common feature of the higher education systems in central and eastern European countries, except Hungary. Not only the existence of private institutions is common, but also the fact that those institutions have gradually become a permanent feature of the higher education systems in these countries in a relatively short period of time. There are also other common particularities among these countries when speaking about the emergence and rising of the private higher education system.

First, in most of these countries none of the private higher institutions existed before 1990. The growth from zero to substantial in the first half of the 1990s is considered the most dramatically concentrated spurt ever seen in any region, Central and Eastern Europe being one of the regions with the highest PHE enrolment shares after Asia and Latin America (Bjarnason et al., 2009). In 2009, the private enrolment share reached 42% in Romania, 33% in Poland, 32% in Latvia, 21% in Bulgaria and 18% in Estonia. Lower shares were registered in Slovakia (13%), Czech Republic and Lithuania (both with 12%), Croatia and Slovenia (7%). For most of these countries, the period between 2008 and 2010 was associated with the highest private enrolment shares.

Another common feature of the PHE in these countries can be correlated with the factors that contributed to this continuously growing process, at least until 2009–2010. After the communism fall, there was a persistent high demand for higher education which has led to the so-called *massification* of higher education. In this context, a gradual *privateness* of the higher education system became a second alternative which offered a fertile ground for the development of the PHE institutions. Most of the newly created private institutions followed a demand-absorbing and non-elite pattern supported by the strong social demand and also by lax regulatory forces. Thus, for many private institutions quantity became more important than quality in their strategies (Levy, 2011). Also, this demand-absorbing pattern has lead private institution to concentrate more on study fields generally associated with low infrastructure costs and little investment, such as social sciences, economics and law (Amaral et al., 2007; OECD, 2009). As a consequence, the PHE institutions are considered to be more oriented to student market than the labor market (Wells et al., 2007). This approach it seems to be outdated nowadays, as the demographic pattern is constantly contributing to the slowing down of demand in most countries. Since 2010, the decline of the PHE is becoming a common feature for most of the central and eastern European countries, except Slovakia, Slovenia, and Croatia where the private enrolment is still growing. Romania registered the highest negative chance, from 42% in 2009 to 23% of enrolment in 2012. A significant decrease was also in Poland, from more than 33% in 2009 to 29% in 2012, and Estonia, from 18% in 2009 to 11% in 2012. The decline seems to be weaker in Bulgaria, Latvia, and Lithuania.

In this new challenging environment the future of the private higher institutions is uncertain. In Poland, under a pessimistic scenario up to 75% of private institutions will gradually disappear by 2020 (Siwinska, 2011). Demographic and financial pressures will make private institutions very vulnerable and it will be increasingly difficult for them to compete with the public sector. Some solutions might come from the policy-makers, even if many private institutions do not rely very much on them. In 2010–2011 some policy proposals in Poland included large-scale public bids for teaching services, open to both public and private sectors in order to stimulate inter-sectoral competition between public and private providers, thus treating on equal footing all higher education institutions (Kwiek, 2010). In Lithuania, under some reforms launched since 2009, the also state finances private institutions' students, implementing the *money follow the student* mechanism. Even if some support measures for the entire higher education sector might come from the policy-makers, private institutions have to concentrate more on finding their own successful survival solutions. This current decline in PHE can determine the emergence of a more innovative behavior of the private institutions, as they were expected to have (Geiger, 1986). Thus, private institution have to concentrate more on raising the quality of their teaching and research activities, finding niche programs, improving attractiveness for foreign students, orientation towards labor market needs instead of student market, improving business and research networks.

3. The Rise and Fall of the Romanian Private Higher Education

The history of the PHE in Romania has started soon after the fall of the communism, in 1989. In 1991 there were already 17 private institutions, the number rising to 40 by the mid-1990s, while the number of public institutions slightly changed from 48 in 1990 to 50 in 1995 (Reisz, 1997). The process was impressive not only in terms of the number of private institutions established, but also in terms of the number of students enrolled. In 1992, about 85,000 students were enrolled in private institutions, representing 36% from the total students enrolment (Wells *et al.*, 2007). The rapid expansion of the private sector makes Romania one of the leaders in the privatizing of higher education, alongside Poland (Lewis *et al.*, 2003). As Reisz (1997) highlighted, the framework for the emergence and development of the private higher education in Romania was characterized by the under-development of the whole higher education sector.

After the communism fall, the higher education landscape has been mostly influenced by an increasing demand for higher education services. The factors that contributed to this expanding demand for higher education can be associated with the large number of high school graduates from past generations who aspired to get access to higher education, an overall liberalization of the system and a general perception that a university diploma was a prerequisite for getting better jobs in the labor market (Nicolescu, 2003). Thus, the individuals' behavior coupled with the lax regulatory forces have made higher education an attractive market first for private institutions, but also for the public institutions, later, when they started to increase the number of tuition-fee-paying students.

The private higher education sector is expected to bring *more, different and better education*, as Geiger noted in 1986, but in Romania, in the first decade of its existence, the private sector was generally perceived as a second-best option for students failing admission to state universities, questionable quality, with many semi-elite and even non-elite institutions, as profit-oriented sector having mainly a demand-absorbing orientation, even if the level of quality and social legitimacy has increased since the introduction of the accreditation system in 1993 (Nicolescu, 2005; Bjarnason *et al.*, 2009). However, the emergence and the development of private institutions brought the most significant differentiation in the Romanian higher education system, the weight of the private sector in higher education sector becoming more and more important after 2000. The private enrolment reached its peak in 2008/2009 academic year, the number of students enrolled in private institutions was 410,859, representing over 46% of the total enrolment in higher education. The student enrolments increased both in private and public institutions, but the number of the students enrolled in private institutions significantly increased starting with 2005/2006 academic year. Since 2009, a decline in higher education has occurred. For private institution the student enrolments dropped from 410,869 students in 2008 to 99,676 in 2012, private institutions contributing only with 21% to higher education. The negative trend in higher education enrolments hit also the public institutions, but the magnitude of the decline has been lower, even if it emerged one year earlier than in the private sector. From 526,844 enrolled students in 2007, the public sector reached 364,916 students in 2012. While for the public institutions the level of enrolments in 2012 was slightly lower than the level registered in 2000, for the private ones the level was close to that registered in the mid-1990s (around 100,000 students). Analyzing the level of enrolments by field of study, those that have been affected by the decline were mainly economics and law. The concentration of the private sector mainly on economics and law, finally made it vulnerable to changes in higher education demand.

The decline that has emerged since 2009 in the student enrolments levels has not affected the number of the private institutions. In 2008 there were 50 private higher institutions, and in 2012 their number reached 51 units. The number remained stable since 2007, after reaching its peak in 2002 when the number of private institutions was 70. Some chances occurred regarding the number of the faculties within the private institutions which decreased from 207 in 2009 to 191 in 2012. The negative impact might be deeper in terms of number of programs offered within different faculties.

The reasons behind the decline that started in 2009, both in private and public higher institutions are mainly related to demographic patterns, like in many other central and eastern European countries. The stagnant low birth rates after 1991 have negatively affected higher education only since 2009, and are expected to have the same impact in the following years. Besides this demographic pattern, there are also other possible factors that have contributed to this decline. One of them can be associated with some degree of market saturation for some study fields, mostly those in which the private sector offered the highest number of graduates since 2007, namely economics, law and humanities. In 2010, the number of the graduates coming from the private institutions reached 97,422, half of them in economics, higher even than the number of public institutions' graduates. In this context, lower levels of enrolments were predictable to some extent taking also into account the labor market needs. Another factor that has negatively influenced higher education is correlated with the number of pupils who graduated the schools leaving examination. In the last three years only around half of them passed the baccalaureate. Thus, the number of potential candidates sharply decreased affecting both private and public institutions. Moreover, an increasing number of Romanian students have chosen to study abroad, especially in western European countries. The above mentioned factors have affected both private and public institutions, but for the private ones another one can be added, namely the gradual privatization of the public sector. The number of the fee-paying-students in public institutions steadily increased to almost 50% of total enrolment, while the other half is subsidized. Thus, the level of privatization of higher education in Romania is much higher. Moreover, in 2011 and 2012 the number of subsidized places in public institution could cover more than half of the baccalaureate graduates. In this context, the competition for students become stronger and the private institutions have to pay more attention to their tuition-fees, as the lower fees was one of the main advantage offered to those students that failed to get a subsidized place in public institutions.

After 20 years of expansion, the future of the Romanian private higher institutions is full of challenges which threaten their existence. This difficult period might be for some of them a survival test. Some might pass, some not, the result mostly depending on their capacity to find innovative responses to all these challenges. Going back to Geiger's approach regarding the role of the private education (*more, different, and better education*) probably during the last 20 years much has been done in terms of *more* higher education and less regarding *different* and *better* education. The shift to different and better education can be a solution for private institutions. For those private institutions that didn't neglected quality during their expansion, the shift will be easier but still requires more orientation towards quality, both in teaching and research activities. To some extent the decline brought also a positive effect on the private higher education. During its peak period, within the private sector the average student/teacher ratio was very high, reaching 84 students/teacher in 2008. In 2012, the average student/teacher ratio decreased to 27, double than the ratios in public sector. However, this new environment of doing education might be the appropriate ground for private institutions to concentrate more on the quality of the educational services they are providing which will differentiate good private universities and eventually will be a good argument for raising tuition fees.

Another trend can be also beneficial for private higher education sector overall. The privatization of the educational services becomes a common feature of other levels of education, especially in pre-school education, but also in primary and secondary education and high schools. This increasing privatization process that takes place at all levels of education, can gradually lead to more widespread acceptance of private education as a better alternative to public education. Especially among kindergartens, the private ones are already perceived as different and better alternative for education. This process will determine an increasing demand sophistication which will be gradually transferred to other levels of education. Thus, greater openness towards private education can be an opportunity for private higher institutions as long as they will be capable to offer different and better education than other institutions.

4. Conclusions

After 20 years of expansion, the Romanian private higher education has gone on a declining path since 2009. The demand-absorbing growth that has characterized the emergence and the development of private institutions is no longer sustainable, due mainly to demographic trends but also to other factors that have made higher education a much more complex environment. However, private higher education remains an important feature of the Romanian higher education landscape, as in other central and eastern European countries. Although the current decline in higher education sector threatens the existence of many private institutions, it can also determine the emergence of a more innovative behavior from them. After almost two decades of doing just more education, the private higher institutions have to concentrate more on doing different and better education through raising the quality of their teaching and research activities, finding niche programs, improving attractiveness for foreign students, more orientation towards labor market needs and improving business and research networks.

References

Bjarnason, S. *et al.* (2009), A new dynamic: Private higher education, World Conference on Higher Education, UNESCO.

EHEA (1999), The Bologna Declaration of 19 June 1999, Joint declaration of the European Ministers of Education.

EHEA (2009), The Bologna Process 2020 — The European Higher Education Area in the new decade, Leuven and Louvain-la-Neuve: Communiqué of the Conference of European Ministers Responsible for Higher Education (April, 28–29).

EHEA (2012), *The European Higher Education Area in 2012: Bologna Process Implementation Report*, Brussels: EACEA P9 Eurydice.

Geiger, R. (1986), *Private Sectors in Higher Education*, Ann Arbor: The University of Michigan Press.

Geiger, R. (1988), Public and private sectors in higher education: A comparison of international patterns, *Higher Education*, 17(6), 699–711.

Kwiek, M. (2010), The public/private dynamics in Polish higher education. Demand-absorbing private sector growth and its implications, *Center for Public Policy Studies*, 20.

Levy, D. C. (2011), The decline of private higher education, PROPHE Working Paper Series No. 16.

Lewis, D. R., Hendel, D., & Demyanchuk, A. (2003), *Private Higher Education in Transition Countries*, Kiev: Publishing House KM Academia.

Nicolescu, L. (2003), Higher education in Romania — evolution and views from the business community, *TEAM Tertiary Education and Management*, 9, 77–95.

Nicolescu, L. (2005), Private versus public in Romania: Consequences for the Market, International Higher Education, *The Boston College Center for International Higher Education*, 39, 12–13.

OECD (2009), *Higher Education to 2030, Volume 2, Globalisation, Centre for Educational Research and Innovation*, Paris: OECD.

Reisz, R. (1997), Private higher education in Romania, *Tertiary Education and Management*, 3(1), 36–43.

Siwinska, S. (2011), Europe: Tired pioneers in Eastern and Central Europe, *University World News* (November 13).

Teixeira, P., Rosa, M. J., & Amaral, A. (2004), Is there a higher education market in Portugal? *Higher Education Dynamics*, 6, 291–310.

Teixeira, P. & Amaral, A. (2008), Can private institutions learn from mistakes? — Some reflections based on the Portuguese experience, *Die Hochschule Journal für Wissenschaft und Bildung*, 17(2), 113–125.

Wells, P. J., Sadlak, J., & L. Vlasceanu (eds.) (2007), *The Rising Role and Relevance of Private Higher Education in Europe*, Bucharest: UNESCO–CEPES.

Part IV

Knowledge-Based Organization, Intellectual Capital, Information, and Management Documents

Chapter 13

Contributions to the Evaluation of e-Learning Processes in Higher Education

Doina Banciu

Institutul National de Cercetare Dezvoltare in Informatica

Monica Florea

Siveco Romania

The chapter refers to general aspects of e-learning processes with focus on the higher education's characteristics. Several models for evaluation of the quality of the e-learning processes are analyzed. As a result of the analysis, a new conceptual model is defined, taking into consideration the characteristics of both learning and teaching processes.

1. Introduction

According to The e-Learning Action plan (2001): Designing tomorrow's education: "e-Learning is the use of new multimedia technologies and the Internet to improve the quality of learning by facilitating access to resources and services as well as remote exchanges and collaboration." Nowadays, e-Learning is of strategic importance for education. The expansion of e-learning initiatives in higher education is driven by the increase of learners who prefer flexibility in geographic location, scheduling, and also access to courses resources.

2. e-Learning Platforms

An e-learning platform is a system for management of content and teaching, being made of several components:

- Learning Management System (LMS);
- Learning Content Management System (LCMS);
- Human and Knowledge Management System (HKMS);
- Virtual class (synchrone learning);
- ePortfolio.

The first model of e-learning was also called e-Learning 1.0. Starting with Web 2.0 technologies ("Web as a platform" was first called web 2.0 by O'Reilly in 2004), the second generation of web development and design, aiming to support and improve the communication, information exchange, information security, interoperability, and collaboration on World Wide Web, a new e-learning model arises: e-Learning 2.0.

As Downes mentioned: WEB 2.0 *is an attitude, not a technology*, meaning that we are not facing a technological revolution, but a social revolution.

e-Learning 2.0 uses Web 2.0 technologies for educational purposes, some of the features used are:

- Social networks;
- Wikis: a webpage or set of web pages that can be easily edited by anyone who is allowed access;
- Chats;
- Blogs: simple webpage consisting of brief paragraphs of opinion, information or links, called posts, arranged chronologically;
- Really Simple Syndication (RSS) reader pages;
- Social bookmarking: allow users to create lists of 'bookmarks' or 'favorites', to store these centrally on a remote service);
- Multimedia-sharing: facilitate the storage and sharing of multimedia content;
- Folksonomy (a collection of tags created by an individual for their own personal use) versus collabulary (collective vocabulary);
- Group work spaces etc.

e-Learning 2.0 is based on the following concepts:

- Standards and technology;
- Sharing local and external resources;
- Process and governance;
- Organization culture and education;
- Abilities and competences.

The new e-learning generation: *e-Learning 3.0*, being called also *Edutainment* or *Entertainment-Education*. e-Learning 3.0 is based on:

- *Cloud computing*: distributed computing, increased data storage and retrieval, easy access to tools and services that enable personalized learning, self-learning;
- *Collaborative Learning*: e-Learning 3.0 will facilitate collaborative learning through predictive intelligent filtering, intelligent agents, multi-user participative features;
- *Mobile intelligent technologies*: the extension of intelligent mobile technologies will play an important role in e-Learning 3.0. Using smart phones and better connected network services (wireless, satellite), education and learning will be accessible to learners anytime and anywhere;
- *3D visualization and interaction*: the development of 3D multi-touch interfaces and multi-gesture devices will facilitate exploration of virtual spaces, manipulation of virtual objects, fine motor skills interaction.

Among the advantages of e-learning systems versus traditional learning, we can mention:

- Accessibility and mobility;
- Flexibility;
- Adaptability;
- New dynamic technologies;
- Reduced costs;
- The courses are organized on the subjects/topics, not on the age groups like traditional courses.

We have noticed some interrelated transformations in the e-learning field over the next few years:

- e-learning becomes more than "e-training";
- e-learning moves to the workplace;
- Blended learning is redefined (combining formal training with non-formal training);
- e-learning is less course-centric and more knowledge-centric;
- e-learning adapts differently to different levels of mastery;
- Technology becomes a secondary issue.

3. e-Learning in Higher Education

More than two-thirds of academic leaders consider that online learning is critical to the long term mission of the institution for institutional growth and increased access. According to a report of EDUCAUSE Center for Analysis and Research, some key finding on the state of e-learning in higher education encounters:

- *Almost all higher education institutions have a major interest in e-learning.* Over 80% of institutions offer at least several courses online and more than half offering a significant number of courses online.

- *For a successfully large-scale implementation of e-learning in mature institutions, a centralized model is more efficient and offers an easier integration of e-learning.* However, for some institutions, a distributed model allows for more innovation and individualization for specific e-learning programs.
- *There is a need to double the number of e-learning staff in central IT.* The most-desired positions include course designers, professional development staff, and app designers. IT is involved in the management of e-learning services in almost two-thirds of institutions.
- The greatest concern about e-learning is the technological know-how of faculty's staff.
- In general, institutions are most mature in their synergy of e-learning systems and are least mature in assessing e-learning outcomes.
- Maturity in e-learning involves seven factors: policies/governance ongoing evaluation, training, synergy, priority, outcomes assessment, readiness and investment in faculty/staff.
- The most important factors in selecting technologies for e-learning are reliability, the security of student data, ease of use for both faculty and students, and effectiveness.

There are different ways to deliver e-learning services in higher education institutions depending on the mission, organization management and the size of the institution:

- Deliver e-learning services through central IT;
- Deliver e-learning services through distributed systems (multiple departments);
- Deliver e-learning services through mixed approach.

Web 2.0 can support learning in various ways:

- Single sign on;
- Students/teachers should decide which application fits the best their purpose;
- LMS provides structured content;
- Blogs offer the possibility to collect, share or to discuss the content;
- Web 2.0 applications are usable via various ways (application program interface (API), Widget, RSS, hyper text transfer protocol (HTTP)).

3.1. Quality in higher education

The problem of quality of e-learning has gained increasing interest due to the widespread use of distance learning in universities, and due to the fact that e-learning has become an instrument of internationalization of education. Quality assurance in higher education is a fundamental aspect of the ongoing internationalization of higher education. Following the recommendation [98/561/EC] in September 1998, the European Union Council began developing a transparent quality assessment and quality assurance in higher education, based on the following principles:

- Bodies responsible for the assessment and quality assurance must be independent.
- Assessment procedures include self — assessment and also external experts' assessment.
- Results should be published.

Success factors for e-learning programs depend on: student characteristics, instructor skills, technological infrastructure, and support of the university.

The European Network for Quality Assurance in Higher Education (**ENQA**) was created in 1999 by the European Union Council of Ministers. The investigation conducted by ENQA shows that eight types of assessment are used in Europe, in descending order of frequency: assessment programs, accreditation programs, institutional audit, evaluation institutional, institutional accreditation, assessment disciplines, reference systems software, and reference systems disciplines. According to the recommendations of the Council of Europe, the four-phase model used by independent agencies has the following characteristics: autonomy and independence of the assessment in relation to institutions, self-evaluation, external evaluation, publication of a report.

4. Assessing Quality in e-learning Platforms

"E-learning platforms" is a term covering a variety of different products, all of which support learning in some way by using electronic media (Ferl).

Quality in e-learning has a twofold significance in Europe:

- First, e-learning is associated with an increase in the quality of educational opportunities, ensuring that the shift to the information society is more successful, namely "*quality through e-learning*".
- Second, there is a separate but associated debate about ways of improving the quality of e-learning itself, referring to "*quality for e-learning*".
- e-learning systems' quality is made of the following components (Garvin, 1988):
- Performance — the e-learning system should perform in a efficient manner, taking in consideration the user's requirements;
- Functionalities according to the requirements;
- Reliability;
- Conformity with the standards (technological standards, industrial standards, educational standards);
- Durability: the e-learning system should be relevant also from pedagogical perspective, and easy to be updated;
- Flexibility: the system should be easy to be repaired and adjusted according to the requirements;
- Aesthetic;
- Perceived quality.

Due to their multidisciplinary nature, the assessment of e-learning platforms requires the collaboration of experts from different domains as: computer science, information systems, psychology, education, educational technology, etc.

The evaluation of e-learning platforms requires a measure of self-review of the institution on the following areas:

- Institutional cultural change towards the adoption of e-learning platform;
- Content management: identification, storage, and retrieval of digital content;
- Communication and collaboration (inside and outside the institution);
- Learner information: assure an effective management of learner data;
- Administration: network access and users and groups management;
- ICT resources: security, access, administration rights, methods of data storage, filtering, etc.

In the literature, there are defined a series of conceptual models (frameworks) to assess the quality of e-learning systems. These conceptual models can be grouped according with the e-learning systems' aspects that are envisaged:

- Models to assess the quality of the content (information)
- Models to assess the quality of the e-learning services
- Models to assess the quality of the e-learning programs
- Models to assess the quality of the e-learning institutions
- Models to evaluate the acceptance of e-learning technologies (extending the general conceptual models of technologies' acceptance to e-learning technologies)
- Models for evaluation of e-learning systems student-centric
- Models for evaluation of e-learning systems using standards specifications (e.g., SCORM specifications).

5. Models to Assess the Information Quality in e-Learning Platforms

5.1. *The five pillars of quality online education* (*Sloan Consortium*) [1]

Sloan Consortium (Sloan-C) is comprised of accredited institutions of higher education and organizations that have interest for quality online education, www.sloan-c.org. The consortium has established five pillars that underpin online education: *learning effectiveness*, *student satisfaction*, *faculty staff satisfaction*, *cost effectiveness*, *access*. Based on these pillars of the Sloan-C, a framework for measuring and improving online education programs for any institution has been developed. Best practices on each pillar of quality are published on the website of the consortium, http://www.sloan-c.org/effectivepractices. The consortium built a tool based on

---

[1] Lorenzo & Moore (2002).

empirical evidence, representing best practices in online education programs for universities.

In the context of user-centric web, e-learning 3.0 faces the great challenge of adapting the evaluation standards, methods of evaluation and metrics to the features of new education era. One of the key issues is the Intellectual Property Rights of the digital content.

5.2. *Model assessment of e-learning systems based on nine categories of quality criteria*

There are many models of quality content for e-learning systems. Under the new generation of e-learning, *e-learning* 3.0 (*Edutainment*), assessing the quality content is a challenge. Although quality is an important content in the evaluation of e-learning, has not reached a consensus on evaluation methods and criteria for assessing the information in e-learning systems. New features should be considered when evaluating the e-learning systems, such as personalized learning, novelty, and attractiveness of content, etc. Based on the analysis of several conceptual models on information quality assessment, quality of electronic services, quality education systems, the author[2] proposed a model that takes into account nine categories of quality, grouped into subcategories, which contain relevant quality criteria e-learning systems.

The model has two components:

- Evaluation of e-learning platforms (LMS), taking into account **quality five categories**: management, collaboration, management and impact of interactive learning objects, the adjustment path of learning, ease of use.
- Evaluation of digital content. To assess the content will be used as the following **four categories**: language, terminology, compliance, pedagogical features, functional features and technical, aesthetic and ergonomic value.

Depending on the parameters above, the weights associated criteria (dimensions) of assessment that take into account the evaluation of e-learning platforms. These criteria can be updated by the institution intends to assess e-learning platform, depending on the objectives it wishes to achieve. However, the criteria must be in accordance with e-learning standards in force, any change in standards resulting in the appropriate update criteria for evaluation. Evaluation criteria are grouped into categories, the weights being given both categories of criteria and each criterion within one group. Each criterion is given a note on a metric measurement, or assessment.

For each of the nine categories is assigned a relative weight reflecting the relative importance of the category for scenarios covered in the assessment.

The first component of the model was applied to evaluate the two platforms for eLearning: Moodle platform (open source) and Advanced eLearning or AeL platform (developed by SIVECO Romania) for three scenarios: a blended learning course, online course evaluation, and a professional training course.

AeL obtained higher scores than the Moodle platform for all categories of criteria, except criterion of *ease of use*, where AeL obtained score 81, while the score obtained Moodle platform 94, but the *utility* criterion score of AeL is 44, being significantly higher score Moodle platform (18). It can be concluded that, once mastered, users of AeL have greater benefits than if they use the Moodle platform. Based on the results following the evaluation platform based on Moodle and AeL first group of five quality criteria (evaluation e-learning platforms), and the weights for each of the five quality criteria in the three scenarios used in the assessment: blended learning, distance learners and professional training, we obtain the following scores for the two platforms:

Platform score	Blended learning	Distance learners	Professional training
Moodle	23.50	28.05	31.00
AeL	26.40	29.70	31.20

5.3. *AeL platform*

Complete integrated platform computer assisted instruction and content management, AeL platform[3] is an integrated teaching, learning and content management based on modern educational principles. AeL is

---

[2] Floera (2011).

[3] www.advancedelearning.com.

the platform developed by SIVECO Romania SA (www.siveco.ro). AeL platform supports teaching and learning, testing and evaluation for content management, monitoring of education and curriculum design. AeL eContent is organized in reusable learning objects (RLOs) that are structured in learning content packages. The main idea of "learning objects" is to break educational content down into small chunks that can be reused in various standard-compliant learning environments. The concept of content re-usage is based on description formats of the XML packing, having the necessary elements, in order to import and export conformable the MathML, SCORM, and IMS standards. AeL eContent library contains over 16,000 interactive lessons covering over 21 subjects. AeL eContent provides teachers and students with true-to-life lab experiences in a safe environment. The digital learning content is pedagogically-sound and makes it easy for teachers to convert any regular computer classroom into an interactive lab, simply by launching the appropriate digital unit for students. The educational software allows students to repeat experiments as many times as needed to understand a certain topic.

5.4. *Moodle platform* (*Modular object-oriented dynamic learning environment*)

Moodle[4] is a platform for open source e-learning, providing support for security and administration by a community of users and developers. Moodle has its origins in an educational project developed by Martin Dougiamas in *Curtin University of Technology*, from idea to improve the management system provided by the WebCT platform.

6. Conclusions

Due to the advantages offers to the users, almost all higher education institutions have a major interest in e-learning services. More than two-thirds of academic leaders consider that online learning is critical to the long term mission of the institution for institutional growth and increased access. The shift to e-learning 3.0 opens a debate on the assessment and assuring the quality in e-learning systems. The quality of the e-learning services and processes in higher education is still a challenge taking into account the standards and methods of evaluation for information quality in such systems.

References

Anderson, P. What is Web 2.0? Ideas, technologies and implications for education, JISC reports. Available at http://www.jisc.ac.uk/media/documents/techwatch/tsw0701b.pdf2007.

Banciu, D. & Florea, M. (2011), Information Quality — A Challenge for e-learning.

Bartolomé, A. (2008), Web 2.0 and new Learning paradigms, eLearning Papers, 8(April). Available at www.advance-delearning.com.

Bichsel, J. (2013), The state of e-learning in higher education: An eye toward growth and increased access (Research report), Louisville, EDUCAUSE Center for Analysis and Research. Available at http://www.educause.edu/library/resources/.

Ebner, M., e-Learning in Higher Education — A Concept for Future?, Graz University of Technology.

Ehlers, Ulf-Daniel, Goertz, L., Hildebrandt, B., & Pawlowski, J. M. (2005), Quality in e-learning. Use and dissemination of quality approaches in European e-learning: A study by the European Quality Observatory.

Ferl, (2005). Evaluating Learning Platforms.

Florea, M. (2011), Contribution to the evaluation of e-learning systems, PhD thesis.

Garvin, D. (1988), *Managing Quality*, New York: Macmillan.

Ikhattabi, M., Neagu, D. & Cullen, A. (2011), Assessing information quality of e-learning systems: a web mining approach, *Computers in Human Behavior*, 27, 862–873.

Kahn, B. K. Strong, D. M., & Wang, R. Y. (2002), Information quality benchmarks: Product and service performance, *Communications of the ACM*, 45(4), 184–192.

Klein, B. D. (2002), When do users detect information quality problems on the World Wide Web? American Conference in Information Systems.

Knight, S. A. & Burn, J. M. (2005), Developing a framework for assessing information quality on the world wide web, *Informing Science*, 8, 159–172.

Lorenzo, G. & Moore, J. (2002), The Sloan Consortium Report to the Nation: Five Pillars of Quality Online Education, November.

---

[4] www.moodle.org.

McGilvray, D. (2008), *Executing Data Quality Projects: Ten Steps to Quality Data and Trusted Information*, Morgan Kaufmann Publishers.

O'Reilly, T. (2007), What Is web 2.0: Design patterns and business models for the next generation of software. Available at http://mpra.ub.uni-muenchen.de/4580/.

Rosenberg, M. J. (2006), Beyond e-learning: Approaches and technologies to enhance organizational knowledge, learning and performance. Available at http://www.marcrosenberg.com/images/What_Lies_Beyond_E-Learning_ASTD.pdf.

Soumplis, A., Koulocheri, E., & Xenos, M. (2011), The twobility factor, the 7th International Conference eLearning and Software for Education, Bucharest.

Wang, R. Y. & Strong, D. M. (1996), Beyond accuracy: What data quality means to data consumers, *Journal of Management Information Systems*, 12(4), 5–34.

Chapter 14

Evaluation of Knowledge Processes Within the Learning Organization

Constantin Bratianu

Bucharest University of Economic Studies

Ruxandra Bejinaru

University "Stefan cel Mare" of Suceava

The purpose of this chapter is to present a synthesis of our research on learning organizations performed in the North-Eastern region of Romania. We go beyond the metaphor of knowledge as an object or flow, considering knowledge as a field. That means that in each organization we may consider a field of cognitive knowledge, a field of emotional knowledge, and a field of spiritual knowledge. These three fields are dynamic and in a continuous interaction. Based on these fields of knowledge we conceived a questionnaire to identify and evaluate the main factors able to influence the organizational learning and to transform a company into a learning organization. We distributed our questionnaires to companies based in the North-Eastern zone of Romania, and then processed the answers using the Statistical Package for Social Science (SPSS) package. We performed a factorial analysis and found that the main factors to influence organizational learning are the following: vision and mission, knowledge transfer, and knowledge creation. Also, the leadership plays an important role as an integrator and fundamental factor in transforming a company into a learning organization.

1. Introduction

Knowledge has been a favorite topic in philosophical discussions and today fulfills a similar role in scientific research. Since the time of ancient Greek philosophers, views regarding knowledge and the concept of knowledge were shared. In Plato's view knowledge that we are convinced, that we have about a particular thing is not absolute knowledge because there is a possibility, however small it may be, to get deceived. In this chapter we consider the following perspective on knowledge: knowledge is processed information in order to better understand the phenomena that occur around us (Brătianu, 2008a, 2008b).

Referring to the concept of knowledge dynamics we approached the description of knowledge conversion phenomenon through every step of conversion (Brătianu, 2013a, 2013b). In the literature, the dynamics of knowledge has become a concept that is identified by four conversion processes that occur between tacit and explicit knowledge. The first process is socialization. Knowledge is gathered from tacit knowledge of another person. Learning occurs not by speech or training, but through observation and imitation. Socialization process is considered, by Nonaka, as the most important type in the knowledge transfer cycle because it involves the transmission and transformation of key knowledge generated at individual level (Polanyi, 1983). Externalization is transforming tacit knowledge into explicit knowledge through the use of metaphors and analogies or gestures and body language. Combination is the third process and is seen as a stage in which knowledge is mixed and new explicit knowledge are structured to integrate the body of explicit knowledge already present (Brătianu & Orzea, 2010). The last process is the internalization, the newly perceived explicit knowledge will be transformed back into tacit knowledge. Internalization closes the cycle of knowledge creation and is an ongoing process that is based on social interaction.

Recently, debates about knowledge dynamics put emphasis on Brătianu's model in terms of which it presents a series of new concepts (cognitive-emotional knowledge dyad, the principle of thermodynamics) that we believe bring an important added value for understanding this phenomenon. This new paradigm is needed in order to integrate the emotional dimension of knowledge within organizational knowledge. If paradigm based on Newtonian dynamics allowed the approach of transfers between tacit and explicit knowledge, the thermodynamic paradigm brings a considerable advantage namely it supports the reflection of another dimension of knowledge, called intensive dimension (Brătianu, 2011).

In essence, the new paradigm of thermodynamics is much stronger and better reflects the knowledge properties and types of processes that occur between them. Knowledge can be better understood through metaphors that have as source field the thermodynamics paradigm. The benefits of this new set of metaphors are: knowledge management can integrate emotional knowledge and emotional intelligence in a new organizational framework; organizational knowledge dynamics can be explained by a more appropriate manner and the decision process can be understood both from the rational and the emotional perspective.

2. Emphasizing the Learning Organization's Dynamic Characteristics

Today we are in a dynamic world, in all aspects of life that is rapidly changing concepts and always challenges us to adapt. It is understandable that economic life is in the same process, except that players are more aggressive than ever, competition is tough, the rules are different, the stakes are getting higher. In a changing world, organizations must continuously reach for adaptation. This becomes much easier if the organizational culture of a company values the knowledge, knowledge that can help employees to follow the company's vision through all their efforts.

The organization is a social invention, a systematic arrangement of people gathered together to achieve specific goals. After more than a century ago, studies about organizations emphasized that there is, or should be, an organization suitable for every purpose designed (Drucker, 2000). Experience has shown that the model of a suitable organization has changed several times, as the business itself has changed. It is this continuous change in the business environment that has led organizations to adopt a lifelong learning process, in order to maintain themselves effective and efficient over time. A learning organization is "an organization that continually expands its capacity to create the future. For such organizations, it is not enough to survive on the market" (Senge, 1990).

Orientation towards knowledge and "learning organization" are not easily achievable steps. Managers need to be leaders, positive personal example should prevail, internal structures must promote sustainable development and exchange of information between employees — in order to obtain a competitive advantage in a highly competitive market. Many researchers and many organizations have recognized the importance of organizational learning — the notion of "learning organization" as the impetus for the progress, development, and achieve competitive advantage. Many authors have tried to create ideal templates or ideal forms according to which organizations may attempt to adapt their own structure. In this sense, the learning organization is an ideal toward which the organization must evolve to meet the different pressures through individual and collective learning (Easterby-Smith et al., 1999).

In this context, for all economic agents, adaptation becomes a condition for survival, and the way this is done is the performance condition. We observe more about the intelligent organization, the learning organization, the networked organization, the democratic organization, the expressive organization, generally an organizational world that values to a much greater extent than in the past knowledge, talents, motivations and innovative spirit. The success of these organizations depends on effective use of talented people and how they are encouraged to develop permanently. Although there have been many discussions on account of this topic is relatively difficult to find examples in practice. This might explain the fact that the results of this concept are not tangible on a short-term, it is a long process that some managers may believe that it is not relevant to the organization requirements and dynamics. Secondly, focus on creating a template and the need to present it in an attractive form for commercial consultants and authors, led to a decrease of the theoretical framework of learning organizations. There is a strong contrast to the study of organizational learning.

For a long time, the learning organization has developed towards the same direction as organizational learning. Writings about organizational learning focused on analysis of processes involved in individual learning and collective/group learning inside organizations; while, literature about the learning organization is action oriented and intends to use specific diagnose instruments and methodological evaluation that may help to identify, promote, and evaluate the quality of learning process in organizations. It may be said that organizational learning is the process and the activity through which organizations eventually reach the ideal of learning organizations. This is why we cannot separate the two concepts that intertwine both in theory and practice (Easterby-Smith & Araujo, 1999).

Since 1960, there have been elaborated more definitions of this concept. Simon (1991) talks about organizations characterized by a more and more profound approach of organizational issues, preoccupied by restructuring through the effort of the individuals inside it; Stata (1989) brings to light an organization characterized as more intuitive and that shows new behaviors; Senge (1990) describes the organization as a group of persons that work together to improve the collective capacities, in order to obtain the desired results.

It has been a while since we do not consider anymore the learning organizations as a physical structure but on the contrary as a theory, a culture, a context, or a paradigm. When the organization concentrates towards purposes as adaptation to change and organizational learning, we may say that the organization has a dynamic perspective. Thus, the learning organization does not refer only to learning. Sommerville & McConnel-Imbriotis (2004) note that a learning organization has eight features. These were formulated as follows: commitment to lifelong learning, a systematic approach to learning, common vision, flexibility and adaptability, participation in a cooperative business environment, a clear management structure, a broad perspective on learning and management acceptance as that work and learning are interrelated/combined.

Considering the fascinating paradigm of the learning organization, it becomes more and more important for the ability of organizations to compete and develop in the actual business environment. Traditionally speaking it was considered that the basic ingredients of success were the impressive quantitative results and rigorous administration. Today, the learning organization defies this view by the fact that it focuses on creating quality and value, involving every member of the organization in this endeavor as it becomes increasingly true that an organization is only as strong as its weakest employee.

In this century characterized by rapid changes and sometimes radical, it is impossible to resist without adaptation, both for people and organizations. Everything is subject to change: law, technology, customer needs, even the system of values. It is therefore necessary, both on behalf of the organization and staff, a new way of thinking based on continuous change through the integration of lifelong learning in the organizational culture. It is necessary in these conditions, the orientation of organizations to lifelong learning, learning that, experts say, is the only way to determine the achievement of significant competitive advantages. Thus, learning must be a way of life for all staff of the organization, regardless of age, background or level of seniority, considering that the new philosophy adopted by the organization is the guarantee of organizational change success.

3. Key Factors Within the Learning Organization

Currently, the identification of the factors with major influence on the success of an organization is based on the well-known perspective of Senge (1990), namely that learning is one of the most important factors for achieving sustainable competitive advantage. According to this theory, organizations succeed to evolve and develop only through learning. Learning within an organization occurs through processes that create new knowledge or processes that use and transform existing knowledge. From this perspective, a vital resource for organizations is knowledge and learning is a vital process. However, learning in an organization will mostly happen under the coordination of leadership. Concern for organizational learning should be initiated from the top of the organization and spread to the bottom of the organizational hierarchy.

An organization's actions must be directed through learning so that they become able to design and create their own future. The vision of these organizations must design their desired future and such their efforts will be directed towards developing those strategic resources and dynamic capabilities needed to generate sustainable competitive advantage. Integrating perspectives on the learning organization and knowledge management we have identified that one of the most important dynamic capabilities is organizational learning. In this view of dynamic capability, organizational learning is the organizational capacity to integrate individual learning of each employee in an organizational process starting with adherence to a common vision and cultural values. Learning outcomes succeed and evolve on an increasing scale. Learning is a dynamic process that is based on its capacity to reinvent itself through innovation and performance by changing coordinates.

At this stage of the work, considering the specific driving forces of knowledge management, we reinvent a variant by identifying and pointing complementarities with the principles of a learning organization. Internal forces acting in support of organizational learning and its amplification of the learning organization are: (i) leadership, (ii) organizational learning processes, and (iii) specific organizational culture. We appreciate that the significance and importance of leadership in the context of a learning organization is to define the vision and motivation that create mechanisms to engage all employees in order to share this vision and work within the gravitational field that it creates. The existence of learning processes and organizational mechanisms is essential though they are different for each business area separately. We believe that it is based on the dynamics of organizational knowledge and teamwork. Regarding organizational culture, the most important is it to support the efforts of management and employees so as to form a convergence towards a common goal.

Dynamic capabilities of the organization can take various forms but the shared key mechanism of organizational learning and learning organization is the translation of knowledge, information and data at the individual, group and organizational level and ultimately be reflected in the success of the business. As a conclusion of the above ideas, dynamic capabilities can be developed only through learning and as result will be obtained sustainable competitive advantage of the organization.

4. Key Research Methodology and Evaluation of Knowledge Processes

Contributions found in the literature are of a mainly theoretical or empirical approach using methodologies based mostly on qualitative data. Therefore the outcome of literature review resulted in the extraction of the main ideas on knowledge processes in organizations that were used as variables in questionnaire design: the vision, motivation, stimulating new ideas and projects, generation/creation of knowledge, the creation of databases, conducting analyzes, training programs, transfer of knowledge, empowerment (participation in decision-making of employees) trust and knowledge acquisition. The questionnaire was constructed in order to assess the level of importance as perceived by each respondent on several factors, variables drawn from the literature, assumed to affect knowledge processes within the learning organization. The section to which we refer in this paper includes administration and knowledge transfer, knowledge creation, and knowledge combination.

The questionnaire was filled by managers and employees of small and medium-sized enterprises (SMEs) in the North-East of Romania. The questionnaire was composed of two parts. The first part of the questionnaire contained statements including factors suspected to affect knowledge processes. Indicators obtained from statistical processing of the questionnaires reflect the respondent's level of agreement on the existence of indicators included in the statements with regard to the respondents' work environment. In this sense it was used a Likert scale measuring six steps, where 1 is strong disagreement and 6 representing strong agreement.

To make it as easy completing the questionnaire, the items were going to be perceived as simple statements about the variables of interest and respondents were faced with expressing the measure/extent of their agreement or disagreement. Research variables have been translated into a common language accessible to most respondents. The second part of the questionnaire aimed profiling respondents and was devoted to identifying details about (age, gender, position in the organization, number of years in the organization) using closed-choice questions with unique choice. The response rate was 42%, being considered by specialists large enough to get relevant results even at regional level. Data collection was done through several methods such as interviewing respondents, distributing questionnaires by mail, telephone and email completing of questionnaires.

Among the reasons that some representatives of organizations refused to participate in the conduct of the study we mention lack of time and/or interest in the field of knowledge management and learning organization and certain policies relating to privacy and information within the organization. Distrust of respondents that data will be used only for academic research could lead to some incorrect answers, to determine the distortion of the results, which is one of the limitations of the research. Through questionnaire, have been assessed personal agreement/disagreement to statements included in the survey, and not the actual situation of the organization. The results thus obtained in the process of collecting data were analyzed using IBM SPSS version 19 and Amos v. 18.

The results of a questionnaire-based survey are considered empirical results, and we have presented these from two perspectives. On the one hand, the analysis of data collected through the descriptive statistics materialized. Descriptive statistics provides a profile of the organizations that participated in the study and also have identified their common aspects. In this work descriptive statistics presents less importance in relation to its size and objectives so that we will not dwell on it.

The second part of the analysis of the data was to identify factors influencing knowledge processes in organizations by means of exploratory and confirmatory factor analysis. Exploratory factor analysis has the role to highlight the factors that may be identified in the claims under review. Confirmatory factor analysis is to confirm the model of the factors identified in the first phase of exploratory factor analysis, and thus to demonstrate/argue based on the correlation between the indicators, assumptions and findings.

Exploratory factor analysis can be achieved through two methods or data analysis options. Principal Component Analysis is based on a mechanism that breaks the original data set into a set of linear variable data. With this method are identified only linear components that belong to the set of data. Principal Factor Analysis uses a derived mathematical model through which estimates some factors. It is considered that only the main factor analysis is able to identify true latent factors in the purview of a data set.

In the second part, the method chosen to investigate whether the forty-five statements are identifiable factors was exploratory factor analysis. Factorial analysis bases on the premise that the variables are correlated. Therefore, the variables measured have a high similar degree of correlation, while those that measure different sizes that have low degree of correlation.

The reviews are based on the values of verification benchmarks for making observations step by step regarding research trajectory. To check the appropriateness of the sample we applied the Kaiser–Meyer–Olkin (KMO) test. Test KMO measures the extent to which

Table 1. KMO and Bartlett's test

Kaiser–Meyer–Olkin Measure of Sampling Adequacy		0.853
Bartlett's Test of Shericity	Approx. Chi-Square	24328,686
	df	0.990
	Sig.	0.000

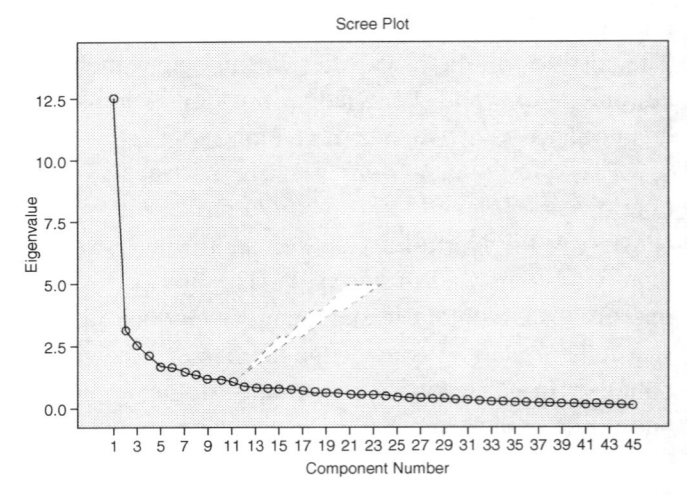

Fig. 1. Influence and pressure groups for public administration
Source: Developed by the authors based on SPSS results.

there are correlations between variables. Its value attests that when applying a factor analysis, the factors extracted explain to a very large extent the variation, thus validating the correctness of using factor analysis.

In Table 1 it can be seen that, just as in the case of the test KMO, spherical Bartlett's test had a high value and a level of significance of less than 0.001 (or Sig. 0.000), confirming the accuracy of the analytical method used. The null hypothesis is rejected, resulting in the matrix of correlations that there are significant correlations between variables. KMO test provides us information on sample size. The minimum value of this test for the sample to be considered adequate is 0.5. Kaiser (1974) provides information on the test values. Thus, values below 0.5 are unacceptable, values between 0.5 and 0.7 are mediocre, values between 0.7 and 0.8 are good, values between 0.8 and 0.9 are excellent, values between 0.9 and 1 are "superb". Therefore, the present sample can be characterized as "excellent", with KMO test value of 0.853 (Table 1).

The objective at this stage was to group the data and obtain a minimum number of factors needed. In this case, it was decided to use the graph (Scree Plot) to extract the number of factors, resulting in 11 factors that correspond to nine dimensions of knowledge management in the learning organization. This decision was made by viewing the inflection point of the curve to which they have found a number of 11 factors (Fig. 1).

At the point indicated by the arrow on the graph, the curve shows the last major peek, then it flattens. As can be seen the curve decreases uniformly after the 11th point, factor. Thus we conclude that the 45 independent variables were grouped into a number of 11 factors, namely groups of variables. Grouping of these items reveals strong similarities in terms of the significance/meaning of the questionnaire in the perception of their respondents.

To represent the original data set we chose the Principal Components extraction method. Examining the number of extracted factors associated with eigenvalues and using the rule to retain only factors with eigenvalues greater than or equal to 1, 11 factors were used for the next step. By running SPSS software were obtained extensive information on factor analysis. Due to the limited structure of this chapter, we present only the very important results, the rest can be discovered in a future chapter. Following factor analysis protocol steps have resulted from running the program matrix correlations between items, matrix level of significance for these correlations and the determinant of the matrix.

In order that the items get grouped in clusters, they must be correlated but do not have their level of correlation very high. If the items are strongly correlated (more than 0.9), they can lead to errors. In our research correlation index is not very strong, and the value of the determinant of the matrix is also within the recommended limits, namely Determinant = 8.29–005 (< 0.00001). Therefore none of items has to be removed. In Table 1 Kaiser–Meyer presents test results — Olkin (KMO) and Bartlett's test. We

Table 2. Influence statistics on internal consistency

FACTOR 1

Reliability Statistics

Cronbach's Alpha	No. of Items
0.861	10

FACTOR 2

Reliability Statistics

Cronbach's Alpha	No. of Items
0.860	11

FACTOR 3

Reliability Statistics

Cronbach's Alpha	No. of Items
0.842	9

processed into SPSS v.19 factor analysis and decided what variables contribute to factors. In our case we see that groups of items are formed and which are the factors of major influence in terms of knowledge processes within a learning organization.

Varimax Rotation optimizes the structure of factors. The relative importance of factors is balanced. After the first Varimax rotation, components matrix after rotation, contains the 11 factors identified by the program and which consistence can be seen in Table 2. Following items' posts that form each factor we note that they converge to a certain idea. Let us consider the statements that are found for Factor 1: in the organization there is a constant concern for her future, Managers are concerned with identifying business opportunities. Managers talk with employees about their vision on the future of the company. We note that these statements convey the concern of managers and employees for the future of the company and on development opportunities. In the same factor we identified items aimed at organizational perspective on creativity, innovation, and free speech.

In this context, to strengthen the structure of factors we decided to run a Varimax rotation with preset number of factors, namely 6. Thus, after rotation, the program will redistribute items that operate on the same principle, namely grouping those items whose responses had similar variations. The advantage of obtaining a lower number of factors is that we can make observations and specific actions to be applicable to the business environment in the region studied. Among the main arguments that led to a second rotation with predetermined number of factors we mention: (a) influence of some items can be found within several factors but in weights significantly different, and (b) the value of Cronbach Alpha was supposed to fall in order to show a better consistency of factors.

In the second-components matrix after rotation we observed that contains grouping items into six factors and that significantly decreased the cases where the same item is under the influence of several factors. We have not included the second-components matrix after rotation within this paper because of space limitations. For items that do arise with weights of influence for two factors is noted that this is not an impediment to decide which factor is assigned to that item, as the difference between the weights of influence is significantly high. For example, if the second item in the matrix (corresponding the statement — employees are stimulated to use some of their time for study and professional training specialization) note that it has a weighting of 0.735 for Factor 1 and a share of 0.342 in Factor 4, which indicates that this item has the most influence for Factor 1. We passed through this filter every item and we concluded the structure of the six influence factors calculated by the rotation matrix.

5. Analysis Results

Factors matrix after rotation shows us in a much more concise and fast manner towards what channel the respondents' options regarding the survey topic. Factors matrix after rotation must be analyzed as follows: must be analyzed questions that are grouped and thus form factor 1 and subsequently must be identified their common aspects. Following we present on which bases were formed the three factors and what do they reveal about the researched sample.

Factor 1: The first column in the "Component" factors matrix after rotation contains a total of 10 values (which are called saturation coefficients) from a total of 10 items of the questionnaire used in the statistical research. Looking closely to saturation coefficient values that were formed to Component 1 or Factor 1 we see that they are higher than most other values that the program calculated for other factors. This is easily observed due to the display in descending order of saturation coefficient values. Also, there is a significant difference between this factor that consists of 10 items and the other five factors. The formula that is found after the factors rotation phase in the exploratory factor analysis procedure leads to the conclusion that the questionnaire was designed to cover a balanced range of organizational issues broad enough to faithfully reflect the reality of the organization but not so large as to dilute the influence of opinions and to disperse into too insignificant factors.

The first factor contains items indicating cohesion of respondents' views regarding the *vision of the organization and encouragement of creativity*. Regarding vision, this is reflected in aspects such as interest of managers for the future of the company, openness of managers for leading the company in direct collaboration with employees, practice of freely discuss issues adopted by the company, etc. The items that make up the first factor contain the fundamental ideas about the existence, the organization and functioning of the company that essentially reflects the vision of the organization. Through the items within this factor we identify the interest and attention shown by managers in terms of creativity and learning processes.

In the context of this research, formation of this factor has brought a real acknowledgment of the importance of learning and creativity within an organization. This factor contains the association of the following items: staff participate in training programs to develop their new skills, managers encourage employees to express their honest opinions and beliefs, and employees are encouraged to use part of their time to study and professional training.

Factor 2: We called this factor — structuring and transfer of knowledge, as it is composed of items that relate precisely the steps and processes of knowledge organization and management within the firm. In the questionnaire there were a number of questions that reflect how the organization manages its databases. The contents of the eight items that have the most significant saturation coefficients, of the second factor, asked respondents their opinion on issues such as whether within the firm are created and updated databases on internal resources and business conducted on competitors, on suppliers and customers, if within the company are held discussions with experts in the business environment for the dissemination of new knowledge in the field or if it provides the necessary support for new technologies acquired by the firm. All these items are following the path of knowledge from outside to inside the organization, between departments within the organization and outside the organization towards the business environment.

Factor 3: The items that are included in this factor have in the foreground the idea of creating knowledge and we named factor 3 — encouragement of knowledge creation. The message that emerges from putting together these items, namely factor analysis 3, is to stimulate awareness and knowledge creation process. In order of decreasing saturation coefficients, we see that the most important aspect that is related to knowledge creation is stimulation of developing methods and production processes. For this research is particularly important and relevant that this item has a value so high for the saturation coefficient of 0.816. The following items retrieved with high values of this factor in considering whether the firm organizes group creative sessions to generate new ideas and solve complex problems (0.639); if the company organizes training programs for managers (0.634); and if the company encourages sharing their own experiences and not their monopoly (0.626).

The grouping items that emerged from the exploratory factor analysis reveal that they correctly pointed concrete issues important to the current work of organizations in the North-East of Romania. The respondents' trend is clear and we can easily see the outcome of factor analysis and of course on the basis of factors rotation matrix. Following discussions and reasoning in the preceding paragraphs, we present below Table 3. Regarding the three factors and items that make them up to be more easily viewed and the relevance of each factor in the composition of the investigation as a whole.

Table 3. Correlation of the three factors and items, according with the components of the matrix after rotation

Factors	Items
1 Vision and encouragement of creativity	The company is preoccupied about its future
	Within the organization is encouraged honest expression of opinions, even diverging ones
	Employees are incentivized to use some of their time for study and professional training
	Managers are preoccupied with identifying business opportunities
	Within the organization is encouraged knowledge transfer between generations
	Managers discuss with employees their vision about the company's future
	Employees participate to training programs in order to develop new abilities
	Within the organization are analyzed both performances and failures in order to learn from others mistakes
	The firm focuses on the acquisition of information and knowledge through subscriptions to magazines and international databases
	The company's employees are not penalized for their mistakes. They are stimulated to analyze such mistakes to learn from them
2 Structuring and transfer knowledge	The company creates and updates databases regarding internal resources and business conducted
	The company creates and updates databases regarding competitors
	The company creates and updates databases regarding customers
	The company organizes discussions with experts from the business environment for the dissemination of latest knowledge in areas of interest
	Technological changes within the company are accompanied by corresponding training programs
	Within the company are organized training programs for professional re-conversion
	The company creates and updates databases regarding suppliers
	Within the organization is encouraged knowledge transfer between different departments
	Within the organization is encouraged the creation of new products and services
	Managers encourage employees to learn from their mistakes and to propose solutions to avoid them in the future
	Managers discuss and analyze business problems with employees
3 Encouragement of knowledge creation	The company organizes creativity group sessions in order to generate new ideas and complex problems solving
	The company stimulates the development of new methods and production processes
	Within the company are organized training programs for managers
	The firm encourages sharing of experiences and knowledge and not their monopoly
	The company creates and updates databases regarding the best practices in the domain
	The company is taking steps to correct operational discrepancies between results and objectives
	The company has achieved a state of transparency for all employees
	Employees are stimulated to consider the problems they have to solve as new opportunities for learning
	Within the organization has developed an atmosphere of trust between employees

6. Conclusions

We consider that knowledge dynamics processes may be a strategic tool for achieving many purposes of the organization. As we presented, each type of knowledge process generates some specific effects which, due to the complexity and dynamics of knowledge, each time are different because for every process the knowledge involved/combined is different. The outcomes of knowledge processes have to be carefully read as, even if they seem alike, they are not identical and this particularity is very important in order to create a strategic and competitive advantage. Knowledge dynamics' processes are real and continuous and they represent an endless source of innovation. We propose that organizations should have a well-determined protocol of monitoring/channeling the knowledge trajectory and effects within the organization and also towards the external environment. Furthermore, the benefits of knowledge thermodynamics principle consist in the fact that, in this view, knowledge management can integrate emotional knowledge and emotional intelligence in a new organizational framework; organizational knowledge dynamics can be explained by a more appropriate manner and the decision process can be understood both from the rational and the emotional perspective.

Knowledge and learning are certainly interdependent in theory and practice. Learning within an organization means to use knowledge (existing knowledge) in order to create knowledge (new knowledge) weather for experienced employees or for new comers. The factors that we discovered that influence knowledge management within a learning organization are real and reveal the power of certain actions that take place within the organization. Considering the previously mentioned, lifelong learning involves more than the formal education system, which, in the wrong way, we call learning. Therefore, the learning organization continually senses and responds to changes in the internal and external environment in order to ensure its survival and development.

Once again it is worth to mention that dynamic capabilities of the organization can take various forms but the shared key mechanism of organizational learning and learning organization is the translation of knowledge, information and data at the individual, group and organizational level and ultimately be reflected in the success of the business. The fascinating theoretical approach and hypothesis with respect to the controlling the influence intensity of factors within an organization lead our research towards investigating the role of dynamic capabilities.

Through this research chapter we aimed to present and highlight specific issues of knowledge management within the learning organizations in the North–East of Romania. In the first instance, based on literature analysis we scaled the principles and processes of a learning organization. Out of these, we bring to your attention the following: principles that support lifelong learning and learning from mistakes; principles that support the sharing of knowledge and not their monopoly; principles supporting confidence and stimulate ideas among employees; principles that support flexibility in thinking and adaptability in any situation of change.

Descriptive analysis, exploratory factor analysis and confirmatory factor analysis showed that there is a major impact of knowledge management factors at the individual and organizational learning within an organization, thus validating the four formulated hypotheses, in accordance with the following:

— Validation of (IP1) and (IP2) is achieved simultaneously since it refers to specific operating principles of a learning organization and processes that take place within it;
— Validation of (IP3) is achieved by confirmatory factor analysis which certifies that a learning organization evolution is in a close interdependence with the implementation of knowledge management and its specific processes;
— Validation of (IP4) is achieved by the fact that the factors derived from exploratory factor analysis have weights that vary according to the variables they contain, hence we deduce that whatever the variables rearrangement within factors, their influence persists per/over the whole organization.

The content of this chapter combines theoretical descriptions and proposals with experimental analysis and argumentation. Throughout intertwining theoretical descriptions and proposals with experimental analysis and argumentation we debated upon concepts like knowledge dynamics, knowledge management or learning organization. Our aim was to shape up a different view upon organizational knowledge processes and of course to point out the critical aspects of these. The discussion sections were also mixed from a theoretical/conceptual view and a pragmatic/statistical perspective. The research results reveal several specific aspects of knowledge transfer processes within the learning organization. The results of the research combined with the conclusions of this paper could successfully contribute to increasing the performance of organization and to help them develop in the direction they want.

Therefore, this chapter might be of interest both for theoreticians and practitioners.

Although problematic, the ideal learning organization seems to promise much to organizations seeking to change the rigid hierarchical structures, communication systems with restrictions and authoritarian leadership, as lifelong learning seems to be a great ideal. Thus we consider that the purpose of knowledge management is to support and guide the processes within the organization, becoming an imperative tool support.

References

Brătianu, C. (2008a), Knowledge dynamics, *Review of Management and Economic Engineering*, 7(5), Special Issue, 103–107.

Brătianu, C. (2008b), A dynamic structure of the organizational intellectual capital. In *Knowledge Management in Organizations*, M. Naaranoja (ed.), pp. 233–243, Vaasa: Vaasan Yliopisto.

Brătianu, C. (2011), Changing paradigm for knowledge metaphors from dynamics to thermodynamics, *Systems Research and Behavioral Science*, 28, 160–169.

Brătianu, C. (2013a), The triple helix of the organizational knowledge, *Management Dynamics in the Knowledge Economy*, 1(2), 207–220.

Brătianu, C. (2013b), Nonlinear integrators of the organizational intellectual capital. In *Integration of Practice-Oriented Knowledge Technology: Trends and Perspectives*, M. Fathi (ed.), pp. 3–16, Heilderberg: Springer.

Brătianu, C. & Orzea, I. (2010), Organizational knowledge creation, *Management & Marketing*, 5(3), 41–62.

Drucker, P. (2000), *Inovare și Spirit Întreprinzător*, București: Teora.

Easterby-Smith, M., Burgoyne, J., & Araujo, L. (eds.) (1999), *Organizational Learning and the Learning Organization*, London: Sage.

Nicolescu, O. & Nicolescu, C. (2011), *Organizația și Managementul Bazate pe Cunoștințe*, București: PRO Universitaria.

Nonaka, I. (1991), The knowledge-creating company, *Harvard Business Review*, 69(6), 96–104.

Polanyi, M. (1983), *The Tacit Dimension*, Gloucester: Peter Smith.

Senge, P. M. (1990), *The Fifth Discipline: The Art and Practice of the Learning Organization*, London: Random House.

Simon, H. A. (1991), Bounded rationality and organizational learning, *Organization Science*, 2(1), 125–134.

Sommerville, M. & McConnel-Imbriotis, A. (2004), Applying the learning organization concept in a resource squeezed organization, *Journal of Workplace Learning: Employee Counselling Today*, 16(4), 1–15.

Stata, R. (1989), Organizational learning — the key to management innovation, *Sloan Management Review*, 30(3), 63–75.

Chapter 15

Universities in Transition: Are Library Directors Facing Changed Demands?*

Arja Mäntykangas

Lucian Blaga University

This chapter focuses on the current re-organization trend among universities in Sweden and other countries. It is also related to the author's ongoing thesis on the contribution of library directors to the information society in different countries. The demands and the pressure on universities to increase their efficiency are highlighted as a driving force. In the academic world, several conferences call for discussions about the role and function of universities, with titles such as "Higher Education: Against all Greater Inequality?", in Finland, "Nordic Model in Times of Crisis: What Is at Stake?", in Norway and "Universities in Transition", in Italy. Obviously, there are demands for reforms. These demands can also be seen as connected to needs for reforms in management in universities with an academic culture. This is an interesting phenomenon, a question of diverse aspects: cultural change in leadership styles resulting from re-organization, and the role of support functions of course as a part of resources of a university. Libraries are often included among support functions, but not necessarily. In this chapter I will propose conceivable implications of re-organization on the changing roles of and qualifications required of library directors. The New Public Management (NPM) movement is used as a theoretical framework of understanding. Even the question of visions and values is mentioned in relation to the idea of breaking with tradition. Some experiences from Sweden, Norway, and Finland are described as done by Almqvist in Sweden, Temmes in Finland, and Frølich in Norway. The idea of reform is central in this context and the term NPM is used to describe the movement. Central themes for NPM are competition exposure and the market, management by contract and internal control and decentralization/management by objectives. In this chapter NPM is discussed from the point of view of management and the use of common resources.

1. Ongoing Change and Issues Discussed in This Chapter

In this chapter, the author aims to describe changes in the thinking on higher education in relation to leadership and management. That a critical change of some degree is under way in current thinking about this function is illustrated by the names of conferences, symposia and the like. One example is the conference "Nordic Model in Times of Crisis: What Is at Stake?" that took place in Norway in 2014. The key issue of this conference is whether it is even possible to still speak of a "Nordic model" such as has been used as a model of a successful welfare state. The forces of change that led to this issue are said to be "the pressure of rising

---

*Thanks to Heather Howey, Certified Translator, for translation and comments.

unemployment amongst young people across the globe, processes of increased privatization, global competition for talent as well as the increasing focus on more excellence in knowledge production push towards greater differentiation". (*Source*: www.nifu.no/en/nfhe).

A Finnish conference highlights a similar issue but in a different light. This conference, which is to take place in August 2014, will focus on the theme of "Higher Education: Against All Greater Inequality?" As pointed out in the conference description, Finnish higher education has undergone significant reform in the past decade. Particular emphasis is now placed on the phenomenon of competition — for rankings between universities, for tenured positions, for better salaries, and for external funding — that undermines collegiality and introduces a focus on individuality-centred managerial approaches (*Source*: https://ktl.jyu.fi/symposium2014).

A third example is from Italy (the 27th Annual Consortium of Higher Education Researchers (CHER) Conference). This conference is called "Universities in Transition". Boundaries serve as the theme of this conference:

> One emerging issue in higher education studies organizations, the institutions and the academic profession is changing organizational boundaries ... Several signals of shifting boundaries can be envisaged, such as the replacement of permanent involvement of firms with research groups, networking with non-academic organizations (e.g., public or private research organizations, firms), as well as universities participating in private companies or agencies ... Shifting boundaries are also investigated as changing relationships between academic scientists and the marketplace ..." (*Source*: http://www.triumphgroupinternational.com/event/27thcher).

The above-mentioned examples touch on many issues. NPM is often mentioned in connection with discussions on management and supervision of universities. In the final analysis it is a matter of a shift in strategy, of wanting to change a university's management. From that it follows that fundamental values and visions are also being reconsidered. This chapter will address the following issues:

- Where does the management orientation often called NPM actually come from?
- What does it entail?
- In what way can the management mentality be reflected in academic libraries?

2. Management in the Spirit of the NPM

Hood (1995) describes the movement toward NPM on the macro level. The doctrines on which management in the public sector is based are guided by NPM. Various approaches based on NPM will be discussed, below. According to Hood, NPM is a question of a movement "from policy-making to management skills, from a stress on process to a stress on output, from orderly hierarchies to an intendedly more competitive basis for providing public services, from fixed to variable pay and from a uniform and inclusive public service to a variant structure with more emphasis on contract provision" (p. 95).

In his conclusions, Hood (1995) finds that much of NPM is based on an idea of homeostatic control, and refers to the "clarification of goals and missions in advance, and then building the accountability systems in relation to those pre-set goals" (p. 107). He explains that the effects of NPM are not unambiguous; rather, they vary from country to country (p. 107).

2.1. *Sweden*

Almqvist (2006: 13) describes NPM as consisting of three primary theories: competition exposure and the market; contract management, and internal control and decentralization/management by objectives. On the basis of practical examples (with support from Hood) and the above, he arrives at seven general observations on NPM. Essentially, his conclusions regarding NPM are that it can work — it can lead to desirable results — but that implementing NPM sometimes backfires and the lack of improvement is worse than before the implementation. According to him, based on empirical observations, it can be safely said that NPM can also have had a positive effect, even though it may not have been expected [2006: 126–127]. This aspect could be designated "unpredictability", which is related to the fact that the interaction of dissimilar factors is complex.

The complexity of the actual circumstances is a complication in the application of theoretical constructs. A theory could reasonably be considered a construction based on available knowledge obtained through studies and proven experience? The aforementioned conclusions can also make it impossible to have a theory of the NPM; instead there must be several locally adapted theories with generalizable knowledge and non-generalizable edge knowledge that must be retrieved from the local context. "Context is King" — an expression that the author of this paper finds neatly summarizes the conclusions described by Almqvist and Hood. The aim of achieving efficiency and better use of common resources is context-dependent. Almqvist claims that is this true not only on the macro level but on the micro level as well. Almqvist addresses another dimension of NPM in his concluding discussion, stressing that NPM is more an icon that has a value as an organizing symbol that helps focus the organization's energy. According to him, competition, contracts and management can be value-laden and symbolize change and operational development (Almqvist: 141).

2.2. *Finland*

Temmes (1998) describes NPM in Finland. In his article he states that NPM "does not describe individual reform projects or ideas but a combination of interconnected reform policies and ideas which, as a whole, form an administrative doctrine" (p. 441). According to Temmes, the scientific basis of this is partly economics — the machinery of the welfare state has not been effective. One of the key ideas is managerization, that is, "the making of managerial know-how one of the central elements of public management" (p. 442).

Temmes identifies further critically reflective views: public administration can undergo significant changes that are ignored by media and even by academic research. He believes it is difficult to judge whether it is politicians or civil servants who have been the driving force behind these reforms, since they frequently work together (p. 443). It is peculiar to Finland, according to Temmes, that it was the civil servants who played an extraordinarily important role in building up and defending the country's autonomy after it had received a guarantee of its own autonomy. According to Temmes, their role and status has remained strong throughout the period of independence (p. 144).

Temmes (p. 449) presents a comparison of administrative policies in 1987 and 1997. It is relevant to the issues addressed by this chapter to look at the situation in 1997 — that is, closer to the first decade after 2000. Temmes and Kiviniemi claim that "the profession of public managers then being created, and there will be emphasis on the development should be placed to public services on customer direction, quality and costs".

Attention should, according to Temmes (1998), be focused on the political administrative whole. He also identifies the culture of administration as the "main issue".

2.3. *Norway*

Frølich (2005: 223–224) describes the implementation of NPM thinking in Norwegian universities. Above, Temmes stressed the importance of culture. Frølich, too, addresses culture and cultural theory to explain value conflicts on the implementation of NPM in Norwegian universities. She believes, taking support from theories that different cultures can never agree as they are based on different premises, but that cultural theory is suitable to analyze the above implementation.

The conclusions that Frølich presents are that different universities use arguments regarding the reform question. She even refers to it as a "normative mismatch between managerialism and academic organizations (p. 228)". The conclusion she reaches by using the framework of cultural theory regarding the implementation of NPM in Norwegian universities is summarized with the following: firstly, promotion of NPM is based on the combination of two discourses — hierarchy and individualism. In her view, the combination gives added value to the established description of NPM as an introduction to market culture in public management. Secondly, she believes that NPM in universities is justified by reference to a third discourse, egalitarianism. It reveals the complexity of the promotion of this reform. It can also be viewed as that this reform could be justified through reasons that would seem to conflict with the primary ideas of NPM. Thirdly, the investigation shows that uniform values gave support to resistance to the reform. In this way, the author came to the assumption that the idea in academic culture seemed to be in conflict with NPM. Fourthly, the analysis shows there is a complexity in academic and administrative decisions to introduce or oppose NPM (pp. 228–229).

3. Library Management

With NPM, it is, as mentioned, about competition exposure and the market, management by contract and internal control and decentralization/management by objectives. The public libraries are — usually, at any rate — attached to their parent organizations. They are often considered as support functions. A support function is operated and monitored by the surrounding organization. How the library/library director asserts his or her role in reforms, or strivings to achieve reform, depends on how well the ideas underlying the reform are understood, and how well the culture surrounding the local context is understood. Contracts imply a management approach; competition is a market force and cannot be excluded regardless of what it is called. Competition exists about libraries as idea, space and financial structure. Internal control and decentralization/management by objectives applies to support functions as well, perhaps to an even higher degree simply because they are support functions. That they are considered as such in many cases may be culture-dependent; to break such a connection in associations entails a change to traditional chains of thought. The library is also an icon. There is actually no self-evident reason why libraries cannot be viewed as core operations. It could simply be a matter of library directors noting a lack of a "language" in an environment characterized by theories from an area of competence rather than management. This requires in-depth "language courses" and a desire to analyze to understand and "localize" the use of resources (human, technical, financial, knowledge-related) in as efficient and effective manner as possible.

One example of reforms in the library world into which NPM thinking seeps is the amalgamations of libraries that are occurring in Finland, with the Tritonia Academic Library in Vaasa, Fellmania Information and Library Services in the Lahti Regional Consortium, and Lappeenranta Academic Library and the Lapland University Consortium. Palonen *et al.* (2013) describes this development as "integration," as "joint libraries." NPM thinking can be discerned in the conclusions. The authors contend as follows:

Joint libraries for universities and polytechnics serve both sectors equally. They produce joint services and especially tailored services according to needs and possibilities. Administratively, the existence of joint libraries is based on contracts between universities and jointly compiled statutes (2013: 240).

The authors' financial discussion also addresses the components of costs, personnel, and decentralization/centralization. All of these are central issues in management.

4. Summary

The term "managerial" has been used above in conference descriptions, management and supervision, and even money, market, private, competition, strategy, set. These terms also naturally belong to management theories and thinking. At the above conferences, it is implicitly all about a threat that must be averted. The averting may take place by opposing the central themes of NPM — competition exposure and the market; contract management and internal control and decentralization/management by objectives simplified, it should be possible to summarize this as the central aspect of the force field in the questions articulated in the aforementioned conferences.

In this chapter, NPM has been the object of close descriptions based on earlier studies. Almqvist and Hood stress that NPM operates in a complex situation, a situation that varies from country to country, as well as on the micro level. Almqvist address NPM as icon and symbol, unifying and focusing. There is of course an opening for another type of interpretation in Almqvist's description. The problems involved in reform demands and demands of efficiency-enhancement may vary from one context to another and be based on different grounds.

NPM identifies and promotes the attitude that there is also a financial reality and that the common resources could be used more efficiently. Research shows and some current conferences suggest, in line with this research, that the NPM movement also generates counter movements. Library management is facing the demands of knowing two libraries: one for management and one for libraries.

References

Almqvist, R. (2006), *New Public Management — Om Konkurrensutsättning, Kontrakt och Kontroll* [New Public Management: Competition, Contracts and Control], Liber: Malmö.

Frølich, N. (2005), Implementation of new public management in Norwegian universities, *European Journal of Education*, 40(2), 223–234.

Hood, C. (1995), The new public management in the 1980s: Variations on a theme, account, *Accounting, Organization and Society*, 20(2/3), 93–109.

Palonen, V., Blinnikka, S., Ohvo, U. & Parikka, S. (2013), Joint academic libraries in Finland: Different models of integration, *Advances in Librarianship*, 37, 223–241.

Temmes, M. (1998), Finland and new public management, *International Review of Administrative Sciences*, 441–456.

Chapter 16

Knowledge Management in the Information Society — Case Study on e-Services

Monica Anghel

National Institute for Research and Development in Informatics — ICI Bucharest

The era we live in is often referred to as the *"age of information"* or the *"age of the information society"*, therefore *"information science"*, *"information management"*, and *"knowledge management"* have emerged as highly valued disciplines, as a logical reaction to the requirements of this age. In this context, universities, learning centers, various educational institutions, and research institutions all over the world, have revised their curricula/adapted their research interest domains in accordance with the demands of the new century and defined the discipline as *"Information and Document Management"*. The most imperative explanation behind this conversion has been the boundless utilization of computerized data and machine based engineering. Nowadays, at the point when a lot of data is made accessible online and when the data engineering relationship is at such a great level as it has never been all around its history, data and report administration divisions throughout learning institutions, hold an extremely imperative place in helping and making the adjustment procedure to these new times a simpler one.

The purpose of the creation and introduction of the "Information and Document Management" discipline (within learning institutions) is to prepare the labor force fundamental for "knowledge administration" that includes the aggregation, association, access, and distribution of data and data assets. This labor force is taught to end up data and report chiefs who will oversee libraries, documents, documentation focuses, data focuses, and so forth; they will seriously utilize data and correspondence innovations (Information Technology and Communications (IT&C)), they will have the capacity to show systems and strategies required to get to data, and they will have the capacity to assess fields with respect to the regulation of and access to data science with a business and administration approach.

1. Context and Premises

Knowledge Management (KM) is a concept and a term that rose to prominence approximately two decades ago, roughly in the 1990s. To put it simply, one might say that it means *organizing an organization's information and knowledge comprehensively*.

Early on within the KM movement, T. Davenport[1] offered the much quoted definition: *"Knowledge management is the process of capturing, distributing, and effectively using knowledge."* Out of the stack of existing definitions, this one has the virtue of being simple, stark, and to the point.

---

[1] Davenport (1994).

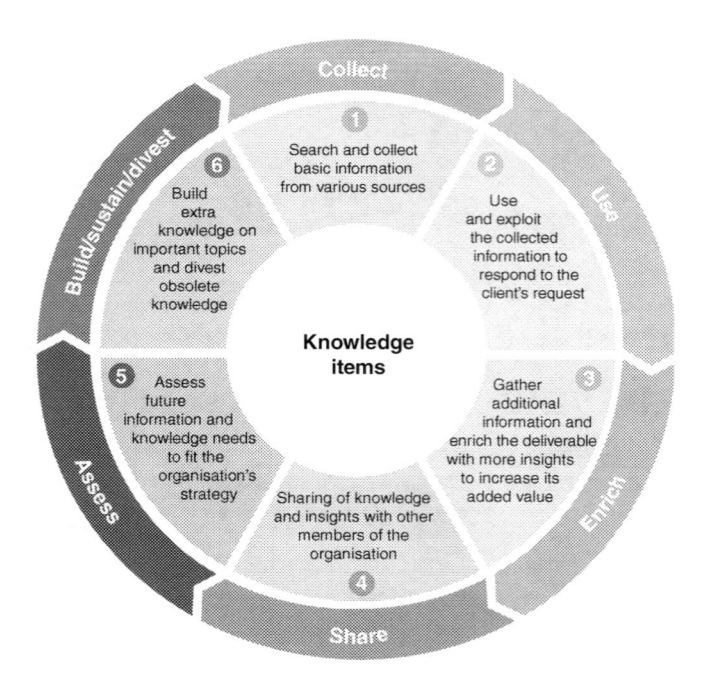

Fig. 1.
Source: http://brainstormingbusiness.files.wordpress.com/2013/11/blog.gif.

A few years later, consultants of the Gartner Group[2] created a second definition of KM, which is perhaps one of the most frequently cited one (Duhon, 1998)[3]: *"Knowledge management is a discipline that promotes an integrated approach to identifying, capturing, evaluating, retrieving, and sharing all of an enterprise's information assets. These assets may include databases, documents, policies, procedures, and previously un-captured expertise and experience in individual workers."*

Both definitions share a very organizational, and very corporate orientation, since KM, verifiably in any event, is basically about dealing with the information of and in associations.

However, in this day and age, in this perpetual paradigm change, we can now argue that KM is not only the attribute of private organizations and/or public institutions, but it is also making an impact within the scholarly world, as many learning institutions within Europe and have included this subject in their curricula. Whether it may be entitled as "knowledge management" or "document management" or "information management", these names all reflect the same purpose: teaching students (the next generations) about the importance of collecting, storing and sharing valuable, re-usable information assets, from which all can benefit from.

The operational birthplace of KM, as the term is seen today, emerged inside the consulting community and from that point the standards of KM were somewhat quickly spread by the counseling associations to different controls. The counseling associations immediately understood the capability of the "intranet" kind of the "internet" by connecting together their topographically scattered and information based associations. When having picked up skill in how to exploit intranets to join over their associations and to impart and oversee data and learning, they then comprehended that the mastery they had picked up was an item that could be sold to different associations. The new result obviously required a name, and the name picked, or in any event the name they landed at, was *Knowledge Management*.

The timing was favorable, as the excitement for intellectual capital in the 1980s, had prepared for the distinguishment of data and information as fundamental stakes for any association.

Perhaps the most central thrust in KM is to capture and make information available, so it can be used by others in the organization, the information and knowledge that is in people's heads as it were, and that has never been explicitly set down.

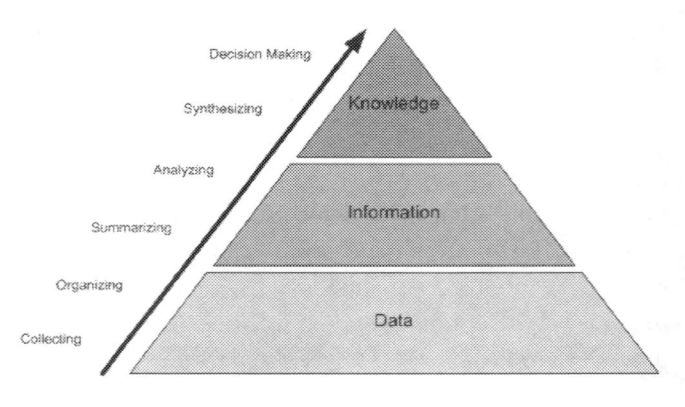

Fig. 2.
Source: "Deloitte" Luxemburg.[4]

---

[2] http://www.gartner.com/it-glossary/km-knowledge-management.
[3] http://management.simplicable.com/management/new/10-knowledge-management-definitions.

[4] http://www.deloitte.com/assets/Dcom-Luxembourg/Local%20Assets/Images/Business%20Graphics/Channels/km/lu_kmgraph_400x400_160412.jpg.

What is still probably the best table to try to set forth what KM is constituted of, is the mnemonic one developed by IBM for the use of their KM consultants, based on the distinction between collecting "stuff" — content and connecting people, presented here with minor modifications:

The mnemonic table is useful because it places a focus on knowledge as an actual asset, rather than as something intangible. In so doing, it enables the organization to better protect and exploit what it knows, and to improve and focus its knowledge development efforts to match its needs.

In other words:

- It helps organizations learn from past mistakes and successes;
- It better exploits existing knowledge assets by re-deploying them in areas where the organization stands to gain something, e.g., using knowledge from one department to improve or create a product in another department, modifying knowledge from a past process to create a new solution, etc.;
- It promotes a long-term focus on developing the right competencies and skills and removing obsolete knowledge;
- It enhances the organization's ability to innovate;
- It enhances the organization's ability to protect its key knowledge and competencies from being lost or copied.

Unfortunately, KM is an area in which organizations/institutions are often reluctant to invest because it can be expensive to implement properly, and it is extremely difficult to determine a specific *return on investment (ROI)*.

Moreover, KM is a concept, the definition of which is not universally accepted, and for example, within IT one often sees a much shallower, information-oriented approach.

However, as stated in the beginning of this article, the very premise of this investigation is the increased degree of introduction of this concept within learning institutions as a course. Therefore, even though KM is not a domain in which firms are willing to invest, universities are (as it seems to appear) the new promoters of the KM concept and are quite interested in teaching students about this discipline, as are students interested in learning about it — as reports have shown, more and more of the young generation take and graduate this course.

2. Knowledge Management in e-Services

2.1. *Context*

Nowadays, more information is uploaded on the World Wide Web than information has been produced since the beginning of recorded human history! Thus, the Internet is literally "bombarded" with over 4Tb of video, audio and written information on a daily basis.

Along with this huge quantity of uploaded information, we are also experiencing the changing of human

Table 1.

	Collecting (Stuff) & Codification	**Connecting (People) & Personalization**
Directed information and knowledge search Exploit	Databases, external and internal content architecture information service support (training required) data mining best practices/ lessons learned/after action analysis (HARVEST)	Community & learning; directories, "yellow pages"; (expertise locators)/findings & facilitating tools, groupware response teams (HARNESS)
Serendipity and browsing Explore	Cultural support current awareness profiles and databases selection of items for alerting purposes/push data mining best practices (HUNTING)	Cultural support spaces — libraries & lounges (literal & virtual), cultural support, groupware travel & meeting attendance (HYPOTHESIZE)

Source: Tom Short, Senior consultant, Knowledge Management, IBM Global Services.

behavior, seen as how, society is changing at a much faster pace and adapting abilities are the most sought after in this day and age. Therefore, we have seen the dawn of the "digital natives"[5] — children younger than 2/3 years of age that can handle an electronic device/gadget much faster and much better than young adults that were born in the 1980s for example.

People from all walks of life, and regardless of age, can now pay taxes on the internet, read their news, and find out important information about the weather on Internet, at a global level.

More than that, within the European Union, thanks to the European Commission's initiatives and co-financing programs, citizens can also benefit from electronic public services. Ever since 2009, the European Commission has co-financed five Large Scale Projects (LSPs) in five different domains that have steadily risen the level of digital awareness and strived to bridge the digital divide within the European Union (EU).

The LSPs develop practical solutions tested in real government service cases across Europe.

Many public services such as personal documents, tax claims, company registration or value added tax (VAT) are available online but this is not always the case across borders. Just like digital services in the private sector, cross-border digital public services are building blocks to a Connected Continent and a real Digital Single Market.

LSPs have been developed and run under the Information and Communications Technology (ICT) Policy Support Program in five main areas; eID, eProcurement, eBusiness, eHealth, and eJustice to engage public authorities, service providers and research centers across the EU.

Seven LSPs are piloting a number of solutions, or building blocks, that enable cross-border digital services in the above-mentioned policy areas. Each block consists of a number of components (common code), uses a number of standards and specifications, and all share a key characteristic: they are intended to be taken up as part of online services which make these online services 'cross-border enabled'. To expand the LSPs and to make the building blocks re-usable in other policy areas is one of the challenges for the future in order to fully implement cross-border digital public services.

Four such LSPs are still currently running:

- e-SENS — moving services forward;
- e-CODEX — making justice faster;
- epSOS — making healthcare better;
- STORK 2.0 — making access smarter through a single European electronic identification and authentication area.

and three are completed:

- SPOCS (making business easier) has finished, and offers its Starter-Kit.
- PEPPOL (eProcurement) has been transferred to the non-profit international association Open PEPPOL AISBL to sustain the developed structures and results.
- STORK (making access smarter) has been finished but results are taken-up by STORK 2.0.

These solutions are bringing down the digital borders in Europe, many years after the physical barriers were already removed.

2.2. Case Study — Electronic Simple European Networked Services (e-SENS)

Motto: *"People and businesses should be able to transact within a borderless Digital Single Market, that is the value of the Internet."*

Neelie Kroes

e-SENS is a new large-scale project that embodies the idea of European Digital Market development through innovative ICT solutions. The project will consolidate, improve, and extend technical solutions to

Fig. 3.
Source: http://www.immigrationpolicy2.eu/sites/default/files/picture.jpg.

---

[5] http://workdesign.co/2012/02/digital-natives-a-tech-savvy-generation-enters-the-workplace.

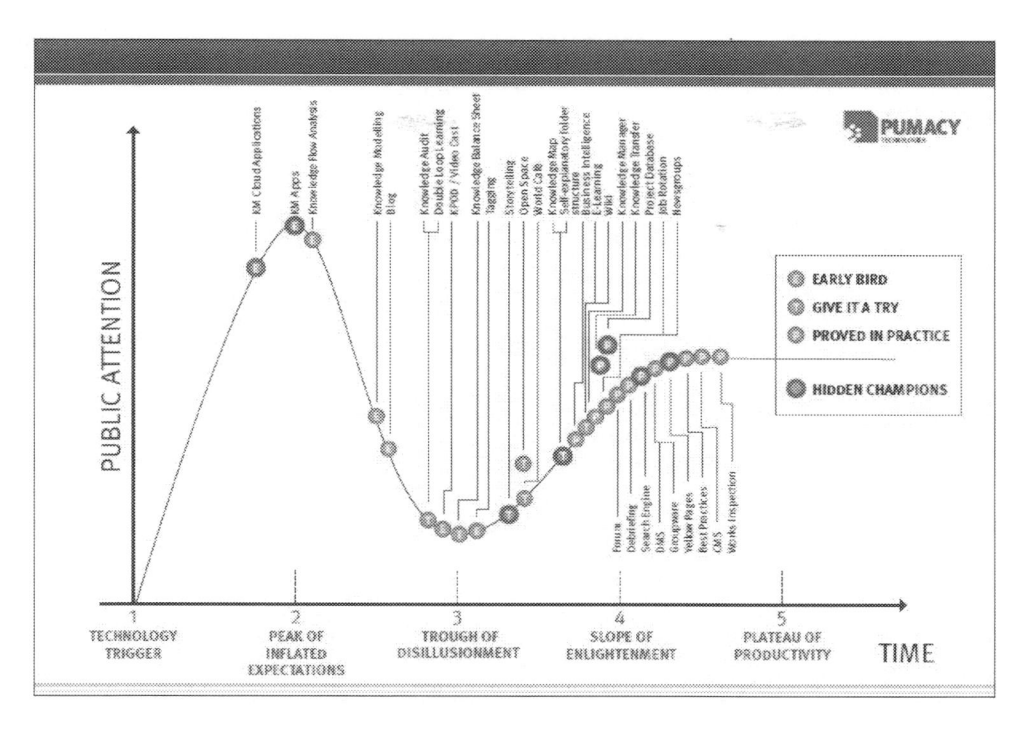

Fig. 4. Knowledge management practices along the hype cycle
Source: http://www.pumacy.de/en/knowledge_management_trends.html.

foster electronic interaction with public administrations across the EU.

Travelling, doing business or living abroad often involves administrative procedures. e-SENS will facilitate cross-border processes within the EU by:

- Making it easier for companies to set up business electronically.
- Enabling electronic procurement procedures for businesses.
- Creating seamless access to EU legal systems.
- Making it easier to use healthcare services abroad in cases of emergency.

The project will develop the digital infrastructure for improving the quality of public services in EU. e-SENS will support the implementation of European policies, in particular the Digital Agenda for Europe.

2.3. *Knowledge Management in e-SENS*

Desire grows to embed KM in the flow of work, as this represents the next step for the efficiency improvement of online collaborative work on European funded projects.

KM's technology portfolio expanded, and within the project, team members use the following platforms for collaborative work:

- Basecamp[6] dominates as a standard KM platform;
- Enterprise social networking (Facebook, LinkedIn) and microblogging (Twitter) are also firmly represented and made use of — with a special team member as a Social Media Officer especially dedicated to this activity;
- Mobile access: BSCW[7] — work document server of the Ministry of Justice of North-Rhine Westphalia is firmly used as a sharing platform regarding confidential documents;
- Using analytics to tie results to KM.

---

[6] https://basecamp.com/.
[7] https://public.bscw.de/pub/.

3. Conclusions

3.1. *Knowledge management trends 2014–2023: What practitioners use and visionaries expect*

The trend study of Pumacy Technologies AG answers the question of which knowledge management approaches have a chance to succeed in practice. The authors have examined all practices for their application and distribution by applying a hype cycle approach. The hype cycle illustrates the different phases of public attention that an innovation goes through during market introduction. For each method and technology the chart shows whether it is already being used in practice or is still subject to development. In addition to this data, the study shows when the different knowledge management trends will become established. The respondents are all knowledge management practitioners and visionaries, most of them in managing or executive positions in large companies.

The Hype-Cycle-Study on knowledge management trends by Pumacy Technologies AG shows that most of the examined knowledge management practices have already reached operative corporate use. The study's authors conclude that the still-young discipline of knowledge management is becoming a part of operational processes across industries — at least in larger companies.

Most practitioners generally agreed about classification of the knowledge management practices. Some practices were subject to high variance (spread of the answers) as illustrated in the respective sub-chapters.

Therefore, four specific categories were developed to classify the practices as follows according to their results on the market — based on the hype cycle of Gartner Inc.

Our new information era is characterized by the exciting transition from single-node to Cloud Computing, from fixed-line to mobile Internet, from discrete to Big Data, and from the physical to the virtual world.

Worldwide, we enjoy 24/7 mobile access regardless of enterprise network boundaries. Cloud Computing technologies enable on-demand service provisioning at lightning speed, and social network technology has turned precision marketing into reality. Security threats are at the very top of the concerns to be considered in this new era.

Visualizing the entire domain of knowledge and tracking the latest developments of an important discipline are challenging tasks for researchers, professors and teachers. Thus, this article tries to build an intellectual structure by examining some publications, blogs and vlogs[8] in the KM field beginning from 1995 up to 2010.

Document co-citation analysis, pathfinder network and strategic diagram techniques are applied to provide a dynamic view of the evolution of knowledge management research trends, as this article aims to provide a systematic and objective means of exploring the development of the KM discipline, and its introduction within various universities across the globe.

This chapter not only drew its findings from a decent amount of data sets, but also presented a longitudinal analysis of the development of the KM related studies. The results of this study reflects that the coverage of key KM papers has expanded into a broad spectrum of disciplines, including European funded research projects in various domains — such as e-Services.

References

Davenport, T. H. (1994), Saving IT's soul: Human-centered information management, *Harvard Business Review*, March–April, 119–131. Available at http://www.knowledge-management-tools.net/about_me.html; http://www.knowledge-management-tools.net/why-is-knowledge-management-useful.html#ixzz2wLHSJVyM; http://www.pumacy.de/en/knowledge_management_trends.html; http://workdesign.co/2012/02/digital-natives-a-tech-savvy-generation-enters-the-workplace/.

Davenport, T. H. & Leibold, S. (2006), Voelpel, Strategic management in the innovation economy. Strategy approaches and tools for dynamic innovation capabilities, Wiley, p. 441.

Davenport, T. H. & Prusak, L. (2000), Working knowledge: How organizations manage what they know, *Harvard Business School Press*, 240.

Davenport, T. H. (2008), Enterprise 2.0: The new, new knowledge management? *Harvard Business Online* (February 19).

Liu, S. (2014), Agile networks providing unmatched intelligent defense, *ICT Insights*, 9 (March).

---

[8] http://en.wikipedia.org/wiki/Video_blog.

Lee, M. R. & Chen, T.T. (2012), Revealing research themes and trends in knowledge management: From 1995 to 2010, *Knowledge-Based Systems Magazine*, 28, pp. 47–58.

Malhotra, Y. From information management to knowledge management: Beyond the "Hi-tech hidebound" systems. In *Knowledge Management for the Information Professional*, K. Srikantaiah & M.E.D. Koenig (eds.), pp. 37–61, Medford: Information Today Inc.

Chapter 17

Risk Awareness as Key Success Factor for more Efficient Management for Local Public Administrations

Markus Bodemann, Marieta Olaru, and Ionela Carmen Pirnea
Bucharest University of Economic Studies

Since the last 30 years public administration is dominated by the notion and realization of reforms and reengineering of objectives, outputs, and processes. Risk management is one of the private sector management tools for evaluating current and future situations for transferring to public sector; it is legally demanded and applied in the most private organizations. Although there are similarities, there are differences between both private and public manager also. Decisions under no uncertainty combined with probabilities and potential damages are often made with inappropriate knowledge or awareness about the consequences. Missing risk awareness and the traditional kind of behavior of public managers are attempts to explain the yearly deficits in the public balance sheets and the rising debt level. Regulations or models similar to private sector are not introduced for risk management, but will contribute if appropriate applied.

1. Introduction

Since the last 30 years public administration is dominated by the notion and realization of reforms and reengineering of objectives, outputs and processes. Risk management is one of the private sector management tools for evaluating current and future situations for transferring to public sector; it is legally demanded and applied in the most private organizations. Although there are similarities but also differences between both private and public manager, decisions under no uncertainty combined with probabilities and potential damages are often made with inappropriate knowledge or awareness about the consequences. Missing risk awareness and the traditional kind of behavior of public managers are attempts to explain the yearly deficits in the public balance sheets and the rising debt level. Regulations or models similar to private sector are not introduced for risk management, but will contribute if appropriate applied.

2. Current Approaches Regarding the Risk Management in Public Sector

New Public Management (NPM) is based on the assumption that within limits characters from private sector could contribute to more effectiveness and efficiency in public sector. O'Flynn (2007: 353–366) described the characters as follows:

- Results and managerial responsibility;
- Economic principles;
- Modern management theory and practices;
- Service delivery.

Bodemann (2011, 2014), Novell (2009), Rainey & Bozeman (2000), and Alison (1980) have shown that according to ongoing comparisons of both sectors, various management tools have been transferred to fit in public sector. Because of the tasks of societies that they depend on, survival and ongoing prosperity the tool of risk management can be used in public administration as well. From different angles different definitions are used for risk: one of the more technical notion comes from Cottin & Döhler (2013: 5): For them risk is a valuable object which is subject to a potential future alteration applying to period of time or the determined decision situation. Buehler et al. (2009: 3) suggest that risk management is considering both sides of a situation with no certainty, recognizing an opportunity to create value.

Efficiency in the context of this work is used in the meaning to consider deviations of public value in the case of potential gains and losses. Risk is used in the meaning of opportunities/chances and dangers/threats as desired or undesired results of a decision under no certainty (Fig. 1).

In private sector risk management is determined by different rules for auditing and for appropriate transparency. For example a rare risk management framework is demanded for New York Stock Exchange (NYSE) enlisted companies by the Sarbanes–Oxley Act (SOX), for German private sector companies it is codified by the German Corporate Sector Supervision and Transparency Act (KonTraG) of 1998. Although in Germany since the beginning of the 21st century, in Switzerland since the 70's of the last century, and currently in Austria the accrual accounting system is introduced, concrete determination of risk management is absent. At least the municipal code (GO) of North Rhine-Westphalia in Germany includes a short notice about content of a risk recognition system. While the strategic management in private sector tries to fit between one's organization and the external environment to operate, main focus in public sector remains the control of tax revenues, sustain operation and justice and fairness according to Moore (2013: 33). So the National Audit Office in the United Kingdom (2000: 3) states that: "the main focus of private sector risk management is on maintaining and enhancing profitability — in contrast in departments the focus is on implementation of objectives and services to the citizenry."

3. Measurement of Risk and Efficiency in Public Administration

The term and the consequences for public administration in the case of decisions under no certainty are similar to private sector. Political and societal outcomes are more important, the utility for society, for the citizenry. Alford & Hughes (2008) considered that public value is a matter of who consumes it. Furthermore Arrow & Lind (1970) mentioned that risk preferences must be established in accordance with other evidence of social objectives. Benefits and costs depend upon how large is each individual's share of these benefits and costs according to Arrow & Lind (1970). Hansson (2002: 27) put the grade on risk in a ranking: the last in the list is the best fitting and reflects the situation an individual stands for: "Nobody should be exposed to risk unless it is part of an equitable social system for risk taking that works to her advantage."

A risk imposition is acceptable in the case that the total benefits that it gives risk outweigh the total costs or disadvantages. The numerical determination will give a better notion of the exposure to risk, with both sides of a possible development. Gomez & Meynhardt (2009) mentioned that the society has to accept that public administration has to search and use new ways to restore trust in the processing the output and the outcome and their measurement of risks. Risk management for public administration will be ineffective without a convergence considering tools to measure expected and undesired outcomes, especially the numerical status. Expressed by a measurable value of public value and/or economic values in currency is useful for an analysis and as orientation for public managers and

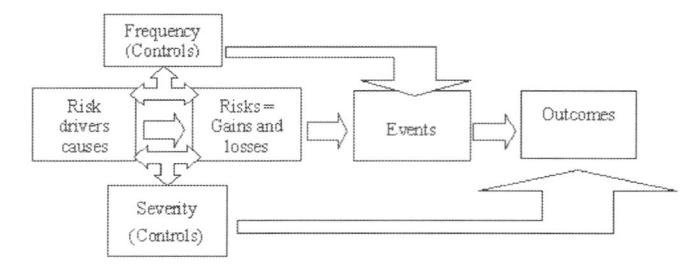

Fig. 1. Relationship of risk and outcomes
Source: Monahan (2008).

politicians. According to Hohan *et al.* (2011: 250) "the manager of risk informs permanently the leaders of the organization and it will brief them on the risks identified and actions seeking approval for the treatment of these risks".

4. Research Methodology Applied for Defining the Limits for Transfers and Loans by Private Sector

In order to analyze the limits for transfers and borrowings by private sector, the following steps have been done:

- Literature review on the current status of scientific literature about risk management in public administration;
- Survey based on a questionnaire during 2009–2012 in 30 selected local public administrations in Austria (5), Germany (23), and Switzerland (2);
- Identification of the limits for transfers and borrowings by private sector.

5. Research Results

(a) *Risk means to have a change to gain something as desired result*

Considering the origin and fundamental objectives and function of the public sector, i.e., to contribute to a steady increase of welfare state, gain and loss have different meanings and consequences. The question occurs what and who are affected. For example the US Public Accounts Committee (1994) predicted in 1994 that reduction of investments in highways will save a lot of money, but on the long run this decision could lead a reduction of the Gross Domestic Product (GDP) by 3.5% and a 2.2% increase in unemployment.

Decisions affect the society as a whole and collectively. Just the results of the decision can affect one as part of the society. The effects of a decision are directed not to the organization itself. Therefore the organization itself is not affected, only the public managers or employees as part of the society but not as part of the organization. The outcome of a decision will not hit the internal construct. That differs from private sector, where decisions of strategy have effects to the organization itself. In addition desired results are directly linked to legal and political determination. Grades of freedom to act freely are very limited.

As Mussari (1996) already 15 years ago stated that the local governments believe to find the reason and the justification for their existence within themselves; he suggested that the ramification of decisions made under no certainty and consequences to bear will not endanger the existence of a department or a local administration, neither the functional leaders nor the politicians. What will be desired and undesired results depends on the expectation on the decision level.

It will be too complex to discuss the relationship of output and outcome and the structure to communicated and process individual and collective values and interests. That should be discussed in further considerations about goals and values for private and public organizations in the context of measuring of the impact of risks of both.

(b) *The manager has to be in a decision situation within a freedom to choose*

Rules and regulation provide a framework, what allows relatively limited freedom to act, based on the Weberian Bureaucratic Model. This model works with fixed and determined processes and the tendency of objectivity and fairness, according to Weber (2006). Without the authorization for fast and autonomous separated decisions, the classical function of a public manager is to execute orders and follow regulations while implementing governmental programs.

Different to private sector urgent and important decision and opportunities are delegated to the priority of the political mandate. This leads to the conclusion that risk management in public administration is more focused to pure risks, in the meaning to avoid and to be prepared for situations with exclusive negative consequences, regarding operations or financials.

One effective improvement would be to determine indicators to provide the managers with appropriate authorization to decide in the parliamentarian or political majored way (Fig. 2).

(c) *Managers focus on rational behavior*

Decisions to make under recognition of uncertain developments and influences have to be based on a rational behavior by the managers. In private sector this is amongst others the sustainable operation and

Influence and pressure groups for public administration

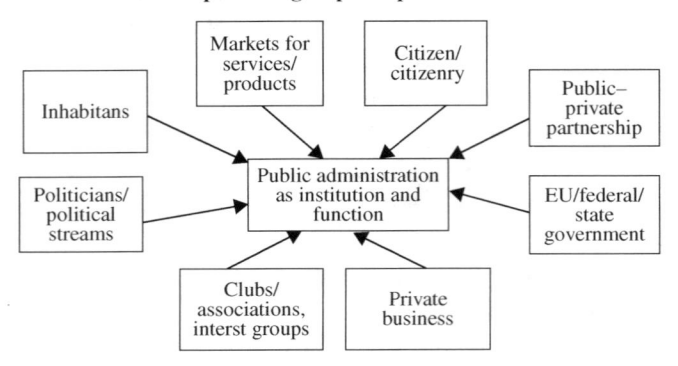

Fig. 2. Influence and pressure groups for public administration
Source: Developed by the authors, based on interviews flanking the questionnaires.

existence of the organization or enterprise. Main focus in private sector is based and measured on yearly profits, increased market shares or other indicators. On governmental level to local administration it has to be increasing welfare and sustainable operations to provide public services and products. These objectives are measurable by economic indicators, like average income, employment rate or economic growth on federal level. Similar to the question of desired results remains the answer to the question what is rational behavior: On a superficial way, following political programs and executing mandatory tasks is a kind of rational behavior, based on the traditional paradigm of implementation of political ground plans, as O'Flynn states (2007: 360). But rational behavior is endangered by a more individual oriented rational behavior. O'Flynn (2007: 355) has also shown that Boyne (1998), Walsh (1995) and Rosly (1995) complain on bureaucracy that leads to resource wastage and budget maximization in the pursuit of power, status, income, ideology, patronage, discretionary power and ease of management. These downsides of bureaucracy produce allocative inefficiency and oversupply.

(d) The manager handles based on a specific information structure and validated inputs

Excuses are partly based on the vision that the public sector has to handle unique projects in unique environments, considering planning, financing, steering, finalizing and controlling. To cope with this situation Flyvberg (2007) advocates the "Reference Class Model" for orientation and for better evaluation of potential threats or ramifications in the case of undesired deviation from the planned path, concerning time and budget. Loevenich (2011) demands a concentration and standard of data processing and publishing, oriented on Basel II or the Standards of the German Minimum Requirements for Risk Management (MaRisk). Knight's (2006) separation is used to distinct between different stages in a decision situation. Risk combines a known probability and an expected gain or loss (Fig. 3).

That leads to a classification of decisions to make and a comparison with already executed steps to get a better estimation of future ramifications. For a situation under uncertainty other ways for estimation are necessary, although all of the results will remain vague.

(e) The manager is forced to decide future-oriented and active

In a case of a decision under no certainty, the manager has to act in a way including freedom to choose. Because of the combination of legal framework, politics and procedural determination that kind of freedom is organization-wide limited. Priority and privilege of politicians are involved in almost every notable decision, partly directly linked to a process of involving politics for further decisions. Because the public administration is an executive organ there is a regulatory reservation to make decision of one's own. This is intentionally given by the privilege of the politicians as representatives of the citizenry by the constituency; further they are elected to compress individual to collective interests. Van der Wal et al. (2008) proved in an empirical research that the values. a public manager applies executing his tasks, differ from the managers in private sector. First accountability is ranked in the meaning of acting willingly to justify and explain actions to the relevant stakeholder, in the kind of demand of an explanation. Similar results Pečarič (2013) presents in his research considering applied

Certainty	Risk	Uncertainty
Certain future developments	known volume of gain or loss and known probability	Not known gain or loss, not known probability

Fig. 3. Distinction between certainty and uncertainty
Source: Knight (2006).

values in private and public sector. But accountability has another meaning than the expected responsibility as the explanation of SOX or KonTraG demands. This specific quality affects the risk awareness as fundamental character for an effective risk management.

(f) *There has to be an acceptable relationship between reward and loss*

Alteration means a deviation from the predicted and desired path. In the case of a decision situation the deviation in a positive way means a reward, in a negative way a loss. Losses in the meaning of risk are human, financial, and material kind, but also nonmaterial significance, for example trust and reputation. All consequences, material or nonmaterial, have to been taken into consideration in the decision process. For private sector, economic values are priority; those provide existence and development. Especially material losses or rewards have another meaning to public administration caused by the model of funding activities and products, and services. In Bozeman's (2007) opinion this leads further to the evaluation and comparison of economic and public values.

(g) *Acceptance of risk has to be oriented to objective and goals of an organization*

The acceptance of risk in public administration is on a cross road: Should the public administration be enabled to search for opportunities under acceptance of a threat in the meaning of loss can occur?

Coupon swaps leasing was publicly discussed in Germany over the last years. The use of this instrument had caused several millions of losses for the public sector. In the discussion about the authorization of public managers, in this case of the Chief Financial Officers (CFO or former treasurer) to invest in that kind of not certain bank transactions, they are not accused and blamed for choosing, but they are mainly accused for an obvious insufficient research and knowledge for that very complex coupon swaps. Similar, but more oriented to increase local public, utility guarantees are given for investing; for example new sport grounds or associations as substitutes of administrative services. The given guarantees are taken as acceptable loss in comparison to an expected potential increase of public utility (Table 1).

Table 1. Given guarantees in proportion to annual budget

	Guarantees given to third persons		
n = 13	Total amount of given guarantees (€)	Annual budget (€)	Proportion to annual budget (%)
1.	10.316	48,781.000	0.1
2.	50.000	4,000.000	1.3
3.	574.000	35,000.000	1.6
4.	7.262838	350,000.000	2.1
5.	2,400.000	86,500.000	2.8
6.	15,000.000	204,000.000	7.4
7.	1,900.000	24,056.000	7.9
8.	23,422.000	200,000.000	117
9.	35,602.724	210,000.000	17.0
10.	4,500.000	20,000.000	22.5
11.	25,100.000	45,000.000	55.8
12.	22,825.471	37,000.000	61.7
13.	99,500.000	76,000.000	130.9

Because of the objectives it sounds inappropriate to discuss reward and loss, because of the statutory task the financial frame should enable to provide the legal obligations. A smaller part should be used for individual, local, and political targets or programs. Losses in the meaning of risk management could be human, financial, and material resources, all direct or indirect. In this abstract consideration all losses will lead, at least, to financial effects; costs for restoration, costs for expanding projects or routine duties.

(h) *The organization uses measurable objectives*

As pointed out above performance measurement is an ongoing discussion according to Van Thiel & Leeuw (2002). Consequences in a concrete numerical value or ranking are hard to measure. First because measurement of output in public sector is hard to define; but on the other hand the outcome of decisions have a different impact to each individual in the citizenry. The citizenry and therefore the representative of public interest is an inhomogeneous complex subject. Sensors and indicators for measurement will lead to diffuse results. Without steady surveys and scientific fitting indicators the ramification of a decision are hard to measure with abstract results. The introduction of quality reports as flanking measurement during the introduction of the German Diagnostic Related Groups (gDRGs) is one example to get information of accomplishment of expectations of customers, in this case patients. O'Flynn (2007) offers the expression of collective preferences. The political level mediates expressions of collectively determined preferences. That leads to the notion what the citizenry determines as valuable. Orientation to pure numerical indicators is an alternative, but it neglects the main focus to improve welfare. Unemployment rate, average income and others are valuable indicators and have to be considered to analyze and process the public interest. Using the term public value and the expected deviations as gain or loss is one alternative for using internal and external benchmarks.

(i) *The manager is held responsible*

Public administration is a system of organized non-responsibility. With this provocative assumption Banner already in 1991 described his impression of responsibility in public organizations. Banner summarizes the personal involvement from the initial point of a decision to the evaluation of the outcomes. Moore (2013) demands in his model of public value a sharper focus to outcomes of government agencies and to call both managers and employees to account for productivity. Similar to Van der Wal *et al.* (2008) and their approach to compare private and public sector managerial values: They use the term accountability as act willingly to justify and explain. In private sector under ideal conditions the manager is held responsible for the ramification of a decision once made. For example, SOX was especially introduced to bind the board; explicit acknowledgement and confirmation in the yearly report is demanded to underline the responsibility and to avoid any evasive action from being held responsible according to some authors like Lander (2004) or Bainbridge (2007). Because of the split authority of politics and administration, responsibility is seldom to locate and to allocate to a function or process.

(j) *There are tools to influence the development and the range of probabilities, rewards, and losses*

The settlement of different strategies is depending on the grade of influence and the grade of variability of the given goals by the influencing framework. The surveyed public administration ranked the influence spheres as it can be seen in Table 2.

Table 2. Ranking of threats for operations

Ranking of influence to public administration		
1.	Declining tax income	2,42
2.	More duties without adequate compensation	4,17
3.	State politics	6,54
4.	Delayed necessary investments	7,00
5.	Limited freedom to act	7,08
6.	Attraction of location	7,35
7.	Federal politics	7,46
8.	Demographic change	7,58
9.	Deficits by shares	8,17
10.	European politics	8,42
11.	Addition political expectation	8,67
12.	Less qualified employees	9,04
13.	Increasing demand by society	9,38
14.	Climatic change	10,87
15.	Negative development of financial transactions	12,95

The ranking shows that most important the resources are. The focus to input for executing remains. Remarkable is the ranking of the influence of the European politics.

On local level the strings to the European Central government are evaluated with less priority. That depends on the one hand to the organizational distance between central government and administration but also on the intermediary role of federal and state governments. Although some mislead financial transaction undermined the trust in the competence to treasurer's influence to the execution by the negative developments in the case of existing financial transactions are lowest ranked.

(k) *Acceptance of risk has to be oriented to objectives and goals of an organization*

Should the public administration be enabled to search for opportunities under acceptance of a threat in the meaning of loss can occur? In the discussion about the authorization of public managers in the case of coupon swaps, the Chief Financial Officers (CFO or former treasurer) are mainly accused for insufficient research and knowledge for that very instrument. Similar, but

Table 3. Investment bottlenecks

Bottlenecks in public administration				
Buildings	Infrastructure	Personnel	Others	N = 30
36.67%	40.00%	20.00%	3.36%	

more oriented to increase that local public utility are guarantees given for example for funding new sports ground or associations. The results later act as substitutes of administrative services as presented in Table 1. The given guarantees are taken as acceptable loss; on the other hand the utility of the supporting of external projects is ranked higher or at least equal.

Investment bottlenecks are on a considerable level. Especially postponing money for infrastructure is wide spread as shown in Table 3. Remarkable is also the human resource development status. All bottlenecks in the declared domains can inflict mayor complications, but are tolerated.

Because of the objectives of public administration it is inappropriate to discuss reward and loss and because of the statutory task the financial frame should enable to provide the legal obligations. A smaller part should be used for individual, local and political targets or programs.

6. Concluding Remarks

The results of the research undertaken showed that more interested citizenry, more and more complex duties, increasing competition with private companies which try to overtake government sponsored duties, and the current financial situation of the public sector in general forces the public sector to react.

Also be noted that public sector has to cope with internal and external events, but neither the legal framework provides help nor it is distinctively formulated. There are lacks in the system of public administrations which prevents to organizations to accept fully value of risk management and the positive effects for operational steering and strategic planning. The case of a realized guarantee in combination of an insufficient grade of reserves is one significant example for necessary change to get a valid status report in finances and potential threats, depict in monetary values for forecasts and planning.

Research results showed that the transfer of risk management as part of a control system from private to public administration will not bring the expected results. Further a company-wide awareness, introduced by personal involvement, accompanied by more and more dynamic authorization, and incentives could transfer existent systems to work properly in the public sector.

On the other hand, a result of the research showed that public managers have to be given more freedom to act and to decide; they have to be held responsible in success as well as fail. This model has to be transferred gradual to all levels and means a rejection of the predetermined model of Weber. In addition it means a drop of political influence to win more dynamic processes and the search for economic opportunities in pursuit of the political goals and objectives. With information lines all over the organization and a personal interest, not only functional interest, internal and external events could be detected and the ramification avoided to better contribution to increase welfare.

These results may provide a starting point for future research to increase the risk awareness so that the local public administrations used it as a key success factor for more efficient management.

References

Alford, J. & Hughes, O. (2008), Public value pragmatism as the next phase of public management, *The American Review of Public Administration*, 38(2), 130–148.

Alison, G. T. (1980), Public and private management: Are they fundamentally alike in all unimportant respects? *Journal of Public Management*, 127(1), 27–38.

Arrow, K. & Lind, R. (1970), Uncertainty and the evaluation of public investment decisions, *American Economic Review*, 60(3), 364–378.

Bainbridge, S. M. (2007), *The Complete Guide to Sarbanes–Oxley*, Avon: Adams Business.

Banner, G. (1991), Von der Behörde zum Dienstleistungsunternehmen: Die Kommunen brauchen ein neues Steuerungsmodell. Verwaltungsführung, Organisation, Personalführung, 1, pp. 6–11.

Benington, J. & Moore, M. H. (eds.) (2011), *Public Value — Theory & Practice*, Basingstoke: Palgrave Macmillan.

Bodemann, M. (2011), Risk Awareness als Schlüssel zum einem erfolgreichen Risikomanagement. In *Risiken im*

Öffentlichen Bereich, A. Niedostadek, R. Riedl, and J. Stember (eds.), Berlin: Lit Verlag.

Bodemann, M. & Olaru, M. (2014), Responsibility to customers in the context of public value management — a German case study, *Amfiteatru Economic*, 35, 171–186.

Bovens, M., Schillemans, T. & Hart, P. (2008), Does public accountability work? An assessment tool, *Public Administration*, 86(1), 225–245.

Bozeman, B. (2007), *Public Values and Public Interest: Counterbalancing Economic Individualism*, Washington, D.C.: Georgetown University Press.

Buehler, K., Freeman, A., & Hulme, R. (2009), The new arsenal of risk management. In *Harvard Business Review on Managing External Risk*, Boston: Harvard Business School Printing.

Cottin, C. & Döhler, S. (2013), *Risikoanalyse*, Wiesbaden: Springer Spektrum.

F. A. Z. Öffentliche Schulden liegen bei 2,058 Billion Euro. [online]. Available at http://www.faz.net/suche/?query=%C3%96ffentliche+Schulden%2B&resultsPerPage=20&suchbegriffImage.x=0&suchbegriffImage.y=0 (Accessed 10 September 2013).

Ferlie, E., Lynn, L. E. Jr., & Pollitt, C. (eds.) (2005), *The Oxford Handbook of Public Management*, Oxford: Oxford University Press.

Flyvberg, B. (2007), Eliminating bias through reference class forecasting and good governance, Norges tekrisk-naturvitenskapelige universitet, Concept Report No. 17.

Flyvberg, B., Holm, M. K., & Buhl, S. L. (2005), How (in)accurate are demand forecasts in Public Works Projects, *Journal of the American Planning Association*, 71(2), 131–146.

Forrer, J., Kee, J. E. Newcomer, K. E., & Boyer, E. (2010), Public–private partnerships and the public accountability question, *Public Administration Review*, May–June, 475–484.

Gomez, P. & Meynhardt, T. (2009), Public value: Gesellschaftliche wertschöpfung im fokus der führung. In *Führung neu denken — Im Spannungsfeld Zwischen Erfolg, Moral und Komplexität*, S. Seiler (ed.), Zurich: Orell Fuessli.

Hansson, S. O. (2002), Philosophical perspectives on risk, Delft University.

Hohan, A., Olaru, M., & Pirnea, C. (2011), Case study regarding the implementation of an integrated risk management system in local public administration, *Supplement of Quality-Access to Success*, II(125), 246–251.

Knight, F. H. (2006), *Risk, Uncertainty and Profit*, New York: Dover Publications.

Lander, G. P. (2004), *What is Sarbanes–Oxley?* New York: McGraw-Hill.

Loevenich, B. (2011), Der Umgang mit operationellen Risiken in Kreditinstituten — vorbild für öffentliche verwaltungen? In *Risiken im Öffentlichen Bereich*, A. Niedostadek, R. Riedl, and J. Stember (eds.), Berlin: Lit Verlag.

Manski, C. F. (2013), *Public Policy in an Uncertain World: Analysis and Decision*, Cambridge: Harvard University Press.

Monahan, G. (2008), *Enterprise Risk Management*, Hoboken: John Wiley & Sons Inc.

Moore, M. H. (2013), *Recognizing Public Value*, Cambridge: Harvard University Press.

Mussari, R. (1996), *Autonomy, Responsibility and New Public Management*, St. Gallen: Conference on New Public Management in International Perspective.

National Audit Office (2000), *Supporting Innovation: Managing Risk in Government Departments*, London: National Audit Office.

Novell, G. (2009), Public vs. private managers: A new perspective, *Journal of Business Economic Research*, 7(3), 1–6.

O'Flynn, J. (2007), From new public management to public value: Paradigmatic change and managerial implications, *The Australian Journal of Public Administration*, 66(3), 353–366.

Pečarič, M. (2013), Personal establishment and accomplishment of public service values, *Transylvanian Review of Administrative Sciences*, 38E, 25–143.

Loosemore A. M. (2006), Risk allocation in the private provision of public infrastructure. *International Journal of Project Management*, 06(005), 2–10.

Rainey, H. G. (2009), *Understanding and Managing Public Organizations*, San Francisco: John Wiley & Sons.

Rainey, H. G. & Bozeman, B. (2000), Comparing public and private organisations: empirical research and the power of the a priori, *Journal of Public Administration Research and Theory*, 10(2), 447–469.

Van der Wal, Z., de Graaf, G. & Lasthuizen, K. (2008), What's valued most? Similarities and differences between the organizational values of the public and private sector, *Public Administration*, 86(2), 465–482.

Van Thiel, S. & Leeuw, F. (2002), The performance paradox in the public sector, *Public Performance & Management Review*, 25(3), 267–281.

Weber, M. (2008), *Wirtschaft und Gesellschaft*, NeuIsenburg: Wunderkammer Verlag.

Chapter 18

Information and its Entropy — A Measure of Market Complexity

Camelia Oprean

Lucian Blaga University of Sibiu

One of the main tasks of managers is to identify sources of information so that, through information-processing, they may secure an edge over other managers. To determine the information available on the market in a more comprehensive and structured manner, we define in this chapter the main informational groups concerned with the production and spreading of information on financial markets.

Charging an ordered structure with a minimum degree of uncertainty (lack of knowledge) and a disordered, chaotic structure with a maximum degree of ignorance, in this chapter we also coined the term *information entropy* as a measure of the degree of uncertainty within a system (the market). The link between a certain level of complexity and the *efficient market hypothesis* is the following: if we consider an efficient market (a weak form one), then prices follow the random-walk pattern. In quantitative terms, such a white noise process has the highest level of complexity; conversely, if the efficient markets hypothesis is not accepted, then prices are not a random-walk process and, therefore, the complexity of the market will be lower. Taking into consideration the explanations aforementioned, in this chapter we see *entropy as a measure of informational efficiency* of markets. In the terms of information entropy, market efficiency is equivalent to having maximum entropy, complexity, or uncertainty levels. To measure the informational efficiency of markets, we use the *Shannon* *Entropy* methodology. We start from the basic assumption that, on an efficient market, prices reflect all available information. The Shannon entropy is assessed for 8 emerging countries, 4 European Union (EU) countries (Romania, Hungary, Estonia, the Czech Republic) and the 4 BRIC emerging countries (Brazil, Russia, India, and China). Using this methodology, we rate these emerging countries on the basis of the entropy value obtained.

1. Asymmetric Information in Financial Markets

Over a decade ago, in 1999, Peter Drucker stated: "*The one thing we can be sure of is that the world that will emerge from the present rearrangement of values [...] will be different from anything today imagines.* That the new society will be both a non-socialist and a non-capitalist society is practically certain. And it is certain also that its primary resource will be knowledge." In fact, in this emerging society, knowledge has become the key to competitive and economic success. The industrial revolution that occurred in the past centuries relied mainly on the traditional factors of production — land, labor, capital, which were chiefly physical. Thus, ever since the earliest times, wealth and power have been associated with the possession of physical resources; hence, the need for knowledge was limited. Unlike in those times, "wealth and power" now derive primarily from intangible intellectual resources, capital of knowledge and information. Nowadays, these assertions are even more pertinent when it comes to the management of stock exchange securities portfolios. One of the main tasks of portfolio managers is to identify sources of information so that, through information-processing, they may secure an edge over other investors.

Financial market information has a number of features (*apud* Duțescu, 2000: 16), such as:

— The very low cost of information transfer due to the use of sophisticated telecommunication technologies that enable the free access of those interested;
— The results of information production are not always the desired ones (the intended information recipients are not the sole users) since there are no laws in this area to provide proper protection. Thus, the analysts who process the information may face real difficulties in obtaining compensation for their work. Even though a specific segment of investors resort to their services, information is also indirectly transferred to the public, who bears no costs. As a result, some investors may mirror the behavior of those who are informed, without the need of obtaining information themselves (Dragotă, 2009: 93);
— Information is often a highly perishable product and this has lately resulted in the increase in the speed of its distribution and use;
— A real information market with supply and demand for information has emerged (Dragotă, 2009: 92). Information supply (including information production, storage, and processing) requires a number of distinctive skills and sophisticated technologies, the degree of specialization in this area being extremely high. Information bidders must be concerned not only with covering information purchasing and processing costs, but also with deriving a profit. Information demand has become increasingly widespread and varied. Information buyers must be interested in purchasing it only insofar as they may benefit from it in the future, by increasing its utility function.

The available information must first be processed and interpreted, since not only the availability of information is important, but also the investors' capacity to use it to the best of its ability to support the most favorable investment decisions. Given that any piece of information may be of use to the portfolio manager, obtaining and processing some pieces of information that later turned out to be inaccurate or useless is at risk of generating loss. Thus, information asymmetry is one of the main causes identified so far for the gaps between the investors' profits and may lead to abnormal returns for some capital market operators. Nevertheless, it is extremely difficult to identify specific situations when certain people have owned an advantageously strategic position in the informational flow with a view to deriving abnormal gains. These are, rather than certitudes, mere suppositions, not validated by statistic tests (Dragotă, 2009: 91).

We have focused so far on those models in which all participants have access to the same information at the same time. Even if the requirements of equal access of investors to the available information have been met, information asymmetries between various agents are real, being the consequence of the differences that occur between the ability to interpret information as well as of the uneven degrees of information. The 2001 Nobel Prize winners in Economics (Akerlof, Spence, Stiglitz, 2001) reiterated the importance of information asymmetry that may lead to adverse selection and moral hazard.

Adverse selection occurs at the stage of investment decision-making. The investors will make the most advantageous decision based on the information they hold, without knowing whether the information is accurate or not; as a result, they may make wrong decisions (agents are incapable of distinguishing between projects characterized by varying performance degrees). In the field of capital markets, an application of the theory of adverse selection is the issue of shares. Managers have an interest to issue shares precisely when these are overvalued on the market. Since following the issue of shares their price will tend to decrease, the investors who have already purchased these shares at a higher price than their intrinsic value will be at a disadvantage as they will obtain a lower return than that forecasted in an accurate essential analysis carried out at the time of the security purchase.

Unlike adverse selection, *moral hazard* occurs after the decision has been made. It consists in changing the behavior of business partners after signing an agreement, which leads to the worsening of their position. Moral hazard may generate abnormal returns for certain market operators. An example of moral hazard occurring on capital markets is that of the investor purchasing shares on the basis of an analysis of the performance indicators that have as yet been registered by the issuing company. If in the future the issuer's behavior as reflected by the indicators at the time of the purchase changes for the worse, shareholders may witness a decrease in their assets (in the case when the management may make hazardous decisions regarding company strategy, etc. in dealing with their business partners).

When they ground their investment decisions, investors are generally tempted to resort to "additional" information, i.e., processed information, such as statistical or feasibility studies. However, this process may turn out to be expensive, the cost of obtaining the information sometimes being higher than the profit derived from using it. Hence, the process of determining the *value of information*, during which one may assess the extent to which the search for information is actually advantageous, seems to be more suitable.

The value of information depends on its impact on future decisions, hence the high degree of subjectivity of its interpretation and use. A piece of information is valuable provided that it its users may turn it to good account in making decisions that lead to the desired results. Thus, to determine the value of a piece of information, one may determine who its user is and what the purpose for using that particular piece of information is. It is virtually impossible to reach consensus by substantiating a general decision-making model since it is difficult to aggregate individual, subjective utilities (each investor may differently assess the importance that a piece of information has in making a decision).

A phenomenon that occurs on financial markets refers to the managers' tendency to improve the appearance of publicly distributed information. Faced with this, the market more often than not fails to distinguish between the actual changes in the state of a company and the "cosmeticized" information. This procedure is common in many countries and shows the manner in which company managers move away from the concept of faithful image by putting their companies in the most advantageous light, for instance by "enhancing" the solvency and profitability ratios by means of accounting policies, but without resorting to any illegal act. Another reality of financial markets refers to the existence of false or "poisoned" information (Stoica, 2002: 36), usually spread by people who are keen on influencing the market (usually majority shareholders). More often than not, most small shareholders are those who fall prey to false rumors. Manipulating exchange rates is considered in many countries an offence and is punished as such, although punitive measures have not been successful in annihilating it completely.

2. Producing and Spreading Information

Even though all information may be useful in the decision-making process, it does not mean that all public or private statements, representations, or data can be regarded as information. First, information requires judgement — i.e., it is vested with authority — that makes it inherently asymmetrical. Secondly, information generates uncertainty (in other words, it generates informational surprises), requiring further action.

To determine the information available on the market in a more comprehensive and structured manner, we define the main informational groups (adapted from Preda, 2010: 122) concerned with the production and spreading of information on financial markets, as follows:

1. Groups specialized in producing and spreading relational and transactional information as a commodity — in other words, groups concerned with producing and selling informational items. These include service providers such as Reuters and Bloomberg, other news agencies, rating agencies, etc.
2. Groups specialized in producing and spreading information in the context of the financial market, in relation to the traded entities: for instance, stock market websites, field-specific websites (e.g., kmarket.ro), or analyst reports. Almost all financial intermediaries offer their customers the analytical reports providing information on the key events occurring on the market, forecasts, etc. These

reports are usually sent free of charge only to the intermediaries' customers, although they may also make available to the general public some of their reports on their own websites.

3. Groups belonging to non-economic organizations, generally specialized in producing and spreading economic information. For instance, information offered by the Romanian National Institute of Statistics, the National Bank of Romania, the Ministry of Economy, valid legal regulations, etc.

4. Groups specialized in producing and spreading information in the context of the financial market, as part of it. These groups include company economic analysts. Thus, the major sources of information are provided by the regular public announcements made by company spokespersons and published in annual balance sheets, related primarily to the following:

— The results of the financial year: the chief question is not whether these announcements are informative to investors, but rather refers to the impact that expected and unexpected announcements regarding returns have on prices. Company announcements regarding returns may or may not be new information to the investors. If the returns are expected, the prices have already been corrected with the notified income margin at the time the announcement is made public. If the notified returns are not expected, the price needs to be adjusted. In this case, if markets are efficient, the price adjustment will be instantaneous. If they are inefficient, there will be a delay in the adjustment and, therefore, the likelihood of speculative profits;

— Management forecasts: the management may occasionally produce forecasts of earnings per share prior to the publication of financial reports. Generally, these forecasts have informative content only if they differ from market expectations, although recent studies have revealed that market rates tend to anticipate favourable and unfavourable announcements.

5. Groups producing informational items with this activity as an end in itself, without necessarily aiming at any immediate application. This is the case of academic economics, whether we refer to specialty books or to scientific studies. These consist in professional approaches to financial market phenomena, the uninformed finding it very difficult to select those that are both useful and relevant for the financial market in question.

6. Groups specialized in producing market information and spreading it to the public at large: for instance, the views of a number of specialists published in various specialized newspapers or broadcast on television. Even if these may act as useful landmarks in making an investment decision, this kind of information is often subjective, the journalistic style sometimes prevailing over scientific accuracy, for reasons that regard the provision of marketability and accessibility of information for as wide an audience as possible.

The informational groups described earlier may be classified in relation to one another by ranking them on the basis of their prestige, which impacts on the information produced by these groups, granting additional legitimacy to the decisions based on them. Thus, this information is endowed with various levels of authority. A statement on inflation made, for instance, by the Chief Economist of the National Bank will carry more weight than the same statement made by the chief economist of a local bank. Since it is vested with authority, the information will pass as a judgment. Nevertheless, not only will the judgment have different influences, but it may also be disputed in various ways. A scientific study may be signed by a renowned economist, yet it may be judged by the public as a rather worthless product.

An important procedure used by all portfolio managers involves their ability to classify publicly available information into information groups that allow for its better management. The professional experience they have accumulated as well as their subjectivism may facilitate the classification of available information according to specific criteria, such as its degree of usefulness (useful/useless) (Dragotă, 2009: 94), and to its legitimacy and level of authority (legitimate/illegitimate). These information groups are illustrated in Fig. 1.

If we assume that money has informative value and that prices are an information medium, then, within the context of the financial market, prices are essential information. Thus, quotations of financial assets are

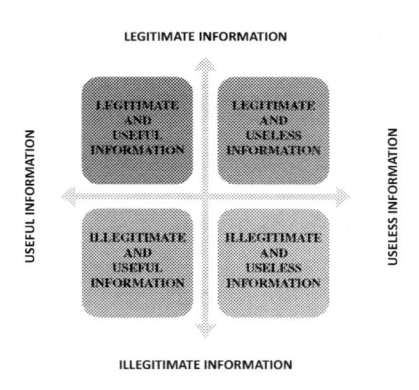

Fig. 1. Classification of financial market information

essential knowledge, particularly to those who use the tools of technical analysis. The quotations are available on the web pages of stock exchanges where these assets are traded.

The information needed to ground decisions of investing into securities must take into account not only the state of the company concerned, but also the state of the business segment and of the entire economy, without losing sight of the global economic situation. The volume of information is much larger for essential analysis users. Essential analysis may comprise information on macroeconomic developments; forecasts on the development of the business sector; the general trend of the capital market; the financial results of the company issuing the securities; the transaction volume; the cyclicity of the business or of the company activities; the analysis of product quality and market outlets; the quality of the analysed company management; the ownership structure; the strategy set for the future, etc. A theoretical rate of the securities based on the financial statements, similar to the market value, may be calculated. This correlation indicates whether the securities are overvalued or undervalued, supporting the investor in making the appropriate decision.

If we assume that prices are information, then, on an efficient market, investors capable of studying prices in a centralized and unified way will have the same type of information. Yet this does not preclude temporary deviations: for instance, in some cases, some investors will access relevant information before others. However, on the whole and in the long run, no investor will constantly secure relevant information so as to have a transactional edge repeatedly. This can be inferred from the impossibility of making a capital out of monopolies of knowledge (Preda, 2010: 137), so that no long-term abnormal returns can be derived on an efficient market.

Market efficiency involves the following elements in terms of available information and its processing:

— Information observation (in the case presented, price information) must be accessible to all investors;
— There must be common procedures to translate information into prices. This means that stories, rumors, data interpretation and other such sources should work to influence share lists through the interaction of market participants. Thus, for information to be reflected in share lists, there must be market-specific interaction procedures which should not be subject to a monopoly (a group can monopolize the contents of a rumor for a while, but not how to spread the rumor). Thus, market efficiency would require the public availability of market interaction authorized procedures;
— To make possible the conceptualizing of the translation of information into prices, it is necessary that we regard certain features of market participants as features of rational agents. The assumption that all agents display the same features (e.g., rationality) and, therefore, should be treated as equals, facilitates general pattern-making, diverting attention from the participants' interaction. The main postulation of this assumption refers to the fact that agents have rational expectations, i.e., they make accurate use of all relevant information. Being a rational market participant means being driven by self-interest and making calculations based on the assumption that the future will not necessarily look like the past.

3. Information Entropy — A Measure of Financial Market Complexity

Entropy is the measure of both the uncertainty and the complexity of a system, with many applications in physics (the second principle of thermodynamics), in information theory, in biology (the complexity of DNA sequences), in economics (system complexity). In other words, high levels of entropy are obtained in situations of deep uncertainty, while low levels of entropy are associated with low uncertainty situations.

3.1. *Entropy-specific issues*

In the context of the physical and mechanical approach to the economic phenomenon, the original meaning of the word entropy has its roots in the second principle of thermodynamics: heat always moves from a warmer body to a cooler body and never the other way round. Thus, in a metaphorical way, to reconnect with thermodynamics, we consider a certain "temperature" of a system, which increases as the complexity increases and vice versa (Dinga, 2009: 49). Simplifying the problem, we further state that an uninsulated system, having a higher temperature than that of the environment, spontaneously and irreversibly tends to reach thermal equilibrium with the environment, in the process leading to an increase in entropy, measurable as heat. The organized energy naturally and irreversibly turns into disorganized energy. Hence, the modern interpretation of the law of entropy, by which in any system there is a tendency of continuous transformation of order into disorder or chaos.

The exception to the rule of entropy exchange described previously is made by *dissipative structures* (a concept coined by the 1977 Nobel Chemistry Prize winner Ilya Prigogine), which are those independent systems that resist the natural tendency to reach equilibrium, managing to keep in a state of imbalance through an exchange of matter and energy with the environment. These far-from-equilibrium systems may maintain their structure as long as the intake of energy/matter from the environment is greater than the entropy exported by the system. Such negative entropy systems, called **negentropy** systems, are living organisms because they need to import low entropy resources (strongly structured energetic elements) from the environment and export high entropy matter (destructured matter).

In information theory, negentropy is used as a measure of the distance to normality. Of all distributions with a given dispersion, normal (or Gaussian) distribution is the one that requires the highest entropy, because the more random the variables are, the higher the entropy will be. Negentropy measures the difference in entropy between a given distribution and the normal distribution with the same dispersion, so we can state that negentropy is a "measure of non-Gaussianicity". Thus, negentropy can also be calculated as the difference between the entropy of the random variable with normal distribution $H(Y_{gauss})$ and the entropy of the random variable $H(Y)$ (we consider how to determine the entropy information through the *Shannon Entropy* further in this chapter) as follows:

$$J(Y) = H(Y_{gauss}) - H(Y) \geq 0. \quad (1)$$

Thus, negentropy will always take positive values and will be equal to zero only provided that variable Y follows a normal Gaussian distribution.

3.2. *Information entropy*

Information, which is essential to the functioning of the stock market, determines the organization of the system and shapes its behavior, counteracting the effects of the law of entropy and preserving the system characteristics: openness, dynamism, complexity, and deterministic chaos.

The link between a certain level of complexity and the *Efficient Market Hypothesis* is quite clear: if we consider an efficient market (a weak form one), then security prices follow the random-walk pattern, i.e., the returns series is a *white noise process*. In quantitative terms, such a white noise process has the highest level of complexity; conversely, if the efficient markets hypothesis is not accepted, then prices are not a random-walk process and, therefore, the complexity of the market will be lower. For instance, if the security price is a purely deterministic, predictable process, the level of complexity is minimal; if price is a completely unpredictable random-walk process, then we are dealing with the highest level of complexity. Taking into consideration the explanations earlier, we can see *entropy as a measure of informational efficiency* of financial markets. In the terms of information entropy, market efficiency is equivalent to having maximum entropy, complexity, or uncertainty levels.

To measure the informational efficiency of financial markets, we use the **Shannon Entropy** (This is the inability to predict, on average, a random-walk variable equivalent to its information content. The concept was coined by Claude E. Shannon in his 1948 work "A Mathematical Theory of Communication".). We start from the basic assumption that, on an efficient market, prices reflect all available information. As a result, we notice that the returns of efficient market securities are not predictable. Measuring efficiency involves two stages. First, we represent returns for us to be easier to detect their changes over the analyzed period. In the second stage, we apply and calculate the Shannon entropy to measure the amount of information contained in the returns series. Using the symbolic time series analysis (Symbolic Time Series Analyses — Daw et al., 2003, *A Review of Symbolic Analysis of Experimental Data*), we can get more data from a normal time series, as we turn the normal data with very different values into a series symbolized by just a few distinct values.

The problem of the symbolic series is that there is no formal method by which to define time series symbols. However, in our case, we are interested in combinations of the positive and negative values of the returns series. Consequently, we denote negative returns by (0) and positive ones by (1). In fact, in this case, the process is a sequence of Bernoulli trials ((0) and (1)).

Thus, we define a time series of size T defined as $(R_1, R_2, R_3, \ldots, R_T)$, R_t being the security returns at time t, where $t = 1, 2, 3, \ldots, T$.

The returns were measured using the first difference of logarithmic values of daily prices (the arithmetic and logarithmic returns are not equal, but they are approximately equal for small returns. The difference between them is high only when the relative change of the rate is high):

$$R_t = d\log_e(C_t) = \log_e(C_t) - \log_e(C_{t-1}). \quad (2)$$

We then turned the series of returns into a symbolic series in accordance with the following notations:

$$\begin{cases} if\ R_t < 0, s_t = 0 \\ if\ R_t \geq 0, s_t = 1 \end{cases} \quad (3)$$

We thus obtained the following symbolic series $(s_1, s_2, s_3, \ldots, s_T)$, which is actually the same original series, but presented as a sequence of 0 and 1, as indicators of price decreases and increases. In an efficient market, the assumption is that it is not possible to forecast future security prices (or their related returns) using historical values. Thus, the probability of having positive (negative) returns the next day is ½ and the Shannon entropy level is the highest.

To analyze the uncertainty level, we implement the Shannon entropy (H) as a measure of informational efficiency. This indicator can take a maximum value of 1, when the process is completely random, and a minimum value of 0, when referring to a sure event. Here is the theoretical expression of H for two events, p (the probability of having negative returns) and 1− p (the probability of having positive probabilities) (we used Risso's methodology, 2008):

$$H = -[p * log_2 p + (1 - p) * log_2(1 - p)]. \quad (4)$$

Since the above-mentioned equation is concave, the maximum (H = 1) is obtained for p = 1/2 (maximum uncertainty) and the minimum is obtained when one of the events is a sure event (p = 0 or p = 1). In the latter case, it means that the market is not efficiently informational and the Shannon Entropy value (H) will be less than 1.

3.3. Applying information entropy to emerging financial markets

The Shannon entropy was assessed for 8 emerging countries, 4 EU countries (Romania, Hungary, Estonia, the Czech Republic) and the 4 emerging countries Brazil, Russia, India, and China (BRIC). The data used in this analysis consists of the main stock indexes traded on the stock exchanges of these countries, so we chose the following indexes: BET for Romania, OMX Tallinn for Estonia, PX for the Czech Republic, BUX for Hungary, IBOVESPA for Brazil, RTSI for Russia, Sensex for India and Shanghai Composite Index for China. The data series cover a period of 10 years, from October 2003 to October 2013. The data sample consists of about 2,500 daily values of the price of each separate stock index.

Using the methodology outlined earlier to determine the Shannon Entropy, we rated these emerging countries on the basis of the entropy value obtained, as shown in Table 1 and Fig. 2.

Table 1. Classification of indices according to recorded entropy value

Rank	Index	Country	Entropy (H)
3	BET	Romania	0.998014
2	BUX	Hungary	0.998616
4	PX	The Czech Republic	0.996222
8	OMX TALLINN	Estonia	0.946398
5	IBOVSPA	Brazil	0.996099
7	RTSI	Russia	0.990961
6	SENSEX	India	0.994193
1	SHANGHAI_C_I	China	0.999945

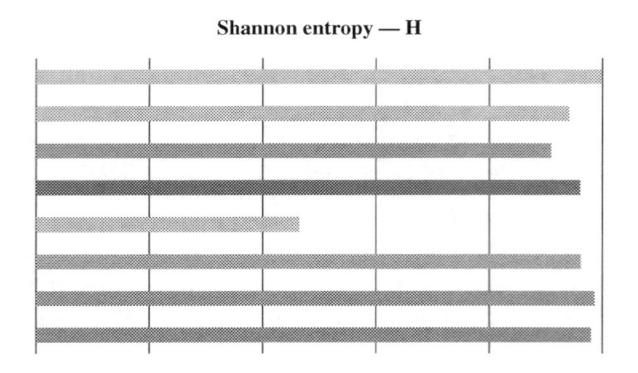

Fig. 2. Value of Shannon entropy from 2003 to 2013

The results obtained indicate that, in general, all eight emerging countries are characterized by weak informational efficiency, if we take into account the value that is quite close to 1 of the Shannon entropy obtained in all cases. However, the most efficient financial market in terms of information seems to be the Chinese market, followed by the Hungarian market. The least effective market in terms of information, using the Shannon entropy as an indicator of appreciation, is the Estonian financial market, which has the lowest entropy value.

4. Concluding Remarks

Charging an ordered structure with a minimum degree of uncertainty (lack of knowledge) and a disordered, chaotic structure with a maximum degree of ignorance, we coined the term ***information entropy*** as a measure of the degree of uncertainty within a system. There is a direct relationship between the degree of organization of a system, the amount of information stored, and information entropy, expressed by the law of negative entropy: within systems, there is a tendency of the degree of organization to increase in direct proportion to the increase in the amount of information stored in the system. In other words, the organization of the system is directly proportional to the amount of information stored and inversely proportional to the entropy information of the system (Ghilic-Micu, 2002: 232).

However, a more comprehensive analysis of the degree of financial market informational efficiency could be produced if we calculated the Shannon Entropy for emerging countries, but compared to that of developed countries. Furthermore, the study could be improved by calculating the entropy in different periods of time in order to draw comparisons of market efficiency in such times as those before the crisis, during the crisis, and after the crisis. Finally, we can extend the analysis by calculating the modified Shannon Entropy (following Risso's methodology, 2008), which involves calculating the entropy for time windows of different lengths (day sequences).

References

Akerlof, G. A., Spence, A. M. & Stiglitz, J. E. (2001), *Markets with Asymmetric Information*, Nobel Prize in Economics documents 2001–2002, Nobel Prize Committee.

Dinga, E. (2009), *Studii de Economie*, București: Editura Economică.

Dragotă, V. (coordinator) (2009), *Gestiunea portofoliului de Valori Mobiliare, Ediția a Doua*, București: Ed. Economică.

Drucker, P. (1999), *Societatea Postcapitalistă* (*traducere după: Post-Capitalist Society*), București: Image.

Duțescu, A. (2000), *Informația Contabilă și Piețele de Capital*, București: Economică.

Ghilic-Micu, B. (2002), *Strategii pe Piața de Capital*, București: Economică.

Preda, A. (2010), *Introducere în Sociologia Piețelor*, Timișoara: Polirom.

Risso, W. (2008), The informational efficiency and the financial crashes, *Research in International Business and Finance*, 22, 396–408.

Stoica, O. (2002), *Mecanisme și Instituții ale Pieței de Capital*, București: Economică.

Part V

Entrepreneurship, Social Enterprise, and SMEs

Chapter 19

SME-Conducive Policy Formulation under Systemic Perspectives

J. Hanns Pichler

Austrian Institute for SME Research
Vienna University of Economics and Business

"Why are SMEs so important ... Because high employment growth in SMEs in the last decade has prevented unemployment rising ... in the European Economy Area".

The European Observatory for SMEs

The very topic raises an ever challenging question: that is, of the role and significance, if not to say "survival" of small and medium-sized enterprises (SMEs) and related structures within an environment of forces which — particularly in the sphere of industry — on first sight tend to favor the "big" rather than the "small". This at the same time points at the underlying aspects and challenges of broader socio-economic and structural dimensions with a concomitant need for appropriate formulation of more differentiated and specifically designed business policies in general.

1. Introduction

The very topic raises an ever challenging question: that is, of the role and significance, if not to say "survival" of small and medium-sized enterprises (SMEs) and related structures within an environment of forces which — particularly in the sphere of industry — an first sight tend to favor the "big" rather than the "small". This at the same time points at underlying aspects and challenges of broader socio-economic and structural dimensions with a concomitant need for appropriate formulation of more differentiated and specifically designed business policies generally.

Such challenges and related problems today are to be seen from an inseparably intertwined and multipronged point of view:

- From a more and more international point of view, not the least, a strategic ingredient of development to be recognized as perception of the role and exposure of SMEs in their sector-related structural significance nationally, regionally and nowadays, in fact, **globally.**
- Then, from a closer to the skin view of developments related to on-going restructuring in our **European** and — when speaking of SMEs — in many ways regionally unique business environment.

Finally, under overriding socio-economic and systems-related aspects of a more comprehensive SME-specific policy formulation.

Globally, evidence of a new and growing recognition of the role of SMEs is provided by a profound reorientation in development policy over the last decades with a distinct change in strategies toward fostering sector-related diversification for more balanced long-term growth and economic welfare under sustainable conditions generally.

In speaking of strategies, there is today an ever growing awareness worldwide of the role of SMEs both as a factor of sustaining economic stability and as simply indispensable a catalyst for fostering economic dynamics and welfare. Experience and recognition thereof has triggered a more broadly based rethinking and change in outlook quite in contrast still to post-war decades, when sustained economic buoyancy, business dynamics, and growth in considerable measure tended to blur the need for any more subtle structural considerations. Yet, underlying economic realities and the very characteristics of any SME structured business environment, in the end, were not to be neglected with impunity indefinitely.

Altogether — and not the least from an European angle — this largely has disproved more orthodox and seemingly ill-conceived notions of any inherent superiority of the "big" vis-à-vis the "small", thus recognizing the specific role of SMEs in the context of a more subtle and diversified approach toward "structural development".

2. Economic and Social Importance of SMEs

In geographically narrowing our focus and taking a closer look now at the specificity of the **European business environment:** a unique, richly structured, and indeed highly diversified SME "landscape" emerges. A landscape with manifold facets is vividly being illustrated again and again by the "European Observatory for SMEs". Thus, in its current (sixth) issue it is being shown that SMEs (defined as up to 250 employees) within the "European Space" in a broader sense number somewhere close to 20 milli-units, against only about 40,000, or just 0.2%, larger firms (with more than 250 employees); this makes for an average of some 50 (non-primary) business establishments per 1,000 inhabitants! Furthermore, these millions of smaller — in considerable part craft dominated micro-enterprises — over the past years continuously have tended to outperform larger enterprises in terms of job creation. This at the same time demonstrates that without such relatively high employment growth and intensity on part of SMEs, the European unemployment syndrome would have been even more pronounced!

While illustrating thereby the economic and social importance of SMEs in a European context, this further implies — as stated in the 1996 "Observatory" — that over the years an estimated 1.5 million Europeans annually decide to start a business of their own; and this way, over half a decade or so, the number of (mostly small to very small) enterprises increased by about 9%, while the European Union (EU) population grew by only some 2%.

In country-specific terms it is quite typical too when, e.g., in Austria — and similarly in Germany, in Switzerland and elsewhere — nearly 99% of all non-agricultural business establishments have less than 100 employees; and of those again close to 90% have less than 10, and just about 2% have 100 or above. Moreover, in terms of sustaining employment the SME sector on the whole — due to its flexibility and adaptability — over the 1980s and well into the 1990s, in a period of profound industrial restructuring, was able to by and large absorb, and thereby compensate for, ongoing layoffs in the larger public sector dominated industries to the tune of some 80,000 employees (or nearly 3% of Austria's total work force).

While recognizing such proven strength not only structurally but also as providing a certain measure of resilience against business cycle volatilities one might take note of the fact that it is exactly in the sphere of SMEs as well where — due to their more immediate socio-economic exposure — conflicts of interest (not free at times from certain partisanship) do arise and are being fought out; conflicts implying both positive and negative repercussions as to sector-related policy formulation with concomitant institutional implications. Frequently, this indeed resembles the arena where in essentially market based systems "the very action" is; where policy challenges and demands are being articulated in ever so many nuances and facets.

Sheer existence and sustained survival of SME structures with their complexities as mirroring the very reality of economic life itself, also contradicts once widely spread "prophecies" of the ultimate demise of small businesses as a predicament under both "classical" and, of course, Marxian doctrines. Historical evidence and today's systemic transformation processes at our doorsteps in Central and Eastern Europe clearly point to the opposite; the very essence of restructuring going on there more than ever calls for speedy creation or revival of sound and diversified SME structures as simply indispensable an ingredient for any sustained recovery as one of the strategically most challenging issues.

All too easy at times, as it seems, the inherent wealth of diversity as so typical for the European business scenario merely is being taken for granted; this perhaps too, because we somehow are used to the fact that SMEs always have been or simply ought to be there anyway. Yet, for any more conscious policy considerations this, in fact, is not really so self-understood; it rather does call for continued awareness to assure that underlying resilience and adjustment capabilities constantly are being safeguarded.

Such adjustment capabilities to changing business conditions and, at times, volatile cyclical movements quite typically are characterized also by structural permeability both upward and downward: that is to say, by way of adjusting — and in today's scenario all the more relevant — to forces of regional (or even global) integration with implicit restructuring of business sizes. Such restructuring, by its very nature, is not one-sidedly to be interpreted as simply a tendency toward "concentration" only; rather, and more objectively so, it is equally to be seen as a process of opening up opportunities also "downstream" in terms of structural deepening as markets and, in particular, size of markets change.

Insights of modern industrial economics give credence to such complexities in the course of structural adjustment with, in part, new evidence as to criteria of "optimal" business sizes being induced, e.g., by technological developments. Thereby, placing emphasis not so much on economies of "scale"; rather more on elements such as SME-specific diversification or differentiation rendering classical returns to "scale" no longer so valid an argument as against economies of "scope". More pointedly still, it implies conscious recognition of such complexities as, e.g., regional specifics and market differentiation, locational spread including relative density of businesses relating to given demand and supply patterns, with implications again for product/market orientation and diversification of size structures as relevant for both forward and backward linkages of respective business activities.

Any SME policy addressing such complexities finally has to do with what one might subsume under contributing to "quality of life" and to conditions of welfare in a broader sense. Endowment with diversified business structures and, thereby, with enhanced economic opportunities, productive capacities and increased potential for catering to differentiated, individualized patterns of demand finally needs to be judged with a view to such qualitative aspects. (A study to this effect conducted in Austria, e.g., depicts regional differences in relative SME density between 40 and 80 per 1,000 inhabitants as clearly correlating with respectively higher or lower levels of economic welfare, incomes and purchasing power.)

3. SMEs Policy

Over and above mere economic considerations, relevance of SMEs, finally, is to be viewed also from a more broadly based **socio-economic** point of view; that is, SMEs being seen as a driving force of structural change on the one hand, and as a stabilizing factor for safeguarding a given economic setting with its institutional framework in the dynamics of change on the other.

For any freedom — and as such market — oriented socio-economic order as a form of life, this unequivocally implies a commitment to entrepreneurial initiative, to guaranteeing both free and autonomous pursuit of business opportunities; implies furthermore a commitment to market criteria of performance with quite legitimate a claim for adequate return under due consideration of social (including environmental) responsibility in the conduct of business as such. It also means that any such policy inescapably becomes part and parcel of shaping socio-economic conditions as conducive a framework wherein SMEs, with their diversified structures and patterns of performance, can thrive as indispensable for guaranteeing and sustaining welfare conditions for society as a whole (as no doubt constituting a policy challenge at any time anywhere).

Such policy ought not to shy away from the very "nitty gritty" either: such as, e.g., avoiding to burden SMEs in a discriminatory manner with unremunerated administrative tasks by public authorities. A more recent study to that effect in Germany demonstrates that the relative impact in terms of cost and manpower to be allocated proves up to 22 times (!) and, thus, quite disproportionately higher for SMEs as compared to larger enterprises. In a somewhat more sarcastic vain, but pointing essentially in the same direction, the US Small Business Administration some time ago pointed out that the then roughly 10 million businesses under its constituency got inundated yearly by well over 300 million forms with up to 1 billion pages containing more than 7 billion questions; altogether entailing unremunerated costs averaging some USD 3,000 — or more per firm. Gracefully perhaps, a similar EU related assessment has not, as yet, been carried out!

If on the other hand — as often quite "liberally" being claimed — it is to be recognized that SMEs indeed represent the mainstay or very "trade mark" of any market oriented economy; and if it is true further, as variously being claimed, that — due to the sheer existence of more diversified SME structures — economies over and over again could prove their adaptive capabilities for both overcoming even severe policy mistakes and at the same time taking on new challenges, then it would be only consequential for any related policy to attain a certain measure of "natural" legitimacy of its own.

4. Conclusions

Upon closer scrutiny of such pronouncements and arguments though, one might be left wondering whether this kind of demands or recommendations not remain pretty much on the surface and, thus, tend to fall way short of recognizing more profound issues involved; whether indeed — if argued from a systems-related point of view — not more deeply probing questions as to the really crucial "building stones" of any SME-specific policy were to be addressed, as e.g.,

○ **Questioning**, with a view not the least to prevailing structures, whether "classically" defined strategies of blatant "marketeering" indeed make for adequate and sensitive enough a policy, taking proper cognizance of underlying diversities and complexities?

○ **Questioning** further, whether sheer prevalence of SME diversification with related institutional structures rather not might call for an equally differentiated policy; a policy which — within an essentially market-based framework — just as well allows for appropriate multiplicity of cooperative (corporatist) or in various ways subsidiary forms of business organization and relationships as a kind of "natural" ingredient, if not enrichment of any economic system pointing beyond simple supply and demand mechanisms at the very micro level?

○ **Considering** finally, and without wanting to seem "heretical", whether or not — and possibly quite legitimately so — to foster and thereby acknowledge also intermediate forms of business association at the meso-level as a reflection or simply inescapable a feature of institutionalization for any sound SME policy recognizing, in principle:

— For one, that competition as a coordinating "mechanism" via markets constitutes only one — but not the only — criterion or instrument governing business conduct and, depending on given sectoral or structural conditions, not necessarily is to take center stage; or in putting it more bluntly: that acceptance of an essentially competitive, market oriented economic order for SMEs equally requires an appropriate framework of institutions going along with;

— Furthermore, that cognizance of such specifics with implicit forms of institutionalization may prove more conducive to SME related business conduct than any undifferentiated plea for cutthroat competition at micro level, by emphasizing and bringing to bear economies of "scope" rather than of "scale"; or in short: considering SMEs not merely as "beautiful", but also as being "efficient" in a more comprehensive sector-specific understanding;

— And finally, that necessary autonomy of SMEs within a spectre of larger entities is to be constantly safeguarded, not the least by way of sector-related forms of institutionalization in duly recognizing role and relevance of the SME sector as a whole from an overriding socio-economic perspective.

Any self-conscious, not to be confused with self-righteous, SME policy conceived under such auspices should — in view of the legitimate claims and issues involved — ultimately be articulated more aggressively still, as quite essential an element within the realm of economic policy formulation generally.

References

Akokangas, P. (1998), Internationalisation and resources: An analysis of processes in Nordic SMEs, *Acta Wasensia No. 64*, Vaasa.

Aiginger, K. & Tichy, G. (1984), *Die Groeße der Kleinen: Die Ueberraschenden Erfolge Kleiner und Mittlerer Unternehmungen in den Achtziger Jahren*, Vienna: Signum Verlag.

Anderson, I. (1982), Small industry in developing countries, World Bank Staff Working Papers 518.

Bamberger, I. & Pleitner, H. J. (eds.) (1988), Strategische ausrichtung kleiner und mittlerer unternehmen, *Internationales Gewerbearchiv*, 2.

Bamberger, I. (ed.) (1994), *Product/Market Strategies of Small and Medium-sized Enterprises*, Avebury: Aldershot.

Becattini, G. (1999), Flourishing small firms and the re-emergence of industrial districts, Keynote, 44th ICSB World Conference, Naples (mimeo).

Belak, J., Kajzer, S., Mugler, J., Senjur, M., Sewing, N., & Thommen, J.-P. (eds.) (1997), *Unternehmensentwicklung und Management Unter Besonderer Beruecksichtigung der Klein-und Mittelbetriebe*, Zurich: Versus.

Buckley, P. & Ghauri, P. (eds.) (1993), *The Internationalization of the Firm: A Reader*, London: Academic Press.

Crauser, G. (1999), Enterprise policy — quo vadis? Challenges and prospects for the year 2000 and beyond, Opening Address, 44th ICSB World Conference, Naples (mimeo).

Dahiya, S. B. (1991), *Theoretical Foundations of Development Planning*, 5 Vols., New Delhi.

de Vries, B. A. (1980), Industrialization and employment:. The role of small and medium-sized manufacturing firms. In *International Economic Development and Resource Transfer*, Kiel: Institute of World Economic.

Donckels, R. & Miettinen, A. (eds.) (1997), *Entrepreneurship and SME Research on its Way to the Next Millennium*, Aldershot: Ashgate Publishing Ltd.

ENSR/EIM (1996, 1997, 2000), *The European Observatory for SMEs*; esp. Fourth to Sixth Annual Reports, Zoetermeer: EIM Business and Policy Research.

Froehlich, E. & Pichler, J. H. (1998), Werte und typen mittelstaendischer Unternehmer. In *Beitraege zur Ganzheitlichen Wirtschafts- und Gesellschaftslehre*, J. H. Pichler (ed.), Berlin: Duncker & Humblodt.

Froehlich, E. A., Hawranek, P. M., Lettmayr, C. F., & Pichler, J. H. (1994), *Manual for Small Industrial Businesses: Project Design and Appraisal*, Vienna: UNIDO Publication, General Studies Series.

Gibb, A. A. (1993), Key factors in the design of policy support for the small and medium enterprise development process: An Overview, *Entrepreneurship and Regional Development*, 5.

Gutersohn, A. (1977), *Das Gewerbe in der Freien Marktwirtschaft*, 3 Vols. (1954–1974), Berlin–Munich–St. Gallen.

Gutersohn, A. (1981), Zur Belastbarkeit der gewerblichen unternehmen mit gesetzlichen vorschriften, administrativen Auflagen und mit abgaben. In *Klein-und Mittelbetriebe: Chancen, Probleme, Loesungen*, W. Kemmetmueller, W. Sertl (eds.), Vienna.

Haahti, A. J. (1993, 1995), INTERSTRATOS. Internationalization of strategic orientations of European small and medium enterprises, EIASM Reports 93-01 and 95-01, Brussels.

Haahti, A., Hall, G., & Donckels, R. (eds.) (1998), *The Internationalization of SMEs: The Interstratos Project*, London: Routledge.

Heinrich, W. *Wirtschaftspolitik*, 2 Vols. (1948–1954) (2nd edn.), Berlin 1964–1967.

Heinrich, W. (1964), *Probleme der Klein- und Mittelbetriebe* (1962) (2nd edn.), Muenster.

Hirschman, A. O. (1958), *The Strategy of Economic Development* (10th edn.), New Haven: Yale University Press.

Institut fuer Gewerbe- und Handwerksforschung (IfG) (1992), Gewerbe und handwerk 2000. Perspektiven und szenarien, schriftenreihe des wirtschaftsfoerderungsinstitutes 216, Vienna.

Institut fuer Gewerbe- und Handwerksforschung (IfG) (1994), Internationalization of strategic orientation in European small businesses. Austrian Results 1991/93, INTERSTRATOS Report, Vienna.

Institut fuer Gewerbe- und Handwerksforschung (IfG) (1998), Das burgenlaendische gewerbe und handwerk, Szenario 2005, Auswirkungen der EU-Osterweiterung, Vienna.

Kailer, N. & Mugler, J. (eds.) (1998), *Entwicklung von Kleinen und Mittleren Unternehmen: Konzepte, Praxiserfahrungen, Perspektiven*, Vienna.

Kao, R. W. Y. (1984), *Small Business Management: A Strategic Emphasis*, Toronto: Holt, Reinhart, and Winston.

Kao, R. W. Y. (1985), *Entrepreneurship: A Wealth-Creation and Value-Adding Process*, New York.

Kemmetmueller, W. & Sertl, W. (eds.) (1981), *Klein- und Mittelbetriebe: Chancen, Probleme, Loesungen*, Vienna.

Larcon, J.-P. (ed.) (1998), *Entrepreneurship and Economic Transition in Central Europe*, Boston: Kluwer Academic Publishers.

Lehtimaeki, A. & Ahokangas, P. (1993), Foreign market orientation and international operations of European SMEs in 1990, Working Paper 7, University of Oulu.

Levy, B. (1993), Obstacles to developing indigenous small and medium enterprises: An empirical assessment, *World Bank Economic Review*, 7(1).

Little, I. M. D. (1987), Small manufacturing enterprises in developing countries, *The World Bank Economic Review*, 1(2).

Muegge, H. (1988), Entwicklungshilfe fuer kleine und mittlere unternehmungen aus der Sicht der UNIDO, IfG Mitteilungen.

Mugler, J. & Schmidt, K.-H. (eds.) (1995), *Klein- und Mittelunternehmen in einer dynamischen Wirtschaft: Ausgewählte Schriften von Hans Jobst Pleitner*, Berlin–Munich–St. Gallen: Duncker und Humblodt.

Mugler, J. (1993), *Betriebswirtschaftslehre der Klein- und Mittelbetriebe* (3rd edn.), Vienna-New York: Springer.

Neck, P. (ed.) (1977), *Small Enterprise Development: Policies and Programmes*, Geneva: ILO.

Pichler, J. H. (1981), Der klein- und mittelbetriebliche Sektor als Herausforderung und Anliegen weltweiter Entwicklungsstrategie. In *Klein- und Mittelbetriebe: Chancen, Probleme, Loesungen*, W. Kemmetmueller and W. Sertl (eds.), Vienna.

Pichler, J. H. (1988), Gewerbe und Entwicklung. Die Rolle der Kleinbetriebe in Entwicklungsländern, lfG Mitteilungen.

Pichler, J. H. (1994), Toward a Technology Scenario: 2000 and beyond. A systems-related approach geared to small business development. In *Small and Medium-sized Enterprises on their Way into the Next Century* (2nd edn.), 20th International Small Business Congress (1993), IGW, St. Gallen.

Pichler, J. H. (1995), Consequences of a Larger Europe for SMEs. In Quest of SMEs Specific Policy Formulation. In *European Yearbook, Vol. XLI*, P. Drillien (ed.), Dordrecht: Council of Europe.

Pichler, J. H. (1996), European Small Businesses Responding to the Larger Market. Entrepreneurial "profiles" in the context of business life cycles. In *Versicherungen, Risiko und Internationalisierung. Herausforderungen fuer Unternehmensfuehrung und Politik, Festschrift fuer H. Stremitzer*, J. Mugler and M. Nitsche (eds.), Vienna.

Pichler, J. H. (1996), SMEs at the frontiers of development: Assessing success factors for policy formulation, The UNIDO Manual as a Guide. An Overview, in *Proceedings*, Vol. 11, 415t ICS13 World Conference, Stockholm.

Pichler, J. H. (1997), KMU als dynamischer erfolgsfaktor im entwicklungsprozeß. In *Unternehmensentwicklung und Managment unter besonderer Beruecksichtigung der Klein- und Mittelbetriebe in den Reformlaendern*, J. Belak and S. Kajzer et al. (eds.), Zurich.

Pichler, J. H. (1998), SME internationalization: Entrepreneurial profiles and patterns of strategic adjustment, *Piccola Impresa*, 2.

Pichler, J. H. (ed.) (1993), *Oekonomische Konsequenzen eines EG-Beitritts Oesterreichs*, Berlin: Duncker & Humblodt.

Pichler, J. H., Pleitner, H. J., & Schmidt, K.-H. (eds.) (2000), Management in KMU: Die Fuehrung von Klein- und Mittelunternehmen (3rd edn.), Bern: Haupt.

Pleitner, H. J. (ed.) (1989), Neue Problemperspektiven und neue erfolgsaussichten fuer kleine und mittlere unternehmen, *Internationales Gewerbearchiv*, 3, Berlin–Munich–St. Gallen.

Pleitner, H. J. (ed.) (1992), *Die Veraenderte Welt — Einwirkungen auf Die Klein- Und Mittelunternehmen, Beitraege Zu Den Rencontres De St-Gall*, IGW, St. Gallen.

Pleitner, H. J. (ed.) (1994), *Small and Medium-Sized Enterprises on Their Way into the Next Century*, 20th International Small Business Congress (1993) (2nd edn.), IGW, St. Gallen.

The STRATOS Group (1990), *Strategic Orientations of Small European Businesses*, Aldershot [etc.].

UNIDO (1979), *Industry 2000 — New Perspectives*, New York.

Van der Burg, B. I. & Nijsen, A. F. M. (1998), *How Can Administrative Burdens of Businesses be Assessed? Different Methods: Advantages and Disadvantages*, Zoetermeer: EIM.

World Bank: World Development Report, Washington D.C. (annually since 1978; in the given context esp. 1987 on "Industrialization", 1991 on "The Challenge of Development", 1996 on "From Plan to Market", 2000/01 on "Attacking Poverty").

World Bank (1978), Employment and development of small enterprises, Sector Policy Paper.

World Bank (1986), Industrial restructuring, Working Paper, Washington, D. C.

World Bank/CFS (1994), Eastern European experience with small-scale privatization, CFS Discussion Paper Series, No. 104, Washington, D. C.

Chapter 20

Particularities of the Procesual Organisation in the Medium Knowledge-Based Enterprise

Ovidiu Nicolescu

Romanian Scientific Management Association (RSMS)

Transition to the knowledge-based economy — the fundamental mutation of the present times — generates a lot of changes in all fields. One of this is the development of the knowledge-based enterprises, which became the main components of the knowledge-based economy.

Knowledge-based enterprise is very different from typical capitalist enterprise (Angela & Oxbrow, 2002; Amaravadi & Lee, 2005). It presents many specific structural, functional, and performance characteristics.

The main objective of our chapter is to identify and to analyze the major characteristics of the medium knowledge-based enterprise from procesual organisation point of view. We select medium enterprise because in this type of company the evolution to the knowledge-based economy is more advanced comparative with micro and small enterprises and, because at the world level they represent the most numerous groups of knowledge-based companies. Our analyse is focused on the procesual organisation because the changes in this field have major influence on all other features of the company and on its management and performance.

The paper is structured in **five parts**:

- The organizational changes occured at the level of all enterprise's functions — research and development (R&D), commercial, production, financial-accounting, and human resources (personnel).

- The new configuration of the functions in the medium sized companies based on knowledge, revealing the apparition of two new organisation functions — knowledge function and training function.
- The presentation of the knowledge function characteristics in medium knowledge-based company and its nine main activities.
- The presentation of the 10 characteristics of the new training function.
- The identification and the presentation of the main particularities of the classical enterprise functions — R&D function, commercial function, production function, finance-accounting function, human resource function — in the medium knowledge-based company.

All mentioned elements represent novelties in the international literature dedicated to the SMEs in the context of the transition to the knowledge-based economy.

1. Introduction

Transition to the knowledge-based economy — the fundamental mutation of the present times — generates a lot of changes in all fields. One of this is the development of the knowledge-based enterprises, which became the main components of the knowledge-based economy.

Knowledge-based enterprise is very different from typical capitalist enterprise (Angela & Oxbrow, 2002; Kessels, 2001). It presents many specific structural, functional, and performance characteristics.

The main objective of our chapter is to identify and analyse the major characteristics of the medium knowledge-based enterprise from procesual organisation point of view. We select medium enterprise because in this type of company the evolution to the knowledge-based economy is more advanced comparative with micro and small enterprises and, because at the world level they represent the most numerous groups of knowledge-based companies. Our analyse is focused on the procesual organisation because the changes in this field have major influence on all other features of the company and on its management and performance.

The paper is structured in **five parts**:

- The organisational changes occured at the level of all enterprise's functions — R&D, commercial, production, financial-accounting, and human resources (personnel).
- The new configuration of the functions in the medium sized companies based on knowledge, revealing the apparition of two new organization functions — knowledge function and training function.
- The presentation of the knowledge function characteristics in medium knowledge-based company and its nine main activities.
- The presentation of the 10 characteristics of the new tarining function.
- The identification and the presentation of the main particularities of the classical enterprise functions — R&D function, commercial function, production function, finance-accounting function, human resource function — in the medium knowledge-based company.

All mentioned elements represent novelties in the international literature dedicated to the SMEs in the context of the transition to the knowledge-based economy.

2. Changes in All Enterprise Functions

Our analysis has identified the following **major changes**:

- Internationalization of work process inside enterprise, of course not all at the same level, but very consistent in each company function.
- Knowledge becames an essential input in the company, representing the strategic raw material for all enterprise activities.
- Increase in the creative dimension of the work process within each enterprise's functions and activities.
- Amplification of the work productivity, which determines much better knowledge-based company's performance, comparative with the previous period.
- Externalization of certain specific enterprise activities which are not part of the value chain in the organization and, concomitently, internalization of certain activities which incorporate the essential knowledge needed in the enterprise chain value.
- Focalization of the enterprise activities on the essential knowledge creation, share, use, and valorification.
- Transfer of the management emphasis from work process to the knowledge involved — both explicit and implicit knowledge — and to their owners" (knowledge-based specialists).
- Intensive informatization of the enterprise work processes determined by the essential role of the knowledge creation, use and valorization, replacing the emphasis on work (cazon) discipline, predominantly in the classic capitalist enterprise.

The synergetic result of all mentioned changes is the superior functionality of companies activities and of their procesual organization.

3. New Organizational Configuration in the Knowledge-Based Medium Enterprises

The systemic dimension of the organization's functions is not only maintainned, but it is even amplified. In the same time, **importance and impact of certain functions** on the company's performance increase comparatively with classical capitalist enterprise.

- R&D function and, especially, technical activity becomes vital for the enterprise. Innovation in product and technology increases and accelerates. As a consequence of this evolution, the role of the technical creativity processes amplifies and, concomitently, their integration with activities of the production and commercial functions.
- In the context of the hyper-concurrence and of the continued modification of the market requirements, the commercial function, in its components, especially marketing activity (Lindsey, 2002) get more impact on the enterprise competitivity.
- Transformation of modern companies in the learning organizations determines a significant increase in the size and in the impact of the human resource function and especially of the training activity. As a consequence, certain specialists (Fisk) have started to consider the training activity as becaming an autonomous function, outside of human resource function.

In parallel — we observe a rapid and consistent development of numerous and heterogeneous processes focused on the knowledge treatment. All these processes constitute a new organization function — **knowledge function**. Processes incorporated in the knowledge function are presented in two ways:

(a) As processes itself, without overlapping with other company's activities. For example, the creation of new knowledge within the design department.
(b) Processes of knowledge treatment integrated in other companies activities — sale, supply, fabrication a.s.a.

In the context of the knowledge-based economy development, in the knowledge-based organisation, both ways intensify, generating more functionality and sustainability.

As we already mentionned, **training activity** amplifies its role, size, impact, and performances and **becames an autonomous function of the enterprise**. This chapter is supported by the scientific work of the International Labour Organisation specialists. The

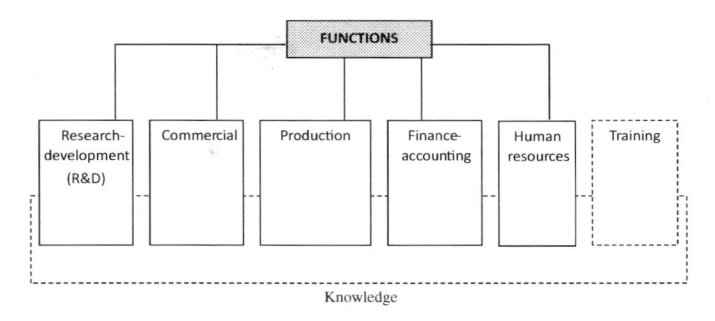

Fig. 1. Specific configuration of organization functions in the knowledge-based enterprise

intensification of the organisational and individual learning processes in knowledge-based company and their increasing impact on the enterprise functionability and performance represent a valuable proof in this aspect. In Fig. 1, we present the specific configuration of the organisation functions in the medium and large knowledge-based enterprises.

4. Knowledge Function

All informations presented so far argues that knowledge represent the determinant element for the functionality of the knowledge-based enterprise.

The **knowledge function could be defined** as the all organization processes focused on the knowledge treatment, which provide the necessary knowledge, use, develop, protect, and valorize them, making a decisive contribution to the generation of the competitive products and to the competitivity and sustainability of the company. In Fig. 2, we present the main activities which make up the knowledge function. In the next paragraphs we shortly present the content of each activity.

- **Identification of the knowledge necessary to the enterprise** and its components, in order to achieve its objectives. Identification of the necessary knowledge is realized both inside and outside of the organization, in its environment. Identification of the knowledge necessary to the company employees involves special actions in certain fields of the company environment, where it is probable and possible to discover these knowledges, in the condition of the best relation price-quality. An important role in this

```
┌─────────────────────────────────┐
│   Knowledge identification      │
└─────────────────────────────────┘
              │
              ▼
┌─────────────────────────────────┐
│     Knowledge purchase          │
└─────────────────────────────────┘
              │
              ▼
┌─────────────────────────────────┐
│ Knowledge learning and assimilation │
└─────────────────────────────────┘
              │
              ▼
┌─────────────────────────────────┐
│      Knowledge creation         │
└─────────────────────────────────┘
              │
              ▼
┌─────────────────────────────────┐
│      Knowledge storage          │
└─────────────────────────────────┘
              │
              ▼
┌─────────────────────────────────┐
│       Knowledge share           │
└─────────────────────────────────┘
              │
              ▼
┌─────────────────────────────────┐
│        Knowledge use            │
└─────────────────────────────────┘
              │
              ▼
┌─────────────────────────────────┐
│     Knowledge protection        │
└─────────────────────────────────┘
              │
              ▼
┌─────────────────────────────────┐
│     Knowledge valorisation      │
└─────────────────────────────────┘
```

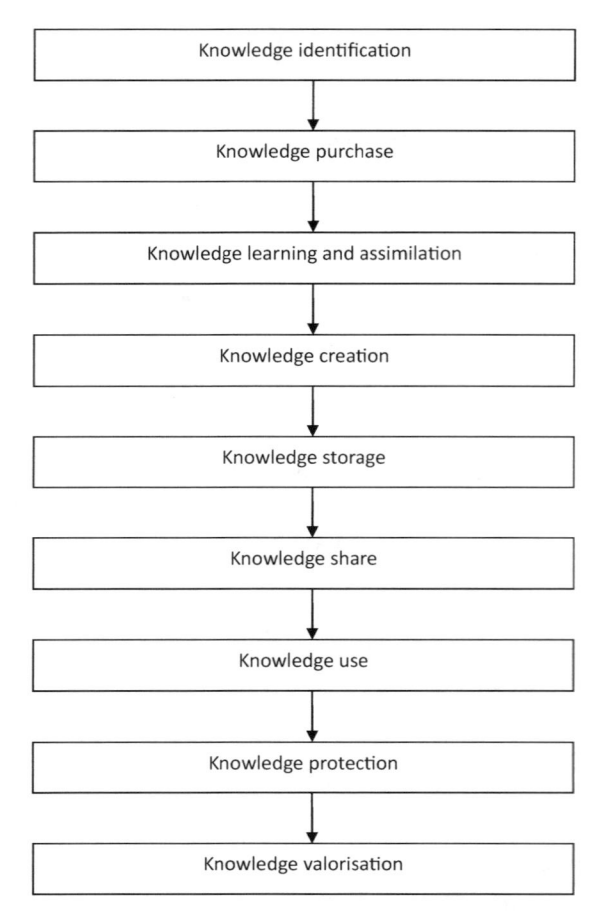

Fig. 2. Activities contained by organization knowledge function

activity is played by the knowledge intermediaries — knowledge stewardesses, knowledge brokers, knowledge researchers a.s.a.

- **Knowledge purchase** is used by company only when the necessary knowledge has been identified in other organizations or to knowledge specialists outside the company. The knowledge aquisition, in order to be successful, should be very well prepared and the knowledge price and other knowledge characteristics should be corelated with the company's necessities, possibilities, and priorities. The main role in the knowledge aquisition should be played by the company specialists in the field of knowledge, who shall use them.

- **Knowledge learning and assimilation** by the company and its employees. Knowledge identification and knowledge purchase are not enough (sufficient) for the organisation. All these knowledges should be assimilated (integrated) using learning processes by the company human resources. Knowledge learning could be a formal process, using special training courses or informal processes, realized by individual specialists efforts, and endeavors. Practices in medium enterprises demonstrate that the most part of new knowledge are obtained by employees using informal ways.

- **Knowledge creation** is necessary for company objectives achievement when the present knowledge is not sufficient and when the knowledge purchase is not possible or is too expensive. Knowledge creation is very common in the knowledge-based enterprises because usually there are focused on innovation and their specialists have high creativity abilities. Knowledge creation in medium knowledge-based companies has a decisive role in getting its competitive advantage and sustainability.

- **Knowledge storage**, refers to the company's own knowledge and the purchased knowledge is a very important activity for the company. Knowledge storage should be very well conceived in order to assure the company specialists and departments easy access to knowledge and the low costs with knowledge store and protection.

- **Knowledge share** represents — according to many specialists (Amaravadi & Lee, 2005; Calrero & Calrero, 2005; Hutzschnreuter & Harstkotte, 2010) one of the most important, difficult, and complex work processes based on knowledge. Knowledge productivity and value depends on their common access, assimilation, debate, analysis, and use of the interested company's specialists and departments. Knowledge share is based both on formal and informal approaches. Formal approach consists in special company messages (announcements) regarding the knowledge existence, knowledge distribution to the specialists interested, organization of special knowledge presentation and discussion a.s.o. Informal approach refers to the spontaneous discussion, exchange of views, and other usually communication ways among the company employees. To large extend it depends on the company culture and the personal example of managers.

- **Knowledge use** is, without any dought, a key process which quantitatively is quite often used, predominantly in the company's work processes. In order to be effective and efficient the knowledge use should be done by competent employees, in the optim period, in the certain company departments, and using right ways and tools.

- **Knowledge protection** is increasingly becoming an important company activity. The main reasons for this evolution are the following: rapid proliferation of the explicit knowledge in company; knowledge essential capacity of demultiplication, which allows the same knowledge to be used in the same time by many specialists; electronic storage of an important part of company's knowledge, which is very difficult to stop the access of unauthorized users. Knowledge protection should be organized (done) without making its access difficult and with the help of the company specialists' involvement.
- **Knowledge valorization** could be done directly inside the company by producing new or better products and services. This is the most used way to valorize the company knowledge. The second way of company's knowledge valorization is to sell them to other companies. The knowledge's high fluidity and the rapid moral depreciation could be faced by company deploying fast feed-back and using performant commercial and technical skills. Knowledge valorization should provide the financial resources necessary to assure company's current work and its sustainability.

5. Training Function

According to our analysis, **the new training function** in the medium knowledge-based companies is different from training activity in classical companies from many points of view (see Fig. 3).

The support for these characteristics is represented to a large extend — **by the sustainable education concept** (Fien *et al.*, 2009) developed during last few years. Strong specificity of the knowledge-based company training is reflected with the appearance of the new knowledge-based specialist — organizational learning agent (Skyrme, 2002) — who has the following features:

- Proactive in action, but reflexive in thinking.
- High aspiration for training and performance, but realistic regarding the company's limits.

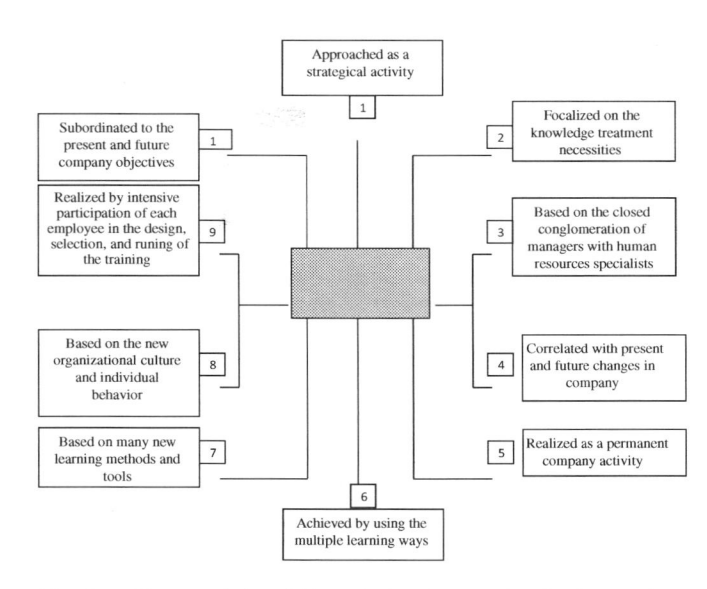

Fig. 3. Characteristics differentiating the training in the medium knowledge-based enterprises and the training activity in the classical medium enterprise

- Critic in analysis, but constructive and dedicate in solutions and actions.
- Independent in thinking, but cooperant with others in training activities.

Company practice demonstrates that organisational learning agents could have a substantial contribution to the high performant training. In training function in the knowledge-based company there are used a large variety of training ways (formal, informal, in company or outside a.s.a.). Naturally, the programs' content is different to a large extend from one company to other, or for the same organization from a period to another. According to the specialists (Dalkir, 2008; Singh, 2009) even in these conditions the following elements should be used in company training programs:

(a) Up-to-date ways and tools to create, purchase, share, use, valorize, protect a.s.a. the knowledge.
(b) Changes in informatics and communication technologies.
(c) Last evolutions in the company markets and its local, regional, national, and international environment.
(d) Recent changes and tendencies in the technical and technological fields of the company and other related branches.

6. Main Particularities of the "Classical" Enterprise Functions

Based on the elements presented in the previous paragraphs and on the other analysis (Boissot, 1998) we shall reveal the main particularities of the five classical functions in the medium knowledge-based enterprise.

6.1. R&D function

Main **particularities of the R&D function** — which contains pre-vision activity, technical design (conception) activity, and organisation activity — within knowledge-based company are the following:

- Size increasement of its three main activities, both absolutely and relatively, based on the intensive participative approach and knowledge-based specialists competence.
- Knowledge-based experts — to a large extent — are working in R&D activities.
- Change speed of the R&D activities; content and ways are higher in the knowledge-based enterprise.
- New products generated by the R&D activities incorporate large knowledge quantity, which are determinant factors for obtaining competitive advantage and enterprise sustainable development.
- R&D activities are quite frequently achieved by enterprise knowledge-based communities.
- Knowledge-based R&D function impact is increasingly an imporatnt determinant on the enterprise's functionality and performance.

6.2. Commercial function

Commercial function, made up of marketing, purchase, and sell activities, presents the following major **particularities**:

- The commercial function's importance and complexity is amplifying constantly, asking for more knowledge with a high specificity, which the smaller size companies are finding it very difficult to have and to develop profitably.
- Externalization of the marketing work processes using very high quality knowledge is a strong tendency in the last decades in medium knowledge-based enterprise.
- Externalization of many purchase and sell activities, especially those using very specialized equipments and knowledge.
- Amplification of the marketing, purchase, and sell actions which focused on the international markets.
- Commercial functional impact on the medium enterprise functionality and performance increases because of the internationalization and the hyper-concurrence.

6.3. Production function

This function is made of several activities — production schedule, fabrication or exploitation, quality control, equipment maintenance and repair, production of the utilities. Its main **particularities** are the followings:

- Size of the work processes has the tendency to decrease because of highly automatized equipments and of very modern technologies used in knowledge medium size companies.
- Rapid intellectualization of work processes within production function; physical work having the tendency to dissappear in production activity.
- Human resource used has high level skills, medium companies using to a large extend knowledge-based specialists, increasingly with university degrees.
- Innovative dimension of the production activities is amplifying, quite often they generate new knowledge integrated in new products, services, and technologies.
- Production activities are focalized on the company chain value and in the same time certain work processes regarding repairing, maintenance, or utilities production are frequently externalized.
- Production function — which in many medium-sized companies in the industry, agriculture, or construction remain predominantly quantitative — continue to have a high impact on their performances.

6.4. Finance — accounting function

This medium company function has three main activities — finance, accounting, and financial-control (audit). According to our analysis, **the main particularities** of finance-accounting function are the followings:

- Size of work processes decreases because of information codification, financial documents standardization, informatization and/or externalization of certain specific work processes, especially in financial audit and accounting.
- Financial activity has the tendency to dominate this function, both qualitatively and quantitatively, using more sophisticated financial, business and mangement knowledge.
- Human resources involved in finance-accounting work processes are very high-skilled and few in number.
- Amplification of information categories are taken into consideration in the design and achievement of financial processes, because of the business internationalization and of the rapid changes in finance and banking systems at national and international level.
- Impact of financial-accounting function on the knowledge-based organization's functionality and performances remains high, having a tendency to increase in periods of economic crisis and during companies' economic stress.

6.5. *Human resources function*

Personnel or human resources company function contains the followings main activities: provision of necessary human resources; enterprise personnel calification; human resources selection; personnel integration in the company; human resources evaluation; personnel motivation; enterprise's employee training; personnel promotion; human resources protection. According to our analysis, the most relevant **particularities** of human resources function in the medium knowledge-based company are:

- Size and complexity of human resources' activities amplify because of the increasing role of human resources mainly made of knowledge-based employees in the obtaining, sharing, using, valorizing a.s.o. of the organization's knowledge.
- Human resource function is extending its actions to the main company stakeholders (clients, buyers, bankers, consultants a.s.a.) in order to atract, share, use and valorize their knowledges.
- Content of each human resource activity is changing because the organization's management is focused more and more on knowledge, the main source of obtaining competitive advantage.
- Training processes have a decisive impact on the knowledge-based company functionality and performance, becoming (as we already mentioned) an autonomus company function in large and medium-sized companies.
- In motivational activity occurs major changes, its framework and content are remodelated, in order to facilitate a better knowledge use, development, and valorization.
- Overall impact of the human resources function in the medium knowledge-based companies increases on organization functionality and competitivity, because they posses the most part of the company knowledge.

7. Concluding Remarks

Based on the elements presented in previous paragraphs we could formulate **several concluding remarks** regarding knowledge-based medium enterprise and its management.

- The numerous and deep changes in organization's functions demonstrate that the medium knowledge-based enterprises is very different from the medium classic capitalist enterprise. We have a new configuration of enterprise functions with many particularities.
- New functions configuration of the knowledge-based medium enterprises demand new types of organization structure, able to facilitate and contribute to a performing organisation system.
- Knowledge-based community is the main component of knowledge-based organization system.
- New functions configuration determines many changes in the company's decisions at the entire organisational level and at the level of each procesual and structural component. As a result, decisional system of knowledge-based medium enterprise should be remodelated.

Management, financial, commercial, juridical a.s.a. methods and tools used in medium enterprises should be changed to a large extent. The specialists already have conceived a lot of new specific methods and techniques focussing on knowledge treatment. Among them we enumerate: Kim model (Kim, 2003) best practice method (Melcrum Research Report, 2002), informational space model elaborated by Boissot, People-Capacity Model (P-CMM), knowledge audit (Nicolescu & Nicolescu, 2011), social network analysis (Nicolescu & Nicolescu, 2005), knowledge matrix (Powell, 2004) a.s.o.

- Concomitantly, most part of management, finance, commercial, informatic a.s.o. methods and techniques started to change in order to be able to valorize the knowledge-based company specificities (Melcrum Research Report, 2002). Practically, in knowledge-based medium enterprise we redesign a new methodologic system.
- Information system in the knowledge-based company also change deeply. Information system is redesigned in order to be able to process large quantity of knowledge, mainly explicit knowledge and especially to valorize them. In order to achieve this, information system should modify deeply its structure and functional characteristics.
- Human resource system of the knowledge-based enterprise should be modified in order to determine the company employees and its main stakeholders to create, learn, obtain, share, use, and valorize the high quality of knowledge necessary to the company.

Redesigning of the five management subsystems — organizational, methodological, decisional, informational, and human resources — demands a new management system, radically different from those of previous period. The principles and basic rules to be used in designing or redesigning the knowledge management system have been already elaborated by management specialists (Friedman, 2002; Jennex; King, 2006; Prothmann & Clarke, 2005; Russ, 2010).

All elements presented in this chapter argues the necessity to promote a new type of management — knowledge-based management — to be able to assure the functionality and the competivity of the knowledge-based medium enterprise.

References

Angela, A. & Oxbrow, N. (2002), *Competing with Knowledge*, pp. 20–24, London: Library Association Publishing.

Amaravadi, C & Lee, I. (2005), The dimensions of process knowledge, *Knowledge and Process Management*, 12(1), pp. 24–25.

Boissot, M. (1998), *Knowledge Assets*, pp. 64–92, Oxford: Oxford University Press.

Calrero, F. & Calrero, A. (2005), Fostering knowledge sharing through people management practices, *International Journal of Human Resource Management*, 6(5).

Dalkir, K. (2008), *Knowledge Management in Theory and Practice*, pp. 94–104, Amsterdam: Elsevier.

Fien, J., McLean, R., & Port, M. (2009), *Work, Learning and Sustenable Development*, pp. 382–392, Tokyo: Springer.

Fisk, P. (2004), *Genii în Marketing*, pp. 18–20, București: Editura Meteor Press.

Friedman, V. (2002), The individual as agent of organizational learning, *California Management Review*, 44(2), pp. 147–150.

Hutzschnreuter, T. & Harstkotte, J. (2010), Knowledge transfer to partners: A firm level perspective, *Journal of Knowledge Management*, 3, pp. 246–252.

Jennex, M. (2002), Knowledge management system succes factors. In D. Schwartz, pp. 436–441.

Kessels, J. (2001), Learning in organization: A corporate curriculum for the knowledge economy, *Futures*, 33(6), pp. 74–77.

Kim, M. (2003), A knowledge management model for SMEs în the knowledge based economy. In xxx, *Entrepreneurship and Innovation in the Knowledge Based Economy: Challenges and Strategies*, pp. 18–19, Tokyo: APO.

King, W. (2006), Knowledge sharing. In *Encyclopedia of Knowledge Management*, D. Swartz (ed.), pp. 493–498, Hershey: Idea Group Reference.

Lindsey, K. (2002), *Knowledge Sharing Barriers*. In D. Swartz, pp. 499–506.

Melcrum Research Report (2002), Learning and Development, in the Electronic Age.

Nicolescu, O. & Nicolescu, L. (2005), *Economia, Organizația și Managementul Bazate pe Cunoștințe*, pp. 103–110, Bucharest: Economica Publishing House.

Nicolescu, O. & Nicolescu, C. (2011), *Organizația și Managementul Bazate pe Cunoștințe*, pp. 110–142, 118–124, 312–317, 222–228, București: ProUniversitaria.

Powell, T. W. (2004), The knowledge matrix: A proposed taxonomy for entreprise knowledge. In *Knowledge Management Lessons Learned — What Works and What*

Doesn't, E. Michael, D. Koenig, and T. Srikantaiah (eds.), pp. 227–237, Medford: Information Today Inc.

Prokopenko, J. (1998), *Management Development, A Guide for Profession*, pp. 340–348, Geneva: ILO.

Prothmann, M. T. & Clarke, S. (2005), Use and methods of social network analysis in knowledge management. In *Encyclopedia of Communities of Practice in Information and Knowledge Management*, E. Coakes (ed.), pp. 565–574, Hershey: Idea Group.

Russ, M. (2010), *Knowledge Management Strategies for Business Development*, pp. 64–83, Hershey: Business Science.

Skyrme, D. J. (2002), *Best Practices in Best Practices*, pp. 10–24, New York: David Skyrme Associates.

Chapter 21

Preparing Our Students for an Entrepreneurial Life: Are Universities Part of the Solution or Part of the Problem

Lester Lloyd-Reason

Anglia Ruskin University

In a report recently produced by the National Council for Graduate Entrepreneurship (NCGE), the National Endowment for Science, Technology and the Arts (NESTA) and the Council for Industry and Higher Education (CIHE) concluded that "Entrepreneurship education is currently taught primarily through modules in business school courses and extra-curricular activities. Higher Education Institutions (HEIs) need to enhance the perception and relevance of entrepreneurship education, so students and staff recognize the value of its combination of innovation, creativity, collaboration, and risk-taking skills to a wide range of disciplines."

This chapter will firstly explore the key issues raised by the policy community and others calling into question the appropriateness of the way in which enterprise and entrepreneurship is taught. It will then look at the way in which universities are responding to these comments. The chapter will call for a change in the way universities around the globe respond to the challenges of the 21st century in terms of entrepreneurship education and will conclude with a number of examples of both pedagogical and projects delivered by academics and entrepreneurs by way of an example of best practice.

1. Introduction

Over the last 20 years or so, there has been an ever increasing level of academic and policy interest in the role of higher education institutions (HEIs) as agents of economic and social development, through not only their research and teaching activities but also their engagement with individuals and businesses in the wider local and regional economy. The 2008 report from the Council for Industry and Higher Education (CIHE), the National Council for Graduate Entrepreneurship and National Endowment for Science, Technology and the Arts (NESTA) in the United Kingdom notes that 'HEIs have increasingly become more involved in regional economic and social development (through closer business, industry, and third sector collaborations …) and activities such as the commercialization of intellectual property' (NESTA, 2008).

Across a range of developed market economies, there have been a number of policy statements which have outlined ways in which the outreach or 'third leg' activities of HEIs can be enhanced and supported. In the United Kingdom, for example, the Innovation White Paper (Department for Innovation, Universities and Skills (DIUS), 2008a), the Enterprise Strategy

(BERR, 2008) and the Employer Engagement Reforms (DIUS, 2008b) all outline different scenarios for HEIs supporting the development of the capabilities and skills of individuals and businesses to survive and thrive. At a Pan-European level, The Oslo Agenda for Entrepreneurship Education in Europe (2006) calls for: better integration across subject areas, improved practice-based pedagogical tools, and better approaches to teamwork, whether internal or external (through collaboration with industry and business). In the UK, in 2008, the department of Business, Enterprise and Regulatory Reform developed a new strategy as part of the UK government's vision to 'make the UK the most enterprising economy in the world and the best place to start and grow a business (BERR, 2008).

In 2010 the current UK administration reiterated this vision leading to the 2011 White Paper for Higher Education 'Students at the Heart of the System' which emphasized entrepreneurship education. At a global level, the need to promote entrepreneurship education has been recognized and promoted by a great number of governmental and non-governmental bodies such as the World Economic Forum report to the Global Education Initiative in 2009 titled *"Educating the Next Wave of Entrepreneurs: Unlocking entrepreneurial capabilities to meet the global challenges of the 21st Century"* and The United National Conference for Trade and Development (UNCTAD) 2010 report "The importance of entrepreneurship".

2. The HEI Response

This policy narrative has manifested itself in programs of support and funding streams including the Higher Education Reach Out into the Business and Community Fund, the Science and Enterprise Challenge Fund, and the Higher Education Innovation Fund. Reflecting this need to encourage small firm activity, universities in the United Kingdom have been encouraged to participate in programs to increase the numbers of students of enterprise and assist them in starting their own business. As a result, HEIs have introduced a range of activities and initiatives to support students and staff in engaging with their community and vice-versa. Incubation spaces, technology transfer offices, business planning competitions and business development programs are now common across the HEI landscape.

Evidence from economies such as the United States highlights the potential contribution of enterprising students to competitiveness and productivity, particularly through facilitating organizational change and business start-up. By the year 2000, business and entrepreneurial development had been listed by Universities UK as one of four strategic goals for British Universities. Hannon *et al.* (2004) report on statistics from the United States that demonstrates that business start-ups by graduates accounts for between 6% and 8% of national GDP. More recently, the European Directorate General for Enterprise and Industry's report, Effects and Impact of Entrepreneurship Programs in Higher Education (2012), presents results that clearly indicate that entrepreneurship education in higher education makes a difference. It has impact on intention, competence and employability and generally benefits society and the economy. The report underlines the importance of developing effective educational capacity across all disciplines.

As a guide to the skills requirement of enterprise students, the QAA Framework for Higher Education Qualifications (England) in General Business and Management states that 'Preparation for business should be taken to mean the development of a range of specific business knowledge and skills, together with the improved self-awareness and personal development appropriate to graduate careers in business with the potential for management positions and to employability in general. This includes the encouragement of positive and critical attitudes towards change and enterprise, so as to reflect the dynamism and vibrancy of the business environment'.

However, despite the policy initiatives, qualification guidelines and a huge increase in enterprise and entrepreneurship provision within HEIs, there is much evidence of a mismatch between the supply of graduates and the skills required to success within the contemporary business environment. Research undertaken by CIHE demonstrates a gap between perceived importance and levels of satisfaction in terms of commercial awareness and communication skills. Archer & Davison (2008) note that:

> *It appears that while many graduates hold satisfactory qualifications, they are lacking in the key "soft" skills and qualities that employers increasingly need in a more customer focused world.*

In their 2008 report, the NCGE, the NESTA and the CIHE concluded that 'Entrepreneurship education is currently taught primarily through modules in business school courses and extra-curricular activities. HEIs need to enhance the perception and relevance of entrepreneurship education, so students and staff recognize the value of its combination of innovation, creativity, collaboration and risk-taking skills to a wide range of disciplines'.

In the intervening years since these reports were published, the groundswell of policy advice, supported by an increasingly sophisticated range of university initiatives and developments in the area of enterprise and entrepreneurship education, does not appear to have adequately addressed the problem of producing graduates with an appropriate enterprising skills set. In the Wilson Report (2012), a review of Business–University collaboration conducted by Prof. Sir Tim Wilson the message was loud and clear, although perhaps somewhat diplomatically expressed:

> "Universities should reflect on the strategies they use to ensure that students have the opportunity to develop enterprise skills both through the formal curriculum and through optional study or practice, and reflect on the integration of enterprise education in the professional development programmed for academic staff."

3. So Where are We Now: The Current State of Play within the Higher Education Sector

The European Commission Green Paper on Entrepreneurship (2008) states that within university entrepreneurship training should not only be for MBA students it should also be available for students in other fields. However, with a few notable exceptions this has not happened within the Higher Education sector. Indeed even within Business schools the whole enterprise agenda has been undervalued resulting in an uneven offering across the sector where in the main enterprise as a subject remains on the periphery offered either as an option elective or at best bolted on to the pervading corporate model of education to create a degree program that has enterprise/entrepreneurship the title, but with little change in the content and none in teaching methodology.

There has in business schools been an attempt to define the subject area for example is teaching for enterprise or about entrepreneurship. These words are often seen as synonymous; however, entrepreneurship is in essence about starting a new venture. Enterprise is the whole concept of how students need to think in a completely different way to face the challenge of work in the 21st century. It is important therefore to define what we mean by "Enterprise Education" and "Entrepreneurship Education" (QAA, 2012).

Enterprise is defined here as the application of creative ideas and innovations to practical situations. This is a generic concept that can be applied across all areas of education. It combines creativity, ideas development and problem solving with expression, communication and practical action. This definition is distinct from the generic use of the word in reference to a project or business venture.

Enterprise education aims to produce graduates with the mindset and skills to come up with original ideas in response to identified needs and shortfalls, and the ability to act on them. In short, having an idea and making it happen. Enterprise skills include taking the initiative, intuitive decision-making, making things happen, networking, identifying opportunities, creative problem solving, innovating, strategic thinking, and personal effectiveness. Enterprise education extends beyond knowledge acquisition to a wide range of emotional, intellectual, social, and practical skills.

Entrepreneurship is defined as the application of enterprise skills specifically to creating and growing organizations in order to identify and build on opportunities.

Entrepreneurship education focuses on the development and application of an enterprising mindset and skills in the specific contexts of setting up a new venture, developing and growing an existing business, or designing an entrepreneurial organization.

Entrepreneurship education aims to produce graduates who are capable of identifying opportunities and developing ventures, through setting up new businesses or developing and growing part of an existing venture. It focuses on encouraging students to apply enterprising skills and attributes to a range of different contexts, including new or existing businesses, charities, non-governmental organizations, the public sector, and social enterprises.

If we accept therefore, that enterprise is about the development of an enterprising skill set, the 'soft' skills so craved by employers, and that entrepreneurship represents the application of that skills set in the recognition and exploitation of business opportunities. In terms of the development of appropriate academic programs within the Higher Education sector, this translates into a need for course that are 'about' rather than the more traditional courses which are more 'about' courses.

"*About*" courses are intended to help students to assimilate and reflect upon existing knowledge and resources that enhance their understanding of a topic or theme, for example, venture creation and business growth strategies. They tend to draw upon a more traditional pedagogy involving lectures and set texts to explore the theoretical underpinnings of enterprise and entrepreneurship. Students may learn how enterprise and entrepreneurship has evolved as a discipline and be able to critically evaluate the relevant literature.

"*For*" courses focus on creating enterprising mindsets in graduates and help them to discover what it is to be enterprising, as well as offering insights into being an entrepreneur. These courses are normally delivered via experiential learning opportunities that engage and enhance the student's abilities and skills, set within a meaningful and relevant context. They challenge the student to think about the future and visualize opportunities. Learners will typically be engaged in scenarios that challenge their thinking and make explicit the need for creativity and innovation. As with all academic disciplines, practice should be underpinned by theory, so an ideal combination is to include learning both "about" and "for" within the curriculum.

In other words, the value of current knowledge and its delivery in an environment where change occurs at great pace and the ability to harvest knowledge as and when needed becomes more important than being reliant on facts and figures. To put it another way, what is a correct solution today may not be a correct solution tomorrow. In this complex learning environment, despite the abundance of information, processing it and linking and connecting becomes the imperative, not merely recalling it. Self-efficacy, for example, the confidence to try something out and to survive repeated failures is often as reliant on motivational drivers as it is knowledge.

We need to help our students to develop an entrepreneurial mindset, to not just feel comfortable with ambiguity, but to thrive in it, to understand the value of creative thinking, and to be able to generate creative solutions. Within our universities, there is a need for enterprise to triumph over process, for innovation to be regarded as more important than systems thinking. Yet the reality is that enterprise and innovation are discouraged, frowned upon and those seeking to promote them at best tolerated and at worst regarded as disruptive influences. The expert psychologist Theresa Amabile has suggested that those of us working within universities need to check what we are doing in terms of motivational activities such as being creative and trying new things out for ourselves:

"Creativity is undermined unintentionally every day in work environments that were established for entirely good reasons to maximize business imperatives such as coordination, productivity and control ... in working toward these imperatives, they may be inadvertently designing organizations that systematically crushes creativity" (Amabile, 1997).

Of course, not everyone will want to start a business, but all students need to be enterprising both for success in the work place and to add value to society. Therefore business schools need to change the way they both structure and deliver enterprise education. They have not thus far taught enterprise skills except where they are seen as relevant to understanding new venture creation, thus making it appear that this "special few" who are entrepreneurial have or need such a capability. Indeed most of such entrepreneurial programs are formulaic in structure and traditionalist in methodology, which only serves to underpin the view that entrepreneurs are different to the rest of mainstream business. This has been and still is a very dangerous weakness in the understanding shown by universities about the enterprise agenda and it is importance to their collective futures.

There has then to be a major cultural change in the way universities operate if they are to face these changes that are coming. Acceptance that there needs to be a move to a model of integrated learning with more student management of the process and a wide and more innovative use of technology is essential.

Universities have to move rapidly from an educational orthodoxy based on separate disciplines being taught in silos and managing the learning process by and arcane approach to teaching and learning that is reliant on didactic teaching approach and the production of ever more obtuse work books to an educational methodology that embraces the concept of enterprise and integrated business skills thus placing them at the center of the curriculum and not on the periphery.

Further there has to be a much deeper understanding that such activities as creativity, problem solving, understanding innovation, risk management and culture change coupled with decision-making and confidence building which in turn leads to self reliance, open minded respect for evidence and a willingness to take on responsibility, are the absolute core issues of the enterprise concept.

In order to achieve this change, universities need to interact more with the entrepreneurial world by bringing successful enterprising people into the development and delivery process. This is something again which many universities have not embraced due to a culture of academic insulation that if not changed will render them increasingly non competitive.

4. Embedding Practitioner Experience: A Case Study — BA (Hons) in Enterprise and Entrepreneurial Management

4.1. Background to the course

The objective behind the development of this course was to address many of the issues identified above through establishing a benchmark program in the area of enterprise and entrepreneurial management. It provides the students with conceptual and theoretical insights into enterprise, innovation and entrepreneurial management, as well as the practical abilities and skills to apply this understanding within a range of different business, community and organizational contexts.

It has been developed by the Centre for Enterprise Development and Research (CEDAR) within the Lord Ashcroft International Business School (LAIBS), Anglia Ruskin University, Cambridge, UK. CEDAR is the first UK Institute for Enterprise and Entrepreneurs (IOEE) Centre for Excellence and has run programs promoting enterprise development and enterprise education across the world.

With regard to curriculum design, CEDAR worked in close conjunction with a wide range of successful entrepreneurs from Cambridge in the UK and elsewhere to ensure that the course from conception to delivery succeeded in blending theory and practice in a meaningful way to develop a coherent academic program. The extensive academic and entrepreneurial networks at CEDAR allowed practitioners to be involved from the outset. An 'entrepreneur in residence' network was established to ensure that leading entrepreneurs were closely embedded in the fabric of the course from the start, playing a very active role in the continued development of the curriculum, content, and delivery of the academic program. In this way the course blends theory and practice to provide graduates of the program with the skills, attitudes and aptitude required if they are to thrive in a highly complex, fast changing business environment.

It is important to stress that the aim in developing the 'entrepreneur in residence' network is to embed enterprise and the experiences of entrepreneurs within the academic program. This allows for the strong, theoretical underpinning of a university academic program to be interlaced with the insights and experiential learning brought into the lecture room by this group of world class entrepreneurs.

A key role of the entrepreneur is one of mentoring the students. In addition to the Personal Tutor appointed under the University Personal Tutoring system, each student on the course is allocated a member of the 'entrepreneur in residence' network who acts as their personal mentor for the duration of the academic program. The Personal Tutor and the entrepreneur will then work closely together to support the ongoing learning needs of the student. This creates a very strong link between the Personal Tutor system and the 'entrepreneur in residence' network whist at the same time providing the student with a very powerful learning support structure.

Before briefly describing the academic program, below is a brief profile of some of the entrepreneurs involved in the course.

Walter Herriot
Director of the Entrepreneur in Residence Network, Managing Director, St. John's Innovation Centre

Walter Herriot built St. John's Innovation Centre into one of the most successful business incubators in the world. Regarded as one of the founders of the Cambridge Phenomenon, Walter is Chair of the Cambridge Chamber of Commerce, Chairs both the EEDA Enterprise Hubs in the East of England and Enterprise East and is a member of the steering committee of the Greater Cambridge Partnership. A former Cambridge Evening News "Businessman of the Year", in 1999 Walter was awarded an OBE for services to enterprise.

Billy Boyle
Co-founder/Director Owlstone Ltd

Billy Boyle is co-founder and director of Owlstone which develops and commercializes MEMS chemical sensors for industrial and military use. Founded in 2004, Owlstone currently employs 30 people, has raised USD 10 mn in the USA and has won a USD 3.7 mn contract from the US Department of Defence. Billy is first and co-author on numerous conference and journal papers, has presented at a number of prestigious international conferences and is co-inventor of 19 patents.

Peter Taylor
Managing Director, TTP Group plc

Peter, a Cambridge physicist, is Managing Director of TTP Group, the holding company for a number of international high-technology companies supplying products, R&D services and venture capital. He is Chairman of The Technology Partnership plc, Europe's leading independent technology development and licensing business and TTP Group's principal operating subsidiary. In 1987, he was one of the founders of TTP and subsequently built the science-based half of the business. Peter has been responsible for product and technology developments in major markets including healthcare, communications, and consumer products, including the formation of several jointly or wholly-owned companies. Peter was responsible for developing the company's business in Japan and in the field of Digital Printing.

Giulio Cinque
Giulio Man and Woman

Having started working on a market stall, Giulio has built his designer clothing retailer business into one of the most highly regarded designer boutiques in the UK. Now part of a 250 strong global designer clothing network, over 30% of all revenues are generated outside of the UK.

Natalie Haywood
Founder of Leaf Tea Shop and Bar

Natalie is the founder and managing director of the Leaf Tea Shop and Bar, an innovative, award winning tea shop and bar concept, based in Liverpool, UK. She has considerable marketing experience working with small and medium-sized enterprises and is a Chartered Marketer and Young Enterprise Ambassador. Natalie has recently opened two further venues — 'The Garden' a vegetarian focused café and meeting place and 'Oh Me Oh My' a Parisian teahouse, wedding venue and events space. Natalie is regarded as one of the leading young entrepreneurs in the UK, and has been the recipient of numerous awards. She was recently featured in the 2013 Accelerate 250 as one of the 250 fastest growing businesses in the UK.

Paddy Bishopp
Co-founder of Paddy and Scotts

"Paddy's and Scott's Seriously good coffee. A guy who shares a passion for great coffee. Paddy used to own a café which was voted The Best Deli/Café in Suffolk in the UK and harbored a longing desire to roast his own coffee. He strongly believes business should be fun, but producing coffee does have a serious side. Being a father he understands the importance of education and nurturing children. In many situations it is the children in the plantation areas who are forgotten and they end up with very little or no education. By working with organizations such as Fair Trade and Utz Certified the company ensures these communities can invest in future generations.

Amy Mokady
Entrepreneur

Amy Mokady is a serial entrepreneur who has held senior sales, marketing and business development roles in start-ups and multinational companies. She was a co-founder and marketing director of STNC Ltd., which was acquired by Microsoft in 1999. Following roles working at the forefront of the mobile industry at Microsoft, QUALCOMM and Hutchison 3G, more recent start-ups include Pogo Mobile Solutions, Light Blue Optics and Mo. Jo. Amy is also a Director and mentor of several early-stage technology start-ups, a Director of the Greater Cambridge Partnership, and a Board Member of the Cambridge Angels.

Micah John Styles
Managing Director CLR Global Group

Micah is founder and Managing Director of the CLR Global Group, a visionary Group of specialist international recruitment consultancy companies, which has been operating on a truly global scale since 2001. A "Born Global" entrepreneurial business, the CLR Global Group has operations in Qatar, China, Brazil and Mauritius. Prior to founding the CLR Global Group Micah worked in senior finance positions in Media companies in the UK and South Africa and currently directs his commercial endeavors and oversees his worldwide interests from his home in the South of France.

4.2. *The academic program*

With regard to the coverage of key academic areas for the subject, the majority of existing enterprise and entrepreneurship degree programs are either highly practical in nature or 'knowledge' based. The 'about' courses. This course takes the approach of marrying these two together through developing an enterprising skills set alongside the practical application of those skills. Schools and Colleges increasingly report that 'enterprise clubs', 'run your own business' schemes and other programs tend to capture the attention of those students alienated from more traditional subjects and who are likely to drift away from education. Having been persuaded to stay within the education system, upon entering University these students again typically encounter traditional functional subjects such as finance, marketing and HRM. For many students this is perfectly appropriate, but for the type of student likely to be attracted to enterprise and entrepreneurship this fails to capture their imagination, their interest is again lost and they tend either to drift out of the educational system or to badly underperform due to lack of interest or motivation.

This course, through a highly innovative and radical approach to curriculum design and delivery aims to capture the passion and imagination of this neglected group of students. At the outset, the students are introduced to the concept of enterprise through two innovative modules 'Foundations of Enterprise' which provides an understanding of enterprise as a discipline and 'Enterprise in Action' which allows for the initial development of core enterprising abilities and skills.

The 'Enterprise in Action' module, as the name suggests, is a very practical, hands on module. To this end, the development team worked in partnership with

Virgin Money to provide the students with an opportunity to work on a real business opportunity. Virgin Money had for some time been exploring the potential market for a new product. Virgin Money provided the students with their market intelligence and provided a dedicated liaison person and the students were required to prepare an outline business plan for the market potential and the best route to market. This plan was then presented to the senior management at Virgin Money in their boardroom at the conclusion of the module. A remarkable opportunity for first year undergraduate students.

In the second semester the students are placed within an entrepreneurial business, not on a traditional student placement where low level tasks are often undertaken, but to provide exposure to the trading realities facing the entrepreneurial enterpriser and to offer opportunities for personal skills development through such mechanisms as mentoring and shadowing. This is the first stage in the students' outside journey and is called 'Learning in Residence'.

Keith Hermann, Deputy Director of the National Council for Education and Entrepreneurship, has described the "Leaning in Residence" module as *"a fabulous invention and although there are numerous schemes which encourage work-based learning for students via placements, the design of this element of the program is fundamental to its success."*

In the final year, rather than having to produce a dissertation, the students have the opportunity to manage a charity event. The students have to engage with the charity of their choice and then select and run a fund raising event. This challenging module requires the students to put into practice many of the 'soft' skills developed over the three years of the course such as, team work, leadership, creative thinking, problem solving, risk assessment and risk management as well as developing a solid understanding of the concept of networks. The most recent group of final year students organized a black tie dinner and auction raising over £7,000 for water aid.

Consistent with the highly innovative nature of this course, an innovative approach is taken to the learning and teaching methods used to achieve the learning outcomes. That is, the differentiator is not 'what', but 'how'. There are no lectures or tutorials, rather, teaching is undertaken in full day blocks, often away from the University within entrepreneurial businesses and other locations. For example, Paul Bourne, Artistic Director of Menagerie Theatre Company, Managing Director of Ensemble Training and Visiting Fellow at CEDAR takes the students to a theater to take part in the creative process of developing a piece of theater from scratch.

5. Some thoughts in Conclusion

This chapter has identified a number of policy initiatives aimed at promoting the development of skills and capabilities required by graduates if they are to survive and thrive within the modern fast paced, highly competitive entrepreneurial environment. Evidence of the contribution made by enterprising students to competitiveness and production, particularly through facilitating organizational change and business start-up has been cited. However, the key issue underpinning this paper is that HEIs have demonstrated relatively few offerings able to provide students with an awareness of the abilities, behaviors and skills required to compete within different employability contexts.

In recent years there has been growing interest in the area of enterprise education, resulting in a huge increase in the academic literature in the area. This body of work appears to suggest that within universities there largely remains a focus on traditional teaching methods and learning pedagogies such as lectures and case studies. In the paper we note that there is a lack of insight as to how practitioners can be embedded within the development and delivery of enterprise education offerings.

The case study presented here is one of many examples of good practice to be found within the Higher Education sector. Such programs, however, that embed practitioners into the teaching of enterprise and entrepreneurship appear to be the exception rather than the rule. This chapter contends that there are significant weaknesses in the way universities in general approach the teaching of enterprise and entrepreneurship.

The writing is on the wall for those universities in the developed world who may think they lead the way with regard to enterprise and entrepreneurship education. The UNCTAD spent three years investigating what makes an entrepreneurial eco system, concluding that education was one of the key six pillars that policy makers needed to address, the prime call being to "Mainstream the development of entrepreneurship awareness and entrepreneurial behaviors starting from primary school level". UNCTAD's Chief of Entrepreneurship reports that many developing countries are more engaged than countries with more traditional approaches to education, and that based on research developed from the Global Economic Monitor, "entrepreneurial dynamism has been shifting to developing countries".

We would argue that if universities in the developed world wish to counteract this shift, they need to move from a model of educational orthodoxy to a more integrated based approach which interacts in a much more meaningful way with the entrepreneurial world. One of the ways this can be achieved is by bringing successful enterprising people into the development and delivery process. The case study above provides an example of how this can be done efficiently and effectively.

References

Amabile, T. (1997), How to kill creativity, *Harvard Business Review*, 77.

An Education System fit for an Entrepreneur (2014), Fifth Report by the All-Party Parliamentary Group for Micro Businesses.

Archer, W. & Davison, J. (2008), *Graduate Employability: What Do Employers Think and Want?* London: Council for Industry and Higher Education.

Department of Business, Enterprise and Regulatory Reform (BERR) (2008), *Enterprise: Unlocking the UK Talent*, London: The Stationery Office.

Department for Innovation, Universities and Skills (2006), *UK Skills: Prosperity for All in the Global Economy — World Class Skills*, London: The Stationery Office.

Department for Innovation, Universities and Skills (2008a), *Innovation Nation*, London: The Stationery Office.

Department for Innovation, Universities and Skills (2008b), *Higher Education at Work: High Skills, High Value*, London: Department for Innovation, Universities and Skills.

European Commission (2012), *Effects and Impact of Entrepreneurship Programmes in Higher Education*, Brussels: Directorate-General for Enterprise and Industry/European Commission.

Gibb, A. A. (2005), Towards the entrepreneurial university, Policy Paper No. 3, NCGE, Birmingham.

Hannon, P. (2004), Making the journey from student to entrepreneur: A review of existing research into graduate entrepreneurship, Final Report for the National Council for Graduate Entrepreneurship, Birmingham: Institute of Small Business Affairs Consortium.

Hannon, P. (2007), Enterprise for all? The fragility of enterprise provision across England HEIs, *Journal of Small Business and Enterprise Development*, 14(2), 183–210.

Hartshorn, C. & Sear, L. (2005), Employability and enterprise: Evidence from the North East, *Urban Studies*, 42(2), 271–283.

Leaning and Skills Development Agency (2002), *The Howard Davies Review of Enterprise and the Economy in Education*, London: HMSO.

NESTA (2008), *Developing Entrepreneurial Graduates: Putting Entrepreneurship at the Centre of Higher Education*, London: NESTA, National Council for Graduate Entrepreneurship and Council for Industry and Higher Education.

National Council for Graduate Entrepreneurship (2007), *Enterprise and Entrepreneurship in Higher Education*, Birmingham: National Council for Graduate Entrepreneurship.

Mugione, F. (2013), *Joint Inter-Governmental Conference Parliamentary Assembly of the Mediterranean & United Nations Inter-Agency on Trade and Productive Capacity*, Geneva.

QAA (2012), *Enterprise and Entrepreneurship Education: Guidance for UK Higher Education Providers*.

The Oslo Agenda for Entrepreneurship Education in Europe (2006), European Commission, Brussels.

Wilson, T. (2011), *The Wilson Review of University–Business Collaboration*.

Chapter 22

Difficulties in Improving Romanian Companies Management

Corneliu Russu

At the current stage of economic development of the countries of the world, firstly the major industrialized ones, professional potential, strategic vision, and creative ability of managers of companies is one of the most effective springs to ensure sustainable development, modernization of economic activity, and significant competitiveness growth. In the era of globalization, global confrontation of economies, companies and their products/services, the role of this resort is decisive, determinant for successful chances of maintaining in the planetary competition.

The present circumstances are profoundly changed in comparison with those specific to the second half of the last century, and impose to managerial activity significant improvements in dynamism, flexibility, approaches rationality, forecasts realism, rapid response to change.

1. Introduction

At the current stage of economic development of the countries of the world, firstly the major industrialized ones, professional potential, strategic vision and creative ability of managers of companies is one of the most effective springs to ensure sustainable development, modernization of economic activity and significant competitiveness growth. In the era of globalization, global confrontation of economies, companies and their products/services, the role of this resort is decisive, determinant for successful chances of maintaining in the planetary competition.

The present circumstances are profoundly changed in comparison with those specific to the second half of the last century, and impose to managerial activity significant improvements in dynamism, flexibility, approaches rationality, forecasts realism, rapid response to change.

2. Management Challenges of Today and Its Responses

The present period of Romanian society and economy evolution is characterized, in terms of company management, by the existence of some **major challenges** to its address:

— **Strategic** — consisting in urgent requirement to have "strategic visions", to anticipate the changes that will occur, and to outline on this basis the most appropriate strategies to be followed: (i) to achieve the critical size necessary of getting a high level of competitiveness (economies of scale), (ii) to de-specialize and re-specialize on a wider and more competitive product range (economy of range),

(iii) to outsource related activities, which includes the development of subcontracting and production services;
- **Technological** — developing the technological capacity of firms, stimulating and appropriate capitalization of their creative potential, in order to improve products and their distribution, and to increase managerial and trade capacity;
- **Social** — ensuring balance between economic and social, collective, and individual objectives, growing and deepening the social responsibility of companies to the immediate community and society in general, adopting corporate governance to generate plus value for all the stakeholders in welfare of firms and society;
- **Organic** — nurturing care for the environment of existence and action of firms, rational use, and preservation of resources, ensuring the conditions for firms sustainable development, intensive promotion of "eco-efficiency";
- **Psychological** — the requirement to imprint a modern spirit of discipline, efficiency and superior productivity to all staff, promoting "the cult of labor", change of passive mentality, specific to assistance role of the State, into an active one, imposed by the company exposure to discipline and rigors conditions on international markets;
- **Cultural** — deepening and strengthening "enterprise culture", its adaptation to general societal evolution, increasing cultural homogeneity of companies by unitary sharing of their staff of superior values reflected in the concepts, attitudes and behaviors.

In relation to these challenges, management activity in Romanian companies presents conflicting aspects, consisting, on the one hand, mainly, in marked differences of quality and competitiveness between that specific to public companies and to private companies, and on the other hand, between that specific to the foreign firms operating in Romania and of the companies with local capital; these contradictory aspects are determined by inertial perpetuating concepts and attitudes specific to centralized economy, and considerable ability of many managers, especially young people, to respond adequately to the mentioned challenges.

In general, the answer of the Romanian medium manager, especially one from the public-owned firms, to these complex and unavoidable challenges, turns out, unfortunately, still disappointing, empirical evidence of worsening economic and financial performance of a large part of firms still in the public sector, but also many in the private sector, being a convincing confirmation in this sense.

Explanations for reduced capacity of a large part of Romanian companies' managers to adequately respond to the mentioned challenges, and achieve inspiring and accelerated restructuring of their units, are multiple.

(a) *The strategic response*: modest results recorded in economic agents restructuring were determined, to a large extent, by the lack of economic and social development strategy of the country, coherent and consistently followed regardless of the electoral cycles, for clarifying government's vision on future configuration of the Romanian economy and how economic and financial tools will be used to gradually forge this configuration. The absence of this strategy and related industrial policy has made the strategic response of firms to be devoid of clear reference landmarks, difficulty emphasized by the onset of the global financial and economic crisis in 2008;

(b) *The legislative and regulatory response*: regulatory framework instability continuously manifested after 1990 and accelerated in recent years, prevents crystallization of strategic visions on which plans and programs of restructuring and modernization of firms activity are set;

(c) *The financial response*: companies restructuring is a process that requires considerable financial resources necessary to achieve certain deep technical, technological, and organizational changes; in the circumstances of drastic contraction of demand in domestic and international markets, a poor or negative cash flow, termination of welfare role of the State, financial resources are insufficient or lacking, which is a formidable obstacle on the path of firms activities modernization;

(d) *The professional response*: despite participation in numerous training programs in business management, a good part of managers are still far from a scientific basis of their managerial actions (methods, techniques, and tools of modern management), indispensable for successful "piloting" companies in a highly competitive environment internally (dealing with imports products and foreign-owned firms) and internationally;

(e) *The psychological response*: mentalities specific to centralized economy, with assistancy role of the State, still remain strong, avoiding risk — consisting in the absence of engaging in aggressive strategies, capital-risk insurance, etc. — continuing to be a negative feature of the Romanian management;

(f) *The moral response*: failure of many managers of public enterprises to observe managerial ethics and professional deontology led, by extension, to form a widely shared opinion about the moral deficit of the "class" of managers; if one add to this authority crisis the painful social impact of the restructuring programs, uncorrelated with those of retraining and regional and local development, clearly appears as one of the reasons for lack of determined commitment of many managers to initiate comprehensive restructuring programs.

It is obvious that in the generation and perpetuation of a good part of these disturbances the role of managers of firms in such situations is crucial, despite liabilities under management contract.

3. Difficulties Faced by the Management of Romanian Companies

Shown responses to the challenges specific to the management of Romanian companies in the current period, many of them poor responses, as well as reviewed disfunctionalities, have, in large part, obvious explanations in existence of endogenous and exogenous dificulties, whose outrunning requires resolute, firm actions, consistent and coherent at the government and the microeconomic level. Highlighting these difficulties provides necessary benchmark to judicious directing efforts to eradicate them, as a *sine qua non* condition of profound restructuring enterprises' activity, in order to achieve significant productivity, effectiveness and efficiency growth.

3.1. *Endogenous difficulties*

(a) **Shortage of skilled managerial knowledge**, which continues to be a critical dimension for a very important segment of Romanian managers at all levels, the effects of this situation being felt more acutely at the upper level. Although the supply of management training programs of state and private universities, under the form of postgraduate courses, and managerial training specialized centers, including presence of training staff from Western countries, is considerable, and programs are attended by a growing number of managers, at global scale, the level of management knowledge is still insufficient in comparison with the companies management requirements under functional market economy and international competition globalization. Moreover, some of the failures in the market conduct of state-owned companies mentioned earlier have their immediate cause or contributory factor in poor management training, which does not provide essential knowledge range for successful piloting companies activity;

(b) **Continued use of a limited, outdated, managerial tools by a large part of Romanian managers** and called with low frequency to make major decisions for the firms activity, as a natural consequence of the scarcity of expertise mentioned in the precedent point. The explanation of this condition are numerous and represent as many obstacles to achieving higher managerial benefits: scarcity in many enterprise of information necessary to support sound decision; the reluctance of many managers to use seemingly complicated methods and techniques; the short time available for major decisions making; perfunctoriness of participation in management training programs of many managers and specialists with promotion prospects, and so on;

(c) **Shortage of managerial culture** that is intertwined in a mutually reinforcing relationship with the managerial expertise, also significantly threaten managerial activity of public-owned companies. Management culture, which means all representations and conceptual, moral and actionable values dominant in a particular managerial environment (Nicolescu & Verboncu, 2007), is currently confusing and contradictory, being very difficult to outline the archetype of such a culture specific to Romanian environment.

The practices specific to centrally planned economy removed managerial culture elements progressively accumulated and sedimented in many reference companies in the interwar period until 1948. Political pressures and ideological dilettantism in the management of State-owned enterprises, the ideological compromising and, especially, misapplication of modern management methods and techniques have emptied driving acts in centralized economy of the content that really had to have, and have gradually outlined a managerial culture" characterized by improvisation, grotesque miming management science and practice, deliberate distortion of economic and financial performance, lack of purpose, and low overall efficiency.

After 1989, the profound transformations experienced by the Romanian society and economy offered few reference landmarks and favorable conditions for recovery of losses over five decades and accelerated crystallization of a managerial culture that draws nearer to Western standards. Efforts devoted to creating appropriate institutional framework and operational mechanisms of a functioning market economy were made in the absence of a clear strategy for the evolution of Romanian society and the national economy. Also, they were slow and much delayed and not accompanied by efforts for crystallization and strengthening a culture of modern management, consistent with the new economic realities and able to provide significantly increase of activity efficiency and competitiveness. In these circumstances, outlining specific type of Romanian management is difficult;

(d) **The importance of power relations, which is much higher compared to the situation in the consolidated market economies**, in the sense that the social status of each person remains preponderant dependent on its relations with the "power", i.e., managers, and much more less dependent on its professional capacity, his/her performance and the role he/she really plays in the organization. "Power" dependence, taken from the centralized economy and inertially continued, caused degradation of managerial authority and the existence of personal value scale unrelated to the real moral and professional value. Moreover, the position of manager has suffered from exaggerated importance of power relations in two ways: on the one hand, managerial activity is not regarded as one specialized, as a profession, but as a true social status, as a privileged position within the firm; on the other hand, the managers themselves perceive their position as one of a leader and not as professional who occupy it a limited period;

(e) **Chronic distrust in the effectiveness of state institutions**, due to the instability of the legislative and institutional framework, the existence of parallel economy, bureaucratic practices that favor bureaucratic relationships customization, abuse, and corruption. This distrust leads to increasing personal relationships role in business management, frequent avoidance of formal, official channels for problem solving in relations with the State institutions, and the deliberate distortion of information conveyed within these relations;

(f) **Cleavage between generations** is becoming increasingly manifested among Romanian managers: young managers, expert of English language, and Anglo-Saxon management literature, attach great importance to the cognitive component of managerial culture that sometimes leads to a high skill carrying out; managers over 45 years show a certain cognitive limitation, maintain theirs adaptive skills learned in the old regime, and capability of simulation managerial roles they must play;

(g) **Instability of leadership styles**, a feature noted by many foreign specialists who have come into contact with the realities of the Romanian economy and the peculiarities of the Romanian management model; it consists of the fact that many Romanian managers readily pass into relations with subordinates from a rigid attitude to one of excessive tolerance; explanation is given for maintaining skills of the old centralized economy regime, professional insecurity and lack of true managerial vocation of many managers;

(h) **Managerial self-training**: many managers have managerial experience acquired through their own effort in the sense of occasional knowledge accumulation, participation in short training programs, and cultivation of native inclination toward entrepreneurial or managerial activities. The typical profile of these self-trained managers presents the following features: are mostly graduates of technical education and people over 45 years; highly appreciate the role of personal experience and talent in resolving current problems, and thoroughly gather evidence when faced with special situations; give small importance to the knowledge regarding economy, human resources and organization of production, considering that they can solve the problems specific to these fields based only on their own experience; believe that through graduation in attended management training programs gained just little or no knowledge; pursue management information disseminated through the media in smaller proportion than other managers; believe that made personal efforts larger than others to train; consider that the main causes of managerial inefficiency are snugness, conservatism and stupidity; consider that the translation and dissemination of published works of successful managers from other countries would substantially contribute to the development of managerial skills;

(i) **Inappropriate organization by many managers of their own activities, irrational use of working time, focusing on secondary, unessential issues, poor delegation of authority to solve problems of secondary importance, unbalanced coverage of the range of managerial roles, misuse of Secretariat and collaborators.** Inappropriate use of these pathways and tools that, in a large measure, determine management "productivity", constitute a formidable obstacle whose overcoming requires appreciable efforts to significantly extend best practices, to assimilate managerial „automatisms" which are common currency in firms management in advanced economies.

3.2. *Exogenous difficulties*

(a) **Lack of national strategy for economic and social development and industrial policy.** The lack of these key documents essential for the future development of any country profoundly affect firms' management in the sense that they do not provide landmarks to guide their business plans, and realistic evolution objectives. Benchmarks provided by the mentioned documents consist of the major coordinates of the Government's vision on economic and social development of the country at national, regional and sectoral level, economic structure configuration perspective, economic and financial instruments to be used for progressively "forging" desired economic structure, international agreements to be concluded, and so on.

These benchmarks should be clear signals given to foreign and domestic investors on Government's intentions, its philosophy, the ways it will follow; in the absence of such guidelines, outlining "strategic vision" of the company management is an approach without full required substantiation, limited, therefore, only to fragmentary estimates of domestic and external demand;

(b) **Legislative instability** is a deficiency with profound adverse effects on the whole society, which also prevents managers to establish strategies, plans and programs for sustainable activities development of their companies. One single example of this is enlightening for the pace and scope of legislative changes facing even organic laws: Labor Code, approved by Law No. 53/2003 (Legea nr. 53/2003 Codul Muncii, 2003), amended and supplemented by Law No. 480/2003, Law No. 541/2003, Government Emergency Ordinance no. 65/2005, Law No. 241/2005, Government Emergency Ordinance No. 55/2006, Law No. 237/2007, Law No. 202/2008, Government Emergency Ordinance No. 148/2008, Law No. 331/2009, Law No. 49/2010. Therefore, in eight years there were 10 changes to a very important and sensitive law for the society, which gives a convincing image on this pernicious practice of the Parliament and the Government, which, although repeatedly condemned by the ruling authorities of the European Union, continues to be manifested and have serious effects at the societal level;

(c) **The existence of many onerous, restrictive provisions of the legislative framework.** Numerous legislative regulations significantly restrict the scope of managerial action, hampers materializing managers initiatives, often reduce their speed of response decisions, and hinders their efforts to restructure the business of firms they run. Requirements to simplify administrative procedures, reduce para-fiscality and the number of permits, notifications, notices, and licenses for businesses were made consistently over the years, but the Government and local authorities reactions were almost nil. A 2010 survey carried out in companies, preponderantly SMEs, signaled the following obstacles and difficulties they faced in running current affairs (Munteanu, 2010): high taxes — 64.7% of respondents; bureaucracy — 64.6%; decrease in domestic demand — 41.6%; high interest rates on loans — 41.3%; difficult access to loans — 38.5%; corruption — 38.1%; delayed payment of invoices — 37.8%; hiring, training, and keeping staff — 33.6%; excessive controls — 30.9%. The situation remained unchanged, despite the politicians' rhetorics who repeatedly promised significant improvements. Illustrative examples can be given in various fields.

Law No. 40/2011 amending and supplementing Law No. 53/2003 — Labour Code (Legea nr. 40/2011 pentru modificarea si completarea Legii nr. 53/2003 — Codul Muncii, 2011) contains many provisions favoring employees and constraining employers, particularly at the conclusion of collective work contracts and dismissal of employees who have professional, disciplinary or ethics deficiencies. Provisions that unbalanced protecting employee, multiple and cumbersome procedures to be strictly followed, the frequent prospect to solve labor disputes by legal way detrimental to employers induce justified reluctance among managers to commit into effective actions for organizational restructuring of companies facing financial difficulties, with drastic reductions in productivity or sales. For example, Article 29, para. 4, provides that "the employer can request information about the person seeking employment from his former employers, but only on the activities performed and the duration of employment, and only with the informing respective person"; the provision is restrictive, preventing the hiring manager to ask all information on the previous performance and behavior of the applicant.

The system of taxes is characterized by: their poor collecting; inefficient management of funds collected accompanied by excessive bureaucracy; relatively low tax base, with many exceptions and statutory deductions; high fiscal evasion; high share of indirect tax revenue in total tax revenue (in 2011 — 46.3% as compared to EU average — 33.1%) and low of direct taxes (21.3% as compared to EU average — 31.8%), while the share of revenue from social contributions was 32.4% as compared to EU average — 27.4%. The tax burden is reduced on income and profit tax, but companies pay one of the highest VAT in the EU.

As for social contributions, Romania is at the top of the hierarchy of countries with the highest taxes on income from work. According to a copublication of The World Bank and the International Finance Corporation (The World Bank & IFC, 2013), a company in Romania makes 41 payments each year to the State on account of taxes, three times more than the EU average, which lost 216 hours for, the bulk of the tax burden is distributed on work; should be added that some charges have a high cost of administration which often exceeds the tax.

High frequency of inspections of different kinds — financial, fiscal, accounting, social, environmental, etc. — hinders considerably the activity of all categories of enterprises, especially SMEs. For companies managers, checks carried out in the current conditions, in addition to being a cause of increased stress, distract them from their current work, forcing them to stay continuously at the disposal of control bodies. Serious failures generated by the current system of corporate control activity determined Economy Ministry to initiate a law draft amending and supplementing Law No. 346/2004 regarding the SMEs stimulation, by proposing their financial and fiscal inspection no more than once in a period of three years. The measure, welcome, must, undoubtedly, be followed by others with the same goal of simplifying and easing control system.

(d) **The arrears** are, by their permanent existence and growth, a formidable difficulty for the efforts of managers of "accurate" companies to improve their work, as they create unequal competitive conditions between companies, especially in relation to the state-owned companies, for which, if they fail to streamline their activity, the Government should intervene to support them with resources. The outbreak of the global crisis in 2008 increased the overall arrears, to higher levels in State-owned companies compared with private ones.

The State-owned companies are the largest debtors to the national social security budget, the remaining debt to consolidated general budget representing 1.9% of GDP in December 2012; moreover, arrears of State-owned companies registered in relations with the private sector create for latter serious problems of liquidity and, hence, development. It is known, in fact, that the profitability of state-owned enterprises is significantly lower than that of private companies: according to calculations made in 2012 by the Fiscal Council (Consiliul Fiscal, 2012), profit margin was — 3.0% for the firsts and 0.7% for seconds, and rates of operations were, respectively, 0.8% and 3.3%. Significantly reduced capacity of state-owned companies to generate profits led to other negative result: reduced ability to pay debts and new investment (in 2012: state-owned companies — 1.3%, the main source of funding is the budget, private companies — 4.8%).

(e) **Tax evasion**. Accounting for 13.8% of GDP in 2012, tax evasion has the same effect on management of "accurate" companies as the previous difficulty, their managers facing, on the one hand, excessive tax they must bear, and on the other hand, the unequal situation in which they are placed in relation to companies that practice tax evasion or register growing arrears. The largest share stands for the evasion of VAT, 8.3% of GDP in 2012, followed by contributions to social assurances, about 3.3%, mainly due to "black labor" (workers in the informal economy).

Related to tax evasion is the degree of compliance with the main duties and taxes, which is the ratio between actual revenues to budget and theoretical revenues (which also include tax evasion and actually received revenues); in 2012, it was of 64.3% (in 2006 it was of 76.1%).

The figures demonstrate the persistence of serious disfunctionalities in the Romanian economy, adversely affecting economic and financial performance of companies that follow the rules of correct market economy functioning, fully and timely pay their debts, behave ethically in the marketplace. For the management of these companies, unfavorable operating environment is characterized by numerous challenges with negative influences, the removal of which the central and local Governments should have the decisive role.

Exogenous difficulties reviewed are the most important from wider range of those facing managers of Romanian companies. Prospects for reducing these difficulties, in which the governmental measures are essential, are nevertheless encouraging, given that it is anticipated that the main engine of economic growth will be the domestic demand, inflation will continue to decline, public investment will increase by improving absorption of the EU funds, the Government and private consumption will increase gradually to accelerate the pace of structural adjustment under increasing pressure of accumulated imbalances (Russu *et al.*, 2008). At the same time, we must take into account the worrying realities of late structural reforms in education, health and management of state-owned companies, failure to timely reach targets set by the IMF, which significantly decrease local and foreign investors' confidence and economic growth potential.

4. Conclusions

Management practiced in Romanian companies reveals contradictory aspects, which clearly differentiate, in terms of activity quality and financial and economic performances, public and private companies, especially foreign companies, by far in favor of the latter.

Numerous difficulties presented by the management of a large part of the Romanian firms, localized, predominantly, in the public sector, are determined by both endogenous difficulties — lack of appropriate expertise of many managers, poor management culture, exaggerated importance of power relations, fluctuating leadership styles, poor self-organizing managerial work, etc. — and exogenous difficulties — instability of the legal framework, existence of numerous restrictions provided by law for business management, phenomena of arrears and tax evasion, widespread corruption, etc.

Exogenous difficulties deeply hinder, especially, right companies management, that behave properly on market and promote higher quality values, being, therefore, disadvantaged in dealing with companies that use shady practices.

To perpetuate many difficulties from the regime of centralized economy and generate new ones in the system of market economy, the main responsibility is incumbent upon the Legislature and the Government, which failed to properly improve the business environment and ensure transparency and fairness for plenary affirming truly efficient company management.

References

Codul Muncii (2003), *Legea nr. 53*, României: Monitorul Oficial.

Codul muncii (2011), *Legea nr. 40 Pentru Modificarea si Completarea Legii nr. 53*, României: Monitorul Oficial.

Consiliul Fiscal (2012), Report Annual 2012, p. 77.

Munteanu, C. (2010), Impactul Crizei Economice Asupra Percepției Întreprinzătorilor Români cu Privire la Mediul de Afaceri, *Sfera Politicii*, 148(Junie).

Nicolescu, O. & Verboncu, I. (2007), *Managementul Organizației*, Biblioteca de Management 20, București: Editura Economică.

Russu, C. (coordinator), Dumitrescu, M., & Pleșoianu, G. (2008), *Calitatea Managementului firmei: Evaluare și Interpretare*, București: Editura Economică.

The World Bank & IFC (2013), *Doing Business 2013: Smarter Regulations for Small and Medium-sized Enterprises. Comparing Business Regulations for Domestic Firms in 185 Economies* (10th edn.), p. 190.

Chapter 23

Contributions to Redesigning the Management System in Medium-Sized Enterprises

Ion Verboncu and Ciprian Nicolescu

Bucharest University of Economic Studies

One major way to change and increase competitiveness of the Romanian organizations is redesigning of the management system — a complex strategic approach to reinforce the decisive role of management in achieving economic performance.

As the most comprehensive way of managerial change, redesigning of the management system starts from the premise that a radical, fundamental, and spectacular change of work processes, based on the principle "all or nothing" is a condition for success. Focusing management on processes "in line" with specific mechanisms for quality management systems is the central idea of reengineering, promoted about two decades by the Americans M. Hammer and J. Champy and other specialists.

For medium-sized enterprises within the small and medium-sized enterprise (SME) sector, such a solution takes into account their characteristics, and through a rigorous methodological scenario — objectives, processes, structures, people, results — provides rethinking and redesigning of the management, overall and at level of components (organizational, decisional, informational, methodological, and human resource management) in terms of efficiency, effectiveness, and competitiveness. We recommend this kind of demarche to medium-sized enterprises that are in economically and managerial declining, to the ones that "are going well", but are threatened by imminent danger that "comes" from inside or outside (national and international environment) or the ones that are "going well" but want to strengthen their position in a particular market or to "enter" in other markets.

1. Introduction

Reengineering or business process reengineering (BPR) has become one of the most commonly used terms by management specialists and managers who want to amplify their business efficiency and effectiveness. Officially launched in the 1990s by Hammer & Champy (1993), reengineering has revolutionized the theory and practice of management at company level, by focusing on the fundamental, spectacular, deep, and radical rethinking and redesign of work processes, especially on those generating added value. The key concept around which gravitates this unique way of change is represented by "the process" to which, we must admit, Romanian management referred too little, until the development and the promotion of the quality management systems.

We will present the most representative contributions, mainly American, regarding the concept, the principles, and especially the reengineering methodology.

Although the term itself was established by the famous work Reengineering the Corporation: A

Manifesto for Business Revolution, (Hammer & Champy, 1993), reengineering has been used in literature since 1990, both by Hammer (1990) and by Davenport & Short (1990). Famous specialists have conferred similar meanings to the reengineering: **the fundamental rethinking and radical redesign of business processes to achieve outstanding improvements of the indicators which today are considered critical in assessing performance, such as cost, quality, service, and speed** (Hammer & Champy, 1993); **critical analysis and design of production flows and processes within the organization and between organizations** (Davenport & Short, 1990); **reengineering business processes consists in radical transformation of organizational processes using information technology in order to achieve major improvements in quality and productivity** (Bergeron & Falardeau, 1994).

The most important principles promoted by this new conception in management, concerns orientation towards process, ambitious management, breaking old rules, and creative use of information technology (Hammer & Champy, 1993).

Methodology of promotion and application of BPR can be found in a variety of variants, most of which are developments or adaptations of the methodological concepts of the two American promoters, Hammer and Champy. Some of them are presented by C.S. Stan in the book *Reengineering — A New Philosophy of Management* (Stan, 2007). Thus:

- Hammer & Champy (1993) propose a methodology structured into six stages: **(i) Reengineering launching**, in the sense of specifying the need and opportunity of reengineering, of major factors requiring restoration of business processes from the perspective of company's efficiency; **(ii) Setting the "map of company's processes"**, which graphically highlights the types of existing work processes at the moment of reengineering launching, the links between them and the impact, positive or negative, on the manner and degree of achieving objectives; **(iii) Establishing the processes subject to reengineering**. From this point of view there can be several situations: processes which are to be redesigned and reengineered refers to the firm as a whole; it is approached only one group of processes (e.g., activities embedded in a function); reengineering aims a single process which is representative and has a high impact on the functionality and efficiency of the company. The fundamental principle of reengineering "all or nothing" has its explanation in the fact that the redesigned process or processes should be addressed in their complexity and entirety; **(iv) Forming overall image on processes or process subject to reengineering**, exploiting the information detached from analysis of its/their viability, weaknesses and strengths which are characteristic to it/them, causes that generated them, links to other processes as shown in the map of processes; **(v) Reengineering of business processes/process**, in the sense of rethinking and redesign. In fact, occurs a redesign of business processes/process in terms of their/its role in achieving some goals, especially strategic, and its/their processual, structural, organizational, and human resizing; **(vi) Operationalizing of the project regarding the processes/process radically changed** by reengineering and hence remaking of processes map;
- Davenport and Short formulated a partially changed version, but we must underline that it was launched in the literature three years earlier than the version which we already mentioned (Davenport & Short, 1990): **developing of business vision and processes objectives, identifying processes that need to be redesigned, understanding and measuring existing processes, identifying facilities offered by new technologies, designing and construction of a prototype for new processes**;
- Beauchemin (2002), a Canadian specialist, has shown that reengineering should be applied based on a methodological scenario structured in nine steps, as follows: **identifying and designing a new process, obtaining the cooperation and involvement of stakeholders (participatory approach), viewing the process and identifying all activities, even the obvious ones, examining the value added by each activity, studying the new process, testing the new process, implementation of the new process, follow-up and evaluation, dissemination of results**;

- Manganelli & Klein (1994) consider that reengineering process should follow several stages such as: **introduction, identification of processes, developing a vision, developing a solution (technically and socially), transformation**;
- Durlik (1998) also believes that reengineering must be done on the following trail: **establishing of project activities, making a graphical representation of the process and deciding on the scope of the project, radical rescheduling of planned processes, simulation and evaluation of options, choosing the best option, implementation**;
- Polish Cempel (2005) identifies in his doctoral thesis, four major phases of the methodology for process reengineering (with focus on logistic process): **the phase of scope and qualification** — understanding the current state, identifying the need for change, setting the team responsible for change at strategic level, introduction of reengineering approach, reinventing or updating the organization's mission and creating the vision, defining the scope of change, selecting the process for reengineering; **the phase of research and modelling optimal solutions** — setting up the team which is responsible for changing at the operational level, modelling a new process, detailing and realigning the new process (engagement/involvement of users); **the phase of creating instructions, diagrams and characteristics** of the new process, project planning and achieving; **phase of verification and evaluation** — measuring results, comparing results with the objective/purpose of changing, changing organizational culture (continuous improvement of the process);
- French specialists Brilman & Herard (2006) insist on the **three key points of reengineering — an objective of rupture, innovation and approach through processes** — as well as on **specific phases and stages** of such an approach: **phase of study and redesign**, in which forming the reengineering team is crucial and the **phase of implantation**, involving restructuring, merging some existing processes, creating new processes, training staff involved in the implementation of these new processes, reducing staff, operationalizing of information systems, so on. Also, the two specialists outline the conditions for reengineering success — total commitment of the company's management within a clear strategy, approach of customer — oriented processes, setting targets of rupture, forming multidisciplinary teams made of the best, stimulating creativity, involving computer scientists from the beginning, careful selection of the first operations which are specific to the processes chosen to be redesigned so on.

2. Contributions of Romanian School to Managerial Redesigning

BPR, as theory and practice, quickly spread to Europe and, consequently, in Romania, through translation and publication of the famous work *Reengineering the Corporation: A Manifesto for Business Revolution*, published in the USA in 1993, under the signature of M. Hammer and J. Champy.

Paradoxically, the first Romanian achievements in the field were recorded before the publishing year of this book and aimed the microeconomic management practice, not theory(!). In 1992, some of the representatives of the School of Management at the Academy of Economic Studies (Prof. PhD O. Nicolescu, Prof. PhD E. Burduș, Prof. PhD I. Verboncu, Prof. PhD G. Căprărescu, Prof. PhD I. Cochină) started a research project for a representative company of the Romanian industry at the time — STEROM SA Câmpina — focused on redesigning management system, but without focusing on business processes.

The methodology used for the first time in Romania was divided into the following steps:

- **Managerial and economic diagnosis;**
- **Formulating the strategy** (fundamentation, elaboration and implementation of the strategy at the level of vision, mission, objectives, strategic options, resources, terms, and competitive advantage);
- **Redesigning management system and each of its components** (methodological, decisional, informational, organizational, and human resource management) following specific methodologies;
- **Implementing the new management system;**

- **Evaluating the efficiency of the redesigned management system.**

The methodology was satisfactory but, during the subsequent approaches of management redesign, in which were involved other large and medium sized companies — S.C. ELECTROPUTERE S.A. Craiova, S.C. IMMUM Baia Mare, S.C. RESIAL S.A. Alba Iulia, S.C. PLEVNEI S.A. Bucharest, S.C. Alro S.A. Slatina, S.C. PRINCO GROUP S.A. Buciumeni so on — it has been improved in the sense of changing the redesign order of some management subsystems or in terms of content enrichment of some phases related to the redesign of methodological component. Pragmatic experience gained along with these companies' managerial redesign, allowed the theoretical completion of this methodological alternative and its insertion in "Management based on profit centres" (Nicolescu & Verboncu, 1998) and later in "Management methodologies" (Nicolescu & Verboncu, 2001; Nicolescu & Verboncu, 2008).

As worldwide the book "Reengineering the Corporation" (1993), published in the USA under the signature M. Hammer and J. Champy, made waves through the new proposed guidance to management, that of management on processes, professor Ion Verboncu considered that the use of these elements in a redesign methodology would be very appropriate. Consequently, **Verboncu has developed and published a new variant of methodology regarding managerial redesign, able to integrate BPR, which we are trying to present in the following paragraphs** (Verboncu, 2008, 2011).

3. New Romanian Methodological Variant to Redesign the Management System of Medium Sized Companies

Although in our country the number of companies subject to management redesign is relatively low and restructuring/reorganization practices outrun this new and modern attitude and approach towards novelty, we consider that especially in times of crisis and post crisis, such organizational change should be reconsidered.

For the success of this complex strategic approach certain **conditions** are needed, such as:

- Reshaping organizational culture by transforming it into a favorable mechanism for managerial change;
- Existence of managers and specialists truly professional;
- Use of consultancy services, which provides the methodology, ensures accomplishment of managerial redesign study and offers expert assistance during the implementation of the new management system.

Regarding medium-sized companies, the redesigning of management system must take into consideration characteristics of their organizational systems, comparative with large enterprises: more reduced size and complexity, typological diversity, intense human dimension, lower formalization, strong interweaving of formal and informal elements, relative processual and structural simplicity, high flexibility, entrepreneurial customization, more intense centralized decision-making, etc.

The methodological scenario to redesign the management system of medium sized companies is structured in **several sequences: objectives — processes — structures — people** (managers and executives) — **results** (performance). In the following we will make a brief presentation of this methodological approach (Verboncu, 2008, 2011).

The starting point in such a complex approach is the diagnosis study, resulted from a rigorous methodological approach, which highlights causal strengths and weaknesses, determine the economic and management viability potential and ends with strategic and tactical recommendations.

3.1. *Objectives*

The first step — objectives — refers to targets of the new management system and takes the form of a system of objectives, resulted from the development of global and partial strategies and policies. Fundamenting and elaborating of fundamental, derived, specific and individual objectives as a result of promoting realistic strategies and policies, involves a radical change of attitude of the organization and its management towards its present and future. Objectives empower individuals and groups of individuals, imposing a strong strategic and tactical dimension, required for a proper positioning on the specific market and — finally — represent very good benchmarks for assessing the functionality and performances.

Objectives must meet simultaneously several conditions: to be specific (S), measurable (M), achievable (A), relevant (R), and timed (T).

SMART requirements translate into the followings:

- The objective must be **specific**, accurately reflecting what we want to achieve; such a requirement is verified through answers to questions like who? what? when? how? or who is the target group?
- Must be **measurable**, quantifiable; questions to which must be answered to verify compliance with this requirement are like how much? or how many?
- The objective should be **affordable/attainable**, that can be achieved;
- It should be relevant, **real**; in other words, the objective allows obtaining the expected results;
- Finally, the objective should be framed in **time**, meaning the time needed to achieve it must to be accurately determined; verifying compliance with this feature is provided by answers to questions like when?, until?, in which period?

In return, professor Popa (2004) considers that the objectives — especially strategic ones — must meet the requirements of **measurability, acceptability, flexibility, comprehensibility, tangibility, and motivability**.

Important clarification is needed: in our opinion, the objectives should not be confused with the purpose or purposes of the organization or of its processual/structural components, because the objectives are the quantitative and/or qualitative expression of the purpose for which it was founded and operates the organization (or a component of it). The "father" of management by objectives, Drucker (2001) pointed out that profitable companies set their goals in several "key areas for performance": position on the market, innovation, productivity, physical and financial resources, profitability, development of management performance, work attitude and performance, public responsibility.

3.2. *Processes*

Processes are defined as logical sequence of activities, attributions or tasks exercised/performed in order to achieve assumed objectives in conditions of efficiency and effectiveness. "Bridge" between strategic management and management redesigning is translated through link between the strategic objectives (plus the other categories of objectives derived from them) and processes needed for their achievement. Such a connection and, especially, its reconsidering, triggered a true revolution in management, through the appearance and development of BPR. This broad movement that comprises both the theory and practice of management has as content the radical, deep and spectacular restoration of work processes so as to create the necessary premises for achieving the objectives.

Delimitating and sizing the processes must be corroborated with the provisions of Organization and Functioning Regulation which approach the organizational structure of the organization by "floors", as follows:

- Upper floor, related to strategic management and occupied by participatory management bodies;
- Medium floor, for the tactical management, includes functional and operational compartments;
- Lower level (operational management) belongs to the compartments which produce true economic substance.

From this perspective, work processes should be treated both on the vertical side of management system (transverse) as well as on horizontal (performed at the level of one compartment or of two or more compartments, depending on their complexity).

Due to the fact that a compartment can be the depositary for a part of a process (irrespective of its type and nature), for a whole process or, frequently, for several processes, it is difficult to associate it (compartment) with an objective. Therefore, the connection objectives — processes is more direct, more realistic, and facilitates the steps for managerial design or redesign.

The arrangement "process-based management" is justified precisely when this link, individual, group and organizational responsibilities become real.

Moreover, **outsourcing decisions** will target processes (obviously auxiliary or support) and not compartments. Please note that in any organization processes are divided into:

- Main processes which give consistency to the object of activity of the organization, creating value, economic substance;
- Secondary processes (support), that support the conducting of main processes and can be executed within or outside the organization;
- Management processes.

Processes that are targeted for outsourcing — to the extent that they are costly or their execution is of low quality — are mainly from the category of supporting processes (auxiliary), although in some cases, even one or another of the basic processes can have such a "fate".

It is important that the main processes to be designed and constructed so that their exercise to generate economic efficiency, to be effective and therefore the targeted objectives to be accomplished.

In order to achieve this, the main, auxiliary and management processes, must meet simultaneously three conditions:

- To be sized accordingly from **processual** point of view (if the process is defined at function level, it must have activities and if it is focused on one activity then it shall include appropriate attributions);
- To be **structural and organizational** dimensioned, exercised by a position/compartment or positions/compartments which have the required official and processual authority;
- To be **human** sized, meaning that people (managers and executives) involved in their ongoing must have professional and managerial competence required by volume, complexity and nature of the respective work processes.

Work processes are not static but, on the contrary, any change in the system of objective causes changes in their typology and manner of exercise. Therefore, not even process map — representative document in the management of business processes — is not a static document/instrument, but a dynamic one, able to reflect and support the changes and achieving objectives.

It is interesting from this perspective, the link between BPR and BPM (management based on processes or Business Process Management), two concepts and at the same time, complex managerial practices, indispensable to organizational change by reengineering and quality management at organization level. Why? Because:

- Both must be approached systemic and together as ways to streamline work processes;
- Both aim the efficiency and effectiveness of processes, increasing managerial and economic performance;
- Processes, defined within the quality management system according to SR EN ISO 9001:2008, are the support of reengineering, of organization as it was described by Americans Hammer & Champy (1993);
- Processes approach allows identification of their contribution to getting value, in achieving performance and continuous improvement, in the context of combining two major trends: increasing value added and improving customer satisfaction;
- The organization has a choice between several approaches regarding the typology of processes: PRAXIOM RESEARCH GROUP limited (2010), the conception of Secretariat ISO TC 176/SC (2009) and TUV CERT conception, the last one being taken into consideration by us, **processes being divided in main processes, auxiliary or support processes and management processes**.

We emphasize that in order to achieve the objectives are required, adequate **working processes** with different degree of aggregation. Their delimitation and dimensioning in business processes (main), support processes and management processes are determined by the complexity of the objectives to whose achievement are directly involved. Due to the fact that building the system of objectives is made "top-down", and processual edifice necessary to its achieving is made from complex to simple. As such, the processual remodeling, reflected in the appearance of new work processes, developing existing ones, reducing or eliminating others, aims to ensure full correspondence between objectives and processes by developing a "process map" where are listed the main activities which generate added value. Will be approached with priority main processes identified as vulnerable in terms of participation to added value, uneconomic or of lower significance in the economy of the firm.

3.3. *Structures*

Work processes, regardless of the degree of aggregation, must have adequate structural — organizational support, namely a favorable **organizational structure** to achieving objectives. This is why the third step in managerial redesign is represented by the **structural redesign** materialized in resizing the need of jobs and functions, regarding to management and execution, functional and operational compartments, along with "arranging" them in a pre-established configuration through the medium of hierarchical levels, hierarchical weights and organizational relationships. It is also necessary to design a convenient organizational formula based on dimensional and functional characteristics of remodeled processes and contextual influences — more flattened structure, holonic type of structure, in which holons can be cost centers delimited mainly processual or structural — organizational. Team of specialists which ensures managerial redesign of the organization has two options: either finalize the organizational formula at this stage, or gives shape to a preliminary version, which is to be completed under sequence 4 ("People"), depending on the changes made in other managerial subsystems but especially in managerial instruments. For example, promoting management based on profit centers causes major organizational — structural changes generated mainly by managerial and economic decentralization at cost centers level.

Regarding organizational documents we insist at this stage on completion of function descriptions and job descriptions, while organizational chart and Regulation of organization and functioning will be final after applying decisional informational and even organizational and structural changes, imposed by the managerial tools used to exercise management processes.

3.4. *People*

The next step is crucial to ensure high viability of the organization as it aims to "equip" management and execution positions with people who have the right competences. Fitting right people with right jobs is done through competence and represents the key element. Personal authority given by knowledge, skills and managerial and professional aptitudes must satisfy formal authority, namely the right to make decisions which is related with managerial positions. Consequently, the next managerial component subject to redesign is **human resource management**, a highly dynamic and vulnerable managerial "area", in which the recruitment, selection, hiring, evaluation, motivation, perfection, promotion and protection of employees and shaping organizational culture are key activities.

Through high quality of human resources is ensured **professionalization of management**, because:

- **Managers** are directly involved in the process of fundamentation and making of decisions; in order to do this, they use managerial tools and relevant information transmitted through rationalized ascendant communication channels;
- **Employees** initiate actions needed for operationalizing decisions, by exploiting information transmitted mainly on descendent routes.

That is why the quality of decisions and actions is dependent on not only the manner and ways of decisional redesign, but also on methodological-managerial and informational redesign solutions.

Regarding the **decisional component** of management there are required fundamental changes, materialized in:

- Rigorous delimitation and sizing of formal authority or competences on hierarchical levels;
- Improving the quality of decisions through their judicious scientific fundamentation, through their

"empowering", through ensuring effectiveness of their adopting and operationalizing and through proper formulation;
- Improving the quality of decisions, by their judicious scientific substantiation by "empowering" them, ensuring timeliness, and formulating appropriate adoption and implementation;
- Typologically improving of decisions taken, raising the weight of strategic and tactical decisions, of decisions taken under risk and uncertainty at superior hierarchical levels.

In turn, **informational redesign** includes:

- Improving the quality and quantity of information;
- Rationalize informational situations and routes of communication;
- Increasing the computerization of business, support, and management processes through the promotion of performing systems;
- Sophistication of informational procedures.

Since without a judicious structured methodological and managerial component cannot be achieved scientification of the managers work, special attention should be paid to **methodological subsystem** redesign by promoting a modern managerial tools — with accent on management by objectives or its upgraded version, management based on profit centers — and on rigorous general or specific methodologies. This fourth step of redesign methodology ensures shaping of the **new management system configuration**, whose functioning has to bring more efficiency and effectiveness.

Operationalization of essential changes, sometimes radical, in the area of processes, requires appropriate changes in structural and organizational configuration in the sense of restoring the organizational structure and promoting specific management tools — job description, Regulation of organization and functioning — with dynamic content. This is possible to determine further changes in the conditions in which is decided the use of management by objectives or management by profit centers or even in situations that produce some significant changes in systems of decision, informational or of human resources management. For each of the aforementioned situations careful monitoring is required to ensure application of advanced solutions and their properly correction when necessary.

3.5. *Results*

Redesigned management based on this methodological and operationalized scenario generates results, which normally should end in managerial performances, which, in turn, causes economic performances. If responsibility in achieving managerial performances lies exclusively to managers, for the accomplishment of economic performance are responsible both managers and employees.

4. Conclusions

Taking into consideration the foreign methodological variants for reengineering, presented at the beginning of the chapter, we elaborate some conclusions:

- Most, if not all of them, are adaptations/developments/diversifications of the Americans Hammer and Champy's methodology, who are considered "parents" of reengineering;
- All have a core axis which gives them the same approach of the complex mechanism of change through reengineering — presentation, analysis, rethinking and redesign (reengineering), implementation, evaluation;
- The essence of change regarding business processes, plus auxiliaries (support) and management processes, although these last two categories are not "attractions" for the promoters of such methodological scenarios. A limitation of reengineering methodologies can be considered the lower focus or, in some cases, neglecting processes that do not contribute directly to achieving economic substance;
- None of the options presented does not "tackle" in depth all components of the organization's management system, at the level at which it happens such a profound change. The focus is explicitly on

processual organization (processes), structural organization (organizational structure) and organizational culture, the latter more through the conditions imposed by the change;
- Each of the methodological concepts known in this domain and presented earlier — some of them significant from our point of view — outlines the difference between reengineering and quality management systems, both based on processes. Reengineering and continuous improvement of quality management are at some points tangential, have much in common, but they are different ways of managerial and organizational modernization and efficiency;
- Putting in place any of presented methodological variants has the same outcome: a significant improvement in managerial, economic and financial performance indicators in the context of obtaining competitive advantage;
- Through their content, complexity and impact, each of the existing reengineering scenarios can be treated as a model for reengineering;
- There is a tendency to generalize the role of BPR and to treat it like some kind of miraculous solution for competitiveness, efficiency and effectiveness. In fact it has indeed many advantages, but also serious limitations and should be approached differently from case to case, depending on the particular structural and functional characteristics of the company and its management.

Regarding the new Romanian methodology, we concluded that a rigorous and serious operationalization of the methodological scenario for managerial redesign of medium-sized enterprises, focused on objectives, processes, structures, people and result, is able to ensure both the effectiveness of this category of SMEs, as well as a revival of the SMEs' sector in terms of contribution to obtained GDP. Redesigning of management system is a way to get out of the crisis, an important way to mitigate or eliminate "vicious circles" encountered in business operation and to replace them with genuine "virtuous circles" generating economic substance/added value. Also, regardless of the economic situation of companies, managerial redesigning is particularly effective within medium enterprises where occur rapidly major changes, with strong innovative character, based on identifying and capitalizing on economic opportunities.

Professionalization of managers in medium-sized companies, enterprises resulting from development of smaller businesses or from the restructuring/reorganization of larger businesses, is one of the conditions to generate success in managerial redesign. Of course, managerial methodologization, continuous managerial training and appealing to management consulting are variables which have to be exploited in this context.

References

Bergeron, F. & Falardeau, J. (1994), *The Reengineering of Business Processes within Canadian Organizations*, Montréal: Les Éditions Transcontinental.

Brilman, J. & Herard, J. (2006), *Best Management Practices in the New World Economic Context*, Paris: Editions d'Organisation.

Cempel, W. (2005), Reengineering methodology in engineering industry, Politechnika Poznańska, Poznań (Doctoral thesis).

Davenport, T. H. & Short, J. E. (1990), The new industrial engineering: Information technology and business process redesign, *Sloan Management Review*, 31(4), 11–27.

Drucker, P. F. (2001), *Management Strategic*, Bucharest: Teora Publishing House.

Durlik, I. (1998), *Restructuring Business Processes: Reengineering, Theory and Practice*, Warszawa: Agencja Wydawnicza Placet.

Hammer, M. (1990), Reengineering work: Don't automate, obliterate, *Harvard Business Review*, July–August, 68(4), 104–112.

Hammer, M. & Champy, J. (1993), *Reengineering the Corporation: A Manifesto for Business Revolution*, New York: Harper Collins.

Manganelli, R. & Klein, M. (1994), *The Reengineering Handbook: A Step-By-Step Guide to Business Transformation*, New York: AMACOM.

Nicolescu, O. & Verboncu, I. (1998), *Management Based on Profit Centres*, Bucharest: Tribuna Economică Publishing House.

Nicolescu, O. & Verboncu, I. (2001), *Management Methodologies*, Bucharest: Tribuna Economică Publishing House.

Nicolescu, O. & Verboncu, I. (2008), *Management Methodologies*, Bucharest: Universitară Publishing House.

Popa, I. (2004), *Strategic Management*, Bucharest: Economică Publishing House.

Stan, C. S. (2007), *Reengineering — A New Philosophy of Management*, Bucharest: Expert Publishing House.

Verboncu, I. (2008), Methodological variants for managerial re-projection of the organisation — compared approach, *Review of General Management*, 2, 33–46.

Verboncu, I. (2011), *Organizational Change by Reengineering*, Bucharest: ASE Publishing House.

Chapter 24

The New Paradigm of Social Enterprise

Ana-Maria Grigore

University of Bucharest

It appears that the world's problems are outstripping our ability to address them, but what may be more accurate is simply that traditional institutions are no longer sufficient.

The idea of social enterprise as an alternative business model has arisen as a response to the relentless and ever-changing economic and political swings the world has endured over the past two centuries. Since the beginning of the Industrial Revolution (and even before), two broad ideological models have been continuously battling against each other for supremacy: capitalism and socialism. The institution of the social enterprise provides us with a viable opportunity to break off from this dizzying swing of extremes, and balance the best of all ideologies.

This solution was not easily reached, because in a way it contradicts human nature, which is individualistic at its core. It was reached dialectically, which is to say at the end of a cause and effect evolution. And it was reached because the alternative to this solution is the control of society through dictatorship and totalitarianism, an alternative both tried and disproved by modern history.

The aims of this chapter are to examine in brief the concepts of the social enterprise and entrepreneurship, and to highlight the role of social entrepreneurship in economic development and for society. The methodological approach is literature review.

1. Introduction

The idea of social enterprise as an alternative business model has arisen as a response to the relentless and ever-changing economic and political swings the world has endured over the past two centuries. Since the beginning of the Industrial Revolution (and even before), two broad ideological models have been continuously fighting each other for supremacy: capitalism and socialism (Serafinn, 2013).

Drucker (1993) introduced the term "social sector" in *"Post-Capitalist Society"* when discussing the need for a sector in addition to the "private sector" of business and the "public sector" of government to satisfy social needs, and provide a meaningful sense of citizenship and community.

Social Enterprise Alliance states that the institution of the social enterprise provides us with a viable opportunity to break from this dizzying swing of extremes, and balance the best of all ideologies. It addresses social concerns, more efficiently than government, which no longer has the mandate or resources to solve every social problem; more sustainably and creatively than the non-profit sector, which faces declining funding streams and increased demands for innovation; and more generously than business, which is mandated to place pre-eminence on shareholder returns, but which also realizes it cannot succeed in a decaying world.

The idea of "social entrepreneurship" has struck a responsive chord. It is a phrase well suited to our times. It combines the passion of a social mission with an image of business-like discipline, innovation, and determination commonly associated with, for instance, the high-tech pioneers of Silicon Valley. The time is certainly ripe for entrepreneurial approaches to social problems. Many governmental and philanthropic efforts have fallen far short of our expectations. Major social sector institutions are often viewed as inefficient, ineffective, and unresponsive. Social entrepreneurs are needed to develop new models for a new century (Dees, 1998).

The language of social entrepreneurship may be new, but the phenomenon is not. We have always had social entrepreneurs, even if we did not call them that. They originally built many of the institutions we now take for granted.

There is a long history of entrepreneurs with social motivations — from the chocolate maker J. Cadbury & Sons with its Quaker values, to the jam maker Wilkin & Sons. More recently Body Shop, Lush, and Timberland have managed to successfully combine business and social values — and in the process, to enhance their brand image. But always the commercial objective came first. In contrast, social entrepreneurship is about putting the social objective first and utilising commercial skills to achieve it, in an entrepreneurial way. This also has a long history from Victorian hospitals to the modern-day hospice movement. Civic entrepreneurship, on the other hand, is to do with putting entrepreneurial behavior into public sector. The two concepts have often been used in an almost interchangeable way, but they are different. This link is through the voluntary, community and not-for-profit sectors that straddle the public and private sectors (Burns, 2011).

It is estimated that in the UK, 3.3% of the population is involved in social entrepreneurial activity. In the USA, the non-profit sector is much larger than in Europe and represents some 7% of GDP, probably twice the size of the UK's (Burns, 2011).

The chapter is structured into five sections. The second section focuses on the literature review about social enterprise. The third section focuses on the social entrepreneurs. The fourth section presents social enterprise as the "missing middle". And the fifth section presents the conclusions of the chapter.

2. Social Enterprise

European Commission states that social enterprises are positioned between the traditional private and public sectors. Although there is no universally accepted definition of a social enterprise, their key distinguishing characteristics are the social and societal purpose combined with the entrepreneurial spirit of the private sector (http://ec.europa.eu/enterprise/policies/sme/promoting-entrepreneurship/social-economy/social-enterprises/index_en.htm).

Social enterprises are businesses whose primary purpose is the common good. They use the methods and discipline of business and the power of the marketplace to advance their social, environmental, and human justice agendas.

Social enterprises devote their activities and reinvest their surpluses to achieving a wider social or community objective either in their members' interest or a wider one. Social enterprises exist in all Member States. However, there is no single legal model for these enterprises. Many social enterprises are registered as private companies, others are in the form of social co-operatives, associations, voluntary organizations, charities or mutuals, and some organizations are unincorporated.

In the UK, the Government defines social enterprises as "businesses with primarily social objectives whose surpluses are principally reinvested for that purpose in the business or in the community, rather than being driven by the need to maximize profit for shareholders and owners." As with all businesses, they compete to deliver goods and services. The difference is that social and environmental purposes are at the very heart of what they do, and the profits they make are reinvested towards achieving those purposes (http://www.socialenterprisemark.org.uk/the-mark/what-is-social-enterprise).

Social enterprises operate in almost every industry, from health and social care to renewable energy, from retail to recycling, from employment to sport, from housing to education. Whatever they do, they do it differently from typical business, because they are driven by a social and environmental mission, and they are focused on the community they serve.

Pearce (2003) characterizes the social enterprise as:

- Having a primarily social purpose, with a secondary commercial activity;
- Achieving that purpose by engaging in trade;
- Not distributing profits to individuals but reinvesting profits either in the enterprise or new social ventures;
- Democratically involving members in its governance;
- Being openly accountable to a defined constituency and a wider community.

Social enterprises' drive, innovation and support for grassroots, home-grown talent are commendable, but overemphasis on them as the sole solution to poverty eradication risks to cast a tricky light over the development landscape: ultimately the politics would and should take responsibility, which is as much about power and social structures as it is about service delivery. Social enterprises are by nature often apolitical, taking an uncritical view of the limitations of markets, and solving short-term needs at the expense of long-term, governance-based transformation. Social enterprises, however, seem to be beyond critique. Instead of being lumped together with the rest of the development sector, they are hailed as the solution.

3. Social Entrepreneurs

"What business entrepreneurs are to the economy, social entrepreneurs are to social change. They are the driven, creative individuals who question the *status quo*, exploit new opportunities, refuse to give up, and remake the world for the better" (Bornstei, 2007).

Though the concept of "social entrepreneurship" is gaining popularity, it means different things to different people. There are many definitions out there for social entrepreneurship. Burns (2011) says that social entrepreneurship is an emerging but ill-defined concept. It can be loosely defined as the use of entrepreneurial behavior for social rather than profit objectives. Social entrepreneurs therefore differ from business entrepreneurs in terms of their mission. Their primary purpose is to "create superior social value for their clients" (Mort *et al.*, 2003).

Social entrepreneurs are those exceptional individuals who dream up and take responsibility for an innovative and untested idea for positive social change, and usher that idea from dream to reality. What enables social entrepreneurs to make lasting impact on the most difficult problems is a special combination of groundbreaking creativity and steadfast execution.

Social entrepreneurs are innovative, resourceful, and results-oriented. They draw upon the best thinking in both the business and non-profit worlds to develop strategies that maximize their social impact. These entrepreneurial leaders operate in all kinds of organizations: large and small; new and old; religious and secular; not-for-profit, for-profit, and hybrid.

On the Ashoka site (the largest network of social entrepreneurs worldwide), social entrepreneurs are individuals with innovative solutions to society's most pressing social problems. They are ambitious and persistent, tackling major social issues and offering new ideas for wide-scale change. Rather than leaving societal needs to the government or business sectors, social entrepreneurs find what is not working and solve the problem by changing the system, spreading the solution, and persuading entire societies to move in different directions. Social entrepreneurs often seem to be possessed by their ideas, committing their lives to changing the direction of their field. They are visionaries, but also realists, and are ultimately concerned with the practical implementation of their vision above all else (https://www.ashoka.org/social_entrepreneur).

Just as entrepreneurs change the face of business, social entrepreneurs act as the change agents for society, seizing the opportunities that others miss to improve systems, invent new approaches, and create solutions to change society for the better. While a business entrepreneur might create entirely new industries, a social entrepreneur develops innovative solutions to social problems and then implements them on a large scale. Social entrepreneurs have many of the same qualities as business entrepreneurs. However, they also need a heightened sense of accountability to the wide range of stakeholders involved in a social enterprise.

Social entrepreneurs identify resources where people only see problems. They view the villagers as the solution, not the passive beneficiary. They begin with the assumption of competence and unleash resources in the communities they are serving (Bornstei, 2007).

A social entrepreneur identifies and solves social problems on a large scale. Just as business entrepreneurs create and transform whole industries, social entrepreneurs act as the change agents for society, seizing opportunities that others miss in order to improve systems, invent, and disseminate new approaches and advance sustainable solutions that create social value.

Unlike traditional business entrepreneurs, social entrepreneurs primarily seek to generate "social value" rather than profits. And unlike the majority of non-profit organizations, their work is targeted not only towards immediate, small-scale effects, but sweeping, long-term change.

The job of a social entrepreneur is to recognize when a part of society is stuck and to provide new ways to get it unstuck. He or she finds what is not working and solves the problem by changing the system, spreading the solution, and persuading entire societies to take new leaps. The past two decades have seen an explosion of entrepreneurship and a healthy competition in the social sector, which has discovered what the business sector learned from the railroad, the stock market, and the digital revolution. Nothing is as powerful as a big new idea if it is in the hands of a first class entrepreneur (http://www.pbs.org/opb/thenewheroes/whatis/).

Social entrepreneurs operate in markets, but these markets often do not provide the right discipline. Many social-purpose organizations charge fees for some of their services. They also compete for donations, volunteers, and other kinds of support. But the discipline of these "markets" is frequently not closely aligned with the social entrepreneur's mission. It depends on who is paying the fees or providing the resources, what their motivations are, and how well they can assess the social value created by the venture. It is inherently difficult to measure social value creation. How much social value is created by reducing pollution in a given stream, by saving the spotted owl, or by providing companionship to the elderly? The calculations are not only hard but also contentious. Even when improvements can be measured, it is often difficult to attribute them to a specific intervention (Dees, 1998).

4. The "Missing Middle"

Social Enterprise Alliance states that social enterprise is emerging as the "missing middle" sector between the traditional worlds of government, non-profits, and business. It addresses social concerns:

- **More efficiently than government**, which no longer has the mandate or resources to solve every social problem;
- **More sustainably and creatively than the non-profit sector**, which faces declining funding streams and increased demands for innovation, proof of what works, and collaboration; and
- **More generously than business,** which is mandated to place pre-eminence on shareholder returns, but which also realizes it cannot succeed in a decaying world.

As social needs continue to spike in light of shrinking government budgets, employment rolls, and social safety nets, social enterprise is emerging as a self-sustaining, market-based, business-like, and highly effective method of meeting social needs.

Social enterprises produce higher social returns on investment than other models. On the other hand, they produce direct, measurable public benefits. A classic employment-focused social enterprise, for example, might serve at least four public aims:

- **Fiscal responsibility** — It reduces the myriad costs of public supports for people facing barriers, by providing a pathway to economic self-sufficiency for those it employs.
- **Public safety** — It makes the community in which it operates safer, by disrupting cycles of poverty, crime, incarceration, chemical dependency, and homelessness.
- **Economic opportunity** — It improves our pool of human capital and creates jobs in communities in need of economic renewal.
- **Social justice** — It gives a chance to those most in need.

Yet, almost magically, social enterprises produce these benefits while *reducing* the draw on public and philanthropic funds.

Social enterprises are revenue-generating businesses with a twist. Whether operated by a non-profit organization or by a for-profit company, a social enterprise has two goals: to achieve social, cultural, community economic, or environmental outcomes; and to earn revenue. On the surface, many social enterprises look, feel, and even operate like traditional businesses. But looking more deeply, one discovers the defining characteristics of the social enterprise: mission is at the centre of business, with income generation playing an important supporting role (Centre for Community Enterprise).

5. Conclusion

In essence, social entrepreneurs are entrepreneurs in a social or not-for-profit context. The difference is that their prime motivation, aims, and mission are social rather than commercial. They still pursue opportunities and continually innovate, but for the purpose of serving their social mission. Social entrepreneurs have many of the same qualities as business entrepreneurs; however they also need a heightened sense of accountability to the wide range of stakeholders involved in a social enterprise.

A social enterprise is a business set up primarily for social objectives whose surpluses are reinvested in the business or in the community for that purpose. The mixing of social and economic objectives within a social enterprise can be dangerous. There are difficulties in accounting for the two objectives and in particular making trade-offs between the two. It should be clearly understood that we speak and we plead for very well defined structures, in the sense that every ambiguous venture should be put apart in order to avoid possible temptations of corruption.

Social enterprise is emerging as the "missing middle" sector between the traditional worlds of government, non-profits, and business. Social enterprises produce higher social returns on investment than other models. They produce direct, measurable public benefits.

This solution was not easily reached, because in a way it contradicts human nature, which is individualistic at its core. It was reached dialectically, which is to say at the end of a cause and effect evolution. And it was reached because the alternative to this solution is the control of society through dictatorship and totalitarianism, an alternative both tried and disproven by modern history.

References

Bornstein, D. (2007), *How to Change the World: Social Entrepreneurs and the Power of New Ideas*, Oxford: Oxford University Press.

Burns, P. (2011), *Entrepreneurship and Small Business*, Palgrave Macmillan.

Dees, G. J., (1998), The meaning of "social entrepreneurship". Available at http://www.caseatduke.org/documents/dees_SE.pdf.

Drucker, P. (1993), *Post-Capitalist Society*, New York: Harper Business.

Mort, G. S., Weerawardena, J., & Carnegie, K. (2003), Social entrepreneurship: Towards conceptualisation, *International Journal of Nonprofit and Voluntary Sector Marketing*, 8(1).

Pearce, J. (2003), *Social Enterprise in any Town*, Calouste Gulbenkian Foundation.

Serafinn, L. (2013), Goodbye old economy — enter the new era of social enterprise. Available at http://the7gracesofmarketing.com/2013/08/goodbye-old-economy-enter-the-new-era-of-social-enterprise/.

xxx Social Enterprise Alliance, Social enterprise: the "missing middle". Available at https://www.se-alliance.org/what-is-social-enterprise.

xxx Centre for community enterprise, What is social enterprise. Available at: http://www.centreforsocialenterprise.com/what.html.

xxx European Comission. Available at http://ec.europa.eu/enterprise/policies/sme/promoting-entrepreneurship/social-economy/social-enterprises/index_en.htm).

xxx Social enterprise. Available at http://www.socialenterprisemark.org.uk/the-mark/what-is-social-enterprise.

xxx Ashoka Innovators for the Public, Available at https://www.ashoka.org/social_entrepreneurMeet the new heroes, What is social entrepreneurship. Available at: http://www.pbs.org/opb/thenewheroes/whatis/Center for advancement of Social Entrepreneurship. Available at http://www.caseatduke.org/about/sedefinition.htm.

Chapter 25

Realities and Peculiarities of the Entrepreneurship in Brasov, Romania

Camelia Dragomir and Stelian Panzaru

"Spiru Haret" University, Faculty of Management

Carmen Lis

"Lucian Blaga" University

Nowadays, the entrepreneur and entrepreneurship terms are becoming better known and used by people who work in the area of economy. The entrepreneurship entails to identify the economic opportunities and to use them by starting a new business or taking over and developing the existing business. In recent years, the terms have been extended to include social and political forms of entrepreneurial activity.

Entrepreneurship refers to an individual's ability to turn ideas into action. The entrepreneurs are committed with resources (innovations, money) in an effort to transform innovations into economic goods. This activity implies creativity, sense of initiative, innovation and risk-taking, as well as the ability to plan and manage projects in order to achieve objectives.

The objective of the chapter is to investigate the perceptions of the entrepreneurs from Brasov County, Romania, about the factors that play an important role in the entrepreneurial development. The importance of entrepreneurship development upon economy was stressed by analyzing the factors that encourage or discourage the entrepreneurship. The following aspects were taken into consideration: (a) the important factors in the decision to start/take over a business; (b) the risks in business development; (c) barriers to entrepreneurship development.

The study is based on interviews with 85 entrepreneurs and managers from Brasov County. The conclusions with regard to the Romanian business environment and the development of entrepreneurship were drawn based on this analysis. The chapter also presents aspects that need to be strengthened for shaping the conditions for the development of entrepreneurial performance.

1. Introduction

The entrepreneurship is regarded as one of the most important sources of competitive advantage for all countries. The development of entrepreneurship has important benefits, both economically and socially. The expression of this reality is represented by the European Union (EU) priority which perceives entrepreneurship as one of the key elements of a sustainable development in economy. The entrepreneurial initiatives are significant at national level for job creation and economic growth. In other words, promotion of entrepreneurial spirit equals promoting investments, new jobs, innovation, and competitiveness of business.

For a long period of time, in Romania, the role of entrepreneurship in economic and social development has often been underestimated. However, in the last years, there has become increasingly apparent that entrepreneurship is core objective helping to increase economic and social development. Based on these aspects, the chapter aims to analyze the main issues concerning the perceptions of the entrepreneurs from Brasov County about the factors that encourage or discourage their activity. The empirical research aims to capture the views of a representative group of 87 entrepreneurs and managers from Brasov County. The main conclusions of the chapter provide interesting and useful data regarding the realities and the peculiarities of the entrepreneurship environment. The importance of entrepreneurship was stressed by analyzing the factors that influence the activity of Brasov County's entrepreneurs.

2. Relevance of Entrepreneurship Concept in the Specialty Literature

The entrepreneurship constituted the topic of several specialty studies. The subject attracts many researchers that have made an important contribution to the development of the entrepreneurship concept. This interest is determined by the importance of entrepreneurship for economic progress. In time, the authors had not only different methods and terms in defining the entrepreneurship, but also various angles of approaching its repercussions on the economic development.

Presented as a generator of economic growth and job creation, the entrepreneurship is a means to make economies more competitive. The relevance of entrepreneurship for national economy is expressed by Michael Porter: "Invention and entrepreneurship are at the heart of national advantage" (Porter, 1990: 125).

In the global competition of economy, the entrepreneurship development is the main factor that will stimulate economic development. In other words, economic growth is bound to slow unless there is an adequate supply of entrepreneurs looking out new ideas, and willing to take the risk of introducing them" (Lewis, 1955: 182).

The European Commission recognizes entrepreneurship as a key vehicle by which a region's competitiveness can be stimulated (Kitson *et al.*, 2004; European Commission, 2009). There are many empirical studies regarding the relation between entrepreneurial activity and economic growth. The Global Entrepreneurship Monitor data (GEM provides annual assessments of the national level of entrepreneurship) suggests that there are no countries with high levels of entrepreneurship and low levels of economic growth (Reynolds *et al.*, 2002: 7, 24). Also, Caree & Thurik (1998), who examine how the share of small firms affects subsequent industry output growth, show that industries with a high share of small enterprises relative to the same industries in other countries performed better in terms of output growth. In other words, smaller firms appear to be better suited to cope with the conditions of increased globalization, since they show higher flexibility and propensity to innovation and are an outstanding vehicle for channeling the entrepreneurial ambitions of individuals (Audretsch & Thurik, 2001; Carree & Thurik, 2002). The impact of entrepreneurship on economic growth is supported by other empirical studies (Nickell, 1996; Nickell *et al.*, 1997; Thurik & Wennekers, 2001), as well. These studies suggest that entrepreneurship has a positive effect on economic growth.

The most authorized points of view of the specialty literature approach the notion of *entrepreneurship* from various perspectives. For Reynolds (2005), entrepreneurship can be conceptualized as the discovery of opportunities and the subsequent creation of new economic activity, often via the creation of a new organization. The functional roles of entrepreneurs include, in Friijsetal *et al.*'s opinion (2002) and Jääskeläinen's (2000), coordination, innovation, neutralization uncertainty, supply of capital, decision-making, property and resource allocation. Summarizing the roles of entrepreneurs, Wennekers & Thurik (1999: 46–47) define the entrepreneurship as "... the ability and willingness of individuals, on their own or in teams, within and outside of existing organizations, to perceive and create new economic opportunities (new products, new production methods, new schemes of organization, and new product-market combinations) and introduce their ideas in the market, despite uncertainty and other obstacles, by making decisions about location, form and use of resources. and institutions." According to Sharma & Chrisman (2007), entrepreneurship covers the occurrence of organizational creation or innovation that occur inside or outside the existing organization, whilst entrepreneurs are individuals or groups of individuals that act independently, or as part of a corporatist system, that create new organizations or instigate renewal or innovation within an existing one. Essentially, entrepreneurs are focused on investments, innovation, development, production increase, new jobs creation.

Many authors consider that entrepreneurship has a determinant role in economic progress by creating new firms, by exploiting business opportunities and by improving life quality. Similar to this is the approach of Schumpeter (1911), that states that "everyone is an entrepreneur when he actually carries out new combinations" by creating new firms, by identifying business opportunities, by job creation. Stevenson & Jarillo (1990: 23) define the entrepreneurship as "a process by which individuals — either on their own or within organizations — pursue opportunities". In fact, the entrepreneurial function implies the discovery, assessment, and exploitation of opportunities, in other words, new products, services, or production processes; new strategies and organizational forms, and new markets for products and inputs that did not previously exist (Shane & Venkataraman, 2000). From the point of view of Knight (1967) and Drucker (1970) the entrepreneurship is defined as the activity of people willing to risk their careers, activity, and funds available to put a new idea into practice. Many entrepreneurs undertake risks as a condition for the business success. Usually, obtained results are proportional with the risks undertaken. The entrepreneurs must adequately respond to the risk and uncertainty situations. The unfavorable business environment contains many threats and difficulties for companies: excessive taxation; high inflation rates; heavy bureaucracy and corruption; low level of internal demand; excessive administrative controls; instability of national currency; poor quality of infrastructure; unpaid invoices by state institutions, etc. (Nicolescu & Nicolescu, 2013). An unfavorable business environment amplifies the action and the consequences of all types of risks the company is exposed to, from the perspective of the diversity of forms under which they appear and due to the magnitude of the effects they generate. Risk and uncertainty can be associated to each and every type of business and also, they can be traced, so that their level should be framed within manageable bounds. It is necessary for entrepreneurs to manifest a strong enterprising spirit, to adopt decisions in a short time, to elaborate anti-risk measures, when facing multitudes of tensions which may appear in their entrepreneurial activity. The risk requires courage, but the offensive spirit itself is not enough for success. Courage means responsibility for the accomplished actions (Dragomir, 2012: 166). Entrepreneurs can learn from both their own activity and others' successes and failures, which enable them to improve their skills and adapt their attitudes (Carree & Thurik, 2002). The capacity of facing the challenges and learning from any defeat is a component part of the entrepreneurial spirit. Additionally, the entrepreneurial spirit signifies innovation, flexibility, adaptability to change, dedication, self-discipline, initiative, and vision. These are essential features in order to survive and develop companies that have business success. From this point of view, entrepreneurial behavior is seen as behavior that manages to combine innovation, risk-taking and pro-activity (Miller, 1983).

Entrepreneurs are highly creative and innovative individuals with a tendency to imagine new solutions. They develop something innovative inside an organization, contributing to its development and improvement. Transforming ideas into economic opportunities is an essential element for economic progress and for improving the wellbeing of society.

Consequently, whatever definition is given to entrepreneurship, it is increasingly apparent that entrepreneurship generates innovation, leads to new job creation and contributes to economic development.

Based on the aforementioned highlighted aspects, we have achieved an empirical research that analyzes the realities and the peculiarities of the entrepreneurship development in Brasov County, Romania. In the next paragraphs we present shortly a part of the results of the research.

3. The Study Regarding the Realities and Peculiarities of Entrepreneurial Activity in the Brasov County, Romania

3.1. *The research purpose*

The purpose of this study was to analyze the realities and peculiarities of entrepreneurial activity in the Brasov

County. We have investigated a representative sample of entrepreneurs regarding their perceptions of the factors that encourage or discourage the activity of the entrepreneurs. A total of 87 entrepreneurs from Brasov County were the respondents of this study. All respondents work in the real economy and are daily confronting different problems of the business environment.

More aspects were targeted. Of these, our analysis focuses on the following elements: (a) the important factors in the decision to start/take over a business; (b) the risks in business development; (c) barriers to entrepreneurship development. We consider that, all the elements mentioned influence the development of the entrepreneurship. The questions were addressed and formulated online, as not to induce subjective responses.

3.2. *The results of research*

(a) *Analysis of the important factors in the decision to start/take over a business*

The objective of the section is to investigate the factors that play an important role *in the decision to* start/take over a business. The decision to start or take over a business is not easy and depends on numerous factors. Of these, the respondents believed that the most important factors relate to:

(1) The funds needed to start/take over the business;
(2) Dissatisfaction with previous work;
(3) Identifying the best business ideas;
(4) Correct prediction of chances of success and risks involved in a business;
(5) Resolution regarding unmet environmental and social needs.

For the entrepreneurs interviewed, the financial means and an appropriate idea are the most important factors in the decision to start or take over a business (Fig. 1).

Difficult access to financing has been reported as a barrier in the decision to start/take over a business. Thus, financial resources are considered important in the decision to start/take over a business for 87% of respondents. A best business idea is important for 18.39% of respondents. This can be identified through

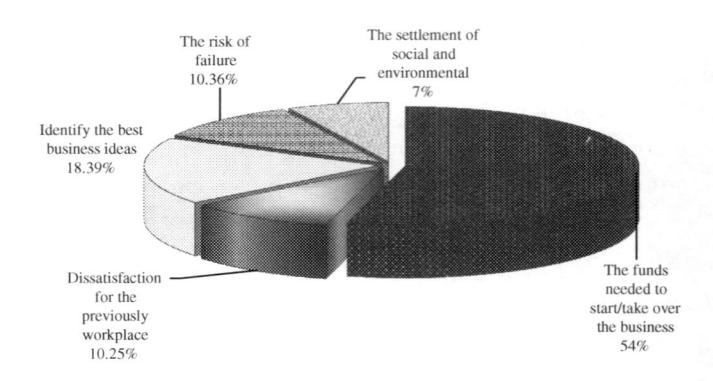

Fig. 1. The important factors in the decision on starting/taking over a business

the complex analysis of the market and identification of consumers' needs which were not satisfied.

Dissatisfaction with the previously workplace is an important factor in the decision to start/take over a business for 10.25% of respondents. Many times, the individuals are trying to start businesses because they have no job options. The risk of failure and its consequences for professional and personal lives are regarded as a serious obstacle in the decision to start a business for 10.36% of the respondents interviewed.

The results of the investigation show that solving social and environmental unmet needs are an important factor in decision to start/take over a business. Around 7% of entrepreneurs interviewed have the opinion that the resolution of unmet social and environmental needs is important in their decision to start a business. The percentage is a proof of interest for the quality of life and for solving the environmental problems. In fact, in Brasov County there are many entrepreneurs who have decided to be actively involved by integration of environmental policies into their business activities and to develop strategies to transform the company into a responsible business from the point of economic and social view (Dragomir *et al.*, 2013: 63).

(b) *Analysis of risks in business development*

The business risk comprises the entire set of threats that can negatively influence the accomplishment of the aimed objectives. The development of the business amplifies the action and the consequences of all types of risks to which the company is exposed. The entrepreneurs must integrate more variables in their managerial decisions, which are difficult to control.

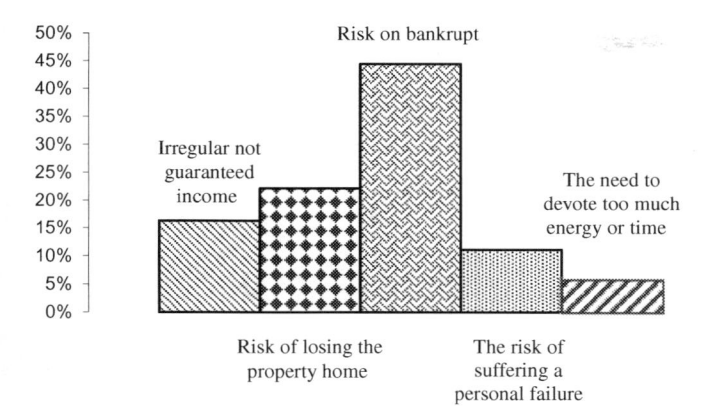

Fig. 2. The risks in business development

Asked to mention the risks that scare them the most, 45.5% of entrepreneurs interviewed noted, in first place, the risk of bankruptcy. The risk of bankruptcy and its consequences are regarded as a serious obstacle for the development of a business (Fig. 2). The risk of losing the property is an obstacle for 22.17% of the respondents and the risk of fluctuating, irregular income gain is an obstacle for 16.33% of the respondents. About 11.15% of the respondents say they the risk of suffering a personal failure worries them.

The entrepreneurs are exposed to uncertainty situations that are strongly felt in their professional and particular lives. The need to devote too much energy or time for business, to the detriment of personal life is particularly worrying for 5.85% of entrepreneurs interviewed.

Survey data reveal a high percentage of respondents who fear the risk of suffering personal failures and their consequences for professional and personal lives (11.15% of respondents). These concerns are explained by the fact that in our entrepreneurial culture we meet a pronounced aversion towards risk-taking and a greater desire for safety and stability. The aversion towards risk-taking is higher especially when it affects the family's expectations of the future. Fear of these risks is more amplified by the economic and financial crisis, which does not encourage the entrepreneurship activity.

Companies, regardless of their size, must face the risks. The risks, which the entrepreneurs are facing, are diverse and difficult to control. The capacity of facing the challenges means courage and responsibility for the accomplished actions. It is necessary for entrepreneurs to manifest a strong enterprising spirit and to elaborate anti-risk measures.

Regarding the fear of risks, the empirical studies (Kan & Tsai, 2006; Sánchez, 2011), show that the school education helped develop some risk tolerance. From this point of view, the entrepreneurs interviewed agree that their entrepreneurial education helped them reduce the fear of risks.

(c) *Analysis of the barriers that mark the development of business*

This section examines the specific issues that constitute direct barriers to entrepreneurial activity. According to the survey conducted, most barriers and difficulties which confront entrepreneurs refer to:

(1) Lack of financial resources, financial blockage, sometimes;
(2) Administrative complexity, bureaucracy;
(3) Insufficient qualified staff;
(4) Difficulties in obtaining the necessary information.

Lack of financial resources is a major barrier to progress/development of business. This is confirmed by the large number of respondents in Brasov County. A total of 54.63% of the entrepreneurs interviewed have mentioned lack of finance as the most important barrier to their entrepreneurial activities (Fig. 3).

The data reveals that the percentages of entrepreneurs that have financial difficulties in their business are extremely high. Regarding the perceived lack of financial support, small businesses rarely meet the conditions for accessing bank loans and other traditional financing instruments. Owing to the risk involved, these firms are rarely supported by the banking sector.

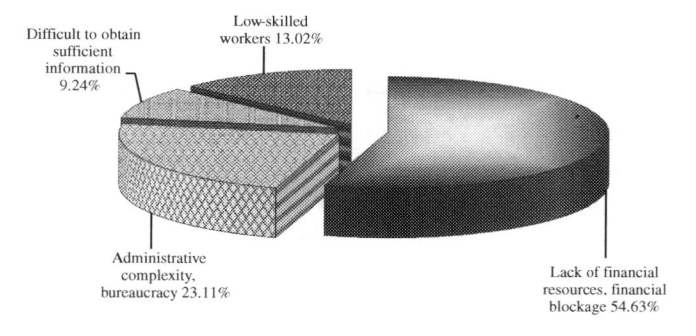

Fig. 3. The barriers in business development

Many entrepreneurs agree that it is difficult to start a business because of the complexity of the administrative process. The administrative complexity and difficult bureaucratic procedures were reported by 23.11% of respondents. Public administration, central and local, determines, to a large extent, the functionality and the performance of the entrepreneurship activity. Two of the major 'diseases' of the business environment — bureaucracy and corruption — are the result of interaction between central and local administration and other components of economy and society (Nicolescu & Nicolescu, 2013).

Insufficient qualified staff is perceived as a barrier in the business development for 13.02% of respondents. Also, regarding the difficulties in obtaining the necessary information, 9.24% of entrepreneurs interviewed see it as a barrier that marks the development of business.

4. Concluding Remarks

Creating a favorable environment for the development of entrepreneurial skills has been a core objective for any country. Romania perceives entrepreneurship as one of the key enablers of sustainable economic growth. Although the role of entrepreneurship has often been underestimated, currently, the status of the entrepreneur enjoys a good reputation. Most of Romanians see entrepreneurship as one of the solutions that can provide economic and social independence. A large majority believes that entrepreneurs are creators of new jobs, products, and services that benefit everyone. For Brasov County the entrepreneurial development has been a powerful engine of economic growth that led to enhanced quality of life in this region. The purpose of the research was to gather information about the factors that encourage or discourage the entrepreneurs' activity in the Brasov County. The recorded data provides interesting information about the entrepreneurial behavior, attitudes, perceptions, and concerns of the entrepreneurs interviewed. The information and the analysis from this study allow us to formulate certain conclusions about the three elements investigated: (a) the important factors in the decision to start/take over a business; (b) the risks in business development; (c) barriers to entrepreneurship development. All of the data explains the necessity to develop a favorable entrepreneurial environment, to determine the good functionality of the economy and social life in Brasov County.

The decision to start or take over a business is a complex process and it involves many aspects that must be taken into account. The recorded data indicates the necessity for reducing administrative burdens, simplifying bureaucratic procedures, and reducing tax obstacles. There are many useless bureaucratic rules that cost time and money and that reduce the efficiency of the entrepreneurial activity. The transition from the conservative and rigid mentalities and practices to the values and attitudes that encourage entrepreneurship is a process to be completed as soon as possible by the Romanian public administration system. Consequently, it is necessary to make the transition from bureaucracy to the new public management, to determine the normal functionality of the business environment.

Regarding the funds needed to start/take over the business, the political and administrative bodies must improve the entrepreneurial framework conditions by increasing access to finance and by creating supportive programs to start up own businesses and by creating a proper environment for entrepreneurial activities. Also, there is need for programs that focus on the small businesses. To have an impact, these programs should be well focused. One way to achieve this is by unlocking the economic resources and entrepreneurial potential.

On the other side, we consider that entrepreneurs need to develop entrepreneurial knowledge and competences. Consequently, education in entrepreneurship can be successfully developed by the involvement of the education system in partnership with the business environment. In Brasov County, there are promoted entrepreneurial skills and attitudes through education and training programs. The entrepreneurs interviewed admit that school education helped them to develop their administrative and financial skills. Also, we consider that there is need to promote entrepreneurship through information programs and through the share experience of best practices among the EU countries.

With all the information taken into account, this study tries to emphasize the idea that Romania needs to make some changes in the economic and administrative environment in order to support the access to financial resources, to reduce the administrative burdens and tax obstacles, and to create a favorable environment for the entrepreneurship development in Brasov County. Without these elements the economic and social prosperity in this region is not possible.

References

Audretsch David, B. & Thurik, R. (2001), *Linking Entrepreneurship to Growth*, Paris: OECD Directorate for Science, Technology and Industry Working Papers.

Carree, M. & Thurik, A. R. (2002), The impact of entrepreneurship on economic growth. In *International Handbook of Entrepreneurship Research*, Z. Acs and D. B. Audretsch (eds.), Boston/Dordrecht: Kluwer Academic Publishers.

Dragomir, C. (2012), Causes generating risks in the business management, *Review of General Management*, 16(2), 160–167.

Dragomir, C., Ionescu, E., & Pânzaru, S. (2013), Economic sustainable development and eco-development, *Review of General Management*, 18(2), 58–68.

Drucker, P. (1970), Entrepreneurship in business enterprise, *Journal of Business Policy*, 1, 59–86.

European Commission (2009), *European Competitiveness Report* 2009, Brussels: DG Enterprise and Industry.

Friijsetal, C., Paulsson, T., & Karlsson, C. (2002), *Entrepreneurship and Economic Growth: A Critical Review of Empirical and Theoretical Research*, Östersund: Institutet för Tillväxtpolitiska Studier.

Jääskeläinen, M. (2000), *Entrepreneurship and Economic Growth*, Helsinki: Institute of Strategy and International Business.

Kan, K. & Tsai, W. D. (2006), Entrepreneurship and risk aversion, *Small Business Economics*, 26, 465–474.

Knight, K. (1967), A descriptive model of the intra-firm innovation process, *Journal of Business of the University of Chicago*, 40, 158–169.

Kitson, M., Martin, R., & Tyler, P. (2004), Regional competitiveness: An elusive yet key concept? *Regional Studies*, 38(9), 991–999.

Lewis, W. A. (1955), *The Theory of Economic Growth*, London: Routledge Publisher.

Miller, L. (1983), The correlates of entrepreneurship in three types of firms, *Management Science*, 29, 770–791.

Nickell, S. J. (1996), Competition and corporate performance, *Journal of Political Economy*, 104(4), 724–746.

Nickell, S. J., Nicolitsas, D., & Dryden, N. (1997), What makes firms perform well? *European Economic Review*, 41, 783–796.

Nicolescu, O. & Nicolescu, C. (2013), Entrepreneurs' perceptions of the state implication in the business environment: Modelling in Romania, *Transylvanian Review of Administrative Sciences*, 38, 106–124.

Organisation for Economic Co-operation and Development (OECD) (2002), *Benchmarking: Fostering Firms Creation and Entrepreneurship*, Paris: OECD.

Porter, M. E. (1990), *The Competitive Advantage of Nations*, New York: Free Press.

Reynolds, P. D., Bygrave, W., Cox, L. W., & Hay, M. (2002), *Global Entrepreneurship Monitor 2002 Executive Report*, Wellesley: Babson College/London Business School.

Reynolds, P. D. (2005), Understanding business creation: Serendipity and scope in two decades of business creation studies, *Small Business Economics*, 24, 359–364.

Sánchez, J. C. (2011), University training for entrepreneurial competencies: Its impact on intention of venture creation, *International Entrepreneurship Management Journal*, 7(2), 239–254.

Schumpeter, J. A. (1911), *The Theory of Economic Development: An Inquiry into Profits, Capital, Credit, Interest and the Business Cycle*, 1934 translation, Cambridge: Harvard University Press.

Shane, S. A. & Venkataraman, S. (2000), The promise of entrepreneurship as a field of research, *Academy of Management Review*, 25, 217–226.

Sharma, P. & Chrisman. J. (2007), Toward a reconciliation of the definitional issues. In *The Field of Corporate Entrepreneurship in Entrepreneurship: Concepts, Theory and Perspective*, A. Cuervo, D. Ribeiro, and S. Roig (eds.), Heidelberg: Springer.

Stevenson, H. H. & Jarillo, J. C. (1990), A paradigm of entrepreneurship research: Entrepreneurial management, *Strategic Management Journal*, 11, 17–27.

Thurik, R. & Wennekers, S. (2001), *A Note on Entrepreneurship, Small Business and Economic Growth*, Rotterdam: Erasmus Research Institute of Management Report Series.

Wennekers, A.R.M. & Thurik, A.R. (1999), Linking entrepreneurship and economic growth, *Small Business Economics*, 13, 46–47.

Chapter 26

ESF Interventions for Promoting Entrepreneurship in Romania

Daniela Manuc
Sectoral Operational Programme Human Resources Development

The chapter examines the role of the European Social Fund (ESF) in promoting entrepreneurial culture and adaptability by supporting skilled, trained, and adaptable labor force and enterprises.

The Sectoral Operational Program Human Resources Development 2007–2013 (SOPHRD) finances projects targeting the objective of making entrepreneurship a career option for everybody, as an important solution for counterbalancing the negative effects of the structural adjustments and industry restructuring process, generating economic and social alternatives, and improving the economic status of a significant number of people.

The chapter focuses on how specific results produced by ESF interventions contribute to increasing competitiveness and modern management systems with emphasis on conceptual human resources management, especially in small and medium enterprises.

The proposed methodology focuses on analyzing different SOPHRD financed projects relevant for promoting entrepreneurship. The key area of intervention (KAI) 3.1 of the SOPHRD — promoting entrepreneurial culture targets both managers who learn how to make best use of the opportunities existing on the market, on the success factors that increase business' competitiveness, management, and marketing strategies, as well as individuals interested in starting up a business as self-employed or employers, in providing the necessary information on business opportunities. However, the examples given will also cover projects financed through other relevant KAIs. Promoting partnership is a specific area of intervention under priority axis 3, but it is encouraged under all other priority axes, as a horizontal principle, wherever deemed relevant.

A key element in the SOPHRD financed projects is the role of partnerships in promoting new methods and models aiming at changing both present traditional arrangements and attitudes towards entrepreneurship.

This chapter concludes that ESF financed interventions contributed to a great extent to developing the entrepreneurial culture as well as to encouraging new start-ups, including in the field of social economy.

1. Introduction

European Social Fund (ESF) is an important instrument used by the Member States to make Europe's workforce and small and medium-sized enterprises (SMEs) better equipped to face new and global challenges. ESF-funded initiatives in the field of entrepreneurship consist in providing career advice, promoting entrepreneurial culture, and training for the self-employed and entrepreneurs. ESF has provided assistance to SMEs through a variety of ways, such as incentives for business start-ups, activities to support organizational changes, and innovation and subsidies for self-employed persons and SMEs. A significant contribution was brought in the field of inclusive entrepreneurship,[1] where the *Community of practice* developed with ESF support played an important role.[2]

The chapter examines the role of the ESF in promoting entrepreneurship and adaptability by supporting skilled, trained, and adaptable labor force and enterprises. The chapter focuses on how specific results produced by ESF interventions in Romania contribute to increasing competitiveness and developing modern management systems with emphasis on human resources management, especially in SMEs, with a special focus on the health sector.

In Romania, the Sectoral Operational Program Human Resources Development (SOPHRD) 2007–2013 finances projects targeting the objective "to make entrepreneurship a career option for everybody, as an important solution for counterbalancing the negative effects of the structural adjustments and industry restructuring process, generating economic and social alternatives and improving the economic status of a significant number of people."[3]

The chapter envisages specific ESF operations, with no intention of stating general conclusions, in the absence of any recent interim evaluation on the implementation of SOPHRD in Romania or of any impact evaluation conducted so far. The purpose is to provide a specific overview on how ESF funding opportunities contribute to promoting entrepreneurship and to improving management systems. At the same time, it is worth mentioning that SOPHRD is currently in Romania one of the main financing instruments for developing the social economy sector.

2. Methodology

The proposed methodology focuses on analyzing different SOPHRD financed projects relevant for promoting entrepreneurship. The choice of this approach is justified by the lack of recent evaluation data regarding the implementation of different interventions funded through SOPHRD.

At the same time, it is not to be argued that the chosen projects are under any criteria representative for the results obtained in the entrepreneurship sector with ESF support. They were chosen on the grounds that they were considered to be successful interventions on the Romanian labor market, with a significant contribution to developing skills and employability of the target group.

The analysis of the case studies was based on desk research. Secondary data was gathered on the basis of official information available on the official project websites.

Given the scope of this chapter, no interviews or questionnaires were conducted with the project managers or project beneficiaries. This approach would be considered necessary in case of an impact evaluation (although no impact indicators are available in the SOPHRD) for this sector, but for the scope of this chapter the questionnaires and interviews would have provided limited results.

3. ESF Interventions Supporting Modern Management and Entrepreneurship

The structure of this chapter is based on the specific outcomes identified in various SOPHRD funded projects, relying primarily on the types of contributions that ESF interventions produced in the area of entrepreneurship and management systems. This approach does not intend to produce any general conclusions at the level of the program (SOPHRD).

The main axes of the analysis focus on: awareness raising measures in the field of entrepreneurship; the role of training programs in support of new start-ups and for developing management skills; the new IT systems in support of modern management and entrepreneurship; inclusive entrepreneurship and supporting women in business.

(a) *Awareness raising measures in the field of entrepreneurship*

The need to foster entrepreneurial mindsets has imposed itself as a priority on the EU political agenda, being a

---

[1] EC, The COPIE Toolkit for Inclusive Entrepreneurship. Available at http://www.cop-ie.eu/sites/default/files/COPIE_Toolkit_ FINAL.pdf.
[2] http://www.cop-ie.eu/.
[3] The Framework Document for the Implementation of the Implementation of the Sectoral Operational Program Human Resources Development 2007–2013.

cornerstone of the employment and education strategies and action plans. In this respect, ESF has contributed to making entrepreneurship a key concept of many awareness campaigns, putting entrepreneurial culture at the heart of the "inclusive growth".

In Romania, SOPHRD has ensured the proper framework for financing awareness raising measures in the field of entrepreneurship, as one of the key eligible actions for many projects implemented under KAI 3.1. A relevant case study is the project called "*DACIE*"[4] (*Entrepreneurial Development for Competitiveness through Innovation and Eco-efficiency*), financed from the SOPHRD 2007–2013 — KAI 3.1. The project partners cover civil society organizations and business environment representatives. The general objective of the project focuses on the development of entrepreneurial culture, managerial skills, and innovative spirit among entrepreneurs, managers, employees, in order to set up new SMEs and to strengthen the existing ones, especially in the new economic sectors, using eco-efficient and information technology and communications (ITC) technologies. The project was implemented in four development regions in Romania. The target group included 75 new entrepreneurs to develop business start-up plans and over 1,000 managers and employees trained. One of the main activities of the project was the implementation of an awareness raising campaign for 1,500 people on the benefits of entrepreneurship. This measure has ensured that entrepreneurship can be understood as a career option for everybody, and that specific instruments are available for addressing individual needs to develop managerial skills and start new businesses.

Besides, the entrepreneurship competence was presented in most ESF campaigns as being more about adaptability and anticipation of labor market trends, meaning thinking employment as constant evolution. This can lead to a great impact in terms of awareness, as not all individuals can imagine themselves business owners, while the idea of becoming more adaptable in the meaning of entrepreneurial spirit and the idea of thus becoming able to cope with the challenges of modern labor markets are things which individuals can easily assimilate. This can trigger a better response to awareness raising measures, making the individuals feel closer to the objectives projected under those specific awareness raising tools. However, this estimated impact is based on direct observation of the specific case studies analyzed, and it is not based on the analysis of a representative sample. All in all, the final SOPHRD evaluation will probably deliver specific conclusions on this point.

(b) *The role of training programs in support of new start-ups and for developing management skills*

Economic growth is influenced both by the number of business start-ups and their adaptability to global challenges. This factor needs to be coupled with a proper understanding of how modern management techniques could contribute to making the most out of the existing human and financial resources. This framework has ensured a specific impetus to making entrepreneurship training a key element in implementing ESF interventions under KAI 3.1. — *promoting entrepreneurial culture*. As mentioned in the SOPHRD, the main output indicator for measures financed under this KAI is the number of trainees in business start-up.

The project "*Entrepreneur in the third millennium*"[5] co-financed through the ESF and implemented by the Foundation "Centre for Entrepreneurship and Executive Development — CEED ROMANIA" and the company MBM Software & Partners SRL during July 2010–April 2013 addressed to a target group of over 1,150 people from urban communities — managers and employees — who wanted to start their own business. The people with disabilities were also considered when selecting the target group, one of the projects objectives being to provide them with training in entrepreneurship, business management, project management, and the introduction of new technologies. In the project management field, the PCM guidelines developed by the EC constituted an important training tool.[6]

The training provided to the target group focused on key issues related to entrepreneurship, such as the legal relevant framework, requirements for setting up a start-up, and how to get funds for developing the start-up,

---

[4] http://www.dacie.ro/index.php.

[5] http://www.im3.ro/.
[6] ECPCM guidelines. Available at http://ec.europa.eu/europeaid/multimedia/publications/documents/tools/europeaid_ adm_pcm_guidelines_2004_en.pdf.

the use of ICT for the business, project management. The theoretical knowledge presented was combined with practical modules in order to contribute to the target group better understanding on how to run a business and how to apply the knowledge into their daily work. Training in business management was conducted as well with the purpose of developing the participant skills in developing and running new established start-ups.

Therefore, it could be concluded that in the context in which the initiatives for setting up new firms are strongly encouraged by the European Commission, Romania financed through SOPHRD 2007–2013 clear measures that increased the number of entrepreneurs. Many SOPHRD beneficiaries provided training courses that improved the knowledge and developed the skills of the individuals that wanted to establish a start-up.

As a result, more individuals were willing to take the risks for setting up a new firm. Administrative requirements which often discourage individuals in setting up a new firm did not seem to be a significant burden any more as trained people knew how to comply with these requirements. In the same time, it could be argued that the projects financing training for promoting better management succeeded to some extent to help managers to adapt their businesses to the competitive and challenging context and even to improve their businesses by applying better management techniques.

(c) *The new IT systems in support of modern management and entrepreneurship*

Many projects financed under KAI 3.1 from the SOPHRD have ensured accompanying measures to tackle the need to develop entrepreneurial skills. These measures included in most cases dedicated IT tools meant to support the access to specialized information regarding business opportunities, dedicated training programs, individualized counseling on business start-ups.

The case study analyzed covered a project implemented by the Foundation "Center for Entrepreneurship and Executive Development — CEED ROMANIA", and the company MBM Software & Partners SRL. The project title was *"Entrepreneur in the Third Millennium"*, co-financed by the European Social Found through the SOPHRD 2007–2013.

The project ran from July 2010 until April 2013 and had the overall objective of developing entrepreneurship, management skills and skills in information technology for Romanian entrepreneurs, in view to foster the establishment and development of new companies and job creation.

The main IT tools developed through this project covered: the Virtual Office for Entrepreneurial Development, as an electronic platform that allowed the target group to consult information resources on fields of expertise relevant to the business community and contribute to its continued development (www.e-birouvirtual.ro); the Virtual SME Demonstrator, as a modern instrument offering an experimental environment for implementation and testing of management systems such as customer relationship management and problem management (www.immvirtual.ro), and online consulting services provided by a team of specialists in business management and information technology, that shared best practices and the knowledge gained in over 10 years of experience, aggregating them into a package of dedicated consultancy, and taking questions from those interested to turn them into solutions.

The impact of the project has been significantly boosted through these electronic platforms. Thus, according to the official project website, approximately 350 beneficiaries were assisted for free via the Virtual SME Demonstrator, more than 750 beneficiaries were assisted with the Virtual Office for Entrepreneurial Development, and of these, approximately 370 have downloaded materials developed during the project and posted on the Virtual Office on topics of interest for business creation and use of ICT in business management.

Over 4,000 beneficiaries have increased awareness and information on the benefits and opportunities offered by ICT in launching and management of a business, through the information campaign: email (2,365 people), telephone (200 persons), electronic platform (1,217 people), awareness events (185).

These results prove that specific ESF projects succeed in targeting a wide audience and delivering specialized management instruments which would not have been accessed by that particular target group in other circumstances, with relevant results in supporting senior entrepreneurship.[7]

---

[7] EC (2012).

(d) Inclusive entrepreneurship and supporting women in business

Social economy is a key pillar in ensuring long term development opportunities for local communities.[8] SOPHRD became over the last years one of the main instruments for promoting social economy in Romania. However, the development of this sector was limited due to the lack of any supporting legal framework during the past years, the potential financing from SOPHRD being to a great extent wasted, as only a limited number of social enterprises were set up through this program. At the same time, it can be argued that partnership was a key element in the implementation of KAI 6.1 — *developing social economy*, with the aim of empowering vulnerable groups "in what concerns promoting positive action for the people belonging to vulnerable groups at community level, as well as gaining financial independence based on the income generating types of activities carried out in social economy entities."[9] The partnerships developed allowed for a better understanding of the shared responsibilities at local level, developing innovative management networks for inclusive entrepreneurship initiatives, and also contributed to raising awareness on the importance of social entrepreneurship.

One of the projects implemented under the KAI 6.1 that focused on creating and promoting social economy structures is the project "*First step to become independent*" implemented by the Foundation "Close to You". The project was implemented starting with October 2008 till October 2011. This non-governmental organization (NGO) addressed the needs of vulnerable groups (such as HIV/AIDS-infected and affected people older than 18 years old) by providing the individuals from the target group with training in order to facilitate their integration into the labor market as well as by establishing social economy structures. Some of the people that followed training programs got jobs in the social economy structures established by this NGO. The products made by the employees as well as their prices were made available on a website in order to be sold. However, without public support and fiscal facilities it is very difficult for the social economy structures to survive the challenges generated by the competitive economic environment.

In the context of the global socio-economic crisis, having in mind the serious difficulties that the people belonging to the vulnerable groups have in finding jobs as well as the challenges faced by the social economic structures to survive and to be competitive on the labor market, it is highly important that the state provide support to the social economy structures.

Another dimension of inclusive entrepreneurship covers measures targeting to empower women in the business sector. SOPHRD had more clear-cut results in this area, with a relatively high number of beneficiaries and success stories. Under KAI 3.1, there were relevant projects targeting women entrepreneurs.

The project "*ANTRES Entrepreneurship and the Equality of Chances an Inter-regional Model of Women School of Entrepreneurship*", financed from SOPHRD, KAI 3.1, was implemented from May 2009 to May 2011. The project beneficiary was the Faculty of Economic Sciences, University of Oradea, and the partners were: West University of Timișoara; "Aurel Vlaicu" University, Arad; North University of Baia-Mare; "Eftimie Murgu" University, Reșița; Commercial Academy of Satu Mare; Management Scientific Society of Romania and The National Agency for Equal Opportunities between Women and Men. This project was considered a success story both by the SOPHRD Managing Authority and the European Commission.[10]

The project was especially designed to address the needs of developing entrepreneurial skills among women, while the selection of the target group rigorously identified those women for whom entrepreneurship was a realistic career option. In this respect, the candidates were subject to an initial screening for the determination of socio-professional and motivational profile. The project covered a large number of women: 1,800 were trained in specific business-related fields, while 108 women participating in the training program were awarded the necessary financing for their business plans.

---

[8] EC (2013).

[9] SOPHRD, p. 106. Available at http://www.fseromania.ro/images/downdocs/sop_hrd11.pdf.

[10] http://ec.europa.eu/regional_policy/projects/stories/details_new.cfm?pay=RO&the=51&sto=2085&lan=7&region=ALL&obj=ALL&per=ALL&defL=EN.

Inclusive entrepreneurship on the two axes presented (social entrepreneurship and supporting women in business) is a key feature of the SOPHRD interventions in Romania, with a visible impact in raising awareness in the business environment. Considering the legal limitations of developing this sector, it can be argued that SOPHRD has laid the foundations for future ESF interventions in the next programming period, and that some of the partnerships developed at local level will benefit from future financing in this area.

4. Conclusions

The impact of ESF interventions in Romania is yet to be established. In terms of relevance, efficiency, and effectiveness, the second interim evaluation and the *ex-post* evaluations of SOPHRD will indicate to what extent this program has produced results which are consistent with the objectives set and in accordance with the socio-economic context. However, considering individual ESF interventions, as it was argued in this analysis, it can be underlined that particular ESF-financed measures have impacted significantly on the specific target group, creating opportunities that could not have been produced in other circumstances.[11] This is the case with measures financed under KAI 3.1 — promoting entrepreneurial culture.

As it was indicated in this chapter, the main measures financed from SOPHRD under KAI 3.1 covered awareness raising measures in the field of entrepreneurship, training programs in support of new start-ups, the development of IT systems in support of modern management and entrepreneurship, promotion of inclusive entrepreneurship, and supporting women in business. For each of these axes of intervention, the specific projects presented in this chapter have proven to impact on a relatively high number of people, creating specific circumstances favorable to entrepreneurship promotion and business development.

ESF has produced a clear shift in understanding how entrepreneurship can be approached, becoming more a "career option for everybody" and less the generic concept applying to a limited number of business owners.

SOPHRD projects have laid the foundations for developing the entrepreneurial culture in Romania, both in the competitive sector of the economy and in the social economy area, allowing for a relatively high number of people to develop skills, build networks, discover business opportunities, overcome traditional ways of thinking about vulnerable groups and approach the labor market with a new understanding of how management principles can be applied to serve the widest range of entrepreneurship opportunities, even in the service of social inclusion.

As a result, SOPHRD supported entrepreneurship and self-employment in the direction of creating jobs, developing skills, and giving unemployed and disadvantaged people an opportunity to fully participate in society and the economy.

The second interim evaluation and the *ex-post* evaluation of SOPHRD will provide further basis for drawing relevant conclusion on this subject. At the same time, it is important to underline that a counter-factual evaluation of the interventions financed through SOPHRD in the entrepreneurship sector would be a very useful tool to draw the relevant conclusions in order to better fine-tune the next operational program.

All in all, in the perspective of the conclusions to be drawn from the *ex-post* evaluation, it is obvious that the SOPHRD will definitely constitute an important input for better designing the new ESF Human Capital Operational Program for the 2014–2020 programming period.

References

ECPCM guidelines. Available at http://ec.europa.eu/europeaid/multimedia/publications/documents/tools/Europeaid_adm_pcm_guidelines_2004_en.pdf.

EC (2012), Policy Brief on Senior Entrepreneurship Entrepreneurial Activities in Europe.

EC (2013), Social economy and social entrepreneurship, Social Europe guide, Vol. 4, March.

EC, The COPIE Toolkit for Inclusive Entrepreneurship. Available at http://www.cop-ie.eu/sites/default/files/COPIE_Toolkit_FINAL.pdf.

---

[11] EC, The European Social Fund and Entrepreneurship, http://ec.europa.eu/employment_social/esf/docs/sf_entrepreneurship_en.pdf.

EC, The European Social Fund and Entrepreneurship. Available at http://ec.europa.eu/employment_social/esf/docs/sf_ entrepreneurship_en.pdf.

http://ec.europa.eu/regional_policy/projects/stories/details_new.cfm?pay=RO&the=51&sto=2085&lan=7&region=ALL&obj=ALL&per=ALL&defL=EN

http://www.cop-ie.eu/

http://www.dacie.ro/index.php

http://www.im3.ro/

Sectoral Operational Programme Human Resources Development, p. 106. Available at http://www.fseromania.ro/images/downdocs/sop_hrd11.pdf.

The Framework Document for the Implementation of the Implementation of the Sectoral Operational Programme Human Resources Development 2007–2013.

Chapter 27

Contributions to the Development and Use of Information Programs Dealing With Human Resources in the Rural Area

Simona Biriescu and Mariana Predişcan

The West University of Timisoara

Marian Năstase

The Bucharest University of Economic Studies

Innovation-based economic renewal evolved geospatial contrary. Advances in knowledge are favored and intimate related to the possibilities of communication. Consequently, they are supported by communication infrastructure and communication technologies. Long history of communication technologies showed the transformation of transmission technologies, leading to solution focused on communication technologies in communication centers that become centers of economic renewal through research, innovation, and technological focus.

Romania's aspiration to integrate all the Community approach for sustainable development is a natural expression of the identity of ideals, values, and principles, therefore his vocation is that of a democratic country deeply rooted in its traditions, culture, and the European civilization.

This chapter's objectives deal with revealing the gap between rural and urban in terms of access and opportunities for education, emphasized by this study and with designing an intervention program in rural areas of Romania, especially in disadvantaged areas, based on an extensive use of informational programs and databases. The program should cover initial education, as well as adult education and community education, and all components. A series of objectives and action directions in education that we propose is already recorded in educational policy and reform benchmarks since education is, also, and objectives of ongoing projects.

The methodology used is based on field research and literatures review that reveals the important role in the county of the information system, as it is for instance the "common database". Common database consists of interconnecting local databases and existing county or in progress. This will allow the effective communication within the network of institutions and an effective promotion of the counties of the region by providing easy access to public information and promoting business opportunities and economic cooperation at regional, county, and local levels.

1. Introduction

The starting point for addressing the criteria of economic reform and its implementation strategy is the analysis, even briefly, of the general characteristics of conducting this process in our country. Based on these characteristics and consequences of current economic reform somebody could draw some conclusions regarding the action of the general principle of "destructive creation", detaching the elements/processes perennial, with a continuing need to traverse the entire current period, of the random, temporary — a result of circumstances national/international economic, social, and unfavorable political or governmental errors.

Growth in natural environmental conditions is marked by efforts to make society avoid degradation of nature. While achieving economic growth is a tendency to increase the external costs they incur first who caused degradation of the natural environment. To speak about education research in areas and trying to develop this subject is one of the most daring and ambitious ideas. In rural area "school" is not a specialized institution for carrying out the pedagogical objectives of education, determined by the policies in education (Porter, 2009), but it is rather embedded in the hearts of children and villagers.

The concern for the analysis of the village education perspective of inequality of opportunity, poverty, and lack of interest is part of a trend already established, especially since Europeanization and globalization after 1989 triggered a series of profound changes. These changes have disrupted the life of Romanian villages, people had to adapt to conditions of a decent life non-specific and often the expectations linked to their efforts — a situation that is characteristic of the current educational system.

The precariousness of specific education in rural areas is due to lack of guidance for development and indifference of Romanian political forces to develop projects affirmative action, as long as insufficient funding is focused on the problem, rather than the correct use of existing funding.

Managers create a plan to attract and retain people with skills needed by the organization. Implementing the plan involves the recruitment, selection, integration, training, rewarding, and choosing the most appropriate benefits and ongoing assessment of performance to verify that organizational targets are met. These activities are components of human resource management. Lack of qualified personnel or under size herd, the age structure of employees within an organization, but many are undesirable situations that arise in business management.

2. The Needs for TIC Tools in the Professional Assessment of Human Resources

Needs assessment and human resource planning is strongly recommended by most specialists, in many competitive organizations or companies. This is part of the long-term success of any organization that can assure a mix of the right people at the right place and right time (Pinder & Stuart, 1997; Turban, 2001). The employment decision is based on information required for a proper selection that has two basic principles.

The first principle claims that the candidate's previous behavior is the best indicator of future behavior. This principle is not determined, an employee who was better than the others in previous employment, a benefit may be mediocre in a new position, and a poor student in the beginning of the year can change and become one of the best by theyear end.

Knowing what people have done in the past, it is not necessarily a very fair indication of what they will do in the future, accepting that people can change (Jolivet, 1996). When it is considered a soft one criterion, it refers to the maintenance of the purposes of adapting to the needs of organizations (Figer, 2007) and at the time, when the unit is considered a quality software product, it must meet two requirements: to be easily implemented and tested, and be easily maintained and modified.

A software and database design can play a critical role in achieving good information about human resources because it is seen as a set of interrelated files. Intercorrelationis identified and represented by links between relations, conceptual, and logical data models (Dalotă, 2000; Dănăiață, 1998). This is the starting point in designing physical database design that preceded the physical files. Computer programming can be accomplished using several methods. Therefore it is necessary to take account of some essential things. When designing database, architecture must be taken into account several aspects of the system size. In fact, architecture highlights ways of defining and structuring data. Selecting appropriate enterprise architecture (rural) is the task where database analysts and system analyst playsan important contribution. Finally, databases evolve as important programs.

The program can be defined either as an entity that can be executed on the computer, or as a means of communication with the computer to solve a problem, a description of an algorithm and associated data for execution on the computer, so their representation given restrictions imposed by the computer.

The time schedule also has other meanings, depending, in particular by the performance of the equipment. A special technical performance is the emergence of computer systems with multiple CPU processors in order to have the possibility of multiple processing programs. An important role in the county information system it is "common database" (Dalotă & Dalotă, 1999). Common database consists of interconnecting local databases and existing county or in progress.

This will allow the effective communication within the network of institutions and an effective promotion of the counties of the region by providing easy access to public information and promoting business opportunities and economic cooperation at regional, county, and local levels (Boddy & Buchanan, 2007).

Transmission of information from county and regional level will be through Internet/intranet. Interconnected equipment and management of data bases and banks at county and regional purchase is provided by the project related to appropriate interconnection supplied by technical solution. Databases of local government and the specialized promotion and economic development are considered mandatory for initial stage and the project will be built up based on the uniformity specifications to be carried out in the project (Dalotă, 1998).

3. Education and Human Resources Management in the Rural Areas

The role of education in a civilized society is very important. First, because education contributes to the formation and development of individual and group personality (Delnet, 2003). So, the economic development of a country depends on the education of citizens, so we need a clear conception of the role of education in society.

Today, the objectives of education and educational processes are so complex that only a concentration of efforts by several institutions, reflected in what some have called "educational city" by "redistribution" of education by several factors, could create actions whose results are satisfactory (Damanpour & Evan, 1984), that a restructuring of work in different sections of the society, on educational requirements, seems to be a good sign. The gap between rural and urban in terms of access and opportunities for education, evident by this study requires an intervention program priority in rural areas of Romania and, especially in disadvantaged areas. The program should cover initial education, as well as adult education and community education, and all components. A series of objectives and action directions in education that we propose is already recorded in educational policy and reform benchmarks since education is, also, and objectives of ongoing projects.

Human Resource (HR) plan for rural is created in accordance with the strategic plan of the organization. As the organization identifies developmental opportunities available, it is necessary to correlate them with skills that will be needed to cover them. Recruiting, training, and reward programs are designed to attract, develop, and retain people with the skills. HR development in rural areas involves a process of training people to perform the tasks needed in the organization.

The problem lies in identifying the type of training that employee's need. All decisions must take into account the training of motivated employees. There are a number of training techniques and elements required for a training program to be effective. The performance evaluation is important as behavior considered appropriate evaluation and those inappropriate and granting equitable rewards. To create healthy relationships between management and employees. HR is conducting a number of activities such as conflict management, strengthening relations with trade unions or employee representatives and counseling employees. As they develop size, any organization faces problems need human resources. If the organization is growing, it has to establish methods for finding and hiring people who possess the required skills (Robinson, 1997). This is usually reflected in a form of human resource planning.

Analyzing the organization's projects and future trends, it is estimated the number of people needed and the type of skills they require for any vacancies. Part of this process is the managerial succession, process that determines the number of managers who will retire and the extent to which the organization has talented people to replace them (Fruja & Jivan, 2006).

After developing a human resource plan it must follow a number of steps required to implement the plan. The first essential part of the implementation is to determine the number of people with specific skills needed at some point. The next step is recruiting — a procedure used to attract qualified people to apply for vacancies within the organization. After people have been drawn from applying, selection procedures are used for determining the persons who will actually perform the tasks in the organization and be engaged.

New employees in rural areas should be taught the rules and standards of the organization and is used for this type of program integration or orientation. After people were integrated into the system, it is usually necessary to help them update their skills, attitudes and powers, bringing them the right to organize are considered through training and development of employees. Then, the people began to work in the organization according to the problem at their appropriate reward (Porter & Robin, 1983).

Considered wages are set correctly for people with certain skills and job responsibilities and appropriate performance evaluation procedure by which management can make informed decisions for granting rewards offered under the form of salary or promotion. As rural people in the organization are established, they become concerned with benefits (health insurance, sick leave and rest, pension funds) are offered. As employees we can choose representatives to join a union to protect the rights and promote the interests and therefore there is a need to employ collaboration with these structures (Deaconu, 2007).

When conflicts arise skilled interventions are necessary to manage and resolve them constructively. Counseling in various aspects should also be granted to employees of the managers or specialists. All these activities constitute the substance of employees — management relations. Human resource management in urban areas should coincide with human resource management in rural areas and should be complex oriented activities efficiency staff use an organization aiming to achieve both objectives and employee needs. The individual country, its structure, the feelings, mentality, culture, motivation, desires, and particularly through self-awareness, is the great unknown of a system, can prevent or, conversely, may potentiate the action, process, activity. Moreover, the nature of social being, he lives and works in the community, part of some group that feels more or less attached to groups which in turn interact with other groups, depending on some and exerting influence on others. Therefore, the successful initiation and conduct of the activities of various organizations depend overwhelmingly on the extent to which it is understood, motivated and coordinated human factor. Human resources are the creative, active and coordinator of the activity within organizations, they decisively influencing efficacy of material, financial and informational (Jaba, 1999). Describing people as "resources" it emphasizes the importance and shows that their management requires high levels of genuine concern for people and their professionalism. The evolution of managerial practice and thinking led to the displacement factor specialists' attention to human resource material. It came to the conclusion that the individual is more than a simple component as a productive factor! And human resource management principles about rigid asset of the management company have to be replaced and the management must take into account a number of features missing in economic calculation. Only taking into account all aspects that define human personality, skills, knowledge, aspirations, temperament, and character traits, the management may be able to lead most precious resource, the only resource equipped with the ability to know and defeat their role limitation. Emphasizing HR does not mean, however, an understatement of other resources. Company's system design involves addressing interdependent resource from fundamental objectives whose achievement contributes together, substantive connections that exist between them. Exacerbation of human resources at the expense of the other resources affects the dynamic equilibrium of the organization (Popescu, 1995). Only by meeting the needs of the employee will be able to get involvement in achieving the organization's objectives and only contributing to the success of the organization's employees will be able to satisfy the needs of the work they perform. Only when those involved understand the relationship of human resource management occupies an important position within the organization and contribute to its success. Essential principles of human resource management in the rural areas are:

- Assessment of the human factor as a vital resource;
- Linking in an integrated manner, policies and human resources systems with the organization's mission and strategy;
- Concern sustained concentration and targeting capabilities and individual efforts to achieve effective mission and objectives set;
- Developing a healthy organizational culture.
  The objectives of HR management are:
- Increase efficiency and effectiveness of staff (increased productivity);
- Reduced absenteeism, turnover, and number scale and strike movement;
- Increase job satisfaction of employees;
- Increase capacity for innovation, problem solving and organization change.

Recruitment and selection of HR in rural areas are complementary activities in the staffing process:

- Recruitment — refers to the confirmation of the need to hire new staff, location, and attract those interested in applying for jobs offered;
- Selection — is the final stage of the recruitment decision, it representing the whole process by which people choose what meets the qualities, knowledge, skills and abilities necessary to achieve the objectives, tasks, powers and responsibilities circumscribed to certain posts.

Phases of this work are:

- Define the job that results in a job description are detailed job requirements and the types of skills needed to meet these requirements and profile of the ideal candidate.
- Attracting candidates — recruitment may be internal or external organization. External recruitment takes place in educational institutions through consulting firms and recruitment (so-called "headhunters"), employment agency employment, advertisements in the media, based on recommendations made by employees of the company.
- Selection — candidates may be asked to send a curriculum vitae (CV), a motivation letter (of intent) and letters of recommendation. CV can be free or standardized format and handwritten letter must necessarily quite often it is subject to handwriting expert.

Among the candidates who have submitted these documents retained as interesting group of candidates for the firm may be asked:

— An interview (telephone or face to face) that may occur after the tests (medical, aptitude, intelligence, training etc.). Many companies use aptitude tests, interest and personality to compare job requirements with certain characteristics of candidates. One of the most known and used such tests is Myers Briggs Type Indicator (MBTI);
— A series of interviews (with the direct, human resources manager, general manager).

In conducting the interview can be approached different strategies: honest and friendly approach, the approach focuses on the candidate's past behavior driven approach to problem solving (situational interview) approach aimed at creating a stressful environment. In practice, a combination of these strategies is used. How selection interview is about meeting people, it does not remove the risk of making decisions based on first impressions, or human error (Abrudan, 2009).

Some candidates with good technical skills can fare poorly in the interview selection, becoming angry or excited, leaving the wrong impression. Research shows that interviewer experience enables him to overcome these factors and take the right decisions. Candidates can expect questions like: What do you know about the industry in which the company operates? What contribution can you make to achieving organizational objectives? What problems do you think the company will face in the coming years? What strengths do you see? Are you satisfied with your career so far? What crisis have recently encountered and how you solved it? What decisions do you find difficult to make? Why do you want to go (you go) to the current (old) job? Why do you want to work in this company? After having considered all the evidence (CV, tests, letters of recommendation, interviews), the final decision is taken. It made a job offer to the selected candidate, which he can accept or reject. The hiring process is attempted harmonization of job candidates with the skills and capabilities to ensure success in the new position of that person (Appleby, 2010).

4. Human Resources Program that Support the HR Strategy in Rural Areas

Recognition and promotion of this strategy involves development of modern tools for knowing about and attracting and keeping the good employees. With such a strategy, the function staff actively contributes to the development and achievement of company strategy.

If we pay attention to the HR strategy, in correlation with different categories of resources, we could ask the following question: What markets could be approached with the human potential from the rural area? In order to demonstrate in a concrete way, it is necessary to have some data and information that are connected to the variables specific to HR in the rural area and that make the object of the use of this elaborated software.

This program can be used, with some adjustments by entrepreneurs and managers from larger companies. It is based on different questionnaires that reveal the characteristics of the personnel that is interested in being employed in the rural and even urban areas.

The application is spread on more sheets within a file where all the macros are grouped in Visual Basic for Application. This is a facility of Microsoft Excel, allowing testing the solutions and analyzing fast the results.

This program works with a database from Access, providing different information about an individual.

Each menu has one or two submenus for introducing the necessary data for HRM in the rural areas.

```
Private Sub MNUEXIT_Click()
Unload Me
End Sub
Private Sub MNUFIS_Click()
Form2.Show
End Sub
Private Sub MNUFISA_Click()
Form3.Show
End Sub
Private Sub MNUPSI_Click()
Form4.Show
End Sub
Private Sub MNUSANAT_Click()
Form5.Show
End Sub
Private Sub Command1_Click()
SPIRIT_DE_OBS = Text1.Text
CAPACITATE = Combo1.Text
GANDIRE = Combo2.Text
INTUITIE = Text2.Text
CUNOASTERE_MET = Text3.Text
VEDERE_SPATIU = Text4.Text
NUME_PRENUME = Text5.Text
Print "NUME SI PRENUME", NUME_PRENUME
Print "SPIRIT DE OBSERVATIE", SPIRIT_DE_OBS
Print "CAPACITATE", CAPACITATE
Print "GANDIRE", GANDIRE
Print "INTUITIE", INTUITIE
Print "CUNOASTERE METODA", CUNOASTERE_MET
Print "VEDERE IN SPATIU", VEDERE_SPATIU
End Sub
Private Sub Command2_Click()
End
End Sub
Private Sub Form_Load()
Combo1.AddItem "CAPACITATE DE ANALIZA"
Combo1.AddItem "CAPACITATE ABSTRACTA"
Combo1.AddItem "CREATIVA"
Combo2.AddItem "GANDIRE ABSTRACTA"
Combo2.AddItem "GANDIRE CONCRETA"
End Sub
Dim INTELIGENTA_GENERALA As Integer
```

```
Dim FLEXIBILITATE_IN_GANDIRE As Integer
Dim PERSEVERENTA As Integer
Private Sub Command1_Click()
INTELIGENTA_GENERALA = Text1.Text
COORDONARE_IDEATICA = Text2.Text
STRUCTURI_OPERATIONALE_ALGORITMICE = Text3.Text
FLEXIBILITATE_IN_GANDIRE = Text4.Text
ASUMARE_DE_RISCURI = Text5.Text
PERSEVERENTA = Text6.Text
RECEPTIVITATE_LA_NOU = Text7.Text
MOTIVATIE_INTRISECA = Text8.Text
APTITUDINI_DE_CONDUCERE = Combo1.Text
If Option1.Value Then TEMPERAMENT = DA
If Option2.Value Then TEMPERAMENT = NU
TRASATURI_DE_CARACTER = Combo2.Text
NUME = Text9.Text
PRENUME = Text10.Text
REZULTAT = INTELIGENTA_GENERALA + FLEXIBILITATE_IN_GANDIRE + PERSEVERENTA
Text11.Text = REZULTAT
If REZULTAT > 100 Then
MsgBox "persoana corespunde"
End If
If REZULTAT < 100 Then
MsgBox "persoana nu corespunde"
End If
End Sub
Private Sub Command2_Click()
End
End Sub
PRIVATE SUB FORM_LOAD()
COMBO1.ADDITEM "PREVIZIONALE"
COMBO1.ADDITEM "DECIZIONALE"
COMBO1.ADDITEM "ORGANIZATORICE"
COMBO1.ADDITEM "COORDONARE SI CONTROL"
COMBO2.ADDITEM "EXIGENTA"
COMBO2.ADDITEM "SUBIECTIVITATE"
COMBO2.ADDITEM "FERMITATE"
COMBO2.ADDITEM "SPIRIT CRITIC"
COMBO2.ADDITEM "MODESTIE"
COMBO2.ADDITEM "CONSECVENTA"
COMBO2.ADDITEM "CINSTE"
End Sub
```

It is very important the relationship between urban and rural areas as these places change the countries all over the world. While some of the issues, like changing agricultural systems are universal, other aspects of the process are specific to certain countries or regions (Abrudan, 1999). Urban and rural land uses in these countries are no longer mutually exclusive, but rather exist on a continuum of community types that are increasingly interconnected. Migration and settlement patterns are changing as new forms of urban, suburban and exurban development alter patterns of community development.

The population is increasingly decentralized as suburbanization is being replaced by exurban development, characterized by low-density growth where households with fewer people are living on larger pieces of land further from urban centers. Development patterns influence national and world views, the vision of governments about the use of natural and financial resources and the development of different systems in order to improve the living standards. This development is largely enhanced by the use of information technology and different programs that are addressed to the rural areas, especially.

Much of this development and the resulting land use and lifestyle clashes occur in peri-urban areas once dominated by agriculture. As non-farm growth in rural and peri-urban areas competes with agriculture for land, tensions arise between farmers and non-farmers.

The focus in many developing countries should also be on rural areas as it is promoted the idea that there is a clear division between urban and rural areas, fact that distorts the realities of urban and rural and the increasingly important peri-urban areas, where both urban and rural characteristics can be found.

Rural areas depend on urban areas for secondary schools, post and telephone, credit, agricultural expansion services, farm equipment, hospitals, and government services. Greater access to information technology, better roads, improved education, and changing economic realities are increasing the movement of people, goods and services, waste and pollution and blurring the boundaries between urban and rural areas.

As incomes from agriculture decrease, rural households are forced to develop new and more complex livelihood strategies that include both agricultural and non-agricultural incomes, including remittances from seasonal and permanent migrants.

At the same time, low income households in urban areas may rely on agricultural goods from rural relatives to supplement their income. Current changes in the global economic, social and political context, including structural adjustment programs and economic reform, have resulted in deepening social polarization and increasing poverty in both urban and rural areas.

As a general conclusion we could say that such software will amplify the knowledge and use of HR potential in the rural areas and will impact both the people' choice for a job, but also the HRM and the competitivity and profitability of companies in this geographical area.

References

Abrudan, I. (1999), *Sisteme Flexibile de Fabricație: Concepte de Proiectare și Management*, Cluj-Napoca: Ed.Dacia.

Abrudan, D. (2009), *Excelența în Managementul Resurselor Umane*, p. 132, Timisoara: Editura Eurobit.

Anonymous (2006), Publications tires a part — corps profesoral du groupe ESC, Bordeaux.

Appleby, R. C. (2010), *Modern Business Administration*, London: Ed. Pitman.

Blake, R. & Mounton, V. (1998), *La Troisieme Dimension de Management*, Paris: Les Edition d'Organisation.

Boddy, D. & Buchanan D. A. (2007), *Managing New Technology*, Oxford: Editura Basil Blackwell Ltd.

Dalotă, S. (2000), Identificarea și selecția metodelor informatice necesare planificării sistemului informațional, Buletin Științific al doctoranzilor, Univ. Politehnica din Timișoara, Ediție omagială, Timișoara.

Dalotă, S. & Dalotă, M. (1998), *Excel in Sprijinul Managerului Modern*, Timișoara: Editura Softlibris Sedona.

Dalotă, S. & Dalotă, M. (1999), Aspecte actuale în managementul recompenselor materiale, Studii Economice, Univ.de Vest din Timișoara, Facultatea de Științe Economice, XX(2).

Dalotă, S. & Dalotă, M. (1999), *Introducere în Planificarea Strategică a Întreprinderii*, Timișoara: Editura Eubeea.

Damanpour, F. & Evan, W. (1984), Organizational innovation and performance: The problem of organizational lag, *Review of Administrative Science Quarterly*, 29(3).

Dănăiață, D. (1998), *Informatica în Sprijinul Managementului*, Timișoara: Mirton.

Deaconu, A. (2007), *Diagnostic și Evaluarea Întreprinderii*, Deva: Editura INTELCREDO.

Delnet (2003), Specialization course in management of local development — October 2003 (Training Units), Centrul Internațional de Instruire ILO.

Figer, J. P. (2007), *Informations et Adaptation de L'Entreprise*, Paris.

Fruja, I. & Jivan, A. (2006), *Economia Serviciilor*, Timisoara: Editura Mirton.

Jaba, O. (1999), *Analiza Strategică a Întreprinderii*, Iași: Sedcom Libris.

Jolivet, F. (1996), *Informatique et Information Aapplique a la Gestion*, Touluse.

Oprea, D., Andone, I., & Airinei, D. (1990), *Bazele Informaticii Economice*, Iași: Univ. Alexandru I. Cuza.

Oprean, D., Racovițan, D., & Oprean, V. (1994), *Informatică de Gestiune și Managerială*, Oradea: Ed.Eurounion.

Otava, M. E. (2006), *Formarea si Utilizarea Resurselor de Munca din Mediul Rural*, Timisoara: Editura Eurostampa.

Otiman, P. I. (2006), *Dezvoltare Rurala Durabila in Romania*, Bucuresti: Editura Academiei Romane.

Otovescu, D. (2010), *Principalele Probleme Sociale ale Comunităților Rurale din România*, Craiova: Editura Beladi.

Pinder, M. & Stuart, M. (1997), *Consultanță în Afaceri*, București: Editura Teora.

Popescu, D. (1995), *Conducerea Afacerilor*, București: Editura Scripta.

Porter, M. (2009), *Competitive Strategy: Techniques for Analysing Industries and Competitors*, London: Editura Free Press.

Porter, M. & Robin, M. (1983), The new programmer — the next wave of computer innovation in North American Business, *Business Quarterly*, 48(4).

Robinson, S. (1997), *Management Financiar*, București: Editura Teora.

Turban, E. (2001), *Decision Support and Expert Systems Managerial Perspectives*, New York.

www.managementul resurselor umane.org

www.managementul resurselor umane.com

www.dezvoltare regionala.ro

www.feaa.uaic.ro/cercetare/simpozioane/24_26_oct_2002/strategii

www.dezvoltare teritoriala.ro

Chapter 28

Management Particularities of the Romanian Social Enterprise

Bibu Nicolae

Faculty of Economics and Business Administration (FEAA), West University

Lisetchi Mihai

Romania Faculty of Economics and Business Administration (FEAA), West University

Nastase Marian

Bucharest University of Economic Studies

The economic and social environment become more and more complex as the human needs diversify and organizations struggle to find new ways to meet them. The globalization process brings together more people and organizations, the cultural values collide, the resources flow freer across the borders, and the speed of innovation and change permanently increase.

The modern leaders have to appropriately face all these challenges that are brought by a fast changing world. One major trend is related to building up a new type of management vision that is translated into practice under the forms of social enterprise (SE), social management, social enterpreneurship, and social economy.

The chapter investigates the main concepts related to the social entrerprise, revealing also the important features of this type of organization through a research carried out in Romania. The research methodology is based on desk and field research and semi-structured interviews that allowed the researchers to draw up valuable conclusions about the topic approached.

1. The SE and Related Concepts

During the last years, in the international academic debate a discussion evolved around a number of interconnected concepts which intrinsically include two apparently contradictory dimensions: social and economic. Among them, the most visible are the social entrepreneurship, social enterprise (SE), and social economy concepts. While the differences between these concepts continue to generate debates, both scholars and practitioners show an increasing interest towards those concepts.

In the USA, SE represents the organizational category with the highest growing (Austin *et al.*, 2006). This could be one of the reasons, among others, generating such an increased interest for social performance, development of the stakeholder approach, spread of the concept of Corporate Social Responsibility, e.a. In the same respect, business schools and universities across the world are nowadays operating a diversity of educational programs (undergraduate, postgraduate, and doctoral studies) on social entrepreneurship and SE (Hulgard, 2010).

As a terminological clarification, within this chapter, we consider "enterprise" and "organization" as synonyms.

1.1. *The concepts of SE and social economy*

Generally, when the economic growth declines, new social forces emerge, reinventing solidarity in production relations, in order to respond to the failures of formal distribution mechanisms (Moulaert & Ailenei, 2005). In this respect, in an attempt to provide appropriate solutions to human needs when the disturbed market or the less flexible state system fail to satisfy them, different initiatives and forms of the social economy, with a considerable impact, emerged during the last two centuries. Different scholars reported the existence of a link between the socio-economic crises and the emergence of different social economy organizations. For instance, according to Monzón Campos (1997), at the end of the 19th century were established the "pillars of the social economy": associations, co-operatives, and mutual support companies, which represent, since then, "the core of the social economy".

Despite the fact that the purpose of all economic activity is the satisfaction of human needs, nor the market or the public sector is able to satisfy them completely (Weisbrod, 1988), especially when the potential beneficiaries are made of vulnerable groups. Actually, all these social needs represents "the sphere of action of the Social Economy" (Monzon & Chaves, 2008). On one hand, these needs can be satisfied by the market, through a commercial business, and this is how almost all the mutual societies and co-operatives get most of their resources. On the other hand, such needs can also be satisfied by non-market services developed by associations and foundations, almost all of which usually get the majority of their resources from donations, membership fees, subsidies, etc. From a structural perspective, the Social Economy is made of two major sub-sectors: (i) the commercial market or business sub-sector and (ii) the non-commercial market or the non-business sub-sector (Monzón & Chaves, 2008).

As a working definition, we consider organizational responsibility as the responsibility of the organization toward accomplishing its organizational fundamental goal. For a graphic presentation, we consider a continuum defined by the organizational responsibility. One end of this continuum (left) is represented by the responsibility towards community, reflected by the organization's stakeholders (social responsibility) while the other end (right) is the responsibility towards shareholders. Private organizations are distributed along this continuum based on their mission and fundamental organizational goals (Fig. 1).

Table 1 presents and overview of the landscape of private organizations structured according to the following criteria: main organizational goal, organizational-juridical form, nature of activities, organizational responsibility, and possibility of profit sharing.

All economic and social sectors are encompassed by the concept of social economy. It includes usually associations, foundations, cooperative enterprises, and mutual societies (Lukkarinen, 2005). The social economy is populated with "people-centered organizations and enterprises companies, owned and run by the members on the basis of their needs", their aims being socially, democratically, and solidarity based. These are civic values and such approach transcends the logic of

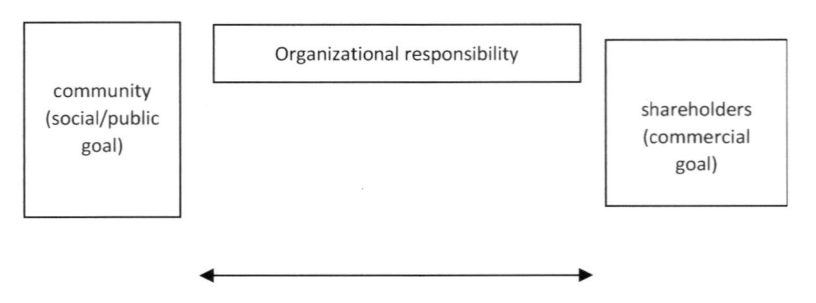

Fig. 1. Organizational responsibility continuum
Source: Own concept.

Table 1. The landscape of private organizations

Main organizational goal	Social/public interest organizations		Socio-commercial (hybrid) organizations		Commercial organizations
	NGOs	NGOs	Mutuals	Cooperatives	Commercial companies
Organizational-juridical form	NGOs	NGOs	Mutuals	Cooperatives	Commercial companies
Nature of activities	Without commercial activities	Including commercial activities (social business)	Without commercial activities	With commercial activities	With commercial activities
Organizational responsibility	Toward stakeholders/members*	Toward stakeholders/members*	Toward members	Toward members (and stakeholders)	Toward stake holders and shareholders**	Toward shareholders and stakeholders***	Toward shareholders****
Possibility of profit sharing	No	No	No	Yes	Yes	Yes

Multitude of social economy organizations (social economy sector)

Social economy | Market economy
Non-commercial subsector | Commercial subsector | Exchange economy

* Priority established based on the type of served interest: private or public.
** Like in the case of the work integration SEs.
*** Social corporate responsibility.
**** "Pure" commercial organizations.
Source: Own concept.

profit-maximization, more important being the valorization of social, cultural, and environmental resources. Therefore, "the fields of the social economy are the social and democratic and participative enterprises, qualitative employment, social inclusion, local development, and social protection" (Lukkarinen, 2005).

There are many definitions of the social economy concept in the literature. We found that some of the most visible are related to the organizational forms belonging to the social economy and not to their activities (e.g., 1998 European conference on social economy titled International Centre of Research and Information on the Public, Social and Cooperative Economy (CIRIEC), Social Economy Charter. See Annex 1). In these respects, we propose the next working definition: *social economy is made of the totality of processes of production, distribution, and consumption developed by the multitude of private organizations aiming at solving a social need, regardless of the commercial or non-commercial nature of their activities.* We emphasize the fact that "social need" concerns the society at large.

Social economy organizations (SEO) are the organizations populating the social economy. Concerning the relation between social enterprise concept and the SEO, from a theoretical perspective and based on different criteria, as we will present further down, *SE are identified as either part of, either the integral multitude of organizational forms used for the incorporation of the social economy organizations.*

1.2. The SE and the social entrepreneurship

Generally, when the economic growth declines, new social forces emerge, reinventing solidarity in production relations, in order to respond to the failures of formal distribution mechanisms (Moulaert & Ailenei, 2005). In this respect, in an attempt to provide appropriate solutions to human needs when the disturbed market or the less flexible state system fail to satisfy them, different initiatives and forms of the social economy, with a considerable impact, emerged during the last two centuries. Different scholars reported the existence of a link between the socio-economic crises and the emergence of different social economy organizations. For instance, according to Campos (1997), at the end of the 19th century were established the "pillars of the social economy": associations, co-operatives and mutual support companies, which represent, since then, "the core of the social economy".

In the development of a social entrepreneurship process, the main element is a problem society is facing. This is why, examples of social entrepreneurship are to be found in all the sectors: non-profit, for-profit, and public.

Based on the typological variety and organizational behavior in the case of SEs, Hulgard (2010) reports "a mixture of common trends and backgrounds" and "a considerable amount of variation in the ways social entrepreneurship is emerging" as a "result of changing balances and relations between state, market, and civil society in the provision of welfare services and work integration".

From a statistical perspective, considering both, their number and their socio-economic impact, the largest category of organizations generated by social entrepreneurship is made of non-profit non-governmental organizations (usually called NGOs), here being included both, associations (i.e., organizations built on persons) and foundations (i.e., organizations built on patrimony) (Bibu *et al.*, 2012). In this respect, according to Hulgard (2010), a relevant aspect of the social entrepreneurship within the non-profit sector, both in

Social entrepreneurship ⇒ Social economy organizations / (SEs included) ⇒ Social economy

Fig. 2. Relation between social entrepreneurship, SE and social economy
Source: Own concept.

Europe and USA, is the transformation of the non-profit organizations into market agents and public welfare services providers. This process leads to increased impact of the sector in society.

1.3. *The social value concept*

As far as it concerns the "social value" concept, not at all surprisingly, there is no unanimously accepted definition. In a common understanding social value is perceived as being opposed to "individual value" (Dees, 1998) and implies expectations concerning the generation of "social, economic, and community development" (Reis, 1999). In other words, social value implies to produce "social change" (Mair & Marti, 2006) through complete or partial satisfaction of the "social need" (*ibid.*). Sometimes is described as "social good" (Cukier et al., 2011) or "collective good" (Murphy & Coombes, 2009). In our view, *social value represents a positive output of solving social needs*. According to Baker et al. (2005), social value is of subjective nature and vary a lot based the context.

In a more restrictive approach, in the case of a specific group of people, the social value is made of principles and standards of human interaction which are considered by the members of the group as being valuable, important or relevant for the group (www.education.com, 2012).

1.4. *The SE concept*

As far as it concerns the "social value" concept, not at all surprisingly, there is no unanimously accepted definition. In a common understanding social value is perceived as being opposed to "individual value" (Dees, 1998) and implies expectations concerning the generation of "social, economic, and community development" (Reis, 1999). In other words, social value implies to produce "social change" (Mair & Marti, 2006) through complete or partial satisfaction of the "social need" (*ibid.*). Sometimes is described as "social good" (Cukier et al., 2011) or "collective good" (Murphy & Coombes, 2009). In our view, *social value represents a positive output of solving social needs*. According to Baker et al. (2005), social value is of subjective nature and vary a lot based the context.

Apparently, Drucker (1979) was the first author who coined the term 'social enterprise' while advocating ethical responsibilities of corporations (Trivedi, 2010). The definition of a SE and its position within the social economy organizational landscape as reflected in the literature vary depending on several criteria: (i) development of commercial activities, (ii) existence of paid staff, (iii) maximal profit sharing limitation, (iv) minimal commercial incomes limitation, (v) existence of a collective property, and (vi) existence of a collective leadership.

Regarding the first criterion, namely the development of commercial activities, there are two approaches: first, a restrictive one, e.g., Finland, Ireland, UK (Defourny & Nyssens, 2010), considering as SE only the organizations developing commercial activities (exclusively or complementary to non-commercial activities) and second, an inclusive one (Monzon & Chaves, 2008), integrating, also, the organizations with only non-commercial activities in the multitude of the social economy organizations.

In other words, in the restrictive approach presented in Table 2, among the social economy organizations, only those developing commercial activities (non-commercial activities not excluded) are considered to be SEs.

For operational reasons, the percentage of the commercial activities incomes within the total incomes of the organization is used by the law as a criterion to determine if an organization fits the "social enterprise" label. Its value may vary from country to country (for instance, in UK is 50%). The question is why, in the case of two organizations with identical goals, identical activities, addressing identical target groups, one would be considered as SE only based on the commercial relations between the organization and its beneficiaries (philanthropic relations not excluded), while the other organization is not qualifying as a SE based on the fact that it develops only philanthropic relations with its beneficiaries.

A similar perspective, implying, also, a restrictive approach (e.g., CIRIEC, EMES) and an inclusive one, may be built considering as a criterion the existence of paid staff operating an organization. And, again, question is why, in the case of two organizations with identical goals, identical activities, addressing identical target

Table 2. Defining "social enterprise" label based on different criteria

Criterion	SEOs status	Restrictive	Inclusive
Commercial activities	Without commercial activities	Non-SE	SE
	With commercial activities	SE	SE
Existence of paid staff (volunteers not excluded)	No paid staff (only volunteers)	Non-SE	SE
	At least a certain number of paid staff	SE	SE
Maximal profit sharing limitation	Comply with profit sharing limitation	Non-SE	SE
	Overpass the profit sharing limitation	SE	SE
Minimal commercial incomes limitation (noncommercial incomes not excluded)	No commercial incomes limitation	Non-SE	SE
Existence of a collective property	Commercial incomes limitation	SE	SE
	No collective property	Non-SE	SE
	Collective property	SE	SE
Existence of a collective leadership	No collective leadership	Non-SE	SE
	Collective leadership	SE	SE

Source: Own concept.

groups, one would be considered as SE based on the existence of paid staff (volunteers not excluded), while the other organization is not qualifying as a SE based on the fact that it develops activities with volunteers only.

A similar perspective, implying, also, a restrictive approach and an inclusive one, may be build considering as a criterion the existence of the maximal limitation of the profit sharing when it comes to incomes from commercial activities. In the same manner, question is why, in the case of two organizations with identical goals, identical activities, addressing identical target groups, when it comes to incomes from commercial activities, one would be considered as SE based on certain value of the profit sharing limitation (e.g., 50% in UK), while the other organization is not qualifying as a SE because overpassing the profit sharing limitation (with 1%, for instance).

Similar perspectives, implying, also, a restrictive approach and an inclusive one, may be build considering other above mentioned criteria (see Table 3). Similar questions could, also, be raised.

As far as it concerns the definition of the SE and the positioning of the concept related to the multitude of social economy organizations, we are advocating for an inclusive approach. Therefore, considering the aforementioned discussion, we propose the next working definition: *social enterprise is a private organization having the explicit organizational goal of aiming at solving a social need, regardless the commercial or non-commercial nature of its activities*. We emphasize the fact that "social need" concerns the society at large.

2. Particularities of the SE Management

For any organization, its primary purpose determines the organizational behavior and accordingly, its management. For example, in the case of the for profit organizations, the primary purpose is to develop services and products to sale to a particular group of consumers in terms of efficiency and effectiveness and having as the main performance criterion the profit maximization (Bibu & Lisetchi, 2011). By

Table 3. The level of practice of specific SE management particularities revealed by theory

	Specific SE management particularities revealed by theory	Level of practice as is (%)
First particularity	*The organizational goal is a social need of a specified or ascertainable group or of the community at large*	100
Second particularity	*The governing board must also assume the role of representative of the market*	0
Third particularity	*The decision-making power is divided equally between the members of the decision-making bodies*	100
Fourth particularity	*The volunteer work of the leaders in favor of the organization*	100
Fifth particularity	A *more balanced power relationship between the executive and governance structure of the organization*	40
Sixth particularity	*Disadvantaged beneficiaries do not pay for their benefit or pay less than the market value*	100
Seventh particularity	To obtain the necessary resources, SE can appeal to a *multiplicity of ways*, including both non-commercial activities and commercial activities	40
Eighth particularity	SE use *a mix of types of human resources: both paid and volunteer staff*	50
Ninth particularity	*Limited or no distribution of the financial profit*	100

comparison, in the case of SEs, development of services and products for sale could be one of the ways to achieve their main organizational goal. This difference is reflected by various aspects of the organizational behavior.

Comparing to the other categories of organizations which operate in the community, we may conclude that SE resemble to private commercial entities concerning the way they function, but their goals and objectives are focused on social needs. On the other hand, like in the case of other types of organizations, SE vary much in terms of mission, size, mode of operation, and impact.

What are the managerial particularities do SE have for performing an independent responsible examination of social problems and the associated approaches to resolve them is an important question to be answered.

2.1. *The research methodology*

No data was available for this study. In order to find the SE specific management particularities, the research methodology includes: documentation (desk and field research), data analysis, non-participant observation, field notes, semi-structured interviews, and analysis of documents and materials.

The target group for this research is made of SE located in the city of Timisoara (over 300,000 inhabitants), Romania.

2.2. *Desk research findings*

No data was available for this study. In order to find the SE specific management particularities, the research methodology includes: documentation (desk and field research), data analysis, non-participant observation, field notes, semi-structured interviews, and analysis of documents and materials.

The target group for this research is made of SE located in the city of Timisoara (over 300,000 inhabitants), Romania.

In the initial phase, our analysis of the literature revealed nine particularities being specific to SE management (development of the model described by Noya & Clarence, 2007).

The first particularity is the organizational goal. In the case of SEs, the organizational goal is a social need of a specified or ascertainable group, relevant to the community, or of the community at large (Noya & Clarence, 2007). In other words, it is a social goal. In the case of commercial activities, the development of services and products for sale is a method that leads to achieving the social goal of the organization. The non-profit social goal increases the public trust in such organizations, generating legitimacy and thus, creating value for these organizations.

Second particularity refers to the role of the governing board. In terms of representation of the clients' interests and needs, SE beneficiaries may not be in a position to reveal their preferences (e.g., people with disabilities, children and older people), nor able to pay prices that cover the cost of service delivery (Anheier, 2000). In this respect, sometimes SE operate in a "muted market". Related to beneficiaries' needs and interest's representation, Carver (1997) suggested that boards should act as the "market" to determine services by setting mission and policies. This is why, sometimes, for a proper design of strategic decision in the case of SEs, *the governing board must also assume the role of representative of the market*.

The third particularity reflects the power distribution within the decision-making bodies (boards, general assembly, etc.). Compared to for-profit companies, generally, within the SE the decision-making process is not based on shares. More precisely, in general, *the decision-making power is divided equally between the members of the decision-making bodies* (Noya & Clarence, 2007). This is determined by the need for organizational legitimacy.

A fourth particularity refers to leaders' compensation. *The SE board members act on a voluntary basis*, with no material compensation for their activity.

The fifth particularity reflects the distinction between the organizational competences of the board and the executive. The governing body is mainly concerned with achieving the mission of the SE, namely monitoring strategic objectives and observing organizational policies (non-financial indicators). By contrast, the executive focuses on operational aspects and financial matters in running the organization. This situation reflects a *more balanced power relationship between the executive and governance structure of the organization*. Meantime, comparing to SEs, for-profit organizations delegate more decision-making power to executives and owners, and less to their employees, consumers, families, boards of directors, and community representatives. Although the differences are, generally, small, they support the hypothesis that decision-making is allocated to different groups based on the broad objectives of the organization (Ben-Ner & Ren, 2010).

The sixth particularity concerns the service-market couple. Many times, the cost of a product or service provided by a SE to a disadvantaged group has not been determined in relation to the cost of product or service delivery so that *disadvantaged beneficiaries do not pay for their benefit or pay less than the market value*. This is possible when there is a third party involved, the funder, which subsidizes, in whole or in part, products or services provided to beneficiaries by the SE. The funder is not a direct beneficiary of the provided products or services. This is determined by the weak financial potential of the SEs' beneficiaries and in connection of the SE with their social goal. Such an approach allows deprived or vulnerable groups to receive with no costs or reduced costs services and products which they would not get other way.

The seventh particularity is about the ways SE is getting resources. To obtain the necessary resources for operating their activities, SE can appeal to a *multiplicity of ways, including both non-commercial activities* (i.e., attracting grants) *and commercial activities* (Noya & Clarence, 2007). This is determined by the week financial potential of the SEs' beneficiaries and in connection with their social goal.

The eights particularity refers to human resources. Comparing to for-profit companies, SE may use *a mix of types of human resources: both paid and volunteer staff*. This implies a complex motivational structure of staff, volunteers and stakeholders, and the interplay between altruistic and egotistical goals (Anheier, 2000). This is determined by the weak financial potential of the SEs' beneficiaries and in connection with their social goal.

The ninth particularity concerns the *limited or no distribution of the financial profit*. It may be obtained from commercial activities or as surplus from non-profit incomes, if they exist. Comparing with for profit firms, such "profit", either cannot be appropriated by owner or associates (the case of absolute restriction), either does exist a regulation limit of "profit" distribution (partial restriction). The difference remains for the social organization to achieve its social goal.

It should be noted that the particularities of the above-mentioned particularities are not absolute, neither in terms of their existence in the entire mass of SEs, nor in terms of their uniqueness only for this category of organizations. For example, working with volunteers can be done in public institutions too, but in this case, volunteers are found only at the operational management level and, more importantly, have no role in the decision-making process. On the other hand, the aforementioned items are the most representative and thus defining for SE operation mode.

2.3. *The Pilot Research*

In order to see how the above-mentioned theoretical findings are reflected in SEs' practice and, simultaneously, to test the proposed research methodology, a pilot research was carried on by a partnership involving the Agency for Information and Development of Nongovernmental Organization (AID–ONG), the Management Department, Faculty of Economics and Business Administration (FEAA) and the Faculty of Political Science, Philosophy and Communication Studies of West University, Timisoara (Romania). The research sample consists of ten organizations (the list is presented in Annex 3) and the structure of the sample is based on the NGO typology described in the International Classification of Non-profit Organizations (ICNPO) (see Annex 4). More precisely, the ten organizations are covering eight of the twelve groups described in ICNPO. The selection of these organizations is based on their public notoriety as identified through phone interviews conducted with relevant leaders of the SE community in Timisoara.

The pilot research objective was the identification of the theoretical SE specific management particularities in the practice of the target group.

Three questionnaire based interviews were conducted (in Romanian) in every organization: one with a board member, one with the CEO, and one with a grassroots staff representative (like volunteers, for example) in order to create a complex perspective on the management process within each organization. A total of 30 filled questionnaires covering 10 organizations were the first results of our field investigation.

The questionnaire was built around the nine particularities revealed by the academic literature as being specific to SE management and included both, closed (multiple choice, all that apply) and open questions.

First of all, data was aggregated for each organization by processing the three questionnaires describing the organization. In the second phase, data was aggregated at the level of the pilot project sample organizations.

The outputs of the calculations are presented in Table 3.

While the findings completely validated some of the particularities revealed by the academic literature as being specific to SE management, some were only partially validated, while some others were not validated at all. There are several comments to be made based on the findings of this research.

First particularity: in the case of SEs, *the organizational goal is a social need of a specified or ascertainable group or of the community at large*. Regardless the size or complexity of their target group, all the organizations are stating a social need as their goal.

Second particularity: *the governing board must also assume the role of representative of the market*. None of the organizations has such role imposed by their bylaws and none of the interviewed representatives mentioned this as a common practice. On the other hand, in a broader context, involving the beneficiaries in the organization's decision is a good practice principle in the case of SE. The present situation might reflect a week participatory culture and it may be related to the former socialist past of the country. In the same time, in the specific case of SE serving vulnerable groups, the governing board might assume the role of representative of the market without a clear norm in their bylaw.

Third particularity: the *decision-making power is divided equally between the members of the decision-making bodies*. Regardless their size or activity domain, all the organizations are reporting an equal distribution of the decision-making power between the members of their decision-making bodies.

Fourth particularity: *the volunteer work of the leaders in favor of the organization*. In all the organizations, board members do not get tangible rewards for their work as leaders of the organization.

Fifth particularity: *a more balanced power relationship between the executive and governance structure of the organization*. Apparently, in more than half of the SE, the role of the board and related activities reflect a mixture of governance and operational activities. The present situation might reflect both an authoritarian behavior of the leadership and/or a lack of trust in delegating authority within the organization and they may be related to the common culture of the society (another heritage of the socialist period).

Sixth particularity: *disadvantaged beneficiaries do not pay for their benefit or pay less than the market value*. Regardless their size or activity domain, all the organizations are reporting that the cost of their provided products or services is subsidized and thus representing less than the cost of product or service delivery.

Seventh particularity: to obtain the necessary resources, SE can appeal to a *multiplicity of ways, including both non-commercial activities* (i.e., *attracting grants*) *and commercial activities*. Apparently, despite the huge need of means to accomplish their mission, less than half of the SE consider commercial activities as a way of obtaining resources. The present situation may be related to the rather week economic entrepreneurship culture in Romania.

Eights particularity: SE use *a mix of types of human resources*: *both paid and volunteer staff*. Apparently, only half of the SE use employed workers to carry on their activities. This situation may be connected to the fact that these organizations have larger incomes than average Romanian SE.

Ninths particularity: *limited or no distribution of the financial profit*. Regardless their size or activity domain, all the organizations are reporting limited or no distribution of the financial profit (if any).

3. Conclusions

Crossing knowledge boundaries determines the development of science and society. Such crossing of boundaries strengthened civil society studies through the time the sub-discipline has existed. The research field has accommodated scholars from different main stream disciplines and has thus gained a much wider perspective of society than what is possible only inside one discipline (Muukkonen, 2009).

As contradictory as they seem, "social economy and commercial economy emerge not as opposite poles to each other but as parts of a continuous spectrum". From this perspective, the study of the social economy implies "studying the commercial aspects of the socially-dominated economy and also the social elements of the commercially-dominated economy". Such conclusions appear to be in conflict with most of the definitions political bodies and scholars are using (Westlund, 2003). Meantime, they are in line with the one saying that everything is related to each other and all the distinctions are only analytical (Muukkonen, 2009).

We can deal the contradictory definitions of SE in two ways. In the restrictive approach, we can try to find what different concepts have in common. In practice, this leaves only a short list of organizations as a core of the social economy sector. It will leave outside majority of the organizations that may be studied under the concept presented above. In an integrative approach, we accept organizations that have some elements in common with the others. In terms of SE environment (i.e., managing diverse constituencies, stakeholders and multiple revenue sources including commercial revenues, donations, fees and charges, and public sector payments like subsidies, grants and contracts), and its internal components (i.e., board, staff, volunteers, clients, and users) the management of SE becomes more complex than the case of a for profit company of similar size. This is why SE are considered to be several organizations or organizational components in one and this heavily impact on SE operation mode.

SE are largely innovating in the way managerial activities are performed by their constituents. At organizational level, SE are solving in new and innovative ways the tasks of planning, organizing, leading, motivating, and controlling resources and people in order to achieve effectively and efficiently/virtuously their social purpose and organizational objectives, and thus creating social value.

The reported SE management particularities come to improve organizational models and management methods. They were determined by an array of factors: public sector and market failure, human solidarity, need for collective empowerment, type of market the SE serve, the need for organizational legitimacy, the SEs' social goal and their implicit operating mode, the week financial potential of the SEs' beneficiaries, etc. They represent changes which increase the public trust in such organizations, generating legitimacy and thus, creating value for these organizations.

Our chapter contributions are the following: first, elaborating the continuum of organizational responsibility model; second, clarifying the rational connections between SE and its complementary concepts: social entrepreneurship and social economy; third, an comprehensive typology of the SEO was elaborated; fourth, clarifying the position of the SE within the multitude of social economy organizations; fifth, inclusive working definitions were elaborated for each of the concepts: social entrepreneurship, SEs, and social economy; sixth, the specific particularities of the SE management were identified and, based on them a new theoretical model was created for the SE management.

4. Appendices

Appendix A: Definitions of social economy

Appendix B: Selected definitions of social entrepreneur and social entrepreneurship

Appendix C: Centralized data on SE consisting the research sample

Appendix A
Definitions of Social Economy

"The social economy brings people together in associative bodies based on free membership and voluntary commitment revolving around a common purpose" *European conference on social economy*, 1998.

[Social economy is made of] "cooperatives, mutual organizations as well as voluntary organizations, associations and foundations which remunerate work" *CIRIEC (International Centre of Research and Information on the Public, Social and Cooperative Economy).*

[Social economy is] "the set of organizations that do not belong to the public sector, operate democratically with the members having equal rights and duties and practice a particular regime of ownership and distribution of profits, employing the surpluses to expand the organization and improve its services to its members and to society" *The Social Economy Charter (Charte de l'économie sociale).*

Appendix B

Selected Definitions of Social Entrepreneur and Social Entrepreneurship

Author(s) & year	Definition of social entrepreneur
Ashoka	Social entrepreneurs are individuals with innovative solutions to society's most pressing social problems. They are ambitious and persistent, tackling major social issues and offering new ideas for wide-scale change.
Bornstein, D. (2004)	A path breaker with a powerful new idea, who combines visionary and real-world problem solving creativity, who has a strong ethical fiber, and who is 'totally possessed' by his or her vision for change.
Dees, J. G. (2001)	Social entrepreneurs play the role of change agents in the social sector, by: Adopting a mission to create and sustain social value (not just private value); Recognizing and relentlessly pursuing new opportunities to serve that mission; Engaging in a process of continuous innovation, adaptation, and learning; Acting boldly without being limited by resources currently in hand; Exhibiting heightened accountability to the constituencies served and for the outcomes created.
Light (2006)	A social entrepreneur is an individual, group, network, organization, or alliance of organizations that seeks sustainable, large-scale change through pattern-breaking ideas in what or how governments, non-profits, and businesses do to address significant social problems.
Martin, R. L. & Osberg, S. (2007)	The social entrepreneur should be understood as someone who targets an unfortunate but stable equilibrium that causes the neglect, marginalization, or suffering of a segment of humanity; who brings to bear on this situation his or her inspiration, direct action, creativity, courage, and fortitude; and who aims for and ultimately affects the establishment of a new stable equilibrium that secures permanent benefit for the targeted group and society at large.
PBS' "The New Heroes"	A social entrepreneur identifies and solves social problems on a large scale. Just as business entrepreneurs create and transform whole industries, social entrepreneurs act as the change agents for society, seizing opportunities others miss in order to improve systems, invent, and disseminate new approaches and advance sustainable solutions that create social value.
Schwab Foundation	What is a Social Entrepreneur? A pragmatic visionary who achieves large scale, systemic and sustainable social change through a new invention, a different approach, a more rigorous application of known technologies or strategies, or a combination of these.
Skoll Foundation	The social entrepreneur as society's change agent: a pioneer of innovation that benefits humanity. Social entrepreneurs are ambitious, mission driven, strategic, resourceful, and results oriented.
Thompson (2002)	People with the qualities and behaviors we associate with the business entrepreneur but who operate in the community and are more concerned with caring and helping than "making money."

(Continued)

(*Continued*)

Author(s) & year	Definition of social entrepreneur
Austin, J., Stephenson, H., & Wei-Skillern, J., (2006)	Social entrepreneurship is an innovative, social value-creating activity that can occur within or across the non-profit, businesses, or government sectors.
Johnson (2000)	Social entrepreneurship is emerging as an innovative approach for dealing with complex social needs. With its emphasis on problem solving and social innovation, socially entrepreneurial activities blur the traditional boundaries between the public, private, and non-profit sector and emphasize hybrid model of for-profit and non-profit activities.
Nichols, A. (2007)	Social entrepreneurship entails innovations designed to explicitly improve societal well-being, housed within entrepreneurial organizations which initiate, guide or contribute to change in society.
Mair, J. & Marti, I. (2006)	Social entrepreneurship: Innovative models of providing products and services that cater to basic needs (rights) that remain unsatisfied by political or economic institutions.

Source: Cukier *et al.* (2011).

Appendix C

Centralized Data on Social Enterprises Consisting the Research Sample

Crt. no.*	Name of the SE**	Internet address	Email	Social character of the goal
1	Eco Club Timisoara	www.ecotimisoara.ro	contact@ecotimisoara.ro	Yes
2	Serviciul de Ajutor Maltez Filiala Timişoara	www.maltez.ro	tmsamr@yahoo.com	Yes
3	Asociatia Timisoara — Capitală Culturală Europeană	http://timisoara2020.wordpress.com/	timisoara2020@gmail.com	Yes
4	Asociaţia Studenţilor Europeni (Aegee) — Timişoara	www.aegeetm.ro	aegee.tim@gmail.com	Yes
5	Asociaţia Generaţia Tânără	www.generatietanara.ro	office@generatietanara.ro	Yes
6	Asociatia Romana Antisida — Filiala Timisoara	www.arasnet.ro	aras.tm@arasnet.ro	Yes
7	Institutul Intercultural Timişoara	http://www.intercultural.ro/rom	iit@intercultural.ro	Yes
8	Fundaţia Filantropia Timişoara	www.fft.ro	adrian.ghiran@yahoo.com	Yes
9	Centrul Euroregional Pentru Democratie	www.regionalnet.org	office@regionalnet.org	Yes
10	Clubul Rotaract Timisoara	http://www.timisoara.rotaract.ro	—***	Yes

Notes:

* The same current number was used to list SEs' names in the following tables of this annex;

** No particular order when listing the SEs' names;

*** Means no data available.

Crt. No.	No. of permanent employees	No. of temporary employees	No. of active volunteers	Last year annual budget [euro]			
				Till 1.000	1.001–10.000	10.001–50.000	Over 50.000
1	0	0	25	No	Yes	No	No
2	28	0	66	—	—	—	—
3	0	1	10	Yes	No	No	No
4	0	0	20	Yes	No	No	No
5	39	0	180	No	No	No	Yes
6	0	0	—	No	Yes	No	No
7	10	20	30	No	No	No	Yes
8	10	12	40	No	No	No	Yes
9	6	0	10	No	No	Yes	No
10	0	0	40	No	Yes	No	No

Crt. No.	Commercial incomes		Non-commercial incomes		Subsidized products		
	Commercial activities	(%)	Non-commercial activities	(%)	No subsidy	Partially	Completely
1	No	0	—	100	No	No	Yes
2	Yes	—	Yes	—	No	Yes	Yes
3	No	0	Yes	100	No	No	Yes
4	No	0	—	100	No	No	Yes
5	No	0	Yes	100	No	No	Yes
6	No	0	Yes	100	No	No	Yes
7	Yes	10	Yes	90	No	No	Yes
8	No	0	Yes	100	No	No	Yes
9	Yes	40	Yes	60	No	No	Yes
10	Yes	50	Yes	50	No	No	Yes

Crt. No.	Role of the board	Distribution of the decision-making power between the members of the decision-making bodies			Board members' rewards		Role of the CEO	Limited or no distribution of the financial profit
		Equal	Unequal	Existence of criterions for unequal distribution	Financial	Non-financial		
1	GO	Yes	No	NA	No	Yes	O	Yes
2	GO	Yes	No	NA	No	Yes	O	Yes
3	GO	Yes	No	NA	No	Yes	O	Yes
4	GO	Yes	No	NA	No	Yes	O	Yes
5	GO	Yes	No	NA	No	No	O	Yes
6	G	Yes	No	NA	No	Yes	O	Yes
7	G	Yes	No	NA	No	No	O	Yes
8	G	Yes	No	NA	No	No	O	Yes
9	G	Yes	No	NA	No	No	O	Yes
10	GO	Yes	No	NA	No	No	O	Yes

Notes:
GO — Governance and operations;
G — Governance;
O — Operations.

References

Austin, J., Stevenson, H. & Wei-Skillern, J. (2006), Social and commercial entrepreneurship: Same, different, or both? *Entrepreneurship: Theory and Practice*, 30(1), 1–22. Available at http://onlinelibrary.wiley.com/doi/10.1111/j.1540-6520.2006.00107.x/full.

Baker, T., Gedjlovic, E., & Lubatkin, M. (2005), A framework for comparing entrepreneurial processes across nations, *Journal of International Business Studies*, 36, 492–504.

Ben-Ner, A. & Ren, T. (2010), A comparative study of allocation of decision-making across stakeholder groups: The case of personal care industries, *Annals of Public and Cooperative Economics*. Available at http://econpapers.repec.org/article/blaannpce/v_3a81_3ay_3a2010_3ai_3a4_3ap_3a611-630.htm (Accessed 13 June 2011).

Bibu, N. & Lisetchi, M. (2011), Particularities of the Strategy Approach within Nongovernmental Organizations: A Literature Review, *Proceedings of international conference "Managerial Challenges of the Contemporary Society"*, June 3–4, 2011, Cluj Napoca, Romania.

Bibu, N., Lisetchi, M. & Nastase, M. (2012). "Socializing" economic concepts: the entrepreneurship, *Proceeding of international conference EURAM 2012: "Social Innovation for Competitiveness, Organisational Performance and Human Excellence"*, Rotterdam, June 6–8, 2012.

Cukier *et al.* (2011), Social entrepreneurship: A content analysis, *Journal of Strategic Innovation and Sustainability*, 7(1), 99–119. Available at http://usasbe.org/knowledge/proceedings/proceedingsDocs/2009/PaperID187.pdf (Accessed February 2012).

Dees, J. G. (1998), Enterprising non-profits: what do you do when traditional sources of funding fall short? *Harvard Business Review*, January–February, 5–11.

Defourny, J. & Nyssens, M. (2010), Conceptions of social enterprise and social entrepreneurship in Europe and the United States: Convergences and divergences, *Journal of Social Entrepreneurship*, 1(1), 32–53.

Drucker, P. (1979), *The Practice of Management*, London: Pan Books. Available at http://www.education.com/definition/social-values/ (Accessed February 2012).

Ghenea, M. (2011), Entrepreneurship (original title: Antreprenoriat. in Romanian), p. 61, Editura Universul Juridic, Colectia Business.

Hulgård, L. (2010), Discourses of social entrepreneurship — variations of the same theme?, Working Papers Series, no. 10/01. EMES European Research Network, Belgium: Liege. Available at http://www.emes.net/fileadmin/emes/PDF_files/Working_Papers/WP_10-01_Hulg_rd__web_pdf (accessed February 2012).

Lukkarinen, M. (2005), Community development, local economic development and the social economy, *Community Development Journal*, 40(4), 419–424.

Mair, J. & Marti, I. (2006), Social entrepreneurship research: A source of explanation, prediction, and delight, *Journal of World Business*, 41(1), 36–44. Available at http://linkinghub.elsevier.com/retrieve/pii/S1090951605000544 (Accessed February 2012).

Monzón Campos, J. (1997). Contributions of the social economy to the general interest, *Annals of Public and Cooperative Economics*, 68, 397–408.

Monzon, J. L. & Chaves, R. (2008), The European social economy: Concept and dimensions of the third sector, *Annals of Public and Cooperative Economics*, 79, 549–577.

Moulaert, F. & Ailenei, O. (2005), Social economy, third sector and solidarity relations: A conceptual synthesis from history to present, *Urban Studies*, 42(11), 2038.

Murphy, P. J. & Coombes, S. M. (2009), A model of social entrepreneurial discovery, *Journal of Business Ethics* (87), 325–336.

Muukkonen, M. (2009), Framing the field: Civil society and related concepts, *Nonprofit and Voluntary Sector Quarterly*, 38(4), 684. Available at http://search.proquest.com/docview/231488153?accountid=30274.

Reis, T. (1999), *Unleashing the New Resources and Entrepreneurship for the Common Good: A Scan, Synthesis and Scenario for Action*, Battle Creek: W. K. Kellogg Foundation.

Trivedi, C. (2010), A Social entrepreneurship bibliography, *Journal of Entrepreneurship*, 19(1), 81–85. Available at http://joe.sagepub.com/content/19/1/81 (Accessed February 2012).

Weisbrod, B. (1988), *The Nonprofit Economy*, Cambridge: Harvard University Press. Available at http://www.newworldencyclopedia.org/entry/NGO.

Westlund, H. (2003), Form or contents? On the concept of social economy, *International Journal of Social Economics*, 30(11), 1192–1206.

Chapter 29

The Evolution of the Romanian SMEs' Perceptions Over the Last Decade

Luminița Nicolescu and Ciprian Nicolescu

Bucharest University of Economic Studies

This chapter aims to highlight key issues regarding the evolution of entrepreneurs' perceptions within small and medium-sized enterprises (SMEs) sector from Romania in the period 2003/2004–2012/2013. Given the fact that the SMEs' sector has a major role in any economy, bringing a considerable contribution to the achievement of GDP, job creation, collection of the revenues for the state budget, generation of technical innovations applicable in the economy, etc., the presentation of the evolution of perceptions associated to SMEs from Romania in the last decade, has a special importance. The dynamic analysis of the perceptions afferent to SMEs sector in Romania is more interesting, considering that the last 10 years were marked by economic boom, the integration of Romania into the European Union (EU), and a period of economic crisis. The research in dynamic of few relevant issues to SMEs — assessments of Romanian business environment, economic opportunities and difficulties encountered, effects of EU integration, impact of economic crisis, training, and using of external consultants — was achieved by studying annual results of nationwide investigations, based on questionnaires and conducted on representative samples of SMEs. Taking in consideration the dynamic approach to the study of entrepreneurs' perceptions, there were identified some trends in the evolution of SMEs and were formulated some proposals and recommendations for the improvement of the Romanian entrepreneurial environment.

1. The Approach of the Research

This research is focused on the small and medium-sized enterprises (SMEs), as they are defined by Romanian Law No. 346/2004, with subsequent amendments. Taking into consideration the European Commission Recommendation 2003/361/EC, Romanian regulations stipulate that SMEs are those entities which have less than 250 employees and, simultaneously, have the turnover up to EUR 50 mn or the total assets up to EUR 43 mn.

We used for documentation of 10 editions of White Charter of Romanian SMEs, from 2004 till 2013, books that are co-authored by one of this chapter's authors. The annual surveys based on questionnaires were conducted on representative samples of SMEs (see Table 1), which incorporated micro, small, and medium enterprises, having all forms of legal organization and of all ages, coming from all branches of activity and development regions of Romania.

During the period of time considered, investigations based on questionnaires have been designed as surveys, on stratified samples. This research method ensures better quality of information and a higher degree of knowledge of the realities investigated. Annually, this kind of

Table 1. Dimension of the SMEs samples in the period 2004–2013

Year	2004	2005	2006	2007	2008	2009	2010	2011	2012	2013
Number of SMEs in the sample	1,378	1,398	1,306	1,178	1,256	1,099	1,485	1,723	1,716	1,858

Sources: Nicolescu et al. (2004, 2005, 2006, 2007, 2008, 2009, 2010, 2011, 2012, 2013a). CNIPMMR, White Charter of SMEs from Romania, Editions 2004–2013.

survey is organized in the first quarter of the year, and therefore, many of the entrepreneurs' answers from the respective year's edition reflect the situations/perceptions corresponding to the previous year. For instance, the results presented in White Charter of Romanian SMEs 2013 are considered as being relevant for the year 2012/2013 and recorded as such.

2. Assessment of Romanian Economic Environment

The evaluations of the Romanian business environment made by entrepreneurs (Table 2) reflect to a large extent the way how the environment actually evolved in the analyzed period. We observe that favorable views on the economic environment registered an ascendant trend until 2008, (the year of the crisis' start), when more than half of deciders from SMEs considered that conditions from Romania were friendly for business. This perception is explained by the positive evolution of Romanian economy during 2004–2008, characterized, as Nicolescu & Nicolescu (2008) shown in "Entrepreneurship and Management of SMEs", through:

- Reviving industrial activity;
- The rapid growth of the service sector;
- Continuing the dynamic evolution of trade and construction;
- Increment of foreign and domestic investments;
- The rapid growth of imports and exports;
- The proliferation of the *acquis communautaire* and the transition to its consistent implementation;
- Rise of the convergence of the Romanian economy and the European Union (EU) economy as a result of the pre-accession process and the effective integration of Romania into the EU;
- Modernization and rapid diversification of the banking system, decreasing substantial differences between Romania and developed countries.

In 2009 and 2010 a decrease in the percentage of favorable assessments took place, generated by the international and national economic crisis, manifested through compressing domestic demand, reduction in the volume of industrial production, decreasing investments, increasing budget deficit, rising unemployment, declining purchasing power of the population, etc. Also, it is worth to be mentioned that in 2009 and 2010 came into force the mandatory minimum tax — a payment obligation for all companies regardless their financial results — resulting in the obligation to pay the minimum tax even when the company had zero income.

Table 2. Entrepreneurs' assessment of the Romanian economic environment 2004–2013

Status of the economic environment	2004 (%)	2005 (%)	2006 (%)	2007 (%)	2008 (%)	2009 (%)	2010 (%)	2011 (%)	2012 (%)	2013 (%)
Favorable to business	16.89	25.50	30.01	42.91	51.61	17.13	3.91	7.73	11.81	15.34
Neutral	28.95	29.86	35.07	35.11	28.56	24.69	17.96	20.66	33.74	41.28
Detrimental to business development	54.17	44.64	34.92	21.98	19.83	58.18	78.13	69.61	54.45	43.38

Sources: Nicolescu et al. (2004, 2005, 2006, 2007, 2008, 2009, 2010, 2011, 2012, 2013a). CNIPMMR, White Charter of SMEs from Romania, Editions 2004–2013.

This led to a substantial growth of SMEs which have suspended business.

We underline that the perceptions of entrepreneurs/managers regarding business environment, have a large impact on the way they act, react, and decide for their firms, influencing functionality, competitiveness and performance at micro, mezzo, and macro level.

3. Main Business Opportunities and Difficulties for SMEs in Romania

Entrepreneurs' perceptions of business opportunities are very important, because they can be starting points for future actions and strategic processes of SMEs.

The surveys point out that the main business opportunities perceived by SMEs for 2003/2004–2012/2013 period were **increasing sales on the internal market, assimilating of new products, entering on new markets, creating business partnerships, using new technologies, obtaining a grant and the growth of exports**. Table 3 shows how the perceptions of SMEs on economic opportunities evolved during the 10 years under study.

The growth of sales in the domestic market was perceived most frequently as the main opportunity in the entire analyzed period, with the exception of the year of Romania's integration in EU (2006/2007), when most of respondents were optimistic and focused towards penetrating new markets.

Whilst, the entering on new markets and assimilating new products were perceived over time in close percentages as being opportunities, other aspects, such as obtaining a grant, increasing exports or operationalization of a business partnership have fluctuated quite significantly.

As far as the opportunity of getting a grant is concerned, we observe that over half of the deciders from SMEs were enthusiastic at the time Romania adhered to EU while in the subsequent years, the perception over this opportunity has known diminishing trends. This situation can be explained by the difficulties related to accessing the European grants: bureaucracy in Romania, deficiencies at the Romanian authorities level on the administration of EU funds (preferential treatment, lack/shortcoming of information, etc.), insufficient know-how of the entrepreneurs/managers from SMEs about the specific aspects of the application process and the requirement to contribute with relatively considerable funds at the project's total budget in order to obtain co-financing.

Considering selling of products/services in other countries, we find low proportions of firms for whom exports' growth is seen as an economic opportunity, with a minimum of 7.28% of the SMEs for 2010/2011. One

Table 3. Business opportunities for SMEs in Romania in 2003/2004–2012/2013

Business opportunities	2003/2004 (%)	2004/2005 (%)	2005/2006 (%)	2006/2007 (%)	2007/2008 (%)	2008/2009 (%)	2009/2010 (%)	2010/2011 (%)	2011/2012 (%)	2012/2013 (%)
Increasing sales in the domestic market	64.01	66.67	64.70	36.93	69.75	64.88	68.01	78.08	64.34	64.67
Assimilating new products	53.05	51.79	54.59	46.60	46.34	40.22	51.3	48.27	45.16	50.75
Penetrating new markets	50.15	46.99	51.15	58.15	44.43	41.77	46.94	47.58	44.99	44.40
Creating a business partnership	38.97	43.99	41.81	15.03	35.27	33.39	33.27	28.54	30.89	26.93
Using a new technology	36.94	38.77	34.53	47.11	34.55	31.94	26.40	28.03	30.01	26.37
Obtaining a grant	11.18	12.59	13.71	55.26	20.30	23.66	16.43	15.12	12.65	11.31
Increasing exports	10.96	8.30	9.34	16.72	8.84	20.56	9.97	7.28	11.77	7.32
Others	2.47	2.72	1.61	2.21	1.51	3.09	2.56	1.53	0.34	2.64

Sources: Nicolescu *et al.* (2004, 2005, 2006, 2007, 2008, 2009, 2010, 2011, 2012, 2013a). CNIPMMR, White Charter of SMEs from Romania, Editions 2004–2013.

explanation can be that most SMEs, especially microenterprises, work at local, and regional levels and do not have the economic power to operate on foreign markets.

Taking into consideration the high percentages of enterprises that assimilated new products (about 40–54% in the last decade) and the only slightly lower proportions of firms that use new technologies (especially in 2012/2013 and 2009/2010 with percentages of 26.37% and 26.4% respectively) we can appreciate that SMEs are open to activities oriented on induction of new, although with few exceptions, they do not have a strong innovative character.

We note that between 0.34% (2011/2012) and 3.09% (2008/2009) of entrepreneurs did not refer at any of the opportunities listed in Table 3 and identified other sources of economic opportunities such as: diversification of products and services, reviving the bank credits, stability/loyalty of customers, subcontracting activities in projects financed by the EU, increasing prices of certain products, stabilizing of the exchange rate, development of real estate market, changes in tax laws, employee stability, increasing imports, renting spaces/equipment on favorable terms, external financing, implementation of mandatory standards, growth of sales in the foreign market, reduced competition in some areas, opening new outlets, transparency of public tenders, developing collaborative relationships with stakeholders, attracting investments for modernization, the existence of staff with high levels of skills, a.s.o.

Perceived business difficulties faced by Romanian SMEs are relevant for entrepreneurs/managers, as they contribute to the design of corresponding actions and strategies, and are relevant for politicians, as knowing them, can contribute to the improvement of public policies. Table 4 presents the frequency with which different aspects have been appreciated to be business difficulties during last 10 years.

The most frequently encountered difficulties by SMEs in 2013/2014 were high taxation, bureaucracy, decrease in the internal demand, inflation, excessive controls, difficult access to credits, raised costs for credits, lack/delays in paying invoices, and corruption.

The examination of the business difficulties perceived by Romanian deciders in the analyzed period reveals that there are a number of aspects that have evolved different over time. Thus:

- Percentages of respondents who faced a decrease in the domestic demand were lower in 2006/2007 (28.61%) and 2007/2008 (31.21%) and reached a maximum of 70.08% in 2012/2013;
- Bureaucracy was indicated in the highest proportion in 2006/2007 (71.65%) and in the lower proportion in 2009/2008 (36.21%) and 2013/2012 (36.33%) as a business difficulty;
- Weights of entrepreneurs who reported excessive fiscal taxes decreased annually till the beginning of the economic crisis, from 72.93% in 2003/2004 to the minimum of 41.40% in 2008/2009;
- Inflation was recorded as a difficulty more frequently in 2003/2004 (51.89%) and rarely in 2006/2007 (19.78%);
- Proportions of SMEs who reclaim excessive controls diminished year by year from 2003/2004 (35.78%) until 2008/2009 (17.83%) and increased afterwards annually until 2012/2013 (41.50%);
- Difficult access to credits, high interest rates, and other costs for credits, delays in paying invoices by private companies and the lack/delay of payment of invoices by the state were registered in lower proportions in 2011/2012 and 2012/2013 as being business difficulties;
- Corruption was claimed less frequently in 2003/2004 (11.18%) but more often in 2011/2012 (41.14%);
- Knowledge about and the compliance with the *acquis communitaire* is perceived less as a business difficulty starting 2008/2009, as compared to the previous periods, due to the intensification of European regulations implementation at country level and the improvement of the level of information of the employers and employees.

At the first glance, it might be interpreted that it is a contradiction between the high proportions of entrepreneurs who considered increasing sales in the internal market as being a major opportunity during 2003/2004–2012/2013 and the raised frequencies of respondents who opined that one of the main business difficulties was the decrease in the domestic demand, especially starting with 2009/2008. On the one hand, augmentation of sales on internal market was the main possible opportunity for many SMEs for the entire investigated

Table 4. Major difficulties for the SMEs activity in Romania: 2003/2004–2012/2013

Major difficulties for SMEs	2003/ 2004 (%)	2004/ 2005 (%)	2005/ 2006 (%)	2006/ 2007 (%)	2007/ 2008 (%)	2008/ 2009 (%)	2009/ 2010 (%)	2010/ 2011 (%)	2011/ 2012 (%)	2012/ 2013 (%)
Excessive fiscal taxes	72.93	68.24	64.70	60.27	42.52	41.40	54.61	48.44	51.69	54.25
Decrease in the domestic demand	46.52	39.13	41.58	28.61	31.21	62.06	66.20	67.77	60.55	70.08
Inflation	51.89	29.33	29.79	19.78	33.92	33.76	36.70	44.40	49.59	50.27
Excessive controls	35.78	34.84	30.93	30.48	24.92	17.83	26.13	31.15	40.56	41.50
Bureaucracy	57.47	66.24	64.62	71.65	47.37	36.21	47.07	41.39	52.86	36.33
Corruption	11.18	38.77	38.13	37.69	33.12	23.20	36.8	36.10	41.14	30.95
High interest rates and other costs for credits	37.74	38.13	41.27	41.51	33.36	35.30	25.86	27.80	19.17	16.58
Difficult access to credits	31.35	42.49	38.51	38.88	23.09	24.57	30.51	25.53	20.22	14.59
Delays in paying invoices by private companies	—	—	—	—	—	36.12	26.80	27.52	15.79	12.92
The lack/delay of payment of invoices by the state	37.95	40.41	37.83	42.44	33.84	14.83	12.32	13.47	7.40	5.49
Competition of imports	23	19.10	24.73	28.10	20.70	20.20	18.11	14.38	22.90	16.95
Hiring, training and maintaining staff	—	36.55	33.61	43.72	35.03	18.84	19.06	22.91	29.94	28.53
Increase in the level of wage expenses	—	—	—	—	29.62	21.47	20.34	19.56	9.62	25.46
The relative instability of the national currency	—	12.59	12.33	8.49	24.36	31.76	18.25	21.15	19.00	17.81
Poor quality of infrastructure	—	—	—	—	13.46	13.47	15.35	15.86	4.90	12.00
Decrease in the export demand	—	—	—	—	—	12.73	6.94	5.06	7.17	5.54
Getting the necessary consultancy and training	—	—	9.65	11.63	7.96	6.46	3.5	4.09	5.24	5.87
The knowledge about and the compliance with the *acquis communautaire*	—	—	7.73	10.87	12.10	4	2.90	1.82	2.27	3.44
Others	5.01	5.01	2.60	1.53	0.56	1.18	1.35	0.97	0.93	0.59

Sources: Nicolescu *et al.* (2004, 2005, 2006, 2007, 2008, 2009, 2010, 2011, 2012, 2013a).

period, due to their difficulty to valorify at superior level other aspects as opportunities (exporting, obtaining grants, using new technologies s.o.). On the other hand — even though few entrepreneurs indicated it before 2008 as a difficulty, the real decrease in the domestic demand for many products and services was an immediate consequence of the economic crisis, a trend that continued in the subsequent years. Therefore, the entrepreneurs put their hopes for economic recovery in the increase of the domestic demand, so that they would reach the pre-crisis levels of sales, considering it among the business opportunities expected to occur in the near future.

4. The Effects of Romania's Integration in the EU

Romania's integration in EU in January 2007, generated changes both before and after adhering, changes that affected SMEs. Investigation reveals that Romania's accession into EU was generally seen positively by entrepreneurs/managers in spite of all inherent difficulties arising from the alignment to European standards and requirements in areas like labor relations, consumer protection, health and safety, environmental preservation, etc.

Analyzing the evolution of the perceptions of SMEs on EU integration (Table 5) we observe the following:

- Weights of deciders from SMEs that considered that EU accession had no significant influence on their activities grown over 50% in 2009/2010–2011/2012, denoting an increasing neutral perceived character of the economic integration process in recession period;
- Percentage of entrepreneurs who perceived European integration as a major opportunity augmented quite enough in 2012/2013 (54%), that can be explained through decisions adopted within EU concerning substantial support for few member states;
- Proportion of respondents who appreciated that EU integration represents a major threat reached a maximum of 26.84% in 2005/2006 and recorded the lowest level in 2012/2013 (3.90%).

The investigations revealed that the main positive effects of Romania's integration in the EU are: higher access to markets, potentially cheaper and better suppliers, improved legislation and regulations, superior access to technologies, accessing structural funds, better cooperation for innovation, and more transparent and fair public acquisitions procedures. Taking into account the evolution of aspects seen within SMEs as being positive effects of Romania's adherance to the EU (Table 6), we can emphasize that:

- The proportion of entrepreneurs who indicated better access to markets decreased annually from 2008/2009 till present;
- Perceptions regarding improved legislation/regulations recorded in generally increasing trends since the integration in EU, comparative with previous years;
- The access to potentially cheaper and better suppliers was reported as a positive effect in the highest proportion in 2012/2013 (42.54%) and in the lower proportion in 2005/2006 (19.76%);
- The percentage of respondents who refer to more transparent and fair public acquisitions procedures peaked in year of Romania's integration and decreased afterwards annually;
- Higher access to technologies was recorded more frequently in 2006/2007 (32.51%) and rarely in 2005/2006 (5.14%);

Table 5. The perceptions of the effects of Romania's integration in the EU

Perception on the effects of EU integration	2004/ 2005 (%)	2005/ 2006 (%)	2006/ 2007 (%)	2007/ 2008 (%)	2008/ 2009 (%)	2009/ 2010 (%)	2010/ 2011 (%)	2011/ 2012 (%)	2012/ 2013 (%)
Major opportunity	40.10	40.19	47.05	46.47	46.67	38.80	40.11	38.46	54.00
Major threat	22.43	26.84	11.28	9.18	10.99	9.18	6.34	6.23	3.90
No significant influence	37.46	32.97	41.67	44.34	42.35	52.02	53.55	55.31	42.10

Sources: Nicolescu et al. (2004, 2005, 2006, 2007, 2008, 2009, 2010, 2011, 2012, 2013a).

Table 6. The positive effects of Romania's integration in the EU for SMEs

The positive effects of Romania's integration in the EU for SMEs	2003/ 2004 (%)	2004/ 2005 (%)	2005/ 2006 (%)	2006/ 2007 (%)	2007/ 2008 (%)	2008/ 2009 (%)	2009/ 2010 (%)	2010/ 2011 (%)	2011/ 2012 (%)	2012/ 2013 (%)
Potentially cheaper and better suppliers	29	25.58	19.76	41.85	38.54	36.49	41.08	32.29	26.22	42.54
Better access to markets	31	36.06	35.67	41.68	43.47	46.41	43.16	42.44	41.32	40.93
Improved legislation and regulations	17	19.48	31.67	32.0	35.35	32.30	32.46	40.82	32.11	35.33
Better access to technologies	10	12.79	5.14	32.51	28.34	22.75	19.73	19.78	13.29	21.16
Accessing structural funds	—	—	—	24.11	32.64	32.85	23.64	24.22	20.40	19.71
Better cooperation for innovation	4	4.91	3.43	11.88	12.02	10.74	8.08	9.04	10.26	19.74
More transparent and fair public acquisitions procedures	—	—	3.76	15.53	12.82	12.19	9.76	8.81	5.83	5.33

Sources: Nicolescu et al. (2004, 2005, 2006, 2007, 2008, 2009, 2010, 2011, 2012, 2013a).

Table 7. The impact of the economic crisis on SMEs

The dynamics of SMEs activity	2008/2009 (%)	2009/2010 (%)	2010/2011 (%)	2011/2012 (%)	2012/2013 (%)
SMEs that have reduced their activity	57.58	43.95	39.22	40.83	37.20
SMEs that bankrupted	14.80	27.91	24.02	20.39	18.98
SMEs that have the same activity	23.39	20.82	27.25	24.32	29.97
SMEs that have increased their activity	4.23	7.32	9.51	9.27	13.85

Sources: Nicolescu et al. (2004, 2005, 2006, 2007, 2008, 2009, 2010, 2011, 2012, 2013a).

- Better cooperation for innovation registered the highest percent in 2012/2013 (19.74%) and the lowest percent in 2005/ 2006 (3.43%);
- The accession of structural funds was indicated in higher percentage in 2008/2009 and less frequently in the last two years.

5. The Impact of the Economic Crisis on SMEs

The economic recession that started in 2008 has generated multiple negative effects in Romania. Many specialists believe that a considerable number of countries are still faced with unfavorable economic evolutions, even if they had increases of Gross Domestic Product in different periods. In this context, revealing the impact of the internal/international economic crisis over the sector of SMEs from Romania is highly significant.

Considering the dynamics of the SMEs activity in 2008/2009–2012/2013 (Table 7) we find the following:

- SMEs which reduced their activity registered the highest proportion in 2008/2009 (57.58%) and the lowest proportion in 2013/2012 (37.20%);
- The companies that have been bankrupted recorded the maximum percentage in 2009/2010 (27.91%) and decreased afterwards annually;
- The frequency of respondents who declared that their firms have increased activity is the most reduced in 2008/2009 (4.23%) and the highest in 2012/2013 (13.85%).

Concerning the psychological influences of the economic crisis on entrepreneurs, we observe that:

- A great majority of respondents declared that they are impacted by the recession.
- Only 4.15–6% of the deciders from SMEs opined that there were no emotional influences.
- With the exception of 2013 over 40% of respondents were affected in medium/large enough extents by the crisis.
- Proportion of persons who felt to a great extent (large or very large) the effects of recession was lowest in 2011/2012 (23.65%) and the highest in 2012/2013 (33.46%).
- Over one-fifth of the entrepreneurs were low/very low affected by the negative contextual evolutions during the investigated period, reaching a maximum percentage of 31.95% in 2012/2013.

Further information is given in the Table 8.

We conclude that, even though Romania registered only in 2009 and 2010 decreases of GDP, the negative economic evolutions at international level, the uncertainties related to current economic situation every year and the unpredictability of the future developments had a considerable impact on the a large part of the entrepreneurs (Nicolescu et al., 2013a).

6. Training and Consultancy in SMEs

Taking into account that training and consultancy could have a considerable positive impact on functionality, sustainability, and performance of enterprises, it is important to point out the frequency in which SMEs have accessed this kind of services during 2004–2013.

Examination of the average number of working days per employee dedicated annually to training by SMEs during period 2003/2004–2012/2013, show the following aspects:

- Percentages of companies that have not invested in training of employees increased year by year after the outset of crisis, respectively from 35.04% in 2008/2009 to 83.13% in 2012/2013 (magnifying by 2.37 times);
- Proportions of SMEs that allocated 1–5 working days to training activities registered a descendent trend, starting with the year of Romanian integration in EU, from 51.12% in 2007/2006 to 12.35% in 2012/2013;
- The proportion of firms which dedicated more than 10 days yearly per person for training decreased in 2013/2012 compared to 2009/2008 by 13.33 times (from 12.27% to 0.92%).

See more information in Table 9.

As far as the dynamics of using consultancy services by SMEs is concerned, during the period 2004–2013 (Fig. 1), the surveys highlight the following:

- Comparing the first and the last year of the analyzed period, it was noticed a reduction of almost three times of the proportions of companies using external consultants (from 30.06% in 2004/2003 to 10.13% in 2012/2013);
- In 2009/2010 it was registered the largest contraction of accessing consultancy services, more than two times compared to the previous year;
- In the period between the year of integration in EU and year of the crisis' start, the trend of consultants' usage was ascendant;

Table 8. The psychological impact of the crisis on entrepreneurs

The psychological impact of the crisis	2008/2009 (%)	2009/2010 (%)	2010/2011 (%)	2011/2012 (%)	2012/2013 (%)
Very large	—	13.95	14.16	10.25	13.51
Large	24.22	18.10	16.51	13.40	19.95
Medium/large enough	42.92	41.77	42.21	47.30	28.59
Low/very low	27.26	20.85	22.75	24.90	31.95
No impact	5.60	5.33	4.36	4.15	6.00

Sources: Nicolescu et al. (2004, 2005, 2006, 2007, 2008, 2009, 2010, 2011, 2012, 2013a).

Table 9. Dynamics of average working days per employee allocated to training within SMEs in Romania during period 2004–2013

Average number of working days, dedicated to training within SMEs	2004/ 2005 (%)	2005/ 2006 (%)	2006/ 2007 (%)	2007/ 2008 (%)	2008/ 2009 (%)	2009/ 2010 (%)	2010/ 2009 (%)	2011/ 2010 (%)	2012/ 2011 (%)	2013/ 2012 (%)
None	45.00	34.17	40.68	34.68	35.04	35.25	60.88	62.52	70.70	83.13
1–5 days	34.00	43.00	41.00	51.12	44.46	36.61	24.88	23.46	21.35	12.35
6–10 days	21.00	22.83	18.32	14.20	11.44	15.87	7.20	7.87	4.34	3.61
More than 10 days					9.06	12.27	7.04	6.16	3.61	0.92

Sources: Nicolescu et al. (2004, 2005, 2006, 2007, 2008, 2009, 2010, 2011, 2012, 2013a).

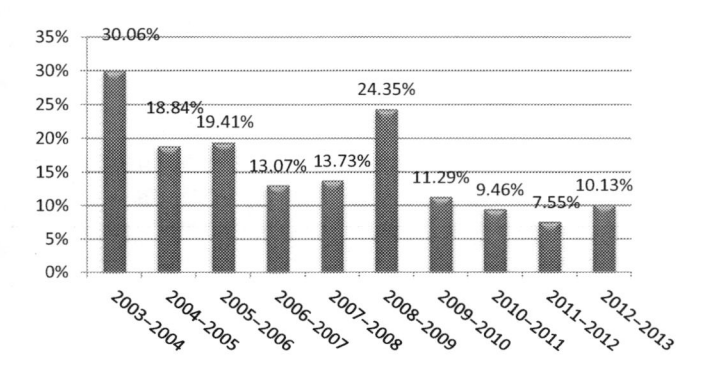

Fig. 1. Dynamics of using consultancy services by SMEs during period 2004–2013

Sources: Nicolescu et al. (2004, 2005, 2006, 2007, 2008, 2009, 2010, 2011, 2012, 2013a).

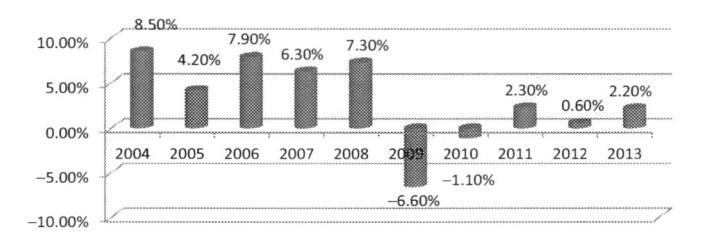

Fig. 2. The evolution of real GDP in Romania in the period 2004–2013

Source: http://www.mdm.ro/2014/evolutia-pib-romaniei-pentru-perioada-2004-2013/.

- In 2011/2012 it was recorded the lowest percent of firms (7.55%) that resort to this kind of services.

It can be seen that in the last years, the frequency of consultancy and training services within SMEs registered a descendent evolution, due to the period of recession, which generated reducing financial potential of many enterprises, but as well due to negative attitudes of some entrepreneurs who do not apprehend the importance and necessity of accessing consultancy/training for them and their employees (Nicolescu, 2013).

7. Conclusions and Recommendations

Taking into account the evolution of the entrepreneurs' perceptions, there were identified few characteristics of the SMEs' sector for the period 2003/2004–2012/2013:

- Assessments of the SMEs on the business environment evolved quite close to dynamics of Romania's GDP. Thus, the favorable evaluations of entrepreneurs about economic environment registered ascendant trend before integration in the EU, a descendent tendency when the crisis began and an upward evolution after GDP started to increase (Fig. 2 and Table 2);
- Regarding business opportunities we observed that some aspects were revealed relative constantly by a considerable number of entrepreneurs (penetrating new markets, assimilating new products) and other aspects have been pointed under the impact of contextual evolutions such as economic recession or integration in EU (increasing exports, obtaining a grant);
- Concerning the views of companies deciders regarding the major difficulties of SMEs, we distinguish different tendencies in the analyzed period, with some aspects of the economic environment deteriorating in recent years (decrease of internal demand, inflation, excessive controls), few problems

remaining more or less alike over time (corruption, excessive fiscal taxes, competition of imports) and some aspects improving (bureaucracy, cost of credits, lack/delays of invoices payments, the knowledge over the *acquis communautaire*);
- Evaluations of entrepreneurs on the European integration effects outline that on overall, the adhering of Romania to EU represents a major opportunity, less respondents considering it without significant influence and only a low part of persons (with tendency of further diminishing), appreciated the integration as a threat;
- The impact of economic recession both on the dynamics of SMEs activities and psychological state of entrepreneurs was higher in the years of decreasing GDP;
- Intensity of training and consultancy registered a negative trend within the sector of SMEs, but noting that in last year increased slightly the proportion of companies which use independent consultants;

Considering the evolution of the entrepreneurs' perceptions, especially of those referring to business difficulties, we formulated few recommendations in order to support development of SMEs sector (Nicolescu & Nicolescu, 2014 and Nicolescu *et al.*, 2013b):

- **Designing of "National Plan for the implementation of the Small Business Act for Europe"** with the purpose to put into practice the 10 principles stipulated by the Small Business Act, a relevant European document and avoiding discrimination of Romanian SMEs as compared to SMEs from countries that apply SBA. Small Business Act for Europe (SBA) aims to improve the overall approach to entrepreneurship and was enacted by the EU Commission in 2008 and revised in 2011. This very important document recognises the central role of SMEs in the EU economy and for the first time puts into place a comprehensive SME policy framework for the EU and its Member States;
- **The amelioration of fiscal conditions** through measures like immediate implementation of reducing/eliminating of taxes on reinvested profit, introducing regulations of payments afferent to VAT in the moment of collection, not on billing/selling, decreasing of taxation levels on social contributions, diminishing of the excise duties, etc.
- **The enhancement of the support for Romanian SMEs in order to access EU structural funds.** Concretely, we recommend: improving information levels concerning the availability of EU structural funds at territorial level through local authorities; perfecting assistance for SMEs to clarify the different aspects of the application process, including specialized consultancy and training; higher correlating between SMEs' necessities and EU programs dedicated to small and medium sized enterprises; ameliorating Romanian administrative processes for accessing EU funds, by means of simplifying procedures, standardizing of eligibility criteria for different programs, better and clearer communication with applicant, etc.; founding a special fund in order to increase SMEs access to finance, by providing co-financing SMEs that access structural funds;
- **Reestablishment of a ministry for SMEs**, with a higher degree of autonomy in elaborating and implementing strategies and policies for small and medium sized companies, conjunction with increasing the number of territorial offices for SMEs so that to get closer to SMEs and their needs at local level;
- **Specific measures focused on SMEs, to support them to cope with business environment difficulties**, such as: assisting the exchanges of best practices and creation of business contacts at national and international level; perfecting the crediting system for SMEs, founding of a state bank dedicated exclusively to SMEs; stipulating regulations to provide postponement of charges/debts toward the state for SMEs that were affected by lack/delays of payments from public/state entities, etc.

Translating into practice these proposals represents in our opinion an urgent necessity, that could contribute to improving the economic environment in which small and medium sized firms operate, taking into account that SMEs, although represent the most dynamic, flexible and innovative sector of economy, are more vulnerable and need specific support in order to survive and develop.

References

Nicolescu, C. (2013), Romanian SMEs in context of national and international complex evolutions, *Proceedings of International Management Conference — New Management for the New Economy*, November 2013, Bucharest, Romania.

Nicolescu, O., Chirovici, E., Dumitrache, B., Maniu, A. I., Maniu, I. I., Nicolescu, C., & Anghel, F. (2005), *White Charter of Romanian SMEs 2005*, Bucharest: Olimp Publishing House.

Nicolescu, O., Chirovici, E., Dumitrache, B., Maniu, A. I., Maniu, I. I., Nicolescu, C., & Anghel, F. (2006), *White Charter of Romanian SMEs 2006*, Bucharest: Olimp Publishing House.

Nicolescu, O., Haiduc, I. C., Nancu, D., Maniu, A. I., Drăgan, I. I., Nicolescu, C., Bâră O. M., Borcoş, M. L. & Anghel, F. (2010), *White Charter of Romanian SMEs 2010*, Bucharest: Olimp Publishing House.

Nicolescu, O., Haiduc, I. C., Nancu, D., Maniu, A. I., Drăgan, I. I., Nicolescu, C., Bâră O. M., Borcoş, M. L. & Anghel, F. (2011), *White Charter of Romanian SMEs 2011*, Bucharest: Sigma Publishing House.

Nicolescu, O., Maniu, A. I., Maniu, I. I., Nicolescu, C. Anghel, F. (2007), *White Charter of Romanian SMEs 2007*, Bucharest: Olimp Publishing House.

Nicolescu, O., Maniu, A. I., Maniu, I. I., Nicolescu, C. Anghel, F. (2008), *White Charter of Romanian SMEs 2008*, Bucharest: Olimp Publishing House.

Nicolescu, O., Maniu, A. I., Maniu, I.I., Nicolescu, C. Anghel, F. (2009), *White Charter of Romanian SMEs 2009*, Bucharest: Lidana Publishing House.

Nicolescu, O., Maniu, A. I., Drăgan, I. I., Nicolescu, C., Bâră O. M., Borcoş, M. L. Lavric, V., Anghel, F. (2012), *White Charter of Romanian SMEs 2012*, Bucharest: Sigma Publishing House.

Nicolescu, O., Maniu, A. I., Drăgan, I. I., Nicolescu, C. Bâră O. M., Borcoş, M. L. Lavric, V. (2013a), *White Charter of Romanian SMEs 2013*, Bucharest: Sigma Publishing House.

Nicolescu, O., Maniu, A. I. Popa, I., Nicolescu, C., & Anghel, F. (2004), *White Charter of Romanian SMEs 2004*, Bucharest: Olimp Publishing House.

Nicolescu, O., Popa, I., & Nicolescu, C. (2013b), *Health Management in Romania 2012*, Bucharest: Pro Universitaria Publishing House.

Nicolescu, O. & Nicolescu, C. (2008), *The Entrepreneurship and Management of SMEs*, Bucharest: Economică Publishing House.

Nicolescu, L. & Nicolescu, C. (2014), Trends in the development of European SMEs. The case of Romanian SMEs, *Proceedings of the International Conference — European Entrepreneurship in the Globalizing Economy*, Preparation of New Generation of Entrepreneurs and Business Leaders, June 2012, Sozopol, Bulgaria, pp. 115–135.

http://www.mdm.ro/2014/evolutia-pib-romaniei-pentru-perioada-2004–2013.

http://ec.europa.eu/enterprise/policies/sme/small-business-act/index_en.htm.

Part VI

Leadership and Human Resources Management

Chapter 30

The Relationship between Leadership Styles, Leader Communication Style, and Impact on Leader–Member Exchange Relationship within the Banking Sector in the United States

Theodore G. Pacleb and Mihai C. Bocarnea

Lincoln Memorial University

School of Business and Leadership

Regent University

Proceeding from the assumption that leadership is a socially constructed relationship, the purpose of the study was to examine (a) the direct causal link between leadership styles and leader communication styles, (b) the direct causal link between leadership styles and quality of leader–member exchange (LMX) relationship as well as (c) the extent to which leader communication styles mediates the relationship between leadership styles and LMX. Using hierarchical multiple regression analysis, three regression models were estimated on data drawn from 213 domestic bank employees in the United States. The findings indicated that the transformational leadership style is negatively related to the communication style of verbal aggressiveness and positively related to preciseness. Furthermore, verbal aggressiveness and preciseness partially mediated the relationship between transformational leadership and LMX. The findings also suggested that verbal aggressiveness leads to low quality of LMX, while preciseness leads to high quality LMX. Finally, results indicated that transactional leadership is significantly related to leader expressiveness, questioningness, and preciseness, which, in turn, explain the relationship of transactional leadership with quality of LMX. The current study concluded that leadership is enacted through different leader communication styles. The implications of the findings draw attention to the importance of leader communication styles in building productive and enduring dyadic relationships with followers in the workplace. Moreover, the findings underscore the role that leader communication plays in influencing the work environment in manners of conveyance that impact proximal and power relationships.

1. Introduction

In a typical communicative discourse on leadership within organizations, the dialogues rarely focus on leadership in terms of how relationships evolve. Only recently have some scholars called for a more integrative and comprehensive definition of leadership that encompasses the main locus of leadership theories (leader, follower, dyad, and context) as well as the mechanisms such as traits, cognitions, behaviors, and affects (Hernandez et al., 2011) that influence the leadership process. Although Hernandez et al. (2011) pushed for a more integrative and comprehensive understanding of where leadership comes from and how it is transmitted, one could lament the fact that the literature on leadership has largely relegated the role of communication as the primary and central enactive mechanism of building relationships along the margins of leadership research. Neufeld, Wan, and Fang (2010) stated, "Without effective communication, leadership is essentially irrelevant" (p. 241). To put it differently, leadership is a communicative process. Leadership theories explain leadership behavior but they do not explain how the leader expresses and conveys the behavior, yet the basis of such expression and conveyance is communicative by nature (Bambacas & Patrickson, 2008, 2009; De Vries et al., 2010; Gaines, 2007; Hamrefors, 2010). The purpose of this quantitative study was to examine the relationship between leadership style (transformational/transactional), leader communication styles, and effect of leader communication style on the quality of LMX relationship among employees drawn from bank organizations. The current study linked the following theories: (a) transformational and transactional leadership, (b) leader communication styles, and (c) LMX theory.

2. Transformational Leadership

Transformational leaders mutually stimulate and elevate in a way "that converts followers into leaders and may convert leaders into moral agents" (Bass, 1990, p. 23). Followers become aware of the importance of their work and induces them to transcend self-interest for organizational (Kovjanic et al., 2012) interest through the activation of their higher-order needs of self-esteem and self-actualization (Yukl, 2010). Transformational leaders accomplish these follower outcomes through articulation and role modeling (Bass, 1990). Bass (1985) and Bass and Avolio (1990, 1997, 1998) identified four measureable behavioral dimensions of transformational leadership: (a) idealized influence, (b) individualized consideration, (c) intellectual stimulation, and (d) inspirational motivation.

The four behavioral dimensions of transformational leadership suggest that it is a relations-oriented leadership approach that focus on the mutual development of the leader and follower (Burns, 1978), and that mutual development depends on interpersonal communication styles (De Vries et al., 2010).

Although the preponderance of studies in transformational leadership focuses on outcomes and effect (e.g., Carmelli et al., 2011; Cheung & Wong, 2011; Dimaculangan & Aguiling, 2012; Jiao et al., 2011; Mitchell & Boyle, 2009) the role of leader rhetoric expressed in different communication styles is a critical factor in the transformational leadership process (Conger, 1991; Den Hartog & Verbug, 1997; Shamir et al., 1994). Rhetoric is the ability of a person to persuade others to "accept new ideas and undertake some specific activities" (Bonet & Sauquet, 2010: 121). Rhetoric is expressed in forms of impression management strategies (Gardner & Cleavenger, 1998; Sosik & Jung, 2003) and other forms involving symbols, slogans, imagery, and metaphors (Amernic et al., 2007; Conger & Kanungo, 1998; Holladay & Coombs, 1994; Yukl, 2010), and may be conveyed in epideictic form (Bonet & Sauquet; Den Hartig & Verbug, 1997; Sheard, 1996; Summers, 2001), which may involve emotional expressivity (Groves, 2006; Riggio, 1992). The use of good rhetorical devises may lead to the attribution of transformational abilities and quality dyadic relationships (Conger, 1991; Sidani, 2007). De Vries et al. (2010) and Bryman (1992) suggested that charismatic-transformational leaders may be attributed certain communication styles differentiated from other forms of leadership styles. Thus, the following hypotheses were tested:

- *H1a*: Transformational leadership style is negatively related to the leader communication style of expressiveness.
- *H1b*: Transformational leadership style is negatively related to the leader communication style of verbal aggressiveness.
- *H1c*: Transformational leadership style is negatively related to the leader communication style of questioningness.
- *H1d*: Transformational leadership style is positively related to the leader communication style of preciseness.

- *H1e*: Transformational leadership style is positively related to the leader communication style of emotionality.
- *H1f*: Transformational leadership style is positively related to the leader communication style of impression manipulativeness.

3. Transactional Leadership

Transactional leadership takes on a different form of dialogic discourse because the emphasis is not on relational building but on behavioral compliance (Whittington *et al.*, 2009), thus communication may be more direct, unambiguous, and less contextual on task performance. Transactional leaders are more task-oriented than relational because the basis of rewards and punishments are on the successful completion of tasks (2009). Bass & Avolio (1990) advanced this leadership concept by identifying three behavior dimensions to measure transactional leadership: (a) contingent reward, (b) active management by exception, and (c) passive management by exception. The forms of communication tend to be directive, controlling, and power oriented (De Vries *et al.*, 2010), which are inversely related to loyalty and innovativeness (Lee, 2008), creative performance (Wei *et al.*, 2010) and quality of LMX (Yrle *et al.*, 2002). De Vries and colleagues (2010) suggested that the communication style of task-oriented leadership approaches tend to be more assuring, precise, and with some level of verbal aggressiveness. Thus, the following hypotheses were tested:

- H2a: Transactional leadership style is positively related to the leader communication style of expressiveness.
- H2b: Transactional leadership style is positively related to the leader communication style of verbal aggressiveness.
- H2c: Transactional leadership style is positively related to the leader communication style of questioningness.
- H2d: Transactional leadership style is positively related to the leader communication style of preciseness.
- H2e: Transactional leadership style is negatively related to the leader communication style of emotionality.
- H2f: Transactional leadership style is positively related to the leader communication style of impression manipulativeness.

4. Communication Styles

Kellerman (1987) stated, "Social interaction depends on communication. The form, the purpose, the outcome, and the participants in social interaction may vary; communication remains the vehicle" (p. 188). The axiom that a person "cannot not communicate" (Watzlawick *et al.*, 1967: 51) captures the autonomic nature of communication. One cannot possibly begin to understand the leadership process unless one understands how the leader communicates; yet, to date, the central role of communication as a key element in leadership as a relational process has only been examined as expressions of personality and predictors of some leader outcomes (Bakker-Pieper & De Vries, 2013; De Vries *et al.*, 2011; De Vries *et al.*, 2010; De Vries *et al.*, 2009, 2013) and, for some, has not been given due importance in the leadership process (Fairhurst & Uhl-Bien, 2012).

Leader communication as a variable is treated as a general construct rather than specific leader communication styles reflecting a positive or supportive communication in a high-LMX situation (Maslyn & Uhl-Bien, 2001) and dominance-like and restricted communication in a low-LMX situation (Fairhurst *et al.*, 1987). De Vries and colleagues (2010), however, found significant support for the importance of communication style in the leadership process. Yet, there remains a critical gap in leadership research that places leader communication style as the central and underlying mechanism of the leadership process in terms of its influence on the quality of the dyadic relationship. Thus, the current study tested the following hypotheses:

- H3a: Lexical leader communication style of expressiveness is negatively related to the quality of LMX relationship among transformational leaders but positively related among transactional leaders.
- H3b: Lexical leader communication style of verbal aggressiveness is negatively related to the quality of LMX among transformational but positively related among transactional leaders.

- H3c: Lexical leader communication style of questioningness is negatively related to the quality of LMX among transformational leaders but positively related among transactional leaders.
- H3d: Lexical leader communication style of preciseness is positively related to the quality of LMX among transformational and transactional leaders.
- H3e: Lexical leader communication style of emotionality is positively related to the quality of LMX among transformational but negatively related among transactional leaders.
- H3f: Lexical leader communication style of impression manipulativeness is positively related to the quality of LMX among transformational leaders and transactional leaders.

5. Leader–Member Exchange Theory

Founded upon social exchange theory (Blau, 1964), LMX theory is the social exchange process in a leadership context where leader and follower define their roles in a reciprocal interaction involving mutual evaluation and exchanges of resources valuable to each party, leading to the development of a relationship (Brandes et al., 2004; Dansereau et al., 1973; Dansereau et al., 1975; Graen & Schiemann, 1978; Graen & Uhl-Bien, 1995; Klein & Kim, 1998). The emphasis is on the construction of a relationship through social interaction built upon communication (Graen & Scandura, 1987; Graen & Uhl-Bien, 1991, 1995; Uhl-Bien, 2006). Proximal relations (close or distant) are essential to LMX relationship (Brandes et al., 2004). The theory suggests that high LMX is a close relationship between supervisor and subordinate in a way that the reciprocal relationship mutually benefits both (Graen & Uhl-Bien, 1995) but low LMX suggest a dysfunctional form of exchange (Othman et al., 2010). In a dysfunctional form of exchange, reciprocity is negative (Uhl-Bien & Maslyn, 2003), which means that the leader and subordinate are exchanging negative behaviors such as restrained and aggressive communication (e.g., disrespect), avoidance and non-commitment, misinterpretations and misunderstanding, marginal follower performance, low commitment, motivation, and productivity. Proceeding from the assumption that LMX is a "communicatively constructed" (Fairhurst, 1993: 322) relationship, the current study examined the mediated relationship of leadership style and LMX by testing the following hypotheses:

- H4a: Transformational leadership style predicts the quality of LMX relationship.
- H4b: Transactional leadership style predicts the quality of LMX relationship.
- H5a: Lexical leader communication styles mediate the relationship between transformational leadership style and quality of LMX.
- H5b: Lexical leader communication styles mediate the relationship between transactional leadership style and quality of LMX.

6. Method

The sample was drawn from domestic banks in the United States. Respondents were invited in person, online through panel services, social networking site (e.g., LinkedIn), and by email to individual social relations (e.g., family, friends) working in domestic banks. The survey instruments were distributed via SurveyGizmo, an Internet based research survey distributor. A total of $N = 213$ usable surveys were collected representing a 37.3% response rate. The age ($M = 2.61$, $SD = 0.88$) distribution shows that 24 (11.3%) were 18 to 24 years old, 67 (31.5%) were 25 to 34 years old, 90 (42.3%) were 35 to 54 years old, and 32 (15%) were above 55 years old. In education ($M = 1.59$, $SD = 1.00$), 167 (78.4%) hold Bachelor's degrees, 41 (19.2%) hold Master's degrees, and 5 (2.4%) hold Doctorate degrees. For employment ($M = 2.51$, $SD = 1.38$), 18 (8.5%) had less than a year with the bank, 42 (19.7%) had 1 to 2 years, 45 (21.1%) had 3 to 4 years, 29 (13.6%) had 5 to 6 years, and 79 (37.1%) had over 6 years. Gender ($M = 1.66$, $SD = 0.47$) shows that 72 (33.8%) were male and 141 (66.2%) were females. Supervisors ($M = 1.63$, $SD = 0.48$) comprised 78 (36.6%) of the respondents and 135 (63.4%) were non-supervisors.

The current study used the Multi-Factor Leadership Questionnaire (MLQ-5X Rater Form) to measure the independent variables, transformational and transactional leadership styles. Internal reliability for TF and TL leadership styles are $\alpha = 0.91$ and $\alpha = 0.71$, respectively. The Communication Style Inventory (CSI Rater Version) was used to measure the mediating variables leader communication styles. All six sub-scales of the CSI demonstrate acceptable internal reliabilities ranging from $\alpha = 0.69$ to $\alpha = 0.87$. The Leader–Member Exchange Questionnaire (LMX-7) was used to measure the dependent variable quality of LMX relationship. Internal reliability is $\alpha = 0.88$.

6.1. Results

Using hierarchical multiple regression, three regression equations were estimated to examine the mediated relationship (Baron & Kenny, 1986) of leadership styles, leader communication styles and LMX, controlling for age, education, employment, gender, and position. The first regression equation (Model 1, Table 1) shows that the model is significant, $F(7, 205) = 14.97$, $p < 0.01$. Leadership styles explained 58% ($R = 0.58$, $p < 0.01$) of the variance in leader communication styles. The second regression equation shows that the model is significant, $F(7, 205) = 33.14$, $p < 0.01$. Leadership styles explained 72% ($R = 0.72$, $p < 0.01$) of the variance in LMX. The third regression equation, which shows that the addition of leader communication styles as mediating variables, is significant, $F(13, 199) = 25.24$, $p < 0.01$. The model explains 79% ($R = 0.72$, $p < 0.01$) of the variance in LMX and indicating the presence of mediation effect. As Hair *et al.* (2010) recommended however, the current study used the estimated regression model for prediction only and examined the bivariate correlations "to understand the independent-dependent variable relationship" (p. 205).

The bivariate correlations show that transformational leadership has significant positive correlations with expressiveness ($r = 0.46$, $p < 0.01$), preciseness ($r = 0.66$, $p < 0.01$) and questioningness ($r = 0.41$, $p < 0.01$) but significant negative correlations with emotionality ($r = -0.17$, $p < 0.05$), impression manipulativeness ($r = -0.26$, $p < 0.01$) and verbal aggressiveness ($r = -0.57$, $p < 0.01$). The results of the correlation with expressiveness and questioningness are in the negative direction of the hypothesized model, thus H1a and H1c are not supported. The results support the proposition that transformational leadership is negatively related to verbal aggressiveness, thus H1b is supported. The results also show that transformational leadership is positively related to preciseness, thus H1d is supported. Emotionality and impression manipulativeness were hypothesized to have a

Table 1. Hierarchical multiple regression models ($N = 213$)

Step		Model 1β	Model 2β	Model 3β
Step 1	(Control variables)			
	Age	−0.20	−0.04	−0.04
	Education	0.10	−0.01	−0.01
	Employment	−0.03	0.15	0.15
	Gender	−0.11	0.05	0.05
	Position	−0.29**	−0.03	−0.03
Step 2	(Unmediated model)			
	Age	−0.18**	0.00	0.00
	Education	0.07	0.03	0.03
	Employment	−0.04	0.09	0.09
	Gender	−0.09	−0.04	−0.04
	Position	−0.20**	0.06	0.06
	Transformational	−0.20**	0.74**	0.74**
	Transactional	0.50**	−0.03	−0.03
Step 3	(Mediated model)			
	Age			0.01
	Education			0.02
	Employment			0.05
	Gender			−0.01
	Position			−0.01
	Transformational			0.31**
	Transactional			0.05
	Emotionality			0.26**
	Expressiveness			0.09
	Impression manipulativeness			−0.16*
	Preciseness			0.18*
	Questioningness			0.11
	Verbal aggressiveness			−0.31**
	R	0.58	0.72	0.79
	F	14.97***	33.14***	25.24***
	df	(7,205)	(7,205)	(13,199)
	R^2 change	0.17***	0.51***	0.09***

Note: Model 1 predicted leader's communication style and represents the first regression equation of the mediation model. Models 2 and 3 predicted LMX and represents the second and third regression equation of the mediation model.
* $p < 0.05$. ** $p < 0.01$. *** $p < 0.001$.

positive relationship with transformational leadership, but the results were significant in the negative direction, thus H1e and H1f are not supported. The results for transactional leadership shows significant positive correlations with expressiveness ($r = 0.37$, $p < 0.01$), questioningness ($r = 0.38$, $p < 0.01$), and preciseness ($r = 0.60$, $p < 0.01$), thus supporting H2a, H2c, and H2d. Significant negative relationships were found on verbal aggressiveness ($r = -0.57$, $p < 0.01$) and impression manipulativeness ($r = -0.28$, $p < 0.01$), thus H2b and H2f are not supported. Emotionality is positive but not significant ($r = 0.06$, $p > 0.05$), thus H2e is not supported.

The causal propositions of the current study argued that the relationships of leader communication styles with LMX would follow the causal (linear) propositions of transformational leadership, H1a to H1f, and transactional leadership styles, H2a to H2f. The results for transformational leadership show that only two of six leader communication styles followed the causal propositions of H1a to H1f (Table 2). Expressiveness is positively related to LMX but significant in the opposite (negative) direction of H1a, thus H3a is not supported. Verbal aggressiveness is negatively related to LMX and follows the direction of H1b, thus H3b is supported. Questioningness is positively related to LMX but significant in the opposite direction of H1c, thus H3c is not supported. Preciseness is positively related to LMX and follows the direction of H1d, thus H3d is supported. Emotionality is not significant, thus H3e is not supported. Lastly, impression manipulativeness is negatively related to LMX but significant in the opposite direction of H1f, thus H3f is not supported.

The results for transactional leadership show that three leader communication styles followed the causal propositions of H2a to H2f for the U.S. sample (Table 3). Expressiveness is significant and followed the causal proposition of H2a, thus H3a is supported. Verbal aggressiveness is not significant, thus H3b is not supported. Both questioningness and preciseness are positively related to LMX, which follows the causal propositions of H2c and H2d, thus H3c and H3d are supported. Emotionality is not significant in relation to LMX, thus H3e is not supported. Lastly, although impression manipulativeness followed the causal proposition of transactional leadership, H2f, it is negatively related to LMX, thus H3f is not supported.

Table 2. Directional results of bivariate correlations

Variable	Causal propositions	Transformational	LMX	Results
H_{1a}/H_{3a} Expressiveness	−	+	+	NS/NS
H_{1b}/H_{3b} Verbal aggressiveness	−	−	−	S/S
H_{1c}/H_{3c} Questioningness	−	+	+	NS/NS
H_{1d}/H_{3d} Preciseness	+	+	+	S/S
H_{1e}/H_{3e} Emotionality	+	−	NS	NS/NS
H_{1f}/H_{3f} Impression manipulativeness	+	−	−	NS/NS

Note: S = Supported, NS = Not Supported.

Table 3. Directional results of bivariate correlations

Variable	Causal propositions	Transactional	LMX	Results
H_{2a}/H_{3a} Expressiveness	+	+	+	S/S
H_{2b}/H_{3b} Verbal aggressiveness	+	ns	−	NS/NS
H_{2c}/H_{3c} Questioningness	+	+	+	S/S
H_{2d}/H_{3d} Preciseness	+	+	+	S/S
H_{2e}/H_{3e} Emotionality	−	+	ns	NS/S
H_{2f}/H_{3f} Impression manipulativeness	+	+	−	S/NS

Note: S = Supported, NS = Not Supported, ns = non-significant.

As shown in Model 2, transformational leadership style predicted LMX, $\beta = 0.74$, $p < 0.01$. Thus, H4a is supported. Although the regression coefficients of transactional leadership, $\beta = -0.03$, $p > 0.05$ was not significant, the bivariate correlations however are significant, thus predictive of LMX, $r = 0.36$, $p < 0.01$. Thus, H4b is supported. In Model 3, leader communication styles partially mediated the relationship between transformational leadership and quality of LMX relationship. Thus, H5a is supported by three leader communication styles. Although transactional leadership was not significant in Model 2 and Model 3, thus no mediation effect, possibly due to high multicollinearity with transformational leadership, the overall models were significant, $F(7, 205) = 33.14$, $p < 0.01$ and $F(13, 199) = 25.24$, $p < 0.01$, respectively. An examination of the correlation of transactional leadership with LMX, $r = 0.36$, $p < 0.01$, and regression coefficient of transactional leadership, $\beta = 0.05$, $p > 0.05$ suggest that in a simple regression with leader communication styles as mediators, a mediation effect would occur and may be attributed to emotionality, impression manipulativeness, and verbal aggressiveness. Thus, H5b is supported.

7. Discussion

Scholars in leadership and communication have agreed that communication is the interactive pathways in a network of social relationships. The findings indicate that leader communication styles enact leadership behavior and have a direct causal effect on respondents' perceptions of their relationship with leaders in a dyadic exchange process. In a series of estimated regression models transformational leadership predicted two leader communication styles — preciseness and verbal aggressiveness — that predicted the quality of LMX relationship. As expected, the positive effect of preciseness increases the variance on LMX, while the negative effect of verbal aggressiveness decreases the variance on LMX, which suggests that preciseness leads to high LMX while verbal aggressiveness leads to low LMX. Transactional leadership also predicted three leader communication styles — questioningness, expressiveness, and preciseness. All three, in turn, predicted the quality of LMX relationship. In contrast to transformational leadership, all the predicted relationship of transactional leadership with these leader communication styles proceeded in the positive direction, which is a clear indication that the increase in variance on LMX suggests that these ways of communicating would lead to high LMX. A general conclusion could be drawn that transformational and transactional styles of leadership are enacted through leader communication styles and that the quality of the dyadic relationship are determined significantly, in part, by certain ways of communicating. The relevance of the findings of this study can be situated in several aspects of leadership studies such as proximal relations and power relations.

a. *Proximal relations*

The current research supports the theory that the quality of dyadic relationship between a leader and follower is determined to a significant extent by the communication style of the leader, more specifically his or her manner of verbal expressions. Leader communication styles determine proximal relations in LMX relationships. The fundamental premise of LMX theory is that the quality of LMX depends on the distance of the leader and follower to each other in terms of relationship. When a follower is close to the leader, he or she gains access to social capital necessary to achieve his or her instrumental objective of career success (Seibert *et al.*, 2001). The leader, however, initiates the proximal relationship in that he or she must convey to the follower that it is worth it to draw close to the leader. The conveyance comes in the form of advice, encouragement, task assistance, rewards, and mutual influence (Fairhurst & Chandler, 1989; Klein & Kim, 1998). In other words, close proximal relations depends on supportive communication (Eisenberg *et al.*, 2007), while non-supportive communication such as verbal aggressiveness, questioningness, and emotionality may push followers to maintain some distance in interacting with the leader. Supportive communication creates a climate of reciprocal behavior, both in-role and out-role, because of the higher quality of LMX (Brandes *et al.*, 2004), but derogatoriness in verbal aggressiveness, argumentativeness in questioningness, and tension in emotionality (De Vries *et al.*, 2009, 2013) creates the opposite condition. The extent to which followers will reciprocate behavior in a climate of fear, conflict, and tension restrain follower motivation, which in effect limit the extent of their performance to the formal requirements of their work (Yukl, 2010). These manners of communication lead to a heightened level of pressure, stress, and insecurity in the workplace, which undermines mutual dependence, loyalty, commitment, and support. The low-level mutual influence perpetuates a work climate where the quality of LMX would be low. Followers will continue to perform despite distant proximal relations, but productivity would correspond with low LMX.

If verbal aggressiveness, questioningness, and emotionality create distance, then preciseness and expressiveness could draw leader and follower toward a closer relationship because these manners of communication promote information exchange, which is essential to creating certainty. When followers know exactly what they need to do, which means they are not confused about responsibilities and priorities, then the probability of high-level performance would be greater (Yukl, 2010), and success at performance brings a sense of accomplishment that spills over toward a favorable view of work and the leader. The structure, thoughtfulness, substance, and conciseness that a leader expresses in communicating with followers creates conditions of reciprocal behavior because they know exactly what to expect, thus drawing leader and follower closer to each other. Expressiveness offers a similar implication on proximal relations. Expressiveness is a way of self-disclosure in the form of talkativeness, humor, conversation, and informality (De Vries *et al.*, 2009, 2013). Social penetration theory describes a means of increasing or escalating intimacy in a relationship (Roloff, 1981). Within the context of LMX, this manner of communicating would permit followers to gain a deeper familiarity with the leader, and when the rewards of self-disclosure exceed the costs of being reserved or distant, they would move to a closer relationship. The information gained in expressiveness is used to predict reward and cost outcomes in the future (Littlejohn & Foss, 2011). For as long as rewards exceed the cost in proximal relations, the relational interaction progresses toward a deeper relationship.

b. *Power relations*

Leader communication styles are expressions of power in the form of compliance-gaining messages or strategies (Marwell & Schmidt, 1967). Compliance-gaining strategies includes making threats, promising rewards, displaying friendliness, calling in a debt, attributing positive and negative feelings, asking for favors, and showing positive esteem by saying to the person that he or she will be liked by others if he or she complies or hated when he or she does not comply (1967). In a power relationship such as LMX, these message strategies are typical communication goals that leaders pursue. The whole idea of compliance-gaining messaging is based on exchange theory. Recognizing that people will comply in exchange for something, individuals in positions of power and authority will attempt to influence compliance through three types of general power: (a) manipulating the consequences or the giving out of rewards and punishments, (b) taking advantage of relational position by being a supervisor, and (c) defining values and obligations or telling followers what is acceptable and not acceptable (Littlejohn & Foss, 2011). When followers perceive any of these powers through any of the specific compliance-gaining messaging strategies they would feel compelled to act or not to act. Thus, as an expression of power, the leader would typically use the verbal manner that invokes his or her power.

The results also support the theory that as an expression of power, the communication style or manner of linguistic form is different between a supervisor and a subordinate. Individuals in positions of power and authority tend to be less polite, and those under the authority tend to be more polite (Morand, 2000). Politeness is a communication goal or a linguistic gesture or behavior that individuals pursue in order to meet the face needs of self and of others. Face is the image that individuals project in public (Ting-Toomey, 1994). In dyadic interactions, face-threatening acts are a normal part of everyday interactions, such as requests or impositions. It is expected that face-threatening acts would flow between leader and follower in either direction, thus both would be sensitive to politeness gesture. Given the results, verbal aggressiveness, questioningness, expressiveness, and emotionality may be considered impolite because some facets of these communication styles are face-threatening acts. Face-threatening acts are serious considerations in intercultural relations because cultures determine the types of identities that are acceptable and unacceptable, thus manners of communication, or communication styles, become the most important element when culture is a factor in building relationships (1994).

c. *Limitations*

Empirical research has several limitations. First, suprious effects cannot be completely removed in *ex-post facto* research (Jarde et al., 2012). In *ex-post facto* research, the conditions or causes that the researcher assumes in the prediction model makes the plausibility of explanation dependent on uncontrolled information, which opens the possibility for other causal explanations outside of the model (Kerlinger & Lee, 2000). The inherent presence of post hoc fallacy derived from ex-post facto data "can and often does, lead to erroneous and misleading interpretations of research data" (Kerlinger & Lee, 2000: 558). Second, in models of prediction, the predicted casual results may not always follow the direction of the causal propositions even when conceptually or theoretically supported. Hair *et al.* (2010) stated that even when the selection of independent and dependent variables are based on empirical evidence and theoretically relevant, the basic tenets of predictive model development might be violated. In the current study, some of the leader communication styles did not follow the direction of the causal predictions, but the bivariate relationships were significant. Lastly, the generalizability of the results is limited to the target population of domestic bank employees, which is a criterion of research design (Kerlinger & Lee, 2000).

d. *Future research*

The causal model investigated in the current study is a modification of the model investigated by De Vries *et al.* (2010) in which leader communication styles were mediators rather than predictors. In the current study leader communication styles were mediators. No implications should be drawn from this divergence in model findings because each study examined different predictors and outcomes. Nevertheless, the divergence in findings suggests that the causal path needs further investigation. In addition, there were twice as many female respondents in the sample. With language as gendered, further investigation is needed to ascertain differences on the impact of feminine communication styles on the quality of dyadic relationships. The results also open opportunities to further research leadership rhetoric. Following a constructivism perspective (Littlejohn & Foss, 2011) such as personal construct theory (Kelly, 1955) personal similarities and differences may be examined to explain how rhetoric may influence the choices of communication strategies and tactics to gain compliance. Lastly, along the same lines of examining rhetoric and perception, examining further the relationship between impression management and compliance-gaining strategies contributes to how it affects the work environment and quality of dyadic relationships. The construction of social realities in the workplace is formed through a system of meaning and discourses that lead to a psychological state destructive to the work enviroment and employees (Lutgen-Sandvik & Tracy, 2012). To the extent that workplace environment has a lot to do with leader behavior, leader communication styles become a primary means of determining workplace environment, thus some communication styles may fall within the category of workplace bullying. This deserves further investigation by extending the current study into the realm of qualitative methods.

8. Conclusions

The findings indicate that certain leader communication styles — preciseness, verbal aggressiveness, expressiveness, and questioningness explains how leadership behavior of transformational and transactional leadership affect the quality of dyadic relationships. It provides a model that builds upon the concept of leadership as relational and contributes to the overall effort to shift the focus of leadership studies from trait-based to examining how leader–member dyadic relationships are built or constructed. The model provides a framework to guide in further investigating the importance of leader communication styles in creating social realities within the workplace that contribute to either productive work or workplace toxicity. The research model highlights the role that leader communication style plays in proximal relations and power relationships. The model upholds the fundamental premise that relationships are built through communication. It affirmatively confirms that leadership is communication.

Communication is the pathway and mechanism by which leadership is enacted.

The enactment of leadership is more pronounced in communicative expressions. Leader communication styles would be the first environment cue that shapes the dyadic interaction, and determines the path of the LMX relationship. A communicative behavior that is precise, aggressive, expressive, or questioning clearly leads to different outcomes of relationships, but in general, one that promotes either a close or distant relationship. Perceptions of leadership and proximal relationships, in this regard, would be dependent on manners of conveyance, and will shape to some extent perceptions of power behavior in terms of deference to politeness and sensitivity to face concerns. Face concerns are particularly important in cross-cultural interactions. The relational effect of manners of conveyance, in verbal and non-verbal forms, will not be universally similar across cultures. Preciseness may be perceived as too directive in a collectivist society but appreciated in an individualistic society. The para-verbal dynamics of how people communicate in one society will elicit a different form of reaction in another. In other words, beyond the choice of words, tonal differences will affect the path and direction of the relationship outcome, that is, whether it draws the interactants closer or farther apart.

How perception of leadership styles, proximal relations, and power relations are influenced by leader communication styles largely depends on the nature of the manner of conveyance itself. The nature of preciseness is uncertainty avoidance. Leader communication behavior that is highly structured, concise, thoughtful, substantive, and expressed in an unambiguously clear manner reduces the amount of uncertainty inherently present in communication. The higher level of certainty of precise communication tends to lead towards a positive and productive interaction. Dealing with and managing uncertainty is one of the most important predictors of leadership outcomes because of the inherent tension that exists in relationships. Inherent in relationships, particularly in the theory of relational dialectics, are tensions involving integration versus separation, closeness versus distance, similarity versus difference, and certainty versus uncertainty. The tension of certainty and uncertainty deals with the interplay of predictability and consistency versus being spontaneous and different. These tensions are complex dynamic of contradictions that defines and redefines relationships. Preciseness of leader communication would influence and shape the outcome of in any transformative effort because the ability of a transformative leader to precisely communicate a sense of urgency, the need for radical change, powerful vision and inspirational goals are necessary in elevating levels of motivation, inspiration, commitment, satisfaction, and productivity. Regardless of the focal emphasis of transformational and transactional leadership styles, precision in the articulation of vision and precision in conveying expectations of task performance have a significant positive effect on the quality of LMX.

Verbal aggressiveness creates a different field of relationship. It creates the conditions that directly affect a follower's inclination for attachment with the leader, and generally considered a form of abusive behavior by the supervisor. The undesirability of this manner of conveyance leads to attachment avoidance and workplace aggression in the form of retaliatory behaviors on the part of the follower. The farther a follower is to the leader in terms of relationship, the less safe and attached the follower is to the leader. The resulting anxiety and fear are psychological threats and barriers that prevent the formation of quality relationships. The intimidation and fear individuals develop removes their sense of security in the relationship. The result is a natural inclination to avoid, but may also lead to counter-aggression or retaliation. Verbal aggression not only pushes individuals away but also directly challenges their self-control capacity by heightening their emotional sensitivity and weakening their capacity for rational thinking and reaction. These negative effects diminish an individual's sense of worth. In the workplace where productivity depends on employee empowerment, lack of self-worth typically leads to feelings of insecurity. Insecure employees manifest counterproductive behaviors cooperation and coordination. They tend to limit and avoid social interactions, thus difficulties in adaptive behaviors. The difficulty of relating or adapting positive and productive behaviors consequently creates conflict in the workplace. The negative chain of effects that verbal aggressiveness creates directly affects the ability of followers to form quality relationship with leaders.

Questioningness forms a different perception of leader behavior. It conveys a broad range of behavior where the quality of the LMX relationship may be high or low, positive or negative. Questioningness is an expressive manner of conveyance. An expressive who, engages in philosophical or inquisitive dialogue reveals more of himself or herself to his or her followers. The self-disclosure gives followers the ability to judge and evaluate the character of the leader, which either draws them closer to the leader or maintains a certain distance. Questioningness also involves being argumentative. The risk of being argumentative is that it tends to create distance or separation when hostility is involve. When argumentative manners of conveyance are confined to exchanges of differences in ideas, it may lead to better understanding, which in turn permits movement or convergence towards mutual agreement and unity. When people argue, they begin the process of working through divergence or disagreements about certain things or may be engaged in trying to resolve interpersonal conflict. Questioningness, in this regard, becomes a positive way of strengthening and deepening a dyadic relationship or resolving relationship problems.

References

Amernic, J., Craig, R. & Tourish, D. (2007), The transformational leader as pedagogue, physician, architect, commander, and saint: Five root metaphors in Jack Welch's letters to stockholders of general electric, *Human Relations*, 60(12), 1839–1872.

Bakker-Pieper, A. & De Vries, R. E. (2013), The incremental validity of communication styles over personality traits for leader outcomes, *Human Performance*, 26(1), 1–19.

Bambacas, M. & Patrickson, M. (2008), Interpersonal communication skills that enhance organisational commitment, *Journal of Communication Management*, 12(1), 51–72.

Baron, R. M. & Kenny, D. A. (1986), The moderator–mediator variable distinction in social psychological research: Conceptual, strategic, and statistical Considerations, *Journal of Personality and Social Psychology*, 51(6), 1173–1182.

Bass, B. M. (1985), *Leadership and Performance beyond Expectations*, New York: Free Press.

Bass, B. M. (1990), *Bass & Stogdill's Handbook of Leadership: Theory, Research, & Managerial Applications* (3rd edn.), New York: The Free Press.

Bass, B. M. & Avolio, B. J. (1990), The implications of transactional and transformational leadership for individual, team and organizational development, *Research in Organizational Change and Development*, 4, 231–272.

Bass, B. M. & Avolio, B. J. (1997), Full range leadership development manual for the multifactor leadership questionnaire, Palo Alto, CA: Mindgarden.

Bass, B. M. & Avolio, B. J. (1998), Improving organizational effectiveness through transformational leadership. In *Leading Organizations: Perspectives for a new era*, G. R. Hickman (ed.) (pp. 135–140). Thousand Oaks, CA: Sage.

Blau, P. M. (1986), *Exchange and Power in Social Life*, New Brunswick, NJ: Transaction Books.

Bonet, E. & Sauquet, A. (2010), Rhetoric in management and in management research, *Journal of Organizational Change Management*, 23(2), 120–133.

Brandes, P., Dharwadkar, R., & Wheatley, K. (2004), Social exchanges within organizations and work outcomes: The importance of local and global relationships, *Group Organization Management*, 29(3), 276–301.

Bryman, A. (1992), *Charisma and Leadership in Organization*, London, UK: Sage.

Burns, J. M. (1978), *Leadership*, New York, NY: Harper & Row.

Carmeli, A., Atwater, L., & Levi, A. (2011), How leadership enhances employees' knowledge sharing: The intervening roles of relational and organizational identification, *Journal of Technology Transfer*, 36(3), 257–274.

Cheung, M. F. & Wong, C. (2011), Transformational leadership, leader support, and employee creativity, *Leadership & Organization Development Journal*, 32(7), 656–672.

Conger, J. A. (1991), Inspiring others: The language of leadership, *Academy of Management Executive*, 5(1), 31–45.

Conger, J. A. & Kanungo, R. N. (1998), *Charismatic Leadership in Organizations*, Thousand Oaks, CA: Sage.

Dansereau, F., Cashman, J., & Graen, G. (1973), Instrumentality theory and equity theory as complementary approaches in predicting the relationship of leadership and turnover among managers, *Organizational Behavior and Human Performance*, 10, 184–200.

Dansereau, F., Graen, G. B., & Haga, W. (1975), A vertical dyad linkage approach to leadership in formal organizations, *Organizational Behavior and Human Performance*, 13(1), 380–397.

De Vries R. E., Bakker-Pieper, A., & Oostenveld, W. (2010), Leadership = communication? The relations of leaders' communication styles with leadership styles, knowledge sharing and leadership outcomes, *Journal of Business and Psychology*, 25(3), 367–380.

De Vries, R. E., Bakker-Pieper, A., Konings, F. E., & Schouten, B. (2011), The Communication Styles Inventory (CSI): A six-dimensional behavioral model of communication styles and its relation with personality, Communication Research. Advance online publication.

De Vries, R. E., Bakker-Pieper, A., Siberg, R. A., van Gameren, K., & Vlug, M. (2009), The content and dimensionality of communication styles, *Communication Research*, 36(2), 178–206.

De Vries, R. E., Bakker-Pieper A., Siberg, R. A., van Gameren, K., & Vlug, M. (2013), The content and dimensionality of communication styles, *Communication Research*, 40(4), 506–532.

Den Hartog, D. W. & Verburg, R. M. (1997), Charisma and rhetoric: Communicative techniques of international business leaders, *Leadership Quarterly*, 8(4), 355–391.

Dimaculangan, E. D. & Aguiling, H. M. (2012), The effects of transformational leadership on salesperson's turnover intention, *International Journal of Business and Social Science*, 3(19), 197–210.

Eisenberg, E. M., Goodall, H. L. Jr., & Trethewey, A. (2007), *Organizational Communication: Balancing Creativity and Constraint* (5th edn.), Boston: Bedford/St. Martin's.

Fairhurst, G. T. (1993), The leader–member exchange patterns of women leaders in industry: A discourse analysis, *Communication Monographs*, 60(4), 321–351.

Fairhurst, G. T. & Chandler, T. A. (1989), Social structure in leader-member interaction, *Communication Monographs*, 56(3), 215–239.

Fairhurst, G. T., Roger, L. E., & Sarr, R. A. (1987), Manager subordinate control patterns and judgments about relationships. In *Communication Yearbook*, M. McLaughlin (ed.), (Vol. 10, pp. 395–415), Beverly Hills: Sage.

Fairhurst, G. T. & Uhl-Bien, M. (2012), Organizational discourse analysis (ODA): Examining leadership as a relational process, *Leadership Quarterly*, 23(6), 1043–1062.

Gaines, K. A. (2007), A communicative theory of leadership practice (Doctoral dissertation). Available from ProQuest Dissertations and Theses database. (UMI No. 3285362)

Gardner, W. L. & Cleavenger, D. (1998), The impression management strategies associated with transformational leadership at the world-class level: A psychohistorical assessment, *Management Communication Quarterly*, 12(3), 3–41.

Graen, G. & Scandura, T. (1987), Toward a psychology of dyadic organizing, *Research in Organizational Behavior*, 9, 175–208.

Graen, G. & Uhl-Bien, M. (1991), The transformation of work group professionals into self-managing and partially self-designing contributors: Toward a theory of leadership-making, *The Journal of Management Systems*, 3(3), 25–39.

Graen, G. B. & Schiemann, W. (1978), Leader–member agreement: A vertical linkage approach, *Journal of Applied Psychology*, 63(2), 206–212.

Graen, G. B. & Uhl-Bien, M. (1995), Relationship-based approach to leadership: Development of a leader–member exchange (LMX) theory of leadership over 25 years. Applying a multi-level domain perspective, *Leadership Quarterly*, 6(2), 219–247.

Groves, K. S. (2006), Leader emotional expressivity, visionary leadership, and organizational change, *Leadership & Organization Development Journal*, 27(7), 565–583.

Hair, J. F., Jr., Black, W. C., Babin, B. J., & Anderson, R. E. (2010), *Multivariate Data Analysis* (7th edn.), Upper Saddle River: Prentice Hall.

Hamrefors, S. (2010), Communicative leadership, *Journal of Communication Management*, 14(2), 141–152.

Hernandez, M., Eberly, M. B., Avolio, B. J., & Johnson, M. D. (2011), The loci and mechanisms of leadership: Exploring a more comprehensive view of leadership theory, *Leadership Quarterly*, 22(6), 1165–1185.

Holladay, S. J. & Coombs, W. T. (1994), Speaking of visions and visions being spoken: An exploration of the effects of content and delivery on perceptions of leader charisma, *Management Communication Quarterly*, 8(2), 165–189.

Hosking, D. (1988), Organizing, leadership, and skillful process, *Journal of Management Studies*, 25(2), 147–166.

Jarde, A., Losilla, J. M., & Vives, J. (2012), Suitability of three different tools for the assessment of methodological quality in ex post facto studies, *International Journal of Clinical Health & Psychology*, 12(1), 97–108.

Jiao, C., Richards, D. A., & Zhang, K. (2011), Leadership and organizational citizenship behavior: OCB-specific meanings as mediators, *Journal of Business and Psychology*, 26(1), 11–25.

Kellerman, K. (1987), Information Exchange in Social Interaction. In *Interpersonal Processes: New Directions in Communication Research*, M. E. Roloff and G. R. Miller (eds.), pp. 188–219, Newbury Park: Sage.

Kelly, G. (1955), *The Psychology of Personal Construct*, New York: North.

Kerlinger, F. N. & Lee, H. B. (2000), *Foundations of Behavioral Research* (4th edn.), Belmont: Cengage.

Klein, H. J. & Kim, J. S. (1998), A field study of the influence of situational constraints, leader member exchange, and goal commitment on performance, *Academy of Management Journal*, 41(1), 88–95.

Kovjavic, S., Schuh, S. C., Jonas, K., Van Quaquebeke, & Van Dick, R. (2012), How do transformational leaders foster positive employee outcomes? A self-determination-based analysis of employees needs as mediating links, *Journal of Organizational Behavior*, 33(8), 1031–1052.

Lee, J. (2008), Effects of leadership and leader–member exchange on innovativeness, *Journal of Managerial Psychology*, 23(6), 670–687.

Littlejohn, S. W. & Foss, K. A. (2011), *Theories of Human Communication* (10th edn.), Long Grove: Waveland Press.

Lutgen-Sandvik, P. & Tracy, S. J. (2012), Answering five key questions about workplace bullying: How communication scholarship provides thought leadership for transforming abuse at work, *Management Communication Quarterly*, 26(3), 3–47.

Marwell, G. & Schmitt, D. R. (1967), Dimensions of compliance-gaining strategies: A dimensional analysis, *Sociometry*, 30(4), 350–364.

Maslyn, J. & Uhl-Bien, M. (2001), Leader–member exchange and its dimensions: Effects of self-effort and other's effort on relationship quality, *Journal of Applied Psychology*, 86(4), 697–708.

Mitchell, R. J. & Boyle, B. (2009), A theoretical model of transformational leadership's role in diverse teams, *Leadership & Organization Development Journal*, 30(5), 455–474.

Morand, D. A. (2000), Language and power: An empirical analysis of linguistic strategies used in superior–subordinate communication, *Journal of Organizational Behavior*, 21(3), 235–248.

Neufeld, D. J., Wan, Z., & Fang, Y. (2010), Remote leadership, communication effectiveness and leader performance, *Group Decision and Negotiation*, 19(3), 227–246.

Othman, R., Ee, F. F., & Shi, N. L. (2010), Understanding dysfunctional leader–member exchange: Antecedents and outcomes, *Leadership & Organization Development Journal*, 31(4), 337–350.

Riggio, R. E. (1992), Social interaction skills and nonverbal behaviors. In *Applications of Nonverbal Behavioral Theories and Research*, R. S. Feldman (ed.), pp. 3–30, Hillsdale: Lawrence Erlbaum.

Roloff, M. E. (1981), *Interpersonal Communication: The Social Exchange Approach*, Beverly Hills: Sage.

Seibert, S. E., Kramer, M. L., & Liden, R. C. (2001), A social capital theory of career success, *Academy of Management Journal*, 44(2), 219–237.

Shamir, B., Arthur, M. B., & House, R. J. (1994), The rhetoric of charismatic leadership: A theoretical extension, a case study, and implications for research, *Leadership Quarterly*, 5(1), 25–42.

Sheard, C. M. (1996), The public value of epideictic rhetoric, *College English*, 58(7), 765–794.

Sidani, Y. M. (2007), Perceptions of leader transformational ability, *The Journal of Management Development*, 26(8), 710–722.

Sosik, J. J. & Jung, D. I. (2003), Impression management strategies and performance in information technology consulting, *Management Communication Quarterly*, 17(2), 233–268.

Summers, K. (2001), Epideictic rhetoric in the "Englishwoman's Review," *Victorian Periodicals Review*, 34(3), 263–281.

Ting-Toomey, S. (ed.) (1994), *The Challenge of Facework: Crosscultural and Interpersonal Issue*, New York: State University of New York Press.

Uhl-Bien, M. (2006), Relational leadership theory: Exploring the social processes of leadership and organizing, *The Leadership Quarterly*, 17(6), 654–676.

Uhl-Bien, M. & Maslyn, J. M. (2003), Reciprocity in manager–subordinate relationships: Components, configurations and outcomes, *Journal of Management*, 29(4), 511–532.

Watzlawick, P., Beavin, J., & Jackson, D. (1967), *Pragmatics of Human Communication: A Study of Interactional Patterns, Pathologies, and Paradoxes*, New York: Norton.

Wei, F., Yuan, X., & Di, Y. (2010), Effects of transactional leadership, psychological empowerment and empowerment climate on creative performance of subordinates: A cross-level study, *Frontiers of Business Research in China*, 4(1), 29–46.

Whittington, J. L., Coker, R. H., Goodwin, V. L., Ickes, W., & Murray, B. (2009), Transactional leadership revisited: Self-other agreement and first consequences, *Journal of Applied Psychology*, 39(8), 1860–1886.

Yrle, A. C., Hartman, S., & Gale, W. P. (2002), An investigation of relationships between communication style and leader-member exchange, *Journal of Communication Management*, 6(3), 257–268.

Yukl, G. (2010). *Leadership in Organizations* (7th edn.), Upper Saddle River: Prentice Hall.

Chapter 31

The Effect of Organizational Culture on the Responsiveness of Small and Medium-Sized Enterprises to Environmental Change: An Empirical Study in Romania

Michael Stoica and Liviu Florea

Washburn University School of Business

Edit Lukacs

Dunarea de Jos' University of Galati

This empirical study examines the relationship between organizational culture and responsiveness, in a special setting: an economic environment in transition to a free market system, in particular the environment of Romanian small and medium-sized enterprises (SMEs). Romania offers a business context with many changes over the last two decades, a challenge and an opportunity for researchers. Firm's responsiveness represents an important concept related to both company performance and market environment. While there are studies that show the relationship between responsiveness, business environment and performance, there is less work done in investigating its relationship with the four archetypes of organizational culture: adhocracy, clan, market driven, and hierarchy. Using multivariate analysis to test the hypotheses, we found that the combination of entrepreneurial cultural characteristics, planning, and goal oriented managerial styles best suits successful companies. A market-driven type of culture, focusing on competitiveness and goal achievement, has the best coordination and is best positioned to deliver customer-centered versatility, while adhocracy, centered on entrepreneurship and creativity, helps businesses respond quickly to changes in the market environment.

1. Introduction

Responsiveness is the action taken in response to the relevant information generated and filtered previously (Kohli *et al.*, 1993). In a system context, responsiveness can be defined as the outcome that can be achieved when institutions and institutional relationships are designed in such a way that they are cognizant and respond appropriately to the legitimate expectations of individuals (Sharma *et al.*, 1999). Responsiveness means speed and coordination with which actions are implemented and periodical reviews product/service development. It also refers to evaluation of over- or under-filling of goals and correcting accordingly, including interdepartmental cooperation and coordination (Kohli *et al.*, 1993).

Garrett et al. (2009) developed a framework in which they hypothesized a relationship between responsiveness and market pioneering. In their model, learning strengthens the relationship. Our study is analyzing responsiveness in an environment characterized by multiple and rapid changes, thus having elements of market pioneering. Garrett et al. (2009) suggested that future research should explore relationships between responsiveness, learning and culture. Accordingly, this study investigates relationships between responsiveness and culture.

Following the Fall of Iron Curtain, the economic development of Central and Eastern Europe countries, such as Romania has been contingent on changes in economic systems and government policies (Hisrich & Drnovsek, 2002; Utsch et al., 1999). Given the rapidly changing competitive positioning and consumer preferences and demand, dependence on obsolete economy, and dramatically changing legal system (Uhlenbruck et al., 2003), Romanian business environment has all the key characteristics of an emergent economy and a high degree of market turbulence. As such, it provides an interesting opportunity to observe and analyze the adaptability of companies to both radical economic and radical social changes.

Researchers have devoted considerable effort to examine the impact of dispositional (e.g., entrepreneurial personality) and contextual variables (e.g., social network, environmental conditions) on the growth and financial performance of companies (Liao et al., 2003). Knowledge, information gathering, learning, and responsiveness are increasingly mentioned as being critical for the survival of SMEs (Chaston et al., 2001). The way knowledge is produced and used is less than adequate (Baker & Sinkula, 2005; Pelham, 2000), especially in the SMEs context.

Meanwhile, organizational culture has an impact on the way companies process information and adapt to changes (Pelham, 2000; Liao et al., 2003). Cultures that emphasize the value of flexibility and have an external focus tend to benefit the creation of information through innovation and its successful implementation. While many studies examine generation and dissemination of information, less attention was paid to responsiveness. Swanson (1999) considered responsiveness, along with responsibility, in an attempt to integrate normative and descriptive approaches to business. Her perspective on responsiveness is value based and qualitative. Responsiveness is often limited to "response time" (Thompson & Strickland, 2001).

From a system perspective, most of existing studies focus on "input–output" links in the context of businesses. Therefore, one of the reasons for the literature's inconclusiveness is the omission of process elements, most importantly the processes of information scanning, knowledge generation and dissemination, and organizational response formulation (Rafaeli et al., 2007). Laden with many contingencies, this research appears to be divergent.

Our empirical research aims to fill the gap by investigating the complexity of the organizational responsiveness concept, identifying factors that determine responsiveness and exploring their relationships to organizational culture. It addresses important research questions: Are culture and responsiveness related? Is there a particular type of culture that favors a high level of responsiveness? What are the relationships between these components and culture?

2. Theoretical Background and Hypotheses Development

2.1. *Organizational responsiveness*

Narver et al. (2004) and Kara et al. (2005) developed scales to measure the concept of market orientation using information processing as key element for their scales. While the concept is one-dimensional for Narver et al. (2004), it is three-dimensional for Kara et al. (2005), developed based on Kohli et al. (1993) market orientation scale, integrating intelligence generation, intelligence dissemination, and responsiveness.

Organizational responsiveness is the action taken in response to the relevant information generated and disseminated previously (Venaik et al., 2004), is related to organizational learning and performance (Luo & Peng, 1999), and is a predictor of SMEs success. Responsiveness, according to Kara et al. (2005), includes the speed and coordination with which actions are implemented and periodical reviews of product/service development.

The MARKOR scale (Kara *et al.*, 2005) measures market orientation, and consists of four parts: general market orientation, intelligence generation, dissemination, and responsiveness. The field findings indicate that responsiveness takes the form of selected target markets, designing and offering products that cater to current and anticipated needs, and producing, distributing and promoting the products in a way that elicits favorable end-customer response. Virtually all departments participate in responding to market trends in the firm. The factor analysis, performed in this study, identified three components of responsiveness: speed (S), coordination (C), and customer-centered versatility (CCV). In Table 1, the extraction method was Principal Component Analysis and Rotation Method was Varimax with Keiser Normalization.

2.2. Organizational Culture

Across management research areas, organizational culture is defined as the pattern of shared values and beliefs that help individuals understand organizational functioning, and provide behavioral norms. Hofstede *et al.* (2010) defined culture as "mental software" (p. 5), emphasizing its role as an interactive aggregate of common characteristics that influence any group's response to the environment.

Culture and tradition represent key factors that may influence SMEs' responsiveness. Jung developed the culture paradigm in 1923, in which he described several archetypes of culture, further developed by Cameron & Quinn (2011). Two key dimensions were used to classify organizational culture: the continuum from organic

Table 1. Factor analysis of organizational responsiveness (alphas = 0.83/0.81/0.85)

Items	Extraction		
	Factor 1	Factor 2	Factor 3
	Speed	Coordination	Customer centered versatility
A. It takes us more time than needed to decide how to respond to our competitors' price changes	0.81	0.20	–0.00
B. For one reason or another we tend to ignore changes in our customers' product or service needs	0.25	–0.01	0.72
C. We periodically review our product development efforts to ensure that they are in line with what customer want	0.022	0.86	–0.03
D. Several departments get together periodically to plan a response to changes taking place in our business environments	0.014	0.65	–0.00
E. If a major competitor were to launch an intensive campaign targeted at our customers, we would implement a response immediately	0.72	0.30	0.03
F. The activities of the different departments in this business unit are well coordinated	0.15	0.62	–0.16
G. Customer complaints fall on deaf ears in this business units	–0.27	0.16	0.69
H. Even if we came up with a great market plan we probably would not be able to implement it in a timely fashion	0.62	0.20	0.19
I. When we find that customers would like us to modify a product or service, the departments involved make concerned efforts to do so	0.20	0.63	0.38
J. We evaluate the over- or under-fulfilling of our goals and adapt accordingly	0.10	0.23	0.75
Cumulative Variance		62.95%	

to mechanistic processes and the relative emphasis on internal maintenance versus external positioning. The resulting quadrants are called market culture, adhocracy, clan, and hierarchy.

The adhocratic culture centers on entrepreneurship, creativity, and adaptability. It represents a composite of risk-propensity and spirit of initiative. Accordingly, adhocracy favors flexibility and tolerance, and values new markets and new sources of growth. The clan culture values cohesiveness, participation and teamwork highly. Correspondingly, employees' commitment is achieved through participation, and cohesiveness and personal satisfaction are more valuable than financial goals. The hierarchic culture stresses order, rules, regulations, administrative procedures, accountability and predictability, as well as tracking and control. Finally, the market-driven culture focuses on competitiveness and goal achievement, and places emphasis on productivity and responsiveness to environmental changes. The number of rules and routines are dependent upon the type of culture (Cameron & Kim, 2011). Speed of response to environmental changes that determine a higher performance is also culturally dependent.

2.3. *Organizational culture and organizational responsiveness*

Information processing and culture are related (Baker & Sinkula, 2005). In traditional bureaucracies and hierarchies learning is based on institutionalized experience rather than market information. In this case, SMEs expect to grow and survive, but at a higher level of efficiency and predictability, and to continue the same behavior that worked in the past (Baker & Sinkula, 2005). By contrast, in SMEs with a market or adhocracy culture, learning is focused on adaptive behavior. However, SMEs with market-driven culture may be more systematic in information search than the adhocracy ones. Also, Cameron & Kim (2011) found that competing values of market culture outperform clan values, while adhocracy outperformed values of the diagonally opposing hierarchy. Entrepreneurial behavior encouraged by adhocracy dominates. Therefore:

Hypothesis 1: Responsiveness is related to organizational culture. SMEs with market driven culture will be more responsive, followed by adhocracy, clan, and hierarchy.

Speed of Response and Culture. The items that define speed relate to the way SMEs respond to competitors' price changes and promotional campaigns, and timely implementation of strategies. For example, the adoption of Quick Response (QR) in textile and apparel industries represents a Just-In-Time system that helps QR to changes in the marketplace (Sullivan & Kang, 1999). Culture and competitive environment determine the speed of response and therefore the QR adoption. A market-focused company responds more quickly than a hierarchical one.

Hypothesis 2: Speed of response to market signals is higher in SMEs with adhocracy, followed by market-driven, clan, and hierarchy.

Coordination and Culture. Coordination refers to the concerted efforts to allow smooth business operations. Components of coordination include periodical review of business practices, cross-departmental meetings, team planning and implementation of projects, team analysis and change. Organizational culture is central for coordination. Although there is no empirical evidence, it appears that a higher level of coordination is characteristic to organizations that have a formal planning system and a hierarchical type of culture. Similarly, goal-driven companies show good coordination (Cameron & Kim, 2011). Market-driven culture focuses on competitiveness and goal achievement. Therefore we hypothesize that:

Hypothesis 3: SMEs with a market-driven culture show a better coordination, followed by hierarchy, clan and adhocracy.

Customer-Centered Versatility (CCV) and Culture. CCV items are shown in Table 2. Culture evolves in relation to its capacity for learning and retention from the external environment (Minguzzi & Passaro, 2001). Organizations with external focus tend to show high level of CCV, whereas market-driven organizations display more CCV than hierarchies. Therefore:

Hypothesis 4: SMEs having a market-driven culture will demonstrate better customer-centered versatility, followed by adhocracy, clan and hierarchy.

Table 2. Corporate culture influence on responsiveness

Dependent variable	Independent variables	Adj. — R square	Beta coefficients (standardized)	ANOVA F — Statistic
Speed	DUMMY_Clan	0.19	−0.16**	11.47*
	DUMMY_Adhocracy		0.22**	
	DUMMY_Hierarchy		−0.28*	
	Constant			
Coordination	DUMMY_Clan	0.12	−0.01	5.67***
	DUMMY_Adhocracy		−0.43**	
	DUMMY_Hierarchy		0.77**	
	Constant			
Customer Centered Versatility	DUMMY_Clan	0.17	0.02	15.80*
	DUMMY_Adhocracy		−0.19*	
	DUMMY_Hierarchy		−0.25*	
	Constant			

Note: ** $p < 0.01$, * $p < 0.05$.

3. Research Methodology

3.1. *Procedure and research sample*

We used mail surveys because of their relative efficiency. For the two mailings used, the response rate is 29% and obtained a sample of 134 businesses. The survey was translated into Romanian with two iterations of translation-back translation. The majority of businesses were registered as limited liability companies (LLC). Almost half of the respondents, 43.3% represent manufacturing businesses, 23.1% are service businesses, 14.4% are retailers, and 5.8% are construction companies.

3.2. *Measures*

Organization responsiveness. This study considers responsiveness as the action taken in response to relevant information previously generated and filtered (Kara *et al.*, 2005). Examples of items used for measuring responsiveness are: speed and coordination with which actions are implemented; the periodical review of product/service development, the evaluation of over-fulfillment or under-fulfillment of goals, and coordination between departments. The perception of the respondent is the main element used so far in the literature to evaluate responsiveness. The scale for responsiveness developed by Kara *et al.* (2005) was adopted for this study. A 12 level Likert scale is used to measure responsiveness.

SMEs' organizational culture. The measure of corporate culture is adopted from Cameron & Kim (2011). Respondents were asked to assess four descriptions for their organization along the four lines given by the four archetypes: adhocracy, clan, market, and hierarchy and to distribute 100 points according to the similarity between their company and the models described. The culture archetype that received the highest scores was coded as the dominant culture of the SME. SMEs that received two equal scores on two or more culture archetypes were subsequently deleted from the sample.

4. Results

The responsiveness scale is robust and reliable, with a value of 0.83 for Cronbach alpha coefficient. A factor analysis was performed (Table 1) that identified three components of responsiveness: speed of response, coordination, and consumer-centered versatility. Regression with dummy variables was adopted to test the hypotheses Tables 2 and 3), using the four culture archetypes as categorical variables.

Significant differences were found across all four culture archetypes in all dimensions of responsiveness. The means for adhocracy and market driven cultures are higher than for clan and hierarchy. Hypothesis 1 stated that SMEs with market driven culture have the highest level of responsiveness, followed by adhocracy, clan, and hierarchy. Results partially support the hypothesis.

Table 3. Types of dominant culture

Variable	Level	Type of culture
Speed	High	ADHOCRACY
		MARKET DRIVEN
		CLAN
	Low	HIERARCHY
Coordination	High	MARKET DRIVEN
		CLAN
	Low	ADHOCRACY
		HIERARCHY
Customer Centered Versatility	High	CLAN, MARKET DRIVEN
		ADHOCRACY
	Low	HIERARCHY

Indeed, the hierarchical type of cultures will display the lowest level for responsiveness. However, the entrepreneurial SMEs, i.e., businesses with adhocracy as their dominant type of culture, showed the highest levels of responsiveness. Market-driven and clan companies are positioned in between adhocratic and hierarchical SMEs. These results provide partial support for Hypothesis 1.

Hypothesis 2 predicted that the speed of response to market signals is higher in SMEs with adhocracy, followed by market-driven, clan, and hierarchy. The hypothesis is fully supported. Speed of response varies significantly among the SMEs' four culture archetypes. While entrepreneurial SMEs have the highest speed of response, clan companies have the lowest speed.

Hypothesis 3 stated that small businesses having a market-driven culture show a better coordination, followed by hierarchy, clan, and adhocracy. The hypothesis is partially supported. Coordination varies significantly with the culture type. However, while market-driven SMEs have the best coordination, hierarchical companies show, surprisingly, the lowest level.

Finally, hypothesis 4 predicted that SMEs with a market-driven culture demonstrate better customer-centered versatility. We also predicted that they are followed in order by adhocracy, clan, and hierarchy. Substantial differences in the degree of customer-focused versatility exist between market-driven, adhocratic, and hierarchical SMEs. However, market-driven and clan SMEs have means that are close to each other.

5. Conclusions and Management Implications

Businesses that have developed a hierarchic type of culture could be considered thinking "inside the box." They are slow to respond to external stimuli, show poor coordination, and display a low level of consumer-centered versatility. Indeed, Baker & Sinkula (2005) mentioned that companies that have an excessive number of rules and routines manifest difficulties in adapting. Responsiveness is part of the adaptation process. Adhocracy, clan and market driven cultures are all "located outside the 'box'" for at least one dimension. However, a closer look indicates that the companies that have developed clan as their dominant type of culture, while displaying good coordination and having high level of customer-focused versatility exhibit low speed of response.

According to Venaik *et al.* (2004) managers of businesses competing in a global environment face the central issue of integration of their operations in the presence of forces for national responsiveness. Locally responsive businesses perceive pressures to respond to local needs. This study extended the analysis of local SMEs, finding relationships between responsiveness and organizational culture. Organizational culture and its transfer overseas are important in the context of corporations that conduct business globally; therefore, the need to understand and analyze local organizational cultures (Hofstede *et al.*, 2010).

Organizational culture differences have been examined by Pothukuchi *et al.* (2002) in a general context of international joint venture performance. This study went one step further and found differences between the ways companies respond to signals from their marketplace based on their dominant type of organizational culture. Companies that developed an entrepreneurial (*adhocratic*) culture are the only ones that show high levels for all three dimensions of responsiveness. However, the best culture mix would be the *adhocratic* — market driven one. The combination of entrepreneurial characteristics and the planning and goal oriented managerial style will suit best companies that want to be successful in the marketplace. Indeed, the market-driven type of culture SMEs will have the best coordination and are best positioned to deliver customer-centered versatility while adhocracy will make businesses respond fast to changes in the market environment. High level of responsiveness will lead to superior performance. Indeed, Minguzzi & Passaro (2001) state that the entrepreneurial culture with its composite of personal values, managerial skills, and risk-propensity combined with a market-driven, goal oriented management and a system of relations between firm and market will determine the firm's competitiveness.

Further research is needed to enhance the understanding of the responsiveness-culture relationship. Other criterion variables for future research include national culture, organizational strategy, and organizational structure. An important area of future research concerns the analysis and evaluation of the interplay between organizational culture and national culture, as well as the meanings that the *responsiveness* concept takes in different cultural environments. Ethnographic studies are particularly useful in evaluating the meaning of this concept in different environments and relationships between responsiveness and culture. There is also need for field experiments to identify and evaluate the effect of extraneous variables, such as organizational strategy and organizational structure on the relationship between responsiveness and culture. It would be also useful to investigate these relationships in cross-cultural study with multinational corporations.

This study extends the analysis of locally responsive firms finding relationships between responsiveness and organizational culture. Limitations of this study include the use of a convenience sample and a relatively small sample size. Still, the results seem to provide strong support to our conclusions.

References

Baker, W. E. & Sinkula, J. M. (2005), Market orientation and the new product paradox, *Journal of Product Innovation Management*, 22, 483–502.

Cameron, K. S. & Quinn, R. E. (2011), *Diagnosing and Changing Organizational Culture: Based on the Competing Values Framework* (3rd edn.). San Francisco: Jossey-Bass.

Chaston, I., Badger, B., & Sadler-Smith, E. (2001). Organizational learning: An empirical assessment of process in small U.K. manufacturing firms, *Journal of Small Business Management*, 39(2), 139–152.

Garrett, R. P., Covin, J. G., & Slevin, D. P. (2009), Market responsiveness, top management risk taking, and the strategic learning as determinants of market pioneering, *Journal of Business Research*, 62(8): 782–788.

Hisrich, R. D. & Drnovsek, M. (2002), Entrepreneurship and small business research: A European perspective, *Journal of Small Business and Enterprise Development*, 9(2), 172–222.

Hofstede, G. H., Hofstede, G. J., & Minkov, M. (2010), *Cultures and Organizations: Software for the Mind* (3rd edn.). New York: McGraw-Hill.

Kara, A., Spillan, J. E., & Kumar, K. (2005), The effect of a market orientation on business performance: A study of small-sized service retailers using MARKOR scale, *Journal of Small Business Management*, 43(2), 105–118.

Kohli, A., Jaworski, B., & Kumar, A. (1993), MARKOR: A measure of market orientation, *Journal of Marketing Research*, 30(3): 467–477.

Liao, J., Welsch, H., & Stoica, M. (2003), Organizational absorptive capacity and responsiveness: An empirical investigation of growth-oriented SMEs, *Entrepreneurship Theory and Practice*, 28(1), 63–85.

Luo, Y. & Peng, M. (1999), Learning to compete in a transition economy: Experience, environment, and performance, *Journal of International Business Studies*, 30, 269–296.

Minguzzi, A., & Passaro, R. (2001). The network of relationships between the economic environment and the entrepreneurial culture in small firms. *Journal of Business Venturing*, 16, 181–207.

Narver, J. C., Slater, S. F., & MacLachlan, D. L. (2004), Responsive and proactive market orientation and new-product success, *Journal of Product Innovation Management*, 21(5), 334–347.

Pelham, A. (2000), Market orientation and other potential influences on performance in small and medium-sized manufacturing firms, *Journal of Small Business Management*, 38(1), 48–67.

Pothukuchi, V., Damanpour, F., Choi, J., Chen, C., & Park (2002), National and organizational culture differences and international joint venture performance, *Journal of International Business Studies*, 33, 243–266.

Rafaeli, S., Raban, D. R., & Ravid, G. (2007), Knowledge sharing market, *International Journal of Knowledge and Learning*, 3(1), 1–11.

Sharma, S., Pablo, A. L., & Vredenburg (1999), Corporate environmental responsiveness strategies, *The Journal of Applied Behavioral Science*, 35(1), 87–108.

Sullivan, P. & Kang, J. (1999), Quick response adoption in the apparel manufacturing industry: Competitive advantage and innovation, *Journal of Small Business Management*, 37(1), 1–15.

Swanson, D. (1999), Toward an integrative theory of business and society: A research strategy for corporate social performance, *Academy of Management Review*, 24, 506–521.

Thompson, A. & Strickland III, A. J. (2001), *Strategic Management*, Boston: McGraw-Hill Irwin.

Uhlenbruck, K., Meyer, K. E., & Hitt, M. A. (2003), Organizational transformation in transition economies: Resource-based and organizational learning perspectives, *Journal of Management Studies*, 40(2), 257–282.

Utsch, A., Rauch, A., Rothfuss, R., & Frese, M. (1999), Who becomes a small scale entrepreneur in a post-socialist environment: On the differences between entrepreneurs and managers in East Germany, *Journal of Small Business Management*, 37(3), 31–43.

Venaik, S., Midgley, D. F., & Devinney, T. M. (2004), A new perspective on the integration-responsiveness pressures confronting multinational firms, *Management International Review*, 44, 15–48.

Chapter 32

Model Proposal for Cluster Implementation in Romania*

Ion Popa and Cristina Vlăsceanu
Bucharest University of Economic Studies

The most prominent objective of the present chapter is to highlight the advantages of cluster implementation in Romania in the context of knowledge based economy. The research method used was based on both a quantitative analysis as well as on a qualitative analysis, which resulted on a series of observations and conclusions that were used to develop a cluster implementation model proposal.

The main result and contribution of the current chapter is the outlining and creation of a model for cluster implementation in Romania (a guide for cluster implementation). The relevance and importance of this particular model is given, on one hand, by the necessity and opportunity of such a project in Romania (since the Romanian economy is currently undergoing a transition process towards a knowledge based economy and is also trying to catch up to the more advanced economies worldwide), and on the other hand, by the fact that clusters have proven to have a great and real impact on the positive outcome of a country's development (in particular, clusters are considered to have a positive influence on competitiveness, innovation, knowledge and know-how transfer, economic growth, regional development, and so on – the impact of strong cluster portfolios improving the outcome of the overall economic performance of the country in which they are present).

The main conclusions of the following chapter revolve around the important role that clusters have and around the fact that a guide for cluster implementation in Romania can only be beneficial, by acting as a foundation of knowledge and aid (assistance) for the economic agents, in their pursuit to create and develop clusters, and ultimately achieve performance.

1. Introduction

In today's context of knowledge-based economy, clusters are becoming increasingly more important and they are being seen as tools for sustainable development. Both at the European Union level and globally, we can see a clear relationship of interdependence between the power of the state economy and the number of clusters in that country. This concept represents a viable tool for development, both in terms of the economic agents and in terms of the national economies.

The desire of creating a cluster implementation guide in Romania had as starting point a necessity felt in the Romanian business environment. Given that

---

*This work was co-financed from the European Social Fund through Sectoral Operational Programme Human Resources Development 2007–2013, project number POSDRU/159/1.5/S/142115 "Performance and excellence in doctoral and postdoctoral research in Romanian economics science domain".

Romania's economy is currently in a process of transition towards a knowledge-based economy and the need for increasingly specialized, refined and capable human resources, and for their utilization in research, development and innovation activities that will bring added value is felt more and more, clusters representing an extremely relevant instrument in terms of facilitating the fulfillment of this need.

2. Clusters — Theoretical Framework

According to Nicolescu & Verboncu (2006) a cluster is a network of firms, inter-correlated at a high level, which enables it to act as an embedded system, accumulating, at a high level, both the advantages of diversification and complementarities of the networks, as well as the intense intertwining between the involved activities, similar to great extent to those of a big company (Nicolescu & Verboncu, 2006: 337).

A cluster is a network of companies that use all forms of knowledge sharing and exchange. Determinant in defining a cluster is knowledge, considered both as a resource and as a key product of the group of companies involved (Popa, 2006: 22).

"By starting activities close to what is already going on in the cluster, all new spin-offs — newcomer or local independent entrepreneur alike — can safely skip the burdensome and costly process of gathering a lot of circumstantial knowledge about the business environment otherwise crucial. When it works for the neighbor why shouldn't it also work for me? New start-ups are thus given for free the advantages of a business environment tailored to their specific needs, even in situations when they might still be unaware of what these needs might be of how they may be best accommodated" (Maskell, 2001: 933).

"Members of a cluster benefit from the complementary products and services. Firms are privy to the new technological developments and information about changing market demands. Successful clusters provide firms with specialized suppliers and a technologically skilled workforce. Innovation is partly driven by the competitive pressures within clusters but firs and institutions also often mitigate risk and lower the costs of innovation through the development of joint R&D projects" (Mackenzie et al., 2005: 8).

Another key player in the development of clusters is the government of a given state. It has the ability to influence cluster creation and development through its policies and strategies.

"By focusing policy tools on clusters, government can better focus on areas where it impacts the competitiveness of several companies simultaneously. And it can reap additional benefits from the spillovers in the cluster that were triggered through the policies. Rather than improving competitiveness company by company (with a danger of intervening in competition), a cluster-based use of economic policy instruments reaches entire groups of companies. Cluster initiatives are a way to organize economic policies in a more efficient and mutually reinforcing way" (Ketels & Memedovic, 2008: 384).

3. Benefits of Clusters

The advantages of these commercial clusters are multiple, some consisting of the following (Vlăsceanu, 2011: 654):

- Reduce individual costs of each cooperative enterprise network;
- Better chances at competing with larger companies;
- Reduce unit costs through economies of scale at the cluster level;
- Network members cover their deficiencies in resources, skills and qualities to each other;
- Perform external economies, working together for a certain purpose (joint resources);
- The potential for obtaining competitive advantage is higher in terms of complementarities and synergy of goods and services between companies;
- A better opportunity for the member companies to invest in research-development;
- Play a decisive role in raising the standards of living among both residents and management bodies;
- Determine the collection of large sums of money to local/central budget, thus creating a positive and competitive national economy, regional and local;
- Can better defend mutual interests based on sustainable and competitive principles;
- Encourages the transfer of managerial know-how between the components;

- Reduce the time needed to manufacture and increase the turnover of companies by jointly providing products;
- Promotes organizational learning;
- Gives the companies a chance to develop and enter new international markets;

What needs to be remembered is that competitive advantage and innovation are more likely to be created by a regional agglomeration of companies, research centers, institutes, universities, institutions and organizations, etc., rather than individual companies or entities; also a region's favorability towards development needs to be taken into account, this being a two-edge knife, meaning, clusters are more likely to appear in a more developed region, but cluster also lead to the development of the region in which they act (Vlăsceanu, 2014: 55).

4. Model Proposal for Cluster Implementation in Romania

The present model (guide) is, essentially, a tool for implementing clusters in Romania, also this proposal providing the economic agents from Romania an informative guidance on the most important steps in the creation and development of clusters. Therefore, **the implementation guide for clusters in Romania includes the following steps:**

Step 1. Popularization of the cluster concept in Romania (Bringing awareness on the importance of clusters in Romania).

Step 2. Identification of potential areas (regions) suitable for the development of clusters in Romania.

Step 3. Identification of industries in Romania, located in the same geographical area, which present opportunities for the development of clusters.

Step 4. Development of policies and strategies for the formation and development of clusters.

Step 5. Implementation.

Step 6. Operationalization.

These six steps (each step containing the methods and actions needed to be achieved in the particular stage of implementation) will be further detailed in the following paragraphs for a better understanding of the phases that need to be followed for a proper development of clusters in Romania:

Step 1. Popularization of the cluster concept in Romania

- Organization of events, conferences, seminars, fairs to inform operators about the benefits and advantages produced by cluster membership (through partnerships with universities, research centers, institutions);
- Reducing resistance to change in Romanian companies in terms of possible associations and collaborative and cooperative activities;
- Conducting outreach programs organized by specialized authorities (Ministry of Economy, Regional Development Agencies, Chambers of Commerce);
- Creating training, mentoring, and coaching programs for managers of Romanian businesses;
- Increasing cooperation between companies and universities, research centers, local authorities;
- Raising awareness on the benefits of belonging to a cluster — by using the experience of existing clusters and by presenting the evolution of the economic agents within the cluster.

Step 2. Identification of potential areas suitable for the development of clusters in Romania

- Identifying the development regions in Romania with the greatest potential for implementation of clusters by regional development agencies;
- Identifying the companies in the same development region that are performing collaborative activities with other firms, universities, research centers, public institutions (research, training, etc.).
- Conducting outreach activities on the benefits of association in the form of clusters for companies located in the same development region;
- Improving regional infrastructure (transport, communication, etc.).

Step 3. Identification of industries in Romania, located in the same geographical area, which present opportunities for the development of clusters

- Identifying companies in the same industry that can conduct collaborative and cooperative activities with

universities and research centers in the same field or related areas;
- Channeling the efforts of regional development agencies in identifying geographical concentrations of firms in the same industry and informing and supporting them in terms of association in the form of clusters;
- Establishing industrial policies and strategies on the 8 development regions in Romania to meet the specific of each area.

Step 4. Development of policies and strategies for the formation and development of clusters

- Adaptation of cluster policies from other countries with successful innovative clusters to the specific of each region in Romania;
- Creating tax incentives for businesses that want to associate in the form of a cluster;
- Increasing state efforts regarding the creation and development of clusters and transparency of the process;
- Developing a business environment that facilitates cooperation and transfer of know-how between firms and entities.

Step 5. Cluster implementation in Romania

- Establishing the founding members of the cluster and their involvement in the implementation process (identifying participating companies, universities, public institutions — regional development agencies, county councils, and research centers);
- Creation of a cluster management, which will deal with the successful implementation of the cluster;
- Establishment of the purpose and objectives of the cluster by the management of the cluster;
- Preparing the implementation plan containing the cluster's core activities, intermediate objectives (milestones) and time horizons;
- Applying the implementation plan of the cluster;
- Intermediate evaluation of the implementation of the cluster.

Step 6. Operationalization of clusters in Romania

- Detailed and objective analysis of the performance of the cluster;
- Adaptation of the cluster development strategy based on objectives and performance;
- Further development of the cluster by attracting new members;
- Implementation of professional development programs for employees of the cluster;
- Development of advanced research and development teams in the areas of interest to all members of the cluster that can produce innovation;
- Designing of projects of interest to the members of the cluster;
- Capitalization of R&D results.

After following the steps proposed in the aforementioned model regarding the implementation of clusters in Romania and therefore, after creating new clusters, a number of advantages appear, directly resulted from this process.

Further we present a series of key benefits felt as a result of cluster implementation in Romania, alongside some observations and conclusions regarding the relevance and actuality of this subject, in terms of the direct effects of each of the six developed steps, of which the guide consists of.

5. Conclusions

The guide for cluster implementation in Romania can be used both as a tool for implementing clusters in Romania and as an informative guide for businesses on the most important steps for the creation and development of clusters.

By popularizing the concept of cluster in Romania we will gradually reach an understanding of the cluster concept at the level of the economic agents in Romania, which will facilitate the implementation and development of clusters.

The identification of areas suitable for the development of clusters in Romania will help to harness to a higher level the opportunities by particularly focusing efforts and attention on these areas. Therefore, the main advantage of cluster mapping is the creation of a data base containing information on areas where there are potential opportunities for implementing clusters. Thus, both companies and public authorities, institutions, research and development centers, universities in the area will be able to identify entities with geographical proximity that are willing to associate in the form of clusters.

Identification of the industries in Romania that are in the same geographical area also creates opportunities for the implementation and development of clusters by facilitating the creation of policies and strategies for the industries identified as being conducive to the creation of clusters.

The major benefit experienced as a result of the development of specific cluster strategies and policies is the improvement and intensification of the efforts of the Romanian Government and Parliament to promote and implement clusters in the country's eight development regions (respectively: North–West region, Centre Region, North–East Region, South–East Region, South–Muntenia Region, Bucharest-Ilfov Region, South-West Oltenia Region, and West Region). Specific cluster strategies and policies are one of the most important ways of supporting businesses that want to form clusters, and this is demonstrated by the experiences of other European countries that have established and implemented such strategies and policies, the direct effect being the increase of the number of clusters and the growth of the strength of cluster portfolios.

The actual implementation of clusters in Romania will result in obtaining the already well-known advantages that are a direct outcome of cluster membership and association. Among these we mention the following, which we consider as being the most important and relevant: economic growth, innovation, regional development, improvement of capacities and resources, reducing costs incurred by enterprises, increased potential for obtaining competitive advantage and synergy between companies.

Another aspect that should not be ignored is that the management of each cluster implemented must conduct continuous evaluation of the performance obtained by the cluster and must also ensure at all times that these results are in line with the objectives of the cluster and the priorities and vision of the cluster members. Operationalization itself protects and enhances the successful development of a cluster, maintaining as the central point the original purpose of the creation of the cluster.

In conclusion, it is without a doubt that clusters bring major benefits in terms of the economic development of a country and proper implementation and further development of this concept in Romania is not only necessary, in the context of knowledge-based economy, but it also causes major advantages for the economic agents and the overall economy.

References

Ketels, C. H. M. & Memedovic, O. (2008), From clusters to cluster-based economic development, *International Journal of Technological Learning, Innovation and Development*, 1(3), 375–392.

Mackenzie, M., Sheldrick, B., & Silver, J. (2005), *State Policies to Enhance the New Economy: A Comparative Analysis*, Winnipeg: Canadian Centre for Policy Alternatives.

Maskell, P. (2001), Towards a knowledge-based theory of the geographical cluster, *Industrial and Corporate Change*, 10(4), 921–943.

Nicolescu, O. & Verboncu, I. (2006), *Metodologii Manageriale*, București: Tribuna Economică.

Popa, I. (2006), Clusterul de firme, *Tribuna Economică*, 17(13), 22.

Vlăsceanu, C. (2011), The advantages of implementing business networking and clusters in Romania, In *Proceedings of the 5th International Conference Modern Approaches in Organisational Management and Economy*, Bucharest: Editura A.S.E.

Vlăsceanu, C. (2014), Impact of clusters on innovation, knowledge and competitiveness in the Romanian economy, *Revista Economia, Seria Management*, 17(1), 50–60.

Chapter 33

Aspects of Human Resources' Management within Organizations in Brașov, Romania

Stelian Panzaru and Camelia-Cristina Dragomir

"Spiru Haret" University

Tudor Pendiuc

Constantin Brancoveanu University

Dan Cojocaru

"George Baritiu" University

The human factor has an important role in the company's growth. In the process of redesigning and rethinking the economic structures it is necessary to know the problems of employment and the effective use of labor.

The problem of knowledge resources, the ways and means to shape employees, to optimize their creative potential, tends to occupy, today, a priority in all the concerns of science and practice management organizations.

Cultivating a spirit of responsibility, motivation and behavior, according to ethical solicitation, can contribute to the increase of the human resources capacity to endure the stressful action of the disturbing factors and to engage the company's human resources in order to participate within the organization's management.

Within the organizations numerous and complex activities take place, mainly aiming at achieving objectives in conditions of feasibility. In this process, relations are formed between employees and working groups who consist of individuals with different personalities, mentalities, educations, value systems and behaviors. In such circumstances, it is difficult to maintain a perfect harmony. There may appear many difficulties, which can transform into conflicts, with numerous and complicated consequences. In this respect, there appears the need for the manager to understand the place and role of conflicts in the human resources management, their nature and form of manifestation, the causes generating conflicts, the consequences and the effective means to prevent them.

This chapter aims to demonstrate, with arguments, the contribution that human resources management has to achieve greater competitiveness organizations in the Brașov County. Also, from the impact of human resources management on economic performance of the company, the chapter wants to emphasize the perspective of internationalization practices of human resources management of the need to ensure convergence, adaptation and integration of markets under the sign of economic globalization.

The chapter analyses the determining role of the management of human resources, through a case study in the organizations within Brasov County.

The drafting methodology of the study aimed to use the specific methods and instruments of the managerial scientific investigation: the observation, the investigation, the analysis, the synthesis and the model.

1. Introduction

1.1. *Purpose of the chapter*

The chapter refers to overall implementation of research results on the peculiarities of human resource management in Brasov. The study was conducted through a questionnaire applied to a total of 78 representatives belonging to organizations from Brasov County. Anonymous questionnaires were used in order to get honest answers and to conduct impartial investigation. The questionnaire contains 20 questions covering the following aspects of human resources in Brasov County: (a) the role of human resources in the organizations; (b) the specificities of human resources' activity at different levels; (c) attitude towards business managers of human resources; (d) continuous professional role; (e) conflict management in human resources activity.

1.2. *Characteristics of the research*

The purpose of the study was to identify shortcomings in the management of human resources is often the organizations Brasov and propose solutions to improve it.

Objectives of the research: identifying the role of human resources in organizations; analyzing the involvement of managers in human resource management; identifying causes of conflict generated by human resource management in organizations from Brasov.

1.3. *The research methodology*

The research methodology involved the use of scientific methods and tools: investigation managerial, observation, questionnaires, surveys, analyses, syntheses, and models.

The questions in the survey had a closed character, with several variants of answers. This type of survey was used for the ease of the recording of the answers, as well as for the subsequent operative manner of analysis and processing of the collected data. For the same reasons, the questionnaire was conceived in a concentrated form that would allow gathering the relevant information for the issue that interested us. The survey was pre-tested on 10 subjects. After the pre-testing, four questions were reformulated.

1.4. *Originality of the research*

Diagnosis consists of human resource management in some organizations in Brasov; in order to propose feasible solutions regarding the implementation of modern models of human resource management in organizations in the County of Brasov.

1.5. *Practical character of the research*

The research has the following practical applications: improving the quality of human resource management in organizations in Brasov County, and can be extended to other communities; development of competence and skills of human resources managers; creating a climate of trust and openness in relations between staff and their supervisors; contribute to the development strategy of modern management in human resources.

2. Considerations Regarding the Management in Human Resources

2.1. *Role of management in human resources*

Human resources designate individuals that make up a system — country region, city, organization
                                                        Nicolescu, 2011: 536

Effective management of an organization's employees is arguably the most difficult task, more complex, ambiguous, but the most important facing managers. Management is an area of policy that is not characterized by the globally accepted professional standards and rigorous. This is true for at least four reasons (Coyle-Shapiro et al., 2013: 13): *human resources policies relate to human behavior as complex and culturally dependent; There are many tools for human resource different policies and practices; success or failure of the various human resources policies, programs and plans are difficult to assess.*

Many managers believe that managing people is just common sense.

An important role in human resources management is playing and ensuring satisfaction at work for the organization members. Job satisfaction attitudes offer different perspectives on this aspect (Naumann, 1993; Maslow, 1987).

Human resource management is defined as a category of management which consists of the whole process of developing and implementing strategies and policies that enables organizations to deliver their preview, providing training, development, evaluation, promotion, protection and use of human

Nicolescu, 2011: 34

Human capital has a duty to find the most appropriate for integration, orientation, and organization objectives (Petrescu, 2006: 399).

Regarding the involvement of human resource management, we outlined some pragmatic approaches, such as increasing the size of the participating employees; content redefining organizational relationships between organizational subdivision located on different levels; human resources' involvement in decision-making; staff evaluation under a system of performance indicators; limiting monopoly on human resource decision-making; promoting efficiency and competitiveness in organizations, etc.

These approaches provide the starting point for some lines of action in organizational change, such as: management professionalization of human resources; establishment and implementation of certain standards and of a performance indicators' system for each employee; monitoring results; extension of the use of the participative management style; rigorous use of human resources (Panzaru, 2012).

Lopez-Nicholas & Merono-Cerdan (2011) have shown that the human resources manager should anticipate that, in the future, employment will determine the human resources on the long term. The need for human resource forecasting is required. Reality shows that, in many organizations, the concerns, in this regard, are almost non-existent.

Strategic planning needs human resources organization and is essential to its economic performance. However, the strategy for estimating human resource requirements should be consistent with changes in the market economy, competition and finance.

Human Resources Management must fulfill the role of a catalyst in order to bring performance in line with the individual talents as for the employees to meet objectives. The vast majority of specialists in this field believes that human resources management, like any other field of scientific research is the result of specialization and entered the already known path, of relatively rapid development and diversification in many fields (Petrescu, 2007: 156).

Human Resources Management is the science and art development and implementation of strategy and staff policy, as to achieve maximum efficiency for the enterprise objectives. Human Resources Management is a science, with formulated concepts, laws, principles, rules, methods, techniques and tools of leadership and arts. For their application in practice, one must take into account the specific conditions of each company (Manolescue et al., 2004: 58).

The contents of human resource management is given and the multitude of activities to be carried out, linked and harmonized human resources, activities that are more or less connected and have a great impact on results. In attempts to specify, as precisely and completely as possible, the main areas of activity of human resource management were many opinions expressed, in their great majority, the country bears the hallmark of origin of authors.

Thus, the American Society for Training and Development (American Society for Training and Development) identifies nine main areas of activity of human resource management: training and development; organization and development; organization/job design; human resource planning; selection of personnel and insurance; research and information systems personnel; rewards/benefits or aid; advice on personal problems of employees; union/labor relations.

Strategies of human resources shall appoint all long-term objectives on human resources, the main ways of achieving them and the necessary resources or appropriations, which ensure that the structure, values and culture of the organization and its staff will be used to help achieve the general objectives of the organization.

The preparation must start from the organizational objectives and the content of human resource management, and use an appropriate methodology of investigation to ensure rational targeting efforts in this area.

Areas where strategies can be established: insurance and selection of staff; development of employees; relationships with employees. The wide variety of organizations and concepts of specialists in this field, is reflected in the diversity of strategies in human resources.

Therefore, an interesting approach to the strategies of human resources is presented by Rolf Buhner who, depending on the degree of dependency on company strategy, three different types of staffing strategies, presented the following (Buhner, 1994: 149): strategy-oriented personal investment; strategy oriented personal value; strategy-oriented personnel resources.

As for the human resources policy to meet the goals the organization it must meet the following requirements: be consistent with the policy and strategy of the organization; cover the most important fields of personnel; ensuring the transmission and understanding of policies at all levels of the organization; comply with legal requirements; be very transparent, clearly defined, preferably in writing, to not allow interpretation.

Stages of drafting a policy for human resources are: analyzing and understanding the culture of existing organizations and the amount accepted it; policy analysis of existing staff; analysis of external influences in the organization; consulting senior manager on their opinions; consulting staff and unions on staff policy.

In order to implement a staff policy one must be accepted by managers to become operational by their decision and dissemination at all levels of the organization.

2.2. *Continuous training of personnel*

The ability of the 21st century organizations to adapt to the contemporary society, characterized by high complexity and change, is generally given by their attitude towards knowledge, as an essential condition of reaching the top. One cannot promote and develop this type of company, focused on the values of knowledge, without developing permanent training programs and the substantial intervention of knowledge based management practices. In conclusion, permanent accumulation of knowledge through continuous training represents one of the main characteristics of the contemporary organizations and a mandatory condition for a competitive economy to function properly.

To build a strong organization, employee competences need to be developed and retained through effective human resources management (Ulrich & Lake, 1991; Pfeffer, 1994; Becker & Gerhart, 1996; Boxall & Purcell, 2003). Sustained competitive advantage can be achieved through human resources management. The achievement of organizational success through people requires an attitudinal change of managers towards their workforce and employment (Pfeffer, 1994).

Continuous training has become an essential requirement in all organizations, regardless of the field in which they operate. The training programs are designed and the needs arising from their internal organization are consistent with its overall objectives. Only in this way, training and upgrading, the two components of the training, can be truly effective, solving current and future problems of the organization.

Further training aims at improving the capacity already held by employees (retraining, acquisition of new skills on the job or in the same field).

Training can be organized in various forms within the organization, in specialized units or institutions of higher education. In developing a training program, the specialist in human resources and other specialists involved in the preparation will be needed.

Determining the results of a training program or refresher training is one last step you will be interested in solving in the evaluation process of the training courses.

In any training, performance evaluation is required. It is distributed throughout a program. Normally, a course evaluation at the beginning and the end is one way that can also set points after completing an evaluation module.

Objectives staff performance evaluation shows a great diversity, given the support of many organizational functions and activities of human resource management. Defining a more precise evaluation of performance objectives and understanding the degree of complexity of them presents a particular importance, and their implementation on a legal basis to protect both the organization and on its employees (Dragomir, 2013).

There are several ways of making the assessment: through the managers, by colleagues who occupy equivalent positions, self-assessment by specialist assessors or a combination.

2.3. Causes of conflict occurrence in human resource management

In human resource management frequently conflicts may occur. The conflict represents an incident provoked by the existing divergences between the attitudes, means and methods of action regarding a situation or a phenomenon which represents the object of the analysis.

The conflict, from a psychological and social point of view, appears as a form of the human interaction through which two or various members partially or totally disagree in one or various economical or social matters of the organization management, by attempting its re-evaluation usually through the concession of one of the party towards the other. The presence and the action of the interpersonal conflictual rapports prove the necessity of their acknowledgement for the continuous improvement of the institution's management and of the human resources management. The conflict is accompanied by an atmosphere of tension and competitions.

Conflict styles are typically seen as a response to particular situations. By contrast, we argue that individual conflict styles may shape an employee's social environment, affecting the level of ongoing conflict and thus his or her experience of stress (Friedman et al., 2000).

There are certain causes in all the specific conflicts of the human resources. The most significant causes are the followings:

— The distribution of the resources which, irrespective of the institution's dimensions, are limited. We are referring mainly to the fact the manager is obliged to distribute the material, the human and financial resources among different subunits and departments and to mobilize the factors which can train them for the achievement of the purposes of the organization. With respect to its meaning and difficulty in the managerial reality, this process constantly generates different types of conflicts;
— Promotion of staff in different functions based on subjective or political aspects;
— The interdependence of the tasks, acknowledged as a possibility of a conflictual state appearance, is present in all the situations in which the personnel depends on the accomplishment of the task by another persons. The consequences of this cause — factor of conflictual states becomes complicated when connected to the systematic characteristic from a horizontal and functional point of view of the organization. As the entire organizational constitutive parts represent the constitutive parts of that specific system, in the case of an inappropriate activity of one of the subunits the independence to which we refer can be constituted as a conflictual state generating factor;
— The different appreciations regarding certain situations or states of the managerial process or of an action conceived by the manager, usually subjective, generated by an analysis of the superficial situation discussed, can lead to the over-appreciation of certain alternative points of view and aspects which can be favorable for the micro-group, but unfavorable for the organization;
— The communication insufficiency, especially the defective transmission of the information, can be considered both the cause and the consequence of the conflictual states;
— The differences encountered in the professional training, the capacity of effort, the stress endurance, present in every organizations lead in reality to the transmission of various and harder tasks to the competent and dedicated persons. As a consequence, there appears a feeling of injustice and revolt which, in the majority of the cases, generates conflicts;
— The differences from the point of view of the character and of the work style influence the compatibility of the employee with his job and his group, due to the fact that the work collectives are formed of shy people, for example melancholic and phlegmatic persons and dynamic, opened and cordial persons, a phenomena which gives birth to states of irritation and conflict during the work period.

— The ambiguous definition of the individual and derived objectives, the ambiguity in the decisions' transmissions, the existence of certain parallelisms between departments and jobs, the imprecision in the establishment of the tasks, authorities or responsibilities of certain jobs or of the activities and attributions can generate conflictual states which accompany the battle for power which appear in the abnormalities of which we are referring;
— The discontent regarding the social status which grants greater and more honorable chances to certain groups;
— The environment differences which impose certain clothing, work hours, special work conditions, attract privations or privileges capable of leading in the end to conflicts;
— The incomplete description of the job or position;
— The unbalanced load of tasks;
— The lack of accordance between the official authority and requested responsibility;
— The discordance between the material and moral rewards and the level of the work results;
— The lack of cohesion inside the informal group;
— The motivation differences between the members of the informal collective.

3. Analysis of Human Resources in the Organizations of Brasov County

The study highlights the key role of human resources in organizations belonging to Brasov County (82.58%). Around 17.42% of the respondents believe that money is the most important aspect in the work of an organization (Fig. 1).

The scientific investigation conducted has pointed out the fact that, at the level of the organization of Brasov Country, the organizational change is achieved through a democratic management of the human resources, favorably perceived by the employees. Thus, the results of the survey by questionnaire carried out on a representative sample of employees show that 69.45% of the employees consider the style of human resources management to be democratic, while only 18.36% perceive it as an authoritarian and autocratic management. Moreover, only 12.19% consider that subordinates have complete freedom of decision and action — permissive style (Fig. 2).

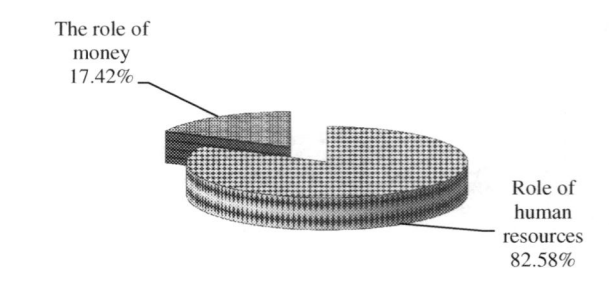

Fig. 1. Role of human resources in organizations within Braşov County

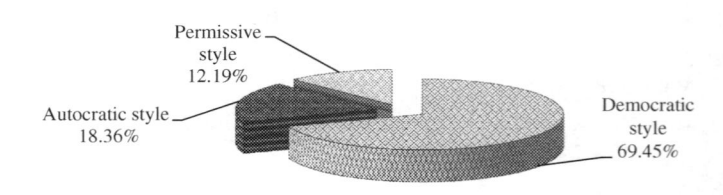

Fig. 2. Styles adopted by the human resources management of the organizations of Braşov County

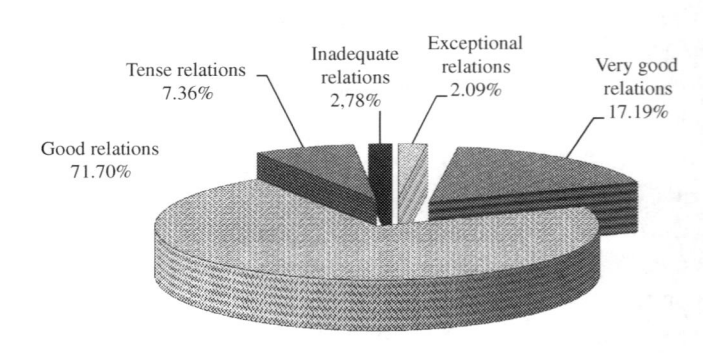

Fig. 3. Types of relations in the human resources management

The relations between the leaders and the employees of subordinated departments are exceptional in proportion of 2.11%, very good in proportion of 17.36% and good in proportion of 72.42%. We have to emphasize that a quite high percentage of the employees — namely 7.43% — have declared that the relations are tensed, and 1.68% of the participants in the survey by questionnaire perceive such relations as being inadequate (Fig. 3).

It should be noted that 6.16% of the questioned samples of employees have declared that the decisions related to human resources have always been made following the consultation of the employees, while 62.74% maintained that such decisions are more often not made following the consultation of the employees. About 28.24% of the questioned employees have declared that

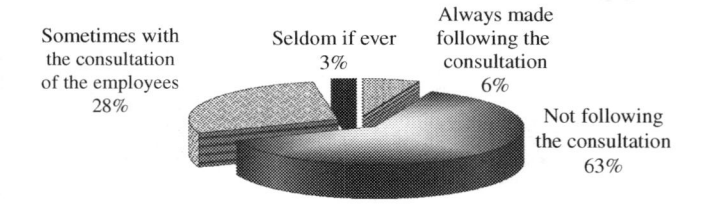

Fig. 4. Opinions of the decision-making process of human resources management

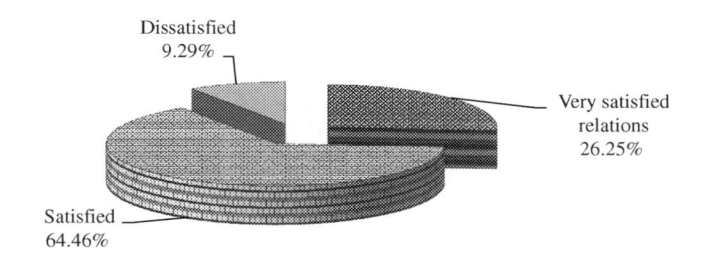

Fig. 5. Assessment training management personnel

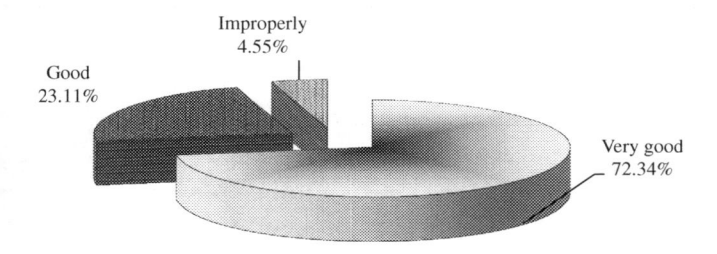

Fig. 6. Conflict management in human resources management

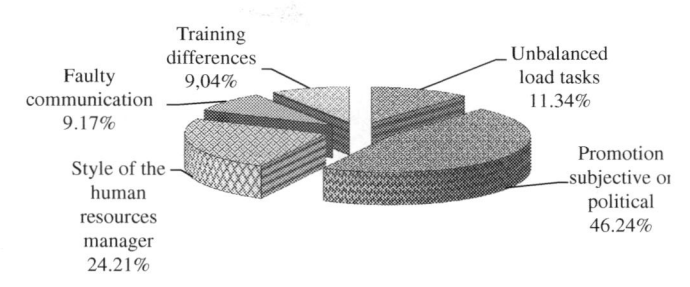

Fig. 7. Causes of conflict in human resource management

decisions are sometimes made with the consultation of the employees and 2.86% of the employees seldom answered, if ever (Fig. 4).

Regarding the training of personnel management 26.25% of the respondents are very satisfied with the way the activity is carried out. 64.46% are satisfied and 9.29% are dissatisfied with the way in which work is performed by training (Fig. 5).

Conflict management is assessed as very good by the respondents (72.34%) in their organizations. 23.11% think that it is well managed and 4.55% believe that this activity is improperly managed (Fig. 6).

The main causes of disputes in organizations were presented as: unbalanced load tasks (11.34%); promotion of staff in different functions based on subjective or political aspects (46.24%); manager's style of the human resources (24.21%); vertically and horizontally faulty communication (9.17%); training differences between members of the organization (9.04%) (Fig. 7).

Focusing on the implications of human resources management on fostering change, the conducted research has pointed out the following lines of action: alignment of human resources management with the institution's management; adjustment of organizational culture to change processes; development of a diversity-friendly culture; correct understanding of the manager's role in human resources; consolidation of a pro-active culture in supporting sustainable performance; creation and maintenance of a climate of confidence and cooperation within the organization; encouraging employees to seek continuous improvement and to develop their potential.

Within the framework of the applicative research, the questioned subjects have pointed out, as relevant for a good human resources manager, the following qualities: competence and professionalism; authority; visionary ability; ability to quickly adapt to changes; responsibility for public welfare; capacity to listen and convey messages, both within the institution and the community, and outside the sphere thereof; correctness and honesty; concern for community and employees.

A series of obstacles to the change of the human resources management of the organizations of Brasov County were identified: inflexibility; conformism; obedience; psychological inhibition in the face of newness; single response; fear of making mistakes.

Another issue taken into consideration within the scope of the research was the extent to which the knowledge of the organizational culture elements determines a greater involvement of the employees in the fulfillment of their tasks. The expressed opinions conveyed the idea that the elements which make up the organizational culture are, to a large extent, known and observed by the employees, these ensuring the rigorous character of the measures adopted at this level of social organization. Changes are also manifested in managerial behavior, being given concrete expression in a clear and deep perception of the need to develop and consolidate an organizational culture intended to fully support and foster the process of modernization and to generate clear-cut and categorical options to achieve organizational change.

4. Conclusions

The purpose of our approach was to come up with feasible managerial solutions regarding the possibility of stimulating human resources management, in such a manner that it could significantly influence the actions and decisions aimed at increasing performance in the sphere of activities of the organization.

The originality of the research resides in the approach of the specificity of human resources management at the level of the County of Brasov.

The results of the research have led us to a series of recommendations which shall give the managers a more qualified and realistic perception of the complex issues raised by human resources management. These recommendations are aimed at:

- Training personnel in view of the transition to a new model of development based on knowledge and innovation;
- Achieving the transfer of knowledge, information and technical solutions at the level of the industrial sector;
- Encouraging continuous education;
- Actions focused on the training and stabilization of the workforce and on the motivation of employees and managers;
- Actions intended to give citizens a sense of responsibility as regards their prevention role and the collaboration with the environmental regulatory agencies;
- Improving the skills of managers;
- Securing the access to European funds destined for personnel organizations training;
- Redefining the content of the relations between organizational subdivisions situated on different hierarchical levels;
- Enhancing transparency in the management of community affairs;
- Creating a climate of confidence and openness towards of the members of the organization;
- Correctly informing members of the organization about actions regarding the human resources management;
- Improving the learning and continuous training processes intended for the members of the organizations of the County Brasov;
- Adopting efficient models of human resources management.

In order to efficiently collaborate with his subordinates and this way to prevent the conflictual states, to acknowledge the following recommendations:

- To grant the collaborators sufficiently large competences in order for them not to feel obliged to continuously demonstrate their need of amplification, but not too large because, in this case, they would often have to justify the unfulfilling of certain tasks;
- To underline with skill the competences of all the subordinated managers, in order to make a simultaneous and equivoque appreciation of the qualities;
- The responsibility degree of the collaborators must be in accordance with the level of their authority, verifying that the attributed tasks are real;
- To grant the department and section managers the liberty of dividing the tasks to people, as they better know each one's possibilities;
- Not to exaggerate in the adoption of his solutions as being optimized;
- The prevention of the conflictual state must be directly connected to the training of the manager in the assuming of the effective responsibility regarding every subordinate and every professional activity developed under his lead. In this matter, the manager must know exactly the processes of service performances as well as the tasks and the capacities of the collaborators asked to develop them;
- In order to avoid the conflict due to failure in meeting the expectations, it is recommended that the manager

receives the number of claims demanded from his collaborators, makes fewer promises, clearly expresses his expectations, reviews and actualizes his expectations and uses them as a basis for a periodical retrospective analysis, for the prevention of the conflictual state;
- The persistence over the detailed knowledge of people, which can be obtained in various manners: with the help of science, with the help of certain observations and systematical verifications, accomplished mainly during the concrete activities and, finally, through impression and intuition;
- Regarding the way to reaction of manager to the disagreements among other persons, he or she should not let himself or herself to be implied in such situations, in which he or she does not deserve to be implied or which can be solved by them. In some cases, the manager is recommended to appeal to a third party for mediation or negotiation. Other measures may also have results, such as: eliminating the situation which produced the conflict, solving of misunderstandings, attracting parties in a general interest, objective or real issues, high lightening that everything is a simple misunderstanding;
- Every manager must analyze by his or her own preoccupation in managing without conflicts, establishing if the organization of the effort corresponds to the aim so that in the end, to be able to combat the conflictual states and ensure the organization's development.

Management without conflicts has as a last objective the mobilizations of all the personnel in order to achieve the economic and social tasks, to take part with maximum efficiency in the organization's economic and social life.

The results of the survey indicate that the managers of organizations have acted for the human resources management's improvement. But, the managers of organizations in the Brasov County should lay more emphasis on the improvement of their managerial skills as a factor likely to enhance performance in the activities carried out.

References

Becker, B., Gerhart, B. (1996), The impact of human resource management on organizational performance: Progress and prospects, *Academy of Management Journal*, 39(4), 779–801.

Boxall, P. & Purcell, J. (2003), Strategy and human resource management, *ILR Review*, 57(1), 145–146.

Bühner, R. (1994), *Personnel Management*. Landsberg: Verlag Moderne Industrie.

Coyle-Shapiro, J., Hoque, K., Kessler, I., Pepper, A., Richardson R., & Walker, L. (2013), *Human Resource Management*, London: University Publishing House.

Dragomir, C. (2013), Role of lifelong learning in development of the organizations based on knowledge, *Review of General Management*, 17(1), 78–84.

Friedman, R., Tidd, T. S., Currall, S., & Tsai, J. (2000), What goes around comes around: The impact of personal conflict style on work conflict and stress, *International Journal of Conflict Management*, 11, 32–55.

Lopez-Nicholas, C. & Merono-Cerdan, A. L. (2011), Strategic knowledge management, innovation and performance, *International Journal of Information Management*, 31(2), 502–509.

Manolescu, A., Marinas, C., & Marin, I. (2004), *Managementul Resurselor Umane: Aplicații*. Bucharest: Economica Publishing House.

Maslow, A. (1987), *Motivation and Personality*, New York: Harper/Row.

Naumann, E. (1993), Organizational predictors of expatriate job satisfaction, *Journal of International Business Studies*, 24(1), 61–80.

Nicolescu, O. (ed.) (2011), *Dicționar de Management*, Bucharest: Pro Universitaria Publishing House.

Pânzaru, S. (2012), Considerations on some factors that influence organizational structures, *Review of General Management*, 16(2), 177–186.

Petrescu, I. (2006), *Managementul Crizelor*, Bucharest: Expert Publishing House.

Petrescu, I. (2007), *Managementul Capitalului Uman*, Bucharest: Expert Publishing House.

Pfeffer, J. (1994), Competitive advantage through people, *California Management Review*, 36, 9–28.

Ulrich, D. & Lake, D. (1991), Organizational capability: Creating competitive advantage, *Academy of Management Executive*, 5(1), pp. 77–92.

Chapter 34

Managing Individual Performance Appraisal in Project Teams

*Florin-Ioan Petean, Bogdan Bâlc, Horațiu Cătălin Sălăgean,
Răzvan Dimitrie Gârbacea, and Diana Sopon*

Babeș-Bolyai University

The business environment in which organizations are struggling today, is a mosaic of transformations and perpetual changes, therefore, in this context of the dynamics of complex business processes, is absolutely necessary the presence of an effective base of performance appraisal to continuous employee motivation for organizations to register success. This chapter is looking at how supporting project teams define and monitor performance, achieves business results, and provides a strong base for good human resource practices, such as performance management and appraisal systems. The processes of performance appraisal are analyzed using the view of organizational justice, as seen by human resource directors, project managers, and project team members in their efforts to increase the engagement and productivity in project-based organizations. More and more, Romanian organizations recognize projects and project management as a strategic tool to optimize strategy execution by reducing product cycle durations and optimizing other critical dimensions as quality and costs. The strong Romanian industries like automotive, energy and the new star, software, are active promoters for modern project management techniques. Multidimensional client pressures — better quality at reduced costs and faster results — are translated into major tensions for organizational programs and projects. Project managers are forced to translate client requirements into project objectives, and the available resources seem to be scarce. There is a large volume of published studies describing the role of performance management approaches, concepts, and tools. However, one question that needs to be asked is how organizations should adapt their classical performance management processes (including appraisal) to the dynamic and fast pace changing realities of project management. This chapter comprises the conclusions related to a research executed in companies from automotive industry (15 project managers and 2 human resource managers), from IT (5 project managers and 1 human resource manager), and consultancy (3 project managers and 1 human resource manager).

1. Changes in Project Management Practices

One of the most productive responses to the rapid speed and rhythm of change seem to be one of the reasons that determined companies to adopt the definition of programs and projects a functional way for implementation of strategic goals.

Successful companies realize that more and more of their activities are unique and temporary, so decided to act at tactical level by projects, where organizational boundaries are more permissive, as they integrate various contractors and clients' representatives and multiple work locations in order to assure success while maximizing the results.

The positive experiences encouraged companies to expanding their learning in project management and to increasingly use portfolios — a diverse range of related and unrelated projects and programs — as a strategic tool to success and as instruments to maximize results within resource and funding constraints.

The project management techniques were valued and turned into a strategic dimension of portfolio management, where companies define and relate, link, and optimize various programs and projects. The link between the critical quality dimension and work in projects (Ilies, 2003) was operationalized by the large companies from the above-mentioned industries that use portfolio management so they extended the scope of their utilization, from monitoring and report progress (oriented on the past) to investment decisions and proactive responses oriented to the future market demands.

1.1. Evolution in strategy — changes in organisational structures

Crawford & Cabanis-Brewin define three stages in the project management evolution:

(1) Individual;
(2) Division or department-level; and
(3) Enterprise/corporate-level (strategic).

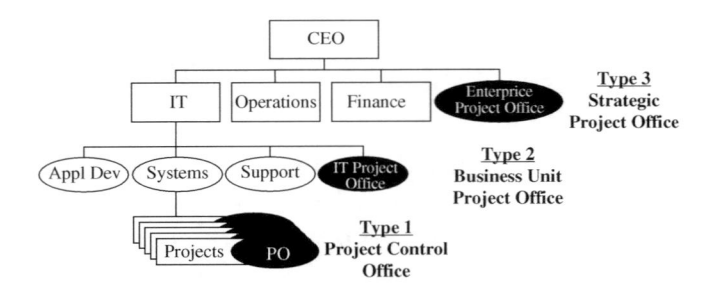

Fig. 1. Stages in the project management evolution — after Crawford

1.1.1. Performance management and organisational justice

Fairness at work, which is known also as the organizational justice (Byrne & Cropanzano, 2001) seems to be a major influencer for individual commitment.

1.1.2. Various dimensions of organisational justice

- **Distributive**: feelings of fairness surrounding the allocation of organizational resources, including pay, bonuses, terminations, or any other resource that an organization can provide to employees (Adams, 1965; Deutsch, 1975).
- **Procedural**: feelings of fairness regarding the procedures (promotions, terminations, performance ratings, bonuses, or anything else of value) used in an organization (Leventhal et al., 1980; Thibaut & Walker, 1975).
- **Interactional**: feelings of fairness regarding how one is treated (truthfully and with respect as they were terminated, given a bonus) Bies & Moag (1986), with two dimensions suggested by Greenberg (1993a).
- **Interpersonal**: based on dignity and respect (Colquitt, 2001) from those in power position (authority, expertise, etc.).
- **Informational**: based on justification and truthfulness (Bies & Moag) and also on adequate

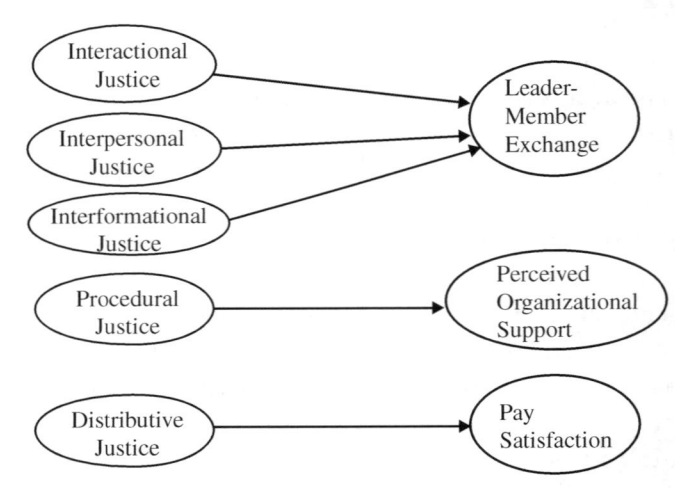

Fig. 2. Dimensions of organisational justice — after Roch & Shanock, 2006: 303

```
┌─────────────────┐
│ Organizational  │
│ justice in      │──────────────────────┐
│ Performance     │                      │
│ Appraisal System│    ┌──────────────┐  ▼
│                 │    │ Performance  │ ┌──────────────┐
│ ▪ Distributive  │───▶│ Appraisal    │▶│ Work         │
│ ▪ Procedural    │    │ Satisfaction │ │ Performance  │
│ ▪ Interactional │    └──────────────┘ └──────────────┘
└─────────────────┘
```

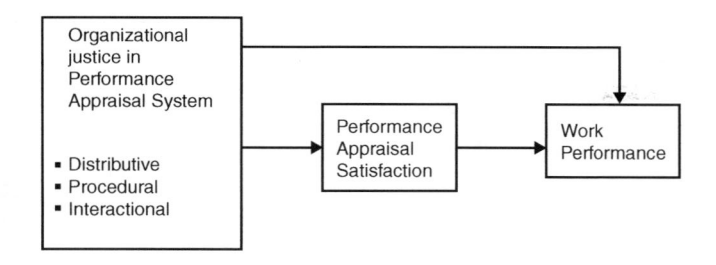

Fig. 3. Conceptual framework for linking organisational justice, appraisal and performance — after Warokka *et al.* 2012

information regarding procedures and outcomes (Colquitt, 2001).

Warokka *et al.* (2012), in a study performed in emerging markets, connected "the employees' perception on fair performance appraisal and organizational justice-considered practices to job satisfaction and work performance", using the following conceptual framework for their study.

2. Performance Management and Appraisal in Projects

In performing interviews and collecting data was used Lockett (Lockett, 1992) definition of performance management as "development of individuals with competence and commitment, working towards the achievement of shared meaningful objectives within an organization which supports and encourages their achievement". It seems that the above-mentioned definition comprise the critical aspects of the performance management process. The aforementioned dimensions were recognized by various managers (from project managers to top executives) as a critical for increasing productivity and to harmonize workplace communications.

Wright (2003) shows that performance management has a critical role in helping companies to ensure competitive advantage. Functional managers declare that at individual and team level, performance appraisal is recognized as a central human resource instrument. An appraisal system that is perceived as fair gets engagement and commitment, and those are the only underutilized reserves all companies seem to have and an important sustainable resource for competitive advantage.

However, the current formal systems to appraise performance in cycles (six months, one year) are seen by most of the interviewed project managers as occasions to generate information for the official organizational systems and to review the performance for the previous cycle (usually six months), and with less influence on performance improvement.

The interviewed project managers recognized their orientation on performance, but many of them reported difficulties (both conceptual — "what should we do" and practical "how to really do it") in managing the individual performance within the coordinated project teams.

Gavrea *et al.* (2011) propose new ways of thinking the project performance management appraisal and other complementary measures are sought by both project managers and other stakeholders, HR managers, and the academic community.

McGregor (1957) was one of the first who proposed a shift in the appraisal methods from one oriented on improving underperformance (past-based) to a future-oriented approach based on strengths.

Different terms were proposed during time, and some companies, in their desire to mark the change in their practices were eager to adapt and promote new concepts and words, like: "analysis" instead of "appraisal" or performance management as a systematic, on-going process, within a performance cycle, instead of performance appraisal, which is seen as more administrative.

The underutilized reserve seems to stay into the skill and will of human resources (including project managers' skill and will).

New ways to define success and appraise individual members are required to improve and define productivity and encourage innovation.

Due to their complex nature, the success of projects depends on the clarity of understanding and acceptance by the team members of the desired outcomes and the readiness to define, adapt, and follow common ways (tools, work procedures, etc.) to accomplish them.

The project team members are more and more specialized in terms of knowledge and they have to face increasingly complex problems, and the increasing interdependency of team members to.

3. Best Practices for Performance Management

Examples Of Best Practices acting as a contextual support for performance management collected from Romanian companies successful in using project management orientation at company level, are the following:

(1) The very existence of the *supporting organizational* structure that contains:
   (a) A strategic committee;
   (b) A strategy management support department.
(2) Well — designed *critical responsibilities* for coordination and implementation at different strategic levels:
   (a) Corporate-level (strategic) — general orientation, operating philosophy, coordination of various programs and major projects;
   (b) department level — tactical dimension of program management and resource optimization;
   (c) individual (project level).
(3) Clear *reporting responsibilities* for project managers (either functional or to higher level projects or programs) within the management structure.
(4) *Pro-active orientation*, long-term based — using the past and current results as a strong base for future decision and implementation.
(5) *Simple mechanisms* for implementation in standardized forms like Plan — Do — Check — Act cycles, milestone analysis.

4. Fairness Associated Difficulties in Performance Management

Some Difficulties in Performance management that are major influences of perceived fairness in project oriented companies were reported by both functional and project managers:

(1) Functional managers
   (a) *Role conflicts* — team members are performing tasks in different simultaneous projects, and an overall performance appraisal is difficult to made;
   (b) *Conflicting priorities* — many task projects have high priority — extra efforts are required to respond (e.g., to quality and time constraints);
   (c) *Competition for resources*;
   (d) *Projects have a life of their own* — the traditional methods of defining objectives (and KPI's attached to them) are very difficult for many domains that are not related to operations (e.g., production).
(2) Project managers
   (a) *Team efficacy* in projects is difficult to be encouraged — it has been shown to positively affect team performance (Knight *et al.*, 2001);
   (b) *Restricted resources to compensate* — project managers have often limited (if any) resources to compensate efforts;
   (c) *Limited formal authority* — team members are often coordinated by their functional managers.

5. Conclusion

Participants interviewed for this research were employees of well-established Romanian companies, with experience in managing and administering performance management systems.

A limitation of the study is the relatively small sample size. However, the findings of this study are still valuable because they offer a base for further research, and by the insights into a less studied fairness dimensions (but critical dimension) of performance management and appraisal in projects.

This research has thrown up many questions in need of further investigation, in some major directions:

(1) How should the strategic levels support fairness (organisational justice) in projects?
(2) What are the new components of the performance management system needed to support a project-oriented organization?

How can be operationalized (in the form of project managerial tools) the above to sustain a team oriented appraisal and reward system.

References

Bies, R. J. & Moag, J. S. (1986), Interactional justice: Communication criteria for fairness. In *Research on Negotiation in Organizations*, B. Sheppard (ed.), pp. 43–55. Greenwich: JAI.

Byrne, Z. S. & Cropanzano, R. (2001), The history of organizational justice: The founders speak. In *Justice in the Workplace: From Theory to Practice*, Cropanzano (ed.), pp. 3–26, Mahwah: Lawrence Erlbaum Associates, Inc.

Colquitt, J. A. (2001), On the dimensionality of organizational justice: A construct validation of a measure, *Journal of Applied Psychology*, 86, 386–400.

Crawford, K. J. & Cabanis-Brewin, J. (2011), The Strategic Project Office, CRC Press, Taylor & Francis Group.

Gavrea, C., Ilies, L., & Stegerean, R. (2011), Determinants of organizational performance: The case of Romania, *Management & Marketing*, 6(2), 285–300.

Ilies, L. (2003), *Managementul Calității Totale*, Cluj-Napoca: Editura Dacia.

Knight, D., Durham, C. C., & Locke, E. A. (2001), The relationship of team goals, incentives, and efficacy to strategic risk, tactical implementation, and performance, *Academy of Management Journal*, 44(2), 326–338.

Lockett, J. (1992), Effective Performance Management, London: Kogan Page.

McGregor, D. (1957), An uneasy look at performance appraisal, *Harvard Business Review*, May–June, 89–94.

Miller, J. S. & Cardy, R. L. (2000), Self-monitoring and performance appraisal: Rating outcomes in project teams, *Journal of Organizational Behavior*, 21(6), 609–626. Available at http://search.proquest.com/docview/224883661?accountid=1553.

Roch, S. G. & Shanock, L. R. (2006), Organizational justice in an exchange framework: Clarifying organizational justice distinctions, *Journal of Management*, 32, 299–322.

Warokka, A., Gallato, C. G., & Moorthy, T. A. (2012), Organizational justice in performance appraisal system and work performance: Evidence from an emerging market, *Journal of Human Resources Management Research*, 1–18. Available at http://search.proquest.com/docview/1446292526?accountid= 15533.

Wright, P. M., Gardner, T. M., & Moynihan, L. M. (2003), The impact of HR practices on the performance of business units, *Human Resource Management Journal*, 13(3), 21–36.

Chapter 35

The Relation between Labor Force Profitability and the Firm's Personnel Policy

*Gabriel Sorin Badea, Constanta Popescu
and Silvia Elena Iacob*

Valahia University of Targoviste
Academy of Economic Studies

Often, in the economic practice, when the decision to diminish the number of employees is not substantiated using calculations and analyses, the increase of both labor productivity and labor volume do not succeed. So, frequently, a firm's leadership — without adequate analyses — believe that they will increase their labor productivity by lowering their number of employees. Applying a personnel policy without rigorous analyses, such leaderships have found themselves faced with an unfavorable situation: both their labor productivity and the physical volume of their production decreased. The evolution of the production process is explained by the fact that the physical production volume largely depends on the labor force volume. The high degree of dependence of the labor productivity and of the physical production on the labor force factor can be the effect of an inadequate technical endowment, i.e., the result of a low level of investments in the modernization of the production process. Labor productivity is a partial efficiency indicator, being considered a main element of the system of economic efficiency indicators. The main flaw of this kind of indicator consists in the fact that it attributes the global result (output), obtained by the combined action of different factors, to a partial effort (input) expressed by one of the production factors that were combined.

1. Introduction: Theoretical Approaches

A firm's personnel policy may sometimes contain measures that do not lead to the increase of the labor force productivity: the increase of the number of employees (T) should occur only in the circumstances of a marginal productivity (W_{mg}) above the average productivity (W), i.e., when the marginal productivity line is above the average productivity line, i.e., $W_{mg} > W$ (see Fig. 1, the area on the left of optimal number of employees (T_M)). In Fig. 1, one can also notice that the optimal number of employees (T_M) is determined by the intersection of the marginal productivity line and the average productivity line, i.e., by the equation $W_{mg} = W$.

The policy of increase of the firm's number of employees leads to positive economic and social consequences, beneficial for the employees' families and/or households.

A special case, given the negative social and economic consequences it determines, is represented by the policy of job cuts.

Fig. 1.

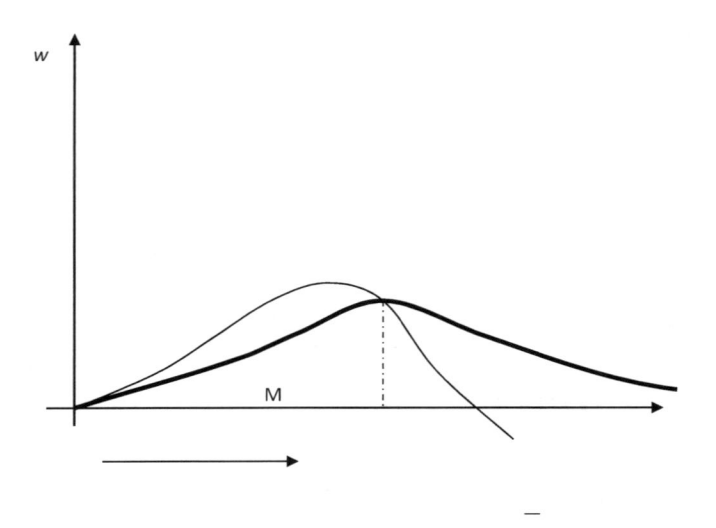

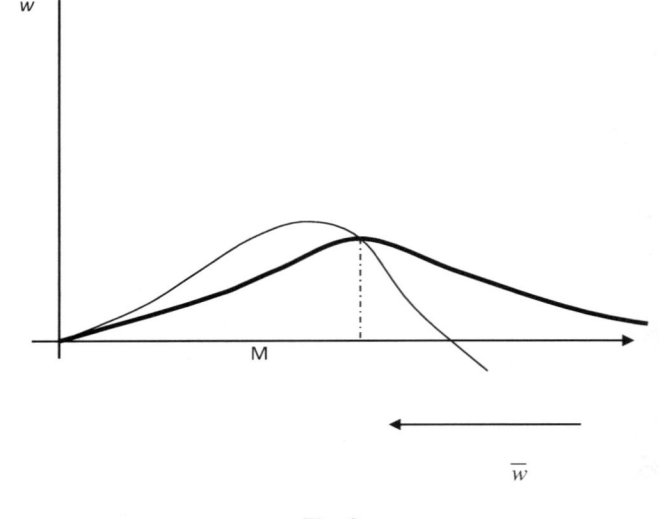

Fig. 2.

The main consequences determined by such a policy are:

— Decrease of the population's (families', households') revenue and standard of living;
— Unsatisfied demand for goods and services because of the decrease in productivity, respectively in the offer of goods and services, if there have been no investments to modernize the production process;
— Increase of the prices for goods and services because of the decrease in the offer of goods compared to the demand;
— Decreased labor productivity, if there has been no investment to modernize the production process.

Consequently, considering the relation between average labor productivity (W) and marginal productivity (W_{mg}) (see Fig. 2, the area on the right of T_M), the decrease of the number of employees must be opted for only when the marginal productivity line, i.e., W_{mg} is situated below the average productivity line (W), i.e., $W_{mg} < W$.

We can see that the optimal number of employees T_M is recorded in conditions similar to the case of the option of increase in the number of employees ($W = W_{mg}$).

Next, we will demonstrate that the employee number increase/decrease policy in a firm has to be realized considering the elasticity of labor productivity in relation to the number of employees (E_{W-T}). The approach is achieved for the case of a homogeneous physical production and, obviously, labor productivity measured in physical units.

It is known that the physical production level (Q) can be established using the relation between labor productivity (W) and the number of employees (T):

$$Q = W * T.$$

The physical production volume is influenced by two factors: an extensive one (T) and an intensive one (W). It can be demonstrated that the policy of modification of the labor force volume (T) can contribute to the increase of the physical production volume if the following conditions are met:

— T increases and productivity is elastic ($E_{W-T} > 1$),
— T decreases and productivity is inelastic ($E_{W-T} < 1$).

On the basis of the relation presented in the previous paragraph, between the physical production volume and the factors that influence this volume, for a given production volume Q_0, between the labor productivity level and the number of employees there is a relation of inverse proportionality:

$$Q_0 = W * T \rightarrow W = \frac{Q_0}{T}.$$

For different values of the physical production (Q_0), the relation $W = \frac{Q_0}{T}$ can be represented graphically (see Fig. 3).

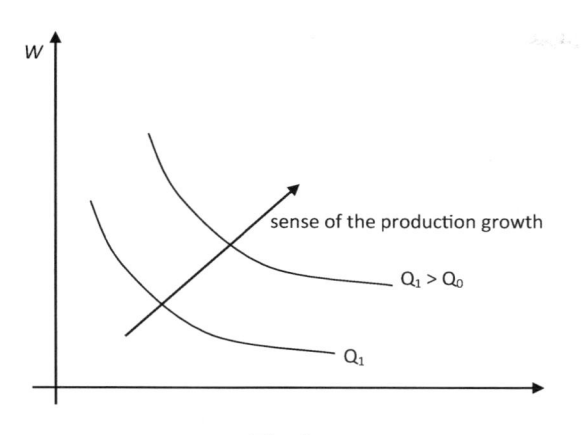

Fig. 3.

The physical production level increases gradually, as the isoquant moves away from the origin of the axes OT and OW.

Analyzing the graph, one can easily notice that the same production level can be achieved with an infinite number of combinations (T, W), with the following consequences:

— The increase of the number of employees (T) can lead to a decrease in productivity;
— The decrease of the number of employees (T) can lead to an increase in productivity.

However, the evolutions in labor productivity also depend on conditions related to the labor productivity elasticity level in relation to the number of employees.

The labor productivity elasticity level is determined by the productivity dynamics and the dynamics of the number of employees measured using the modification rhythm (R).

$$E_{W-T} = \frac{R_W}{R_T}.$$

If there is a relation of inverse proportionality between productivity and the number of employees, then the elasticity level will acquire negative values, while if the relationship between these indicators is directly proportional, then the elasticity level will be positive.

Previously, it has been stated that the labor productivity elasticity influences the dynamics of the physical production. In order to demonstrate it, we will do the following calculations.

From the relationship $Q = W * T$, we deduce a dynamics relationship expressed using dynamics indicators expressed as a decimal:

$$i_Q = i_W * i_T.$$

Between the dynamics indicator and the modification rhythm there is the relationship:

$$i = R + 1.$$

Replacing the modification indicators with the rhythms, the dynamics relationship between physical production, labor productivity, and number of employees can be written as follows:

$$R_Q + 1 = (R_W + 1)(R_T + 1).$$

From the last relationship, we deduce that an increase in physical production will be recorded if the physical production rhythm is positive, i.e., $R_Q > 0$.

Since R_W and R_T represent very low values, then the product of $R_W * R_T$ is much lower than any of the terms of the equation and it can be neglected ($R_W * R_T \to 0$) and the relation becomes: $R_Q \approx R_W + R_T$.

Taking into account that $E_{W-T} = \frac{R_W}{R_T}$ we can write that: $R_W = E_{W-T} * R_T$, and the dynamics relationship deduced previously becomes:

$$R_Q = R_T + R_W = R_T + \frac{R_W}{R_T} * R_T = R_T + E_{W-T} * R_T$$
$$= R_T(1 + E_{W-T}).$$

The final dynamics relationship is:

$$R_Q = R_T * (1 + E_{W-T}).$$

The above-mentioned formula can be used to determine the relationship between production elasticity (E_{Q-T}) and productivity elasticity (E_{W-T}) measured in relation to the volume of the labor factor (T):

$$R_Q = R_T * (1 + E_{W-T}) / : R_T \to \frac{R_Q}{R_T} = 1 + E_{W-T}$$
$$\to E_{Q-T} = 1 + E_{W-T} \to R_Q = E_{Q-T} * R_T.$$

The calculation formula for productivity elasticity will be submitted to an analysis that will allow us to draw vital conclusions on the consequences of the personnel policy on the labor force volume.

Depending on the values of the elasticities E_{Q-T} and E_{W-T}, several cases can be delineated.

(a) The case $(1 + E_{W-T}) = 0$:
 → $E_{Q-T} = 0$, rigid production,
 → $E_{W-T} = -1$, productivity with an elasticity equal to one and having a relation of inverse proportionality with the labor force factor.

(b) The case $0 < (1 + E_{W-T}) < 1$:
 → $0 < E_{Q-T} < 1$, inelastic production and in a relation of direct proportionality with the labor force factor,
 → $-1 < E_{W-T}) < 0$, inelastic productivity and in a relation of inverse proportionality with the labor force factor.

(c) The case $(1 + E_{W-T}) = 1$:
 → $E_{Q-T} = 1$, production with an elasticity equal to one and in a relation of direct proportionality with the labor force factor,
 → $E_{W-T} = 0$, rigid productivity.

(d) The case $2 > (1 + E_{W-T}) > 1$:
 → $2 > E_{Q-T} > 1$, elastic production and in a relation of direct proportionality with the labor force factor,
 → $1 > E_{W-T} > 0$, inelastic productivity and in a relation of direct proportionality with the labor force factor.

(e) The case $(1 + E_{W-T}) = 2$:
 → $E_{Q-T} > 2$, elastic production and in a relation of direct proportionality with the labor force factor,
 → $E_{W-T} = 1$, productivity with an elasticity equal to one and in a relation of direct proportionality with the labor force factor.

(f) The case $(1 + E_{W-T}) > 2$:
 → $E_{Q-T} > 2$, elastic production and in a relation of direct proportionality with the labor force factor,
 → $E_{W-T} > 1$, elastic productivity and in a relation of direct proportionality with the labor force factor.

(g) The case $-1 < (1 + E_{W-T}) < 0$:
 → $-1 < E_{Q-T} < 0$, inelastic production and in a relation of inverse proportionality with the labor force factor,
 → $-2 < E_{W-T}) < -1$, elastic productivity and in a relation of inverse proportionality with the labor force factor.

(h) The case $(1 + E_{W-T}) = -1$:
 → $E_{Q-T} = -1$, production with an elasticity equal to one and in a relation of inverse proportionality with the labor force factor,
 → $E_{W-T} = -2$, elastic productivity and in a relation of inverse proportionality with the labor force factor.

(i) The case $-2 < (1 + E_{W-T}) < -1$:
 → $-2 < E_{Q-T} < -1$, elastic production and in a relation of inverse proportionality with the labor force factor,
 → $-3 < E_{W-T} < -2$, elastic productivity and in a relation of inverse proportionality with the labor force factor.

(j) The case $(1 + E_{W-T}) = -2$
 → $E_{Q-T} = -2$, elastic production and in a relation of inverse proportionality with the labor force factor,
 → $E_{W-T} = -3$, elastic productivity and in a relation of inverse proportionality with the labor force factor.

(k) The case $(1 + E_{W-T}) < -2$:
 → $E_{Q-T} < -2$, elastic production and in a relation of inverse proportionality with the labor force factor,
 → $E_{W-T} < -3$, elastic productivity and in a relation of inverse proportionality with the labor force factor.

Taking into account the cases presented above, the tendencies of the physical production and of the labor productivity have been determined (see Table 1) based on the relationships below:

$$R_Q = E_{Q-T} * R_T, \quad R_W = E_{W-T} * R_T.$$

Table 1. Effects of the labor productivity elasticity on the physical production dynamics

Indicators	Indicator level										
E_{W-T}	<−3	−3	−3→−2	−2	−2→−1	−1	−1→0	0	0→1	1	>1
E_{Q-T}	<−2	−2	−2→−1	−1	−1→0	0	0→1	1	1→2	2	>2
R_Q for $R_T<0$	>0	>0	>0	>0	>0	0	<0	<0	<0	<0	<0
R_W for $R_T<0$	>0	>0	>0	>0	>0	>0	>0	0	<0	<0	<0
R_Q for $R_T>0$	<0	<0	<0	<0	<0	0	>0	>0	>0	>0	>0
R_W for $R_T>0$	<0	<0	<0	<0	<0	<0	<0	0	>0	>0	>0

From the analysis of the values recorded in Table 1, it can be noticed that the physical production and labor productivity increase simultaneously ($R_Q > 0$, $R_W > 0$) under the following circumstances:

(a) For $R_T < 0 \rightarrow E_{w-T} < -1$, respectively $E_{Q-T} < 0$ (the number of employees will be reduced if productivity elasticity is negative and productivity is elastic),

(b) For $R_T > 0 \rightarrow E_{w-T} > 0$, respectively $E_{Q-T} > 1$ (the number of employees will be increased if productivity elasticity is positive and productivity is inelastic or elastic).

If the values of the productivity elasticity are between −1 and 0, i.e., $-1 \leq E_{W-T} \leq 0$, then there is no simultaneous increase in physical production and labor productivity.

Such situations can be explained based on the reasoning in the following paragraph. In order to achieve it, dynamics calculations have been used, where the modifications have been expressed using the dynamics indicators:

$$i_W = \frac{i_Q}{i_T}.$$

The intensity and sense of the modification in physical production and number of employees will determine the sense and intensity of the modification in labor force productivity. The intensity and sense of modification of the indicators analyzed are measured using the dynamics indicators (i) or the rhythm of modification (R).

The relationships between the dynamics of the physical production (i_Q) and the number of employees (i_T) will influence the dynamics of labor productivity (i_w).

⇒ When physical production increases ($i_Q > 1$), while the number of employees is kept constant or decreases ($i_T = 1$, $i_T < 1$), labor productivity will increase, as the value of the fraction increases, i.e., the indicator of dynamics for labor productivity becomes bigger than one ($i_w > 1$).

⇒ When the production volume increases ($i_Q > 1$), and the number of employees is maintained constant or increases ($i_T = 1$, $i_T > 1$), in order for the labor productivity level to increase ($i_W > 1$) it is necessary for the physical production dynamics to be bigger than the dynamics of the number of employees ($i_Q > i_T$).

⇒ If the production volume decreases ($i_Q < 1$), and the number of employees is kept constant or increases ($i_T = 1$, $i_T > 1$), the labor productivity level will decrease, as the value of the fraction decreases, respectively the dynamics indicator becomes lower than one ($i_w < 1$).

Next, we will analyze the cases when the physical production level and the number of employees decrease. In the case when both the number of employees and the physical production decrease ($i_T < 1$, $i_Q < 1$), the rhythms of modification of the two indicators acquire negative values ($R_T < 0$ and $R_Q < 0$). It is obvious that the intensity and sense of modification in physical production and number of employees will determine the sense and intensity of the modification in labor force productivity.

⇒ If the production volume is kept constant ($i_Q = 1$), and the number of employees is decreased ($i_T < 1$), the labor force productivity level will decrease ($i_W < 1$).

⇒ If the decrease of the physical production volume is more intense than the reduction of the labor force level ($\dot{R}_Q > \dot{R}_T$, $R_Q < 0$, $R_T < 0 \to R_T > R_Q$), then the labor force productivity level will decrease ($R_W < 0$);

$$i_W = \frac{i_Q}{i_T} < 1 \to R_w + 1 = \frac{R_Q + 1}{R_T + 1} < 1$$
$$\to R_Q + 1 < R_T + 1 \to R_w + 1 < 1 \to R_w < 0.$$

This case is the most unfavorable in the firm's personnel policy because it triggers a decrease in physical production, a decrease of the economically active population, a decrease in labor productivity, a lowering of the population's revenues and consequently a decrease of the population's standard of living.

⇒ If the decrease of the labor force volume is higher than the decrease of the production level ($\dot{R}_T > \dot{R}_Q$, $R_Q < 0$, $R_T < 0 \to R_T < R_Q$), that will trigger an increase in the labor productivity level ($R_w > 0$);

$$i_W = \frac{i_Q}{i_T} > 1 \to R_w + 1 = \frac{R_Q + 1}{R_T + 1} > 1$$
$$\to R_Q + 1 > R_T + 1 \to R_w + 1 > 1 \to R_w > 0.$$

This last case of the firm's personnel policy represents a *false revitalization in economy*. We have characterized this condition of the economic activity as a *false revitalization in economy because the increase of the labor productivity level under these circumstances is only a result of calculations, without generating beneficial effects for society.*

2. Case Study: Labor Productivity at the Branch Petrom S.A. Târgoviște

2.1. *Labor productivity level and dynamics at the Branch Petrom S.A. Târgoviște*

In the equations presented in the theoretical part and used in the analyses carried out for the **Branch Petrom S.A. Târgoviște**, the following notations have been used:

→ 0 for the indicator of the year 2009;
→ 1 for the indicator of the year 2011.

Because the productivity level includes as well the influence of the prices from one year to the next, it is advisable either to calculate productivity in real terms (by deflating the production value or the productivity value), or by calculating labor force productivity based on physical production.

In the present study, we have chosen to calculate labor force productivity based on physical production.

As far as the dynamics of the physical production on production sections is concerned (see Table 2) a decrease of the physical production for all the sections has been recorded, the most significant decreases being recorded at Gura Ocniței (−29.42%) and Ochiuri (−28.58%) while at Mănești the decrease was lower (−15.79%).

In relation to the negative evolution of the physical production, the evolution of the number of employees in the production sections also has a decreasing tendency.

Table 2. Evolution in physical production (Q) and number of employees (T) on production sections during the years 2009 and 2011

Section	Production volume — TO*		Employee number — T*		I_Q (%)	R_Q (%)	I_T (%)	R_T (%)
	2009	2011	2009	2011				
Ochiuri	51,100	36,500	230	205	71.42	−28.58	89.13	−10.87
G. Ocniței	62,050	43,800	264	212	70.58	−29.42	80.30	−19.70
Mănești	69,350	58,400	135	99	84.21	−15.79	73.33	−26.67
Total	182,500	138,700	629	516	76.00	−24.00	82.03	−17.97

Source: *Data from the accountancy of the Branch Petrom S.A. Târgoviște.

The most significant personnel decrease was recorded at Mănești section (−26.67%). For the whole economic unit, the personnel decrease was of −17.97%, while the production decrease was of −24%.

For the calculation of the physical productivity we have used data that are part of the firm's accountancy, and in order to analyze labor productivity (measured in physical units) in the production sections and for the entire company (Branch Petrom S.A. Târgoviște) we have used the data of the years 2009 and 2011 (Table 3).

The negative evolutions of the physical production and of the number of employees influenced the level and dynamics of labor productivity. The only section where an increase in labor productivity has been recorded was the section from Mănești (+14.83%).

For the other sections, the decrease in labor productivity was much higher than the one recorded for the entire company. So, on the whole, the firm's productivity recorded a decrease of −7.36%, and below this negative rhythm we find the sections of Ochiuri (−19.87%) and Gura Ocniței (−12.1%).

The increase in productivity from Mănești section can be explained by the very significant decrease in the number of employees (−26.67%), and the less significant decrease in the physical production (−15.78%). The increase in labor productivity from Mănești section was not able to compensate for the very significant productivity decreases from the other production sections (Ochiuri and Gura Ocniței).

The dynamics in labor productivity for the period 2009–2011 was influenced by the modifications in volume and structure both concerning physical production (Q) and concerning the number of employees (T). Analyzing the centralized data from Table 3, we can notice different evolutions in the production structure and in the structure of the employees.

Table 3. Physical productivity level and dynamics for each production section during the years 2009 and 2011

Section	W (TO/ employee) 2009	W (TO/ employee) 2011	I_w (%)	R_w (%)	I_Q (%)	I_T (%)
Ochiuri	222.17	178.04	80.13	−19.87	71.42	89.13
G. Ocniței	235.03	206.60	87.90	−12.10	70.58	80.30
Mănești	513.70	589.89	114.83	14.83	84.21	73.33
Total	290.14	268.79	92.64	−7.36	76.00	82.03

Table 4. Structure in point of physical production (g_Q) and employees (g_T) for each production section during the years 2009 and 2011

Section	g_Q _% 2009	g_Q _% 2011	g_T _% 2009	g_T _% 2011
Ochiuri	28	26.33	36.56	39.72
G. Ocniței	34	31.57	41.97	41.09
Mănești	38	42.10	21.57	19.19
Total	100	100.00	100.00	100.00

Concerning the structure of the labor force on sections, according to the data presented in Table 4, we can notice an increase of the share of employees from Ochiuri, while for the sections of Gura Ocniței and Mănești, the share of employees decreased.

Concerning the physical production, for the sections of Ochiuri and Gura Ocniței, the production share decreased, while for the section of Mănești the production share increased.

For the period 2009–2011, the physical production shares of each production section changed as follows:

— For the section of Ochiuri, a decrease from 28% to 26.33% was recorded;
— For the section of Gura Ocnitei, a decrease from 34% to 31.57% was recorded;
— For the section of Manesti, an increase from 38% to 42.10% was recorded.

2.2. Correlation marginal productivity — average productivity

The marginal productivity is an indicator explaining the tendency of the average labor force productivity and at the same time influencing the production elasticity in relation to the labor force factor.

In order to calculate the marginal productivity, we used the data from Table 2.

A specific feature of the company under analysis is the decrease in the number of employees and production. That is why the evolution of the average productivity (calculated for the production sections and for the entire company) will be influenced by the existing relationship between the average productivity (w_0) and the marginal productivity of the period analyzed (w_{mg}) and

Table 5. Marginal productivity level and its effects on the average productivity

Section	ΔQ	ΔT	W_{mg} $\Delta Q/\Delta T)$	W_0	W_1
Ochiuri	−14600	−25	584.00	222.17	178.04
G. Ocniței	−18250	−52	350.96	235.03	206.60
Mănești	−10950	−36	304.16	513.70	589.89
Total	−43800	−113	387.61	290.14	268.79

by the descending tendency in the number of employees.

The data in Table 5 highlight the following evolutions of the average productivity:

— For the sections of Ochiuri, Gura Ocniței and for the whole company, because the marginal labor productivity is above the average productivity of the year analyzed — 2009(w_0), and the number of employees is decreasing, the average productivity will decrease during the following period ($w_1 < w_0$);
— For the section of Mănești, because the marginal labor force productivity is below the average productivity (w_0), and the number of employees is decreasing, the average productivity will increase during the following period ($w_1 > w_0$).

In order to evaluate the influence of the labor force using production elasticity we have used the data in Table 6.

Labor force productivity is the intensive factor that influences the production volume, while the number of employees is the extensive factor.

In order to highlight the sensitivity of the production in relation to the labor production factor, we calculated the production elasticity in correlation to this factor (E_{Q-T}) both on production sections and for the entire company.

$$E_{Q-T} = \frac{R_Q}{R_T} = \frac{\Delta Q/Q_0}{\Delta T/T_0} = \frac{\Delta Q/\Delta T}{Q_0/T_0} = \frac{w_{mg}}{w_0}$$
$$\rightarrow w_{mg} = E_{Q-T} * w_0.$$

While for the sections of Ochiuri, Gura Ocniței and for the entire company the production is elastic in relation to the labor force (E_{Q-T} is bigger than one), for the section of Mănești the production is inelastic (E_{Q-T} is below one).

The highest elasticity level was recorded at the section of Ochiuri (2.62), and the lowest at the section of Mănești (0.59). For the whole company, an average elasticity of 1.33 was recorded.

We must notice the fact that the calculated elasticity level is recorded under the circumstances of a decrease both in point of production and in point of the number of employees. The largest production decrease was recorded at the section of Gura Ocniței (−29.42%), and the most significant decrease in the number of employees was recorded at the section of Mănești (−26.67%).

The production elasticity level in relation to the labor force factor explains as well the difference of productivity (difference between the average productivity measured for the year 2009 and the marginal productivity calculated for the period 2009–2011).

The differences between the average productivity and the marginal productivity determine the production elasticity level in relation to the labor force factor:

$$E_{Q-T} = \frac{w_{mg}}{w_0}.$$

The fact that the average labor force productivity for the production sections of Ochiuri, Gura Ocniței and for the whole company for the year 2009 is lower than the corresponding marginal productivity will trigger high production elasticity levels.

Table 6. Table for the calculation of E_{Q-T}

Section	I_Q (%)	I_T (%)	$R_Q = I_Q - 100$ (%)	$R_T = I_T - 100$ (%)	$E_{Q-T} = R_Q/R_T$	$\overline{W}_0 = Q_{2007}/T_{2007}$
Ochiuri	71.42	89.13	−28.58	−10.87	2.62	222.17
G. Ocniței	70.58	80.30	−29.42	−19.70	1.49	235.03
Mănești	84.21	73.33	−15.79	−26.67	0.59	513.70
Total	76.00	82.03	−24.00	−17.97	1.33	290.14

For the section of Mănești, the productivity for the year 2009 is higher than the marginal productivity, determining the lowest level of the production elasticity as well.

The sections' (average and marginal) productivities, as well as the negative rhythms of modification in the number of employees triggered modifications in the average productivity of the following period, as follows (see Fig. 1):

— When the marginal productivity was higher than the average productivity of the base period, and the number of employees decreased, this created the necessary grounds for the average productivity of the current period to decrease (see the sections of Ochiuri, Gura Ocniței and the whole company).
— When the average productivity of the base period was higher than the marginal productivity, and the number of employees decreased, this created the necessary grounds for the average productivity of the current period to increase (see the section of Mănești).

2.3. *Productivity elasticity*

The analysis in point of labor productivity can be deepened using productivity elasticity. So, on the basis of the data obtained from the firm, we calculated the productivity elasticity level on production sections and for the whole economic unit (see Table 7). The results of the calculations for the productivity elasticity level (E_{W-T}) will be used to substantiate from a theoretical viewpoint the adequate personnel policy. The personnel policy adopted will substantiate the modification of the number of employees (R_T), so as to assure a positive dynamics for the labor force productivity level (R_W) and the physical production volume (R_Q). The policy related to the number of employees is substantiated using the formulas below:

$$E_{W-T} = \frac{R_W}{R_T} \rightarrow R_W = E_{W-T} * R_T,$$

$$R_Q = R_T * (1 + E_{W-T}), \quad R_W > 0, \quad R_Q > 0.$$

Naturally, between labor force productivity and labor force level there has to be a relation of inverse proportionality, when the physical production level is kept constant. However, concerning the firm under analysis, we can notice that a directly proportional relationship appeared between the two indicators, a fact that contributed to the decrease in physical production and labor productivity when the labor force volume decreased. The directly proportional relationship determined as well the existence of the negative values of the labor productivity elasticity, contrary to the hypothesis emitted in the theoretical part of this chapter.

The analysis of the data obtained following the calculations allows us to notice that the personnel policies were sometimes non-beneficial for some production sections and for the whole company.

The leadership of the company practiced the reduction of personnel in all the subunits of the branch, which led to a decrease in physical production in all these subunits, the only subunit that recorded an increase in labor productivity being the section of Mănești. This evolution of the production process is explained by the fact that the physical production volume is largely dependent on the labor force volume (the production is elastic in relation to the labor force factor for all the sections and for the entire branch except for the section of Mănești — see Table 7). The high degree of dependence of the labor

Table 7. Table for calculating productivity elasticity (E_{W-T})

Section	Practical personnel policy					Theoretical personnel policy	
	$R_W(\%)$	$R_T(\%)$	$E_{W-T} = R_W/R_T$	$1 + E_{W-T}$	$R_Q(\%)$	R_T for $R_W > 0 \rightarrow R_T * E_{W-T} > 0$	R_T for $R_Q > 0 \rightarrow R_T * (1 + E_{W-T}) > 0$
Ochiuri	−19.87	−10.87	1.827	2.827	−28.58	$R_T > 0$	$R_T > 0$
G. Ocniței	−12.10	−19.70	0.614	1.614	−29.42	$R_T > 0$	$R_T > 0$
Mănești	14.83	−26.67	−0.556	0.444	−15.79	$R_T < 0$	$R_T > 0$
Total	−7.36	−17.97	0.409	1.409	−24.00	$R_T > 0$	$R_T > 0$

productivity and of the physical production on the labor force factor can be the effect of an inadequate technical endowment, i.e., the result of a low level of the investments for the modernization of the production process.

Positive dynamics in labor productivity and physical production would have been recorded if the firm's management would have ensured, according to the data from Table 6, an increase in the number of employees. A decrease of the number of employees should have been achieved only if some funds had been allotted for the modernization of the production process, which in turn would have contributed to a decrease of the high level of the production elasticity in relation to the labor force factor (see Table 7).

3. Conclusions

Labor productivity is a partial efficiency indicator, being considered a main element of the system of indicators concerning economic efficiency. The main deficiency of this type of indicator consists in the fact that it attributes the global result (output), obtained through the combined action of different factors, to a partial effort (input) expressed by one of the production factors that were combined.

In essence, the activity deployed by such a firm leads to a decrease of the internal offer of goods and services and to the decrease of the number of the economically active population, with serious socio-economic consequences on the population's standard of living. The economic activity being a form of human activity, it is determined by human needs, and its results should have a beneficial character for society. It is not acceptable for the economic activity to be generated by human needs, and yet by its effects to have a negative influence on the bearers of human needs by lowering their standard of living.

References

Andrei, L. (2011), *Economie*, Bucuresti: Economica.

Badea, G. S. (2006), *Resursele de Muncă-Măsurare și Analiză Statistică*: Bibliotheca.

Badea, G. S. (2009), *Microeconomie*, Târgoviște: Valahia University Press.

Mayeur, d' A. (Coordinator) (2013), *Microeconomie*, France: Nathan.

Popescu, C. (Coordinator), Badea, G. S., & Croitoru, G. (2006), *Microeconomie: Teorie si Aplicatii*, Târgoviște: Bibliotheca.

Popescu, C. (2009), *Economie*, Târgoviște: Bibliotheca.

Sowell, T. (2011), *Basic Economics*, New York: Basic Books.

Schiller, B. (Coordinator) (2012), *The Micro Economy Today*, New York: McGraw-Hill Series Economics/Irwin.

Chapter 36

Analysis of Multinational Companies in Romania*

Eduard Ceptureanu and Sebastian Ceptureanu

Bucharest University of Economic Studies

Multinational companies generate a substantial contribution to the development of the world economy by integrating their systems to the trade, the production process, and the monetary and financial structures.

This chapter aims at investigating the impact of multinational companies in the Romanian economy, by customizing effects on some important economic indicators. Functioning of the global economy, characterized by the expression of a tendency to open national markets can be better explained by analyzing the formation process of multinational companies, the causes of this process, the size and, location of their problems related to the functioning, as well as presenting the effects generated on the national economy.

Multinational companies generate a substantial contribution to the development of the world economy by integrating their systems to the trade, the production process and the monetary and financial structures.

Occurred since the late 19th century, in time, multinational companies have imposed relatively fast becoming the next period of the Second World War not insignificant factor in the world economy, often they are presented as such representative organization for post-industrial thinking. Complexity of this process of internationalization of firms as is proven by the large number of names and ways of defining their specialized of renowned experts in the field.

This chapter aims at investigating the impact of multinational companies in the Romanian economy, by customizing effects on some important economic indicators.

In the context of increased globalization and the growing interest shown for multinational companies, which tend to be a "fashionable concept", management field is constantly growing during the past decade gaining a significant scale among theorists and practitioners in Management Science and enjoying the attention of the visible and administrative bodies and public sector in developed countries through the great amount of human, financial, and material taken from this area.

1. Introduction

Functioning of the global economy, characterized by the expression of a tendency to open national markets can be better explained by analyzing the formation process of multinational companies, the causes of this process, the size, and location of their problems related

---

*This work was co-financed from the European Social Fund through Sectoral Operational Programme Human Resources Development 2007–2013, project number POSDRU/159/1.5/S/142115 "Performance and excellence in doctoral and postdoctoral research in Romanian economics science domain".

to the functioning, as well as presenting the effects generated on the national economy.

Multinational companies generate a substantial contribution to the development of the world economy by integrating their systems to the trade, the production process and the monetary and financial structures.

Occurred since the late 19th century, in time, multinational companies have imposed relatively fast becoming the next period of the Second World War not insignificant factor in the world economy, often they are presented as such representative organization for post-industrial thinking. Complexity of this process of internationalization of firms and is proven by the large number of names and ways of defining their specialized of renowned experts in the field.

This paper aims at investigating the impact of multinational companies in the Romanian economy, by customizing effects on some important economic indicators.

In the context of increased globalization and the growing interest shown for multinational companies, which tend to be "fashionable concept" management field is constantly growing during the past decade gaining a significant scale among theorists and practitioners in Management Science and enjoying the attention of the visible and administrative bodies and public sector in developed countries through the great amount of human, financial and material taken from this area.

2. Analysis of Multinational Companies

2.1. *Evolution of turnover (2002–2013)*

In the analyzed multinationals, global turnover in the period 2002–2013 was at the EUR 281,255,7 mn. If we want to do a ranking according to Activity-Based-Costing (ABC) methodology, we find that the first 10% of companies as turnover (OMV Petrom SA, Arcelor Mittal Galati SA, Rompetrol Rafinare SA, METRO CASH & CARRY ROMANIA SRL, Automobile Dacia SA, Romtelecom SA) contributes with 38% (EUR 107,661.7 mn) to generate the results above-mentioned. The next 20% of companies (ORANGE ROMANIA SA, Vodafone Romania SA, GDF Suez Energy Romania SA LUKOIL ROMANIA SRL, Rompetrol Downstream, PETROTEL LUKOIL SA, British American Tobacco (ROMANIA) TRADING, Porsche Romania SRL, CARREFOUR ROMANIA SA, SELGROS CASH & CARRY Ltd., Coca Cola HBC Romania SRL, OMV ROMANIA MINERALOEL SRL) generates 30.4% of total turnover (EUR 85,639,38 mns). In quadrant C we included the remaining 70% of companies that contributes only in a proportion of 31.6% to generate the global turnover.

2.2. *Ranking multinational companies by turnover*

Table 1.

No.	Company	Field of activity	Total turnover — EUR in mns
1.	OMV PETROM SA	Oil	36324,22
2.	AUTOMOBILE DACIA SA	Auto	16652,86
3.	ROMPETROL RAFINARE S.A.	Oil	16596,15
4.	ARCELOR MITTAL GALATI SA	Industry	14773,06
5.	METRO CASH & CARRY ROMANIA SRL	Retail	13193,46
6.	ROMTELECOM S.A.	IT	10121,96
7.	ORANGE ROMANIA SA	IT	9535,63
8.	ROMPETROL DOWNSTREAM SRL	Oil	9153,33
9.	VODAFONE ROMANIA SA	IT	8908,69
10.	LUKOIL ROMANIA SRL	Oil	8348,54

(Continued)

Table 1. (*Continued*)

No.	Company	Field of activity	Total turnover — EUR in mns
11.	GDF SUEZ ENERGY ROMANIA S.A	Energy	8302,65
12.	BRITISH AMERICAN TOBACCO (ROMANIA) TRADING	Retail	7653,44
13.	PETROTEL LUKOIL SA	Oil	6625,75
14.	CARREFOUR ROMANIA SA	Retail	6614,69
15.	SELGROS CASH&CARRY SRL	Retail	5552,93
16.	PORSCHE ROMANIA SRL	Auto	5340,44
17.	KAUFLAND ROMANIA SOCIETATE IN COMANDITA SIMPLA	Retail	5001,18
18.	NOKIA ROMANIA SRL	IT	4602,11
19.	JT INTERNATIONAL (ROMANIA) SRL	Retail	4257,9
20.	JTI MANUFACTURING SA	Retail	3983,55
21.	COCA COLA HBC ROMANIA SRL	Retail	3777,2
22.	CONTINENTAL AUTOMOTIVE PRODUCTS SRL	Auto	3519,85
23.	MEDIPLUS EXIM SRL	Pharma	3432,1
24.	MOL ROMANIA PETROLEUM PRODUCTS SRL	Oil	3425,6
25.	E.ON GAZ ROMANIA S.A.	Energy	3369,59
26.	REAL,- HYPERMARKET ROMANIA S.R.L.	Retail	3306,71
27.	CEZ DISTRIBUTIE SA	Energy	3123,97
28.	ENEL ENERGIE SA	Energy	3034,75
29.	OMV ROMANIA MINERALOEL SRL	Oil	2795,96
30.	PHILIP MORRIS TRADING S.R.L.	Retail	2731,09
31.	MICHELIN ROMANIA SA	Auto	2651,73
32.	DAEWOO-MANGALIA HEAVY INDUSTRIES SA	Industry	2567,99
33.	ROMANIA HYPERMARCHE SA	Retail	2408,63
34.	BILLA ROMANIA SRL	Retail	2335,14
35.	RENAULT INDUSTRIE ROUMANIE SRL	Industry	2131,37
36.	LAFARGE CIMENT (ROMANIA)SA	Retail	2097,19
37.	HEINEKEN ROMANIA SA	Industry	2093,85
38.	TOP BRANDS DISTRIBUTION SRL	Retail	2078,59
39.	HOLCIM (ROMANIA) SA	Industry	2071,71
40.	COSMOTE ROMANIAN MOBILE TELECOMMUNICATIONS SA	IT	1908,86
41.	URSUS BREWERIES S A	Industry	1905,41
42.	ARCTIC SA	Industry	1887,59
43.	TAKATA-PETRI ROMANIA	Auto	1799,54
44.	CEZ VANZARE	Energy	1701,52
45.	CARPATCEMENT HOLDING SA	Industry	1678,79
46.	FARMEXPERT DCI SA	Pharma	1645,49
47.	PROCTER & GAMBLE DISTRIBUTION SRL	Retail	1600,81
48.	PRAKTIKER ROMANIA SRL	Retail	1530,4
49.	ALFRED C.TOEPFER INTERNATIONAL (ROMANIA) SRL	Agriculture	1507,69
50.	SCHAEFFLER ROMANIA SRL	Auto	1503,57

(*Continued*)

Table 1. (Continued)

No.	Company	Field of activity	Total turnover — EUR in mns
51.	BUNGE ROMANIA SRL	Agriculture	1469,98
52.	CARGILL AGRICULTURA SRL	Agriculture	1398,74
53.	REWE ROMANIA SRL	Energy	1341,56
54.	E.ON MOLDOVA FURNIZARE SA	Energy	1046,15
55.	SENSIBLU SRL	Pharma	980,18
56.	HOLZINDUSTRIE SCHWEIGHOFER SRL	Industry	772,93
57.	ENEL ENERGIE MUNTENIA S.A.	Energy	637,55
58.	DISTRIGAZ SUD RETELE SRL	Energy	443,38

Compared to the field, it appears that the most multinational companies are operating in trade (16 companies), followed by energy and industrial areas (by 9 companies), and oil (6 companies). The situation reflects the structure of the Romanian economy, oriented mainly to areas with low added value and exploitation of natural resources.

Table 2.

No.	Domain	Number of companies
1.	Agriculture	3
2.	Auto	6
3.	Energy	9
4.	Industry	9
5.	IT	5
6.	Oil	7
7.	Pharma	3
8.	Retail	16

To increase the relevance of our analysis, we also consider the issue by the field of activity for the sample of the analyzed companies.

It can be ascertained that the largest weight in developing the global turnover of the 58 multinational analyzed is in the oil area (29.6%), which indicates relatively low level of development of the national economy, based mainly on primary operation natural resources, to which multinationals were oriented. The retail domain is following (24.2%), then IT (12.5%), and industry (10.6%). Although the situation may seems surprising, the change of positions held by retail and industry is caused by the change of orientation of the Romanian economy from one of production to one of consuption. It can be seen the very low percentage in agriculture domain (1.6%) to create overall turnover.

2.3. *Variation of turnover at the analyzed multinational companies*

Regarding to this criterion, it can be observed that the highest positive change for the entire analyzed period is at the company called CONTINENTAL AUROMOTIVE PRODUCTS SRL (678571%) due to expanding business in Romania by opening new factories especially in Transylvania, followed by ROMPETROL DOWNSTREAM SRL (274559%) — this is caused by the expansion of retail activity (opening of new stations), entering in the markets of neighboring countries and even in France by acquiring a chain of gas stations. CARPATCEMENT HOLDING SA is holding the third position (130 176%), its increase is due to the acquisition and modernization of production facilities and exports to the regional market. In the fourth position is the back network of retailers SELGROS CASH & CARRY SRL (53,793%) — increase in turnover, in this case, is generated by the increasing of Romanian customer's purchasing power and the expanding in national distribution. It is important to note that 30 companies (51.72% of the analyzed sample structure) recorded, in the period of 10 years, a growth in turnover below 10%, which indicates the hardships faced in domestic business development.

2.4. The evolution of gross profit for the sample of analyzed companies

It appears that 42 companies, representing 72.41% of the sample size were recorded profit in the analyzed period, the cumulative volume for all companies in the sample during the analyzed period being EUR 16,465,15 mn. Around 16 companies recorded operating loss in this period, the estimated volume being EUR 3169,37 mn.

Among the performers we would particularly highlight OMV PETROM SA with a level of EUR 4.275 mn, representing 25.96% of the total profit of the analyzed companies in those 10 years. In fact, if we were to classify firms according to the principle of ABC, the first five companies that make profits generates a contribution of 66.86% (EUR 11,009,22 mn) to complete this indicator. When referring to losses, we find that the highest loss record is at ROMPETROL RAFINARE (EUR −1122,247 mn) followed by COSMOTE ROMANIAN MOBILE TELECOMMUNICATIONS SA (EUR −418,291 mn), and PETROTEL LUKOIL SA (EUR −396,121 mn). Total losses in the analyzed companies are EUR −3169,37 mn.

2.5. Profitability ranking

Table 3.

No.	Company name	Level of the profit/ loss EUR mn
1.	OMV PETROM SA	4275,023
2.	ORANGE ROMANIA SA	3108,308
3.	VODAFONE ROMANIA SA	2269,092
4.	LAFARGE CIMENT (ROMANIA)SA	811,229
5.	PORSCHE ROMANIA SRL	545,57
6.	CARPATCEMENT HOLDING SA	509,962
7.	ROMTELECOM S.A.	500,086
8.	GDF SUEZ ENERGY ROMANIA S.A	461,856
9.	METRO CASH & CARRY ROMANIA SRL	448,044
10.	COCA COLA HBC ROMANIA SRL	424,044
11.	BRITISH AMERICAN TOBACCO (ROMANIA) TRADING	414,812
12.	AUTOMOBILE DACIA SA	257,032
13.	HOLCIM (ROMANIA) SA	252,262
14.	CEZ DISTRIBUTIE SA	243,479
15.	HEINEKEN ROMANIA SA	215,439
16.	ENEL ENERGIE SA	191,211
17.	SELGROS CASH&CARRY SRL	159,339
18.	URSUS BREWERIES S A	144,455
19.	CONTINENTAL AUTOMOTIVE PRODUCTS SRL	143,766
20.	ARCTIC SA	132,814
21.	NOKIA ROMANIA SRL	104,501

(*Continued*)

Table 3. (*Continued*)

No.	Company name	Level of the profit/loss EUR mn
22.	CARREFOUR ROMANIA SA	101,166
23.	MEDIPLUS EXIM SRL	100,341
24.	BILLA ROMANIA SRL	83,715
25.	MOL ROMANIA PETROLEUM PRODUCTS SRL	78,808
26.	ROMANIA HYPERMARCHE SA (CORA)	61,413
27.	OMV ROMANIA MINERALOEL SRL	47,789
28.	HOLZINDUSTRIE SCHWEIGHOFER SRL	46,288
29.	FARMEXPERT DCI SA	45,236
30.	E.ON MOLDOVA FURNIZARE SA	42,25
31.	PHILIP MORRIS TRADING S.R.L.	36,659
32.	PRAKTIKER ROMANIA SRL	35,386
33.	REWE ROMANIA SRL	34,93
34.	ENEL ENERGIE MUNTENIA S.A.	32,075
35.	KAUFLAND ROMANIA SOCIETATE IN COMANDITA SIMPLA	28,294
36.	PROCTER & GAMBLE DISTRIBUTION SRL	23,943
37.	LUKOIL ROMANIA SRL	20,002
38.	E.ON GAZ ROMANIA S.A.	11,051
39.	RENAULT INDUSTRIE ROUMANIE SRL	9,772
40.	TOP BRANDS DISTRIBUTION SRL	8,159
41.	DISTRIGAZ SUD RETELE SRL	4,831
42.	ALFRED C.TOEPFER INTERNATIONAL (ROMANIA) SRL	0,72
43.	CEZ VANZARE	−1,085
44.	SENSIBLU SRL	−7,834
45.	JTI MANUFACTURING SA	−14,715
46.	TAKATA-PETRI ROMANIA	−23,703
47.	CARGILL AGRICULTURA SRL	−31,729
48.	JT INTERNATIONAL (ROMANIA) SRL	−32,127
49.	SCHAEFFLER ROMANIA SRL	−54,698
50.	BUNGE ROMANIA SRL	−58,373
51.	ROMPETROL DOWNSTREAM SRL	−79,43
52.	MICHELIN ROMANIA SA	−99,985
53.	REAL,-HYPERMARKET ROMANIA SRL	−175,023
54.	DAEWOO-MANGALIA HEAVY INDUSTRIES SA	−278,539
55.	ARCELORMITTAL GALATI SA	−339,466
56.	PETROTEL LUKOIL SA	−369,121
57.	COSMOTE ROMANIAN MOBILE TELECOMMUNICATIONS SA	−481,291
58.	ROMPETROL RAFINARE S.A.	−1,122,247

2.6. Losses ranking

Table 4.

No.	Field name	Profit — in mn EUR	%	Loss — in mn EUR	%
1.	Agriculture	—	—	−234,113	7.39
2.	Auto	3437,344	20.92	−59,458	1.88
3.	Energy	587,697	.58	−2064,93	65.15
4.	Industry	910,234	5.54	−383,836	12.11
5.	IT	1610,706	9.80	—	—
6.	Oil	7811,228	47.53	—	—
7.	Pharma	100,341	0.61	−363,169	11.46
8.	Retail	1975,527	12.02	−63,856	2.01
	TOTAL	**16433,077**	**100**	**−3169,362**	**100**

As shown in Table 3, the highest proportion in creating global profits of analyzed multinational companies is held by the oil field (47.53%), followed by Auto sector (20.92%), and Retail (12.02%). The Table 5, relative to the turnover is illustrative:

Regarding the correlation of the turnover and profitability contribution in generating the total output is a contradictory situation.

So, the oil field maintain its supremacy in terms of contributing to the overall turnover for the analyzed multinational companies and has a correlation in profitability level also. Auto field, even if it has only the fourth contribution to the creation of annual global turnover is growing rapidly in terms of profitability.

An evolution of the same type with the record of oil field is also in the *retail field*, which ranks third in the ranking of profitability with the second contribution to the creation of global turnover.

Regarding the *correlation of the turnover with the losses*, we can observe that the energy field is on trend of increased risk (1st at loss) in the conditions of generating an average contribution to the formation of overall turnover (6th), and level of profit is also medium (position 6). This position is surprising because the literature considers that this area is one of the most active in generating higher added value.

A high level of risk (2nd at losses) associated with a higher profitability (1st place at profit), is recorded by the industry field, in the conditions of an average contribution to the creation of total turnover (5th), identical with the profitability ranking. It appears that two fields (IT and Oil) does not have companies with losses.

Table 5.

No.	Field	Turnover — places	Profit — places	Loss — places
1.	Agriculture	PLACE 8	PLACE 8	PLACE 4
2.	Auto	PLACE 4	**PLACE 2**	PLACE 6
3.	Energy	PLACE 6	PLACE 6	**PLACE 1**
4.	Industry	PLACE 5	PLACE 5	**PLACE 2**
5.	IT	**PLACE 3**	PLACE 4	PLACE 7-8
6.	Oil	**PLACE 1**	**PLACE 1**	PLACE 7-8
7.	Pharma	PLACE 7	PLACE 7	**PLACE 3**
8.	Retail	**PLACE 2**	**PLACE 3**	PLACE 5

2.7. *Top of the profitability rate*

It appears that only a total of 11 companies representing 18.9% of the sample size showed a profit rate higher than 10%. Among them stands out a group of companies (Lafarge Ciment (Romania) SA, ORANGE ROMANIA SA, CARPATCEMENT HOLDING SA, VODAFONE ROMANIA SA) which recorded a higher level of profitability of 30%. If at first sight is surprising the case of LAFARGE CIMENT (ROMANIA) SA and CARPACEMENT HOLDING SA, because they come from an industry where traditionally, the profitability rate is lower compared to the level achieved. I think it is better to rethink the position of this companies in the context in which they were involved, according to the Competition Council, in a monopoly investigation made in national market. A similar situation is recorded also for ORANGE ROMANIA SA and VODAFONE ROMANIA SA, investigated by the institution aforementioned.

After this is a group of seven companies with a profit rate situated between 10–15% (Holcim (Romania) SA, Coca Cola HBC Romania SRL, HEINEKEN ROMANIA SA, Ursus Breweries SA, PORSCHE ROMANIA SRL, OMV Petrom SA, CEZ DISTRIBUTION SA) which are operating in heterogeneous domains (industry, retail, energy).

Note the presence of a group of 17 companies (29.3% of the sample) which did not make profits in the analyzed period, and also the existence of a group of 26 companies (44.8% of total sample) with a profit rate between 1–5%.

On economic sectors, the situation is as follows:

Table 7.

	Profit rate%			
	[38–16]	[15–10]	[9–1]	Companies with losses
COMPANIES TOTAL	4	7	30	17
Agriculture	—	—	1	2
Auto	—	1	2	3
Energy	—	1	6	2
Industry	1	3	3	2
IT	2	—	2	1
Oil	—	1	3	3
Pharma	—	—	2	1
Retail	1	1	11	3

3. Conclusions

- It appears that there is a considerable disproportion between Bucharest (53% of representative multinational companies) and the rest of the country. On the second place is situated the Ilfov county (14%) receiving position near the capital and easy access to its infrastructure. The following is an array of five heterogeneous counties in terms of geographical location (Arges, Brasov, Constanta, Cluj, Dolj) which shows an appetite of some companies for some local opportunities generated by the aforementioned cities.
- Analyzing the territorial distribution of multinationals reported to the number of counties in the country we find that only 16 counties (38% of the national total) benefit from the presence of these powerful organizations, creating jobs and generating synergy at local level by subcontracting activities through the Romanian companies.
- In the multinationals analyzed, the global turnover between 2002–2013 was situated at EUR 206.712,22 mn. It is found that the top 10% of the companies like turnover contributes with 45% (EUR 89958,1 mn) to generate the final result. Next 20% of the companies generates 30% of global turnover (EUR 62092,88 mn). The remaining 70% of companies contributes with only 25% to create global turnover.
- In terms of the object of activity, 28% of multinational companies are operating in the Retail, followed by the energy and industry with 15%. Lowest interest is in the fields of agriculture and Pharma (3%).
- Contribution of the activity fields to create global turnover for analyzed period shows that oil has the highest contribution (31.1%), followed by retail industry (22.8%), and IT (12.6%). The lowest recorded contributions are in the Pharma (1.9%) and Agriculture (1.4%).
- It is important to note that 41 companies (70.6% of the analyzed sample structure) recorded in the period of 10 years a growth in turnover below 10%, which indicates the hardships faced in business development on local market.
- Around 43 companies, representing 74.1% of the sample size were recorded profit in the analyzed

period, this volume cumulated for all the companies from the sample in the analyzed period being EUR 13506,73 mn.
- A total of 15 companies recorded operating losses in the mentioned period, their volume is estimated at EUR -2273,38 mn.
- Top five companies that make profits generates a contribution of 65.83% (EUR 8891,49 mn) to achieve the global profit for the analyzed period.
- The highest share of global profit creation of the analyzed multinational companies is in oil field (31%), followed by energy (25%), and Pharma (17%).
- Regarding the correlation contribution in turnover and profitability in generating total output, the situation is contradictory. So, while the oil field maintains its supremacy in terms of contributing to overall turnover for analyzed multinational companies and it has a correlation in the level of profitability, the energy, even if it contributes only in a small proportion to create the global turnover, it has a rapid growth in terms of profitability. An evolution of the same type is also recording by the Pharma field, which is ranked No. 3 in our rankings even if it contributes only to a limited extent in creating turnover.
- Regarding the correlation of turnover and losses in activity is found that the IT field has a trend of increased risk (1st at loss) in condition of generating a significant contribution to create global turnover (No. 3) and registering a level of profit below expectations (8th). A high risk (No. 2 at losses) associated with a higher profitability (1st place at profit), is recorded by the energy, in condition of a modest contribution to create the global turnover (No. 6).
- As profit rate, it appears that only a total of 11 companies representing 18.9% of the sample size showed a profit rate higher than 10%. After them is a group of seven companies with a profit rate between 10–15%.
- Note the presence of a group of 17 companies (29.3% of the sample) did not make profit in the analyzed period, and the existence of a group of 26 companies (44.8% of total sample) with a profit rate between 1–5%.

References

Andreff, W. (1996), *Les Multinationales Globales*, Paris: Editions La Decouverte.

Caves, R. (1982), *Multinational Enterprise and Economic Analysis*, Cambridge: Cambridge University Press.

Ceptureanu, S. I. & Ceptureanu, E. G. (2012), Knowledge based management trends in Romanian companies, Knowledge Based Organization The 18th International Conference, Academia Fortelor Terestre Sibiu, Iunie 14–16.

Cowling, K. & Sugden, R.(1996), Capacity, transnational and industrial strategy. In *Creating Industrial Capacity*, J. Mitchie and J. Grieve Smith (eds.), Oxford: Oxford University Press.

Dunning, J. (1997), *Alliance Capitalism and Global Business*, London: Routledge.

Dunning, J. (1993), *Multinational Enterprises and the Global Economy*, Addison-Wesley.

Kessels, J. (2001), Learning in organisations: A corporate curriculum for the knowledge economy, *Futures*, 33.

Lawrence, R. (1994), Multinationals, trade and labour, Discussion Paper 4836, National Bureau of Economic Research, New York.

Mazilu, A. (2002), *Multinaționalele și Competitivitatea: O Perspectivă Est-Europeană*, București: Editura Economică.

Mereuță, C. (2004), *Analiza Nodală a Sistemelor de Companii*, București: Editura Economică.

Mereuță, C. (2006), Model de analiză a dinamicii performanțelor sistemului național de companii: Proiectul Centre de Excelență, Ministerul Educației și Cercetării.

Mereuță, C. (2009), Particularități ale repartițiilor cotelor de piață ale companiilor active pe piețele clasificate din perspectiva gradului de concentrare, Seminarul de Macromodelare Economică Nr. 102301.

Mereuță, C. și colab. (2003), *Sistemul Național de Companii și Performanța Acestora în Dezvoltarea Economică a României*, București: Editura Academiei Române.

Mereuță, C. et al. (2003), *România 2007: Industria Prelucrătoare Românească. Piețe și Potențial*. București: Editura Finmedia.

Mereuță, C. & Ciupagea, C. ș.a. (2000), *Industria Prelucrătoare Românească 1990–1998: Diagnostic Structural*. București: Editura Expert.

Nicolescu, O., Plumb, I., Pricop, M., Vasilescu, I., & Verboncu, I. (2003), *Abordări Moderne în Managementul si Economia Organizației*, București: Editura Economică.

Pfeffer, J. (2005), Working alone: Whatever happened to the idea of organisations as communities. In *America at Work — Choises and Challenges*, E. Lawer III and J. O'Toole, London: Palgrave MacMillan.

Popa, I. (2003), Rețele de firme și clustere. In *Sistemul Organizatoric al Firmei*, O. Nicolescu (ed.), București: Editura Economica.

Porter, M. (1980), *Competitive Strategies*, New York: Free Press.

Puiu, A. (1996), *Management în Afacerile Economice Internaționale*, București: Independenta Economica.

Rieder, W. J. (2006), Corporate dealings with network economy, *Futures*, 38.

Rugman, A. & Hodgets, R. (1995), International Business — a strategic approach, International edition, New York: Mc-Graw Hill Publisher.

Part VII

Management of Change, Innovation, and Quality

Chapter 37

Study Regarding the Correlation between the Changes in the Energy Economy and the Competitiveness of Companies in Germany and Romania

Gregor Johannes Weber, Marieta Olaru and Georgiana Marin

Bucharest University of Economic Studies

This chapter is part of a first year doctoral research of current state of knowledge in energy economics and its impacts to enterprises in Europe. Its aim is to highlight the relationship between the changes in the energy economics and the competitiveness of the companies in Germany and Romania.

In order to show this relationship, feedback of companies in Germany and Romania were gathered through a questionnaire-based field study in June 2013 with 2,394 replies in Germany and 103 in Romania.

In the first section, the interviewees were asked to provide general data as well as a general judgment of the changes in the energy economics to their business. The second section focused on the importance of the changes of selected energy factors during the last 12 months. To conclude, the companies were asked to judge the changes in the energy economy during the observation period generally.

The collected data was evaluated following a quantitative one dimensional frequency scale, a methodology recommended for such researches by several authors in the literature.

It was found out that, correlation between the amount of energy prices and the importance of energy efficiency measures exists; especially in Germany with its much higher energy price levels. For energy supply interruptions on the other hand no direct correlation was recognized.

The impact of the changes in the energy economics on the competitiveness of their company was generally rated *neutral with a slight trend to negative* by the German respondents; the Romanian enterprises however, assessed this impact much more *negatively*.

Concluding, correlations between the changes in the energy economy and the competitiveness of companies could be confirmed in both countries. The higher the electricity prices are the more important energy efficiency measures become.

1. Introduction

The German energy transition is in the worldwide focus and is differently assessed. Some researchers believe it is a risky journey; others rate it as a reverent power, and as an opportunity.

The energy economics in Germany started a long journey of change, starting with the establishment of the EU policy for the privatization of the power industry into the national law (Kemfert, 2013: 44). This process of change finally turned 2010 into a national energy concept. The government based this plan on several studies, which confirmed that the German energy transition can be realized. The energy concept of the German government (Prognos, EWI, GWS, 2010: 188–193) presented scenarios confirming the technical feasibility for a change to a primary renewable energy production by 2050, also being confirmed by additional studies.[1] Furthermore, the mentioned scenarios confirmed that compared to other energy sourcing strategies, this process also offers benefits to the national economy. The decision to pull-out from the nuclear energy production was followed by studies researching electricity cost, greenhouse gas development, and the projected electricity imports (BET, *Ökoinstitut*, ZNES, Greenpeace, R2B Energy Consulting).[2]

In the following years, the feed-in-tariff system had to undergo several minor changes accompanied by a debate on high electricity prices. Right now, the EEG 2.0 (major change to the renewable energy law in Germany) is being debated strongly with the objective for parliament approval by August 01, 2014 (BMWi, 2014); changes to the levels of electricity prices are hereby again to be expected.

Whereas the renewable energy labor market in Germany was called to be a rising star in the job market, a booster for economic growth and employment (BMU, 2012: 18) during the earlier years (BMU, 2012), company close-downs, and a decrease in employment resulted from the political activities during the following years (BMU, 2013). A high electricity price level combined with decreasing feed-in-tariffs caused a major problem for the competitiveness of such enterprises being active in the construction business for power plants for renewable energies in Germany. This effect was caused by the reluctance of investors and banks to finance such power plants within the uncertain financial frame. As a study, IZA recently detected (IZA, 2013) the long-term development of this trend needs to be further observed in order to be confirmed.

Another result of the activities in changing the energy system, are the steadily increasing electricity prices in Germany, currently among the highest in Europe (statista, 2012), (BDEW, 2013). Compared to Romania, the electricity prices for German enterprises are in average 50% higher. This pressure to the German industry is partially caused by Germany being one of the countries with the highest levels for electricity tax in Europe, as researched by the BDI (German association of the industry) in 2011 (BDI & VCI, 2011: 31). Whilst the prices for electricity in Germany are on this uncompetitive high level, direct neighbor states can offer a much more competitive position (Bureau, *et al.*, 2013: 4). Enterprises in France and the United Kingdom for example, benefit from much lower prices for electricity mainly produced through nuclear power plants.

The discussion on energy prices for the industry however should be seen in the correct context (Bureau *et al.*, 2013). Energy prices for the industry consist of several components. On one hand there are direct and fixed costs for the production process, on the other hand, there are the so called add-on-cost; the latter ones being taxes, grid usage cost, VAT (Value Added Tax), and various additional allocations (BMWi, 2013). A market that is influenced by artificially controlled electricity prices (regulated prices) is reflecting a false image of the real cost situation. Enterprises acting in such a man-made environment will base their management decisions on wrong assumptions leading to inefficient energy sourcing choices on one hand and to uneconomic decisions on energy efficiency measures on the other hand; furthermore, strategically these enterprises will struggle to changes to that regulated system.

This is the case currently in Germany. The pressure on the German industry is being strongly debated in the context of uncompetitiveness comparing the electricity prices in the industry amongst its European partners. A comparison of the electricity tax level by the BDI (German association of the industry) in 2011 (BDI & VCI, 2011: 31) highlights Germany with a substantial electricity tax disadvantage to its partners. In order not to overstress companies, exceptions from the EEG-allocation[3] were approved by the German government for those companies with large electricity consumption

---

[1] (Ökoinstitut, Prognos, 2009), (SRU — Sachverständigenrat für Umweltfragen, 2011), (DLR, Fraunhofer IWES, IfnE, 2010), (Umweltbundesamt, 2010).

[2] (BET, 2010), (ZNES (*Zentrum für nachhaltige Energiesysteme*), 2011), (Greenpeace, 2011), (R2B, 2011), (*Ökoinstitut e.V.*, 2010).

[3] EEG-allocation: With the introduction of renewable energies in Germany, the EEG (law for renewable energies) defined the feed-in tariffs. The EEG-allocation was introduced in order to finance the feed-in-tariff system.

to help them stay internationally competitive. Consequently, the remaining companies and public consumers have to compensate the value/amount of these exceptions. The European Commission recently opened a case against the German government with the objective to evaluate whether these exceptions to the EEG-allocation allow a competitive advantage to German companies in the European context, which would be acceptable, being a market distortion. In this context, it is very important to ensure a European wide coordination for such activities and exceptions, especially once grid costs are concerned (Bureau *et al.*, 2013: 6).

The gas market appears in a similar situation with gas prices in Germany being double the level of the prices in Romania (AHK Germany-Romania, 2013: 22) turning the energy price levels for Germany generally to an extraordinary uncompetitive level not only compared to Romania.

There are many studies available already. An investigation on the perception of the changes in the energy economics comparing the enterprises in Germany and Romania was so far not performed though. Filling that gap, a questionnaire-based field research was performed interviewing the members of the German DIHK[4] and the corresponding German–Romanian Chamber of Commerce and Industry (AHK) Bucharest in Romania. The resulting 2,394 answered questionnaires in Germany and 103 in Romania were analyzed regarding whether the changes in the energy economics over a 12 months period were perceived more as a risk, or an opportunity by the participating enterprises in the selected countries as well as on the correlation between the changes in the energy economy and the competitiveness of companies in Germany and Romania.

2. Current Trends Regarding Changes in the Energy Economy

The changing conditions in the energy economics combined with the accompanying measures in the political surroundings clearly illustrate a high level of impact on competitive objectives. Interruptions in the energy supply also need to be considered in the context of the level of supply security.

Price competiveness is a key element for enterprises to be successful in the market. Factors that influence this increase in production can be labor cost, transport cost, distribution cost, as well as energy cost. In the short-term, the increase in production costs negatively affects the price of the companies activities (Bureau *et al.*, 2013: 7) and with that their competitiveness. If the enterprise follows a revenue focused strategy, the result will be a reduction in sales volume. In case the market share is the driving element for their business decisions, a decreased margin will come out. In both cases, at one point, the decision needs to be taken whether to stop the activities or not.

One option during this process is to take measures to reduce energy costs by reducing the energy consumption. This can be realized by a more conscious consumption of energy on one hand; another option is to push for energy efficiency measures. As mentioned before, this effect could be observed in the case of the respondent enterprises in Germany. With the uncompetitive level of the electricity price in Germany compared to Romania, energy saving measures became more important than ever to the German companies, which also proves the direct correlation between these two elements.

A high level of energy prices (electricity as well as gas) is forcing companies to counteracting measures in the area of energy efficiency activities. In Romania, however, this trend is due to the low level of energy prices. Caused by the high level of energy prices, being among the highest in Europe, especially Germany, the amount of the energy prices plays a very important factor. The effect of the rising energy prices in Germany naturally, also has negative effects on the labor market, which is confirmed by a recent study of (IZA, 2013).

Changes of energy prices in general should be announced in a reliable way. On one hand, planning and building of power plants is a long-lasting process. Reliability, here is very important for planners as well as credit institutes for their feasibility studies and calculations. On the other hand, enterprises also need planning security through long-term energy price levels, to

---

[4] DIHK — Association of German Chambers of Commerce and Industry (*Deutscher Industrie und Handelskammertag*, DIHK (DIHK, 2014)) representing 80 Chambers of Commerce and Industry, CCI (*Industrie und Handelskammern*, IHKs) in Germany with more than three million entrepreneurs of companies of all sizes.

be able to properly plan their production processes and pricing/positioning strategies in a global market place.

In order to counteract the negative effects of energy price increases, appropriate measures on energy efficiency are to be undertaken. On the other hand, activities in R&D are also required, in order to keep the level of innovation high (Bureau *et al.*, 2013: 12; Berk *et al.*, 2006: 4). This will ensure a high level of competitiveness, as well as an advantage of being a leader in key technology, which will strengthen the economies position towards competing economies.

In a study performed by the Netherlands Environmental Assessment Agency (PBL), (Berk *et al.*, 2006) several impacts of technological options on various policy objectives were investigated. One of the mentioned policy objectives was the competitiveness, detailed in the two factors costs and EU-innovation. The technological options were clustered in the groups such as efficiency, energy production forms (nuclear, renewable, fossil), carbon capture and storage, fuel switch, and others (public transport, emission controls, etc.).

From the cost point of view, the impacts were mainly rated insignificant with a trend to negative, which needs to be compared to the analysis performed in this chapterfor the German and Romanian enterprises in the context of the lower level of energy costs in the Romanian market compared to Germany. From an EU-innovation point of view, most of the impacts were rated neutral with a trend towards positive. All elements with the highest cost / investment requirements were rated positively regarding innovation (advanced cars, hydrogen, photovoltaic energy, and emission controls). This study is already eight years old,its results are still accurate today. They also indicate that a financial effort through R&D into innovative energy production and efficiency measures in the short-term, is perceived as a negative impact to the competiveness of an economy. In the long-term however, this investment will pay out and ensure a lower cost level through competitive advantage (Berk *et al.*, 2006: 7).

3. Research Methodology

In order to highlight the relationship between the changes in the energy economics and the competitiveness of the companies in Germany and Romania, a questionnaire based research has been carried out by the German DIHK (*Deutscher Industrie und Handelskammertag*) and the German–Romanian Chamber of Commerce and Industry (AHK), Bucharest in Romania in June 2013 with 2,394 replies in Germany and 103 in Romania. The questionnaires focused on several aspects.

One aspect addressed the collection of general data concerning branch of activity, number of employees, the share of energy costs in general and the electricity costs in particular on the overall turnover, as well as the general judgment of the changes in the energy economics.

The second section focused on the importance of selected factors during the last 12 months.

To conclude, the companies were asked to judge selected political measures according to their energy supply security, affordability, and environmental friendliness.

The data was evaluated following a quantitative one dimensional frequency scale, a methodology recommended by several authors in the literature.[5]

For the performed analysis, the relative frequencies $[p_i]$ of the selected elements and their related subcategories were calculated based on the absolute frequencies $[n_i]$ and the sample size $[n]$ following the context "$p_i = \frac{n_i}{n}$" and transferred into visual bar diagrams for interpretation.

4. Research Results

4.1. *Change of importance selected elements of the energy market*

In order to understand the importance of the energy market evolution, selected elements have been analyzed, namely:

- Amount of electricity price;
- Amount of energy price;
- Fluctuation of energy prices;
- Energy savings;
- Interruptions in electricity supply;
- Interruptions in gas supply.

---

[5] Koch (2012, p. 194), Herrmann & Homburg (2000), Olbrich *et al.* (2012), Christof & Pepels (1999), Grunwald & Hempelmann (2012), Altobelli & Hoffmann (2011), Homburg & Krohmer (2009), Wöhe (1986), Kotler (1982).

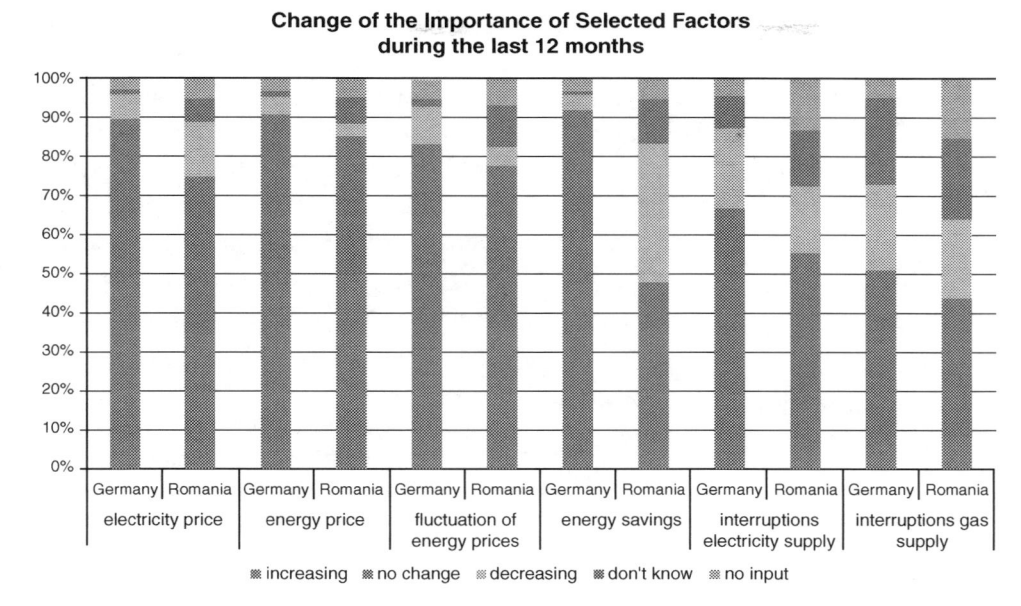

Fig. 1. Change of the importance of the energy market selected elements
Source: Developed by the authors.

Focusing on the lower three pillars in Fig. 1, in all cases, the *decreasing importance* is the least distinctive. Only in the case of supply interruptions (gas and electricity) the decreasing pillar is handing a little share to the increasing pillar. The only big exception is the element of energy savings: whereas in Germany, energy savings became more important, Romania shows an unchanged level of importance.

Supply interruptions do not show remarkable changes.

Fluctuations of energy prices as well the levels of energy prices (be it the amount for energy in general or electricity) show a trend towards *increased importance* for enterprises in both countries. On top, electricity prices and energy savings are more distinctive in Germany compared to Romania, which is a result of the much higher energy prices in Germany compared to Romania as outlined earlier.

4.2. *The impact of changes in the energy economics on the competitiveness of the company*

Being asked to provide a general statement of the changes in the energy systems during the last 12 months on the competitiveness of the companies, the German respondents provided mainly a neutral (41.2%) to negative (26.6%) rating, with the industry branch pushing the overall trend towards negative (34.7%). Comparing the enterprises by the number of employees in the German companies, a significant impact could not be discovered.

In Romania, a negative judgment became with 42.7% apparent and more significant, being mainly driven by the branches Industry (46.9%) and Service (50%). The companies with a larger number of employees indicated with 50% a higher level of negative judgment.

The fact that the changes in the energy system are already for a longer period of time present and publicly discussed in Germany, the companies already were in a

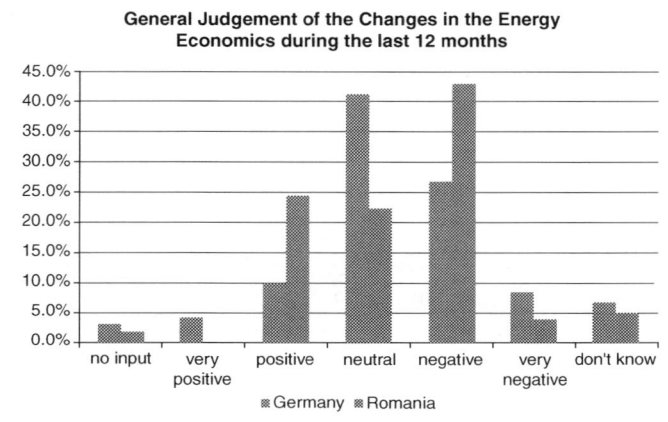

Fig. 2. Impact of the changes in the energy economics on the competitiveness of the company
Source: Developed by the authors.

position to adjust to the changing energy, economy system, and prices. Consequently, they are already a step ahead and the system changes are rated already with a higher level of "normality" compared to Romania. This is resulting into a less extreme judgment of the energy transition. However, the pendulum still is tending to be on the negative side.

5. Conclusion

The research carried out that electricity prices and energy savings are more distinctive in Germany compared to Romania. This is the result of much higher energy prices in Germany compared to Romania.

Another finding highlights the need to take measures in order to reduce energy costs by reducing the energy consumption. This can be realized by a more conscious consumption of energy. Another way of reducing the energy consumption is to undertake selected procedures in the production processes as well as the use of energy efficient equipment and the introduction of an energy management system according to ISO 50001.

The results showed that interruptions in the energy supply are not the major concern of the respondents. Fluctuating energy prices and a high the price level for energy are causing headaches to the entrepreneurs in both countries; Germany more than in Romania, due to its higher energy price levels.

Being asked on their judgment on the changes in the energy economy, the respondents in both countries indicated different trends. In Germany, the opinion on the changing energy environment is predominantly neutral, mainly as the energy transition is already on everyones' schedule for some time. In Romania however, these changes are still new, which explains a more concerned feedback from the Romanian enterprises.

In general, the atmosphere concerning the changes in the energy economics tends to be negative for both countries. In Germany, where these changes have some history, the enterprises are already more prepared/used to these challenges. In Romania, where the energy system also starts to undergo changes during the adaptation process with the rest of Europe, the enterprises are facing a new situation.

Summarizing, it could be confirmed that changes in energy economics are very important to the competitiveness of the enterprises in both countries. These findings directionally also confirmed the outcome of the NEAA-study on trade-offs and synergies between energy security, competitiveness, and environment mentioned in Chapter 1 (Berk *et al.*, 2006).

The information gained from this research will be used in a later stage in order to develop recommendations to politics and well to the enterprises for a smoother and sustainable rebuild of the energy systems in both countries as well as in Europe. In order to reach to that level, the replies to several additional questions will be analyzed throughout this doctoral research and reported in additional chapters.

References

AHK Germany–Romania (2013), Industrieeffizienz, prozessindustrie und logistik in rumänien [pdf]. Bucharest: Deutsch-Rumänische industrie- und handelskammer. Available at http://www.efficiency-from-germany.info/EIE/Redaktion/Datenmigration/marktanalyse-rumaenien-2013-industrie,property=pdf,bereich=eie,sprache=de,rwb=true.pdf (Accessed 10 March 2014).

Altobelli, C. F. & Hoffmann, S. (2011), *Grundlagen der Marktforschung*, Konstanz: UVK *Verlagsgesellschaft* mbH. BDEW, (2013), *Strompreisanalyse Mai* (2013), [pdf] Available at http://www.bdew.de/internet.nsf/id/123176ABDD9ECE5DC1257AA20040E368/$file/13%2005%2027%20BDEW_Strompreisanalyze_Mai%202013.pdf (Accessed 02 March 2014).

BDI & VCI, (2011), *Die Steuerbelastung der unternehmen in deutschland — fakten für die politische diskussion* 2011 [pdf], Köln, Germany: *institut der deutschen wirtschaft köln medien* GmbH. Available at http://www.bdi.eu/download_content/BDI_VCI__Steuerbelastung_der_Unternehmen_2011.pdf (Accessed 10 March 2014).

Berk, M. M., Bollen J. C., Eerens, H. C., Manders, A. J. G., & van Vuuren, D. P. (2006), MNP report 500116001/2006, Sustainable energy: Trade-offs and synergies between energy security, competitiveness, and environment. Available at http://pblweb10.prolocation.net/sites/default/files/cms/publicaties/500116001.pdf (Accessed 11 March 2014).

BET, (2010), Marktplatz energie — kernkraftwerk laufzeitverlängerung. Available at https://www.yumpu.com/de/document/view/2944268/marktplatz-energie-10-2010-bet-aachen (Accessed 05 July 2013).

BMU, (2012a), Erneuerbare energien — Motor der energiewende. [pdf] Berlin: Bundesministerium für umwelt, naturschutz und rektorsicherheit. Available at http://www.erneuerbare-energien.de/fileadmin/Daten_EE/Dokumente__PDFs_/Motor_der_Energiewende_bf.pdf (Accessed 10 March 2014).

BMU, (2012b), Erneuerbar beschäftigt! Kurz — und langfristige wirkungen des ausbaus erneuerbarer energien auf den deutschen arbeitsmarkt [pdf] Berlin: Bundesministerium für umwelt, naturschutz und reaktorsicherheit. Available at http://www.bmub.bund.de/fileadmin/Daten_BMU/Pools/Broschueren/EE_beschaeftigt_bf.pdf (Accessed 10 March 2014).

BMU, (2013), Renewable employed — impacts of the expansion of renewable energy on the German labour market [pdf]. Available at http://www.bmub.bund.de/fileadmin/Daten_BMU/Pools/Broschueren/erneuerbar_beschaeftigt_faltblatt_en_bf.pdf (Accessed 10 March 2014).

BMWi, (2013), Energiedaten: Ausgewählte grafiken [pdf]. Available at http://www.bmwi.de/BMWi/Redaktion/PDF/E/energiedaten-ausgewaehlte-grafiken,property=pdf,bereich=bmwi2012,sprache=de,rwb=true.pdf (Accessed 11 March 2014).

BMWi, (2014), Eckpunkte für die reform des EEG [pdf]. Available at www.bmwi.de/DE/Themen/energie,did=617196.html (Accessed 10 March 2014).

Bureau, D., Fontagné, L., & Martin, P. (2013), Energy and competitiveness [pdf]. Available at http://www.cae-eco.fr/IMG/pdf/cae-note006-en.pdf (Accessed 11 March 2014).

Christof, K. & Pepels, W. (1999), *Praktische quantitaive marktforschung*, München: Verlag Franz Vahlen GmbH.

DIHK, (2013), Faktenpapier — Strompreie in Deutschland [pdf]. Available at http://www.ihk-energieeffizienz.de/media/upload/initiativerheinlandengerie/imap/20121129/121129DIHKFaktenpapier_Strompreise.PDF (Accessed 14 March 2014).

DIHK, (2014), DIHK Facts. Available at http://www.dihk.de/en (Accessed 03 March 2014).

DLR, Fraunhofer IWES, IfnE, (2010), *Leitstudie* 2010 [pdf]. Available at http://www.fvee.de/fileadmin/politik/bmu_leitstudie2010.pdf (Accessed 14 March 2014).

Greenpeace, (2011), Der Plan — *Deutschland ist erneurbar* [pdf]. Available at http://www.greenpeace.de/fileadmin/gpd/user_upload/themen/energie/20110501-Der-Plan-Energiewende-ohne-Atom-und-Kohle.pdf (Accessed 17 February 2014).

Grunwald, G. & Hempelmann, B. (2012), *Angewandte Marktforschung*, München: Oldenbourg verlag.

Herrmann, A. & Homburg, C. (2000), *Marktforschung*, Wiesbaden: Betriebswirtschaftlicher verlag gabler GmbH.

Homburg, C. & Krohmer, H. (2009), *Marketing management*, Wiesbaden: Gabler GWV fachverlage GmbH.

IZA (Institute for the Study of Labour), (2013), Labor demand effects of rising electricity prices: Evidence for Germany [pdf].Available at http://ftp.iza.org/pp74.pdf (Accessed 10 March 2014).

Kemfert, C. (2013), *Kampf um Strom*, Hamburg: Murmann-Verlag.

Koch, J. (2012), *Marktforschung*, Nürnberg: Oldenbourg wissenschaftsverlag GmbH.

Kotler, P. (1982), *Marketing management*, Stuttgart: J.B. Metzlersche verlagsbuchhandlung und carl ernst poeschel verlag GmbH.

Ökoinstitut, E.V. (2010), Erste auswertungen der "Energieszenarien für ein energie-konzept der bundesregierung". Available at http://www.oeko.de/publikationen/forschungsberichte/studien/dok/657.php (Accessed 17 February 2014).

Ökoinstitut, P. (2009), Modell Deutschland, Klimaschutz bis 2050 [pdf]. Available at http://www.wwf.de/fileadmin/fm-wwf/Publikationen-PDF/WWF_Modell_Deutschland_Endbericht.pdf (Accessed 17 February 2014).

Olbrich, R., Battenfeld, D., & Buhr, C.C. (2012), *Marktforschung*, Berlin, Heidelberg: Springer Gabler Verlag.

Prognos, ewi, gws. (2010), *Energieszenarien für ein energiekonzept der bundesregierung*, Basel, Köln, Osnabrück: BMWi.

R2B, (2011), *Energieökonomische analyze eines ausstiegs aus der kernenergie in Deutschland bis zum Jahr 2017*, Köln: BDI e.v.

SRU Sachverständigenrat für Umweltfragen, (2011), *Wege zur 100% erneuerbaren stromversorgung*, Berlin: Erich Schmidt Verlag GmbH.

Statista, (2012), Strompreise für industriekunden in Europa 2012. Available at http://de.statista.com/statistik/daten/studie/151260/umfrage/strompreise-fuer-industriekunden-in-europa/ (Accessed 02 March 2014).

Umweltbundesamt, (2010), (2050): *100% Strom aus erneurbaren energien*, Dessau-Roßlau: Umweltbundesamt.

Wöhe, G. (1986), *Einführung in die allgemeine betriebswirtschaftslehre*, München: Verlag franz vahlen GmbH.

ZNES (Zentrum für nachhaltige Energiesysteme), (2011), *Atomausstieg 2015 und regionale versorgungssicherheit*, Flensburg/Berlin: Deutsche umwelthilfe, universität flensburg.

Chapter 38

Management of Intangible Assets Valorization in Small and Medium Enterprises

Constantin Oprean, Mihail Aurel Țîțu, and Claudiu Vasile Kifor

Lucian Blaga University

In the context of the knowledge-based economy, investment in intangible assets represents the successful alternative for attaining economic growth and increasing the quality of economic performances. SMEs represent the main worldwide drive for economic development, innovation and flexibility.

The aim of this study is to draw up an EU approved methodology for intangible assets valorization in SMEs. Such a methodology is the outcome of analyses and proposals submitted by representatives of the research community like HEIs, State Office for Inventions and Trademarks, Chambers of Commerce, Industry and Agriculture, Financial and Banking institutions, as well as representatives of SMEs.

The main goal is to facilitate funding, based on thorough criteria for SMEs evaluation in view of achieving a significant increase in the absorptive capacity of the knowhow generated by the research community in order to support the innovation process of new products and technologies, and, on the long run, lead to economic growth.

1. Introduction

Market economy represents that competitive economy based on the market laws generated by the plurality of the ownership forms in which private property is predominant, and which determines organizations to take part in a global competition. In order to become competitive, organizations are forced to mandatorily promote entrepreneurship and innovation, to significantly use the intangible assets, meaning the information and to transform it into knowledge.

The level of the organizations' steps for innovation can be taken into account and evaluated. A global indicator of innovation, which would represent a sum of the global indicators of the organizations in a country, can also constitute an image of the steps for innovation of that country.

In the context of meeting the Europe 2020 Strategy and the objectives aimed at, the European Parliament, The Council, The European, and Social Committee and the Committee of the Regions 2013 show that the focus of efforts on innovation constitute a rational undertaking of the organizations' sustainability and of the countries in question (The Commision to the European Parliament, the Council, the European Economic and Social Committee and the Commitee of the Regions 2003. Brussels: COM). Improving these performances will contribute to the intelligent growth. Such an indicator of measuring the results of innovation at country level (Fig. 1) or at organizational level (Fig. 2), refers to: *technological innovation measured in patents*, which shows the ability of an economy to transform knowledge into technologies and the increased accessibility to the values of the intellectual property (IP) system; *the investment in education and training* that will ensure the human resource with skills and competences to generate innovation; *the competitive level of the goods and services made* based on knowledge and *the volume of employees from the innovative sectors in companies characterized by rapid growth.*

The present chapter aims at estimating the potential value of the intangible capital, represented especially by the invention patents in the small and medium enterprises through facilitation procedures accepted by all interested parties: research institutions, banks, small, and medium enterprises, etc.

2. The Win–Win Partnership in Processing the Intangible Assets

The partnership represents a correlation between parties, with rights and obligations to accomplish a common objective, from which all parties will win according to their level of participation and contribution.

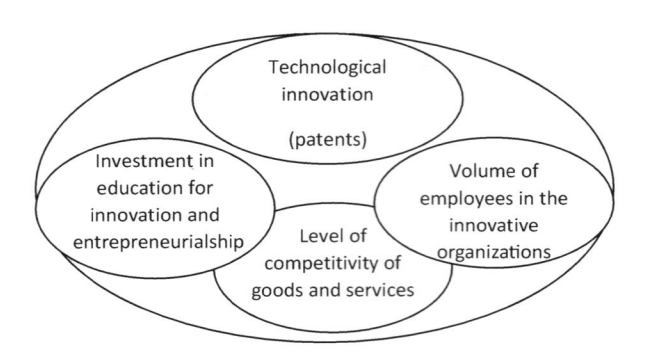

Fig. 1. Degree of innovation at living standards

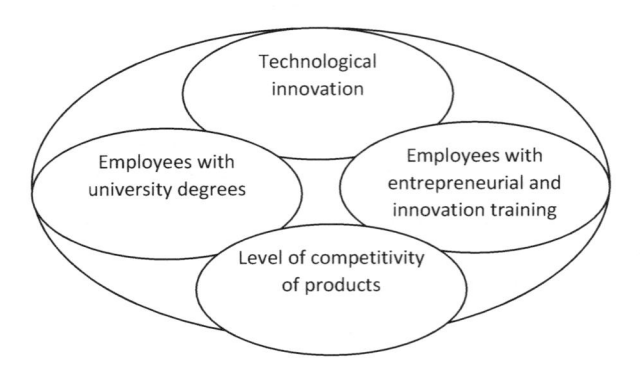

Fig. 2. Degree of innovation at organizational level

When the knowhow transfer occurs, regarding intangible assets, it is necessary for us to approach the identification of all partners that intervene in the life cycle of such an intangible asset, out of which, the most representative is, the invention, whose owner is certified by the invention patent which ensures the intellectual ownership right represented by the exclusive right of producing and commercializing it.

A graphic representation of the life cycle of evaluating the intangible asset, such as the invention patent from its creation to its transformation into a product that is useful to the society, with all involved partners, is represented in Fig. 3.

However, one must mention that together with the IP (patents, codified knowledge, data bases, procedures, commercial marks and brands, drawings and models) in the complete understanding of intangible assets *the human resources* (entrepreneurial experience, education and the competences of the staff, the know-how and the tacit knowledge, the motivation, and loyalty of the staff) must also be considered. *The organizational capital* (methods and production procedures, supply of services, certifications, tools, and management systems, the administrative system) and *the relational capital* (attracting the client, management of the client portfolio, suppliers' management, cooperation and networks).

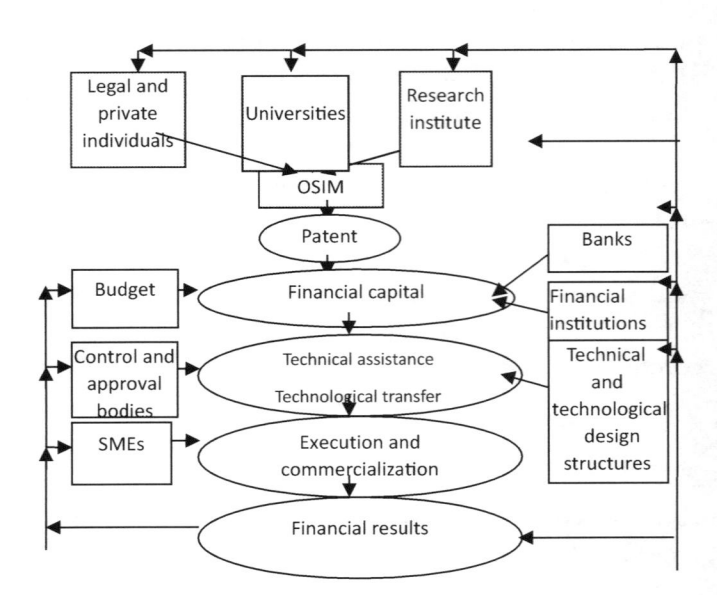

Fig. 3. The life cycle of evaluating the intangible assets

3. Valorization of the Intellectual Property in the SMEs

The chapter aims at offering rapid and efficient solutions of know-how transfer represented by the invention patent, the most representative element of IP in the small and medium enterprises, organizations that constitite the motor of the economy of any country. Their ability to grow constitutes the determinant key of the economic health for the future of any country.

In the last years the investments in businesses in the field of intangible assets, especially in the IP, have increased, much more than in the fixed and physical assets (Tomlison & Fai, 2013).

As opposed to the material resources, which have the tendency of growing, the intangible resources are inexhaustible and increasing. This is the reason why the investment in the intangible assets is the best solution for the sustainability of the organizations and of the entire society.

The SMEs that have the capacity to absorb the knowhow and even to create inventions and new processes are known as *innovative SMEs*. "These organizations have the potential of substantially contributing to the increase of competitiveness, productivity and technological progress in their sectors of activity and in the entire economy" (Pederzoli *et al.*, 2013) and "they can be identified through their patenting activities and through the high degree of flexibility which allows them to answer more actively the market demands" (Thomä & Bizer, 2013).

In the innovation process the SMEs need collaboration and pragmatic partnerships with the representatives and suppliers of scientific research, such as universities and research institutes (Zeng *et al.* 2010) but also with the financial institutes and banks that can ensure the financial support for transforming ideas into a real, commercial product.

Additionally, the country governments need to offer subsidies for the investments in those inventions that ensure development and commercialization (Brant & Lohse, 2013).

In order to ensure the framework necessary for the rapid and efficient transfer of the IP at the SME level and transforming it in competitive products, a methodology dedicated to the financial and economic evaluation of the intangible assets of the SMEs in partnership with the financial institutions in the vision of the researches done within the European project EVLIA (South East Europe Transnational Cooperation Programme, 2012). EVLIA-Making full value of good ideas by leveraging intellectual assets for financing SMEs in SEE), in which Lucian Blaga University of Sibiu is partner, is suggested.

Generally, in the case of the loans for the valorisation of a project, the warranties are ensured through the tangible assets because their value is easier to quantify than the value of the intangible assets. In this case, the banks and the financial institutions aim at considerably reducing the risk of getting the loan back. However, in the past years the intangible assets start to play the role of loan warranties for banks and financial institutions in the case of the SMEs and the patent markets are growing.

The patent market can become one of the main elements of innovation because it facilitates the spreading of innovative ideas through its capacity to encourage the circulation of patents between a large number of organizations.

Generally, banks are reluctant in accepting intangible assets as warranties to the loan, as foreseen by the Basel Regulations.

The investment in knowhow remains the most important success strategy even if the risks are considerable. That is why, the manner in which we evaluate this risk cannot lead to extraordinary results based on a performant risk management, taking into account the market, cost, and income approaches.

The utility of all evaluation approaches and the frequency of using them vary according to the scope aimed at.

The cost approach is the most suitable for evaluating out of financial accounting and profit taxation reasons, the income approach is chosen with the purpose of evaluating inheritance taxes and for collaterals that concentrate on the future generated income, the market approach is for the evaluation of an internal management purpose which usually requires the monetary value of the IP in order to allocate some resources and to evaluate the performances.

According to the EVLIA analysis, the intangible assets can be divided into:

- Relevant and available assets;
- Relevant and unavailable assets;
- Irrelevant and available assets;
- Irrelevant and unavailable assets.

The management phases of the intangible assets refer to:

- Creation (how was the asset obtained);
- Functioning (it is being presently used and what benefits it supplies);
- Planning (is the regeneration of assets being managed);
- Transferability (the value transferred to another entity).

From the point of view of the creation the evaluation aims at:

- The investments in the research-development (time and financial capital);
- The ability to create inventions;
- The number of patents reported to years;
- The number of patents registered;
- The number of valid patents;
- Geographical coverage;
- The context of implementation.

From the point of view of the functioning the evaluation refers to:

- The management and the protection of inventions;
- The effect of the inventions on the volume of sales (%);
- Exploitation of the inventions according to the potential (%).

In evaluating the level of programming one follows:

- The management and the updating and monitoring level;
- The control activities on the competition;
- Planning the activities in order to complete or to make the exploitation more effective and more efficient.

Regarding the evaluation from the point of view of transferability one looks if:

- The inventions are related to certain special goods of the enterprise;
- If there is interest for the competitive organizations;
- If there is interest for the non-competitive organizations or for other sectors.

In the SME evaluation by the financial institutions and banks, drawing up and presenting the business plan is a mandatory condition in order to know their level of sustainability. The evaluation of the innovative organization has in its center the evaluation of the patents, which requires for several questions to be answered. These are related to:

— Legal status:

- Which is the legal status of the patents' family?
- Which is the validity of the patent?
- Is there a protection term for the patents' family?
- How extended and comprehensive are the demands?
- Does the patents' family ensure geographical coverage for relevant markets?
- Are the patents monitored regarding infringements?
- Is there opposition or legal procedures (infringements/invalidity) widely spread in the patented field?
- Is the patent used for licensing?
- Is the patent intended to be used as a tool of the business?
- Is the patent destined to: block the technological developments of the competitors in this field; secure room for one's own development activities?
- Is the exploitation of technology dependent on licensing agreements with third parties?
- Is the solution of the patent or the technology related to a product or service specific to the organization?
- Do you make the agreement known when you negotiate the solution of the patent or technology?
- Do you want a continued existence until the end of the project?
- Do you know of any legal risk verification about the patent?

— Status from a technological point of view:

- Does the invention constitute a key technology?
- Is the invention technical superior from the alternative technologies?
- In what phase was the invention tested?
- Does the patented technology require new skills, qualification or production facilities?
- How much time does the patented technology need in order to be commercialized?
- Is it easy to make counterfeits?
- Can the counterfeited products be easily defected?
- Does the technology offer benefits to the client or does it raise problems for the client?
- Based on the available documentation of intellectual assets, how feasible is the reproduction of the intellectual asset?
- Can the type of technological problems raised by the intellectual assets be defined?
- What percentage does the technological part represent?
- How feasible is the technology?
- What percentage does human security represents by using the technology?
- What percentage does environmental protection represent by using the technology?
- What percentage does the economical part represent by using the technology?
- What type of technical problems does the application of technology raise?

— The market related status:

- How high is the market increasing rate in the business segment in which the patented technology is applied?
- How big is the potential income in the respective business segment?
- Are special licences required for the commercial activities?
- Is the patent related to the basic activities of the applying organization?
- How big is the contribution of the patented technology to the value of the profit?
- How big is the market in the business segment in which the patented technology is applied?
- How high is the competitiveness of the market existing products in the business segment in which the patented technology is applied?
- How easy is the market access?
- Is there a list of licensed potential?
- Is there a plan of exploiting the patent?
- How detailed is the exploitation plan?

— The status related to the strategy:

- Which are the marketing options for the patented technology?
- Which is the duration of the life cycle of the patented technology in the market?
- Are there competitive products or substitutes in the market?
- Does the patented technology offer a potential income?
- The patent intends to broaden the existing markets from a technological point of view?
- Does the patent intend to open new markets?
- Does the patent intend to build an image of the organization?
- Is there an interaction between the patent and the organization's business strategy?
- Does the organization have an image and a mission?
- Does the organization have a strategy for the next 3 years?
- Does the organization have a business plan?
- Does the organization have a financial strategy?
- Does the organization have a marketing strategy?
- Who is involved in approaching the strategy?
- How often was the strategy revised in the last 5 years?
- Can you list the first 5 competences of the organization?
- Do you expect changes in the management?
- Does the organization have a clear organizational structure?
- Do the employees have their job tasks clearly defined?

The answers to these questions are quantifiable for everyone on a scale from 0 to 100 points. The maxim score corresponds to the most favoring aspect for the pragmatism and effects of applying the patent. By summing up a score is ensured which offers a clear image regarding the organization's sustainability. The higher the score, the more sustainable is the organization.

4. Conclusions

The intangible assets created in the innovation processes represent the important part of the value of today's businesses. The evaluation of these intangible assets gives the investors the opportunity to better understand the business and the value of the organization and the key to ensure the decision-making based on the concrete information and to decide if the IP applies or it needs to be patented. (European Commision. Directorate General for Research and Innovation, 2014: 5).

In the center of the intangible assets of an organization the intellectual property represented mainly by the patented invention is found.

The evaluation of the innovative organization through the prism of the IP, represented by the patented invention and suggested in this chapter, represents a complete approach under legal and technological aspect, of the position on the market and the strategy, that can constitute a model of an evaluation procedure, which can be generalized.

It can be stressed again the fact that the knowledge based society capitalizes the innovative organization which possesses an important percentage of intangible assets.

The development of the intangible assets represents the real support of the organizations' and society sustainability.

Both the need to increase the level of credibility and to encourage banks and the financial institutions to award credits based on the results of the correct evaluation of the intangible assets, arise. It has to be sustained through a chart of warranting the risk divided between the creditor and the credited.

Elaborating an evaluation methodology of the intangible assets standardized at international level can be a solution in a globalized world and it can lead to the inclusion of the intangible assets portfolio in the organization's balance.

In order to make a correct evaluation, the creation of a professional organization for evaluating the intangible assets, that will enclose accredited evaluating experts, is required, and, last but not least, the mission of the universities in the future is to introduce in the university curriculum subjects that will tackle in detail the intangible assets of an organization.

References

Brant, J. & Lohse, S. (2013), Enhancing intellectual property management and appropriation by innovative SMEs. *Innovation and intellectual property series*, 1, 31–39.

European Comision, Directorate General for Research and Innovation, (2014), *Final Report from the Expert Group on Intellectual Property Valuation*, Luxembourg: Publications Office of the European Union.

Pederzoli, C., Thoma, G., & Torricelli, C. (2013), Modelling credit risk for innovative SMEs: The role of innovation measures, *Journal of Financial Services Research*, 44, 111–129.

South East Europe Transnational Cooperation Programme, (2012), EVLIA — Making full value of good ideas by leveraging intellectual assets for financing SMEs in SEE Project Code SEE/D/0237/1.2/x.

The Commision to the European Parliament, The Council, The European Economic and Social Committee, and the Commitee of the Regions, (2013), *Measuring Innovation Output in Europe: Towards a New Indicator*, Bruxelles: COM.

Thomä, J. & Bizer, R. (2013), To protect or not protect? Modes of appropriability in the small enterprise sector, *Research Policy*, 42, 35–49.

Tomlison, P. R. & Fai, F. M. (2013), The nature of SME co-operation and innovation: A multi scalar and multi-dimensional analysis, *International Journal of Production Economics*, 141, 316–326.

Zeng, S. X., Xie, X. M., & Tom, C. M. (2010), Relationship between cooperation networks and innovation performance of SMEs, *Technovation*, 30, 181–194.

Chapter 39

Comparative Management in the Field of Extracurricular Activities, Highlighting Instrument of Potential Change*

Oana Dumitraşcu and Emanoil Muscalu

Lucian Blaga University

The purpose of this chapter is to present the similarities and differences in the field of extracurricular activities, comparing universities from Germany with those from Romania, with a purpose to identify the potential innovative leisure activities that can be implemented at the Romanian universities. Also the influence of the extracurricular activities on the attractiveness of the university and the potential factors that could increase the university image will be identified. This study gives recommendations for increasing the attractiveness of the study area through the development of extracurricular activities at Romanian universities. The study has been accomplished using the bibliographic study, using various secondary and primary sources and using the methodology of qualitative research and of quantitative research, based on a questionnaire.

This chapter includes a research, based on a questionnaire realized at the German university environment. Thus, the northern region of Germany is analyzed, including University of Applied Sciences Flensburg, University of Applied Sciences: Technology, Business and Design Wismar and University of Applied Sciences Kiel. A research based on the Romanian university environment is also realized, where the University "1 Decembrie 1918" Alba Iulia, the University "Lucian Blaga" Sibiu and the University "Petru Maior" Târgu Mureş are studied.

Using the methodology of comparative management, the region of northern Germany is analyzed in comparison with the center region of Romania. The work highlights the similarities and differences between regions and between the studied universities, their characteristics, and especially their concerns. Qualitative studies define the nuances of the issues identified, and the quantitative studies confirm or infirm the hypotheses.

Through quantitative analysis based on the questionnaire and comparative management method the major problems identified during the research are highlighted and studied. Identifying the gaps regarding the extracurricular activities offer at Romanian universities compared to that of German universities basically identifies achievable goals through an efficient, effective change management and adapted to the conditions in Romania.

---

*This work was supported by the strategic grand POSDRU/159/1.5/S/133255, Project ID 133255 (2014), co-financed by the European Social Fund within the Sectorial Operational Program Human Resources Development 2007–2013.

1. Introduction

According to the bibliographical results of studies that were the basis of this chapter, like Heine (2008: 23) also mentioned, the attractiveness of the study location is influenced by the good reputation of a university, its facilities, study offer, but also by the extracurricular activities offer and the university atmosphere. These aspects influence the potential student's decision in choosing a study location.

Therefore, we consider appropriate that among the targeted objectives, this article should also analyze the effect of extracurricular activities on the attractiveness of the location study, capturing aspects of compared management in the case of universities from northern Germany, the University of Applied Sciences Flensburg, the University of Applied Sciences: Technology, Business and Design Wismar and the University of Applied Sciences Kiel and in the case of universities in the central area of Romania, the University "1 Decembrie 1918" Alba Iulia, the University "Lucian Blaga" Sibiu and the University "Petru Maior" Târgu Mureş. The data were collected in the year 2012 with the aid of the questionnaire and analyzed using univariate and bivariate analysis. Capturing similarities and differences between Germany and Romania recommendations were issued, which contribute to a change management leading to performance.

In the analysis the students' participation at extracurricular activities has been captured, in general but also by category, as such the extracurricular activities offer was evaluated in the field of sport and recreation. The students' opinion has been identified in regards to these fields and likewise their potential of improvement.

From our point of view, concerns on this topic are necessary and appropriate also out of the desire to identify the cultural, economic, social and education differences for the two countries, such studies, bringing new contributions to the field knowledge. Hence, the comparative method applied in management is the perfect method, helpful and necessary for this work, in which the availability of the data from Germany was facilitated by studies undertaken by us in 2012–2013. Dumitraşcu & Grünwald (2012), Dumitraşcu & Şerban (2013) and Grünwald & Dumitraşcu (2012) mention that, they do not consider the comparison between the two regions (Northern Germany and Central Region Romania) forced, because there are many similarities: a part of the concerned German region has been part of Democratic Germany, its development is still precarious, the culture, mentality, and values of citizens still having influences from the old regime. From the economic point of view, differences between the two regions exist, are untestable, but are not very large, and perhaps the most important aspect, found through observation and direct implication, the quality of education (its aspects of curricular order) is similar.

Nicolescu (1997: 30) stated that "Comparative management is the science that studies processes and managerial relations from organizations operating in different national cultural contexts, focusing on identifying and analyzing the similarities and differences of management in order to facilitate the international transfer of managerial know-how and increase usability, effectiveness and efficiency organizations". This definition can be characterized by the fact that just the elements of management constitutes the subject which lies at the base of the comparison, the multinational cultural vision represents the specific of the analysis, requiring that management be approached differently, depending on the cultural context of each country. Comparative analysis focuses on some similarities and differences between the theoretical and practical aspects of management, and the objectives followed within a comparative management study are of a pragmatic nature.

In regards to this chapter, the utility of comparative management, is given by the availability of information from outside the country, from different cultures, with larger and longer experience in extracurricular activities. Comparison as a method and comparative evaluation as an instrument enable experience take over, sometimes adaptation of them to the environment and culture in which the implementation is desired. It is also our case, by comparing the extracurricular activities offer in universities from Romania and Germany and identifying ways to change in the sense of development.

2. Result Description and Evaluation Based on the Comparative Management Method

2.1. *Description of the sample analyzed in Germany*

The analyzed sample from Germany is formed by students enroled at the university from Wismar, at the university from Kiel and the one from Flensburg, was taken at random. In total 120 responders have been interviewed, from which 40 from the University from Wismar, 40 from the one in Kiel and 40 from the one from Flensburg. Out of these 120 subjects, 41.7% were female and 58.3% male.

Flensburg is situated in the north of Germany, in the Schleswig-Holstein region, at the border with Denmark. At the University of Applied Sciences Flensburg are approximately 4,000 students enrolled. The study offer is focused on technics and economics (University of Applied Sciences Flensburg).

Kiel is the capital of the Schleswig-Holstein region and has direct access to the North Sea–Baltic Sea Canal. The University of Applied Sciences Kiel was established in 1969 as a merger of several state owned engineering schools and technical schools. This is the largest university from Schleswig-Holstein, with approximately 6,400 students (University of Applied Sciences Kiel).

The city of Wismar is a port city on the Baltic Sea. Baldauf (2010) and Borowski (2010) mention that, the University of Applied Sciences: Technology, Business and Design Wismar comprises three faculties, the Faculty of Engineering, Faculty of Economics and Faculty of Design where approximately 6,900 students are enroled.

2.2. *Description of the sample analyzed in Romania*

The sample from Romania is composed of students of the "Lucian Blaga" University Sibiu, "Petru Maior" University Târgu Mureş and "1 Decembrie 1918" University Alba Iulia, and it was chosen randomly. In total 146 students were surveyed, of which 51 from the "Lucian Blaga" University Sibiu, 50 from the "Petru Maior" University Târgu Mureş and 46 from the "1 Decembrie 1918" University Alba Iulia. Of the students surveyed, 43% are female and 57% male.

At the "Lucian Blaga" University Sibiu there are approximately 14,500 students enrolled, the university being split into nine faculties. In the study of "Lucian Blaga" University Sibiu (2011–2012: 4), is stated that the majority of students study within the Faculty of Engineering or at the Faculty of Economic Sciences. The "Petru Maior" University from Târgu Mureş is composed of three faculties, Faculty of Engineering, Faculty of Sciences and Letters and the Faculty of Economics, Law, and Administration Sciences. This university was established in 1960 and has approximately 5,200 enrolled students. (Romanian Agency for Quality Assurance in Higher Education: 12).

At the "1 Decembrie 1918" University from Alba Iulia there are approximately 4,500 students enrolled, and it is divided into four faculties, Faculty of History and Philology, Faculty of Science, Faculty of Law and Social Sciences and the Faculty of Orthodox Theology. ("1 Decembrie 1918" University Alba Iulia).

2.3. *Students' implication in extracurricular activities — Comparison between Romania and Germany*

The analyzed data shows that 37% from the Romanian students participate in extracurricular activities, in comparison with 50.8% of the German students. For both samples the preferred extracurricular activity is sport, this being often practiced in Germany. German students participate in students' organizations or volunteer activities less, compared with those from Romania. In line with the previous finding, nearly a third of Romanian students prefer attending student events, in comparison with not even 10% of German students.

In general, the main cause of non-participation to extracurricular activities is time. Students are occupied with study, courses, job and friends. But, in the same time, as the study reveals, the lack of involvement may be caused by the low attractiveness of the extracurricular activities offer and the lack of students' information in regards to this bid. Specifically, lower involvement of the Romanian students in such activities, comparative with German students, may be due to a much lower diversity and attractiveness of the extracurricular offer and a poorer media coverage, compared to Germany.

Generally the reason of Romanian students' implication in extracurricular activities is for them to complete their professional experience, specially the professional one, the majority of them consider extracurricular activities important in their personal development.

2.4. *Comparison of extracurricular activities offered in the field of sports between Romania and Germany*

Similarly with the students from the Romanian universities, two thirds of the German students consider sports to be important or even very important.

Students' participation is low in regards to sports activities, most of them being uninformed about the offer. The study shows that neither the German students do not seem to be fully aware of the sports activities, although they are more informed than the Romanian ones.

Most of the Romanian students are willing to pay for activities such as swimming, football, fitness, dances in comparison with German students who would prefer to pay for sailing, surf, fitness and swimming. But perhaps the type of activity is not important in this case, because it depends on the study area and natural possibilities offered. Instead, an aspect we consider to be relevant, is the fact that the average amount Romanian students would like to pay for practicing sport activities is between RON51–100, the amount that can be found in equal proportions also at the German students. Taking into consideration, the financial opportunities of Romanian students in comparison with German students, it can be noted that the interest of Romanian students to participate in sports activities is higher than of German students, which may be due to the lack of some sports activities until present time at their university, or of the general low attractiveness of the offer.

The fact that 80% of students from the "Lucian Blaga" University consider sport as being important or very important indicate that they are very interested in regards to these activities. Although, their participation is low, the most likely cause being the poor information on the sports activities offered. Regarding the payment of some activities, students from the "Lucian Blaga" University are willing to pay a fee for fitness, swimming and football. For "Lucian Blaga" University to stand up to the standards of other universities and ideally to the standards of those from Germany, strictly for this one it is recommended to provide the basic sports activities: volleyball, basketball, football, table tennis. And because students would be willing to

	"Lucian Blaga" University Sibiu	"Petru Maior" University Tg.Mureș	"1 Decembrie 1918" University Alba Iulia
VERY FAVOURABLE	12%	2%	9%
FAVOURABLE	22%	26%	51%
NEUTRAL	37%	30%	29%
UNFAVOURABLE	22%	22%	7%
TOTALLY UNFAVOURABLE	8%	20%	4%

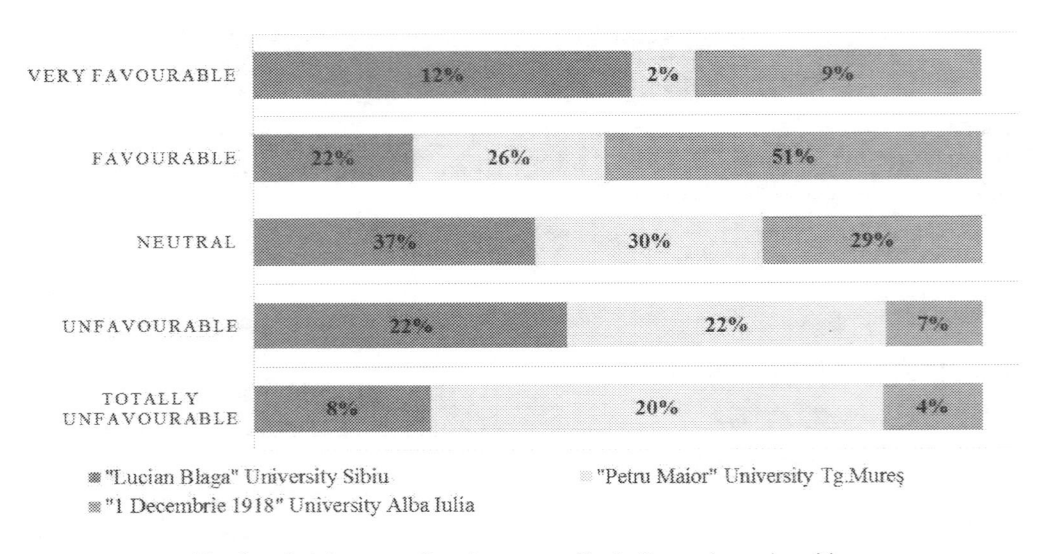

Fig. 1. Opinion regarding the sports offer in Romanian universities

Notes:
Lucian Blaga University Sibiu = 51.
Petru Maior University Tg.Mureș = 50.

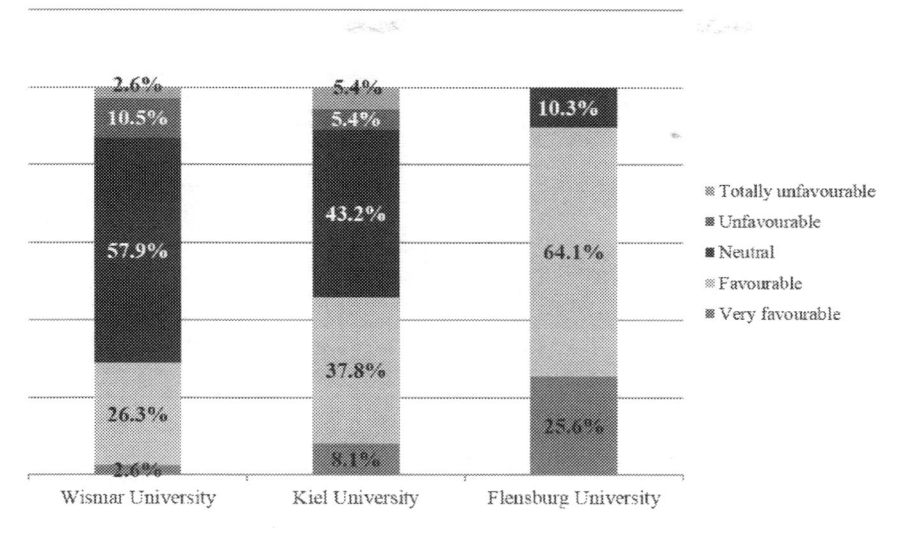

Fig. 2. Opinion regarding the sports offer in German universities

Notes:
University Wismar = 40.
University Flensburg = 40.
University Kiel = 40.

pay a monthly fee between RON 51 and 100 for participating to sports activities, it is recommended to implement a charge for additional sport activities, respectively swimming, fitness, dances, and aerobics. To increase demand, this offer has to be well publicized especially on the website of the faculties and universities with the purpose of promoting student involvement.

Among the analyzed German universities, the offer of the Flensburg University is the most appreciated. From the Romanian universities, "1 Decembrie 1918" University from Alba Iulia is the most appreciated, 60% of the questioned students having a favorable or very favorable opinion in comparison with approximately one third of students from other universities.

2.5. *Comparison Romania — Germany regarding the extracurricular activities offered in the field of recreation*

In general, the participation of students from the analyzed Romanian universities is lower than of German students. Romanian students wish for more trips as well as organizing parties and recreational activities, the majority of Romanian students surveyed being very interested to participate in such activities. The most favorable opinion out of the analyzed Romanian universities about this offer is found at the University of Alba Iulia, followed by Târgu Mureş, University of Sibiu was ranked last. The number of students in Romania which have appreciated this offer as favorable or very favorable is higher than in Germany.

Information, and as a result the participation of students at the "Lucian Blaga" University Sibiu is much lower in terms of theatrical activities, musical activities or competitions, compared to that of other Romanian universities. In return, they have heard and participate to the orientation program for 1st year, the opening festivity of the academic year, trips and carnivals. Surprising is that the University from Sibiu is the last among the analyzed Romanian universities in terms of students' opinion in regards to the extracurricular activities offer in the field of recreation. We consider this finding as a negative one that can be improved in a further research, as in a city as Sibiu, as former European Capital of Culture in 2007, in which the cultural activity is a strategic priority at city and county level, the offer is very large from a quantitative point of view, spread as deployment of time and diverse as typology.

3. Conclusions and Recommendations

From the analysis it is shown that in general, Romanian students' involvement in extracurricular activities is

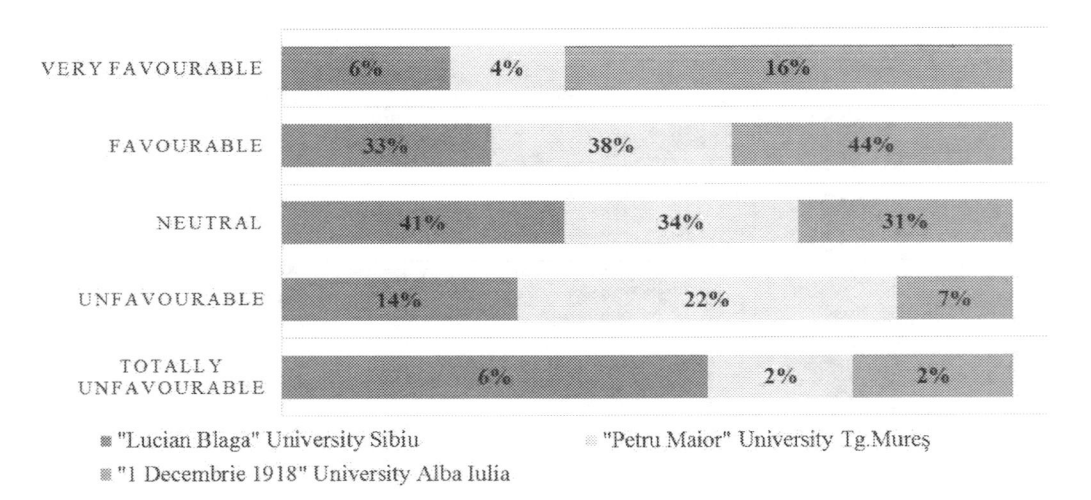

Fig. 3. Opinion regarding extracurricular activities offer in the field of recreation at Romanian universities

Notes:
N"Lucian Blaga" University Sibiu = 51.
N"Petru Maior" University Tg. Mureş = 50.

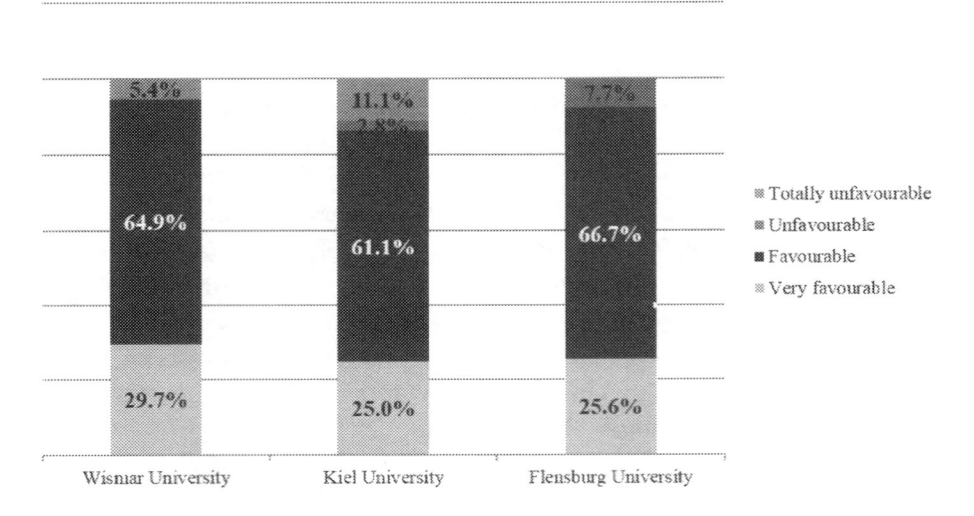

Fig. 4. Opinion regarding extracurricular activities offer in the field of recreation at German universities

Notes:
NUniversity Wismar = 40.
NUniversity Flensburg = 40.
NUniversity Kiel = 40.

lower than that of German students. The majority of students with an unfavorable or totally unfavorable opinion about the extracurricular activities offer are students from "Lucian Blaga" University from Sibiu. This may be due to the low attractiveness of the extracurricular activities offer and the lack of students' information, on one hand and on the other hand to the increased demand, greater willingness to participate in such activities, thus the offer demand rapport being disproportionately in favour of the demand. The comparative analysis shows that a university offer that is more diverse, more attractive and better mediatized can influence students' involvement. For example, the offer in Germany is more diversified and better promoted as the one in Romania, students' implication being thus higher. Romanian students are more interested to participate in extracurricular activities, probably because they did not have the possibility so far, due to the reduced extracurricular offer. Especially the sports offer is very different in Romania as to Germany. Thus, also the desire of students to participate and introduce some new activities is different.

For, in terms of extracurricular activities, Romanian universities to get closer to the standards of the German ones, and consequently the general students' implication in such activities to rise, it is recommended to increase the supply of extracurricular activities by diversification and increasing the attractiveness, a more performing marketing and management of them, a change of organizational culture, in which the social relations and activities involving teams to be restored as important. As suggested by students to increase their interest it is particularly recommended to promote extracurricular activities, involvement of professors in these activities among students, development of sports activities, career guidance activities, but also various seminars, and professional trainings.

Generally, perhaps Sibiu less, which has a rich offer, the offer in the field of recreation should be improved towards developing cultural, musical, and theatrical activities. In cooperation with related organizations and student clubs, diverse events can be organized, competitions and exhibitions, in which students with common interests may assert their ideas, potential and develop their talents. Likewise, the development of summer schools is extremely beneficial and is recommended as a way to develop new skills, because within them, programs can be conceived that blend various types of extracurricular activities.

A very important conclusion, through which foresees a targeting of research towards the correlation of extracurricular activities — academic performance — performance management, is that, students with higher academic averages participate at such activities, more than students with lower averages, from which we can deduce that either extracurricular activities have a positive influence on academic performance, either that only students above the performance average have the capacity and desire to engage in such activities. We do not exclude and we even believe that the assumptions made are synergic in nature, they are supporting and developing each other. It remains for this statement to be proven in a subsequent step of our research.

A recommendation with a purpose to improve the quality of extracurricular activities and satisfying students' needs, refers to the fact that satisfaction studies in regards to extracurricular activities should be carried out periodically (half-yearly) thus, as a result of the findings, through improving the offer of extracurricular activities, in the sense of its attractiveness, through an effective management of marketing, given by a management of change, in the sense of continuous improvement, the university image can be improved, the attractiveness for good students will rise, and as such the quality spiralling towards academic performance.

References

Romanian Agency for Quality Assurance in Higher Education (2010), Petru Maior University Targu Mures; translated from

"Agenţ ia Română de Asigurare a Calităţ ii în Învăţ ământul Superior" (2010), Universitatea Petru Maior din Târgu Mureş.

Agenţia Română de Asigurare a Calităţii în Învăţământul Superior, (2010), Universitatea Petru Maior din Târgu Mureş, Available at http://proiecte.aracis.ro/fileadmin/ARACIS/Publicatii_Aracis/Brosuri_proiect/Etapa_II/Brosuri_proiect/002_Interior_Brosura_UPM_27_preview.pdf (Accessed 8 March 2014).

Baldauf, K. (2010), Hochschule Wismar, Available at http://hs-wismar.de/index.php?id=leitbild&L=0 (Accessed 8 March 2014).

Borowski, K. (2011), Hochschule Wismar, Available at http://hswismar.de/index.php?id=4901&L=0 (Accessed 8 March 2014).

Dumitraşcu, O. & Şerban, A. (2013), Present state of research regarding university choice and attractiveness of the study area, *20th International Economic Conference — IECS* 2013, Sibiu.

Dumitraşcu, O., Grünwald, N., & Bassus, O. (2012), Wirkung der Freizeitangebote auf die Attraktivität des Studienstandortes und der Studienmotivation der Studierenden, Master Thesis, Germania: University Wismar.

Fachhochschule Flensburg. Available at http://www.fh-flensburg.de/fhfl/hochschule.html (Accessed 8 March 2014).

Fachhochschule, K. Available at http://www.fh-kiel.de/index.php?id=28 (Accessed 08 March 2014).

Grünwald, N. & Dumitraşcu, O. (2012), Influence of leisure activities on the attractiveness of the study region, *MSD Journal*, 4. Available at http://www.cedc.ro/media/MSD/Papers/Volume%204%20no%202%202012/Grunwald.pdf (Accessed 8 March 2014).

Heine, C. (2008), Studienanfänger in den alten und neuen Ländern: Gründe der Hochschulwahl und Bewertungen der Hochschulregionen West- und Ostdeutschland. Available at http://www.hochschulkampagne-ost.de/dateien/HIS-Studienanfaenger-Hochschulwahl-und-bewertung.pdf (Accessed 8 March 2014).

Nicolescu, O. (1997), Management Comparat, Uniunea Europeană, Japonia şi S.U.A., Bucureşti, Editura Economică.

"Lucian Blaga" University Sibiu. (2011–2012), translated from "Universitatea Lucian Blaga Sibiu, Departamentul integrat de comunicaț ii şi marketing biroul de marketing, 2011–2012, Studiu privind profilul studenț ilor din cadrul ULBS", Available at http://www.ulbsibiu.ro/ro/universitate/publ_interne/documente/raportprofilul-studentilor_2011-2012.pdf (Accessed 8 March 2014); in "Lucian Blaga" University Sibiu (2011–2012), Department of integrated marketing communications and marketing office, Study regarding ULBS students' profile. Available at http://www.ulbsibiu.ro/ro/universitate/publ_ interne/documente/raport-profilul-studentilor_2011–2012.pdf (Accessed 8 March 2014).

"1 Decembrie 1918" University Alba Iulia", translated from "Universitatea, 1 Decembrie 1918", Alba Iulia, Available at http://www.uab.ro/despre/index.php (Accessed 8 March 2014).

Chapter 40

Study for Creating and Developing Regional Agrifood Markets in Romania

Nicolae Istudor, George Plesoianu, Bogdan Bazga,
Oana Georgiana Stanila, and St. Alexandru Costin Cirstea

Bucharest University of Economic Studies

Taking into account the present context in which the global joint efforts are directed towards identifying feasible and pragmatic solutions for transfer to a new model of development — a sustainable one — and after long debates with specialists in food chain, we have considered as being neccessary to study and implement a new sustainable model for food production, and consumption, adapted to the Romanian specific conditions.

This study primarily aims to analyze the opportunities for creating and developing regional agrifood markets in Romania, as an alternative to the negative effects of globalization and as a pre-requisite for ensuring the food security and safety through local and regional food production. A second objective consists in analyzing the current situation of the level of food markets functioning in Romania, compared to the developed countries of the EU. The third pragmatic objective of the study is creating a pilot model of Regional Agro-Food System, integrated in the food chain and based on best practices from developed countries.

The main research methods used in this study are: Synthesis documentation of the recent reports and studies conducted by international organizations Food and Agriculture Organisation of the United Nations (FAO), Organisation for Economic Co-operation and Development (OECD), World Health Organisation (WHO), which studied the importance of small and medium farms reorientation in ensuring food security and safety at the local/regional levels, models of existing regional food markets at European and international level (Germany, France, Polandand USA); statistical analysis to identify the current situation in Romania, compared with the EU and simulation of socio-economic effects to create a pilot model of Regional Agro-Food System, adapted to the specific situation of Romania.

1. The Opportunities of Creating and Developing Regional Agrifood Markets (RAM)

In the current context of Romania when the food markets are dominated by super and hypermarkets and traditional markets had a strong fall, is required a careful analysis of the effects of this situation and design a new model of integrated development of food production and consumption, which has to be sustainable. This premise is supported by the fact that Romania has a high agricultural potential, which can meet demand of agricultural products from local and regional agricultural production.

From our documentation resulted that currently, international organizations involved in agriculture and food, such as FAO and OECD orient their efforts toward finding solutions for ensuring food security and safety in Europe and globally. These efforts are concentrated especially in the small and medium-sized farms, which can satisfy the local and regional food needs. This justifies studying the opportunity of creating a new Model of Agrifood System in Romania, oriented to promote integrated agricultural production at regional level.

The first part of the study presents the opportunity to analyze the creation and development of regional agrifood markets in response to the negative effects of globalization, which generated dependence with large global networks of agricultural products suppliers, the inability to ensure food security and safety from local and regional products. In our opinion, the main opportunities and advantages of designing and developing regional agrifood markets in Romania are:

- High potential of revival the agricultural and food production that can ensure — qualitative and quantitative — the domestic need for food and may gradually shrink super and hypermarkets competition through strict control of product quality and traceability;
- The possibility and necessity of easy monitoring and traceability of the food products origin, thus leading to increase their quality and to an effective management of activities within the food chain;
- Reorganization of activities within the food chain and the possibility of using and upgrading existing infrastructure by local manufacturers/processors;
- Creating professional networks for product confirmity verification through independent laboratories to confirm the quality of local food products;
- Ability to access European projects funded through the National Rural Development Program 2014–2020, which supports the need for better integration of agrifood producers in the market, through short supply chains. For smaller producers, emphasis will be placed on encouraging association and improving access to credits for investments, while the big players need to invest in modernization and in compliance with EU requirements, focusing on sectors that have the highest added value and the greatest potential for export (Ministry of Agriculture and Rural Development, 2014);
- A premise and opportunity that can be exploited in order to create and develop RAM is also the international initiatives to promote and support small family farmers who produce for local, and/or, regional markets. Thus, according to the resolution of the European Council of Young Farmers, promoting small farms at the European level has many advantages, both in terms of ensuring food security and safety, diversity of food products, and the increased competition on the market, adding value in food sector and increasing the number of jobs for rural young people (European Council of Young Farmers, 2013).
- At the same time, at european level is aimed the rejuvenation of population occupied in agriculture, as a prerequisite for the creation and development of regional food markets, especially as, on average, young farmers are more productive, oriented to technological innovation and better informed (European Council of Young Farmers, 2013).

Based on recent studies conducted by a group of professors and consultants from Bucharest University of Economic Studies was found that this new approach is appropriate and is within the vision and directions of the new Common Agricultural Policy (CAP) 2014–2020 (European Commission, 2013) recently launched by the EU and has a significant importance in:

- Harnessing natural resources at local/regional level by local producers;
- Stimulating rural farmers to associate in production and conditioning products in centers of collecting, sorting, and packaging that contribute to revenue growth of small and medium farms and, consequently, the growth of quality life in rural areas. Also required is the establishment and operation of marketing and sales associations, to provide raw materials for food processing units and final products for supermarkets and other local and regional retail chains, especially stable and moving market places, retail units and e-commerce;

- Strong decrease in the level of imports of agricultural products due to the establishment and development of units which offer local and regional products in regional agrifood markets and including small and medium-sized farms as providers of these networks;
- Increasing food safety and ensuring traceability on the whole agricultural chain, from producer to consumer;
- Development of SMEs for processing natural and healthy food products, with small and medium processing capabilities, operating in the proximity of agricultural production basins and urban localities;
- Development with strategic projects of regional transport and storage, proper for agricultural products and food, including support services for regional agrifood markets development (credit unions, laboratories for product certification, IT systems and advertising).

By implementing the above measures will create prerequisites for developing a new model of sustainable food production and consumption, which will effectively exploit the natural resources available at local and regional level and will provide safe and sufficient food products for domestic needs. Furthermore, this new model of sustainable development can lead to the modernization of food sector, increasing innovation through new technologies and promoting research, development and innovation in the field, and use of best practices for production and processing of agricultural products in accordance with the requirements of environmental conservation.

2. The Comparative Analysis of the Actual Situation of RAM between Romania and Developed Countries in EU

Further in the study, an analysis of the current state of international trade with food products in Romania, compared to the developed countries of the European Union is presented.

Table 1 gives an overview of the evolution of imports with agricultural products in Romania compared with some developed countries in the European Union (France, Germany, Poland, UK, Austria).

From the analysis of data presented in Table 1, it is found that all the analyzed countries have registered ascending values of agrifood imports. The highest import on food products is recorded by Germany, with values exceeding 50 billion across the analyzed period, followed by France and the UK, which recorded values over 30 billion across the analyzed period. On the opposite side is Romania, the country with the lowest level of agricultural products imports, with maximum values of about 4 billion euros (in 2012).

To ensure the relevance of this analysis in Table 2 is presented, an overview of the evolution of agrifood exports in the same states discussed.

From the analysis of data presented in Table 2, it is found that, unlike imports, exports of agricultural products in most countries analyzed have been oscillating. Thus, in Germany, France, Poland, UK, and Austria, 2009 represented a year of decrease in the level of exports with agricultural products, one of the reasons being represented by the manifestation of

Table 1. The evolution of imports with agrifood products (mn EUR)

	2007	2008	2009	2010	2011	2012
Romania	2,975	3,764	3,364	3,288	3,743	4,105
France	32,877	35,420	34,638	36,687	39,911	41,558
Germany	50,602	53,620	51,554	55,421	61,036	63,610
Poland	7,091	—	8,066	9,599	10,739	11,546
UK	38,231	38,214	35,961	39,115	41,627	45,525
Austria	7,322	7,959	7,693	8,250	8,973	9,620

Source: Eurostat.

Table 2. The evolution of exports with agrifood products (mn EUR).

	2007	2008	2009	2010	2011	2012
Romania	854	1,582	1,755	2,352	2,917	3,353
France	42,498	45,480	40,815	44,758	51,778	53,406
Germany	43,432	48,002	46,050	49,495	54,722	58,123
Poland	9,451	10,899	10,788	12,708	14,280	16,671
UK	16,967	17,094	16,259	18,679	20,869	22,082
Austria	7,469	8,067	7,356	7,959	8,755	9,212

Source: Eurostat.

financial crisis in the EU countries, which recorded its maximum in 2009.

Similar to imports, France and Germany have the highest levels of exports throughout the period analyzed, with values exceeding EUR 40 bn in each of the analyzed years. On the opposite side is Romania, which recorded the lowest levels of exports of agricultural products in the analyzed period.

Next on the study will be presented the evolution of agrifood trade balance in Romania and analyzed EU countries, as the difference between the exports and the imports (Table 3 and Fig. 1).

From the analysis of data presented in Table 3 and Fig. 1, it is found that from all the states analyzed, only France and Poland registered during 2007–2012 levels of positive trade balance with food products, which highlights the high performance of food systems practiced in these states and capitalization of local and regional natural resources available for agricultural production. We consider that these patterns should be taken also in our country in order to increase the competitiveness of the agrifood sector and decrease dependence on imports and on big providers of food products.

Although Germany and UK had negative trade balance with food products, the high value of imports and exports indicate the existence of a strong and dynamic food system based on exploitation of local and regional resources that help ensure food security and safety.

In Romania there is a steady reduction in the trade deficit from EUR 2,121 mn (as it was in 2007) to EUR 752 mn (as reached in 2012), which is a positive phenomenon that gives us hope that in the near future, Romania will have a positive trade balance for food products.

For Romania to be able to align the performances of the developed EU countries, we consider absolutely necessary taking good practices from other developed countries in the EU and the world, as for example, the USA case.

3. The Model of USA Regional Food Hubs

One of the priorities of public policies promoted by the USA is to improve the access of small farmers to the food market and strengthen their position in the food chain in response to the disappearance of small farms because of large corporations and the need to ensure food security and safety.

In these conditions, lately, various models have been developed to streamline the agro chain from producer to consumer in the US regional food system, which are called food hubs. These are entities that manage the collection, storage, processing, distribution, and marketing of locally and regional produced food but also provides technical assistance to small farmers working in other vital areas of their business: Marketing, farm management, consulting for start-ups (Toderita, 2013).

Food hubs is an innovative tool for developing regional food systems as an intermediary between producer and consumer, operating both in the area of supply and demand.

In the food supply area, hubs advise farmers for production planning, offer technical consulting, marketing consulting, organic certification, verifying product confirmity, so that farmers can adapt to market demands and achieve satisfactory income from agricultural activity.

Table 3. The evolution of trade balance with agrifood products (mn EUR)

	2007	2008	2009	2010	2011	2012
Romania	−2,121	−2,182	−1,608	−936	−826	−752
France	9,621	10,060	6,177	8,071	11,867	11,848
Germany	−7,170	−5,618	−5,504	−5,927	−6,314	−5,487
Poland	2,359	10,899	2,723	3,109	3,541	5,125
UK	−21,264	−21,120	−19,702	−20,435	−20,758	−23,443
Austria	147	108	−336	−291	−218	−408

Source: Eurostat.

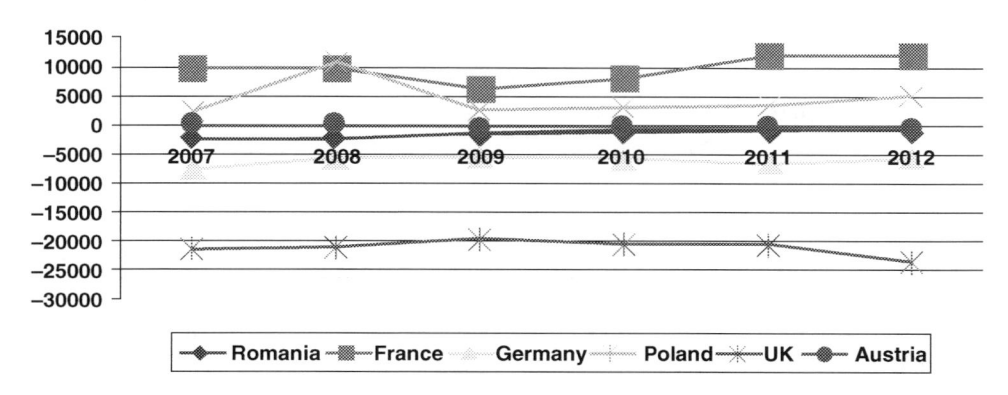

Fig. 1. The evolution of trade balance with agrifood products (mn EUR)

In terms of meeting the demand for food products, food hubs conducts contracting with distributors, processors, wholesalers and direct to consumers, so there are three areas/levels at which they operate:

- **Farm to business/institution (commercial and logistics support services).** This category collects agricultural products from farmers and distribute them to large retail chains, SMEs processing of agricultural products, public institutions, restaurants. Thus, the small farmers have access to new markets that they would not be able to access without association in food hub.
- **Farm to Consumer (conditioning and distribution services).** This category collects agricultural products from farmers and distribute them (after preparation and packaging) directly to consumers. This model includes local and regional commercial networks, online platforms, home delivering companies, and regional mobile markets.
- **The hybrid model.** This category conducts sales both to intermediaries and consumers.

Food hubs are financed by government through federal agencies in both start-up and subsequent operation phase. Also, food hubs are financed by various philanthropic foundations and private donors (those who finance these activities). They have a number of facilities such as tax breaks and low-interest loans and subsidized interest for equipment purchasing.

Next, a few examples of food hubs will be presented in the category of Farm to business/Institution that we consider appropriate for Romania too.

3.1. *Farm-to-table-Co-Packers (F2TCP) (Toderita, 2014)*

Set in a former IBM cafeteria, F2TCP is a private food hub which buys various products (especially fruits and vegetables) from small and medium farmers in New York State and gives them added value by freezing, preservation and/or processing.

F2TCP is also an incubator for agrifood industry, as it gives farmers consulting services for recipes and phytosanitary procedures, marketing and provides warehouse and refrigeration equipment for hire. The Food hub is totally owned by a consortium of companies and obtained a loan in the amount of USD 230,000 from the State of New York.

3.2. *Philadelphia wholesale produce market (Toderita, 2014)*

This is the second wholesale market in the US in size, extending over an area of 65,000 sqm. The construction, privately owned, was funded through a mix of public funds, both federal and local. The space is split and rented by 26 wholesalers, 13 of them being part on the Board of Directors. The market space contains also refrigerated containers, cooking rooms and offers re-packaging, brokerage, and sales of food products from local producers.

3.3. *Common market (Toderita, 2014)*

Common Market is a non-profit social enterprise that collects crop and animal production of over 100 small farmers from local and regional level, within a distance of 120 km from Philadelphia. The purpose of this food hub is to support local agriculture and provide quality food at affordable prices to low-income population in the suburbs of Philadelphia through public institutions and traders serving the disadvantaged population in the area.

The food hub enroll in the "Farm to Institution" category, as it distribute fresh food to a network of 240 clients which are public institutions: schools, colleges, universities, hospitals, some restaurants, and food cooperatives.

Basically, the food hub regularly buys agricultural products from local farmers at a negotiated price. The relationship is not validated through written contracts, but by verbal agreements, operating on trust that the hub has developed in time with the farmers, and also due to the flexibility in price negotiations. Common Market farmer pays to the farmers on average 76% of the sale price — compared to only 20–30% as they receive through conventional distribution networks.

3.4. *Reading terminal market (Toderita, 2014)*

Reading Terminal Market is a market located in a former train depot in the center of Philadelphia, which rents 'stands' at advantageous tariffs to local and regional producers and traders for valuing agricultural output directly to final consumers.

4. The Regulatory Impact Assessment of RAM Needs in Romania

In the efforts to transfer to a food system model based on regional food markets functioning in Romania, there are required the promotion and processing of pragmatic approaches based on the methodology of Regulatory Impact Assessment (RIA), through interdisciplinary studies of emphasizing needs to create regional food markets. Although there are formally accepted in governmental and sectoral structures, currently no regulations impact studies are done following internationally established methodology, in order to commensurate opportunities and needs of the population, farmers, and processors in the food chain.

We also state that Romanian law generally, and the food sector, in particular, is still in a continuous change and accepts too many exceptions, which led to a inconsistent legislative conglomerate affecting the food business environment, especially small farmers, generating excessive bureaucracy, with negative effects on stakeholders from the entire agrifood chain.

All these loopholes and the lack of a strategy for industrialization of food products contributed indirectly but essentially, to major investments in the processing of agricultural products in Romania, without being related to the possibility of obtaining materials for covering these capabilities (far reaching to cover less than 40% of processing capacity), which resulted to the drawn of food sector in our country. This phenomenon is accompanied with poor quality landowners and foreign investors in agriculture and food industry, and refusal of foreign banks to provide loans to support agriculture, which transformed Romania from an exporter into a net importer of agricultural and food products (with a comeback in recent years, but which hasn't stopped the trade deficit).

There is, however, a positive aspect regarding food sector in our country, represented by Romanian investors who have created integrated production systems able to cope with the tough competition in the European Union and beyond, such as: *Insula Mare a Brăilei,*

Interagro, Agroindustriala Vaslui, Comcereal Dolj. Yet, as shown above, the problems arise from small and medium farmers for whom it have to be found solutions for marketing in terms of economic efficiency, to be stimulated in agricultural production.

This situation necessarily requires the development of macroeconomic impact studies, to properly assess the directions of development of Romania's agricultural sector in the medium and long term.

Currently, although Regulatory Impact Assessment (RIA) was performed through technical assistance with international financing, there is not yet a body of professionals specialized in interdisciplinary RIA studies at the macroeconomic level who know the issues facing the agrifood sector. Also, existing bodies dealing with public policies within relevant ministries are still in a phase of bureaucratic hesitation, consisting in apprehending details of laws provisions of the Articles and some post factum warnings, which are rarely considered by experts in the field.

In our opinion, the aforementioned elements can be a challenge to institutionalize consistent and professionally elaborate studies on impact assessment, in accordance with the methodology agreed at EU level to substantiate all strategic requirements, as a prerequisite for moving to a food system model based on exploitation of natural resources, and products locally and regionally, according to international best practices implemented in the field.

5. Model of Integrated Regional Agrifood System

Based on the above considerations and proposals, we have designed an integrated model of Regional Agrifood System, similar to those in the US, and developed countries in Europe, which consider all the links in the chain, starting from providing necessary inputs for agricultural production, primary production, transport and storage of agricultural products, processing and trading on various channels and providing support services for each link of the chain (management consulting, legal and financial consulting, independent laboratories for analysis, and certification of food products).

Also, we consider that in Romania it is necessary to create associations, such as food hubs, to provide to small farmers a number of basic services for the development of their activities. It is necessary, first, providing technical advice for acquisition and use of agricultural inputs required to obtain good quality primary products. Next, is needed transportation, storage, packaging, and transport to the next link, which is needed to broker the sale of agricultural products.

To increase the added value, are required processing units of agricultural products in small and medium capacities, in accordance with Hazard Analysis and Critical Control Points (HACCP) standards specific for food system. Implementation of HACCP and the creation of independent professional networks of public and private surveillance is one of the priority in the functioning of regional food markets, in order to monitor compliance and quality of food products and thus to increase food safety.

Implementation of HACCP is promoted at the European level through Directive 178/2002 which contains a number of principles and general requirements for food safety. The priority objectives of this regulation are (Craciunescu & Ciobanu, 2009):

- The availability of safe and healthy food products that come from local and regional sources;
- Ensure a high level of human life and health protection, through product quality monitoring on the whole food chain.

For the creation and development of agricultural processing units, we propose accessing European funded projects through the new National Rural Development Program 2014–2020, measure: "Support for investments in processing and marketing of agricultural products" — as a dedicated tool to implement a new model based on the creation and operation of regional agrifood markets.

The next link in the chain — food marketing — can be achieved through several local and regional channels such as:

- Networks of supermarkets locally and/or regionally;
- Networks of small shops locally and/or regionally;
- Stable and mouving market places;
- Online, with home delivery;
- Schools and other institutions and private companies.

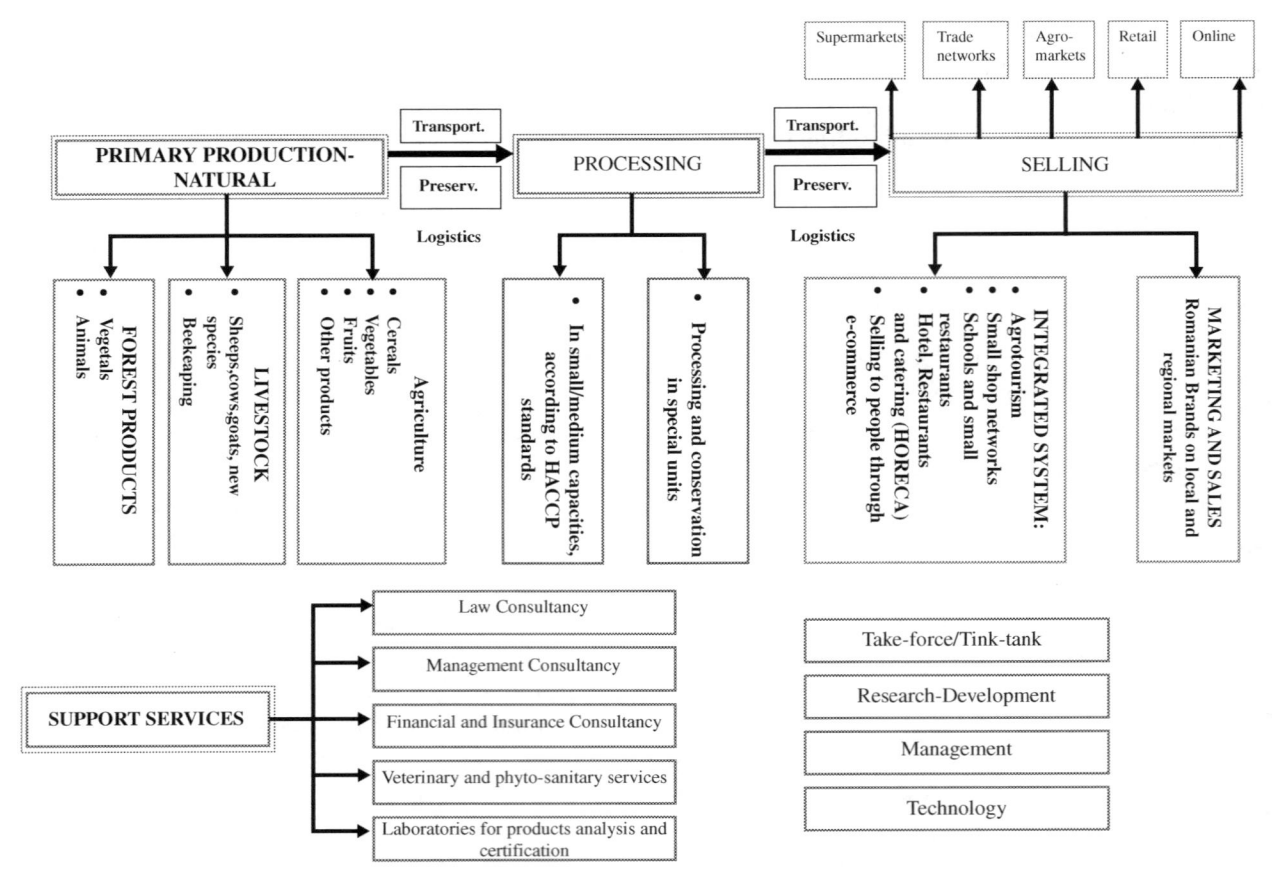

Fig. 2. Model of Integrated Regional Agrifood System

For the proper functioning of the new regional agrifood system, it is necessary that each link of the chain to benefit from a number of underlying services, such as management consulting, legal consulting, financial advisory, audit and assurance services, veterinary and phytosanitary services, independent laboratories for analysis and quality certification of agricultural and food products provided locally and/or regionally.

Fig. 2. shows a template of our contribution to creating a pilot Model of Integrated Regional Agrifood System.

6. Conclusions

In conclusion, future functioning, in Romania, of the Integrated Regional Agrifood System, which includes all links in the food chain from the local/regional level may lead to a more efficient use of natural resources and a gradual reduction in food trade dependence from international suppliers. This has the condition of providing support networks of cooperation between producers/processors/sellers and promote pragmatic quantifiable and stimulating policies of bridging facilities and agricultural subsidies with the need to develop production and sales of food commodities.

To implement this synergic project of agrifood system development in Romania are required joint efforts from the Government and authorities (all actors involved in food policies in Romania).

In this context it becomes obvious that all food market players must contribute to finding solutions for the production, collection and marketing of these products, mainly for small and medium producers. Of these, worthy of consideration are the following:

- Valorification of the agricultural potential of the country, which is able to provide quality raw materials to processors, for which can be achieved traceability and reduce dependence on imports of agricultural products with questionable quality;

- Participation of integrating economic organizations (the sphere of distribution and processing of agricultural products) to support small and medium farmers through win–win contracts between the two sides;
- Create new collection systems that can bring on private consumer market, food products made in the classical system (without allocation of pollutant inputs) by small and medium farmers, as shown in the proposed model;
- Create marketing chains composed of small shops that sell mainly fresh local products;
- Forbid the supermarkets opening in the inner cities and keeping them at a reasonable distance from populated areas, correlated with their orientation towards the purchase of local food products;
- EU funding of integrated projects in which funds are allocated to traders and processors, if they stimulate domestic production (in this way the production capacity can effectively be used and the domestic production is stimulated);
- Conversion to authorized individuals (at least, if not economic) of all "so called direct producers" who sell on the traditional markets, which will help reduce tax evasion and encourage the establishment of producer groups.

References

Brown, L. R. (Earth Policy Institute), (2011), *Lumea pe marginea prăpastiei — Cum să prevenim colapsul ecologic și economic*, Bucharest: Ed. Tehnică.

Craciunescu, V. & Ciobanu, E. (2009), Siguranta alimentului pe intelesul tuturor. Ghid realizat prin proiectul PHARE 2006/018-147.04.02.02.01.713 *Finantat de Uniunea Europeana si Guvernul Romaniei*, Bucharest: COMETAM Ltd.

European Comission (2002), General food law regulation. Available at http://www.aptus.ro/images/stories/Regulamentul-CE-nr._178_2002.pdf (Accessed 1–10 April 2014).

European Commission (2013), *Overview of CAP Reform 2014–2020*. Available at http://ec.europa.eu/agriculture/policy-perspectives/policy-briefs/05_en.pdf (Accessed 1–10 April 2014).

European Council of Young Farmers (2013), Draft supporting chapter for family farming consultation. Available at http://ec.europa.eu/agriculture/consultations/family-farming/contributions/ceja_en.pdf (Accessed 1–10 April, 2014).

Chapter 41

Comparative Analysis of the Factors Influencing the Development and Implementation of European Projects

Diana Elena Ranf and Liana Marcu

Romanian-German University of Sibiu

Dănuț Dumitru Dumitrașcu

Lucian Blaga University of Sibiu

The chapter is a conclusive part of a complex work that attempted to identify the factors of negative influence on the two stages of the cycle of European projects: Initiating European projects and implementation of European projects. The main objectives of the article are: Identifying the weights of each environmental factor into the influence on European projects, prioritizing them according to the degree of influence and making a comparison between the two stages analyzed from the factors identified.

The information that has enabled this analysis were obtained by conducting a research to identify the main problems and shortcomings encountered by beneficiaries of projects financed by European funds due to the negative influence of certain categories of factors. This research has resulted in an analysis of the practice of project management in public institutions in Region 7 Center and how it has resulted in successful projects.

This chapter is an ordering of the original results obtained from the research conducted on the topic, the validation of certain assumptions and awareness of deficiencies in the previous approach to the sector under investigation and suggesting new areas of research. Therefore, the data processed by means of statistical methods such as frequency analysis, correspondence analysis, and correlation analysis of the independent variables with the dependent variables allowed to obtain information that would lead to the development of models to increase performance in European projects.

One of the most relevant conclusion of the article resulted from the comparative analysis of the stages of European projects based on the degree of influence of environmental factors. There has thus been identified a decrease in the degree of influence of the absorption phase of the projects, with percentages up to 300%, therefore an improvement in the ability to combat negative factors with overcoming the stage of accessing projects.

1. Introduction

A preliminary study of literature in the field of projects in general, is shown in an abundance of books, studies and researches conducted in projects. From foreign literature, especially the American authors (Lewis, PJ,

Morris, P., Portny, E., Kerzner, H., etc.) and continuing with Romanian literature (Mocanu, M. & Schuster, C. Neagu, C. Dumitrascu, D. & Pascu, VR) we have identified a variety of books in project management. But, very few authors have touched the issue of European funded projects. European projects have a specificity that makes them different from other projects and they have been the subject of study for a small number of authors. The author Bârgăoan Alina treated European projects in a number of books and studies that have contributed both in the practice and theory of projects.

The need for a study to evaluate the results obtained at the end of the 2007–2013 funding period occurred as a result of reduced performance registered since then. Therefore, our country has a degree of absorption that has not crossed the threshold of 30%, remaining at the bottom of the classification of Community countries. Each funding period 2007–2013, 2014–2020, and so on, can be designed to help increase experience in the field. Thus, these periods may be associated with development cycles of six years in which Romania has the chance to improve certain skills, starting from the stage of development of strategic documents that program the funding process for the preparation of administrative structures that will become responsible for managing funds until improving skills in project management, which have a great contribution in accessing and absorbing European funds.

At the end of each period, particular importance is given to an analysis of the positive and negative diagnosis that led to the obtained results. This analysis is intended to help improve the results that Romania might get in the future in this area.

The population of interest for the study, namely the population from which the sample was selected, is made up of public institutions (municipalities, county councils, foundations, government, prefectures) or NGOs located in Region 7 Center. From this sample, two target groups were formed: institutions that have accessed European funds for identifying problems and difficulties in accessing and implementing and institutions that have not accessed European funds to identify potential causes of low level of access.

These two studies have allowed the identification of categories of environmental factors that have influenced the planning and implementation of projects, and on whose analysis and control may depend on the results that will be obtained in the funding period starting in 2014.

2. Share of the Influence of Environmental Factors on the Implementation of European Projects Developed by the Social Actors from Region 7 Center

This share occurs by identifying the degree of influence that environmental factors have had on each stage of the cycle of European projects, namely the definition, planning and implementation stages. Table 1 correlates the influence factors with the stages of the project through the problems in each stage and which were caused by one of the factors. The table contains only those factors from the internal and external environment whose influence has contributed to problems in the implementation of projects by the social actors in Region 7 Center.

To identify the factors of influence listed in the table, the problems faced by institutions were grouped according to of factors that caused them, namely:

- Problems like the lack of specialists in the field of projects, budgetary restrictions, understaffing, etc. encountered in the planning phase of projects are considered to be the result of internal environmental influence factors and were classified in the category "resources";
- Problems like poor legislation, mismatch between the guide and the law in force, long periods of time required to obtain permits, etc. have been classified as external environmental factors, specifically the "political and legislative factors."

Following this method, the classification of problems into categories of environmental factors, information that have allowed comparing the phases of the European projects depending on the action of the influence factors was obtained. As it can be seen from Fig. 1, internal factors outperform the external factors in terms of the influence on European funded projects. Resources have the most obvious influence and the categories of financial and human resources should be

Table 1. Influence of the environmental factors on the development of projects

		Filling in the application form	Contracting	Technical and financial reporting	Total problems/ factor
Internal environment	Resources	19	15	15	**49**
	Management	2	2	3	**7**
	Organisational culture	2	—	—	**2**
	Total	23	17	18	—
External environment (Micro-environment + Macro-environment)	Suppliers	9	10	8	**27**
	Economic factors	—	3	—	**3**
	Political and legislative factors	20	6	3	**29**
	Socio-cultural factors	1	—	—	**1**
	Technological factors	2	—	—	**2**
	Total	32	19	3	—
	Total problems	**55**	**36**	**21**	—

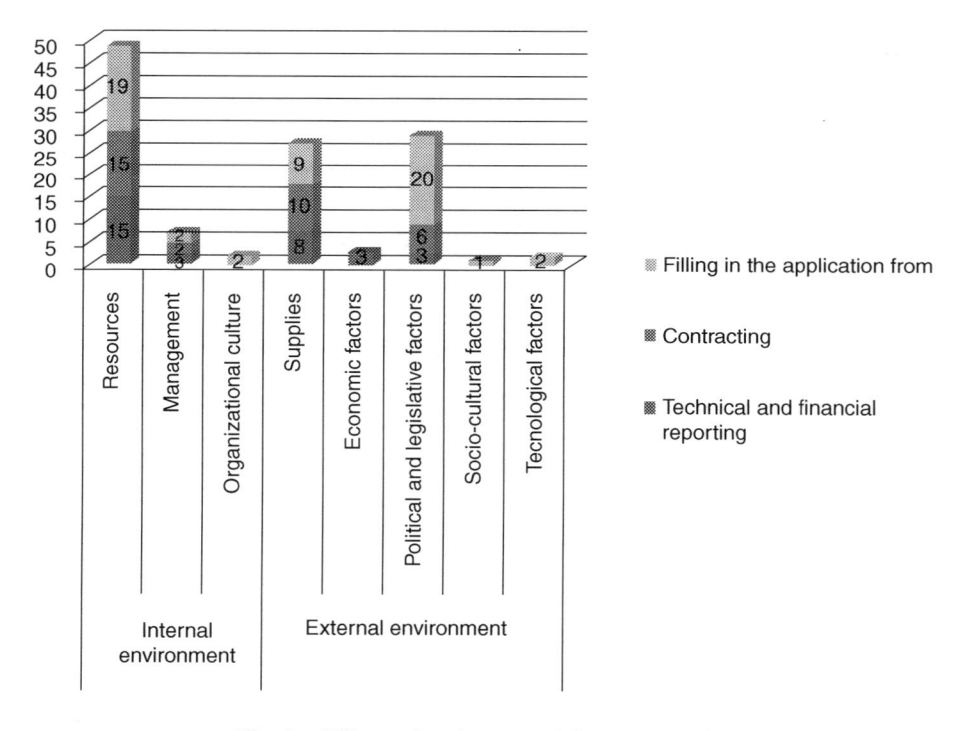

Fig. 1. Effects of environmental factors on projects

emphasized. It is actually quite known the lack of funds from public institutions, personnel restructuring that took place and the large number of vacancies that are still blocked. They have all brought a fairly high intake on the performance of these institutions in various fields, including European projects. It should be mentioned here, the lack of financial motivation, especially of existing staff who increasingly manifest disinterest in engaging in activities, which require extra work and effort.

From the external environmental factors, the highest share is held by the political and legislative factors, the effects of their influence being highlighted in the research conducted in chapters six and seven. Suppliers are an important source of problems, generating a fairly high number of problems.

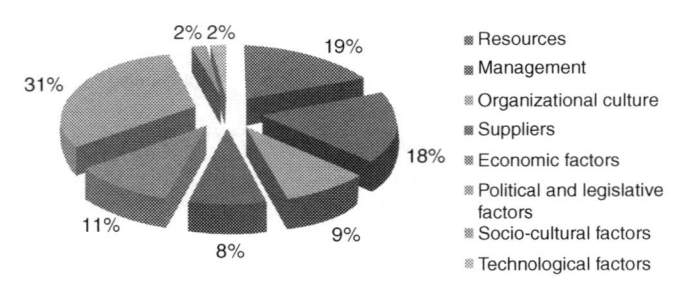

Fig. 2. Share of influence that environmental factors have on the carrying out of projects

In the category of suppliers, there were included the companies providing services, including consulting services and state institutions dealing with the coordination of European funds in Romania, namely the Intermediary Bodies which keep direct contact with project beneficiaries. They were blamed quite frequently by respondents for poor communication, damaging important projects undertaken by them. Also, consulting firms contracted by the institutions have been accused of lack of professionalism and fairness.

Figure 3 contains a hierarchy of influence factors from the general and specific external environment in regard to the action of the institutions in Region 7 Center. The ranking of external factors was based on the results of the research through which the problems faced by social actors in Region 7 Center and their shares carried out above have been identified.

Figure 4 outlines the influence of political and legislative factors, external factors that have a strong influence on institutions having accessed European funds in Region 7 Center based on problems reported by respondents in the research.

According to the answers of respondents who represent the institutions in the development Region 7 Center, political and legislative factors represented the category of external factors with the strongest negative influence on the running of projects by them. This conclusion results from the multitude of problems they have encountered, most of them having as cause the poor legislation and heavy bureaucracy, some with disastrous effects on projects. The disparity between legislation and guide entails a number of shortcomings both in the access and in project implementation.

Another category of factors influencing projects are, the stakeholders. Even by definition, these are factors that influence or are influenced, whether we refer to the context of an organization or of a project. Chapter five of the thesis deals with the categories of stakeholders who can have an impact on projects.

Figure 5 examines both the positive and negative effects that partners can have on the project. Partners are a group of stakeholders with significant importance in the projects developed from European funds, this also being obvious because a large number of problems encountered by the social actors from Region 7 Center.

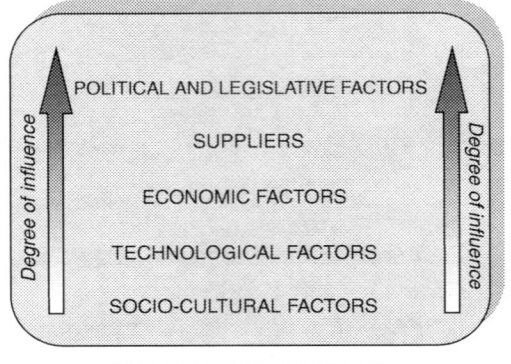

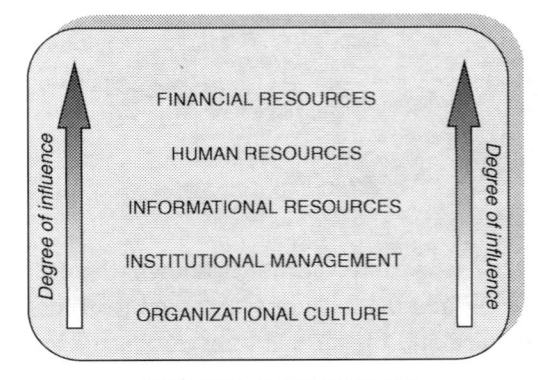

Fig. 3. Hierarchy of factors depending on the influence on running projects of social factors from Region 7 Center

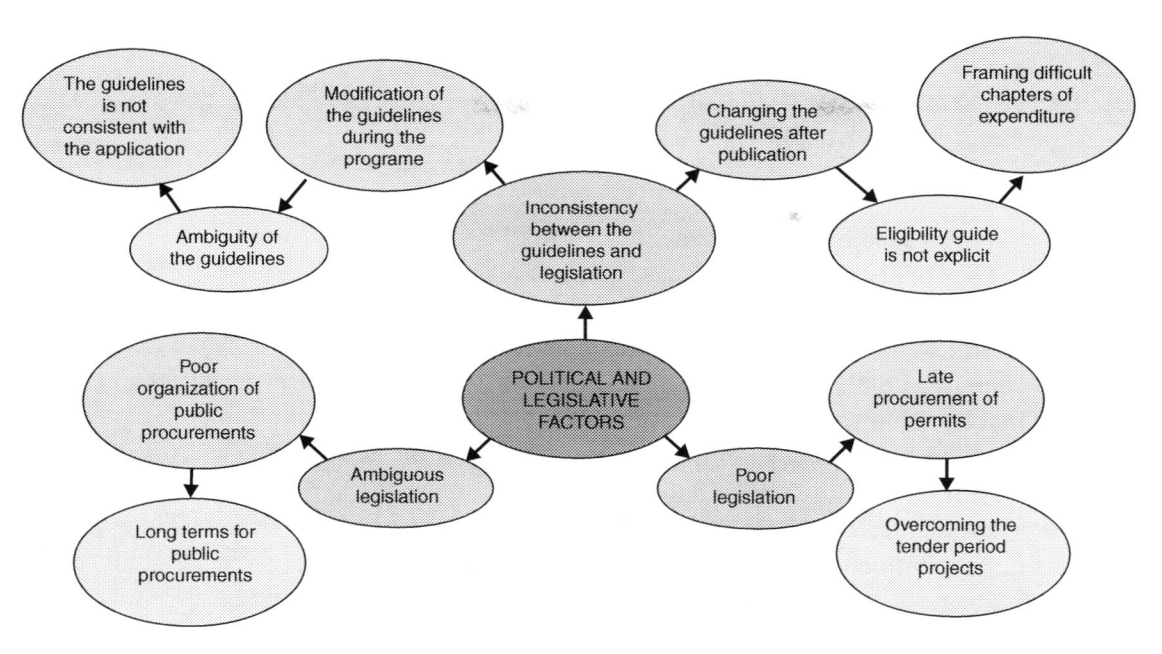

Fig. 4. The negative effect of the political and legislative factors' influence on the course of the European projects developed by the social actors in Region 7 Center

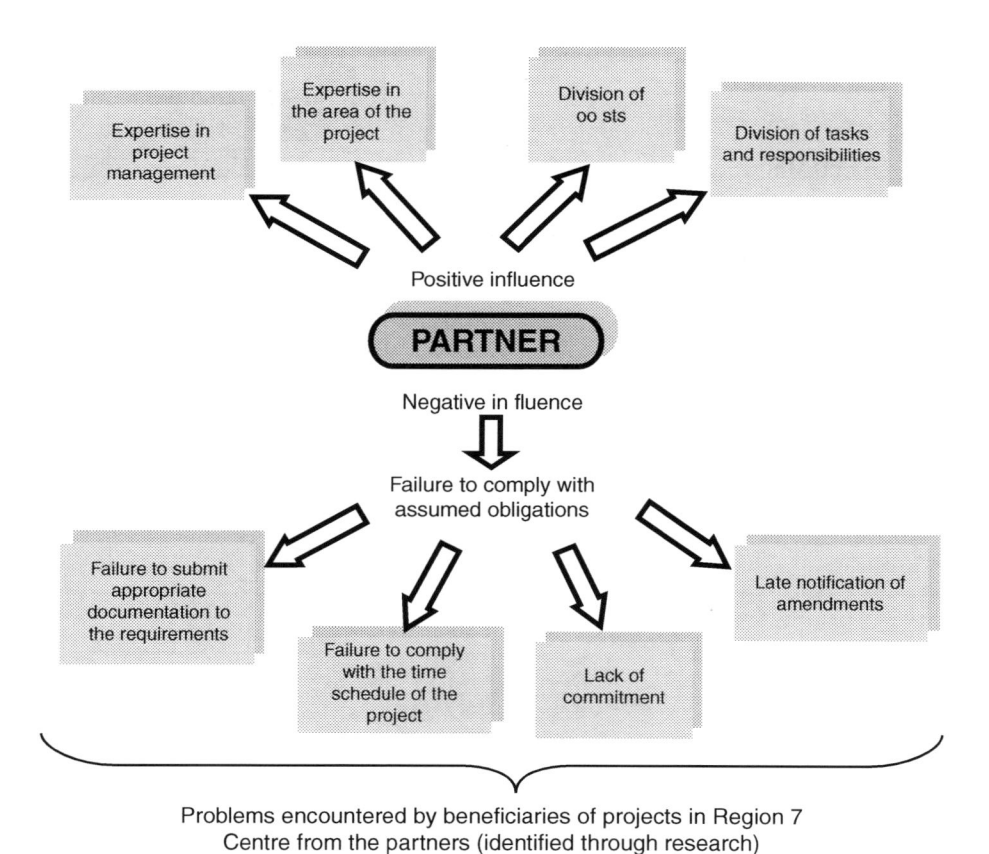

Fig. 5. The influence partners may have on the projects in which they were involved

3. Comparison between the Stages of Planning and Implementation of Projects Based on the Degree of Influence of Environmental Factors

The identification of the negative influence of environmental factors on the small degree of accessing European funds allows us a comparison of the extent to which they will influence the absorption of funds and access to funding. Therefore, Table 2 contains the percentages of factors that have influenced the decision to access funds and European funds absorption, percentages identified according to the methodologies described.

Table 2 shows that the influence that environmental factors have on the decision to access European funds is also maintained on the development of projects. In some cases there is emphasized, for example, the lack of resources affecting 19% of access to funds, which is felt more acutely in the implementation of projects, their influence having increased to 41% and affecting project implementation by causing various problems.

The influence of suppliers of services is felt also in the implementation of projects, but there are categories of factors whose influence decreases, for example, the institution's management reduces its negative influence and also the organizational culture improves, and the political and legislative factors are no longer perceived as negative, though, they are still the sources of multiple problems, as highlighted in the previous chapter.

Figure 6 highlights the evolution of the influence factors in the two stages of projects: access of projects (planning) and absorption of funds (project implementation). As it can be noticed, the categories of factors that remain constant in the two stages are the technological factors. Resources and suppliers are two categories whose influence grows in the stage of accessing the projects. The rest of the factors analyzed are characterized by a decrease in the degree of influence projects in the absorption stage, with a percentage of up to 300% (the economic factors).

4. Concluding Remarks

It can thus be concluded that, once the institutions manage to write projects and extend beyond the access period, they improve their ability to resist the negative impact of certain categories of factors.

Investigations made, can be helped identify certain aspects that may contribute to increased performance in European projects, but which have been neglected by the target group investigated, becoming the cause of a large number of problems in the implementation of projects. Therefore, Fig. 7 highlights ways that applicants for projects can follow to develop successful projects.

The recommendations from these reviews take into account the entire community of projects analyzed in the scientific enterprise approach, namely: project

Table 2. Comparison between access and absorption of funds according to the degree of influence of environmental factors

	Internal environment			Total	External environment					Total
	Resources (%)	Institutional management (%)	Organiational culture (%)		Suppliers (%)	Economic factors (%)	Political and legislative factors(%)	Socio-cultural factors (%)	Technological factors (%)	(%)
Accessing European funds	19	18	9	46	9	8	32	3	2	54
Absorption of European funds	41	6	2	49	22	2	24	1	2	51

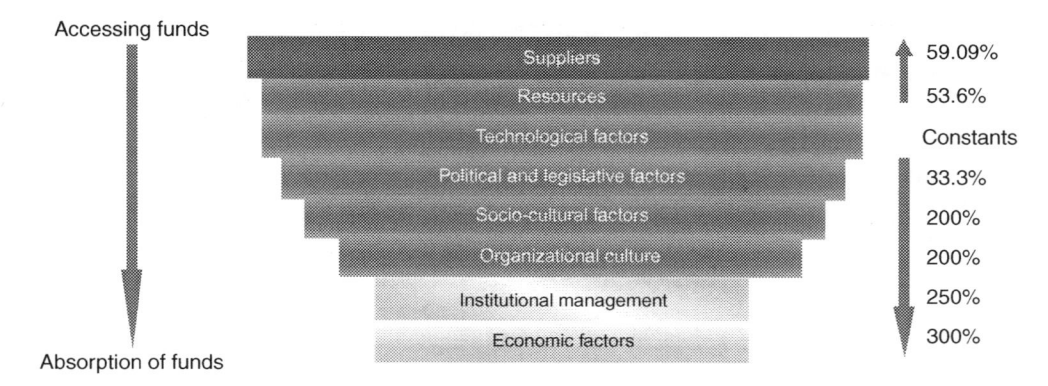

Fig. 6. Evolution of the influence of factors on projects from the stage of accessing the projects to the absorption stage of funds

Accessing funds → Absorption of funds

- Suppliers — ↑ 59.09%
- Resources — 53.6%
- Technological factors — Constants
- Political and legislative factors — 33.3%
- Socio-cultural factors — 200%
- Organizational culture — 200%
- Institutional management — 250%
- Economic factors — ↓ 300%

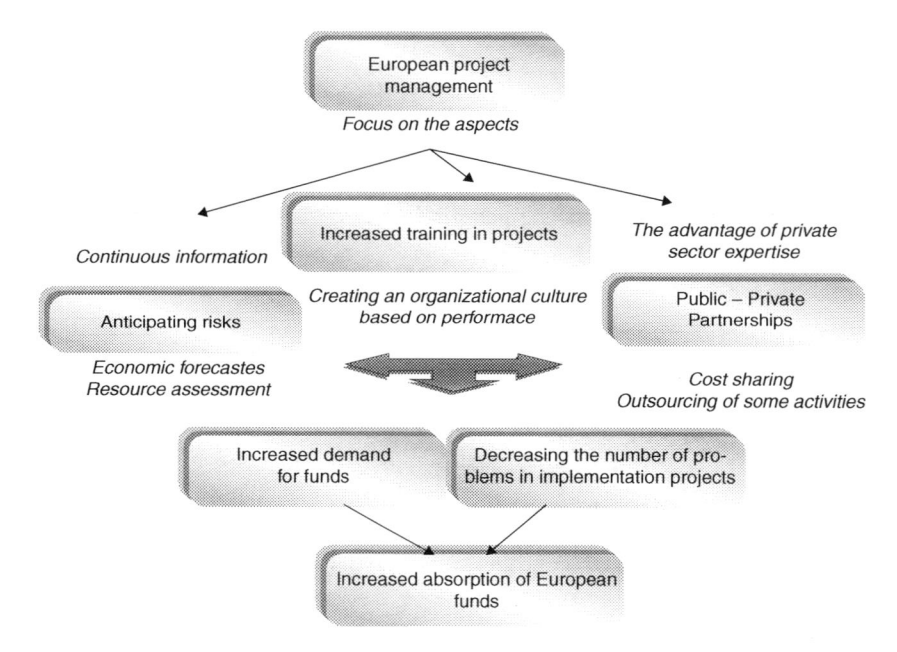

Fig. 7. Aspects which contribute to increased performance in European projects

developers, institutions managing European funds in Romania and other stakeholders (state, consulting companies, etc.):

- Awareness of the funding opportunities and hence the development opportunities that European funds offer to national and institutional levels, a condition of modernization and progress in Romania;
- Formulating and defining an investment policy in line with the strategic development coordinates set by institutions that would materialize in fine fundable European funds (eligible);
- Training and professional training of the staff involved in public institutions for the accumulation of skills on several levels, including project management;
- Adoption of a high level of professionalism at the institutional level and particularly in the field of project management through rigorous application of methods and techniques depending on the requirements of each project;
- Identifying ways to motivate employees to increase institutional performance, an example that could be the development of a career management

- professional or plotting an explicit occupational path for those working on projects;
- Since projects in the public field show an increased risk, being developed in a hostile environment, it is vital to make a preliminary analysis of potential negative factors that may affect the success of the project and to identify means to counteract risk generating factors;
- Decentralization of state institutions by reducing bureaucratic regulations and rigid hierarchical structures to help the document workflow implied by the project management cycle become more flexible;
- Simplification of procedures for accessing European funds to facilitate access to a growing number of institutions both in the public and private sector which would receive support and assistance throughout the project;
- Increasing the level of professionalism in negotiating priority areas investment by covering investment real needs of our country;
- To reach a level of maturity in projects at company level, it is important that the contribution made by each institution whose specific activity allows it to organize projects, but very important is the support of state institutions, which carry out the most complex projects, may provide examples of good practice and may involve private organizations in the implementation of projects.

The combination of projects and European funds meant to help improve the practice of project management based on the experiences made in the field of social actors from Region 7 Center. Achieving project management maturity contributes to the ability to face the dynamism and complexity of the environment in which we live and operate.

References

Bârgăoan, A. (2009), *European Funds — Strategies to Promote and Use*, Bucureşti: Tritonic Publisher House.

Dumitrascu, D. & Pascu, V. R. (2005), *Project Management*, Sibiu: ULBS Publisher House.

Kerzner, H. (2005), *Proiect Management — Planning, Scheduling and Control*, Milano: Italian Edition by Ulrico Hoelipi Publisher House.

Mocanu, M. & Schuster, C. (2004), *Project Management*, Bucuresti: All Beck Publisher House.

Lewis, P. J. (2010), *Project Planning, Scheduling and Control*, SUA: McGraw Hill Publisher House.

Morris, P. & Pinto, J. K. (2007), *The Wiley Guide to Project Program and Portofolio Management*, New Jersey: Wiley & Sons Publisher House.

Neagu, C. (2007), *Project Management*, Bucuresti: Tritonic Publisher House.

Portny, E. S. (2010), *Project Management for Dummies*, SUA: Wiley Publishing.

Ranf, D. & Dumitraşcu, D. (2012a), Study on the problems in the stages of filling out the application form and technical-financial reporting encountered by the public institutions in the center region in accessing european funds, annals of the University of Oradea. *Economics*, No.1/156/2012, pp. 1059–1065.

Ranf, D. & Dumitraşcu, D. (2012b), Case study on the state of projects accessed by public institutions in center region, *Studies in Business and Economics*, 64(6), 96–106.

Chapter 42

Organizational Change — Managing Employees Resistance

Viorel Cornescu

"Nicolae Titulescu" University

Roxana Adam

National Institute of Economic Research
Romanian Academy

This chapter presents a theoretical perspective concerning the management of change and innovation and correlates it with aspects of employees' reactions to change. The central proposal of the chapter is that resistance to change is a basic human characteristic and it strongly depends on every individual's nature. Each organizational change induces a certain level of resistance in employee behavior which may in turn affect its implementation and the smooth running of things. The review shows that change is uncomfortable and managers need to find new ways of thinking and doing it, ways that should lead the organization to solve its problems in the most efficient manner. The chapter derives its originality from the fact that it exceed the focus on the technical elements of change and it brings to the forefront the key human element which is central to the successful implementation of change in organizations. The case study presents the orientation of a Romanian university towards organizational change. It reveals the most common types of organizational change among faculties and some significant factors that could contribute to block the change. Analyzing the nature of the successful methods used in producing new ideas or to increase individuals' creativity, the study reveals the importance of financial and non-financial incentives in motivating employees.

1. Introduction

Organizational change emerges from the dynamics of the environment and is inevitable in a society based on fast technological development. Organizations change when the market demands it and often represents the organizations' intention to grow and or to achieve its objectives. Managing organizational change is a difficult phase in an organizations life, because it involves a transfer from a "known" to an "unknown" situation. Starting from the assumption that these changes are not once-in-a-lifetime technological or structural revolutions that involve mass layoffs or the elimination of traditional professions, we consider that organizational changes lead on to an increase in productivity which, in a competitive market, may be vital to business progress.

Rieley & Clarkson (2001) suggested that if organizations were not constantly changing, its performance could not be effective or improved. However, during the past years, due to the large number of new or improved products and services for more and more organizations change is vital. Let's think a little bit to the story of Kodak Company. A considerable number of authors wrote about Kodak and its years of success and also about its failure. Gavetti *et al.* (2004) analyzed the situation of Kodak Company through time. Starting from 1993, when George Fisher was chosen as chief executive, the Kodak Company was oriented to an organizational change process, yet in 1997 *"the old-line manufacturing culture continues to impede Fisher's efforts to turn Kodak into a high-tech growth company. Fisher has been able to change the culture at the very top. But he hasn't been able to change the huge mass of middle managers, and they just don't understand this [digital] world."* (Gavetti *et al.*, 2004). The company tried also an open discussion in the Motorola style, *Kodak executives tended to be very polite and things looked much easier than they actually were. Kodak's employees didn't like confrontation and venerated authority [...] Fisher tried to introduce the Motorola-style of open discussion, but change was difficult* (Gavetti et al., 2004).

Luecke (2003) claimed that to be effective and able to improve performance people need routines, therefore we consider that people need habits to become acquainted with a new process, but at the same time, in the new era of fast technology, change is a requirement, it's the way to performance. Organizational change is a process that should come as a response to the organizations' needs, while taking account of its employees and in accordance with a well-established schedule. Organizational change is influenced by contextual factors and there is not a recipe for success to prescribe the amount of time needed since an organizational change took place before another organizational change. Change is not about regularity in time, it's about organizational and employee's needs, about performing or surviving in a competitive market. It is wrong to consider change itself to be inherently good (Hultman, 1979), or bad, because change can only be evaluated after its goals were or not achieved and its consequences. However, sometimes employees predict consequences based on the perceived information or on their past experiences.

From a theoretical perspective, change is characterized most often by how it comes about. When change is being characterized, a large number of chapters refer to planned and emergent change (Bamford & Forrester, 2003). Planned change refers to a premeditated, agent-acilitated intervention intended to modify organizational functioning for a more favorable outcome (Lippit *et al.*, 1958) and it is the most common type of change. The planned action of a change agent (individual or group) to create something new is characterized by: A main and rational purpose, The method used in the change process influences the quality and Direction of change and in any change process, the adoption rate is different. According to the Emergent approach, change is a continuous, dynamic and contested process that emerges in an unpredictable and unplanned fashion. For Weick (2000), the advantages of Emergent change include: *"... sensitivity to local contingencies; suitability for on-line real-time experimentation, learning, and sense making; comprehensibility and manageability; likelihood of satisfying needs for autonomy, control, and expression; proneness to swift implementation; resistance to unraveling; ability to exploit existing tacit knowledge; and tightened and shortened feedback loops from results to action"* (Burnes, 2009).

According to Burnes (2004), the two approaches share a common, and major, difficulty, which is that whilst both claim to be universally applicable; they were developed with particular change situations, organisations types and environments in mind. The Planned approach appears to be predicated on the assumption that organisations operate in stable or relatively predictable environment, the managers can identify where change is required, that change projects are concerned primarily with group attitudes and behaviors, and the change is about moving from one fixed point and that the steps or phases in between are relatively clear and realisable. He also claims that the Emergent approach, on the other hand, assumes that organisations are open and fluid systems that operate in unpredictable and uncertain conditions over which they have little control. It further assumes that change is a continuous process of adaptation which, because of its speed and frequency, managers can neither fully identify nor effectively control centrally (Burnes, 2004).

With minor differences, both theories consider that managers and employees are oriented towards change. They are characterized as willing to change, competent and adaptable, ready to implement change. Skipping the theoretical aspects, what actually happens is that no matter the type of change, change creates challenges for us all. It brings stress and anxiety, as well as the possibility for optimism (Carnall, 2007). Due to its uncertainty, change creates challenges for employee and managers, being a difficult process also for those who are managing change.

2. Resistance to Change

Although change is intended to be a benefit for the organization or its employees, the employees' behavior it is not always *for* change. Resistance to change is the employees' natural reaction to the change process. When a change is introduced in organization, it produces a range of reactions due to the inherent uncertainty or to the incentives that alter human behavioral patterns such as: *status quo*, anxiety, lack of tolerance, etc.

Frequent resistance to change is defined as, a reaction of human behavior against undesired consequence of change, in other words a natural reaction caused by losing control — *anxiety*. Ford *et al.* (2002) in a review of the literature say that resistance occurs because it threatens the *status quo*, or increases fear and the anxiety of real or imagined consequences including threats to personal security and confidence in an ability to perform.

Resistance is a natural phenomenon in the change process; it is not necessarily towards change itself, but towards the implications of the change. The process of passing from known to unknown implies uncertainty, therefore individuals' perceived threats towards a state which they knew, controlled and it was a satisfactory stage. Change menaces the way people make sense of their actions, bringing into question their rationality, values and their understanding or assessment of the situation at different stages. In organizations, moreover, people resist change because they: Perceive negative effects to their interests; the uncertainty of the future situation determines a high degree of discomfort; are attached to the organizational culture, lack of convention or clarity to what is needed; they just dislike the change or due other contextual situations, personal characteristics, and organizational goals.

Resistance to change represents an obstacle to in any change initiatives. The specific features of change, a high degree of ambiguity or risky parameter, can lead to a lack of participation and transmission of correct information among those involved. Resistance to change is divided into three groups of factors (Mabin *et al.*, 2001): Individual, roup and Organizational.

An interesting approach to the individual's resistance is Kotter & Schlesinger's (1979) research, the authors suggest that people resist change for various reasons, but the most common reasons for resisting change are:

— Individuals interests, people are characterized by their own interests and by the desire not to give up something of value;
— A misunderstanding of the change and its implications;
— A belief that the change does not make sense for the organization;
— Low tolerance for change.

From the literature, Coch & French (1948) focused their research on individual factors by analyzing psychological factors such as — fear, feelings of failure, resentment, frustration, and low motivation. Other studies have approached factors like — habit, tradition, stability, insecurity (Watson, 1969) or selective perception, economic implications, fear of the unknown, loss of freedom (Mullins, 1999) and other auxiliary factors.

According to Mabin *et al.* (2001) divisions of resistance to change into three groups of factors, we associate the Watson orientation on conformity to norms, systemic and cultural coherence, vested interests, sacred values, and rejection of outsiders (Gravenhorst, 2003) to the group factors approach and Mullins orientation on organization culture, maintaining stability, investment in resources, past contracts and agreements, and threats to power or influence (Gravenhorst, 2003) to the organizational factors approach. Resistance is a normal stage in change progress, it is a natural defense mechanism. Regarding human behavior, resistance is a common reaction of individuals because people are naturally wary of change.

Individuals' reactions to change are a result of their emotions with respect to change (Liu & Perrewe, 2005). Also, recent studies have provided evidence of a complex relationship between employees' emotions and their reactions to change (Avey et al., 2008; Hareli & Rafaeli, 2008). Starting from the conceptual framework of the operationalizing cognitions of Bovey & Hede (2001), we have schematized the individual's cognitive process at the impact of the change (See Fig. 1).

Research indicates that irrational ideas are significantly and positively correlated with employees' resistance to change. Individuals tend to have automatic thoughts that incorporate what has been described as faulty, irrational, or "crooked thinking" (Bovey & Hede, 2001; Wittig, 2012). The individual's cognitive process at the impact of the change shows that employees have their own ideas of what it means the particular change. The ideas might be rational, as well as irrational. Ellis and Harper (1975) defined irrational ideas through examples, some of them are: the approval from all important people in a person's life; fears of failure request a high degree of competency; the individual is preoccupied with anxiety, self-blame or that people are acting unfairly; they don't control their own feelings and destiny; it is easier to avoid life's difficulties than facing them, today behaviors' and feelings of individuals are influenced by their own past experiences, etc.

Starting from individual cognition and passing through the information offered by the organization regarding the change, leads each employee to draw a personal map, according to his perception about the change process. The designed map of the change impact together with the individuals' ideas creates powerful emotions. Later, based on these emotions, employees will decide to adopt or to resist organizational change. Eisenberger et al. (1990) in their empirical study have demonstrated that employees' perceived organizational support is related to various attitudes and behaviors. Other authors (Vakola et al., 2004) identified multiple studies in which the positive attitudes of employees toward change were vital in achieving successful organizational change initiatives.

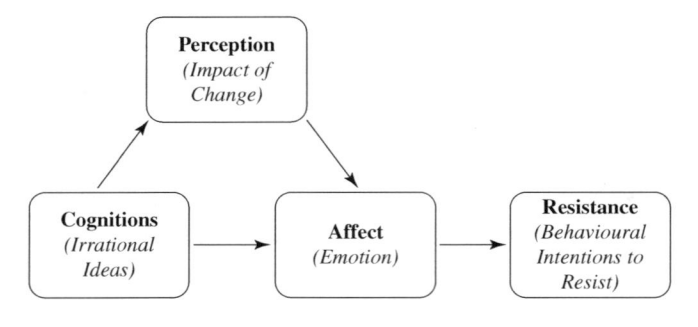

3. Managers, Employees, and Organizational Change

Organizational change is an ambitious objective which involves different actors of organizations, often employees and managers. From the managements' perspective resistance is the behavior of organization's members who refuse to adopt an organizational change (Chew et al., 2006; Cheng & Petrovic-Lazarevic, 2004; Coghlan, 1993).

Resistance to change was studied through various models of resistance and the two most important are: a psychological model and a systems model. The psychological model of resistance states that in basic human characteristics resides the source of resistance to change: personalities, perceptions, and needs. The idea of change suggests itself for most people a kind of manifestation of resistance response, often caused by uncertainty, lack of tolerance and threatened self-importance. The basic principle of the systems model of resistance is that resistance to change shows that the members of the organization feel uncomfortable with the modifications required by the change, it is not a change *per se* that people resist but the changes associated with it, such as losing their comfort or something that are satisfied with.

There are also others models which study resistance to change, such as: organization's culture, institutionalized resistance to change, and so on. When it comes to the organizations' culture, employees are sharing common organizational standards and norms which influence their behavior and any attempt to change its core elements must be thoroughly designed because other ways might meet employee resistance. While the institutionalized resistance to change explains that the organizational members perceive the change as being unnecessary and therefore they manifest resistance to it.

Besides these theoretical models, in reality resistance may be summarized as any employee actions perceived as attempting to stop, delay, or alter change (Bemmels & Reshef, 1991). Resistance to change is not

Fig. 1. Individual's cognitive process at the impact of the change.

the fundamental problem to be solved. Rather, any resistance is usually a symptom for more basic problems underlying a particular situation (Singh & Waddell, 2004). Resistance can therefore serve as a warning signal (Judson, 1966) for managers. There are a variety of factors which can lead to resistant behavior, according to their nature we can classify in: psychological, economic, and social factors. An important role in organizational change it is played by social factors, furthermore by the management factors. Inappropriate or poor management style also contributes to resistance (Judson, 1966).

Ansoff (1988) defined resistance as a multifaceted phenomenon which introduces unanticipated delays, costs, and instabilities into the process of a strategic change, therefore management may greatly benefit from techniques that prudently manage resistance, by utilizing or overcoming it.

In the managerial context, at the beginning, resistance was presented as an enemy of positive changes that were to bring organizational progress and growth (Azad et al., 2013), later more advanced sociological and psychological researches have approached positively the concept, in a strong contrast to the traditional viewpoint, revealing its utility as a way to actually improve management of change in modern organization (Azad et al., 2013).

Resistance can reveal aspects of change which may prove to be inappropriate, or they might reveal a problem in the organization's method of communication. The big issue for managers is not how to eliminate resistance, rather to identify its cause.

According to Singh & Waddell (2004), managers must be aware that employees manifest resistance due to the different aspects of the change, in addition they should be encouraged to re-evaluate the change and its implications. They should regularly communicate and consult the organizations' employees, to search alternative methods of introducing change. An important role in the change process is that managers should involve employees in the change project, requiring feedback to ensure support. Therefore the natural outcome of people's internal defense mechanism (Bovey & Hede, 2001) could be used by management in the favor of the change process.

As Yue (2008) mentioned, some employees will find developing a broader set of relationships at work to be a stimulating new challenge and personally fulfilling; however, others may find these new relationships to be incompatible with their more restricted concept of self, and experience increased role strain and stress.

When the organization is on the verge of implementing change, the employees' behavior must be analyzeddand monitored by managers. Through a brief passing in specialized literature, we have selected the most three common recommended methods to overcome or manage the resistant behavior:

(a) Improving information and communication — the best alternative when managers identify that the primary cause of resistance is lack of information;
(b) Employees involvement and participation — employees' involvement in the change process leads to promotion of the change process, a promotion made by organizations' employees. Resistance is unlikely to come from employees that took part in the change process and they provide useful information to improve the implementation of desired change;
(c) Management assistance and support — when employees encounter problems adapting to change, leading to a resistant behavior, in order to facilitate the transition management representatives should guide employees in this regard.

An effective change requires management approaches that enhance change through employees' participation, motivation, and a correct perception of information. To encourage employees' participation, managers have to offer material, moral, and emotional support according to the circumstances encountered. In a change process, managers also ought to attempt to know what can influence employees' behavior, the most important ways to motivate them, such as: Job satisfactions, gains or other intrinsic or extrinsic motivation. Another sensitive part is that managers should be able to interpret the inputs of the employees' black box and to ensure the information and organization objectives have been correctly perceived. We can conclude that, depending on the relationship between managers and subordinates, resistance may be managed in favor of change and overcome. Is this a problem about rules, about skills about managers' characteristics? We can't claim one or another, theoretically it's about all that implies this relationship, and in reality it's a complex process depending on many factors, circumstances, and most important, human characteristics. Moreover resistance to change in organizations occurs when it creates too much role incapability for employees.

Zeffane (1996) argues that change can only succeed if it is based solidly on an understanding of how people behave, what motivates them, and how improved positive attitudes can be developed. In organizational change good communication between managers and employees should be developed, it is preferable that everyone who is affected by change to be involved in planning and implementing change. As we have already mentioned, employees are an important component in organizational change, it is useful to know their concerns and fears, because, through an appropriate management style, it is possible to diminish the impact of change in order to avoid loss of productivity and decreased performance.

4. Case Study

Purpose: This study presents the organizational change in the academic environment. It presents the profile of a Romanian university regarding the process of change, the management approach towards change and the main factors which influence organizational change.

Research limitations/implications: This study assumes that universities are similar to companies, with various hierarchical levels. It examines the organizational change at only one time point in faculties of one university. The reference period is the currently mandate and perceptions of the change may differ over time.

Methodology: Participants include the faculty governing body, one representative for each faculty of the studied university. An online questionnaire was used in order to obtain representative data, by identifying different aspects of the organizational change in faculties to describe the university orientation towards organizational change.

A preliminary study showed that the university is a promoter of the "new" and "change". The preliminary study took the *form* of informal interviews with 20 Romanian professors from different universities and was *conducted* as a *preliminary* step to the present work, therefore, after the interviews we designed the framework of the current research. The University is an institution which produces ideas and knowledge. It generates new insights, which in one way or another will inevitably lead to change. Romanian higher education system is oriented toward a knowledge-based society and the universities are pursuing the valorization of staff (professors) creativity, and also to train young specialists with an opening towards: apply the "new", create the "new", and mitigate,or eliminate resistance to change of organization members.

We have divided the main organizational change which can be found in universities into three groups: changing the occupational area and content of staff faculty duties (e.g., new tasks, new working methods, equipment and new programs, etc.), changing the status of university employees (e.g., didactic promotion, salary increase, delegating managerial, professional development, etc.) and changing the formal and informal social relations within the faculty staff (e.g., restructuring the micro-groups, informal leaders revaluation, increasing cohesion between groups, reducing conflicts, modify faculty employees value, etc.).

The University, as an organization, is not exempted from resistance to change, which may take the form of: The university management's resistance to faculty's employees' proposals (faculty management or professors), employee resistance to management's proposal or to students' proposal. Since universities are operating at different hierarchical levels, we have associated universities' structure with a pyramid at the top of which the Academic Senate and the Rector can be found, in the middle are the university faculties and at the bottom are all the departments of each faculty. The tip of the pyramid is represented by the legal provisions which are limiting the university activities, and the pyramid base line is represented by students. Because the general operating diagram of Romanian universities is too complex, and resistance to change can manifest from the bottom up, and also in the other direction, from the top of the pyramid down, we have chosen to investigate only the changes that may occur within the university, the main influence factors and the employee (professors) resistance.

Findings: Based on the survey response from the faculty governing body of 13 faculties of the same

Romanian university, the results of the statistical analysis show that the studied university is oriented towards change, all the faculties acted to change the occupational area and content of staff faculty duties, 85% of faculties claimed to change the status of university employees and more than 90% claimed to change the formal and informal social relations within the faculty staff.

For the organizational change within the university's faculties, the most important objectives were: improving learning conditions for students and improving communication and information exchange across the university or with other institutions or organizations. Other significant objectives have been: to improve teaching methods, to improve learning conditions for students, and to improve the ability to develop new educational approaches.

During the reference period of the study, the implementations of changes within the three change categories were:

— Aim to change the occupational area and content of staff faculty duties: 54% have been accepted and in a proportion of 46% have been implemented;
— Aim to change the status of university employees: 77% have been implemented, 15% have been accepted and 8% refused;
— Aim to change the formal and informal social relations within the faculty staff: a proportion of 46% have been implemented, 38% accepted, 8% refused, while for a proportion of 8% no change were necessary.

Most of the changes regarding the content of teaching and staff duties introduced in university were: the addition of new tasks for employees with the same career positions, significantly improved or new working methods and new bachelor/master programs. In most of the cases, changes were initiated and supported by faculty heads and professors.

Regarding the change of employees' position within university, most of the introduced changes were: the collaboration with external experts, employees' promotion, attracting new employees for new positions and investments in research and development. Also this time, the changes were initiated and supported mostly by faculty heads and professors.

For the third organizational change type, changing the formal and informal social relations within the faculty, the most common changes within university were: to reduce the within-group conflicts and increase cohesion between groups. The actions were initiated and supported mostly by faculty heads and professors.

Most of the changes at faculty level already existed in other university's faculties; the organizational changes that have been recorded in faculties with no precedent in university mostly were focused on the formal and informal social relations change, within the faculty staff.

The most significant factors that have prevented the university's faculties to accept change or which have blocked it were cost factors, such as: lack of university or faculty funds and lack of funding from external sources. Another significant factor was the discouraging legislative regulation, while employees though lack of motivation and complacency had a significant impact.

Of the analyzed faculties 92% used various methods to stimulate new ideas and creativity among professors. The nature of the successful methods used in producing new ideas or to increase creativity have been: financial incentives for the creation and development of new ideas and non-financial incentives such as free time, public recognition, mobility, honorary titles, etc.

Practical implications: These findings suggest that the main problems encountered in achieving organizational change were determined by higher cost, discouraging legislative regulations and human capital. We also observed that financial and non-financial incentives were successful methods used in producing new ideas and increase creativity. Therefore, we consider that a possible cause of employee resistance or disinterest toward organizational change within university may be low motivation due to lack of financial and non-financial incentives.

Originality: This study shows that the analyzed university is oriented toward change, by adopting several organizational changes. A nationwide study may bring to the forefront important factors for the Romanian education system which may contribute to the development of a knowledge-based society.

5. Conclusions

The organizational change creates challenges for managers and employees, and therefore change has a big impact on individuals in the organization. The theoretical aspects characterize individuals as willing to change and adapt, moreover ready to implement change. We consider that effective management of change is based on a clear understanding of human behavior in the organization.

Through the *literature review* presented we have shown that some of the organizational change issue and a positive perspective regarding resistance to change. Due to the challenge of change, individuals may have a defensive or negative attitude and to resist to change. Therefore, successful implementation of change in organization demands a good knowledge of the features and a high orientation towards analyzing the employees' behavior.

The case study has shown the orientation of a Romanian university towards organisational change. Analyzing the three organisational change types, the factors that could lead to a resistance to change or which may block it and, by identifying the change promoters, we have created the profile towards organisational change of one university. The study also suggests an assumption for future research: Increasing employees' motivation to get involved in the organizational change process, minimize employees resistance to change. Considering that in most of the cases, changes were initiated and supported by faculty heads and professors, we consider that the proper employees' motivation may contribute in a constructive manner to a positive organizational change.

In conclusion, involving individuals directly in the organizational change process may bring out good change ideas and contribute towards organizational change acceptance. Therefore change agents should consider the behavior characteristics of individuals in order to achieve effective and successful organizational change.

References

Ansoff, H. I. (1988), *The New Corporate Strategy*, New York: John Wiley and Sons, Revised-Edition (February, 1988), 202–217.

Avey, J. B., Wernsing, T. S., & Luthans, F. (2008), Can positive employees help positive organizational change? *Journal of Applied Behavioral Science*, 44(1), 48–70.

Azad et al. (2013), Resistance to change: A blessing or a curse? *Interdisciplinary Journal of Contemporary Research In Business*, 4(12), April.

Bamford, D. R. & Forrester, P. L. (2003), Managing planned and emergent change within an operations management environment, *International Journal of Operations & Production Management*, 23(5), 546–564.

Bernard Burnes, (2004), *Managing Change: A Strategic Approach to Organisational Dynamics*, Harlow: Financial Times Prentice Hall.

Bernard Burnes, (2009), *Managing Change*, Harlow: Financial Times Prentice Hall.

Bemmels & Reshef, (1991), Manufactoring employees and technological change, *Journal of Labour Research*, 12 (3), 231–246.

Bovey, Wayne, H., & Hede, A. (2001), Resistance to organizational change: the role of cognitive and affective process, *Leadership & Organization Development Journal*, 22(8), 372–382.

Cheng, J. S. L. & Petrovic-Lazarevic, S. (2004), The role of effective leadership in doing more with less in public universities, Chapter presented at Global Business and Technology Association Sixth Annual Conference, Cape Town, South Africa, June.

Chew, M. M. M., Cheng, J. S. L., & Petrovic-Lazarevic, S. (2006), Managers' role in implementing organizational change, *Journal of Global Business and Technology*, 2(1), 58–67.

Coch, L. & French, J. R. P., Jr. (1948), Overcoming resistance to change, *Human Relations*, 1, 512–532.

Coghlan, D. (1993), A person-centerd approach to dealing with resistance to change, *Leadership & Organization Development Journal*, 14(4), 10–14.

Carnall, C.A. (2007), *Managing Change in Organization* (5th edn.), London, UK: Prentice Hall.

Eisenberger, R., Fasolo, P., & Davis-LaMastro, V. (1990), Perceived organizational support and employee diligence, commitment, and innovation, *Journal of Applied Psychology*, 75, 51–59.

Ellis, A. & Harper, R.A. (1994), *A new guide to rational living*, North Hollywood, CA: Wilshire Book Company.

Gavetti, G., Henderson, R., & Giorgi, S. (2004), Kodak (A), February 18, Harvard Bussiness School.

Gravenhorst, K. M. B. (2003), A different view on resistance to change, Chapter for "Power Dynamics and Organizational Change IV" Symposium at the 11th EAWOP Conference in Lisbon, Portugal, 14–17 May.

Hultman, K. (1979), *The Path of Least Resistance, Learning Concepts*, Denton, TX.

Hareli, S., & Rafaeli, A. (2008), Emotion cycles: On the social influence of emotion in organizations, *Research in Organizational Behavior*, 28, 35–59.

Ford, J. D., Ford, L. W., & McNamara, R. T. (2002), Resistance and the background conversations of change, *Journal of Organizational Change Management*, 15(2), 105–121.

Judson (1966), *A Managers Guide to Making Changes*, London: John Wiley & Sons.

Kotter, J. P. & Schlesinger, L. A. (1979), Choosing strategies for change, *Harvard Business Review*, 57, 106–114.

Lippit, R., Watson, J., & Westley, B. (1958), *The Dynamics of Planned Change*, New York: Harcourt Brace.

Liu, Y. & Perrewe, P. L. (2005), Another look at the role of emotion in the organizational change: A process model, *Human Resource Management Review*, 15, 263–280.

Mabin, V. J., Forgeson, S., & Green, L. (2001), Harnessing resistance: using the theory of constraints to assist change management, *Journal of European Industrial Training*, 25(2/3), 168–191.

Mullins, L. J. (1999), Management and organisational behavior (5th edn.), London: Financial Times/Prentice Hall.

Rieley, J. B. and Clarkson, I. (2001), The impact of change on performance, *Journal of Change Management,* 2(2), 160–172.

Singh, M. & Waddell, D. (2004), E-Business Innovation and Change Management, PaperBack, Waddell, Idea Group Inc.

Vakola, M., Tsaousis, I., & Nikolaou, I. (2004), The role of emotional intelligence and personality variables on attitudes toward organizational change, *Journal of Managerial Psychology*, 19(2), 88–110.

Watson, G. (1969), Resistance to change. In *The Planning of Change*, W. G. Bennis, K. D. Benne & R. Chin (eds.), (2nd edn., pp. 488–498), New York: Holt, Rinehart & Winston.

Wittig, C. (2012), Employees' reactions to organizational change, *OdPractioner*, 44(2), 23–28.

Zeffane, R. (1996), Dynamics of strategic change: critical issues in fostering positive organizational change, *Leadership & Organization Development Journal*, 17(7).

Chapter 43

How to Reduce Supplemental Claims in Construction Industry — Selected Management Tools to Implement a Systematic Anti-Claim Management

Martin Heinisch

MHI Ingenieurgesellschaft mbH;

ULBS Sibiu Department of Industrial
Engineering and Management

Jörg-U. Muckenfuß

MHI Ingenieurgesellschaft mbH

Dan Miricescu

"Lucian Blaga" University of Sibiu, Industrial Engineering
and Management Department, Romania

Contemporary anti-claim management requires a permanent collection of actual data. Only those who are aware of the projects status and all relevant interfaces within the project may take early effective action to minimize deviations. In case of disrupted planning and processes, changes, and additions to the project, one can provide solutions to minimize damage as well as testing and evaluating contractors claims. Only few construction projects can be realized without changes and disruptions of the construction schedule. To make them transparent and to counteract them, a functioning system of measures and control mechanisms is called for. The case of the new Kaiser Wilhelm tunnel (NKWT) is used as an example to demonstrate various aspects of anti-claim management on the client's side.

1. Introduction

Only few construction projects can be realized without changes and disruptions of the construction schedule. To make them transparent and to counteract them, a functioning system of measures and control mechanisms is called for. The new Kaiser Wilhelm tunnel (NKWT) is used as an example to demonstrate various aspects of anti-claim management on the client's side.

The terms "claim management" and "anti-claim management" are not part of the VOB-oriented terminology (VOB: German Standard Building Contract). This terminology derives from the Anglo-American language regions, where often other forms of contracts dominate than the unit price contract favored in Germany.

Nevertheless, these terms can be found frequently in many construction projects, both on the client's and the contractor's side. Particularly the internationally operating construction companies have so-called "claims teams", which exclusively deal with the identification, preparation, and enforcement of claims.

2. Definitions

Claims management is the collective term for all measures taken to identify and record deviations, modifications, and amendments of a construction and to enforce them on an economic scale.

Therefore, anti-claim management comprises all measures taken by the client on the one hand to have as few deviations and modifications of the contract as possible and on the other hand to process inevitable claims such that optimal, economic, and schedule-related results are achieved.

3. Constructing the "New Kaiser Wilhelm Tunnel" (NKWT)

The existing, double-tracked Kaiser Wilhelm tunnel (length: 4,205 m) is located on the Koblenz–Perl line, on the Koblenz–Mosel–(Ehrang) line section between the Cochem station (Bf) and the corresponding sub-station (Bft) in Ediger–Eller. Due to railroad operation and safety reasons, a second tunnel tube with a connection to the existing tunnel is presently under construction and will mainly run in parallel to the existing tunnel.

The planning segment has an overall length of approximately 5 km. The conversion project starts north of the Cochem station area. The line crosses a bridge and leads to the Northern Portal of the Kaiser Wilhelm tunnel which is located in an elevated position in the Cochem urban area and passes a tunnel through the "Cochemer Krampen" mountain ridge towards the South. The southern tunnel portal is located in the unpopulated area north of the Ediger–Eller substation. The remaining track section of about 400 m is using an overground track.

Parts of the NKWT construction project are preliminary measures, various services for the development of the construction site, the construction of the new tunnel tube with connecting structures, various bridge constructions and the expansion of the tunnel's superstructure and electro-technical systems.

4. Anti-Claim Management — Implementing Tools of Preventive and Active Anti-Claim Management

4.1. *Framework of implementing anti-claim management*

Only few building projects can be realized without modifications and amendments of the scope of service, and without disruptions to the construction schedule. The approach of planning, tendering, and contracting the construction target exactly as the actual building is planned and specified, is a rather theoretical one.

The reasons for this also derives from the spheres of risks on the client's side. They comprise, in particular, risks related to quantities, completeness, coordination, interfaces and subsoil, as well as technical or official requirements, third-party influences, but also incomplete or faulty planning services and inadequate service descriptions and modifications due to own additional requests. Investigations conducted by our engineering company confirm the causes for supplemental claims referred to in relevant literature so far. Significant variations can be established with regard to the supplemental claims volume in respect of the original order total. These range between 5–100%. No valid statements can be made as to the extent of claims that were approved.

It is quite common that contractors find it difficult to submit supplemental claims before or during the construction work, that comply with the required formal quality. This applies to both modified services according to VOB, Part B, Paragraph 2, Sec. 5 and to any additional services according to VOB, Part B, Paragraph 2, Sec. 6.

With regard to additionally required tasks, contractors in most cases just inform the client of the need for further services without quantifying the amount. Such notification is not required in case of changed services. In this case, the client is deemed not to be in need of protection. This circumstance results in the fact that a large number of claims (often more than half of all claims) will have to be dealt with, after the construction works are completed and are only submitted belatedly, and in some cases together with the final invoice. For the client, this means that on-site cost updating is not possible.

Anti-claim management can be organized in two stages: Preventive anti-claim management in the run-up to the proper construction work and Active anti-claim management during the execution of the construction up to final accounting.

4.2. *Preventive anti-claim management*

When using anti-claim management, the emergence of possible claims is detected and reduced during the run-up to the project realization phase, and contributes to improving the initial situation. First of all, this includes a critical analysis of the contractual conditions, the choice of project partners, existing management structures, possible risks, and own weak points.

The main focus of the activities is on the contractual conditions or — to be more precise — on scrutinizing the quality of tender documents submitted by the planning experts with regard to their practicability, inconsistencies, and completeness as well as on the analysis of any required services, which might have been described twice or forgotten altogether.

One of the principal reasons for supplemental claims is an inadequate planning implementation in the service description. This calls for monitoring

Fig. 1. Portal on the Eller side, construction works for the New Kaiser Wilhelm tunnel extension, mid of May, 2012, © R. Pellenz/nkwt.de

measures in order to gain as much as possible from a high potential for optimization.

The aim is preventing additional costs deriving from an insufficiently determined quantity structure of costs and from gaps or errors in the construction task descriptions. Further potential for supplemental claims arises from faulty or incomplete as-built documents, and from the realization of the so-called subsoil risk.

A structured approach towards preventing claims in advance can take place both in the tendering and planning sector and during the execution of the construction work, but the impact is considerably higher when the measures are applied before the start of the construction works.

During the preliminary planning and preparation of the tender, it is necessary to conduct an ongoing analysis of the project-specific requirements on planners and to elaborate work Phases 1 to 3. The planning must be conducted on the basis of guaranteed approvals. Preventive anti-claim management can be applied by setting up control functions responsible for the supervision of planning quality. Another important principle is the strict separation of work Phases 1 to 7 and of object monitoring in work Phases 8 and 9.

Supplemental performance claims can be prevented by: formulating of clear project fundamentals, assessment of the quality of the as-built documentation, safe implementation of project contracting in project planning, analysis of how permit issues are implemented in the planning, comparison of planning documents with tender documents, examination of the tendered quantity structure of costs, strategic handling of risk potentials (e.g., sub-soil risk), and prevention of intervention in the construction schedule.

Supplemental performance claims can be prevented by: imposing an adequate construction schedule (with buffer time) — which also includes the service schedule of contractors involved before project start — sufficient exploitation of optimization potential based on the contractors' know-how (alternative proposals), limitations only to those milestones that are absolutely necessary, start of construction works based on permits and safe implementation of structured decision-making processes, minimization of risks in advance.

Further areas of work are the assessment of variant solutions during the tender phase, providing advice in the contract awarding proposal and the verification of the contract awarding specifications. At the end of the process, unavoidable supplemental risks shall be identified and assessed.

On the part of the contractors, the investigation of existing supplemental claims potentials is also conducted during the quotation processing phase. This is done by studying the contract, surveying the site, determining and checking the tendered quantities, checking specifications for completeness and inconsistencies, and by checking the calculation of direct and indirect costs. A common situation is to draw up two order calculations — one for submittal to the client and a more detailed version for future supplemental claims.

On both the client's and contractor's side, a review of the price-determining main quantities is absolutely essential.

Preventive anti-claim management ends with the conclusion of the construction contract and passes into the active anti-claim management phase.

In the presented example of NKWT, an active preventive anti-claim management was implemented as early as the invitation to tender for the first contract packages.

The construction task described was subdivided to the effect that the construction services were split up into several contract packages, which assigns all construction tasks to site-related or time-related segments.

Therefore, one of the key tasks in preventive anti-claim management is to define the relevant interfaces between the individual contract packages in close coordination with the project management on the client's side, to implement them in the corresponding performance description and to check the whole tender documents for completeness.

Moreover, anti-claim management had a positive effect on the tendering process to the effect that tender documents were critically assessed with regard to possible inconsistencies, double entries, and omissions. In this case, the use of comparable methods currently in use in the construction industry led to the publication of a high-quality invitation to tender.

4.3. *Active anti-claim management*

In the context of active anti-claim management, the first step is to assess if the submitted supplemental claims comply with formal requirements. The term of supplemental claim is not part of the VOB. The contractual construction targets are determined by the sum of all construction services to be rendered by the contractor in accordance with the tendered conditions and construction circumstances.

The supplemental claims processing commences with the notification of order changes and requires careful justification of grounds for the supplemental claim including the description of the additional/changed services. The description shall be comprehensible and shall describe the issue in a clear, unambiguous, and an obvious manner.

5. Requirements for Supplemental Claims

5.1. *Requirements for supplemental claims justification*

Anti-claim management begins with checking whether, and to, what extent the submitted claim is complete and verifiable. The examination of claim basis starts with establishing deviations from the contractually agreed

Fig. 2. Portal on the Eller side, construction works for the tunnel extension, mid of May, 2012, © R. Pellenz/nkwt.de

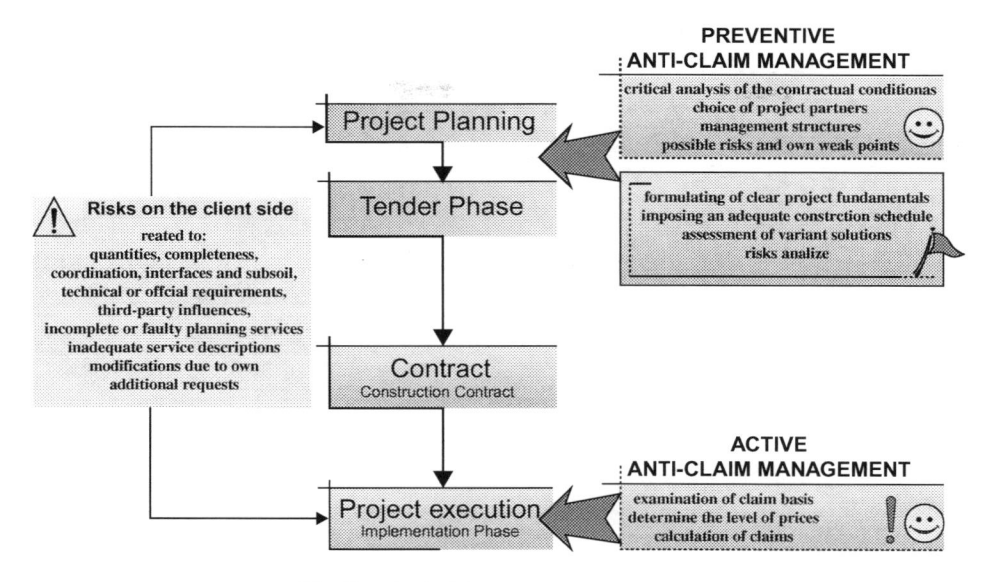

Fig. 3. Anti-claim management process

construction targets and the corresponding legal basis. Moreover, it is necessary to determine if the contractor has submitted cost notifications in due time and if the client has issued orders to that effect. The next step is to determine the level of prices for the contract and possible process risks.

The verifiability of the claim "on the grounds of" requires a documentation of the modified services (the additional, omitted, or changed services) with a description of the effects. This documentation shall contain a reference to a contractual position together with the determination of possible similar contractual services.

5.2. Requirements for supplemental claims calculations

The calculation of claims shall be based on the order calculation and must be plausible. The implementation and use of factors determining the contractual performance level ensures that the quoted services meet with the contractual level stipulated by the order calculation.

We recommend the following calculation systematic:

- Determination of the difference regarding the scope of service and conditions.
- Determination of the new scope of service, comparison of tendered and new services.
- Recording of the difference.
- Determination of individual costs of the partial service based on the order calculation, either as a claimed supplement or as a replacement item.
- It must be determined whether the omission or change of certain services will result in the accrual of individual costs from the scope of partial service, which cannot be avoided — direct costs that cannot be reduced.
- It must be determined whether the modified services have an impact on the direct costs for other items or whether the construction conditions will change, thus resulting in additional costs.

Fig. 4. Cochem side: From the Pinnerkreuz side, early June, 2012, © R. Pellenz/nkwt.de

Fig. 5. Tunnel breakthrough in the year 2011, © Alpine

- Adoption of the surcharge rates as previously determined in the order calculation for the allocation and addition to the direct costs of the partial services of the supplemental claim.

In a claim calculation review, the contractual price level is verified and an impact forecast for the claim is drawn up, which covers possible process risks.

The stipulation that claims shall be closely related to a construction contract prevents claims being formulated as a mere cost reimbursement.

In the NKWT construction project examined here, the client's project management was, and is still being provided, with support in the assessment of the submitted claims. In discussions with the contractor, an adequate assessment of the grounds for, and amounts of the submitted claims based on the construction contract could be substantiated with regard to the technical or contractual reasons.

6. Supplemental Claims Due to Hindrance Issues

Claims due to hindrance issues result from a change of the construction circumstances, which do not allow a direct recourse to the construction contract and construction target; where appropriate, construction site facilities are an exception.

Hindrance issues result from complications, disruptions, postponement of construction start, construction period extension and from acceleration orders.

Further grounds are project-related claims due to changes of the scope of delivery, belated planned deliveries, delays in the construction-related decision-making processes, missing or faulty preliminary work, faulty material orders, hindrances due to parallel works or external incidents such as weather, changes of rules or regulations, and pending clearances.

When dealing with claims on the grounds of hindrances in the context of anti-claim management, it is essential to establish whether formal requirements were complied with during the construction period (such as submission of qualified hindrance notifications, or if certain issues were addressed in the reports). This also includes *provisos* and the consideration of disruptions in the updating of schedules. The hindrance notifications have to be clearly distinguished from one another to be able to rule out overtaking causality.

The extension of the construction period can be evidenced through critical path analysis. It serves to enhance transparency of the details of a local disruption, but requires a clear delimitation of case-related disruption periods and the presence of hindrance notifications.

Each disruption incident requires precise costing based on the order calculation or the ascertainment of damage. At first, proof of an adequate and sufficient order calculation has to be furnished. Alternatively, it is also possible to utilize conclusive derivation of determining factors in the event of missing calculation elements. The following cost elements are frequently a part of claims on the grounds of hindrance issues:

Fig. 6. At the Cochem side: View from above on the large-scale construction site, early June 2012, © R. Pellenz/nkwt.de

- Site overhead costs.
- Overhead expenses.
- Expenses for downtime shifts (staff/equipment).
- Costs for underperformance.
- Costs for acceleration performances.

In anti-claim management, the assessment and refutation of such claims require, that the hindrance notifications are processed promptly and that the indicated causes are either eliminated or refused. Furthermore, it is necessary to put the contractor (if possible) in default. Schedule tracking in conjunction with an active project management is absolutely essential as a final step.

Thus, the assessment of "soft claims" starts with a preliminary check that involves an overall analysis for a comparison of schedule and budget. This is followed by a plausibility check to assess the relationship between the supplemental claim and the main contract. A preliminary check shall be conducted to differentiate between issues that are to be attributed to the client and such issues that have arisen due to the contractor's own negligence.

Then a detailed verification serves to check formal requirements and to analyze the main contract (with regard to schedules, owed performances, shutdown periods agreed with the contractor) for a determination of claims (in view of the claimed remuneration, compensation, or damages). The following step serves to determine if the order calculation is based on correct assumptions.

Based on these results and in due consideration of the limiting conditions of the construction contract it is now possible to conduct a parallel calculation of an acceptable claim for remuneration. Due to the fact that the examination of such claims will often be conducted at the end of a construction project, the ongoing documentation of the construction work is of the essence.

The main documentation means for a building site are:

- Documentation of performance changes as a cause for hindrances.
- Determination of schedule.
- Monitoring of the scheduled list of deliveries.
- Statements in the daily construction reports.

Fig. 7. At the Cochem side: The backfilling work between the mountainside and building structure is nearly finished; early June 2012, © R. Pellenz/nkwt.de

- Photo documentation.
- Construction meeting reports.
- Hindrance notifications.

Monitoring is very important because in most (and often contractually agreed) cases, the contractor submits a construction schedule within an appropriate period following the awarding of the contract, which shall be updated — if possible — on a monthly basis and shall include all disruptions and hindrances.

In addition to processing of the supplemental claims, the systematic identification, development and enforcement of counterclaims is a central task. Therefore, the regulations of DB AG include the following measures (according to directive 134 300):

- Early detection.
- Documentation.
- Tracking.
- Negotiation.
- Use of existing forms.
- Maintaining a supplemental claims database.

7. Conclusions

The development of an effective counterclaims management cannot prevent the cause for claims, but they can be significantly reduced. On the client's part, this calls for a detailed documentation of the construction process, as the basis for counterclaims management and also for the assessment of claims, to prevent having to rely on third-party records only.

References

Dumitrascu, D. & Pascu, R. (2008), *Managementul Proiectelor*, Romania: Editura Universității Lucian Blaga din Sibiu.

Heinisch, M. (2013), Systematic anti-claim management reduces supplemental claims, *Proceedings of the 6th International Conference on Manufacturing Science and Education*, MSE 2013.

Heinisch, M. (2007), Faires nachtragsmanagement durch das bilden von vertragsniveaufaktoren bei der fortschreibung der auftragskalkulation für geänderte und zusätzliche leistungen, *Der Eisenbahningenieur*, No. 03/2007.

Heinisch, M. (2006), *Grundlagen des Bauvertrags/Nachträge beim Bauvertrag*, Romania: Eigenverlag.

Miricescu, D. (2011), Study on temporal influences on management and managers of business organizations, *Proceedings of the 2nd Review of Management and Economic Engineering Management Conference (RMEE)*, 15th–17th September, 479–490, Romania: Todesco Publising House.

Țuțurea, M., Miricescu, D., Moraru, G., & Grecu, V. (2010), *Leadership în Organizații*, Romania: Editura Universității Lucian Blaga din Sibiu.

VOB, (2012), German Construction Contract Procedures, DIN, DVD, April.

Chapter 44

Implementation of Quality Management for Ecotouristic Operators in the Danube Delta

Virgil Nicula and Simona Spânu

"Lucian Blaga" University of Sibiu

The present chapter is analyzing the way in which the elements/processes of a quality system contribute to obtaining some quality ecotouristic products.

This chapter aims at identifying the main particularities of the quality management with ecotouristic operators, outlining the role, and importance of quality management in organizing and functioning of ecotouristic operators in the Danube Delta in view of drawing up a performant system of implementing the quality management in a touristic agency.

The implementation of quality management is the most adequate way to ensure the competitivity of products and services for the touristic firm on the market. The quality of the touristic services depends on the training of the employees, of their managerial quality, of that "culture" regarding the firm and which gives flexibility, velocity, initiative in activities.

The methodology and research techniques used aimed at putting into force the politics and strategies of quality management within tourism agencies in order to highlighted the degree of knowledge and use of elements specific for quality management and to propose a performant system of implementing quality management.

The necessity to focus the attention on the quality of the touristic product relies on at least three aspects: the increase of the offer for touristic products in each country and at the level of world economy and this determines an increase regarding the number of users, the growth in quality within the competition of touristic products on the national and international market, the decisive influence of quality on the other economic indicators of the touristic firm.

The implementation of the quality management to an ecotouristic operator insures the coordination of the activity in the direction of performance and implicitly to obtain the sustainable competitive advantage.

1. Introduction

Diversity and quality are the main factors of competitiveness and, as logical consequence they also represent the fundamental problems facing the tourism industry in general, and reception of international tourism in particular (Cosmescu & Nicula, 2004).

At this time, current tourism consumer demands grow continuously, particularly concerning quality, but also such characteristics as technical, psycho-sensory economic issues related to the availability of products on interrelations, Sanogenesis characteristics, and the relationship with environment. Through a seemingly globalized care for the local environment, lately, it is several international organizations, such as the (World Travel & Tourism Council) WTTC, the Green Globe Program, the (International Hotels Environment Initiative) IHEI, (International Hotel & Restaurant Association) IH & RA,

(European Confederation of National Associations of Hotels and Restaurants of the European Union) HOTREC have voiced concerns for a proper application of quality requirements in ecotourism, ensuring greater protection and conservation of tourism resources, some of which are unique worldwide.

Increasing competition in terms of prices as well as an organized network of destinations and cheaper offers from other continents has emphasized pressure on the European tourism sector and traditional tourism destinations, as in the case of the Danube Delta.

Based on the role and importance of quality management in the organization and functioning eco-tour operators, an efficient system of quality management in the travel agencies or tour operators can be devised and implemented as this system can also include reception and accommodation structures located in Delta.

The introduction of a new quality management system in eco-tourism services aims to improve the quality of services provided in establishments of this kind; such a system can help to increase customer satisfaction and the possibility of using this symbol for the promotion and recognition of units on a national and international level.

2. Danube Delta — General Coordinates

The Danube Delta covers 2.5% of the country. The reservoir is situated in the territory of Tulcea county (51.88% of the county), Constanta county (2.89% of the county) and Galati (0.098% of the county). Within this perimeter, 18 strictly protected areas have been identified, occupying an area of 50,600 ha (8.7%), consisting of natural ecosystems, terrestrial, and aquatic reserves and buffer zone — a total area of 223,300 ha. Landscape is valued by tourism activities, both by specialized companies and through local population.

The Delta's complexity is determined primarily by its biodiversity, containing a third of the number of plant species that live in Romania. Natural habitats in the Delta are the most varied in Romania and are home to a great diversity of plant and animal communities, whose numbers were estimated at 30 types of ecosystems with 5,429 species, 1,839 of which are flora and 3,590 of which are fauna.

In the Danube Delta, we can find many medicinal plants, and large areas are covered with reeds — the largest area in the world. Letea and Caraorman consists of secular trees and Mediterranean lianas, which are unique in Europe. However, the greatest wealth is the bird fauna, found within the reserve, either coming to this area during migration, as birds chose the Delta as a place of feeding, nesting, and rearing. These unique elements make the Delta an invaluable space for the world's natural heritage, a research laboratory and observation point for researchers around the world, as well as a place for nature lovers and tourists visiting the Delta in search of natural areas and unique species.

The Delta's protected area status prompted a reorganization of tourism that takes place in this region, in the context of a required sustainable exploitation of natural resources and in particular landscape resources, so as to have a minimal impact on the integrity of natural ecosystems. The main components of Delta's landscape are nearly 400 lakes of various sizes, reeds, forests of oak and ash, sand dunes, beaches, seaside marine deltaic environments; all this gives a particular spatial diversity and variety. However, human settlements, through their unique and specific architecture, make for outstanding attractions.

The diversity of these resources makes it possible to practice biosphere conservation in the Danube Delta, but also tourism, in its various forms:

— Travel for leisure and recreation, tourism practiced by companies through hotels, through reservation, and even floating hotels, combining trips on scenic canals, lakes and seawater, sunbathing on the beaches located along the Black Sea coast;
— Knowledge tours (itinerant), practiced either individually or through organized tours, suitable for smaller groups of visitors who have the opportunity to explore the variety of wild landscapes, combining boating channels through manually propelled boats with scenic hiking along the canals or fluvial and marine ways, etc.
— Specialized tourism (Scientific) for ornithologists, specialists, researchers, students;
— Special programs for youth, for knowledge, understanding, and appreciation of nature;

- Ecotourism, with a role in promoting sustainable use of biodiversity, by generating income, jobs and business opportunities, along with an equitable distribution of the benefits to the population and the local community;
- Rural tourism (in which guests are hosted and guided by locals) and which has tradition in the Danube Delta Biosphere Reserve, home to many local families and visitors coming to the Danube Delta. This type of tourism has an important potential to improve incomes of local people;
- Travel for water sports, photography, safaris;
- Travel for fishing, which is highly appreciated by visitors of all ages, in any season, for any species of fish, and hunting.

3. General Considerations Concerning the Quality System Certification of Ecotourism Services

The objective of quality certification of ecotourism services is to implement a new set of regulations concerning the quality of services in the tourism related activities for: equipping them with systems of internal and external services, so to act as effective tools for management and quality assurance; providing a basis for continuous improvement, adapting to the new management system needs, but also to satisfy customer requirements and expectations. (Hornoiu, 2009).

Since the issue of service quality of tourist facilities is a matter of survival for them, managers in the hospitality industry should provide quality services on the market, at various prices, so that they can retain customers and even gain new customers in order to increase turnover, profit, and customer loyalty. Ecotourism providers to obtain a differential advantage must consider improving service quality, so as to exceed customer expectations and improve their perception. To this end, tourism structures must identify the determinants of service quality expectations of customers who use their services and the appropriate way to measure customers' satisfaction. (Honey, 2002).

Quality means meeting the needs of tourists, and for this, tourism enterprises need to study the market (segments of tourists, competition, *etc.*), then try to adapt their services to the requirements of their environment (level of ambition and needs of tourists).

In conducting all necessary stages in implementing this quality management system, ecotourism operators must involve all members of the organization.

The first step is to analyze the current situation (quality audit). At this stage, they evaluate all relevant aspects of a product. The methods that can be used are: analysis through management quality levels, obtaining customer feedback, which is achieved through questionnaires of opinion and registration of customer, employee or supplier complaints; they must also value opinion makers, using boxes for suggestions and employee feedback, observations concerning leadership, management, customer interaction, management of employees through internal benchmarking (activity/process), functional (activities), general activities (processes, products/services, procedures in relation to leaders, indirect competitors and/or non-competitors) and compared analysis (relative to direct competitors).

The second step is to develop a quality strategy; however it is necessary to first establish a quality level, in order to meet the target consumer groups' expectations. Secondly, actions must be taken to achieve the desired level and the third step is to control the level of performance, through a series of actions to address identified deficiencies.

Next, they must formulate an improvement plan that aims to: raise awareness and education for quality and quality management improvement actions based on priorities, internal and external communication through the development of an effective intra-departmental network; inter-departmental, customers, and public linking. They must introduce and integrate the quality problem, accompanied by a communication plan and monitoring system, to conclude the presented steps.

Applying technology in determining the quality of tourism services has proven to be difficult, as the quality of provided services cannot be separated from the unit which produces them. It is therefore necessary to define and verify the quality of management processes and required procedures to ensure the ultimate quality of tourism services.

When developing a quality system, the first step is to set standards of product/service, according to application needs.

The development of quality systems ensures: the designing of specific rules for each unit, specific procedures for maintaining and improving quality planning and analysis procedures for making decisions about the gathered information, assessment tools and training of human resources.

The ultimate goal is the mark of quality systems, standards and procedures that certifies the final fulfilment: a system that should define a unit of the hospitality industry. Quality of services should be popularized, to be used as a criterion in choosing the right service provider, as appropriate homologation of ecotourism operators and ecotourism products (Classification Acorns).

The National Tourism Authority has proposed the program to improve the quality of tourism services and a new approach to the development of the tourism sector, based on the principles of quality management, aiming to design and implement quality management systems on a pilot group of tourism units in Romania, in order to align with European requirements for development, requirements for sustainable development. Also, it aims to increase the attractiveness and competitiveness of Romania as a tourist destination. (Nicula, 2012).

The new guidelines and requirements acknowledged internationally and in the European Union recommend, in order to ensure and improve the quality of tourism services, a voluntary implementation of standardized management systems — quality, food safety, environmental protection and information security — which proves their efficiency and effectiveness in time, such as (quality management system) ISO 9001, (Food Safety Management System), ISO 22000, (Environmental Management System) ISO 14001, (Information Security Management System) ISO 27000. The implementation of such quality management systems is the only national management approach that can help to align tourism facilities in Romania (compatibility, reliability, competitiveness), to European ones.

Certification of quality management system must be done in accordance with the international standard SR EN ISO 9001:2001 and should be the same for all participants within the industry, including tour operators and agencies, as a confirmation that all processes in the organization are in compliance with the aforementioned standard. Based on this standard, a quality management system can be implemented in any tourism organization (travel agency, hotel, restaurant), so also for ecotourism operators.

The introduction of a quality system benefits all parties involved (tourist destination, entrepreneurs, consumers, and intermediaries and will result in the improvement of marketing: higher customer loyalty which will lead to their establishment and repeated visits due to increased satisfaction levels; new sales through recommendations from satisfied customers, a competitive advantage over competitors by improving image quality, higher revenues by increasing sales prices and attracting a clientele less sensitive to price.

In turn, consumers and intermediaries, as well as travel agencies that sell ecotourism will benefit from the application of quality systems as follows: information regarding products and services which the client can expect, the quality guarantee system which is proof of the quality of products and services, ensuring that the product and service is sold as norms and standards mention it; this would represent an important milestone in the process of comparing similar vacation offers, as it is also critical to inform the customer as he/she wants to be sure he/she made a good choice to spend the most important period of the year. The implementation of such a quality management system in ecotourism operators shall coordinate work, towards higher performance and therefore obtaining a sustainable competitive advantage. Tourists demand to purchase products/services at prices related to the quality of the supply, and so ecotourism operators can answer the increasingly higher demands by optimizing the quality/price ratio. Small and medium tourism enterprises are forced to fight for survival in the face of competition, promoting embedded destinations, working with world-class professionals of tourism, and which have a strong functional organization which can achieve significant savings, superior to those of any small, isolated businesses. On the other hand, these small businesses have to cope with increasing pressure, must move towards cooperation, innovation, specialization, and creation of brand products of high quality.

The Romanian Ecotourism Association (AER) has approved the Ecotourism Guesthouses Initiative, as a measure to counter such effects. The Ecotourism Certification System of AER adapts international experience in Romania's context. It was developed in accordance with the Program for Nature and Ecotourism Accreditation, promoted by the Australian Association of Ecotourism (NEAP is the first accreditation system in ecotourism) and Nature's Best of the Swedish Association of Ecotourism (the first accreditation system in ecotourism in the Northern hemisphere). The Ecotourism Certification System applies to two different categories: ecotourism programs offered by tour operators or guides (maximum 15 participants); small hostels in rural areas and natural areas (maximum 25 rooms) (Rondelli & Cojocariu, 2005).

AER has identified a number of benefits that may result from the implementation of the certification system, such as allowing customers to better identify those products that can offer amazing experiences related to nature and rural culture, contributing to higher levels of trust in eco products in Romania on the international market, becoming a marketing tool for tour operators and owners of guesthouses, which ensures a higher level of service quality and actively contributes to nature conservation and sustainable development at the local level along with supporting local governments in areas protected with minimal impact on tourism development. It provides a platform for joint activities between the business sector and nature conservation organizations.

4. Implementation of Quality Management for Ecotourism Operators in the Danube Delta

Romanian ecotourism product quality requires the application of flexible strategies, diversification of tourism benefits, and differentiation of the tourism product offered compared to competitive offerings (Tuclea, Padureanu & Hornoiu, 2008). The strategy allows flexibility and adaptation following the evolution of tourism and demand tourism benefits depending on the specific variations, as well as being consistent with the natural environment and tourist vocation of the area. The role of the product differentiation strategy in ecotourism versus competitive offerings related to other forms of tourism is to enable the development of ecotourism product originality through creative ways of living space and tourism with spiritual meanings and country specific characteristic applied to regions or localities.

The development of tourism in the Danube Delta calls for special attention to be paid to environmental demands, representing the "raw material" scope and conduct of business travel.

The AER has approved two tourism products in the Delta: "House of Willows" and Canoeing tour operated by groups such as Tioc Nature & Study Travel.

"House of the Willows", located in the village of Uzlina Murighiol, has 12 rooms, terraces, two waterfront gazebos, patio, swimming pool, children's playground, fishing pond, parking on shore and boats (catamaran, motor boats, rowing boats). The initial building was intended to be a holiday home for family and friends relaxing at the pond, but also intended for fish lovers and has become, in just a few years, a small guesthouse that wants to personalize human contact with nature, bringing tourists closer to the spirit and peaceful life of these places. The daily menu includes fish dishes, prepared through site-specific recipes, and meals based on other products, established by agreement with the tourists. The Canoeing tour operated by Tioc Nature & Travel Study suggests canoe trips through wildlife on request and is subject to availability.

Specialized studies carried out by UNWTO have identified key megatrends that are recorded in the tourism sector which will enhance the perspective of the 2020s. Among the most significant aspects are: the number of tourists concerned about environmental issues is constantly increasing, while the demand for new destinations increases as well; also, tourists become more experienced and sophisticated, expect good quality attractions, facilities and services at high quality and suitable prices in their travels.

The existing literature (Chafe, 2005), notes that is a close connection between eco-label and consumer behavior. For example, 69% of Dutch tourists stay in hotels labelled as Green Key, and stated they would be willing to pay more to benefit from facilities that have implemented an eco-label. Meanwhile, 86% of Dutch tourists prefer a star rating system that combines environmental performance and quality of services. Over 62% of Italian tourists and 42% of German tourists believe that environmental performance is a key factor for a successful holiday.

The Danube Delta has all the ingredients necessary for the development of ecotourism, but the essential condition for the sustainability of the tourism phenomenon is the existence of quality certification of ecotourism services.

An analysis of the number of tourist arrivals in Romania in the Danube Delta demonstrates a preference for this destination, especially for tourists from Germany, Norway and Poland.

The European Commission (EC) presented in early February 2014 a Euro Barometer result entitled "Towards Preferences of European Tourism" (EuroBarometer, 2014). The tourism based Euro Barometer consists of telephone surveys made on samples of more than 26,500 people across the European Union from January 10th to January 14th, out of which 1003 people are Romanian. From the analysis of this report regarding

Table 1. Number of tourist arrivals in Romania in Danube Delta

Country/Total Tourists	Total tourists from abroad	No. abroad tourists in Danube Delta, including city of Tulcea
Germany	228,592	6,146
Italy	181,894	1,223
France	118,649	1,710
Hungary	99,261	146
Israel	96,615	203
UK	92,756	369
USA	91,625	288
Spain	66,375	997
Poland	64,152	3,074
Austria	58,765	707
Holland	47,378	240
Bulgaria	43,751	408
Greece	39,360	142
Turkey	38,375	131
Republic of Moldavia	33,668	76
Belgium	30,299	168
Russian Federation	29,302	62
Czech Republic	22,246	160
Switzerland	20,556	292
Ukraine	17,227	109
Japan	16,974	76
Sweden	15,049	126
Norway	14,242	3,865
Canada	13,967	22
Serbia	13,959	125
China	13,329	142
Slovakia	11,678	32
Denmark	11,004	510
Albania	10,884	154
Portugal	10,145	472
Other countries	162,461	615
Total tourists from abroad	1,714,538	22,790

Source: Eurostat, 2014.

Romanians' preferences in terms of tourism and the forecast for 2014, we notice a series of conclusions from which we selected those for choosing a valence for ecotourism destinations such as Danube Delta.

— Among the reasons for which most Romanians traveled in 2013, we have sunny destinations (seaside, beach), a reunion with family and friends (37%), and spending time in nature (34%).
— Natural resources of a destination would cause most Romanians to return to a destination (40%).
— Recommendations from friends, family and colleagues are the most important source of inspiration Romanians when deciding their travel planning (48%), followed by travel websites (23%). The Romanian market is somewhat atypical compared to other European markets, meaning that tourism websites, brochures and catalogues matters less in travel decisions.
— Romanians most used the Internet (35%) to organize the trip and have enlisted the help of a friend (22%).
— Romanians (34%) bought isolated travel packages (up 9% compared to 2012), and purchased tour packages (27%), which saw an increase of 3%, while the purchases of services of all-inclusive type (27%), saw an increase of 6%.
— Romania is among the countries that grew most in terms of tourists' satisfaction on the quality of tourist services (8%), followed by satisfaction with the purchase of accommodation (5%).
— Increased satisfaction lead Romanians to appreciate the general price level (11%), but Romania was the country which fell the most in terms of satisfaction about such services for people with disabilities.
— Most Romanian made short trips of 1–3 nights, and Romania is among the countries whose citizens are the least to travel for 13 or more consecutive nights.
— Romanians are amongst the least staying Europeans in accommodations, with more than 20 seats (27%), the majority preferring small accommodation units (44%). The number of Romanians who opt to stay in camping also decreased by 6%.

Analysis of these preferences reveals opportunities to develop ecotourism in the Danube Delta and the implementation of quality system would generate an increase in tourist arrivals in the area.

Statistical data on the evolution of tourism indicators in Tulcea County, in 2009–2013, shows increasing interest manifested both among tourists from Romania and abroad (International Standards Office, 2008).

From the analysis of this data, it is obvious that tourists are increasing demands for tourism products in the Danube Delta. The ecotourism sector's development and prosperity will lead simultaneously to increases in other sectors of the economy: food, trade, transport, etc. As the demand for ecotourism is permanent and on a steady global growth, and as a continuing trend that influences the tourism market and local communities, it is the interest of local communities to promote the creation of sustainable development models.

The positive effects or what determines the correct application and implementation of quality management in any establishment providing travel services are more likely to repeat visits, increase financial performance, given that attracting new customers is 5–10 times more expensive than keeping customers at existing costs and avoiding complaints; better employee motivation, positive external effects chain (promotion, consistency in business and winning new markets).

The strategy of major service providers in terms of the quality of provided services is limited to the following three steps:

— First, to divide the market very carefully and develop services to meet customer needs as they noticed that not all customers who buy the same product or service have the same needs;
— Second, they realized that only the client knows what he wants, so they pay attention to what the customer says;
— Third, they are careful to meet customer expectations at optimum levels; they promise less and offer more.

Service providers should not try to guess the wishes of the customer, nor his/her expectations, but must try to determine them as accurately as possible, by referring directly to the consumer in connection with his perception of quality, satisfaction, value of tourism product — through surveys. The next step is to harmonize this

Table 2. Tourist arrivals in units with functions of tourists' accommodation guesthouses and agro type

Units with functions of tourists' accommodation	Jan.	Feb.	Mar.	Apr.	May	Jun.	Jul.	Aug.	Sep.	Oct.	Nov.	Dec.
2009												
Guest houses	216	279	—	270	223	343	723	511	402	206	242	114
Agritouristic guest houses	—	—	—	949	491	859	47	315	160	105	—	—
2010												
Guest houses	239	45	158	140	466	193	306	240	116	96	15	5
Agritouristic guest houses	—	—	—	24	391	211	107	302	452	19	55	—
2011												
Guest houses	—	37	1	3	5	149	148	157	75	26	10	27
Agritouristic guest houses	—	—	5	59	151	235	377	1291	700	198	92	14
2012												
Guest houses	11	25	31	29	75	174	206	102	61	41	25	11
Agritouristic guest houses	—	—	—	28	125	279	546	592	490	92	—	—
2013												
Guest houses	9	10	—	—	—	—	58	62	57	38	27	—
Agritouristic guest houses	—	—	—	20	608	948	787	853	156	109	20	—

Table 3. Establishments of tourists' facilities with functions of tourist accommodation, such as guesthouses and agro type

Units with functions of tourists' accommodation	Jan.	Feb.	Mar.	Apr.	May	Jun.	Jul.	Aug.	Sep.	Oct.	Nov.	Dec.
2009												
Guest houses	244	356	—	373	271	343	930	619	515	247	290	126
Agritouristic guest houses	—	—	—	1979	1039	1928	47	861	467	115	—	—
2010												
Guest houses	305	47	185	163	630	249	440	295	144	116	15	5
Agritouristic guest houses	—	—	—	38	671	478	246	999	1161	44	139	—
2011												
Guest houses	—	45	5	20	12	196	206	157	75	45	11	27
Agritouristic guest houses	—	—	10	149	149	530	935	3,011	1621	647	298	42
2012												
Guest houses	11	32	37	35	87	230	395	246	73	52	28	11
Agritouristic guest houses	—	—	—	77	318	640	1,792	1,372	1,138	231	—	—
2013												
Guest houses	—	25	—	—	—	—	58	62	57	38	27	—
Agritouristic guest houses	—	—	—	28	1,842	2,001	2,624	2,818	367	284	59	—

Table 4. Net use index of accommodation places

Units with functions of tourists' accommodation	Jan.	Feb.	Mar.	Apr.	May	Jun.	Jul.	Aug.	Sep.	Oct.	Nov.	Dec.
2009												
Total county	10.5	12.8	15.6	22.9	20.9	28.0	30.8	39.1	25.1	13.9	16.9	11.7
2010												
Total county	8.2	9.5	11.4	15.5	24.2	19.8	25.8	32.4	21.5	17.5	15.9	11.4
2011												
Total county	9.4	10.2	11.5	14.0	28.2	25.6	28.6	34.6	31.4	20.0	18.6	12.4
2012												
Total county	9.0	9.4	18.2	18.4	25.1	20.0	22.4	32.1	27.7	18.7	16.6	8.1
2013												
Total county	9.1	10.1	11.9	18.0	28.8	34.4	39.7	46.2	36.5	30.1	23.2	—

data with the quality perception of the management team to improve service quality.

Tourist companies should establish a permanent evaluation and measuring of customer satisfaction. This assessment must identify reactions, both positive and negative, and their likely incidence on future activities of the company (Ioncica, 2006). Both the blog and the forum are very useful for communication within tourist accommodation structures and beyond: the company can interact with potential clients can exchange information, they can learn new things. One advantage of using them as integral parts to a web site is that visitors can express their ideas, opinions, or provide solutions to solving problems. Another advantage is the ease with which information can be accessed.

5. Conclusion

It can be concluded that the performance is due to the ongoing concern of managers to improve the quality of products and customer service. For these companies, quality is not only a requirement, but has become a value, an essential component of organizational culture.

Quality assurance as part of quality management means creating confidence among tourists interested in purchasing ecotourism programs, and can be considered as an evaluation of different perspectives on how a tourism business operates and the way it needs to provide quality products to its customers.

We can state that the majority of tourists consider tourism products within the following quality parameters: competence, safety, hygiene, availability for the customer, accurate and timely information, timeliness, reliability, trust, safety, etc. Management methods and techniques of quality management are scientifically based on management tools, organizations which promote the marketing of quality products that meet present and future needs of customers.

References

Chafe, Z. (2005), Ecotourism and sustainable development, www.ecotourismcesd.org. (Accessed 19 March 2013).

Cosmescu, I. & Nicula,V. (2004), *Diversitatea și Calitatea Serviciilor Turistice în Bazinul Mării Negre*, Sibiu: Constant.

Honey, M. (2002), *Ecotourism and Certification: Setting Standards in Practice*, Washington, D.C: Island Press.

Hornoiu, R. I. (2009), *Ecoturismul — Orientare Prioritară în Dezvoltarea Durabilă a Comunităților Locale*, București: ASE.

Ioncică, M. (2006), *Economia Serviciilor*, București: Uranus.

Nicula, V., Simona, S., & Ciotea G. (2012), *Ghidul Ecopensiunii Agroturostice*, Sibiu: ULB.

Parasuraman, A., Zeithaml, V., & Berry, L. (1988), SERVQUAL: A multiple item scale for measuring customer perceptions of service quality, *Journal of Retailing*, 64 (1), pp. 12–43.

Rondelli, V. & Cojocariu, S. (2005), *Managementul Calității Serviciilor Dinturism și Industria Ospitalității*, București: THR–CG.

Țuclea, C., Pădureanu, M., & Hornoiu, R. (2008), A certification system for ecoturism servicies in romania, encuentros 2nd days of touristica, Portoroz, New Europe — New Tourist Destination, Colegge of Tourism, Slovenia.

INCDT (2009), *Strategia de Dezvoltare a Ecoturismului in Romania*, București.

International Standards Office (2008), ISO 9001 — *Quality management systems — Requirements*, Geneva: ISO.

International Standards Office (2009), ISO 9004 — *Managing for the Sustained Success of an Organization. A Quality Management Approach*. Geneva: ISO.

Eurobarometer, www.ec.europa.eu/ (Accessed 20 March 2014).

Eurostat, http://epp.eurostat.ec.europa.eu/portal/page/portal/statistics/search_database.

Chapter 45

Romanian Pre-University Educational Management in the Context of European Integration

*Ana Tuşa, Claudiu Sorin Voinia,
and Oana Dumitraşcu*

"Lucian Blaga" University of Sibiu

The issue of educational management has become significant in the current social environment in which all aspects of education begin with quality and efficiency of the systems and, above all, educational activities.

The research objectives were aimed at analyzing and explaining the phenomena of the school management in order to improve intervention techniques and thus improve the quality and performance of the management process.

Research methods are combined, such as exploratory, qualitative, and quantitative methods. Subjects interviewed and surveyed belong to decision-makers from the analyzedd systems, namely of schools in EU countries. Using the comparison method of management systems, some data were obtained on the state and trajectory of European countries in terms of school education and were used to establish lines of action for our country. Thus, the logical line of this chapter consists of the following steps:

- Identifying factors determining the performance management role in school education;
- Analyzing them within the systems performing EU countries and determining specific aspects;
- Determining the defining aspects of the Romanian system of educational management, and in comparison with the systems' performance;
- Establishing the necessary recommendations in systemic improvement process.

The bibliographical study undertaken in the university management based research was completed with performed comparative studies on various management systems practices in pre-university education institutions in EU countries.

One of the most important factors with determining role in achieving managerial performance is the school manager himself.

Considering the previously analyzed determinants of performance, but not being a model taken literally for Romanian pre-university education, some key elements of the management for Romanian education were highlighted and afterwards compared with other European educational systems from the point of view of systems and resources and concerning the quality of management.

Out of all, the recommendations resulting from the comparison of the Romanian university management system with that existing in various EU countries, we emphasized those relating to:

- Development of partnerships between schools and public institutions, businesses, institutions abroad;
- Financial resources of the school unit;
- Human Resources Management;

- Strategic planning process and preparation of the Institutional Development Plan;
- Internal and external evaluation process;
- Decentralization of school education;
- Improve managers.

1. Introduction

In the recent years, educational management, in general, and specificifically secondary education have gained increasing importance, both in Romania and in European society, so that the role of school management has become an important topic of debate at European level.

This chapter aim to obtain a better picture of school education management in Romania compared to EU countries. Moreover, the issue of school education management has become significant in the current social environment in which all aspects of education begin with quality, efficiency systems and educational activities.

This chapter addresses the pre-university educational management, analyzing performance of the functions, relations management, analysis methods and techniques, design strategies, determining the position of the Romanian educational management in regards to European requirements, their needs and finding ways to share in order to enhance performance.

In the development of school education, both at national and at European level, a particularly important question is the appropriate management framework typology in this field. Therefore, choosing the appropriate undergraduate management models constitute one of the fundamental factors of efficiency and performance objectives.

Consistent with these goals, this chapter attempts to find applicable ways and tools, in order that educational management meet its current needs in relation to the requirements of European university education, requirements identified through studies and direct measurements on subjects from various countries of the European Union.

The research objectives were aimed at analyzing and explaining the phenomena of the school management in order to improve intervention techniques and thus improve the quality and performance of the management process. Research methods are combined, such as exploratory qualitative methods and quantitative methods. Subjects interviewed and surveyed belong to the decision-makers from the analyzed systems namely, of schools in EU countries. By comparison method, management systems data were obtained on the state and trajectory of European countries in terms of school education. The data were then used to establish lines of action for Romania.

2. Conceptual Elements Regarding the Management of Pre-University Education

Educational management is evidenced by the ability to reflect the art and science of management and the scheme to create an effective action concerning the problem identification, solution preparation, implementation, evaluation, and development of a new decision.

Educational management performance is given by the efficiency and effectiveness of the process, providing resources and effective coordination of activities within it.

Dragomir states that educational management can be defined as both "science and art" to prepare human resources to train staff, according to the individual and finally accepted by society or a particular community. (2001: 23).

According to Jinga (2003: 400), educational management comprises a set of principles and functions of management standards and methods for achieving the objectives of the educational system (as a whole or the components), the quality and efficiency as high as possible.

The concept of management of school education, component of the educational process, has acquired multiple meanings and is used frequently in theory and practice. Analyzing this concept means the determination and the elements and directions that define it. Management education is presented as an action performed in an organized manner for processing learners personality according to finality, initially established. In full accordance with management education, pre-university management shall focus on the quality of education, i.e., the ratio between the results obtained and those shown and its effectiveness conceived as the ratio between the results obtained and those used.

These concepts create the logical line of this chapter, namely:

(1) Identifying factors with determining role of performance management in pre-university education;
(2) Their analysis in systems performing EU countries and determining specific aspects;
(3) Determining the defining aspects of the Romanian system of pre-university management, and in comparison with the systems performance;
(4) Establish necessary recommendations in a systemic improvement process.

3. Determinant Elements of Managerial Performance in Pre-University Education

3.1. *Regarding the system and resources*

Bibliographical study undertaken in the management of pre-university made the research base, completed then, by the performed comparative studies on various management systems practiced in pre-school education in the European Union. Thus, Hallinger (2003: 67) noticed that, in Europe different practice management systems are applied in schools namely:

- Partnerships between school systems — various agencies and organizations — very important to "put school into the community service";
- A modernization of curricula;
- Systems that provide centralization of attributions by the school management;
- Situations that encourage expansion of extracurricular activities, their achievement involving other stakeholders;
- Systems with very limited autonomy — cases where schools do not set their own goals to achieve their curricula (in Europe there are still a sufficient number of schools in the selection, remuneration of staff or implementing changes required in transformations from the external environment are limited as power of decision).

- Systems with some autonomy, which award grants to the management teams for the results (e.g., facilitating open communication, stimulating creative thinking and innovation, motivate staff and students to achieve competitive results, motivating lifelong learning, etc.).

In the pre-university education, the management relationships are very complex. Besides general management relations presented in any organization, in pre-university school units, some specific types are crystalized which focus on student attention as Stan N. stated (1999: 9).

The management relations are conditioned by variables influenced partly and influenced totally, namely:

- Degree of automation of processing the information;
- Characteristics of the educational process;
- Design managers on the school board;
- Human resources;
- Provided material;
- School size;
- Law school;
- Type of school.

3.2. *Regarding the quality of management*

One of the most important factors with determining role in achieving managerial performance is the school manager himself. Compared with other managers, the school occupies a distinct place, its specificity is given by occupational category in which it is formed, namely the teacher. According to studies, in the majority of EU Member States, the school manager is a teacher, but his title varies depending on the education system decentralization and the type of school.

The work efficiency of a school manager depends on the knowledge and proper application of methods, techniques, and principles of general management, knowledge and education domain specificity. A school manager must have the ability to understand educational policies at the macro-social trends of integration with the European–Romanian education.

Porter & Lawer have shown in *Managerial Attitudes and Performance* (2008: 112) that the ability to lead effectively is influenced by: the personality of the manager, the intellectual and behavioral structure, the educational manager being a model. According to another study by Joiță E. (2000: 312) students' achievement and teachers' performances are influenced by global business school manager, so that the selection, training and promotion of school managers are of utmost importance and priority.

Boboc (2002: 3) discussed the fact that a Romanian pre-university education manager is different from the managers in the European Union as he is not just a manager but also the administrative coordinator of the entire business establishment, both of the educational and the actual administration.

In Romania, school managers have administrative, financial, educational, and school responsibilities to society. Given the complexity of the tasks and responsibilities of school managers, the areas of its work comprise at the same time:

➢ Curriculum: application, development, and evaluation;
➢ Human resources: recruitment, use, motivation, training, assessment, availability, setting an appropriate organizational climate;
➢ Non-human resources: physical, financial, informational, time;
➢ Organizational performance, organizational development, and community relations.

Therefore to achieve the performance, skills, and capabilities of the school manager will be required in accordance with the duties listed above and to be acquired through specialized education in school management. As Mintzberg (1983: 149) specified, "managerial competence highlights broadly the ability of management to perform specific activities of expected performance". He also stated that high performance managerial skills are as follows:

➢ Search for information;
➢ Concept formation;
➢ Conceptual flexibility;
➢ Interpersonal research;
➢ Interaction management;
➢ Development orientation;
➢ Impact;
➢ Self-confidence;
➢ Communication;
➢ Putting into practice;
➢ Orientation towards success.

As we have already mentioned in our study, the key element of managerial performance is, in fact, the manager. His designation is particularly important and, as mention in the Eurydice Report in 2010, differs in each EU country.

Most countries apply a consistent set of criteria to designate one person as the head or director of an educational institution, as mention by Neacșu & Felea (2005: 11) taking into account the:

➢ Professional experience in education;
➢ Experience in administrative/managerial posts;
➢ Special vocational training;
➢ Moral qualities;
➢ Health estate.

4. Conclusions from Romanian Pre-University Education Assessment Management

Considering the previously analyzed determinants of performance, but without a model being taken literally for Romanian pre-university education, the study is further trying to emphasize some key elements of the management of Romanian pre-university education and then compare them with those existing in other European educational systems.

4.1. *Regarding the system and resources*

Out of the total amount of Romanian school managers interviewed, a proportion of 92% felt that they have very little autonomy in the management process, which is due to poor management of schools. According to the respondents, as a solution to revive the Romanian pre-university education and implicitly the managerial activity, a decentralization of education and increasing autonomy are needed.

The transition of education to the financing of local budgets generally led to a close collaboration with local schools, yet in some cases it appeared that there was no real communication between school managers and local authority representatives.

Regarding the resource management, the study revealed a lack of resources in general, and, especially, in human resource issues such as the inability to select the human resources in a strong connection with the lack of autonomy. This finding comes, somewhat, inconsistent compared with the findings of a strong point, as 88% of managers highlighted the importance of the quality of human resources, appropriate level of qualifications, training and performance of good teachers. In fact, the study shows that highly qualified teachers played an important role in the management of classroom and school management in general.

4.2. *Regarding the quality of management*

Our study also revealed that, in Romania, the biggest criticism of the school manager is that, managerial activity is carried out by directors who do not have knowledge of management, which is clearly visible in poor leadership and lower quality of education. The study shows that school managers' knowledge of school management goes towards a percentage of 35.50%.

Directors therefore exercise managerial act intuitively, without scientific basis, although in general they are interested in the system undertaking specialized training to ensure the appropriate qualifications.

The study shows that the activity in schools functions from inertia, observing that very few schools have a strategic management thinking. We can state that because of the decline of the demographic index, many schools will disappear and only those who are interested in designing strategies and translating them into practice, knowing very well their potential and objectives will remain.

Following the assessment of management in pre-university education by aligning performance indicators and descriptors of the European framework, this scientific approach revealed that Romanian pre-university education management values are fully compatible with those promoted by the European educational management, some changes being necessary.

5. Recommendations

Knowing that a copy of European models is impossible and sometimes dangerous for the system to be redesigned, improvement proposals are only the result of benchmarking, without claiming to sketch a general model.

Comparison method was found to be particularly useful in identifying strengths and weaknesses, specificities and common elements, all of which form the basis of departure for subsequent determination of appropriate methods and tools to implement European policies, following as results obtained in undergraduate units, an efficient management, comparable to European countries. In conclusion, our study provides the following recommendations on a real basis:

Developing partnerships between schools and public institutions, businesses, institutions from abroad:

➢ Increasing stakeholder involvement at the local or regional level of school activities and adapting curriculum to community needs. Developing professional skills of students through internships conducted in economic activity whose area corresponds to the interests of the school;
➢ Identifying funding sources by accessing European funds and European programs such as Comenius, Leonardo, cross border cooperation programs financed by the European Social Fund (ESF).

Regarding the financial resources of the school:

➢ Modernization of educational activity is directly influenced by the existence of an incentive system for allocating funds. That is why the distribution by schools and levels is needed to be made, depending on the specific training of students in each school. Allocation of funds in this way would lead to autonomy and thus to the responsibility of each school on the effective use of received funds;
➢ Compliance with the methodology of the income and expenditure budgets and compliance with all phases of the budget process leads to an efficient use of funds available to the school.

Human Resources Management:

- Due to rapid and permanent changes in Romanian society, optimum use of existing staff in each unit, training and development, establish collaborative relationships and promote educational experiences are required;
- The practice of scientific management, based on a correct and complete set long-term goals and rewards based on continuous assessment and performance indicators;
- Compliance with legislation regarding the preparation of job descriptions, performance evaluation sheets of the staff;
- The need for professional development must take into account both the needs of the school and the needs of each person;
- Completing the continuing education required for specific training sessions to solve problems arising in each school and not on the purely theoretical basis.

Strategic planning process and preparation of the Institutional Development Plan:

- Effective communication both inside and outside the school unit and participation in human resources team in the preparation of the Institutional Development Plan (IDP). IDP strategy approaches to start from the tradition of each school and the means of action that should be chosen based on the resources of the school unit.

Internal and external evaluation process:

- Self-evaluation is the basis of culture, and the management should enable schools to identify strengths and weaknesses by comparing performance year after year. Internal assessment is based on the interpretation of evidence and not of the views of those involved in the educational process;
- The external evaluation starting point represent the findings and data obtained from internal evaluation. If self-evaluation is performed incorrectly also external assessment results are as erroneous. Following an evaluation based on real and objective situations, the true weaknesses can be identified and thus measures can be taken to improve them;
- Creating their own textbooks, formalized operational procedures, approved by management unit systems and the creation of risk registers at each school;
- Creating and developing their systems of internal control/management and development of their development programs, according to the 25 management standards approved by the (Ministry of Finance Order) O.M.P.F. No. 946/2005 amended and supplemented by O.M.F.P. No. 1649/2011;
- Participation of employees involved in the creation and development of internal control/ management, forms of training in this field.

Decentralization of pre-university education:

- Decentralization aims to create an organized educational system, managed and financed according to the European requirements, so that the power of decision should be shared, clearly defined and well balanced between local communities and the ministry of education coordinated institutions.

Increasing the quality of managers:

- Qualification of managers through the specialization in educational management by studying specific elements of educational management;
- Through all recommendations resulting from the comparison of the Romanian school management system with the one practiced in different countries of the European Union, results a programmatic and practical nature of the work, both in the management of schools, local authorities, and the upper level of the field. Expected results are to improve quality and production performance system operation.

Acknowledgment

This work was supported by the strategic grand POSDRU/159/1.5/S/ 133255, Project ID 133255 (2014), co-financed by the European Social Fund within the Sectorial Operational Program Human Resources Development 2007–2013.

References

Boboc, I. (2002), Management reform in the European Schools, *Education Tribune* December 17.

Building Europe of Knowledge, Innovation and Technology Transfer 1, (1999).

Dragomir, M. (2001), *Glossary of Educational Management*, Cluj Napoca: Publishing House Hyperbora.

Eurydice, Report (2010), The information network on education in Europe, European Glossary on Education, 3. Available at: http://eacea.ec.europa.eu/education/eurydice/ documents/all_publications.pdf. (Accessed March 2014).

Hallinger, P. (2003), *Reshaping the Landscape of School Leadership Development*, Amsterdam: Swets and Zeitlinger.

Jinga, I. (2003), *Management Education*, Bucharest: ASE Publishing House.

Joiţă, E. (2000), *Teacher–manager Roles and Methodology*, Bucureşti: EDP.

Mintzberg, H. (1983), *The Nature of Managerial Work*, New York: Harper&Row.

Neacşu, I. & Felea, G. (2005), Romanian European Values and Projects in Quality Assurance in Higher Education (2nd edn.), Galati Publishing House. Galati.

Porter, L. W. & Lawer, E. E. (2008), *Managerial Attitudes and Performance*, Homewood: Irwin.

Stan, N. (1999), *Elements of the School Management*, Olt CSI Publishing House.

Chapter 46

Study on the Promotion and Implementation of Sustainable Development in Modern Management in National and Regional Economies. Case Study: Romania as EU Member

George Plesoianu and St. Alexandru Costin Cirstea
Bucharest University of Economic Studies

The study's main objective is to highlight the stringent need to implement a model of sustainable development at the societal level, based on the efficient use of available local resources, recovery the main economic sectors, with modern and environmental friendly technologies and maintenance of national and regional specific through: the homogeneity and the characteristics of each population, the own needs of development, production and consumption, the environmental and socio-economic system peculiarities through a sustainable development positive approach, and also the traditions and aspirations of the populations living in the EU countries. As a final objective, we intend to elaborate a feasible scenario for the application of these concepts in the case of Romania.

For the research study were used analysis and selective documentation synthesis of a series of recent and innovative works of the most renowned specialists and promoters of sustainable development and studies on the economic sectors, but also the strategy documents at EU and national level. On this basis, it was elaborated a comparative analysis between the international, the EU and the national approaches, in the implementation of sustainable development.

The results have led to a set of priority measures and strategic actions, as case studies for Romania, in the four integrated policies for sustainable development, considered in the study. In our opinion it is necessary to harmonize these policies through pragmatic approaches of Regulatory Impact Assessment (RIA), by developing interdisciplinary studies, to highlight the specific policy priorities and quantify their impact on the social groups and stakeholders.

The professional elaboration of these studies, according to the methodology promoted and supported at EU level, with special attention on those which cause discrimination in business environment and in the legitimate rights of citizens, is an absolutely necessary premise for the promotion of sustainable development policies.

1. Introduction

Sustainable development is a complex reality, a major challenge to human society, based on a relatively new concept and a stable model of integrated development of human civilization, and the natural environment in sustainable conditions. Modern concepts of sustainable development can be considered as a new paradigm (Soderbaum, 2004), driven by the need to perpetuate and development of human society in a healthy natural environment, with maintaining the national and regional specificities in each country and geographical areas, the homogeneity, and the characteristics of each population, the needs of development, production and consumption, the environmental peculiarities the traditions and aspirations of life, etc., which can be a pragmatic criteria for modeling and implementation the concept of sustainable development.

In this context, sustainable development must ensure the maintenance and improvement of living conditions for the vast majority of the community members in terms of a dynamic equilibrium and flexible macro system components ecosphere, including macrosystem itself. (Leca & State 1997).

Sustainable development is a relatively new concept in the world, appeared in the last decades of the second millennium, designed primarily as a process that relies on positive changes in people's mentality, in pursuit of a new vision for resource management and economic development (Smith & Fistung, 2005).

As it is evident that the existence of significant differences between countries and geographical areas, both in terms of natural conditions and cultural and linguistic levels, it appears obvious the need for configuration, development and implementation of "sustainable development policies" specific to each country or region, in a climate of rational international cooperation — from positions of equal partnership and honest decision — to solve mutual problems by implementation of sustainable development programs. Thus it will be ensured a uniform and gradual implementation of the common objectives of sustainable development for the medium and long term.

The progresses in sustainable development management led us, on the basis of a comparative analysis, to support comprehensive and integrated approach of this concept, which aims to integrate four systems: Economic, Social, Environmental, and Technological in sustainable integrated public policies (Fig. 1).

2. Sustainable Economic Policies

One of the most redoubtable experts and promoters of sustainable development, Lester Brown, notes that

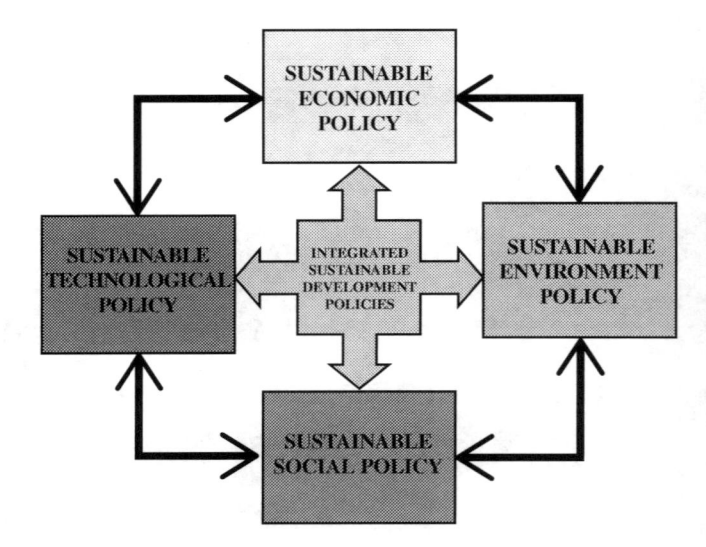

Fig. 1. The integration of sustainable development policies

during the 6,000 years since civilization began, mankind has lived on sustainable productivity of the natural systems of the Earth. In recent decades, however, human society has exceeded the consumption of natural resources that can support these natural systems, which may soon affect the continuity of human civilization that is threatened to become unsustainable (Brown, 2011).

The impact of these new challenges is thought to be differentiated from one sector or area of activity to another, so that some areas will have to "reinvent" or gradually disappear, while others will benefit from new business opportunities generated from these challenges.

Currently, worldwide there is a triple crisis: the global financial crisis, the economic crises of countries with large budget deficits, high unemployment and significantly public debts, and also the irrational and vicious crisis of environment management (Wijkman, Rockström, 2013). To these three will add a fourth, the food sector, which we believe it has an equally negative impact at global level.

This situation with a lot of obvious imbalances lead clearly to the conclusion that the current socio-economic model fails to fulfill its role. The way that international organizations and national governments acted in the past 20 years on climate and natural environment protection, environmental issues, and on. Economic and social sustainability has become a major topic of debate and one of the most important and most frequently subject commented by analysts and researchers.

These analyses show that the current economic model is based on economic and social policies that originated in the early stages of the industrial age, although it is obvious that, now, we face urgent and crucial economic and social demands for the rebalancing of human civilization but we have technological solutions able to support another reality. The population is over seven times higher and is estimated to increase by at least two billion people by the year 2050. Meanwhile, various long-term economic forecasts show that the world economy will continue to grow rapidly to reach by the year 2100, 15 up to 20 times its current size, given that the planetary resources are still limited.

In these circumstances, the use of non-conventional energy transfer acceleration and stopping waste and inefficiency in resource management are keys for developing a new economic model, in agreement with the principles of sustainable development.

At European level, the EU proposes to work with all stakeholders both on a European and global consensus for developing a methodological framework of feasible scenarios for launching a modern industrial policy, to support entrepreneurship and to curb corporate and financial abuses. These strategic actions are considering the design of sustainable and environmentally friendly industrial policies that promote competitiveness of primary industries, to the processing and services ones, to take advantage of the opportunities created by globalization and the green economy, integrated into a programmatic document called Europe 2020. Europe 2020 is launching a new vision for Europe's economy this decade, based on enhanced coordination of economic policies in the EU, in order to obtain growth and an increase in labor employment, to help economic recovery and EU financial sustainability.

This new strategy focuses on the following key areas: knowledge and innovation, a viable and sustainable economy, high employment rate and social inclusion of disadvantaged categories.

The role of external representation of the Europe 2020 strategy is essential to ensure an adequate response to the challenges of the globalization. It requires a strong EU support on solving urgent issues of vital interest and priority, such as the sharp decrease in carbon dioxide emissions, regulation of financial markets, energy security, and intellectual property law.

Europe 2020 Strategy focuses on three priorities:

- Developing an economy based on knowledge and innovation, so a rational and intelligent increase, which is also a sustainable;
- Promoting an efficient economy in terms of resource used, greener and more competitive, so a sustinable increase;
- Promoting an economy that ensure a substantial increase in corporate and SMEs social responsibility, with a high rate of employment, able to ensure economic, social, and territorial cohesion, accompanied by accelerated growth of social inclusion.

2.1. Case-Study at National Level — Romania

From the analysis of the existing situation in implementing the strategies and policies of industrialization and de-industrialization in Romania, resulted, in our opinion, some priorities to be aligned with the Europe 2020 objectives and that we consider necessary and feasible:

1. Drastic simplification and reduction of obligations and administrative documents that currently stifles small and medium businesses by taking over the best practices used in the developed European countries, so that the costs of these activities to be transferred in technological innovation;
2. Reconsidering with EU funded programs, the priority sectors producing added value, such as agriculture and forestry, sectors in which natural resources are wasted. The social component of these programs is essential for Romania and have the effect of the gradual return of emigrants that serve agriculture in other European countries and their participation in maintaining biodiversity and restore the natural potential of land, and thus combating extreme weather events in Romania;
3. Reforming and relaunching the tourism sector in Romania, which really put the potential of a generous and attractive nature for all kind of tourism, which currently is in a state of crisis. Through focused actions, supported by EU funding programs for travel

and tourism in collaboration with major networks from Europe, significant progress can be made in a relatively short time with consistent contributions that will sustain investment in increasing protected areas and creating a healthy natural environment.

3. Sustainable Social Policies

Global vision of sustainable development indicators should relate to the quantification of clear human welfare — for example, increasing the number of jobs, adequate health services, reliable education systems in agreement with labor market needs, equitable distribution of income and so on. A favorable increase of social inclusion involves ensuring self-sustaining for citizens and communities through higher rates of employment, so gradually to reach almost complete occupation rate of the active population.

To achieve this goal, are required coordinated education programs and lifelong learning skills and hence, poverty reduction, ensuring an acceptable standard of living for all citizens.

It is envisaged the rational restructuring of local and regional labor markets through sociological research opportunities and needs for products and services on this basis, planning and organization of training systems and integrated social protection, allowing people to focus training correlated with market requirements. In this way, it will get progressively balancing the supply of labor in the communities and regions and will be enhanced solidarity and efficient movement of labor as much as possible close to communities.

At European level, the EU strategic objective is to harness the full potential of workforce development, managing to cope with the challenges of an aging population and rising global competition. Special attention should be given to the trend of chaotic mass population transhumance in EU countries only because of too large differences of gains in developed countries to emerging new EU entrants. This phenomenon, which seems to be favorable for the economy of developed countries, whereas in certain sectors and categories of hard and polluting activities benefit from cheap labor force, is a violation of international principles of business ethics. A good example of this phenomenon is that in Romania, the agricultural lands are uncultivated, while hundreds of thousands of Romanian people working in the same sector, in Western countries (especially in Spain and Italy). A second wave is the construction workers who arrived in Britain. Therefore will be required active policies to promote equal opportunities between women and men in the labor market, which will also contribute to enhance social cohesion.

3.1. Case-Study at National Level — Romania

In Romania, for the implementation of sustainable development programs with greater economic efficiency and sustainable on medium and long term, are required some priorities related on social initiative that we consider feasible:

1. Creation and implementation of effective models of work organization in companies assisted by digital systems, especially in the SMEs sector, leading to increased productivity and significantly increase the level of security assurance work. It is envisaged exchange of experience from developed countries in Europe where such models have already been implemented. Putting into practice these measures will have the advantage that workers in Romania will have skills compatible with their peers from developed EU countries;
2. Promoting monitoring systems of the labor movement on fields and specialties between the EU countries and design "win–win" patterns for ensuring fairness and reciprocity benefits between partners;
3. Acquiring learning skills required in the labor market trades, which must be achieved through a close collaboration between schools and SMEs, by creating workshops, laboratories, simulators where practitioners directly transfer these skills and abilities to young workers;
4. Improving regulations on minorities, particularly the Rome minority, requiring emergency assistance by local authorities (municipalities) primarily by official registration and their inclusion in the legal market labor;
5. Improving through restructuring the public systems of social protection — currently bushy, inconsistent and unproductive — for sustaining the creation of new jobs in Romania;
6. Launching campaigns that promote the development of SMEs in rural areas and small towns by

providing special facilities, so they should be able to provide self-administration, thereby also creating new jobs.

4. Sustainable Technological Policies

Worldwide, a sufficient supply of affordable energy is essential for any economic activity. An example is the rapid growth of living standards that occurred during the 20th century due to cheap oil resources. But if access to high quality energy will shrink gradually — which is a likely consequence of the depletion of oil and other conventional resources worldwide — a negative impact on economic development would be immediate and catastrophic. Analyses made by the Pentagon, the Ministry of Defence in Germany and the (International Monetary Fund) IMF suggest that the world economy is extremely vulnerable both to disruptions in energy supply and the continuous increase in energy prices (Wijkman & Rockström, 2013).

Conclusion is that efforts should be intensified to broaden both the range of alternatives to conventional energy sources and energy efficiency measures for the development of new innovative technologies, environmentally friendly, which plans to become a strategic priority in sustainable development.

To achieve smart growth by enhancing the transfer of knowledge and innovation as drivers of sustainable growth in Europe was found to be needed improvements in education and educational research performance growth, promote innovation and knowledge transfer between EU countries, rational use of modern information and communication technologies and the transfer of research results and innovative ideas into practice. These measures have to generate new technologies and reliable products and services, which in turn generates economic growth, new jobs and help tackle structured challenges currently facing both European countries and international human society.

4.1. Case-Study at National Level — Romania

In Romania, we consider it necessary several priorities related to technological component of sustainable development, of which we mention:

1. Substantial improvement of business structure, paying particular attention to the entrepreneurship and innovative SMEs, creating "clean" technologies or providing environmentally friendly products, which are given tax incentives and reasonably financing, comparable to those granted in the developed European countries;
2. Develop joint partnership of modern technological parks, operating on the principles of sustainability (solar parks, wind energy, plant cultivation energy etc.);
3. Developing technological clusters on economic chains with pilot projects funded with support from European funds.

5. Sustainable Environmental Policies

Global awareness of the intensifying human activity increases the pressures on the environment, either through the uncontrolled consumption of resources and space, and by producing of waste that nature can not absorb without major negative effects, has led the international community to pass the initiation and supporting concrete actions to prevent, counteract, and eliminate disturbing factors repercussions of ecological balance. Because the main causes of degradation of the ecosphere are related to production systems and consumption of industrial society, it is imperative that solutions be initiated by the technical, economic and social positions integrated, giving it more importance and all other stakeholders, such as the social, moral and cultural ones. Unfortunately, in the technological and economic development, the environment and natural resources were considered as mere instruments serving growth and not as a natural support which needs maintenance and preservation. (Adapted from Smith et al., 2005.)

In Europe, economic recovery in the EU countries and sustainable socio-economic growth needs the existence of a competitive, long-term sustainable and effective economy, through rational use and conservation of natural resources, strong open to the introduction of ecological approaches and "clean" technologies, assisted by "smart" digital networks for communication and operation.

Special attention should also be given to extensive manufacturing and service sectors in SMEs to quickly transfer at large scale the R&D results and digital technology to the entire population.

A strategic importance have also activities against natural environmental degradation, leading to biodiversity loss as a result of the reckless use of fossil resources.

Another strategic priority is to accelerate the transition to an efficient economy based on judicious use of natural resources and reduce pollution drastically, mainly carbon dioxide emissions. An essential objective is to give up economic growth based on irresponsible use and focus on renewable natural resources (mainly solar, wind, geothermal, biomass), thereby achieving a drastic reduction in CO_2 emissions. All these actions will ensure economic competitiveness and energy security of EU countries.

5.1. Case-Study at National Level — Romania

From the analysis of the existing situation in implementing the strategies and policies for sustainable development in Romania resulted several priorities aligned with the Europe 2020 objectives, that we consider feasible for the environmental policy (Decalogue for Romania):

1. Ensure effective and coordinated implementation of infrastructure projects, harmonized with existing networks in Central European countries, which will make a decisive contribution to increasing the efficiency of transport systems in Romania, both for smooth movement of goods and people;
2. Launch pilot projects to optimize urban transport in an intermodal effective approach that actually contribute to streamlining the transport of persons and goods and the drastic reduction of carbon dioxide emissions generated by conventional vehicles;
3. Priority development of energy infrastructure and intelligent transport, upgraded and fully interconnected, assisted by digital monitoring systems, ensuring optimization of energy use;
4. Regulation and implementation of stringent energy performance standards on urban constructions, civil engineering and monitoring through new market instruments that continuously monitor the level of pollution and waste generated by these activities, to be taxed as additional costs for environment;
5. Promoting organic farming biomass generators through priority allocation of European funds for agriculture and rural development and the gradual reduction of the allocation of funds to large industrial farms that can sustain themselves. In this way, it will provide significant support to action of relaunching small and medium farms, which is the target of the new Common Agricultural Policy;
6. Creating an integrated ecological and urban settlement with systems of industrial and domestic waste collection and processing in biomass as alternative energy sources at the local level;
7. Campaigns for accelerate the re-forestation, especially in the areas endangered by desertification and other vulnerable areas of the hill–mountain or around major towns;
8. Provision of special facilities for SMEs active in environmental, biodiversity, non-conventional energy, "clean" technologies, the design and implementation of "green" as well as engineering design and consulting firm specializing in sustainable development and sustainable enterprise;
9. Promoting new market-based instruments to phase out subsidies for environmentally harmful emissions activities and providing some documented cases of minorities exceptions and disadvantaged areas;
10. Implementing a set of coherent and flexible fiscal mechanisms, to stimulate oriented greening production technologies, processing and consumption and rewarding SMEs by facilitating organic processing of their products or services.

6. Comparative Analysis of Sustainable Development Models between Romania and Global Vision

Next, we present a comparative analysis between the TSA Earth Policy Institute in Washington USA, presented in the report "Plan B" and the Sustainable Development Strategy of Romania — Horizons 2013–2020–2030, in effect, developed in 2008.

A synoptic and synthetic presentation of this analysis is shown in the table below, developed by the authors, which has considered as comparison criteria the vision, overall strategy and priority objectives.

Table 1: Comparative analysis of sustainable developments models between Romania and global vision

Plan B — Lester brown earth policy institute	Romanian sustainable development strategy 2013–2020–2030
VISION Global vision, pragmatic, and operational oriented sustainable solutions.	**VISION** Detailed bureaucratic approach of the EU Sustainable Development Strategy, the 2006 version with some specific elements for Romania.
STRATEGY Pragmatic strategies for four major interconnected strategic areas that can become reality.	**STRATEGY** General strategic assessments and qualitative measures and levels below the EU, even in 2030.
OBJECTIVES **I. Environment** 1. 80% reduction in CO_2 emissions by 2020, ➢ Increase energy efficiency by restructuring the transport sector; ➢ Stopping emissions from the energy sector classic fossil fuels, (oil, coal, natural gas) and the gradual replacement with renewable energy (wind, solar, geothermal). 2. Restoring natural systems of the planet by: reforestation, soil conservation, regeneration of fish shoals, stabilize groundwater.	**OBJECTIVES** **I. Environment** 1. Skyline 2020. National Objective: To reach the average level of EU countries on the main parameters for responsible management of natural resources. 2. Skyline 2030. National Objective: Approximation significant environmental performance of other EU Member States.
II. Social component 1. Stabilizing population and eradicating poverty through community action and recovery of natural systems of the planet, which will help eradicate poverty by creating jobs. Eradicating poverty leads to stabilization of population and cultural efforts to accelerate the sizing of families (less numerous). Final indicator: The ability to feed 8 Billion people and reach a balance eco-food in 2020.	**II. Social component** 1. Skyline 2020. National Objective: To promote consistency in the new legislative and institutional framework, the EU norms and standards relating to social inclusion, equal opportunities and actively supporting disadvantaged categories 2. Skyline 2030. National Objective: To come close to the average level of other EU member states in terms of social cohesion and quality of social services.
III. Economic component 1. Assigning additional expenditure of about $ 200 billion annually to restore the natural systems of the planet. Sources may come entirely from updating the concept of national security and the reallocation of a portion of the security budget of the major powers; only the reduction of military arsenals currently unworkable and unnecessary.	**III. Economic component** 1. Skyline 2020. National Objective: Decoupling growth from environmental degradation by reversing the relationship between resource consumption and value creation. 2. Skyline 2030. National Objective: Proximity to the average level of EU countries in terms of sustainable production and consumption.
IV. Technological component 1. Restructuring the energy sector based on "clean" energy and renewable energy through green certificates, additional carbon taxation, economic offset by lower income taxes. 2. Proposal to introduce a carbon tax of $200/t by 2020, accompanied by gradual clearing taxation.	**IV. Technological component** 1. Skyline 2020. To ensure the efficient and safe of national energy system, reaching the current average level of the EU in the intensity and energy efficiency. 2. Skyline 2030. National Objective: Align the average performance of the EU climate and energy indicators, fulfilling commitments for reducing emissions of greenhouse gas emissions in line with international agreements and Community rules and implement adaptation measures to climate change.

In the present context, the main lines of action for ensuring in Romania the economic recovery and for our country to become an active, competitive and respected partner, are related to the existence of a Sustainable Development Strategy for boost the economic crisis and stimulate domestic and foreign investors' participation in implementing social and economic policies for sustainable development.

Developing an own strategy for sustainable development by involving real macroeconomic authorities is necessary because in this way, every investor will know the details of the offer investment, the economic sectors considered as priorities for economic recovery and sustainable development concept by Romanian creating sustainable business in the medium and long term.

Based on these approaches and consistent measures of support, investors may participate on equal terms in various development projects whose goals are known and accepted.

In conclusion, the investment policy of our country should be so oriented as to ensure macroeconomic stability, sustainable economic growth based on sustainable business environment and oriented on rational and efficient growth rates.

We believe that a competitive advantage can be preserved in Romania, especially because it have a relatively cheap labor force and skilled environment, an advantage that should not be missed in the promotion of economic and social recovery process.

Also, in the context of the transfer to a model of sustainable development Romania needs to promote a set of pragmatic approaches based on the methodology of (Regulatory Impact Assessment) RIA, by developing interdisciplinary impact studies for policies in Romania.

Romanian legislation is still in constant change and accept too many exceptions and changes, which led to a inconsistent conglomerate in legislation, affecting business and citizens, creating excessive bureaucracy with chain effects on stakeholders to all levels of society.

A representative example is the bushy and restrictive tax system with changes almost daily, which is very hard to bear, both for businesses and citizens. Tax Code is changing and complicating in a nearly frantic pace, based on lobbying influences without preliminary assessment in practice through impact assessment RIA, generating adverse effects, such as excessive consumption of time for taxpayers, accompanied by significant unnecessary expense, translated into an unsustainable and inefficient model. This situation indirectly contributed significantly to the deindustrialization of Romania and to the fall of agro-food sector, the appearance of landlords and poor quality foreign investors and foreign banks, which turned Romania from an exporter in an importer of goods and services.

This situation necessarily requires the development of macroeconomic impact studies that substantiate judicious directions of future development in Romania.

Currently, although RIA has been proposed by international assistance, there is not yet a professional body, specialized in interdisciplinary RIA studies impact at the macroeconomic level and existing bodies empowered as the Legislative Council and the Government General Secretary and Public Policy Units within ministries are still in a phase of bureaucratic hesitation in apprehending details of laws impact. A representative example can be the aggressive and changing tax system, with strong effects on SMEs, which are not encouraged to develop profitable manufacturing and service activities.

In our opinion, the aforementioned elements can be a challenge to institutionalize the elaboration of professionally consistent regulatory impact assessment studies, in accordance with the methodology agreed at EU level to substantiate all strategic requirements and/or all those causing discrimination among both businesses and citizens, as a pre-requisite for moving to a model of sustainable development, in accordance with internationally accepted principles in the field.

7. Concluding Remarks

In this new approach to sustainable development as a public policy that promotes performance, modern and sustainable management, which we consider a premise for a priority strategic vision for Romania, we present below some opinions and proposals that emerged from our research:

1. Progress in studying the evolution of the concept of "sustainable development" has led us, on the basis of a comparative analysis, to complex and integrated approach of this concept, which aims to integrate four systems: economic, social, natural,

and technological concept unanimously accepted by experts politicians and business;
2. Interpretation of the evolution of "sustainable development" concept has led us to opt for an integrated strategy, agreed during the 40 years of debate, which aggregate between the four aforementioned systems;
3. Review by updating and completing the National Strategy for Sustainable Development of Romania — Horizons 2013–2020–2030, by introducing the concept of the four integrated systems and the elaboration of benchmarking analysis for assessing the progress achieved to date, and on this basis, development of a new cross-sectors development program, updated and aggregated for Sustainable Development of Romania until 2030;
4. Designing a strategic model and its implementation methodology with interdisciplinary approach that takes into account the socio-economic, environment and natural resources as well as existing and potential technological system, as a new paradigm devoted to implementation of the new sectoral and aggregate Sustainable Development of Romania with horizons in 2020–2030;
5. Following our research revealed that in Romania macroeconomic and regulatory stability is a prerequisite for the implementation of a Sustainable Development Program as a key factor for achieving the goal of a sustainable economy and efficiency modern market, in microeconomic and social practice;
6. Recent developments in the socio-economic environment in Romania, under international financial crisis and especially those in Europe, raises serious issues and imperative requirements to effectively manage human resources available and require coherent and appropriate strategies under the responsibility of the Government to counteract poverty and social disparities that affect health and work capacity of disadvantaged populations.

For enhancement of the natural resources and strengthening of sustainable consumption and production, we believe that Romania will have to consider these strategic development axes:

- Reinforce agriculture sector; In this area, the sources provided by the structural funds are relatively generous and should be directed primarily to small and medium-sized farms to produce crops and livestock, ensuring the domestic regional market share of food needed for household consumption from national sources, in accordance, and consensus with recently launched Common Agricultural Policy of the EU;
- To launch campaigns for reforestation on surfaces exposed to degradation by erosion, which will make an important contribution to maintaining temperate climate and reducing carbon emissions, and promoting rational use of diversified products that ensure their professional exploitation of forests;
- To stimulate the development of non-agricultural activities in rural communities and small towns, mainly using cohesion and development funds from the EU budget and contributions in order to rejuvenate and re-populate these areas, taking into account the benefits of returning to a number of Romanian citizens who have emigrated and will be interested to return, if they have secured and attractive jobs in Romania.

Another important issue for the operation of these genuine strategic growth engines of Romania, absolutely necessary and requested by civil society is cutting red tape and modernize business and investment systems by taking models of best practices from the developed countries of Europe, such as the UK, Germany, France, etc.

All these examples show that, in a pragmatic and sustainable approach with relatively little investment and substantial contributions from European funds can revive and complete the programs of vital importance for sustainable development.

References

Barac, L. (2009), *Management Judiciar*, Bucharest: Ed Hamangiu.

Brown, L. R. (Earth Policy Institute), (2011), *Lumea pe marginea prăpastiei — Cum să prevenim colapsul ecologic și economic*, Bucharest: Ed. Tehnică.

Leca, A. & Statie, E. (1997), Dezvoltarea durabilă, *Aspecte conceptuale și elemente de strategie*, (15), 39–51.

Soderbaum, P. (2004), Democracy, markets and sustainable development: The european union as an example, *Journal of European Enviroment*, Wiley InterScience, 14(16), p. 343.

Wijkman, A. & Rockstrom, J. (2013), *Falimentarea naturii — negarea limitelor planetei*, Bucharest: Ed. Compania.

Index

Symbols
2020 strategy, 19

Academic library management, 140
active anti-claim management, 392–394
adoption readiness, 89, 93
average productivity, 319, 320, 325–327

Banking Sector, 275
Bologna Process, 79–81, 83–86
Brasov, 219–225
business environment, 261–263, 269, 270
business opportunities, 263, 266, 269
business process reengineering, 203–205, 208, 210

case study, 3, 4, 9
challenges, 79, 82–85, 87
change management, 355, 356
cluster, 47–51, 297–301
combination, 126, 129
communication style, 275–284
community, 25, 26, 28, 30, 31
comparative management, 355–357, 409, 411
competitive advantage, 89–92, 94
competitiveness, 297, 298, 341–346
conflicts, 303, 307, 308, 311
consultancy, 265, 268–270
corporate alumni, 55–61
corporate culture, 35–40, 42
corporate management, 329, 330
corporate social responsibility, 25, 26
corporate sustainability, 25, 26
creativity, 19, 21, 23
crisis, 261, 262, 264, 266–269
culture, 35–42

database, 235–237, 240
developing study programs, 97, 105
difficulties, 261–264, 266, 269, 270
digital age, 146
digital natives, 146
diversity management, 19, 23

economic development, 213
economic growth, 297, 301
ecotourism, 400–405, 407
Eco touristic operator, 399
ecotouristic product, 399
educational management, 409, 410, 413, 414
effectiveness, 203, 207, 208, 210, 211
efficiency, 151, 152, 203, 204, 206–208, 210, 211
efficient market hypothesis, 159, 164
e-learning process, 117
emergent economy, 290
employees, 381–388
energy economy, 341, 343, 346
energy market, 344, 345
English as a lingua franca, 98, 105
enterprise, 341–346
entrepreneurial education, 185–187
entrepreneurs, 219–224
entrepreneurship, 167, 185–188, 191–193, 213–216, 219–225, 227–232
entrepreneurship education, 192
environment, 25–29, 31, 32
environment business, 219, 224
equal opportunities, 22, 23
e-Services, 143, 145, 148
European, 373–376, 378–380
European Commission Initiatives, 146
European integration, 266, 270, 409
European Social Fund, 227, 232

evaluation, 410, 412, 414
Externalization, 126
extracurricular activities, 355–361

factors, 373–376, 378, 380
financial incentives, 381, 387
food-hubs, 366–369
food safety, 365, 369
food security, 363, 364
forecasts, 157

Germany, 341–346
globalization, 3, 4, 9, 11, 14, 15, 67–70, 73–76

higher education, 67–70, 72, 75, 76, 107–113, 117–120, 122
Higher education governance, 97, 99
Human resource, 181, 182
human resource management, 175–178, 180, 236–239, 303–311

Impact Assessment, 47, 52
implementation guide, 297, 299
Individual Performance Appraisal, 313
inequality, 14
influence, 373–376, 378
influence factors, 386
information, 159–166
information entropy, 159, 163–166
information society, 143
information system, 235, 237
innovation, 297–301
intangible assets, 349–352, 354
integrated alumni management, 55
Integrated Model of RAM, 369
internalization, 126
internationalization, 67–74, 76, 77
international strategy, 67, 70, 76

knowledge based economy, 175–177, 297, 298, 301
Knowledge based enterprise, 175–178, 180–182
knowledge based function, 175–177
knowledge based management, 182
knowledge dynamics, 125, 126, 133, 134
knowledge management, 126, 128–130, 134, 135, 143–145, 147, 148

large Corporate Boards, 3, 10
leadership, 89, 91, 92, 95, 96, 273, 275–281, 283, 284
leadership styles, 275, 276, 278–280, 284

learning, 81–86
learning organization, 125–131, 134, 135

management, 35–37, 40–42, 195–202, 227–232, 243, 248, 249, 251–253, 329, 330, 374, 379, 380
Management Challenges, 195
managerial difficulties, 197, 198, 201
marginal productivity, 319, 320, 325–327
measurement, 47, 49, 51
medium sized enterprise, 203, 211
multilingualism, 104, 105
multinational companies, 329, 330, 332, 335–337
mutation of capitalism, 16

neo liberalism, 11, 14
new firms, 221
new Kaiser Wilhelm tunnel, 391, 392
New Public Management, 137
number of employees, 319–321, 323–328

objectives, 203–211
oligarchs, 11, 16
organizational behaviour, 93, 95
organizational change, 381, 382, 384–388
Organization Culture, 289–295

paradigm shift in education, 85, 86
performance, 36, 41, 203–208, 210, 211, 303, 305, 306, 309–311, 373–375, 378, 379, 409–414
performance management, 313–316
personnel management, 309
personnel policy, 319, 321, 324, 327
physical production, 319–325, 327, 328
Preventive anti-claim management, 393, 394
private institutions, 108–113
processual, 204, 206–209, 211
project management, 313, 314, 316
projects, 373–376, 378, 380
project teams, 313, 315
protected area, 400
public administration, 151–157
public institutions, 373, 374, 379
public value, 152, 155, 156

quality culture, 86
quality evaluation models, 117
quality management, 399–403, 405, 407

railway tunnel, 392
R&D function, 175–177, 180

redesign of management system, 203, 205, 206, 211
reform, 137–140
Regional Agrifood Markets (RAM), 363
regional development, 237, 297, 299–301
Regulatory Impact Assessment, 368, 369
resistance to change, 381, 383, 384, 386, 388
responsiveness, 289–295
risk management, 151–155, 157
Romania, 25–30, 110–112, 219, 221, 224, 341–346
Romania business environment, 329, 330, 332, 333, 336
Romania's higher education sector, 89
rural area, 235–242

school education, 409, 410
school manager, 409, 411–413
small and medium-sized enterprises, 289, 290
Smart Economy, 3
SME policy, 171–173
SMEs, 167, 169–173, 261–264, 266–270
SMEs evaluation, 349
social capital, 47–50
social economy, 227, 228, 231, 232, 243–248, 252, 253, 255
social economy organizations, 244, 246–248, 253
social enterprise, 213–217, 243, 246–248, 258
social entrepreneurship, 243, 244, 246, 253, 256, 257
socialization, 125, 126

Strategic planning, 305
supplemental claims calculation, 391–394, 396, 397
sustainability, 45, 47–52
sustainable business, 47, 50
sustainable development, 25, 26, 29, 402, 403, 405, 417, 419–422, 424, 425
sustainable economic policy, 418
sustainable environment policy, 421
sustainable social policy, 420
sustainable technological policy, 421
system, 36–42
systemic approach to organizations, 40

tax evasion, 12, 14–16
training, 261, 268–270, 305–307, 309, 310
training function, 175, 176, 179

universities, 137–140
university, 381, 386–388
university alumni, 55–61
university governance, 89, 90, 95, 96
university management, 101, 356, 361

work force productivity, 319–321, 323, 324
work productivity elasticity, 321, 323, 327

young entrepreneurs, 190

Printed in the United States
By Bookmasters